MW01120390

ISBN: 9781314279924

Published by:
HardPress Publishing
8345 NW 66TH ST #2561
MIAMI FL 33166-2626

Email: info@hardpress.net
Web: http://www.hardpress.net

Prolegomena to the Study of Greek Religion

CAMBRIDGE UNIVERSITY PRESS WAREHOUSE,
C. F. CLAY, MANAGER.
London: FETTER LANE, E.C.
Glasgow: 50, WELLINGTON STREET.

Leipzig: F. A. BROCKHAUS.
New York: G. P. PUTNAM'S SONS.
Bombay and Calcutta: MACMILLAN AND CO., LTD.

Prolegomena to the Study of Greek Religion

by

JANE ELLEN HARRISON,

HON. D.LITT. (DURHAM), HON. LL.D. ABERDEEN,
STAFF LECTURER AND SOMETIME FELLOW OF NEWNHAM COLLEGE, CAMBRIDGE,
CORRESPONDING MEMBER OF THE GERMAN ARCHAEOLOGICAL INSTITUTE

SECOND EDITION

Cambridge:
at the University Press
1908

First Edition 1903.

Second Edition 1908.

ARTURO ET MARGARITAE VERRALL

HUIC AMICAE MEAE CONSTANTISSIMAE
ILLI ET AMICO ET MAGISTRO

HUNC LIBRUM DEDICO

INTRODUCTION.

THE object of the following pages is to draw attention to some neglected aspects of Greek religion.

Greek religion, as set forth in popular handbooks and even in more ambitious treatises, is an affair mainly of mythology, and moreover of mythology as seen through the medium of literature. In England, so far as I am aware, no serious attempt has been made to examine Greek ritual. Yet the facts of ritual are more easy definitely to ascertain, more permanent, and at least equally significant. What a people *does* in relation to its gods must always be one clue, and perhaps the safest, to what it *thinks*. The first preliminary to any scientific understanding of Greek religion is a minute examination of its ritual.

This habit of viewing Greek religion exclusively through the medium of Greek literature has brought with it an initial and fundamental error in method—an error which in England, where scholarship is mainly literary, is likely to die hard. For literature Homer is the beginning, though every scholar is aware that he is nowise primitive; for theology, or—if we prefer so to call it—mythology, Homer presents, not a starting-point, but a culmination, a complete achievement, an almost mechanical accomplishment, with scarcely a hint of *origines*, an accomplishment moreover, which is essentially literary rather than religious, sceptical and moribund already in its very perfection. The Olympians of Homer are no more primitive than his hexameters. Beneath this splendid surface lies a stratum of religious conceptions, ideas of evil, of purification, of atonement, ignored or suppressed by Homer, but reappearing in later poets and notably in Aeschylus. It is this substratum of religious conceptions, at once more primitive and more permanent, that I am concerned to investigate. Had ritual received its due share of attention, it had not remained so long neglected.

I would guard against misapprehension. Literature as a starting-point for investigation, and especially the poems of Homer, I am compelled to disallow; yet literature is really my goal. I have tried to understand primitive rites, not from love of their archaism, nor yet wholly from a single-minded devotion to science, but with the definite hope that I might come to a better understanding of some forms of Greek poetry. Religious convention compelled the tragic poets to draw their plots from traditional mythology, from stories whose religious content and motive were already in Homer's days obsolete. A knowledge of, a certain sympathy with, the *milieu* of this primitive material is one step to the realization of its final form in tragedy. It is then in the temple of literature, if but as a hewer of wood and drawer of water, that I still hope to serve.

As the evidence to be set before the reader is necessarily somewhat complex in detail, and the arguments of the successive chapters closely interdependent, it may be well at the outset to state, as simply as may be, the conclusions at which I have arrived, and to summarize briefly the steps of the discussion.

In Chapter I. it is established that the Greeks themselves in classical times recognized two forms of ritual, Olympian and Chthonic. It is further seen that the characteristic ritual of Homeric days was of the kind known to them as Olympian. Sacrifice in Homer takes the form of an offering to the god to induce his favour. Its formulary is *do ut des.* Moreover the sacrificial banquet to which the god is bidden is shared by the worshipper. In sharp contradistinction to this cheerful sacrificial feast, when we examine the supposed festival of Zeus at Athens, the Diasia, we find rites of quite other significance; the sacrifice is a holocaust, it is *devoted,* made over entirely to the god, unshared by the worshipper, and its associations are gloomy. The rites of the Diasia, though ostensibly in honour of Zeus, are found really to be addressed to an underworld snake on whose worship that of Zeus has been superimposed.

In the three chapters that follow, on the festivals of the

Anthesteria, Thargelia, and Thesmophoria, held respectively in the spring, summer, and autumn, the Olympian ritual superimposed is taken as known and only alluded to in passing. The attention is focussed on the rites of the underlying stratum.

In the Anthesteria, ostensibly sacred to Dionysos, the main ritual is found to be that of the placation of ghosts. Ghosts, it is found, were placated in order that they might be kept away; the formulary for these rites is not, as with the Olympians, *do ut des*, but *do ut abeas*. The object of these rites of Aversion, practised in the spring, is found to be strictly practical; it is the promotion of fertility by the purgation of evil influences.

The ritual of the Thargelia is even more primitive and plain-spoken. In this festival of the early summer, ostensibly dedicated to Apollo, the first-fruits of the harvest are gathered in. The main gist of the festival is purification, necessary as a preliminary to this ingathering. Purification is effected by the ceremonial of the pharmakos. Though the festival in classical days was 'sacred to' Apollo, the pharmakos is nowise a 'human sacrifice' to a god, but a direct means of physical and moral purgation, with a view to the promotion and conservation of fertility.

Thus far it will be seen that the rites of the lower stratum are characterized by a deep and constant sense of evil to be removed and of the need of purification for its removal; that the means of purification adopted are primitive and mainly magical nowise affects this religious content.

This practical end of primitive ceremonies, the promotion of fertility by magical rites, comes out still more strongly in the autumn sowing festival of the Thesmophoria. Here the women attempt, by carrying certain magical *sacra*, the direct impulsion of nature. In connection with these *sacra* of the Thesmophoria the subject of 'mysteries' falls to be examined. The gist of all primitive mysteries is found to be the handling or tasting of certain *sacra* after elaborate purification. The *sacra* are conceived of as having magical, i.e. divine, properties. Contact with them is contact with a superhuman potency, which is taboo to the unpurified. The gist of a mystery is often the removal of a taboo. From the Olympian religion 'mysteries' appear to have been wholly absent.

In Chapter V. we pass from ritual to theology, from an examination of rites performed to the examination of the beings to whom these rites were addressed. These beings, it is found, are of the order of sprites, ghosts, and bogeys, rather than of completely articulate gods, their study that of demonology rather than theology. As their ritual has been shown to be mainly that of the Aversion of evil, so they and their shifting attributes are mainly of malevolent character. Man makes his demons in the image of his own savage and irrational passions. Aeschylus attempts, and the normal man fails, to convert his Erinyes into Semnai Theai.

In Chapter VI. the advance is noted from demonology to theology, from the sprite and ghost to the human and humane god. The god begins to reflect not only human passions but humane relations. The primitive association of women with agriculture is seen to issue in the figures of the Mother and the Maid, and later of the Mother and the Daughter, later still in the numerous female trinities that arose out of this duality. In Chapter VII. the passage from ghost to god is clearly seen, and the humane relation between descendant and ancestor begets a kindliness which mollifies and humanizes the old religion of Aversion. The culminating point of the natural development of an anthropomorphic theology is here reached, and it is seen that the goddesses and the 'hero-gods' of the old order are, in their simple, non-mystic humanity, very near to the Olympians.

At this point comes the great significant moment for Greece, the intrusion of a new and missionary faith, the religion of an immigrant god, Dionysos.

In Chapter VIII. the Thracian origin of Dionysos is established. In his religion two elements are seen to coexist, the worship of an old god of vegetation on which was grafted the worship of a spirit of intoxication. The new impulse that he brought to Greece was the belief in *enthusiasm*, the belief that a man through physical intoxication at first, later through spiritual ecstasy, could pass from the human to the divine.

This faith might have remained in its primitive savagery, and therefore for Greece ineffective, but for another religious impulse, that known to us under the name of Orpheus. To the discussion of Orphism the last four chapters IX.—XII. are devoted.

In Chapter IX. I have attempted to show that the name Orpheus stands for a real personality. I have hazarded the conjecture that Orpheus came from Crete bringing with him, perhaps ultimately from Egypt, a religion of spiritual asceticism which yet included the ecstasy of the religion of Dionysos. Chapter X. is devoted to the examination of the Orphic and Dionysiac mysteries. It has been shown that before the coming of the Orphic and Dionysiac religion the mysteries consisted mainly in the handling of certain *sacra* after elaborate purification. By handling these *sacra* man came into contact with some divine potency. To this rudimentary mysticism Orphism added the doctrine of the possibility of complete union with the divine. This union was effected in the primitive Cretan rite of the Omophagia by the physical eating of the god; union with the divine was further symbolically effected by the rite of the Sacred Marriage, and union by adoption by the rite of the Sacred Birth. The mission of Orphism was to take these primitive rites, originally of the crudest sympathetic magic, and inform them with a deep spiritual mysticism. The rite of the Omophagia found no place at Eleusis, but the other two sacramental rites of union, the Sacred Marriage and the Sacred Birth, formed ultimately its central mysteries.

With the doctrine and ritual of union with the divine there came as a necessary corollary the doctrine that man could attain the divine attribute of immortality. Orphic eschatology is the subject of Chapter XI. Its highest spiritual form, the belief that perfect purity issued in divinity and hence in immortality, is found expressed in the Orphic tablets. Its lower expression, the belief in a Hades of eternal punishment as contrasted with the shadowy after-world of Homer, is seen in the vases of Lower Italy and the eschatology denounced by Plato.

Finally in Chapter XII. it is shown how, as a concomitant to their Eschatology, the Orphics, unlike Homer, developed a Cosmogony, and with this Cosmogony was ultimately bound up a peculiar and philosophic theology. In the fifth century B.C. the puppet-show of the Olympians was well-nigh played out, but the two gods of the Orphics remained potent. In ritual they worshipped Dionysos, but their theoretical theology recognized

Eros as source of all things. The Eros of the Orphics was a mystery-being, a *daimon* rather than a *theos*, a potency wholly alien to the clear-cut humanities of Olympus.

With the consideration of Orphism it has become, I hope, abundantly clear why at the outset attention was focussed on the primitive rites of Aversion and Purification rather than on the Service of the Olympians. The ritual embodied in the formulary *do ut des* is barren of spiritual content. The ritual embodied in *do ut abeas* contains at least the recognition of one great mystery of life, the existence of evil. The rites of the Olympians were left untouched by the Orphics; the rites of purification and of sympathetic magic lent them just the symbolism they needed. Moreover in theology the crude forms of demons were more pliant material for mysticism than the clear-cut limitations and vivid personality of the Olympians. Orphism was the last word of Greek religion, and the ritual of Orphism was but the revival of ancient practices with a new significance.

The reader will note that in the pages that follow, two authors, Plutarch and Euripides, have been laid under special contribution. Plutarch's gentle conservatism made him cling tenaciously to antique faith. According to him, one function of religion was to explain and justify established rites, and in the course of his attempted justification he tells us many valuable ritual facts. Euripides, instant in his attack on the Olympian gods, yet treats with respect the two divinities of Orphism, Dionysos and Eros. I have suggested that, born as he was at Phlya, the ancient home of Orphic mysteries, his attitude on this matter may have been influenced by early associations. In any case, a religion whose chief divinities were reverently handled by Euripides cannot be dismissed as a decadent maleficent superstition.

I would ask that the chapters I have written be taken strictly as they are meant, as Prolegomena. I am deeply conscious that in surveying so wide a field I have left much of interest untouched, still more only roughly sketched in. I wished to present my general theory in broad outline for criticism before filling in details, and I hope in the future to achieve a study of Orphism that may have more claim to completeness. If here I have dwelt almost exclusively on its strength and beauty, I am not unaware that it has, like all mystical religions, a weak and ugly side.

If in these Prolegomena I have accomplished anything, this is very largely due to the many friends who have helped me; the pleasant task remains of acknowledging my obligations.

My grateful thanks are offered to the Syndics of the University Press for undertaking the publication of this book; to the Syndics of the University Library and the Fitzwilliam Museum for the courtesy they have shown in allowing me free access to their libraries; to my own College, which, by electing me to a Fellowship, has given me for three years the means and leisure to devote myself to writing.

For the illustrations they have placed at my disposal I must record my debt to the Trustees of the British Museum, to the Hellenic Society, the German Archaeological Institute, and the École Française of Athens. The sources of particular plates are acknowledged in the notes. The troublesome task of drawing from photographs and transcribing inscriptions has been most kindly undertaken for me by Mrs Hugh Stewart.

Passing to literary obligations, it will be evident that in the two first chapters I owe much, as regards philology, to the late Mr R. A. Neil. His friendship and his help were lost to me midway in my work, and that loss has been irreparable.

It is a pleasure to me to remember gratefully that to Sir Richard Jebb I owe my first impulse to the study of Orphism. The notes in his edition of the *Characters* of Theophrastos first led me as a student into the by-paths of Orphic literature, and since those days the problem of Orphism, though often of necessity set aside, has never ceased to haunt me.

To Professor Ridgeway I owe much more than can appear on the surface. The material for the early portion of my book was collected many years ago, but, baffled by the ethnological problems it suggested, I laid it aside in despair. The appearance of Professor Ridgeway's article, 'What people made the objects called Mycenaean?' threw to me an instant flood of light on the problems of ritual and mythology that perplexed me, and I returned to my work with fresh courage. Since then he has, with the utmost kindness, allowed me to attend his professorial lectures and frequently to refer to him my difficulties. I have thought it best finally to state my own argument independently of his ethnological conclusions, first because those conclusions are, at the time I write, only in part before the public, but chiefly because I hoped that by stating my evidence independently it might, in the comparatively narrow sphere in which I work, offer some slight testimony to the truth of his illuminating theories.

To all workers in the field of primitive religion Dr Frazer's writings have become so part and parcel of their mental furniture that special acknowledgement has become almost superfluous. But I cannot deny myself the pleasure of acknowledging a deep and frequent debt, the more as from time to time I have been allowed to ask for criticism on individual points, and my request, as the notes will show, has always met with generous response.

Mr F. M. Cornford of Trinity College has, with a kindness and patience for which I can offer no adequate thanks, undertaken the revision of my proof-sheets. To him I owe not only any degree of verbal accuracy attained, but also, which is much more, countless valuable suggestions made from time to time in the course of my work. Many other scholars have allowed me to refer to them on matters outside my own competency. Some of these debts are acknowledged in the notes, but I wish specially to thank Dr A. S. Murray, Mr Cecil Smith and Mr A. H. Smith of the British Museum for constant facilities afforded to me in my work there, and Mr R. C. Bosanquet and Mr M. Tod for help in Athens; and, in Cambridge, Dr Haddon, Dr Hans Gadow, Mr Francis Darwin, Mr H. G. Dakyns and Mr A. B. Cook.

My debt to Dr A. W. Verrall is so great and constant that it is hard to formulate. If in one part of my book more than another I am indebted to him it is in the discussion of the Erinyes. Chapter V. indeed owes its inception to Dr Verrall's notes in his edition of the *Choephoroi*, and its final form to his unwearied criticism. Throughout the book there is scarcely a literary difficulty that he has not allowed me to refer to him, and his sure scholarship and luminous perception have dissipated for me many a mental fog.

Mr Gilbert Murray has written for me the critical Appendix on the text of the Orphic tablets, a matter beyond my competence. Many verse translations, acknowledged in their place, are also by him, and uniformly those from the *Bacchae* and *Hippolytus* of Euripides. It is to Mr Murray's translation of the *Bacchae* that finally, as regards the religion of Dionysos, I owe most. The beauty of that translation, which he kindly allowed me to use before its publication, turned the arduous task of investigation into a labour of delight, and throughout the later chapters of the book, the whole of which he has read for me in proof, it will be evident that, in many difficult places, his sensitive and wise imagination has been my guide.

JANE ELLEN HARRISON.

NEWNHAM COLLEGE, CAMBRIDGE,
September 9, 1903.

IN the second edition, errors to which the kindness of friends and reviewers has drawn my attention have been corrected. The tedious task of proof-revision has been again undertaken for me by Mr Cornford. For the index of Classical Passages I have to thank Mr F. C. Green of Trinity College. In the notes many new references have been added to literature that has appeared since my first edition. I would mention especially Dr Frazer's *Early History of the Kingship* and the invaluable *Archiv für Religionswissenschaft*, the issue of which in new form since 1904 marks a fresh departure in the study of religion. In my second edition however new material has been indicated rather than incorporated. Save for obvious corrections and added references the book remains substantially unaltered—not, I would ask my friends to believe, because in the lapse of four years my views remain the same, but because on some matters, especially on magic, mimetic ritual and the mysteries, I hope before long, in a volume of *Epilegomena*, to develope certain suggestions and to remedy many shortcomings.

JANE ELLEN HARRISON.

NEWNHAM COLLEGE, CAMBRIDGE.
December, 1907.

TABLE OF CONTENTS.

CHAPTER I.

Olympian and Chthonic Ritual.

CHAPTER II.

The Anthesteria. The Ritual of Ghosts and Sprites.

CHAPTER III.

Harvest Festivals. The Thargelia, Kallynteria, Plynteria.

CHAPTER IV.

The Women's Festivals. Thesmophoria, Arrephoria, Skirophoria, Stenia, Haloa.

CHAPTER VII.

The Making of a God.

CHAPTER VIII.

Dionysos.

CHAPTER XI.

Orphic Eschatology.

CHAPTER XII.

Orphic Cosmogony.

CHAPTER I.

OLYMPIAN AND CHTHONIC RITUAL.

'δαίμοϲι μειλιχίοιϲιν ἱλάϲματα καὶ μακάρεϲϲιν οὐρανίοιϲ.'

In characterizing the genius of the Greeks Mr Ruskin says: '*there is no dread in their hearts; pensiveness, amazement, often deepest grief and desolation, but terror never. Everlasting calm in the presence of all Fate, and joy such as they might win, not indeed from perfect beauty, but from beauty at perfect rest.*' The lovely words are spoken of course mainly with reference to art, but they are meant also to characterize the Greek in his attitude towards the invisible, in his religion—meant to show that the Greek, the favoured child of fortune yet ever unspoilt, was exempt from the discipline to which the rest of mankind has been subject, never needed to learn the lesson that in the Fear of the Lord is the beginning of Wisdom.

At first sight it seems as though the statement were broadly true. Greek writers of the fifth century B.C. have a way of speaking of, an attitude towards, religion, as though it were wholly a thing of joyful confidence, a friendly fellowship with the gods, whose service is but a high festival for man. In Homer sacrifice is but, as it were, the signal for a banquet of abundant roast flesh and sweet wine; we hear nothing of fasting, of cleansing, and atonement. This we might perhaps explain as part of the general splendid unreality of the heroic saga, but sober historians of the fifth century B.C. express the same spirit. Thucydides is assuredly by nature no reveller, yet religion is to him in the main 'a rest from toil' He makes Pericles say[1]: 'Moreover we have

[1] Thuc. II. 38, and in the same spirit Plato (*Legg.* 653 D) writes θεοὶ δὲ οἰκτείραντες τὸ τῶν ἀνθρώπων ἐπίπονον πεφυκὸς γένος ἀναπαύλας τε αὐτοῖς τῶν πόνων ἐτάξαντο τὰς τῶν ἑορτῶν ἀμοιβὰς τοῖς θεοῖς.

provided for our spirit very many opportunities of recreation, by the celebration of games and sacrifices throughout the year.'

Much the same external, quasi-political, and always cheerful attitude towards religion is taken by the 'Old Oligarch[1].' He is of course thoroughly orthodox and even pious, yet to him the main gist of religion appears to be a decorous social enjoyment. In easy aristocratic fashion he rejoices that religious ceremonials exist to provide for the less well-to-do citizens suitable amusements that they would otherwise lack. 'As to sacrifices and sanctuaries and festivals and precincts, the People, knowing that it is impossible for each poor man individually to sacrifice and feast and have sanctuaries and a beautiful and ample city, has discovered by what means he may enjoy these privileges. The whole state accordingly at the common cost sacrifices many victims, while it is the People who feast on them and divide them among themselves by lot'; and again[2], as part of the splendour of Athens, he notes that 'she celebrates twice as many religious holidays as any other city.' The very language used by this typical Athenian gentleman speaks for itself. Burnt-sacrifice (θυσία), feasting, agonistic games, stately temples are to him the essence of religion; the word sacrifice brings to his mind not renunciation but a social banquet; the temple is not to him so much the awful dwelling-place of a divinity as an integral part of a 'beautiful and ample city.'

Thucydides and Xenophon need and attempt no searching analysis of religion. Socrates of course sought a definition, a definition that left him himself sad and dissatisfied, but that adequately embodied popular sentiment and is of importance for our enquiry. The end of the *Euthyphron* is the most disappointing thing in Plato; Socrates extracts from Euthyphron what he thinks religion is; what Socrates thought he cannot or will not tell[3].

Socrates in his enquiry uses not one abstract term for religion —the Greeks have in fact no one word that covers the whole field—he uses two[4], piety (τὸ εὐσεβές) and holiness (τὸ ὅσιον).

[1] Ps.-Xen. *Rep. Athen.* II. 99. [2] Ps.-Xen. *Rep. Athen.* III. 8.

[3] Plat. *Euthyph.* 15 D.

[4] So far as it is possible to distinguish the two, τὸ εὐσεβές is religion from man's side, his attitude towards the gods, τὸ ὅσιον religion from the gods' side, the claim they make on man. τὸ ὅσιον is the field of what is made over, consecrated to the gods. The further connotations of the word as employed by Orphism will be discussed later. 'Holiness' is perhaps the nearest equivalent to τὸ ὅσιον in the *Euthyphron*.

Euthyphron of course begins with cheerful confidence: he and all other respectable men know quite well what piety and holiness are. He willingly admits that 'holiness is a part of justice,' that part of justice that appertains to the gods; it is giving the gods their due. He also allows, not quite seeing to what the argument is tending, that piety and holiness are 'a sort of tendance (θεραπεία) of the gods.' This 'tendance,' Socrates presses on, 'must be of the nature of service or ministration,' and Euthyphron adds that it is the sort of service that servants show their masters. Socrates wants to know in what particular work and operation the gods need help and ministration. Euthyphron answers with some impatience that, to put it plainly and cut the matter short, holiness consists in 'a man understanding how to do what is pleasing to the gods in word and deed, i.e. by prayer and sacrifice.' Socrates eagerly seizes his advantage and asks: 'You mean then that holiness is a sort of art of praying and sacrificing?' 'Further,' he adds, 'sacrifice is giving to the gods, prayer is asking of them, holiness then is a art of asking and giving.' If we give to the gods they must want something of us, they must want to 'do business with us.' 'Holiness is then an art in which gods and men do business with each other.' So Socrates triumphantly concludes, to the manifest discomfort of Euthyphron, who however can urge no tenable objection. He feels as a pious man that the essence of the service or tendance he owes to the gods is of the nature of a freewill tribute of honour, but he cannot deny that the gods demand this as a *quid pro quo*.

Socrates, obviously unfair though he is, puts his finger on the weak spot of Greek religion as orthodoxly conceived in the fifth century B.C. Its formula is *do ut des*. It is, as Socrates says, a 'business transaction' and one in which, because god is greater than man, man gets on the whole the best of it. The argument of the *Euthyphron* is of importance to us because it clearly defines one, and a prominent, factor in Greek religion, that of *service* (θεραπεία); and in this service, this kindly 'tendance,' there is no element of fear. If man does his part in the friendly transaction, the gods will do theirs. None of the deeper problems of what we moderns call religion are even touched: there is no question of sin, repentance, sacrificial atonement, purification, no fear of judgment to come, no longing after a future complete beatitude.

Man offers what seems to him in his ignorance a reasonable service to gods conceived of as human and rational. There is no trace of scepticism: the gods certainly exist, otherwise as Sextus Empiricus[1] quaintly argues 'you could not serve them': and they have human natures. 'You do not serve Hippocentauri, because Hippocentauri are non-existent.'

To the average orthodox Greek the word θεραπεία, service, tendance, covered a large, perhaps the largest, area of his conception of religion. It was a word expressing, not indeed in the Christian sense a religion whose mainspring was love, but at least a religion based on a rational and quite cheerful mutual confidence. The Greeks have however another word expressive of religion, which embodies a quite other attitude of mind, the word δεισιδαιμονία, *fear of spirits*; fear, not tendance, fear not of gods but of spirit-things, or, to put it abstractly, of the supernatural.

It is certainly characteristic of the Greek mind that the word δεισιδαιμονία and its cognates early began to be used in a bad sense, and this to some extent bears out Mr Ruskin's assertion. By the time of Theophrastos ὁ δεισιδαίμων is frankly in our sense 'the superstitious man,' and superstition Theophrastos defines as not just and proper reverence but simply 'cowardice in regard to the supernatural.' Professor Jebb[2] has pointed out that already in Aristotle the word δεισιδαίμων has about it a suspicion of its weaker side. An absolute ruler, Aristotle[3] says, will be the more powerful 'if his subjects believe that he fears the spiritual beings' (ἐὰν δεισιδαίμονα νομίζωσιν εἶναι) but he adds significantly 'he must show himself such *without fatuity*' (ἄνευ ἀβελτερίας).

Plutarch has left us an instructive treatise on 'the fear of the supernatural.' He saw in this fear, this superstition, the great element of danger and weakness in the religion that he loved so well. His intellect steeped in Platonism revolted from its unmeaning folly, and his gentle gracious temperament shrank from its cruelty. He sees[4] in superstition not only an error, a wrong judgment of the mind, but that worse thing a 'wrong judgment inflamed by passion.' Atheism is a cold error, a mere dislocation of the mind: superstition is a 'dislocation complicated, inflamed,

[1] Sext. Empir. *adv. Math.* IX. 123.

[2] *The Characters of Theophrastus*, p. 264.

[3] Arist. *Polit.* p. 1315 a 1.

[4] Plut. *de Superstit.* I.

by a bruise.' 'Atheism is an apathy towards the divine which fails to perceive the good: superstition is an excess of passion which suspects the good to be evil; the superstitious are afraid of the gods yet fly to them for refuge, flatter and yet revile them, invoke them and yet heap blame upon them.'

Superstition grieved Plutarch in two ways. He saw that it terrified men and made them miserable, and he wanted all men to be as cheerful and kindly as himself; it also made men think evil of the gods, fear them as harsh and cruel. He knew that the canonical religion of the poets was an adequate basis for superstitious fear, but he had made for himself a way out of the difficulty, a way he explains in his treatise on 'How the poets ought to be taken.' 'If Ares be evil spoken of we must imagine it to be said of War, if Hephaistos of Fire, if Zeus of Fate, but if anything honourable it is said of the real gods[1].' Plutarch was too gentle to say sharply and frankly:

> 'If gods do aught that's shameful, they are no gods[2],'

but he shifted the element of evil, of fear and hate, from his theological ideals to the natural and purely human phenomena from which they had emerged. He wants to treat the gods and regard them as he himself would be treated and regarded, as kindly civilized men. 'What!' he says[3], 'is he who thinks there are no gods an impious man, while he who describes them as the superstitious man does, does he not hold views much more impious? Well anyhow I for my part would rather people would say of me there never was or is any such a man as Plutarch, than that they should say Plutarch is an unstable, changeable fellow, irritable. vindictive, and touchy about trifles; if you invite friends to dinner and leave out Plutarch, or if you are busy and omit to call on him, or if you do not stop to speak to him, he will fasten on you and bite you, or he will catch your child and beat him, or turn his beast loose into your crops and spoil your harvest.'

But though he is concerned for the reputation of the gods, his chief care and pity are for man. Atheism shuts out a man, he says, from the pleasant things of life. 'These most pleasant things,' he adds[4] in characteristic fashion, 'are festivals and feastings in

[1] Plut. *de aud. poet.* 4.
[2] Eur. frg. 292.
[3] Plut. *de Superstit.* x.
[4] Plut. *de Superstit.* ix.

connection with sacred things, and initiations and orgiastic festivals, and invocations and adorations of the gods. At these most pleasant things the atheist can but laugh his sardonic laugh, but the superstitious man would fain rejoice and cannot, his soul is like the city of Thebes:

> "It brims with incense and burnt sacrifice
> And brims with paeans and with lamentations."

A garland is on his head and pallor on his face, he offers sacrifice and is afraid, he prays and yet his tongue falters, he offers incense and his hand trembles, he turns the saying of Pythagoras into foolishness: "Then we become best when we approach the gods, for those who fear spirits when they approach the shrines and dwellings of the gods make as though they came to the dens of bears and the holes of snakes and the lairs of sea-monsters."' In his protest against the religion of fear Plutarch rises to a real eloquence[1]. 'He that dreads the gods dreads all things, earth and sea, air and heaven, darkness and light, a voice, a silence, a dream. Slaves forget their masters in sleep, sleep looses their fetters, salves their gangrened sores, but for the superstitious man his reason is always adreaming but his fear always awake.'

Plutarch is by temperament, and perhaps also by the decadent time in which he lived, unable to see the good side of the religion of fear, unable to realize that in it was implicit a real truth, the consciousness that all is not well with the world, that there is such a thing as evil. Tinged with Orphism as he was, he took it by its gentle side and never realized that it was this religion of fear, of consciousness of evil and sin and the need of purification, of which Orphism took hold and which it transformed to new issues. The cheerful religion of 'tendance' had in it no seeds of spiritual development; by Plutarch's time, though he failed to see this, it had done its work for civilization.

Still less could Plutarch realize that what in his mind was a degradation, superstition in our sense, had been to his predecessors a vital reality, the real gist of their only possible religion. He deprecates the attitude of the superstitious man who enters the presence of his gods as though he were approaching the hole of a snake, and forgets that the hole of a snake had been to his ancestors,

[1] Plut. *de Superstit.* III.

and indeed was still to many of his contemporaries, literally and actually the sanctuary of a god. He has explained and mysticized away all the primitive realities of his own beloved religion. It can, I think, be shown that what Plutarch regards as superstition was in the sixth and even the fifth century before the Christian era the *real* religion of the main bulk of the people, a religion not of cheerful tendance but of fear and deprecation. The formula of that religion was not *do ut des* 'I give that you may give,' but *do ut abeas* 'I give that you may go, and keep away.' The beings worshipped were not rational, human, law-abiding *gods*, but vague, irrational, mainly malevolent *δαίμονες*, spirit-things, ghosts and bogeys and the like, not yet formulated and enclosed into god-head. The word *δεισιδαιμονία* tells its own tale, but the thing itself was born long before it was baptized.

Arguments drawn from the use of the word *δεισιδαιμονία* by particular authors are of necessity vague and somewhat unsatisfactory; the use of the word depends much on the attitude of mind of the writer. Xenophon[1] for example uses *δεισιδαιμονία* in a good sense, as of a bracing confidence rather than a degrading fear. 'The more men are god-fearing, spirit-fearing (*δεισιδαίμονες*), the less do they fear man.' It would be impossible to deduce from such a statement anything as to the existence of a lower and more 'fearful' stratum of religion.

Fortunately however we have evidence, drawn not from the terminology of religion, but from the certain facts of ritual, evidence which shows beyond the possibility of doubt that the Greeks of the classical period recognised two different classes of rites, one of the nature of 'service' addressed to the Olympians, the other of the nature of 'riddance' or 'aversion' addressed to an order of beings wholly alien. It is this second class of rites which haunts the mind of Plutarch in his protest against the 'fear of spirits'; it is to this second class of rites that the 'Superstitious Man' of Theophrastos was unduly addicted; and this second class of rites, which we are apt to regard as merely decadent, superstitious, and as such unworthy of more than a passing notice and condemnation, is primitive and lies at the very root and base of Greek religion.

[1] Xen. *Cyropaed.* III. 3. 58.

First it must clearly be established that the Greeks themselves recognised two diverse elements in the ritual of their state. The evidence of the orator Isocrates[1] on this point is indefeasible. He is extolling the mildness and humanity of the Greeks. In this respect they are, he points out, 'like the better sort of gods.' 'Some of the gods are mild and humane, others harsh and unpleasant.' He then goes on to make a significant statement: '*Those of the gods who are the source to us of good things have the title of Olympians, those whose department is that of calamities and punishments have harsher titles; to the first class both private persons and states erect altars and temples, the second is not worshipped either with prayers or burnt-sacrifices, but in their case we perform ceremonies of riddance.*' Had Isocrates commented merely on the *titles* of the gods, we might fairly have said that these titles only represent diverse aspects of the same divinities, that Zeus who is Maimaktes, the Raging One, is also Meilichios, Easy-to-be-entreated, a god of vengeance and a god of love. But happily Isocrates is more explicit; he states that the two classes of gods have not only diverse natures but definitely *different rituals*, and that these rituals not only vary for the individual but are also different by the definite prescription of the state. The ritual of the gods called Olympian is of burnt-sacrifice and prayer, it is conducted in temples and on altars: the ritual of the other class has neither burnt-sacrifice nor prayer nor, it would seem, temple or altar, but consists in ceremonies apparently familiar to the Greek under the name of *ἀποπομπαί*, 'sendings away.'

For *ἀποπομπαί* the English language has no convenient word. Our religion still countenances the fear of the supernatural, but we have outgrown the stage in which we perform definite ceremonies to rid ourselves of the gods. Our nearest equivalent to *ἀποπομπαί* is 'exorcisms,' but as the word has connotations of magic and degraded superstition I prefer to use the somewhat awkward term 'ceremonies of riddance.'

Plato more than once refers to these ceremonies of riddance. In the *Laws*[2] he bids the citizen, if some prompting intolerably

[1] Isocr. *Or.* v. 117.

[2] Plat. *Legg.* 854 B *ἴθι ἐπὶ τὰς ἀποδιοπομπήσεις, ἴθι ἐπὶ θεῶν ἀποτροπαίων ἱερὰ ἱκέτης...τὰς δὲ τῶν κακῶν ξυνουσίας φεῦγε ἀμεταστρεπτί.*

base occur to his mind, as e.g. the desire to commit sacrilege, 'betake yourself to ceremonies of riddance, go as suppliant to the shrines of the gods of aversion, fly from the company of wicked men without turning back.' The reference to a peculiar set of rites presided over by special gods is clear. These gods were variously called *ἀποτρόπαιοι* and *ἀποπομπαῖοι*, the gods of Aversion and of Sending-away.

Harpocration[1] tells us that Apollodorus devoted the sixth book of his treatise *Concerning the gods* to the discussion of the *θεοὶ ἀποπομπαῖοι*, the gods of Sending-away. The loss of this treatise is a grave one for the history of ritual, but scattered notices enable us to see in broad outline what the character of these gods of Aversion was. Pausanias[2] at Titane saw an altar, and in front of it a barrow erected to the hero Epopeus, and 'near to the tomb,' he says, 'are the gods of Aversion, beside whom are performed the ceremonies which the Greeks observe for the averting of evils.' Here it is at least probable, though from the vagueness of the statement of Pausanias not certain, that the ceremonies were of an underworld character such as it will be seen were performed at the graves of heroes. The gods of Aversion by the time of Pausanias, and probably long before, were regarded as gods who presided over the aversion of evil; there is little doubt that to begin with these gods were the very evil men sought to avert. The domain of the spirits of the underworld was confined to things evil. Babrius[3] tells us that in the courtyard of a pious man there was a precinct of a hero, and the pious man was wont to sacrifice and pour libations to the hero, and pray to him for a return for his hospitality. But the ghost of the dead hero knew better; only the regular Olympians are the givers of good, his province as a hero was limited to evil only. He appeared in the middle of the night and expounded to the pious man this truly Olympian theology:

> 'Good Sir, no hero may give aught of good;
> For *that* pray to the gods. We are the givers
> Of all things evil that exist for men.'

It will be seen, when we come to the subject of hero-worship, that this is a very one-sided view of the activity of heroes. Still it remains, broadly speaking, true that dead men and the powers of the underworld were the objects of fear rather than love, their cult was of 'aversion' rather than 'tendance.'

[1] Harpocrat. s.v. ἀποπομπάς. [2] P. II. 11. 1. [3] Babr. *Fab.* 63.

A like distinction is drawn by Hippocrates[1] between the attributes, spheres, and ritual of Olympian and chthonic divinities. He says: 'we ought to pray to the gods, for good things to Helios, to Zeus Ouranios, to Zeus Ktesias, to Athene Ktesia, to Hermes, to Apollo; but in the case of things that are the reverse we must pray to Earth and the heroes, that all hostile things may be averted.'

It is clear then that Greek religion contained two diverse, even opposite, factors: on the one hand the element of *service* (*θεραπεία*), on the other the element of *aversion*[2] (*ἀποτροπή*). The rites of *service* were connected by ancient tradition with the Olympians, or as they are sometimes called the Ouranians: the rites of *aversion* with ghosts, heroes, underworld divinities. The rites of service were of a cheerful and rational character, the rites of aversion gloomy and tending to superstition. The particular characteristics of each set of rites will be discussed more in detail later; for the present it is sufficient to have established the fact that Greek religion for all its superficial serenity had within it and beneath it elements of a darker and deeper significance.

So far we have been content with the general statements of Greek writers as to the nature of their national religion, and the evidence of these writers has been remarkably clear. But, in order to form any really just estimate, it is necessary to examine in detail the actual ritual of some at least of the national festivals. To such an examination the next three chapters will be devoted.

The main result of such an examination, a result which for clearness' sake may be stated at the outset, is surprising. We shall find a series of festivals which are nominally connected with, or as the handbooks say, 'celebrated in honour of' various Olympians; the Diasia in honour of Zeus, the Thargelia of Apollo and Artemis, the Anthesteria of Dionysos. The service of these Olympians we should expect to be of the nature of joyous 'tendance.' To our surprise, when the actual rites are examined,

[1] Hippocr. *περὶ ἐνυπνίων* 639, *ἐπὶ δὲ τοῖσιν ἐναντίοισιν καὶ γῇ καὶ ἥρωσιν ἀποτρόπαια γενέσθαι τὰ χαλεπὰ πάντα.*

[2] English has no convenient equivalent for *ἀποτροπή*, which may mean either turning ourselves away from the thing or turning the thing away from us. *Aversion*, which for lack of a better word I have been obliged to adopt, has too much personal and no ritual connotation. Exorcism is nearer, but too limited and explicit. Dr Oldenberg in apparent unconsciousness of *θεραπεία* and *ἀποτροπή* uses in conjunction the two words Cultus and Abwehr. To his book, *Die Religion des Veda*, though he hardly touches on Greek matters, I owe much.

we shall find that they have little or nothing to do with the particular Olympian to whom they are supposed to be addressed: that they are not in the main rites of burnt-sacrifice, of joy and feasting and agonistic contests, but rites of a gloomy underworld character, connected mainly with purification and the worship of ghosts. The conclusion is almost forced upon us that we have here a theological stratification, that the rites of the Olympians have been superimposed on another order of worship. The constrast between the two classes of rites is so marked, so sharp, that the unbroken development from one to the other is felt to be almost impossible.

To make this clear, before we examine a series of festivals in regular calendar order, one typical case will be taken, the Diasia, the supposed festival of Zeus; and to make the argument intelligible, before the Diasia is examined, a word must be said as to the regular ritual of this particular Olympian. The ritual of the several Olympian deities does not vary in essentials; an instance of sacrifice to Zeus is selected because we are about to examine the Diasia, a festival of Zeus, and thereby uniformity is secured.

Agamemnon[1], beguiled by Zeus in a dream, is about to go forth to battle. Zeus intends to play him false, but all the same he accepts the sacrifice. It is a clear instance of *do ut des*.

The first act is of prayer and the scattering of barley grains; the victim, a bull, is present but not yet slain:

'They gathered round the bull and straight the barley grain did take,
And 'mid them Agamemnon stood and prayed, and thus he spake:
O Zeus most great, most glorious, Thou who dwellest in the sky
And storm-black cloud, oh grant the dark of evening come not nigh
At sunset ere I blast the house of Priam to black ash,
And burn his doorways with fierce fire, and with my sword-blade gash
His doublet upon Hector's breast, his comrades many a one
Grant that they bite the dust of earth ere yet the day be done.'

Next follows the slaying and elaborate carving of the bull for the banquet of gods and men:

'When they had scattered barley grain and thus their prayer had made,
The bull's head backward drew they, and slew him, and they flayed
His body and cut slices from the thighs, and these in fat
They wrapped and made a double fold, and gobbets raw thereat
They laid and these they burnt straightway with leafless billets dry
And held the spitted vitals Hephaistos' flame anigh
The thighs they burnt; the spitted vitals next they taste, anon
The rest they slice and heedfully they roast till all is done—
When they had rested from their task and all the banquet dight,
They feasted, in their hearts no stint of feasting and delight.'

[1] Hom. *Il.* II. 421.

Dr Leaf[1] observes on the passage: 'The significance of the various acts of the sacrifice evidently refers to a supposed invitation to the gods to take part in a banquet. Barley meal is scattered on the victim's head that the gods may share in the fruits of the earth as well as in the meat. Slices from the thigh as the best part are wrapped in fat to make them burn and thus ascend in sweet savour to heaven. The sacrificers after roasting the vitals taste them as a symbolical sign that they are actually eating with the gods. When this religious act has been done, the rest of the victim is consumed as a merely human meal.'

Nothing could be simpler, clearer. There is no mystic communion, no eating of the body of the god incarnate in the victim, no awful taboo upon what has been offered to, made over to, the gods, no holocaust. Homer knows of victims slain to revive by their blood the ghosts of those below, knows of victims on which oaths have been taken and which are utterly consumed and abolished, but the normal service of the Olympians is a *meal shared*. The gods are as Plato[2] would say 'fellow guests' with man. The god is Ouranios, so his share is burnt, and the object of the burning is manifestly sublimation not destruction.

With the burnt-sacrifice and the joyous banquet in our minds we turn to the supposed festival of Zeus at Athens and mark the contrast, a contrast it will be seen so great that it compels us to suppose that the ritual of the festival of the Diasia had primarily nothing whatever to do with the worship of Olympian Zeus.

THE DIASIA.

Our investigation begins with a festival which at first sight seems of all others for our purpose most unpromising, the Diasia[3]. Pollux, in his chapter[4] on 'Festivals which take their names from the divinities worshipped,' cites the Diasia as an instance—'the

[1] *Companion to the Iliad*, p. 77. I have advisedly translated οὐλοχύται by barley *grain*, not meal, because I believe the οὐλοχύται to be a primitive survival of the custom of offering actual grain, but this disputed question is here irrelevant. I follow Dr H. von Fritze, *Hermes* XXXII. 1897, p. 236.

[2] *Legg.* 653 ξυνεορταστάς.

[3] The sources for the Diasia are all collected in the useful and so far as I am aware complete work, Oskar Band, *Die Attischen Diasien—ein Beitrag zur Griechischen Heortologie*, Wissenschaftliche Beilage zum Programm der Victoriaschule, Ostern 1883 (Berlin). Many of the more important sources are easily accessible in Mr Farnell's *Cults of the Greek States*, vol. I. pp. 171, 172. Mr Farnell regards Zeus Meilichios as merely a form of the Olympian Zeus, not as a *contaminatio* of two primarily distinct religious conceptions.

[4] *On.* I. 37.

Mouseia are from the Muses, the Hermaia from Hermes, the Diasia and Pandia from Zeus (Διός), the Panathenaia from Athene.' What could be clearer? It is true that the modern philologist observes what naturally escaped the attention of Pollux, i.e. that the *i* in Diasia is long, that in Διός short, but what is the quantity of a vowel as against the accredited worship of an Olympian?

To the question of derivation it will be necessary to return later, the nature of the cult must first be examined. Again at the outset facts seem against us. It must frankly be owned that as early as the middle of the seventh century B.C. in common as well as professional parlance, the Diasia was a festival of Zeus, of Zeus with the title Meilichios.

Our first notice of the Diasia comes to us in a bit of religious history as amusing as it is instructive, the story of the unworthy trick played by the Delphic oracle on Cylon. Thucydides[1] tells how Cylon took counsel of the oracle how he might seize the Acropolis, and the priestess made answer that he should attempt it 'on the greatest festival of Zeus.' Cylon never doubted that 'the greatest festival of Zeus' was the Olympian festival, and having been (B.C. 640) an Olympian victor himself, he felt that there was about the oracle 'a certain appropriateness.' But in fine oracular fashion the god had laid a trap for the unwary egotist, intending all the while not the Olympian festival but the Attic Diasia, 'for,' Thucydides explains, 'the Athenians too have what is called the Diasia, the greatest festival of Zeus, of Zeus Meilichios.' The passage is of paramount importance because it shows clearly that the obscurity lay in the intentional omission by the priestess of the cultus epithet Meilichios, and in that epithet as will be presently seen lies the whole significance of the cult. Had Zeus *Meilichios* been named no normal Athenian would have blundered.

Thucydides goes on to note some particulars of the ritual of the Diasia; the ceremonies took place outside the citadel, sacrifices were offered by the whole people collectively, and many

[1] Thucyd. I. 126 *ἔστι γὰρ καὶ 'Αθηναίοις Διάσια ἃ καλεῖται Διὸς ἑορτὴ Μειλιχίου μεγίστη, ἔξω τῆς πόλεως ἐν ᾗ πανδημεὶ θύουσι πολλὰ οὐχ ἱερεῖα ἀλλ' · ἁγνὰ · θύματα ἐπιχώρια.*

Schol. ad loc. *θύματα· τινὰ πέμματα εἰς ζῴων μορφὰς τετυπωμένα ἔθυον.*

of those who sacrificed offered not animal sacrifices but offerings in accordance with local custom. The word *ἱερεῖα*, the regular ritual term for *animal* sacrifices, is here opposed to *θύματα ἐπιχώρια*, local sacrifices. But for the Scholiast the meaning of 'local sacrifices' would have remained dubious; he explains, and no doubt rightly, that these customary 'local sacrifices' were cakes made in the shape of animals. The principle *in sacris simulata pro veris accipi* was and is still of wide application, and as there is nothing in it specially characteristic of the Diasia it need not be further exemplified.

Two notices of the Diasia in the *Clouds* of Aristophanes[1] yield nothing. The fact that Strepsiades bought a little cart at the Diasia for his boy or even cooked a sausage for his relations is of no significance. Wherever any sort of religious ceremony goes on, there among primitive peoples a fair will be set up and outlying relations will come in and must be fed, nor does it concern us to decide whether the cart bought by Strepsiades was a real cart or as the Scholiast suggests a cake-cart. Cakes in every conceivable form belong to the common fund of *quod semper quod ubique*. Of capital importance however is the notice of the Scholiast on line 408 where the exact date of the Diasia is given. It was celebrated on the 8th day of the last decade of the month Anthesterion—i.e. about the 14th of March. The Diasia was a Spring festival and therein as will be shown later (p. 52) lies its true significance.

From Lucian we learn that by his time the Diasia had fallen somewhat into abeyance; in the *Icaro-Menippos* Zeus complains that his altars are as cold as the syllogisms of Chrysippos. Worn out old god as he was, men thought it sufficient if they sacrificed every six years at Olympia. 'Why is it,' he asks ruefully, 'that for so many years the Athenians have left out the Diasia?' It is significant that here again, as in the case of Cylon, the Olympian Zeus has tended to efface from men's mind the ritual of him who bore the title Meilichios. The Scholiast[2] feels that some explanation of an obsolete festival is desirable, and explains: 'the Diasia, a festival at Athens, which they keep with a certain element of

[1] *vv.* 864 and 408.

[2] Luc. *Icaro-Menip.* 24 schol. ad loc. *Διάσια ἑορτὴ Ἀθήνησιν, ἣν ἐπετέλουν μετά τινος στυγνότητος, θύοντες ἐν αὐτῇ Διὶ Μειλιχίῳ.*

chilly gloom (*στυγνότης*), offering sacrifices to Zeus Meilichios.' This 'chilly gloom' arrests attention at once. What has Zeus of the high heaven, of the upper air, to do with 'chilly gloom,' with things abhorrent and abominable? Styx is the chill cold water of death, Hades and the Erinyes are 'chilly ones' (*στυγεροί*), the epithet is utterly aloof from Zeus. The Scholiast implies that the 'chilly gloom' comes in from the sacrifice to Zeus *Meilichios*. Zeus *quâ* Zeus gives no clue, it remains to examine the title Meilichios.

Xenophon in returning from his Asiatic expedition was hindered, we are told[1], by lack of funds. He piously consulted a religious specialist and was informed that 'Zeus Meilichios' stood in his way and that he must sacrifice to the god as he was wont to do at home. Accordingly on the following day Xenophon 'sacrificed and offered a holocaust of pigs in accordance with ancestral custom and the omens were favourable.'

The regular ancestral ritual to Zeus Meilichios was a holocaust of pigs, and the god himself was regarded as a source of wealth, a sort of Ploutos. Taken by itself this last point could not be pressed, as probably by Xenophon's time men would pray to Zeus pure and simple for anything and everything; taken in conjunction with the holocaust and the title Meilichios, the fact, it will presently be seen, is significant. There is of course nothing to prove that Xenophon sacrificed at the time of the Diasia, though this is possible; we are concerned now with the cult of Zeus Meilichios in general, not with the particular festival of the Diasia. It may be noted that the Scholiast, on the passage of Thucydides already discussed, says that the 'animal sacrifices' at the Diasia were *πρόβατα*, a word usually rendered 'sheep'; but if he is basing his statement on any earlier authority *πρόβατα* may quite well have meant pig or any four-legged household animal; the meaning of the word was only gradually narrowed down to 'sheep.'

It may be said once for all that the exact animal sacrificed is not of the first importance in determining the nature of the god. Pigs came to be associated with Demeter and the underworld

[1] Xen. *Anab.* VII. 8. 4 *τῇ δὲ ὑστεραίᾳ ὁ Ξενοφῶν...ἐθύετο καὶ ὡλοκαύτει χοίρους τῷ πατρῴῳ νόμῳ καὶ ἐκαλλιέρει.* The incident probably took place in February, the month of the Diasia. See Mr H. G. Dakyns, *Xen.* vol. I. p. 315.

divinities, but that is because these divinities belong to a primitive stratum, and the pig then as now was cheap to rear and a standby to the poor. The animal sacrificed is significant of the *status* of the worshipper rather than of the content of the god. The argument from the pig must not be pressed, though undoubtedly the cheap pig as a sacrifice to Zeus is exceptional.

The manner of the sacrifice, not the material, is the real clue to the significance of the title Meilichios. Zeus as Meilichios demanded a holocaust, a whole burnt-offering. The Zeus of Homer demanded and received the tit-bits of the victim, though even these in token of friendly communion were shared by the worshippers. Such was the custom of the Ouranioi, the Olympians in general. Zeus Meilichios will have all or nothing. His sacrifice is not a happy common feast, it is a dread renunciation to a dreadful power; hence the atmosphere of 'chilly gloom.' It will later be seen that these *un*-eaten sacrifices are characteristic of angry ghosts demanding placation and of a whole class of underworld divinities in general, divinities who belong to a stratum of thought more primitive than Homer. For the present it is enough to mark that the service of Zeus Meilichios is wholly alien to that of the Zeus of Homer. The next passage makes still clearer the nature of this service.

Most fortunately for us Pausanias, when at Myonia in Locris, visited[1] a sanctuary, not indeed of Zeus Meilichios, but of 'the Meilichians.' He saw there no temple, only a grove and an altar, and he learnt the nature of the ritual. 'The sacrifices to "the Meilichians" are at night-time and it is customary to consume the flesh on the spot before the sun is up.' Here is no question of Zeus; we have independent divinities worshipped on their own account and with nocturnal ceremonies. The suspicion begins to take shape that Zeus must have taken over the worship of these dread Meilichian divinities with its nocturnal ceremonial. The suspicion is confirmed when we find that Zeus Meilichios is, like the Erinyes, the avenger of kindred blood. Pausanias[2] saw near the Kephissos 'an ancient altar of Zeus Meilichios; on it Theseus received purification from the descendants of Phytalos after he had slain among other robbers Sinis who was related to himself through Pittheus.'

[1] P. x. 38. 8. [2] P. I. 37. 4.

Again Pausanias[1] tells us that, after an internecine fray, the Argives took measures to purify themselves from the guilt of kindred blood, and one measure was that they set up an image of Zeus Meilichios. Meilichios, Easy-to-be-entreated, the Gentle, the Gracious One, is naturally the divinity of purification, but he is also naturally the other euphemistic face of *Maimaktes*, he who rages eager, panting and thirsting for blood. This Hesychius[2] tells us in an instructive gloss. Maimaktes-Meilichios is double-faced like the Erinyes-Eumenides. Such undoubtedly would have been the explanation of the worship of Zeus Meilichios by any educated Greek of the fifth century B.C. with his monotheistic tendencies. Zeus he would have said is all in all, Zeus Meilichios is Zeus in his underworld aspect—Zeus-Hades.

Pausanias[3] saw at Corinth three images of Zeus, all under the open sky. One he says had no title, another was called He of the underworld (χθόνιος), the third The Highest. What earlier cults this triple Zeus had absorbed into himself it is impossible to say.

Such a determined monotheism is obviously no primitive conception, and it is interesting to ask on what facts and fusion of facts it was primarily based. Happily where literature and even ritual leave us with suspicions only, art compels a clearer definition.

The two reliefs in figs. 1 and 2 were found at the Peiraeus and are now in the Berlin Museum[4]. From the inscription on the relief in fig. 1 and from numerous other inscribed reliefs found with it, it is practically certain that at the place in which they were found Zeus Meilichios was worshipped. In any case the relief in fig. 1 is clearly dedicated to him. Above the splendid coiled beast is plainly inscribed 'to Zeus Meilichios'

[1] P. II. 20. 1. [2] Hesych. s.v. Μαιμάκτης· μειλίχιος, καθάρσιος.

[3] P. II. 2. 8.

[4] Permission to republish the two reliefs figured here and that in fig. 5 has been courteously granted me by Professor Kekulé von Stradowitz, Director of the Berlin Museum, and I owe to his kindness the excellent photographs from which the reproductions are made. From the official catalogue (*Beschreibung der Antiken Skulpturen in Berlin*) I quote the following particulars as to material, provenance &c.

1. *Cat.* 722, H. 0·58, Br. 0·31. Hymettus marble found with No. 723 at the Zea harbour not far from Ziller's house. Taken to Berlin 1879. Inscribed ΔΙΙ ΜΕΙΛΙΧΙΩΙ. Date fourth century B.C., see *C.I.A.* II. 3, 1581, cf. *C.I.A.* II. 3. 1578, 1582, 1583.

2. *Cat.* 723, material, provenance, date, same as 722.

(Διὶ Μειλιχίῳ). We are brought face to face with the astounding fact that Zeus, father of gods and men, is figured by his worshippers as a snake.

So astonishing is the inscription that M. Foucart[1], who first discussed these reliefs, suggested that in Zeus Meilichios we have merely a Hellenic rendering of a Phenician divinity, Baal Melek or Moloch. The worship of such a divinity would be well in place at the harbour of Munychia, and as M. Foucart points out, the names of the dedicators lack the demotic. Unfortunately for this interesting theory we have no evidence that 'Moloch' was ever worshipped in snake form. Another way out of the difficulty was sought; the snake it was suggested was, not the god himself, but his attribute. But this solution does not square with facts. Zeus is one of the few Greek gods who never appear attended by a snake. Asklepios, Hermes, Apollo, even Demeter and Athene have their snakes,

FIG. 1.

[1] *Bull. de Corr. Hell.* VII. p. 507. I regret that in the first edition of my book I treated M. Foucart's theory with, I fear, scant ceremony. The possibility of a *contaminatio* between the Phenician Baal and Zeus Meilichios cannot be lightly dismissed. For a discussion of the subject see especially Clermont-Ganneau, *Le dieu Satrape*, p. 65, on the river Meilichos at Patrae, and Lagrange, *Etudes sur les Religions Sémitiques*, p. 105. But until evidence is forthcoming of the snake-form of Moloch it is simpler to see in the snake Meilichios an indigenous snake demon of the under world.

Zeus never. Moreover when the god developed from snake form to human form, as, it will later be shown, was the case with Asklepios, *the snake he once was* remains coiled about his staff or attendant at his throne. In the case of Zeus Meilichios in human form *the snake he once was not* disappears clean and clear.

The explanation of the snake as merely an attribute is indeed impossible to any unbiassed critic who looks at the relief in fig. 2. Here clearly the snake is the object worshipped by the woman and two men who approach with gestures of adoration. The colossal size of the beast as it towers above its human adorers is the *Magnificat* of the artist echoed by the worshippers. When we confront the relief in fig. 3, also found at the Peiraeus, with those in figs. 1 and 2, the secret is out at last. In fig. 3 a man followed by a woman and child approaches an altar, behind which is seated a bearded god holding a sceptre and patera for libation. Above is clearly inscribed 'Aristarche to Zeus Meilichios' (Ἀριστάρχη Διὶ Μειλιχίῳ). And the truth is nothing more or less than this. The human-shaped Zeus has slipped himself quietly into the place of the old snake-god. Art sets plainly forth what has been dimly shadowed in ritual and mythology. It is not that Zeus the Olympian has 'an underworld aspect': it is the cruder fact that he of the upper air, of the thunder and lightning, extrudes an ancient serpent-demon of the lower world, Meilichios. Meilichios is no foreign Moloch, he is home-grown, autochthonous before the formulation of Zeus.

Fig. 2.

How the shift may have been effected art again helps us to

FIG. 3.

conjecture. In the same sanctuary at the Peiraeus that yielded the reliefs in figs. 1 and 2 was found the inscribed relief[1] in fig. 4. We have a similar bearded snake and above is inscribed 'Heracleides to the god.' The worshipper is not fencing, uncertain whether he means Meilichios or Zeus; he brings his offering to the local precinct where the god is a snake and dedicates it to *the* god, the god of that precinct. It is not monotheism, rather it is parochialism, but it is a conception tending towards a later monotheism. When and where the snake is simply 'the god,' the fusion with Zeus is made easy.

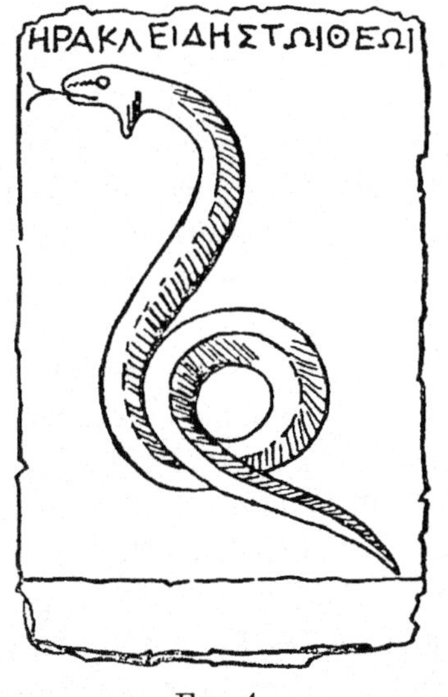

FIG. 4.

In fig. 5 is figured advisedly a monument of snake worship, which it must be distinctly noted comes, not from the precinct of Zeus Meilichios at the Peiraeus, but from Eteonos in Boeotia. When we come to the discussion of hero-worship, it will be seen that all over Greece the dead hero was worshipped in snake form

[1] *Bull. de Corr. Hell.* 1883, p. 510.

and addressed by euphemistic titles akin to that of Meilichios. The relief from Boeotia is a good instance of such worship and is

Fig. 5.

chosen because of the striking parallelism of its art type with that of the Peiraeus relief in fig. 3. The maker of this class of votive reliefs seems to have kept in stock designs of groups of pious worshippers which he could modify as required and to which the necessary god or snake and the appropriate victim could easily be appended. Midway in conception between the Olympian Zeus with his sceptre and the snake demon stands another relief[1] (fig. 6), also from the Peiraeus sanctuary. Meilichios is human, a snake no longer, but he is an earth god, he bears the cornucopia[2], his victim is the pig. He is that Meilichios to whom Xenophon offered the holocaust of pigs, praying for wealth; he is also the Zeus-Hades of Euripides. We might have been tempted to call him simply Hades or Ploutos but for the inscription [Κριτο]βόλη Διὶ Μειλιχίῳ, 'Kritoboule to Zeus Meilichios,' which makes the dedication certain.

By the light then of these reliefs the duality, the inner discrepancy of Zeus Meilichios admits of a simple and straightforward solution. It is the monument of a superposition of cults.

[1] From a photograph (Peiraeus 12) published by kind permission of the German Archaeological Institute, see *Eph. Arch.* 1886, p. 47.

[2] The cornucopia would be a natural attribute for Zeus Ktesios who Dr Martin Nilsson kindly tells me appears in snake form (inscribed) on a votive relief in the local Museum at Thebes.

But the difficulty of the name of the festival, *Diasia*, remains. There is no reason to suppose that the name was given late; and, if primitive, how can we sever it from Διός?

Fig. 6.

It is interesting to note that the ancients themselves were not quite at ease in deriving Diasia from Διός. Naturally they were not troubled by difficulties as to long and short vowels, but they had their misgivings as to the connotation of the word, and they try round uneasily for etymologies of quite other significance. The Scholiast on Lucian's *Timon*[1] says the word is probably derived from διασαίνειν 'to fawn on,' 'to propitiate.' Suidas[2] says it comes from διαφυγεῖν αὐτοὺς εὐχαῖς τὰς ἄσας, because in the Diasia 'men escaped from curses by prayers.' If etymologically absurd, certainly, as will be seen, a happy guess.

Such derivations are of course only worth citing to show that even in ancient minds as regards the derivation of Diasia from Διός misgiving lurked.

The misgiving is emphasized by the modern philologist. The derivation of Diasia with its long from Διός with its short *i* is scientifically improbable if not impossible. Happily another derivation that at least satisfies scientific conditions has been suggested by Mr R. A. Neil. Not only does it satisfy scientific conditions but it also confirms the view arrived at by independent

[1] Lucian, *Tim.* c. 7. [2] Suidas s.v. Διάσια.

investigation of the ritual and art representations of Zeus Meilichios. Mr Neil[1] suggests that in several Greek words showing the stem *δῖο* this stem may stand by the regular falling away of the medial *σ* for *δῖσο* and is identical with the Latin *dīro*[2]. *dirus*, he notes, was originally a purely religious word. Such words would be the Dīasia, whatever the termination may be, the *Δῖα* of Teos, and perhaps the *Πάνδια* of Athens. Seen in the light of this new etymology the Diasia becomes intelligible: it is the festival of curses, imprecations; it is nocturnal and associated with rites of placation and purgation, two notions inextricably linked in the minds of the ancients.

We further understand why Meilichios seems the male double of Erinys and why his rites are associated with 'chilly gloom.' The Diasia has primarily and necessarily nothing to do with *Διός*, with Zeus; it has everything to do with 'dirae,' magical curses, exorcisms and the like. The keynote of primitive ritual, it will become increasingly clear, is exorcism.

In the light of this new derivation it is possible further to explain another element in the cult of Zeus Meilichios hitherto purposely left unnoticed, the famous *Διὸς κώδιον*, the supposed 'fleece of Zeus.' The *Διὸς κώδιον* is, I think, no more the fleece of Zeus than the Diasia is his festival.

Polemon, writing at the beginning of the second century B.C., undoubtedly accepted the current derivation, and on the statement of Polemon most of our notices of 'the fleece of Zeus' appear to be based. Hesychius[3] writes thus: 'The fleece of Zeus: they use this expression when the victim has been sacrificed to Zeus, and those who were being purified stood on it with their left foot.

[1] *J.H.S.* xix. p. 114, note 1.

[2] Mr P. Giles kindly tells me that a rare Sanskrit word *dreshas* meaning 'hate' and the like exists and phonetically would nearly correspond to the Latin *dirus*. The corresponding form in Greek would appear as *δειος*, unless in late Greek. But from the end of the fifth century B.C. onwards the pronunciation would be the same as *δῖος*, and if the word survived only in ritual terms it would naturally be confused with *δῖος*. Almost all authorities on Latin however regard the *ru* in *dirus* as a suffix containing an original *r* as in *mirus*, *durus* etc. This view, which would be fatal to the etymology of *dirus* proposed in the text, seems supported by a statement of Servius (if the statement be accurate) on *Aen.* III. 235 'Sabini et Umbri quae nos mala *dira* appellant,' as, though *s* between vowels passes in Latin and Umbrian into *r*, it remains an *s* sound in Sabine.

[3] Hesych. s.v. *ὁ δὲ Πολέμων τὸ ἐκ τοῦ Διὶ τεθυμένου ἱερείου.* From Athenaeus also we learn that Polemon had treated in some detail of the 'fleece of Zeus'; Athenaeus says (XI. p. 478 c), *Πολέμων δ' ἐν τῷ περὶ τοῦ δίου κωδίου φησί*...

Some say it means a great and perfect fleece. But Polemon says it is the fleece of the victim sacrificed to Zeus.

But Polemon is by no means infallible in the matter of etymology, though invaluable as reflecting the current impression of his day. Our conviction that the *Διὸς κώδιον* is necessarily 'the fleece of Zeus' is somewhat loosened when we find that this fleece was by no means confined to the ritual of Zeus, and in so far as it was connected with Zeus, was used in the ritual only of a Zeus who bore the titles Meilichios and Ktesios. Suidas[1] expressly states that 'they sacrifice to Meilichios and to Zeus Ktesios and they keep the fleeces of these (victims) and call them "Dian," and they use them when they send out the procession in the month of Skirophorion, and the Dadouchos at Eleusis uses them, and others use them for purifications by strewing them under the feet of those who are polluted.'

It is abundantly clear that Zeus had no monopoly in the fleece supposed to be his; it was a sacred fleece used for purification ceremonies in general. He himself had taken over the cult of Meilichios, the Placable One, the spirit of purification; we conjecture that he had also taken over the fleece of purification.

Final conviction comes from a passage in the commentary of Eustathius[2] on the purification of the house of Odysseus after the slaying of the suitors. Odysseus purges his house by two things, first after the slaying of the suitors by water, then after the hang-

[1] Suidas s.v. *θύουσί τε τῷ τε Μειλιχίῳ καὶ τῷ Κτησίῳ Διί, τὰ δὲ κώδια τούτων φυλάσσουσι καὶ Δία (δῖα) προσαγορεύονται, χρῶνται δ' αὐτοῖς οἵ τε Σκιροφορίων τὴν πομπὴν στέλλοντες καὶ ὁ δᾳδοῦχος ἐν Ἐλευσῖνι καὶ ἄλλοι τινὲς πρὸς καθαρμοὺς ὑποστορνύντες αὐτὰ τοῖς ποσὶ τῶν ἐναγῶν.* For *Δία* Gaisford conjectures *Διὸς* but from the passage of Eustathius (see infr.) it is clear that we must read *δῖα*.

[2] Eustath. ad *Od.* XXII. 481 § 1934—5 *ἐδόκουν γὰρ οἱ Ἕλληνες οὕτω τὰ τοιαῦτα μύση καθαίρεσθαι διοπομπούμενα. καὶ ἕτεροι μὲν δηλοῦσι τρόπους καθαρσίων ἑτέρους, ἃ καὶ ἐξάγοντες τῶν οἴκων μετὰ τὰς ἐθίμους ἐπαοιδὰς προσέῤῥιπτον ἀμφόδοις ἔμπαλιν τὰ πρόσωπα στρέφοντες καὶ ἐπανιόντες ἀμεταστρεπτί. ὁ δέ γε ποιητικὸς Ὀδυσσεὺς οὐχ οὕτω ποιεῖ ἀλλ' ἑτέρως ἁπλούστερον. φησὶ γοῦν· οἶσε θέειον γρῆυ κακῶν ἄκος...πλέον ποιήσας οὐδέν...θέειον δὲ θυμιάματος εἶδος καθαίρειν δοκοῦντος τοὺς μιασμούς. διὸ καὶ διαστείλας κακῶν ἄκος αὐτό φησιν ὁ ποιητής, οὔτε δέ τινες ἐνταῦθα ἐπῳδαὶ συνήθεις τοῖς παλαιοῖς οὔτε στενωπὸς ἐν ᾧ ἄνθρακες ἀπαγόμενοι αὐτῷ ἀγγείῳ ἐῤῥίπτοντο ὀπισθοφανῶς. ἰστέον δὲ ὅτι οὐ μόνον διὰ θείου ἐγίνοντο καθαρμοὶ καθὰ προσεχῶς ἐγράφη ἀλλὰ καὶ φυτά τινα εἰς τοῦτο χρήσιμα ἦν. ἀριστερεὼν γοῦν, φυτὸν κατὰ Παυσανίαν ἐπιτήδειον εἰς καθαρμόν· καὶ σῦς δὲ εἰς τοιαῦτα, ἐστὶν οὗ, παρελαμβάνετο, ὡς ἐν Ἰλιάδι φαίνεται. καὶ οἱ τὸ διοπομπεῖν δὲ ἑρμηνεύοντές φασιν ὅτι δῖον ἐκάλουν κώδιον ἱερείου τυθέντος Διῒ μειλιχίῳ ἐν τοῖς καθαρμοῖς, φθίνοντος Μαιμακτηριῶνος μηνὸς ὅτε ἤγοντο τὰ πομπαῖα, καὶ καθαρμῶν ἐκβολαὶ εἰς τὰς τριόδους ἐγίνοντο. εἶχον δὲ μετὰ χεῖρας πομπόν· ὅπερ ἦν, φασί, κηρύκιον, σέβας Ἑρμοῦ. καὶ ἐκ τοῦ τοιούτου πομποῦ καὶ τοῦ ῥηθέντος δίου τὸ διοπομπεῖν...ἄλλως δὲ κοινότερον διοπομπεῖν καὶ ἀποδιοπομπεῖν ἐφαίνετο τὸ Διὸς ἀλεξικάκου ἐπικλήσει ἐκπέμπειν τὰ φαῦλα.* Eustathius passes on to speak of purification by blood and the *φαρμακοί*, see p. 95.

ing of the maidens by fire and brimstone. His method of purifying is a simple and natural one, it might be adopted to-day in the disinfecting of a polluted house. This Eustathius notes, and contrasts it with the complex magical apparatus in use among the ancients and very possibly still employed by the pagans of his own day. He comments as follows: 'The Greeks thought such pollutions were purified by being "sent away." Some describe one sort of purifications some others, and these purifications they carried out of houses after the customary incantations and they cast them forth in the streets with averted faces and returned without looking backwards. But the Odysseus of the poet does not act thus, but performs a different and a simpler act, for he says:

> "Bring brimstone, ancient dame, the cure of ills, and bring me fire
> That I the hall may fumigate."'

In the confused fashion of his day and of his own mind Eustathius sees there is a real distinction but does not recognise wherein it lies. He does not see that Homer's purification is actual, physical, rational, not magical. He goes on: 'Brimstone is a sort of incense which is reputed to cleanse pollutions. Hence the poet distinguishes it, calling it "cure of ills." In this passage there are none of the incantations usual among the ancients, nor is there the small vessel in which the live coals were carried and thrown away vessel and all backwards.'

What half occurs to Eustathius and would strike any intelligent modern observer acquainted with ancient ritual is that the purification of the house of Odysseus is as it were scientific; there is none of the apparatus of magical 'riddance.' Dimly and darkly he puts a hesitating finger on the cardinal difference between the religion of Homer and that of later (and earlier) Greece, that Homer is innocent, save for an occasional labelled magician, of magic. The Archbishop seems to feel this as something of a defect, a shortcoming. He goes on: 'It must be understood that purifications were effected not only as has just been described, by means of sulphur, but there are also certain plants that were useful for this purpose; at least according to Pausanias there is verbena, a plant in use for purification, and the pig was sometimes employed for such purposes, as appears in the *Iliad*.' This mention of means of purification in general brings irresistibly to the mind of Eustathius a salient instance, the very fleece we are discussing. He continues: 'Those who interpret the word διοπομπεῖν say that they applied the term δῖον to the fleece of the animal that had been sacrificed to Zeus Meilichios in purifications at the end of the month of Maimakterion[1] when they performed the Sendings and when the castings out of pollutions at the triple ways took place: and they held in their hands a sender which was they say the kerukeion, the attribute of Hermes, and from a sender of this sort, *pompos*, and from the δῖον, the fleece called "Dian," they get the word διοπομπεῖν, divine sending.'

From this crude and tentative etymological guessing two important points emerge. Eustathius does not speak of the 'fleece of Zeus,' but of the *Dian* or perhaps we may translate *divine* fleece. δῖος is with him an adjective to be declined, not the genitive of Ζεύς. This loosens somewhat the connection of the fleece with Zeus, as the adjective δῖος could be used of anything divine or even magical in its wonder and perfection. Further, and this is of supreme importance, he connects the Dian fleece with the difficult word διοπομπεῖν, and in this lies the clue to its real interpretation. 'That this,' he goes on—meaning his derivation of διοπομπεῖν from πομπός the kerukeion of Hermes and δῖον the divine fleece—'is so we find from special investigation, but in more general parlance by διοπομπεῖν and ἀποδιοπομπεῖν is meant the sending away of unclean things in the name of Zeus Averter of Evil.' Eustathius evidently gets nervous; his 'special investigation' is leading him uncomfortably near the real truth, uncomfortably far from the orthodox Zeus, so he pulls himself up instinctively.

The explanation of the strange word ἀποδιοπομπεῖν, to which Eustathius at the close of his remarks piously reverts, is still accredited by modern lexicons. ἀποδιοπομπεῖσθαι—the middle form is the more usual—means, we are told, 'to avert threatened evils by offerings to Zeus[2].' Are scholars really prepared to believe that ἀποδιοπομπεῖσθαι means, to put it shortly, 'to Zeus things away'? The lexicons after this desperate etymology proceed: 'hence, to conjure away, to reject with abhorrence,' and finally, under a heading apart, 'ἀποδιοπομπεῖσθαι οἶκον, to purify a house.' Surely from beginning to end the meaning inherent in the word

[1] Maimaktes, it will be remembered, is the other face of Meilichios, see supra.
[2] See Liddell and Scott, s.v.

is simply 'to rid of pollution'; *ἀποδιοπομπεῖσθαι* is substantially the same as *ἀποπέμπειν*, to send away, to get rid of, but—and this is the important point—the element *διο* emphasizes the means and method of the 'sending.' The quantity of the *ι* in *ἀποδιοπομπεῖσθαι* we have no means of knowing, the *ι* in Diasia the feast of Zeus Meilichios is long, the *ι* in the *δῖον κώδιον* used in his service is long, the *δῖον κώδιον* is used in ritual concerned with *διοπομπούμενα*, its purpose is *ἀποδιοπομπεῖσθαι*. Is it too bold to see in the mysterious *διο* the same root as has been seen in *Diasia* and to understand *ἀποδιοπομπεῖσθαι* as 'to effect riddance by magical imprecation or deprecation'?

The word *dirus* is charged with magic, and this lives on in the Greek word *δῖος* which is more magical than divine. It has that doubleness, for cursing and for blessing, that haunts all inchoate religious terms. The fleece is not divine in our sense, not definitely either for blessing or for cursing; it is taboo, it is 'medicine,' it is magical. As magical medicine it had power to purify, i.e. in the ancient sense, not to cleanse physically or purge morally, but to rid of evil influences, of ghostly infection.

Magical fleeces were of use in ceremonies apparently the most diverse, but at the bottom of each usage lies the same thought, that the skin of the victim has magical efficacy as medicine against impurities. Dicaearchus[1] tells us that at the rising of the dog-star, when the heat was greatest, young men in the flower of their age and of the noblest families went to a cave called the sanctuary of Zeus Aktaios, and also (very significantly it would seem) called the Cheironion; they were girded about with fresh fleeces of triple wool. Dicaearchus says that this was because it was so cold on the mountain; but if so, why must the fleeces be fresh? Zeus Aktaios, it is abundantly clear, has taken over the cave of the old Centaur Cheiron; the magic fleeces, newly slain because all 'medicine' must be fresh, belong to his order as they belonged to the order of Meilichios.

Again we learn that whoever would take counsel of the oracle of Amphiaraos[2] must first purify himself, and Pausanias himself

[1] Dicaearch. *Frg. Hist.* II. 262.

[2] P. I. 34. 2—5. Strabo (VI. p. 284) says that the Daunians when they consulted the oracle of the hero Calchas sacrificed a black ram to him and slept on the fleece. The worshippers of the 'Syrian Goddess,' Lucian says (*De Syr. Dea* 35), knelt on the

adds the explanatory words, 'Sacrificing to the god is a ceremony of purification.' But the purification ceremony did not, it would appear, end with the actual sacrifice, for he explains, 'Having sacrificed a ram they spread the skin beneath them and go to sleep, awaiting the revelation of a dream'; here again, though the name is not used, we have a *δῖον κώδιον*, a magic fleece with purifying properties. It is curious to note that Zeus made an effort to take over the cult of Amphiaraos, as he had taken that of Meilichios; we hear of a Zeus Amphiaraos[1], but the attempt was not a great success; probably the local hero Amphiaraos, himself all but a god, was too strong for the Olympian.

The results of our examination of the festival of the Diasia are then briefly this. The cult of the Olympian Zeus has overlaid the cult of a being called Meilichios, a being who was figured as a snake, who was a sort of Ploutos, but who had also some of the characteristics of an Erinys; he was an avenger of kindred blood, his sacrifice was a holocaust offered by night, his festival a time of 'chilly gloom.' A further element in his cult was a magical fleece used in ceremonies of purification and in the service of heroes. The cult of Meilichios is unlike that of the Olympian Zeus as described in Homer, and the methods of purification characteristic of him wholly alien. The name of his festival means 'the ceremonies of imprecation.'

The next step in our investigation will be to take in order certain well-known Athenian festivals, and examine the ceremonies that actually took place at each. In each case it will be found that, though the several festivals are ostensibly consecrated to various Olympians, and though there is in each an element of prayer and praise and sacrificial feasting such as is familiar to us in Homer, yet, when the ritual is closely examined, the main part of the ceremonies will be seen to be magical rather than what we should term religious. Further, this ritual is addressed, in so far as it is addressed to any one, not to the Olympians of the upper air, but to snakes and ghosts and underworld beings; its

ground and put the feet and the head of the victim on their heads. He probably means that they got inside the skin and wore it with the front paws tied round the neck as Heracles wears the lion-skin.

[1] Dicaearchus I. 6.

main gist is purification, the riddance of evil influences, this riddance being naturally prompted not by cheerful confidence but by an ever imminent fear.

In the pages that follow but little attention will be paid to the familiar rites of the Olympians, the burnt-sacrifice and its attendant feast, the dance and song; our whole attention will be focussed on the rites belonging to the lower stratum. This course is adopted for two reasons. First, the rites of sacrifice as described by Homer are simple and familiar, needing but little elucidation and having already received superabundant commentary, whereas the rites of the lower stratum are often obscure and have met with little attention. Second, it is these rites of purification belonging to the lower stratum, primitive and barbarous, even repulsive as they often are, that furnished ultimately the material out of which 'mysteries' were made—mysteries which, as will be seen, when informed by the new spirit of the religions of Dionysos and Orpheus, lent to Greece its deepest and most enduring religious impulse.

ATTIC CALENDAR.

NOTE. Names of Festivals selected for special discussion are printed in large type. Names of Festivals incidentally discussed in italics.

1.	Hecatombaion	July, August	Kronia, Panathenaia
2.	Metageitnion	Aug., September	Metageitnia
3.	Boedromion	Sept., October	Eleusinia and *Greater Mysteries*
4.	Pyanepsion	Oct., November	THESMOPHORIA. Pyanepsia and Oschophoria [Id. Oct. (Oct. 15) October Horse]
5.	Maimakterion	Nov., December	'Διὸς κῴδιον'
6.	Poseideon	Dec., January	*Haloa*
7.	Gamelion	Jan., February	Gamelia (Lenaia?)
8.	Anthesterion	Feb., March	ANTHESTERIA, DIASIA, *Lesser Mysteries* [xv. Kal. Mart. (Feb. 15) Lupercalia] [(Feb. 21) Feralia]
9.	Elaphebolion	March, April	Dionysia
10.	Munychion	April, May	Munychia, Brauronia
11.	Thargelion	May, June	THARGELIA, *Kallynteria, Plynteria* (May 15 Argei, June 15 Vestalia, Q. St. D. F.)
12.	Skirophorion	June, July	*Skirophoria, Arrephoria*, Dipolia, Bouphonia

The Athenian official calendar began in the month Hecatombaion (July—August) at the summer's height. In it was celebrated the great festival of the Panathenaia, whose very name marks its political import. Such political festivals, however magnificent and socially prominent, it is not my purpose to examine; concerning the gist of primitive religious conceptions they yield us little. The Panathenaia is sacred rather to a city than a goddess. Behind the Panathenaia lay the more elementary festival of the Kronia, which undoubtedly took its name from the faded divinity Kronos; but of the Kronia the details known are not adequate for its fruitful examination.

A cursory glance at the other festivals noted in our list shows that some, though not all, gave their names to the months in which they were celebrated, and (a fact of high significance) shows also that with one exception, the Dionysia, these festivals are not named after Olympian or indeed after any divinities. Metageitnia, the festival of 'changing your neighbours,' is obviously social or political. The Eleusinia are named after a place, so are the Munychia and Brauronia. The Thesmophoria, Oschophoria, Skirophoria and Arrephoria are festivals of *carrying something*; the Anthesteria, Kallynteria, Plynteria festivals of persons who *do something*; the Haloa a festival of *threshing-floors*, the Thargelia of *first-fruits*, the Bouphonia of *ox-slaying*, the Pyanepsia of *bean-cooking*. In the matter of nomenclature the Olympians are much to seek.

The festivals in the table appended are arranged according to the official calendar for convenience of reference, but it should be noted that the agricultural year, on which the festivals primarily depend, begins in the autumn with sowing, i.e. in Pyanepsion. The Greek agricultural year fell into three main divisions, the autumn sowing season followed by the winter, the spring with its first blossoming of fruits and flowers beginning in Anthesterion, and the early summer harvest (ὀπώρα) beginning in Thargelion, the month of first-fruits; to this early harvest of grain and fruits was added with the coming of the vine the vintage in Boedromion, and the gathering in of the later fruits, e.g. the fig. All the festivals fall necessarily much earlier than the dates familiar to us in the North. In Greece to-day the wheat harvest is over by the middle or end of June.

No attempt will be made to examine all the festivals, for two practical reasons, lack of space and lack of material; but fortunately for us we have adequate material for the examination of one characteristic festival in each of the agricultural seasons, the Thesmophoria for autumn, the Anthesteria for spring, the Thargelia for early summer, and in each case the ceremonies of the several seasons can be further elucidated by the examination of the like ceremonies in the Roman calendar. To make clear the superposition of the two strata[1], which for convenience' sake may be called Olympian and chthonic, the Diasia has already been examined. In the typical festivals now to be discussed a like superposition will be made apparent, and from the detailed examination of the lower chthonic stratum it will be possible to determine the main outlines of Greek religious thought on such essential points as e.g. purification and sacrifice.

It would perhaps be more methodical to begin the investigation with the autumn, with the sowing festival of the Thesmophoria, but as the Thesmophoria leads more directly to the consummation of Greek religion in the Mysteries it will be taken last. The reason for this will become more apparent in the further course of the argument. We shall begin with the *Anthesteria*.

[1] As regards the ethnography of these two strata, I accept Prof. Ridgeway's view that the earlier stratum, which I have called chthonic, belongs to the primitive population of the Mediterranean to which he gives the name Pelasgian; the later stratum, to which belongs the manner of sacrifice I have called 'Olympian,' is characteristic of the Achaean population coming from the North. But, as I have no personal competency in the matter of ethnography and as Prof. Ridgeway's second volume is as yet unpublished, I have thought it best to state the argument as it appeared to me independently, i.e. that there are two factors in religion, one primitive, one later. Recent study has led me to feel that these factors are themselves, specially in the case of the primitive stratum, far more complex than I at first thought.

CHAPTER II.

THE ANTHESTERIA.

THE RITUAL OF GHOSTS AND SPIRITS.

OUR examination of the unpromising Diasia has so far led us to the following significant, if somewhat vague, results. The festival in all probability did not originally belong to Zeus, but to a being called Meilichios, a snake god or demon. The worship of this being was characterized by nightly ceremonies, holocausts which the sun might not behold; it was gloomy in character, potent for purification. The name of the festival is probably associated with *dirae*, curses, imprecations.

The Diasia, gloomy though it is, is a spring festival and its significance will be yet more plainly apparent if we examine another, *the* other spring festival of the Greeks, i.e. the Anthesteria, which gives its name to the first spring month Anthesterion.

If we know little about the Diasia, about the Anthesteria[1] we know much. Apollodorus, quoted by Harpocration, tells us that the whole festival collectively was called *Anthesteria*, that it was celebrated in honour of Dionysos, and that its several parts, i.e. its successive days, were known as Pithoigia (cask-opening), Choes (cups), Chytroi (pots). The exact date of the festival is fixed, the three successive days falling from the 11th to the 13th of Anthesterion[2].

[1] The sources for the Anthesteria are collected and discussed in the Lexicons of Pauly-Wissowa and of Daremberg and Saglio and more completely in Dr Martin Nilsson's *Studia de Dionysiis Atticis* (Lundae, 1900), which has been of great service to me.

[2] Harpocrat. s.v.

On the first day, the 11th of Anthesterion, i.e. the Pithoigia, Plutarch[1] tells us 'they broached the new wine at Athens. It was an ancient custom,' he adds, 'to offer some of it as a libation before they drank it, praying at the same time that the use of the drug (φαρμάκου) might be rendered harmless and beneficial to them.' This is a clear case of the offering of first-fruits[2]. Among his own people, the Boeotians, Plutarch adds, 'the day was called the day of the Good Spirit[3], the Agathos Daimon, and to him they made offerings. The month itself was known as Prostaterios.' The scholiast to Hesiod[4] tells us that the festival was an ancestral one (ἐν τοῖς πατρίοις), and that it was not allowable to hinder either household slaves or hired servants from partaking of the wine.

The casks once opened, the revel set in and lasted through the next day (the Choes or Cups) and on through the third (the Chytroi or Pots). The day of the Choes seems to have been the climax, and sometimes gave its name to the whole festival.

It is needless to dwell on all the details of what was in intent a three days' fair. A 'Pardon' in the Brittany of to-day affords perhaps the nearest modern analogy. The children have holidays, fairings are bought, friends are feasted, the sophists get their fees, the servants generally are disorganized, and every one down to the small boys, as many a vase-painting tells us, is more or less drunk. There is a drinking contest presided over by the King Archon, he who first drains his cup gets a cake, each man crowns his cup with a garland and deposits the wreath in keeping of the priestess of the sanctuary of Dionysos in the Marshes. On the day of the *Cups* takes place the august ceremony of the wedding of the wife of the King Archon to the god Dionysos. On that day alone in all the year the temple of Dionysos is opened[5].

On the third day, the *Chytroi* or Pots, there was a dramatic contest[6] known as Χύτρινοι, Pot-contests. During this third day the revel went on; Aristophanes[7] has left us the

[1] Plut. *Q. Symp.* III. 7. 1.
[2] The gist of such offerings will be considered under the *Thargelia*.
[3] Plut. *Q. Symp.* VIII. 3.
[4] *Op.* 368.
[5] Discussed in relation to Dionysos, see infra, Chapter VIII.
[6] See p. 76.
[7] Ar. *Ran.* 212, trans. Mr Gilbert Murray.

picture of the drunken mob thronging the streets at the holy Pot-Feast:

'O brood of the mere and the spring,
Gather together and sing
From the depths of your throat
By the side of the boat
Coäx, as we move in a ring.

As in Limnae we sang the divine
Nyseïan Giver of Wine,
When the people in lots
With their sanctified Pots
Came reeling around my shrine.'

The scholiast on the *Acharnians*[1], a play which gives us a lively picture of the festival, says that the Choes and the Chytroi were celebrated on one day. The different days and acts of the whole Anthesteria were doubtless not sharply divided, and if each day was reckoned from sunrise to sunset confusion would easily arise.

So far a cursory inspection clearly shows that the Anthesteria was a wine-festival in honour of Dionysos. Moreover we have the definite statement of Thucydides[2] that 'the more ancient Dionysia were celebrated on the 12th day of the month Anthesterion in the temple of Dionysos in the Marshes.' The reference can only be to the Choes, so that the festival of the Choes seems actually to have borne the name Dionysia. Harpocration[3] goes even further; he says, quoting Apollodorus, that 'the whole month was sacred to Dionysos.'

A more searching examination of the sources reveals beneath the surface rejoicings, as in the case of the Diasia, another and more primitive ritual, and a ritual of widely different significance. It has escaped no student of Greek festivals that through the Anthesteria there ran 'a note of sadness.' Things were not altogether so merry as they seemed. This has been variously explained, as due to the 'natural melancholy of the spring,' or more recently as evidence of the fact that Dionysos had his 'chthonic side' and was the 'Lord of souls.' A simpler explanation lies at the door.

The clue to the real gist of the Anthesteria is afforded by

[1] Aristoph. *Ach.* 1076, schol. ad loc.
[2] Thucyd. II. 15.
[3] Harpocrat. s.v. Χόες.

a piece of ritual performed on the last day, the *Chytroi*. The Greeks had a proverbial expression spoken, we are told, of those who 'on all occasions demand a repetition of favours received.' It ran as follows: 'Out of the doors! ye Keres; it is no longer Anthesteria.' Suidas[1] has preserved for us its true signification; it was spoken, he says, 'implying that in the Anthesteria the ghosts are going about in the city.' From this fragmentary statement the mandate, it is clear, must have been spoken at the close of the festival, so we cannot be wrong in placing it as the last act of the Chytroi.

The statement of Suidas in itself makes the significance of the words abundantly clear, but close parallels are not wanting in the ritual of other races. The Lemuria at Rome is a case in point. According to Ovid[2] each father of a family as the festival came round had to lay the ghosts of his house after a curious and complex fashion. When midnight was come and all was still, he arose and standing with bare feet he made a special sign with his fingers and thumb to keep off any ghost. Thrice he washes his hands in spring water, then he turns round and takes black beans into his mouth; with face averted he spits them away, and as he spits them says, 'These I send forth, with these beans I redeem myself and mine.' Nine times he speaks, and looks not back. The ghost, they believe, picks them up and follows behind if no one looks. Again he touches the water and strikes the brass of Temesa and begs the ghost to leave his house. When nine times he has said, 'Shades of my fathers, depart' (Manes exite paterni!),

[1] Suidas s.v. *θύραζε· ἔξω τῆς θύρας·*

θύραζε Κᾶρες, *οὐκ ἔτ' Ἀνθεστήρια,*

οἱ μὲν διὰ πλῆθος οἰκετῶν Καρικῶν *εἰρῆσθαί φασιν, ὡς ἐν τοῖς Ἀνθεστηρίοις εὐωχουμένων αὐτῶν καὶ οὐκ ἐργαζομένων. τῆς οὖν ἑορτῆς τελεσθείσης λέγειν ἐπὶ τὰ ἔργα ἐκπέμποντας αὐτούς·*

θύραζε Κᾶρες, *οὐκ ἔτ' Ἀνθεστήρια.*

τινὲς δὲ οὕτω τὴν παροιμίαν φασί·

θύραζε κῆρες, οὐκ ἔνι Ἀνθεστήρια,

ὡς κατὰ τὴν πόλιν τοῖς Ἀνθεστηρίοις τῶν ψυχῶν περιερχομένων.

Photius s.v. substantially identical.

To the information here given Zenobius (*Cent. Paroimiogr.*) adds: *Εἴρηται δὲ ἡ παροιμία ἐπὶ τῶν τὰ αὐτὰ ἐπιζητούντων πάντοτε λαμβάνειν.* It is fortunate that Suidas records his second conjecture, as his first is rendered plausible by the fact that we know the household servants were admitted to the Pithoigia. Probably in classical days *κῆρες* had already become an old fashioned word for souls and the formulary may have been easily misunderstood. Mommsen in his second edition (*Feste der Stadt Athen*, p. 386) argues that the form *κῆρες* is impossible because 'Gespenstern zeigt man nicht die Thür wie einem Bettler,' a difficulty that will scarcely be felt by any one acquainted with primitive customs.

[2] Ovid, *Fasti* v. 443.

he looks back and holds that the rite has been duly done. We cannot impute to the Anthesteria all the crude minutiae of the Lemuria, but the content is clearly the same—the expulsion of ancestral ghosts. The Lemuria took place not in the spring but in the early summer, May—a time at which ceremonies of purification were much needed.

A second striking parallel is recorded by Mr Tylor[1]. He says of a like Sclavonic custom, 'when the meal was over the priest rose from the table and hunted out the souls of the dead like fleas with these words: "Ye have eaten and drunk, souls, now go, now go".' Dr Oldenberg[2] calls attention to another analogy. In sacrifices in India to the dead the souls of ancestors are first invoked, then bidden to depart, and even invited to return again after the prescribed lapse of a month.

The formula used at the close of the Anthesteria is in itself ample proof that the Anthesteria was a festival of All Souls; here at last we know for certain what was dimly shadowed in the Diasia, that some portion at least of the ritual of the month Anthesterion was addressed to the powers of the underworld, and that these powers were primarily the ghosts of the dead. The evidence is not however confined to an isolated proverbial formulary. The remaining ritual of the Chytroi confirms it. Before they were bidden to depart the ghosts were feasted and after significant fashion.

The scholiast on Aristophanes[3] commenting on the words *τοῖς ἱεροῖσι Χύτροισι*, 'at the holy Pot-feast,' explains the ceremonies as follows: 'The Chytroi is a feast among the Athenians; the cause on account of which it is celebrated is explained by Theopompos who writes thus: ......"They have the custom of sacrificing at this feast, not to any of the Olympian gods at all, but to Hermes Chthonios"; and again in explaining the word *χύτρα*, pot: "And of the pot which all the citizens cook none of the priests tastes,

[1] *Primitive Culture* II. p. 40.

[2] *Religion des Vedas*, p. 553.

[3] Schol. ad Ar. *Ran.* 218 τοῖς ἱεροῖσι Χύτροισι· Χύτροι ἑορτὴ παρ' Ἀθηναίοις· ἄγεται δὲ παρὰ ταύτην τὴν αἰτίαν, ἣν καὶ Θεόπομπος ἐκτίθεται γράφων οὕτως· <   >...ἔπειτα· θύειν αὐτοῖς ἔθος ἔχουσι τῶν μὲν Ὀλυμπίων θεῶν οὐδενὶ τὸ παράπαν, Ἑρμῇ δὲ χθονίῳ. καὶ τῆς χύτρας, ἣν ἕψουσι πάντες οἱ κατὰ τὴν πόλιν, οὐδεὶς γεύεται τῶν ἱερέων· τοῦτο δὲ ποιοῦσι τῇ <ιγ′> ἡμέρᾳ. καί· τοὺς τότε παραγινομένους ὑπὲρ τῶν ἀποθανόντων ἱλάσασθαι τὸν Ἑρμῆν. ἱερῶν Rav., ἱερέων Ven.: whichever be followed, the mandate of not tasting is clear.

they do this on the (13th) day"; and again: "Those present appease Hermes on behalf of the dead".' The scholiast on another passage in Aristophanes[1] says substantially the same, but adds, again on the authority of Theopompos, that the practice of cooking the dish of seeds was observed by those who were saved from the deluge on behalf of those who perished. The deluge is of course introduced from a desire to get mythological precedent; the all-important points are that the *χύτρα*, the dish of grain and seeds, was offered to none of the Olympians, not even to Dionysos in whose honour the festival was ostensibly celebrated, but only to Hermes Chthonios, Hermes of the Underworld, and that of this sacrifice *no man tasted.* It was no sacrifice of communion, but like the holocaust made over utterly to dread chthonic powers, and behind this notion of sacrifice to the underworld deities lay the still earlier notion that it was dead men's food, a supper for the souls.

Before we leave the *χύτρα* it is necessary to examine more precisely the name of the day, Chytroi. August Mommsen[2] has emphasized the fact, too much neglected, that the name of the festival is masculine, *οἱ χύτροι* not *αἱ χύτραι*. The feminine form *χύτραι* means pots artificially made; the masculine form *χύτροι*, which occurs far less frequently, means in ordinary parlance natural pots, i.e. holes in the ground. Pausanias[3] speaks of a certain natural bath at Thermopylae which the country people called 'the Chytroi of the women'; and Herodotos[4] describes it in the same terms. Theophrastos[5] in his *History of Plants* speaks of a certain plant as growing in a place between the Kephisos and the Melas, 'the place being called Pelekania, i.e. certain hollows in the marsh, the so-called Pot-holes.' Hesychius[6], interpreting *οἱ χύτρινοι*, says they are 'the hollow places of the earth through which springs come up.' The word *κολυμβήθρα* itself, in classical Greek a natural pool, became in mediaeval Greek a font, and it may be

[1] Schol. ad Ar. *Ach.* 1076 *Χύτρους· Θεόπομπος τοὺς διασωθέντας ἐκ τοῦ κατακλυσμοῦ ἑψῆσαί φησι χύτρας πανσπερμίας ὅθεν οὕτω κληθῆναι τὴν ἑορτήν...τῆς δὲ χύτρας οὐδένα γεύσασθαι.*

[2] *Feste der Stadt Athen*, p. 385.

[3] P. IV. 35. 9 *κολυμβήθρα ἥντινα ὀνομάζουσιν οἱ ἐπιχώριοι χύτρους γυναικείους.*

[4] Herod. VIII. 176.

[5] Theoph. *Hist. Plant.* IV. 11. 8 *οὗτος δὲ ὁ τόπος προσαγορεύεται μὲν Πελεκανία, τοῦτο δ' ἐστὶν ἄττα χύτροι καλούμενοι βαθύσματα τῆς λίμνης.*

[6] Hesych. s.v. *οἱ χύτρινοι.*

noted that the natural chasms that occur in western Yorkshire still locally bear the name of 'Pots.'

It is possible therefore that the festival took its name from natural holes in the ground in the district of the Limnae where it was celebrated, a district to this day riddled with Turkish cisterns made of great earthen jars (πίθοι). Such holes may have been used for graves, and were in many parts of Greece regarded as the constant haunt of ghosts going up and down. They were perhaps the prototypes of the 'chasms in the earth' seen in the vision of Er[1]. Near akin were the megara or chasms of Demeter at Potniae[2], and the clefts on and about the Pnyx where the women celebrated the Thesmophoria (p. 125). Such chasms would be the natural sanctuaries of a Ge and ghost cult.

It is obvious that the two forms χύτροι and χύτραι would easily pass over into each other, and it is hard to say which came first. It is also to be noted that, though the masculine form more often means natural hole, it is also used for artificial pot. Pollux[3], in discussing 'the vessels used by cooks,' says that when Delphilos speaks of the big pot (χύτρον μέγαν) at the cook's, he clearly means the χύτρα, not the foot-pan (χυτρόποδα). Though the form χύτροι ultimately established itself, the associations of χύτρα, artificial pot, seem to have prevailed, and these associations are important and must be noted.

Hesychius[4] says that by φαρμακή is meant the χύτρα which they prepared for those who cleansed the cities. From the scholiast on the *Choephoroi* of Aeschylus[5] we learn that the Athenians purified their houses with a censer made of a pot; 'this they threw away at the meeting of three ways and went away without turning back.' Here we have of course the origin of 'Hecate's suppers.' These were primarily not feasts for the goddess but purification ceremonies, of which, as no mortal might taste them, it was supposed an infernal goddess partook. The day of the Chytroi was a day of such purifications. From some such notion arose the Aristophanic word ἐγχυτρίζειν, 'to pot,' i.e. to utterly ruin and destroy, to make away with. The scholiast[6] explains it as

[1] Plato, *Rep.* 614 c. [2] P. IX. 8. [3] *On.* x. 99.
[4] Hesych. s.v. φαρμακή· ἡ χύτρα ἣν ἡτοίμαζον τοῖς καθαίρουσι τὰς πόλεις.
[5] *v.* 96.
[6] Schol. ad Ar. *Vesp.* 289.

referring to the practice of exposing children, but Suidas[1] knows of another meaning; he says the *ἐγχυτρίστριαι* were those 'women who purified the unclean, pouring upon them the blood of the victim,' and also those who 'poured libations to the dead,' those in a word who performed ceremonies of placation and purgation.

It is curious that, though most modern writers from Crusius onwards have recognised that the Chytroi was a *dies nefastus* and in the main a festival of ghosts, this day has been separated off from the rest of the Anthesteria, and the two previous days have been regarded as purely drinking festivals:—the Pithoigia the opening of the wine-cask, the Choes the drinking of the wine-cups. And yet for the second day, the Choes, literary testimony is explicit. Spite of the drinking contest, the flower-wreathed cups and the wedding of Dionysos, all joyful elements of the service of the wine-god, the Choes was a *dies nefastus,* an unlucky day, a day to be observed with apotropaic precautions. Photius[2], in explaining the words *μιαρὰ ἡμέρα*, 'day of pollution,' says such a day occurred 'in the Choes in the month of Anthesterion, in which (i.e. during the Choes) they believed that the spirits of the dead rose up again. From early morning they used to chew buckthorn and anointed their doors with pitch.' Buckthorn, known to modern botanists as *Rhamnus catharticus,* is a plant of purgative properties. The ancient Athenian, like the modern savage, believed that such plants have the power of keeping off evil spirits, or rather perhaps of ejecting them when already in possession. Chewing a substance was naturally a thorough and efficient way of assimilating its virtues. The priestess of Apollo chewed the laurel leaf. It seems possible that she may have primarily had to do this rather as a means of ejecting the bad spirits than to obtain inspiration from the good. Fasting is a substantial safe-guard, but purgation more drastically effective. The prophylactic properties of *rhamnus,* buckthorn, were well known to the ancients. Dioscorides[3] in his *Materia Medica*

[1] Suidas s.v. *ἐγχυτρίστριαι· αἱ τὰς χοὰς τοῖς τετελευτηκόσιν ἐπιφέρουσαι...ἐγχυτρι-στρίας δὲ λέγεσθαι καὶ ὅσαι τοὺς ἐναγεῖς καθαίρουσιν, αἷμα ἐπιχέουσαι ἱερείου.*

[2] Photius s.v. *μιαρὰ ἡμέρα· ἐν τοῖς Χουσὶν Ἀνθεστηριῶνος μηνός, ἐν ᾧ δοκοῦσιν αἱ ψυχαὶ τῶν τελευτησάντων ἀνιέναι, ῥάμνων ἕωθεν ἐμασῶντο καὶ πίττῃ τὰς θύρας ἔχριον.*

[3] Diosc. *De mat. med.* I. 119 *λέγεται δὲ καὶ κλῶνας αὐτῆς θύραις ἢ θύρασι προστε-θέντας ἀποκρούειν τὰς τῶν φαρμακῶν κακουργίας.* For this reference I am indebted to the kindness of Dr Frazer, who also notes that in Ovid *spina alba*, white thorn, is

writes, 'it is said that branches of this plant attached to doors or hung up outside repel the evil arts of magicians.' Possibly, in addition to the chewing of buckthorn, branches of it were fastened to doors at the festival of the Choes, and served the same purpose as the pitch. Pitch, Photius tells us in commenting on *rhamnus*, was on account of its special purity used also to drive away sprites at the birth of a child—always a perilous moment[1].

It is not easy to imagine an enlightened citizen of the Athens of the fifth century B.C., an Aeschylus, a Pericles, chewing buckthorn from early dawn to keep off the ghosts of his ancestors, but custom in such matters has an iron hand. If the masters of the house shirked the chewing of buckthorn, the servants would see to it that the doors were at least anointed with pitch; it is best to be on the safe side in these matters, and there is the public opinion of conservative neighbours to be considered. Be this as it may, it is quite clear that the day of the *Choes* was a day of ghosts like the day of the *Chytroi*.

But, if the ceremonies of the Choes clearly indicate the 'unlucky' nature of the day, what is to be made of the name? Nothing, as it stands. *Choes*, *Cups*, are undeniably cheerful. But, as in the case of Chytroi, there *may* have been a confusion between approximate forms; the two words *χοή*, funeral libation, and *χοῦς*, cup, have a common stem *χοϝ*. May not *χόες* have superimposed itself on *χοαί*, wine-cups upon funeral libations? A scholiast on Aristophanes[2] seems to indicate some such a *contaminatio*. In explaining the word *χοάς*, he says the meaning is 'pourings forth, offerings to the dead or libations. An oracle was issued that they must offer libations (*χοάς*) yearly to those of the Aetolians who had died, and celebrate the festival so called.' Here the name of a festival *Χοάς* is oxytone, and though we cannot

placed in a window to keep off *tristes noxas* and *striges* (Ovid, *Fasti* VI. 129—163), and compares the English notion that hawthorn keeps off witches (see *Golden Bough*, second edit. vol. I. p. 124, note 3). Miss M. C. Harrison tells me that to this day rue (*ruta*) is eaten on Ascension Day at Pratola Peligna and other places in the Abruzzi, "that the witches may not come to torment our children" (noi mangiamo la ruta affinche le streghe non vengano a tormentare le creature nostre); see A. De Nino, *Usi Abruzzesi* I. p. 168.

[1] Phot. s.v. *ῥάμνος· φυτὸν ὃ ἐν τοῖς Χουσὶν ὡς ἀλεξιφάρμακον ἐμασῶντο ἕωθεν, καὶ πίττῃ ἐχρίοντο τὰ δώματα, ἀμίαντος γὰρ αὕτη· διὸ καὶ ἐν ταῖς γενέσεσι τῶν παιδίων χρίουσι τὰς οἰκίας εἰς ἀπέλασιν τῶν δαιμόνων.*

[2] Schol. ad Ar. *Ach.* 961 *Χοάς· ἐγχύσεις, ἐναγίσματα ἐπὶ νεκροῖς ἢ σπονδάς. ἐκπίπτει χρησμὸς δεῖν χοὰς τοῖς τεθνεῶσι τῶν Αἰτωλῶν ἐπάγειν ἀνὰ πᾶν ἔτος καὶ ἑορτὴν Χοὰς ἄγειν.*

assume that it was identical with the Athenian Choes, it looks as if there was some confusion as to the two analogous forms.

If we view the Choes as *Χοαί*, the Cups as *Libations*, the anomalous and, as it stands, artificial connection of Orestes with the festival becomes at once clear. At the drinking bout of the Choes, we learn from Athenaeus[1] and other authorities, the singular custom prevailed that each man should drink by himself. A mythological reason was sought to account for this, and the story was told[2] that Orestes, polluted by the blood of his mother, came to Athens at the time of the celebration of the Choes. The reigning king, variously called Pandion and Phanodemus, wished to show him hospitality, but religious scruple forbade him to let a man polluted enter the Sanctuaries or drink with those ceremonially clean. He therefore ordered the Sanctuaries to be shut and a measure of wine (*χοῦς*) to be set before each man severally, and bade them, when they had finished drinking, not to offer up the garlands with which they had been crowned in the Sanctuaries, because they had been under the same roof with Orestes; but he bade each man place his wreath round his own cup, and so bring them to the priestess at the precinct of the Limnae. That done, they were to perform the remaining sacrifices in the Sanctuary. From this, Athenaeus adds, the festival got the name of *Cups*. The mad Orestes in the *Iphigenia in Tauris*[3] tells the same tale and naïvely states that, though he was hurt by the procedure, he dare not ask the reason, knowing it all too well.

The whole account is transparently aetiological. Some mythological precedent is desired for the drinking bout of the Choes, based as it was on a ceremony of funeral libations; it is sought and found or rather invented in the canonical story of Orestes, and he is made to say in a fashion almost too foolish even for a madman:

> 'And this I learn, that my mishaps became
> A rite for the Athenians; and Pallas' folk
> Have still this custom that they reverence
> The Choan vessel.'

If we suppose that the Cups (*χόες*) were originally Libations (*χοαί*), the somewhat strained punctilio of the host becomes at least intelligible. Orestes is polluted by the guilt (*ἄγος*) of his

[1] Athen. VII. 2, p. 276.
[2] Athen. X. 49, p. 437 and Suidas s.v. *Χόες*.
[3] Eur. *Iph. in T.* 953 seq.

mother's blood, he finds the people in the Limnae[1], close to the Areopagos, celebrating the *Χοαί*, the libations to the dead; till he is purified from kindred blood he cannot join: all is simple and clear.

If the Choes were in intent *χοαί*, the Cups *Libations*, the ceremony has an interesting parallel in a rite performed at the Eleusinian mysteries. Athenaeus[2], in discussing various shapes of cups says: 'The plemochoë is an earthen vessel shaped like a top that stands fairly steady; some call it, Pamphilos tells us, the cotyliscus. And they use it at Eleusis on the last day of the mysteries, which takes its name Plemochoai from the cup. On this day they fill two plemochoae and set them up, the one towards the East, the other towards the West, and pronounce over them a magic formula. The author of the *Peirithous* mentions them, whether he be Ktesias the Tyrant or Euripides, as follows:

> "That these plemochoae down the Chthonian chasm
> With words well-omened we may pour."'

It is at least significant that a compound of the word *χοή* should both give its name to a festival day and to a vessel used in chthonic ritual.

The Chytroi and Choes then bear unmistakeably a character of gloom, and in their primary content are festivals of ghosts. But what of the Pithoigia? Surely this day is all revel and jollity, all for Dionysos?

Had we been dependent on literature alone, such would have been our inevitable conclusion. In Plutarch's account of the Pithoigia (p. 33), the earliest and fullest we possess, there is no hint of any worship other than that of the wine-god, no hint of possible gloom. Eustathius[3] indeed tells of a Pithoigia or Jar-opening which was 'not of a festal character, but in every respect unlucky,' but this is the Pithoigia, the Jar-opening, of Pandora. Here we have a hint that a Pithoigia need not be an opening of wine-jars; there are other jars, other openings, but save for the existence of one small fragile monument the significance of the hint would have escaped us.

[1] For the topographical question see my *Primitive Athens*, p. 83.
[2] Athen. XI. 93, p. 496.
[3] Eustath. ad *Il.* XXIV. 526, p. 1363. 26 οὐχ ἑορτάσιμος...ἀλλ' ἐς τὸ πᾶν ἀποφράς.

In the vase-painting in fig. 7 from a lekythos in the University Museum of Jena[1] we see a Pithoigia of quite other and more solemn intent. A large *pithos* is sunk deep into the ground. It has served as a grave. In primitive days many a man, Diogenes-like, lived the 'life of the jar' (ζωὴ πίθου), but not from philosophy, rather from dire necessity. During the Peloponnesian war, when the city was crowded with refugees, a jar (πιθάκνη) was a welcome shelter[2]. A man's home during his life is apt to be his grave in death. In the Dipylon Cemetery at Athens, at Aphidna[3], at Corfu, at Thoricus, and in many another burying place, such grave *pithoi* have come to light. From the grave-jar in fig. 7 the lid has been removed; out of it have escaped, fluttering upward, two winged Keres or souls, a third soul is in the act of emerging, a fourth is diving headlong back into the jar. Hermes Psychopompos, with his magic staff in his hand, is evoking, *re*voking the souls. The picture is a speaking commentary on the Anthesteria; we seem to hear the mandate 'Out of the doors! ye souls; it is no longer Anthesteria!' The Pithoigia of the Anthesteria is the primitive Pithoigia of the *grave*-jars, later overlaid by the Pithoigia of the *wine*-jars.

Fig. 7.

The vase-painting in fig. 7 must not be regarded as an actual conscious representation of the Athenian rite performed on the first day of the *Anthesteria*. It is more general in content; it is in fact simply a representation of ideas familiar to every Greek, that the *pithos* was a grave-jar, that from such grave-jars souls

[1] First published by Dr Paul Schadow, *Eine Attische Grablekythos*, Inaugural-Dissertation (Jena, 1897), reproduced and discussed by the present writer *J.H.S.* xx. p. 101.

[2] Ar. *Eq.* 792. Mr R. A. Neil ad loc. points out that πίθος answers to *fidelia* in etymology, to *dolium* in meaning.

[3] Dr Sam. Wide, 'Aphidna in Nord-Attica,' *A. Mitt.* 1896, p. 398.

escaped and to them necessarily returned, and that Hermes was Psychopompos, Evoker and Revoker of souls. The vase-painting is in fact only another form of the scene so often represented on Athenian white lekythoi, in which the souls flutter round the grave-stele. The grave-jar is but the earlier form of sepulture; the little winged figures, the Keres, are identical in both classes of vase-painting.

The nature of these Keres will be further analysed when we come to the discussion of primitive demonology. For the present it is enough to note that the Keres in the vase-paintings and the Keres of the Anthesteria are regarded as simply souls of dead men, whereas the little winged phantoms that escape from Pandora's jar are indeed ghosts, but ghosts regarded rather as noisome sprites than as spirits; they are the source of disease and death rather than dead men's souls. The jar of Pandora is not so much a grave as a store-house of evil; the *pithos* as store-house not only of wine but of grain and all manner of provisions was familiar to the Greeks. The ordinary *pithos* was pointed at the base and buried permanently in the earth like a Turkish cistern; a row of such pithoi, like those recently unearthed at Cnossus, might serve equally as a wine-cellar or a granary or a cemetery.

The attributes of Hermes in the vase-painting in fig. 7 are noticeable. In one hand he holds his familiar herald's staff, the kerykeion. But, and this is the interesting point, he is not using it; it is held in the left hand, inert; it is merely attributive, present out of convention. The real implement of his agency in revoking the souls is held uplifted in the right hand; it is his rhabdos, his magic wand.

This *rhabdos* is, I think, clearly to be distinguished from the kerykeion, though ultimately the two became contaminated. The kerykeion or herald's staff is in intent a king's sceptre held by the herald as deputy; it is a staff, a walking-stick, a *βάκτρον*, by which you are supported; the *rhabdos* is a simple rod, even a pliable twig, a thing not by which you are supported but with which you sway others. It is in a word the enchanter's wand.

It is with a rhabdos that Circe[1] transforms the comrades of

[1] *Od.* x. 236.

Odysseus into swine; it is as magical as the magic potion they drink:

'Straight with her rhabdos smote she them and penned them in the sties.'

With the rhabdos Hermes[1] led the ghosts of the slain suitors to Hades. He held in his hand

'His rhabdos fair and golden wherewith he lulls to rest
The eyes of men whoso he will, and others by his hest
He wakes from sleep. He stirred the ghosts; they followed to their doom
And gibbered like the bats that throng and gibber in the gloom.'

This magic wand became the attribute of all who hold sway over the dead. It is the wand, not the sceptre, that is the token of life or death, as Pindar[2] shows:

'Nor did Hades the king
Forget his wand to wave
Whereby he doth bring
Shapes of men dying
Adown the hollow roadway of the grave.'

The rhabdos as magic wand was *πεισίβροτος*, *enchanter* of the dead, before it became as sceptre *πεισίβροτος*, *ruler* of mortals.

Eustathius tells us in the passage already discussed[3], that the kerykeion was also called *πομπός*, conductor, and that it was carried in the hands of those who performed ceremonies of purification. He is trying, it will be remembered, to derive the words *διοπομπεῖν* and *ἀποδιοπομπεῖν*. When an ancient author is trying to derive words, we are bound to accept his statements only with the utmost caution; still in this particular instance there seems no reason for suspecting the statement that the kerykeion was called *πομπός*; it is dragged in quite gratuitously, and does not help out the proposed derivation. What Eustathius says is this: 'At the end of the month Maimakterion they perform ceremonies of sending, among which was the carrying of the magic fleece, and there take

[1] *Od.* XXIV. 1—9.

[2] Pind. *Ol.* IX. 33

οὐδ' Ἀΐδας ἀκινήταν ἔχε ῥάβδον
βρότεα σώμαθ' ᾇ κατάγει κοίλαν πρὸς ἀγυιὰν
θνασκόντων.

ἀκινήταν is usually rendered 'unraised' as though the sceptre were lifted in token of kingly power. I translate by 'wave' because I believe the action denoted is the waving or moving of a wand, not the raising of a sceptre. The verb *κινέω* is, I believe, characteristic of this wand-waving. *κινέω* is used in Homer (loc. cit.) *τῇ δ' ἄγε κινήσας.* By Pindar's time the wand and the sceptre were fused, but he is haunted by the old connotation of magic.

[3] For text, see p. 24, note 2.

place then throwings out of purifications at the crossways, and they hold in their hands the *pompos* (i.e. conductor), which they say is the kerykeion, the attribute of Hermes.' The object of the whole ceremony is 'to send out polluted things.' It is, I think, significant that the kerykeion, or rather to be strictly accurate the rhabdos[1], was carried in apotropaic ceremonies, presumably with a view to exorcise bad spirits, which as will appear later were regarded as the source of all impurities. It is the other face of revocation; the rhabdos is used either for the raising or the laying of ghosts, for the induction (ἐπαγωγή) of good spirits, for the exorcism (ἀποτροπή) of bad.

In discussing the Anthesteria on a previous occasion[2], I felt confident that in the opening of the grave-jars we had the complete solution of the difficulty of the unlucky character of the day Pithoigia. It seems to me now in the light of further investigation that another ritual element may have gone to its determination.

Plutarch[3], in discussing the nature of the sacred objects committed to the care of the Vestal Virgins, makes the following notable statement: 'Those who pretend to have most special knowledge about them (i.e. the Vestal Virgins) assert that there are set there two jars (πίθοι) of no great size, of which the one is open and empty, the other full and sealed up, and neither of them may be seen except by these all-holy virgins. But others think that this is false, and that the idea arose from the fact that the maidens then placed most of their sacred things in two jars, and hid them underground below the temple of Quirinus, and that the place even now is called from that by the title *Pithisci* (Doliola).' We have two other notices of these Doliola. Varro[4] says: 'The place which is called Doliola is at the Cloaca Maxuma, where people are not allowed to spit. It is so called from the jars beneath the earth. Two accounts are given of these jars: some

[1] Space forbids the discussion of the whole evolution of the kerykeion. It contains elements drawn from both sceptre and rhabdos. The rhabdos is sometimes forked like a divining rod: the forks were entwined in various shapes. Round the rhabdos a snake, symbol of the underworld, was sometimes curled as the snake is curled round the staff of Aesculapius. Ultimately the twisted ends of the rhabdos were crystallized into curled decorative snakes. In like fashion the frayed fringe of the leather aegis of Athene is misunderstood and rendered as snakes. By the time of Eustathius, kerykeion and rhabdos are not clearly differentiated.

[2] *J.H.S.* xx. p. 101.

[3] Plut. *Vit. Cam.* xx.

[4] *Ling. Lat.* 5 § 157.

say they contain the bones of dead bodies, others that after the death of Numa Pompilius certain sacred objects (religiosa quaedam) were buried there.' Festus[1] gives substantially the same account, but he says that the sacred objects were buried there when the Gauls invaded the city.

Of jars containing 'sacra' we have in Greece no knowledge, but it is significant to find that Zeus, who was the heir to so much antique ritual, had on his threshold in Olympus two jars, one containing good the other evil[2]:

> 'Jars twain upon Zeus' threshold ever stood;
> One holds his gifts of evil, one of good.'

With some such notion as that of the Pithoigia must have been connected the ceremony of the opening of the *mundus* or round pit on the Palatine. Festus[3] tells us that on three days in the year, August 24, October 5, November 6, the *lapis manalis* that covered it was removed. Varro, quoted by Macrobius[4], adds: 'when the *mundus* is open, the gate of the doleful underworld gods is open.'

It has been shown that the ritual of each of the several days points determinedly ghost-wards. The names in each case *admit* at least of chthonic interpretation. It remains to examine the collective name *Anthesteria*.

The ancients sought and found what was to them a satisfactory etymology. Istros, writing in the third century B.C. and quoted by Harpocration, says that Anthesterion is the blossoming month because then 'the most of the things that spring from the earth blossom forth[5].' The *Etymologicon Magnum*[6] offers an easy-going alternative: feast and month bear their names either because the earth then began to blossom, or because they offered flowers at the festival.

It was not the habit of those days to trouble about 'verb-stems' and 'nouns of the agent in τηρ,' but it is surprising to find that the dubious guess hazarded by Istros should have passed so long

[1] *Pauli excerpta ex Lib. Pomp.* Fest. s.v. doliola.

[2] *Iliad* XXIV. 527

δοιοὶ γάρ τε πίθοι κατακείαται ἐν Διὸς οὔδῳ
δώρων οἷα δίδωσι κακῶν ἕτερος δὲ ἑάων.

[3] Fest. 154.

[4] Macr. *Sat.* I. 16. 18.

[5] Harpocrat. s.v. Ἀνθεστ. διὰ τὸ πλεῖστα τῶν ἐκ τῆς γῆς ἀνθεῖν τότε.

[6] *Etym. Mag.* s.v. Ἀνθεστήρια.

unchallenged by modern science, the more so as flowers have but a general and accidental connection with the ritual of the feast. Are scholars really content with an etymology that makes of the Anthesteria the festival of those who 'did the flowers'?

In a recent paper in the *Hellenic Journal*[1] Dr A. W. Verrall has faced the difficulty and offered a new solution. The names of festivals, he points out, are no exception to the rule that nouns in *τηριο* are normally formed from verb-stems through the 'noun of the agent' in *τηρ*, and take their sense from the action described by the verb, as *σωτήριος, λυτήριος, βουλευτήριον*. In like fashion the names of festivals ending in *τηρια* describe the action in which the ceremony consisted, or with which it was chiefly connected. Thus *ἀνακλητήρια* is a feast or ceremony of *ἀνάκλησις, ἀνακαλυπτήρια* of *ἀνακάλυψις* and so on. *Prima facie* then a derivation of *Anthesteria* should start from the assumption that the stem is verbal.

'But we need not assume that the verbal stem is *ἀνθεσ-*. Perhaps *ἀνθεσ-* itself needs analysis; and for the first syllable there is an obviously possible origin in the preposition *ἀν-* (*ἀνά*), of which so many examples (e.g. *ἄνθεμα* = *ἀνάθεμα*) are preserved in the poets. The verb-stem will then be *θεσ-*, which is in fact a verb-stem and has more than one meaning. The meaning which would perhaps in any case have suggested itself first, and which now seems especially attractive, is that which appears in the archaic verb *θέσασθαι* or *θέσσασθαι* *to pray* or *pray for*[2], and in the adjectives *πολύθεστος* and *ἀπόθεστος*. Prayers and invocations addressed to the dead were a regular part of the proceedings by which they were brought back to the world of the living. The compound *ἀναθέσσασθαι* would, after the analogy of *ἀνακαλεῖν* and the like, bear the sense *to raise by prayer* or *to recall by prayer*, literally "to pray up" or "pray back." And *ἀνθεστήρια*, derived from *ἀναθέσσασθαι*, would be the *feast of revocation*, the name, as usual, signifying the action in which the ceremony consisted and which was the object of it[3].'

In connection with this new and illuminating etymology, it is interesting to note that even in their misguided derivation from

[1] *J.H.S.* xx. 115. [2] *Od.* x. 526.

[3] My view of the primitive significance of the root *θεσ*, which is perhaps primarily rather *to conjure* than *to pray*, will appear more clearly when we come to the discussion of the Thesmophoria.

ἄνθος the ancients themselves lay stress not so much on the flowers as on the rising up[1], the *ἀνθεῖν ἐκ τῆς γῆς*. Under the word *Ἄνθεια* the *Etymologicon Magnum* says 'a title of Hera when she sends up (*ἀνίησι*) fruits,' where there seems a haunting of the true meaning though none of the *form*[2].

Dr Verrall declines to assert positively the derivation of *Anthesteria* he propounds, but a second philological argument brings certain conviction. Mr R. A. Neil suggests that the root which appears in Greek as *θες* may appear as *fes fer* in Latin. This gives us the delightful equation or rather analogy *ἀν-θεσ-τήρια, in-fer-iae.* Of course *inferiae* is usually taken as from *inferi, infra* etc., but no Latin word ought to have medial *f* except when preceded by a separable prefix. To make certainty more certain we have the Feralia, the festival of All Souls, kept from the 13th to the 21st of the month of Fe(b)ruary. The month of *purification* is the month of rites to the dead, in a word *purgation is the placation of souls.* This is true for Latin and Greek alike and will emerge more clearly when we come to study in detail the ritual of the month of February.

ANTHESTERION AND FEBRUARY.

The general analogy between the months of Anthesterion and February, and the fact that both alike were unlucky and given over to the service of the dead, was clear to the ancients themselves. The scholiast on Lucian's *Timon*[3], commenting on the word *Diasia*, says: 'The day is unlucky...there were among the Greeks certain days which brought with them complete idleness

[1] Dr Wuensch in his instructive pamphlet *Ein Frühlingsfest auf Malta* (Leipzig, 1902) discusses a spring festival of the flowering of beans which he believes to be analogous to the *Anthesteria*, but the rites practised are wholly different. Dr Hiller von Gaertringen (*Festschrift für O. Benndorf*) calls attention to the title *Anthister* which occurs in an inscription found on Thera, but the inscription is of the second century B.C., the festival of the 'Anthesteria' was celebrated on Thera, as indeed wherever there was a primitive population, and *Anthister* must have borrowed rather than lent his name.

[2] Archbishop Eustathius may have had a dim consciousness of the separable *ἀνα* when he says *ἄνθος ὅτι ἐκ τοῦ ἀναθέειν παρῆκται κατὰ συγκοπήν.*

[3] Schol. ad Luc. *Tim.* 43 *ἀποφρὰς ἡ ἡμέρα*]...*ἦσαν παρ' Ἕλλησιν ἡμέραι ἀπραξίαν εἰσηγούμεναι παντὸς καὶ ἀργίαν, ἃς ἀποφράδας ἐκάλουν. ἐν ταύταις οὐδὲ προσεῖπεν ἄν τις τινα, οὐδὲ καθάπαξ φίλος ἐπεμίγνυτο φίλῳ, ἀλλὰ καὶ τὰ ἱερὰ ἀχρημάτιστα ἦν αὐτοις. ἐκαλεῖτο δὲ ταῦτα αὐτοῖς κατὰ τὸν Φευρουάριον μῆνα ὅτε καὶ ἐνήγιζον τοῖς καταχθονιοις· καὶ πᾶς οὗτος ὁ μὴν ἀνεῖτο κατοιχομένοις μετὰ στυγνότητος πάντων προϊόντων ἕτερον τρόπον ὃν καὶ τὰ Διάσια στυγνάζοντες ἦγον Ἀθηναῖοι.*

and cessation of business, and which were called unlucky (*ἀποφράδες*). On these days no one would accost any one else, and friends would positively have no dealings with each other, and even sanctuaries were not used. These times were so accounted on the analogy of the month of February, when also it was the custom to sacrifice to those below, and all that month was dedicated to the dead and accompanied by gloom, everything going on in an unusual fashion just as the Athenians celebrated the Diasia in gloom.' Clearly to the scholiast the Diasia is but one element of a month given over to the dead.

The meaning of Anthesterion, the significance of its ceremonies, have been effectively overlaid by the wine-god and his flower garlands, but with the Romans there was no such superposition and consequently no misunderstanding. They clearly realized two things, that February was the month of the dead, and that it was the month of purification. Plutarch in his *Roman Questions*[1] asks 'Why was Decimus Brutus wont to sacrifice to the dead in December, whereas all other Romans offered libations and sacrifices to the dead in the month of February?' In his twenty-fifth Question[2], while discussing the reasons why the days following respectively the Calends, Nones and Ides of each month were unlucky, he tells us that the Romans 'used to consecrate the first month of the year to the Olympian gods, but the second to the gods of the earth, and in this second month (February) they were wont to practise certain purifications and to sacrifice to the dead.' Athenaeus[3] states that 'Juba the Mauretanian said that the month of February was so called from the terrors of the lower world, with regard to means taken for riddance from such alarms at the time when the winter is at its height, and it is the custom to offer libations to the dead on several days.' Juba the Mauretanian must have known quite well that in February the winter was not at its height. He states correctly the fact that February was a month devoted to ceremonies for the riddance of terrors from the under-

[1] Plut. *Q. R.* XXXIV. *διὰ τί, τῶν ἄλλων Ῥωμαίων ἐν τῷ Φεβρουαρίῳ μηνὶ ποιουμένων χοὰς καὶ ἐναγισμοὺς τοῖς τεθνηκόσι, Δέκιμος Βροῦτος (ὡς Κικέρων ἱστόρηκεν) ἐν τῷ Δεκεμβρίῳ τοῦτ' ἔπραττεν;*

[2] Plut. *Q. R.* XXV. *τῶν μηνῶν τὸν μὲν πρῶτον Ὀλυμπίοις θεοῖς ἱέρωσαν τὸν δὲ δεύτερον χθονίοις ἐν ᾧ καὶ καθαρμούς τινας τελοῦσι καὶ τοῖς κατοιχομένοις ἐναγίζουσιν.*

[3] Athen. III. 53 p. 98 *τὸν δὲ μῆνα τοῦτον κληθῆναί φησιν ὁ Μαυρόσιος Ἰόβας ἀπὸ τῶν κατουδαίων φόβων κατ' ἀναίρεσιν τῶν δειμάτων ἐν ᾧ τοῦ χειμῶνός ἐστι τὸ ἀκμαιότατον καὶ ἔθος τότε τοῖς κατοιχομένοις τὰς χοὰς ἐπιφέρειν πολλαῖς ἡμέραις.*

world, but carelessly adds an impossible reason for the selection of this particular month.

Ovid is of all witnesses the most weighty because his testimony is in part unconscious. In the opening words of the second book of the *Fasti*[1], after an invocation to Janus, he goes straight to the question of what the Romans meant by the word *februum*; he notes that the term was applied to many things, wool, a branch from a pine-tree, grain roasted with salt, and finally concludes that 'any thing by which the soul was purged was called by his rude ancestors *februum*.'

> 'Denique quodcumque est, quo pectora nostra piantur,
> Hoc apud intonsos nomen habebat avos.'

The month he feels sure got its name from these 'februa' or purifications, but he asks 'was it because the Luperci purified all the soil with the strips of skin and accounted that a purification or atonement, or was it because when the *dies ferales* were accomplished then *owing to the fact that the dead were appeased* there was a season of purity?'

> 'Mensis ab his dictus secta quia pelle Luperci
> Omne solum lustrant idque piamen habent?
> Aut quia placatis sunt tempora pura sepulcris,
> Tunc cum ferales praeteriere dies?'

Both the ceremonials, the Lupercalia and the Feralia, were, he knows, cathartic: that Fe(b)rua and Feralia were etymologically and significantly the same naturally he does not guess. Still less could he conjecture that etymologically February and Anthesterion are in substance one.

The two great February festivals[2] to which Ovid alludes are of course the Feralia and the Lupercalia, celebrated respectively on the 21st and 15th of February.

The Feralia was but the climax of a series of days beginning on Feb. 13th and devoted to ceremonies of the worship of ancestors, Parentalia. It is curious that, though the Lemuria (May 9—13) were marked as Nefasti, none of the days of the Parentalia were so marked: still from the 13th to the 21st marriages were forbidden,

[1] Ovid, *Fasti* II. 19.

[2] The ceremonies of the Lupercalia have been fully discussed by Warde-Fowler, *The Roman Festivals*, p. 310, and very fully by Mannhardt, *Mythologische Forschungen*, p. 72.

temples closed, and magistrates appeared without their insignia; clearly there was some lingering dread of ghosts that might be about. Parentalia and Feralia alike were ceremonies wholly devoted to the placation of ghosts.

In the Lupercalia, on the other hand, it is purification rather than placation that is the prominent feature in the rites. Much in the Lupercalia is obscure, and especially the origin of its name, but one ritual element is quite certain. Goats and a dog were sacrificed, two youths girt themselves in the skins of the slain goats, they held in their hands strips of the hides of the victims. They ran round a certain prescribed portion of the city, and as they ran smote the women they met with the strips of skin. These strips of skin were among the things known as *februa*, *purifiers*, and by their purifying power they became fertility charms.

> 'Forget not in your speed, Antonius,
> To touch Calpurnia, for our elders say
> The barren touchèd in this holy chase
> Shake off their sterile curse[1].'

There has been much needless discussion as to whether in ceremonies where striking and beating occur the object is to drive out evil spirits or to stimulate the powers of fertility. Primitive man does not so narrowly scrutinize and analyse his motives. To strike with a sacred thing, whether with a strip of skin from a victim or a twig from a holy tree, was to apply what the savage of to-day would call 'good medicine.' Precisely how it worked, whether by expulsion or impulsion, is no business of his.

When the Catholic makes the sacred sign of the Cross over his food, is he, need he be, quite clear as to whether he does it to induce good or to exorcise evil? The peasant mother of to-day may beat her boy partly with a view to stirring his dormant moral impulses, but it is also, as she is careful to explain, with intent to 'beat the mischief out of him.' In the third Mime of Herondas[2] the mother is explicit as to the expulsive virtue of beating. Her boy is a gambler and a dunce, so she begs the schoolmaster to

> 'Thrash him upon his shoulders till his spirit,
> Bad thing, is left just hovering on his lips.'

[1] *Julius Caesar*, Act I. Sc. 2, *v.* 6.
[2] Herond. *Mim.* III. 3.

She is in the usual primitive dilemma: his spirit is bad but it is his life; it is kill and cure.

The strips of goat-skin were *februa*[1], purifying, and thereby fertility charms. As such they cast sudden illumination on the 'magic fleece' already discussed. The animal sacrificed, be it sheep or goat or dog, is itself a placation to ghosts or underworld powers; hence its skin becomes of magical effect: the deduction is easy, almost inevitable. The primary gist of the sacrifice is to appease and hence keep off evil spirits; it is these evil spirits that impair fertility: in a word *purification is the placation of ghosts.*

The question 'What was purity to the ancients?' is thus seen to be answered almost before it is asked. Purity was not *spiritual* purity in our sense—that is foreign to any primitive habit of thought, nor was it physical purity or cleanliness—it was possible to be covered from head to foot with mud and yet be ceremonially pure. But so oddly does the cycle of thought come round, that the purity of which the ancients knew *was*, though in a widely different sense, *spiritual* purity, i.e. freedom from bad spirits and their maleficent influence. To get rid of these spirits was to undergo purification. In the month of February and Anthesterion the Roman or Greek might, *mutatis mutandis*, have chanted our Lenten hymn:

'Christian, dost thou see them
On the holy ground
How the hosts of Midian
Prowl and prowl around?
Christian, up and smite them!'

Till the coming of the new religion of Dionysos, the Greek notion of purity seems not to have advanced beyond this negative combative attitude, this notion of spiritual forces outside and against them.

The question yet remains 'Why did this purification need to take place in the spring?' The answer is clear. Why did our own near ancestors have spring cleanings?

'Winter rains and ruins are over
And all the season of snows and sins,...
While in green underwood and cover
Blossom by blossom the Spring begins.'

[1] Serv. ad Verg. *Aen.* VIII. 343 nam pellem ipsam capri veteres *februum* vocabant. Varro (*Ling. Lat.* VI. 13) says that *februum* was Sabine for *purgamentum.*

Winter is a reckless time with its Christmas and its Saturnalia. There is little for the primitive agriculturist to do and less to fear. The fruits of the earth have died down, the gods have done their worst. But when the dead earth begins to awake and put forth bud and blossom, then the ghosts too have their spring time, then is the moment to propitiate the dead below the earth. Ghosts were placated that fertility might be promoted, fertility of the earth and of man himself.

It is true that the primitive rites of February and Anthesterion, of Romans and Greeks, were in the main of 'riddance.' The ghosts, it would seem from the ritual of the Choes and Chytroi, the chewing of buckthorn, anointing with pitch, the mandate to depart, were feared as evil influences to be averted; but there is curious evidence to show that at the time of the Anthesteria the coming of the ghosts was regarded as a direct promotion of fertility. Athenaeus[1], quoting the Commentaries of Hegesander[2], tells us of a curious tradition among the natives of Apollonia in Chalkis. 'Around Apollonia of Chalkidike there flow two rivers, the Ammites and the Olynthiacus and both fall into the lake Bolbe. And on the river Olynthiacus stands a monument of Olynthus, son of Herakles and Bolbe. And the natives say that in the months of Elaphebolion and Anthesterion the river rises because Bolbe sends the fish apopyris to Olynthus, and at that season an immense shoal of fish passes from the lake to the river Olynthus. The river is a shallow one, scarcely overpassing the ankles, but nevertheless so great a shoal of the fish arrives that the inhabitants round about can all of them lay up sufficient store of salt fish for their needs. And it is a wonderful fact that they never pass by the monument of Olynthus. They say that formerly the people of Apollonia used to perform the accustomed rites to the dead in the month of Elaphebolion, but now they do them in Anthesterion, and that on this account the fish come up in those months only in which they are wont to do honour to the dead.' Here clearly the dead hero is the source of national wealth, the honours done him are the direct impulsion to fertility. The gloomy rites of *aversion* tend to pass over into a cheerful, hopeful ceremonial of 'tendance.'

[1] Athen. VIII. 11 p. 334 F.

[2] 3rd cent. B.C.

To resume, the Anthesteria was primarily a Feast of All Souls: it later[1] became a revel of Dionysos, and at the revel men wreathed their cups with flowers, but, save for a vague and unscientific etymology, we have no particle of evidence that the Anthesteria was ever a Feast of Flowers. The transition from the revocation of ghosts with its dire association to a drunken revel may seem harsh, but human nature is always ready for the shift from Fast to Feast, witness our own Good Friday holiday.

THE RITUAL OF 'Εναγισμοί.

In the light of the ceremonies of the spring month February and Anthesterion, it is now possible to advance a step in the understanding of Greek ritual terminology and through it of Greek religious thought.

In the first chapter the broad distinction was established between sacrifice to the Olympians of the upper air—sacrifice which involved communion with the worshipper, and sacrifice to chthonic powers which forbade this communion—in which the sacrifice was wholly made over to the object of sacrifice. The first, the Olympian sacrifice, is expressed by two terms, *θύειν* and *ἱερεύειν*; the second, if the sacrifice is burnt, by *ὁλοκαυτεῖν*, and as will presently be seen by *σφάζειν*, also more generally by the term *ἐναγίζειν*.

As regards the Olympian terms, it is only necessary to say definitely what has already been implied, that *θύειν* strictly is applicable only to the portion of the sacrifice that was actually burnt with a view to sublimation, that it might reach the gods in the upper air; whilst *ἱερεύειν* applies rather to the portion unburnt, which was sacred indeed, as its name implies, to the gods, but was actually eaten in communion by the worshipper. With the growing prevalence of burnt sacrifice and the increasing popularity of the Olympians and their service, the word *θύειν* came to cover the whole field of sacrifice, and in late and careless writers is used for any form of sacrifice burnt or unburnt without any consciousness of its primary meaning.

The term *ἱερεύειν* is strictly used only of the sacrifice of an animal; *ἱερεῖον* is the animal victim. Among the Homeric Greeks

[1] That the religion of Dionysos came to Greece at a comparatively late date will be shown in Chapter VIII.

sacrifice and the flesh feast that followed were so intimately connected that the one almost implied the other; the *ἱερεῖον*, the animal victim, was the material for the *κρεοδαισία*, the flesh feast. So prominent in the Homeric mind was the element of feasting the worshipper that the feast is sometimes the only stated object. Thus Odysseus[1] gives command to Telemachus and his thralls:

> 'Now get you to my well-built house, the best of all the swine
> Take you and quickly *sacrifice* that straightway we may dine.'

Here the object is the meal, though incidentally sacrifice to the gods is implied. It is not that on the occasion of sacrifice to the gods man solemnly communicates, but that when man would eat his fill of flesh food he piously remembers the gods and burns a little of it that it may reach them and incline their hearts to beneficence.

In the Homeric sacrifice there is communion, but not of any mystical kind; there is no question of partaking of the life and body of the god, only of dining with him. Mystical communion existed in Greece, but, as will be later seen, it was part of the worship of a god quite other than these Homeric Olympians, the god Dionysos.

Before we leave the *ἱερεῖον*, the animal sacrificed and eaten, one word of caution is necessary. It is sometimes argued that animal sacrifice, as contrasted with the simpler offerings of grain and fruits, is the mark of a later and more luxurious social state. Such was the view of Porphyry[2] the vegetarian. Flesh-eating and flesh sacrifice is to him the mark of a cruel and barbarous licence. Such too was the view of Eustathius[3]. In commenting on the *οὐλοχύται*, the barley grain scattered, he says, 'after the offering of barley grain came sacrifices and the eating of meat at sacrifices, because after the discovery of necessary foods the luxury of a meat diet and imported innovations in food were invented.' As a generalization this is false to facts; it depends on the environment of a race whether man will first eat vegetable or animal food; but as regards the particular case of the Greeks themselves, the observations of Porphyry and Eustathius are broadly true. The primitive

[1] *Od.* xxiv. 215
δεῖπνον δ' αἶψα συῶν ἱερεύσατε ὅς τις ἄριστος.

[2] Porph. *de Abst.* II. passim.

[3] Eust. ad *Il.* I. 449 § 132 *μετὰ δὲ τὰς οὐλοχύτας αἱ θυσίαι καὶ ἡ ἐν αὐταῖς κρεωφαγία διότι καὶ μετὰ τὴν τῶν ἀναγκαίων τροφῶν εὕρεσιν ἡ τῆς κρεωδαισίας πολυτέλεια καὶ τὸ τῆς τροφῆς ἐπείσακτον εὕρηται.*

dwellers in Greece and round the Mediterranean generally lived mainly on vegetarian diet, diversified by fish, and the custom of flesh-eating in large quantities was an innovation brought from without[1] (*ἐπείσακτον*). Athenaeus[2] in his first book discusses the various kinds of food, and dwells with constant astonishment on the flesh-eating habits of the Achaean heroes of Homer. He quotes the comic poet Eubulos as asking

> 'I pray you, when did Homer ever make
> An Achaean chief eat fish? 'tis always flesh,
> And roasted too, not boiled.'

Achaean chiefs, he notes—and in this they resemble their northern descendants—'do not care for made-dishes, kickshaws and the like. Homer sets before them only roast meat, and for the most part beef, such as would put life into them, body and soul.' It is true Athenaeus is arguing about the simplicity of the Homeric as contrasted with later Greek life, but the fact he states is beyond dispute, i.e. that the Homeric diet was mainly of flesh and unlike the vegetarian and fish diet of the ordinary Greek. Given a flesh diet for man, and the sacrifice of flesh to the gods he makes in his own image follows.

The terms *θύειν* and *ἱερεύειν* belong then to sacrifice regarded as a feast; it remains to consider the term *ἐναγίζειν*, in the definition of which we come, I think, to the fullest understanding of the ideas of the lower stratum of Greek religion.

First it is necessary to establish the fact that in usage the terms *θύειν* and *ἐναγίζειν* are clearly distinguished. A passage in Pausanias is for this purpose of capital importance. Pausanias is visiting a sanctuary of Herakles at Sicyon. He makes the following observations[3]: 'In the matter of sacrifice they are accustomed

[1] Prof. Ridgeway (*Early Age of Greece*, vol. I. p. 524) has shown (to me conclusively) that these Homeric Achaeans were of Celtic origin and brought with them from central Europe the flesh-*roasting* and flesh-eating habits of their northern ancestors.

[2] Athen. I. 46 p. 25.

[3] P. II. 10. 1 *ἐπὶ δὲ τῇ θυσίᾳ τοιάδε δρᾶν νομίζουσι. Φαῖστον ἐν Σικυωνίᾳ λέγουσιν ἐλθόντα καταλαβεῖν Ἡρακλεῖ σφᾶς ὡς ἥρωϊ ἐναγίζοντας· οὔκουν ἠξίου δρᾶν οὐδὲν ὁ Φαῖστος τῶν αὐτῶν, ἀλλ' ὡς θεῷ θύειν. καὶ νῦν ἔτι ἄρνα οἱ Σικυώνιοι σφάξαντες καὶ τοὺς μηροὺς ἐπὶ τοῦ βωμοῦ καύσαντες τὰ μὲν ἐσθίουσιν ὡς ἀπὸ ἱερείου τὰ δὲ ὡς ἥρωϊ τῶν κρεῶν ἐναγίζουσι.* That the distinction between *θύειν* and *ἐναγίζειν* is no late invention of Pausanias is shown by the fact that Herodotos (II. 43) uses the same words and draws the same distinction though with less explicit detail. Speaking of Herakles as god and hero, he says: *τῷ μὲν ἀθανάτῳ Ὀλυμπίῳ δὲ ἐπωνυμίην θύουσι, τῷ δ' ἑτέρῳ ὡς ἥρωϊ ἐναγίζουσι.*

to do as follows. They say that Phaestos, when he came to Sicyon, found the Sicyonians devoting offerings to Heracles as to a hero. But Phaestos would do nothing of the kind, but would sacrifice to him as to a god. And even now the Sicyonians, when they slay a lamb and burn the thighs upon the altar, eat a portion of the flesh as though it were a sacrificial victim, and another part of the flesh they make over as to a hero.' The passage is not easy to translate, because we have no English equivalent for *ἐναγίζειν*. I have translated the word by 'devote' because it connotes entire dedication—part of the sacrifice is shared, eaten by the worshipper in common with Heracles regarded as a *god*, the other part is utterly consecrated to Heracles as a hero; it is dead men's food. Pausanias, who is often careless in his use of *θύειν*, here carefully marks the distinction. The victim is an animal: part of it is offered to an Olympian—that portion is shared; part of it is offered, like the offerings at the *Chytroi*, to no Olympian, but to a ghost, and of that portion no man eats.

A second passage from Pausanias adds a further element of differentiation. At Megalopolis, Pausanias visited a sanctuary of the Eumenides. Of their ritual he speaks as follows[1]: 'They say that when these goddesses would drive Orestes mad they appeared to him black, but that after he had bitten off his finger they seemed to him white, and his senses returned to him, and therefore he made over an offering to the black goddesses to turn away their wrath, but to the white ones he did sacrifice.'

Language and ritual could scarcely speak more plainly: *θύειν* is to the Olympians, a joyous thanksgiving to gods who are all white and bright, beneficent, of the upper air; *ἐναγίζειν* is to those below, who are black and bad and malignant: *θύειν* is for *θεραπεία*, tendance; *ἐναγίζειν* for *ἀποτροπή*, riddance.

The distinction between the two forms of ritual having been thus definitely established, it remains to examine more closely the word *ἐναγίζειν* and the ritual it expresses, that of the dead—a ritual which, it must at this point be remembered, is also concerned with purification.

The word *ἐναγίζειν* can only mean the making of or dealing

[1] P. VIII. 34. 3 καὶ οὕτω ταῖς μὲν (ταῖς μελαίναις) ἐνήγισεν, ἀποτρέπων τὸ μήνιμα αὐτῶν, ταῖς δὲ ἔθυσε ταῖς λευκαῖς.

with something that is of the nature of an *ἄγος*, or, as the word sometimes appears, a *ἅγος*. It did not escape that acute observer of man and his language, Archbishop Eustathius[1], that this word and its cognate *ἅγιος*, holy, had in ancient days a double significance, that holy was not only pure but also polluted; this, he says, 'is on account of the double meaning of *ἄγος*.' To put the matter into modern phraseology, *ἄγος* is the thing that is *taboo*, the thing consecrated to the gods, and hence forbidden to man, the thing 'devoted.' The word lies deep down in the ritual of ancient sacrifice and of ancient religious thought; it is the very antithesis of communion; it is tinged with, though not quite the equivalent of, expiation.

Fortunately we are not left to conjecture as to what was the precise nature of the ceremonies covered by the word *ἐναγίζειν*. We know what was done, though we have no English word fully to express that doing. This fact may well remind us that we have lost not only the word but the thought, and must be at some pains to recover it. In the discussion that follows no translation of *ἐναγίζειν* will be attempted: I shall frankly use the Greek word and thereby avoid all danger from misleading modern connotations[2].

Quite accidentally, in the middle of a discourse on the various sorts of soap and washing basins, Athenaeus[3] has preserved for us a record of the exact ritual of *ἐναγισμοί*. After stating that the word *ἀπόνιπτρον*, washing off, is applied alike to the water in which either feet or hands are washed, he goes on to note that the

[1] Eust. ad *Il.* XXIII. 429, 1357. 59 οὕτω καὶ ἅγιος παρὰ τοῖς παλαιοῖς οὐ μόνον ὁ καθαρὸς ἀλλὰ καὶ ὁ μιαρὸς διὰ τὸ τοῦ ἄγους διπλόσημον.

[2] I do not deny that the word can be translated if we are content to vary our rendering in each various case. In the passages already discussed 'devote' is perhaps a fair equivalent, because the contrast emphasized is with a sacrifice shared. Sometimes the word may be rendered simply 'sacrifice to the dead', sometimes 'purificatory sacrifice', sometimes 'expiatory sacrifice'. No one word covers the whole field. It is this lost union of many diverse elements that has to be recovered and is nameless.

[3] Athen. IX. 78 p. 409 E ff. ἰδίως δὲ καλεῖται παρ' Ἀθηναίοις ἀπόνιμμα ἐπὶ τῶν εἰς τιμὴν τοῖς νεκροῖς γινομένων καὶ ἐπὶ τῶν τοὺς ἐναγεῖς καθαιρόντων ὡς καὶ Κλείδημος ἐν τῷ ἐπιγραφομένῳ Ἐξηγητικῷ. Προθεὶς γὰρ περὶ ἐναγισμῶν γράφει τάδε· "Ὄρυξαι βόθυνον πρὸς ἑσπέραν τοῦ σήματος. Ἔπειτα παρὰ τὸν βόθυνον πρὸς ἑσπέραν βλέπε, ὕδωρ κατάχει, λέγων τάδε· 'Ὑμῖν ἀπόνιμμα οἷς χρὴ καὶ οἷς θέμις.' Ἔπειτα αὖθις μύρον κατάχει." Παρέθετο ταῦτα καὶ Δωρόθεος φάσκων καὶ ἐν τοῖς Εὐπατριδῶν πατρίοις τάδε γεγράφθαι περὶ τῆς τῶν ἱκετῶν καθάρσεως. Ἔπειτ' ἀπονιψάμενος αὐτὸς καὶ οἱ ἄλλοι οἱ σπλαγχνεύοντες, ὕδωρ λαβὼν κάθαιρε ἀπόνιζε τὸ αἷμα τοῦ καθαιρομένου καὶ μετὰ τὸ ἀπόνιμμα ἀνακινήσας εἰς ταὐτὸ ἔγχεε.

word ἀπόνιμμα, 'offscouring,' slightly different in form but substantially the same in meaning, has among the Athenians a technical ritual usage. 'The term ἀπόνιμμα is specially applied *to the ceremonies in honour of the dead* and to *those that take place in the purification of the polluted.*' The word translated 'polluted' is ἐναγεῖς, i.e. under or in a state of ἄγος. He then proceeds to quote from a lost treatise on ceremonies of ἐναγισμός, the exact details of the ritual. 'Kleidemos, in his treatise called *Exegeticus,* writes on the subject of ἐναγισμοί as follows: "Dig a trench to the west of the tomb. Then, look along the trench towards the west, pour down water, saying these words: A purification for you to whom it is meet and right. Next pour down a second time myrrh." Dorotheos adds these particulars, alleging that the following prescription is written also in the ancestral rites of the Eupatridae concerning the purification of suppliants: "Next having washed himself, and the others who had disembowelled the victim having done the same, let him take water and make purification and wash off the blood from the suppliant who is being purified, and afterwards, having stirred up the washing, pour it into the same place".'

The conjoint testimony of the two writers is abundantly clear: either alone would have left us in doubt as to the real gist of the ceremony. Kleidemos tells us that it was addressed to the dead; the trench near the tomb, the western aspect of the setting sun, the cautious formulary, 'To you to whom it is meet and right,' all tell the same tale. It is safest not even to name the dead, lest you stir their swift wrath. But Kleidemos leaves us in the dark as to why they want an ἀπόνιμμα, 'an offscouring,' water defiled: why will not pure water or water and myrrh suffice? Dorotheos supplies the clue—those who have slain the victim wash the blood from their hands and *wash it off him who has been purified,* and then stirring it all up pour it into the trench. The ghost below demands the *blood of the victim washed off from the polluted suppliant*: when the ghost has drunk of this, then, and not till then, there is placation and purification.

That the ghost should demand the blood of the victim is natural enough; the ghosts in the Nekuia of the *Odyssey* 'drink the black blood' and thereby renew their life; but in ceremonies of purification they demand polluted water, the 'offscourings,' and why? The reason is clear. The victim is a surrogate for the polluted suppliant, the blood is put upon him that he may be identified with the victim, the ghost is deceived and placated. The ghost demands blood, not to satisfy a physical but so to speak a spiritual thirst, the thirst for vengeance. This thirst can only be quenched by the water polluted, the 'offscourings'[1] of the suppliant.

The suppliant for purification in the ritual just described was identified with the victim, or rather perhaps we should say the victim with the suppliant, by pouring over the suppliant the victim's blood. There were other means of identification. It has already been seen (p. 27) that the suppliant sometimes put on the whole skin of the victim, sometimes merely stood with his foot on the fleece. Another and more attenuated form of identification was the wearing of fillets, i.e. strands of wool confined at intervals by knots to make them stronger. Such fillets were normally worn by suppliants and by seers: the symbolism for suppliants is obvious, for seers evident on a closer inspection. The seer himself was powerless, but he could by the offering of a sacrifice to ghosts or heroes invoke the mantic dead; he wears the symbols of this sacrifice, the wreath and the fillets. Later their significance was forgotten, and they became mere symbols of office. The omphalos at Delphi, itself a mantic tomb, was covered with a net-work of wool-fillets, renewed no doubt at first with the offering of each new victim, later copied in stone[2], but always the symbol of recurring sacrifice.

The dread ceremonial of *ἐναγισμός* in its crudest, most barbarous form, is very clearly shown on the vase-painting in fig. 8, from a 'Tyrrhenian' amphora now in the British Museum[3]. The scene depicted is the sacrifice of Polyxena on the tomb of Achilles. In the *Hecuba* of Euripides[4], Neoptolemos takes Polyxena by the hand and leads her to the top of the

[1] Hesych. λουτρόν· τὸ ῥύπαρον ὕδωρ ἤγουν ἀπόνιμμα.
[2] *Bull. de Corr. Hell.* XXIV. p. 258.
[3] Published by Mr H. B. Walters, *J.H.S.* XVIII. 1898, p. 281, pl. XV. The class of vases known sometimes as 'Tyrrhenian,' sometimes as Corintho-Attic, all belong to the same period, about the middle of the sixth century B.C., and are apparently from the same workshop.
[4] Eur. *Hec.* 535.

mound, pours libations to his father, praying him to accept the 'soothing draughts,' and then cries

> 'Come thou and drink the maiden's blood
> Black and unmixed.'

In the centre of the design in fig. 8 is the omphalos-shaped grave[1], which is in fact the altar. Right over it the sacrifice takes

FIG. 8.

place. Neoptolemos, as next of kin to the slain man, is the sacrificer; Polyxena, as next of kin to the slayer, is the sacrifice. The ghost of the slain man drinks her blood and is appeased, and thereby the army is purged.

The blood only is offered to the ghost—the blood is the life, and it is vengeance, not food, the ghost cries for. It is so with the Erinyes, who are but angry ghosts[2]; when they hunt Orestes they cry[3],

> 'The smell of human blood smiles wooingly.'

Earth polluted has drunk a mother's blood, and they in turn

> 'Will gulp the living gore red from his limbs[4].'

When the ghost of Achilles has drunk the fresh blood of the maiden her body will be burnt, not that it may rise as a sweet savour to the gods above, but as a holocaust; it is a θυσία

[1] Omphalos and tomb are in intent the same, see *J.H.S.* XIX. p. 225.
[2] The genesis of the Erinys is discussed later, in Chapter V.
[3] Aesch. *Eum.* 253.
[4] Aesch. *Eum.* 264.

ἄδαιτος, a sacrifice without feast. It will be burnt on the low-lying *eschara* or portable hearth that stands on the grave. The *eschara* was by the ancients clearly distinguished from the altar proper, the *βωμός*. The *eschara*, says the scholiast on the *Phoenissae*[1] of Euripides, is 'accurately speaking the trench in the earth where they offer *ἐναγισμοί* to those who are gone below; the altar is that on which they sacrifice to the heavenly gods.'

Porphyry[2], who is learned in ritual matters, draws the same distinction. 'To the Olympian gods they set up temples and shrines and altars, but to the Earth-gods and to heroes, escharas, while for those below the earth there are trenches and megara.'

It is on an *eschara* that Clytaemnestra does her infernal service to the Erinyes[3]. She cries to them in bitter reproach:

> 'How oft have ye from out my hands licked up
> Wineless libations, sober offerings,
> And on the hearth of fire banquets grim
> By night, an hour unshared of any god!'

Her ritual was the ritual of the underworld abhorred of the Olympians.

The eschara on which the holocaust to the underworld gods is burnt lies low upon the ground; the *βωμός*, the altar of the Olympians, rises higher and higher heavenwards. There is the like symbolism in the actual manner of the slaying of the victim. Eustathius[4], in commenting on the sacrifice of Chryses to Phoebus Apollo, when they 'drew back the victims' heads,' says 'according to the custom of the Greeks, for if they are sacrificing to those above they bend back the neck of the sacrificial animal so that it may look away towards the sky, but if to heroes or to the dead in general the victim is sacrificed looking downwards.' Eustathius[5] again says of the prayer of Achilles, 'by looking heavenwards he expresses vividly whither the prayer is directed, for Achilles is not praying to Zeus of the underworld, but to Zeus of the sky.' The Christian of to-day, though he believes his God is everywhere, yet

[1] Schol. ad Eur. *Phoen.* 284 *διαφέρει βωμὸς καὶ ἐσχάρα.* ad 274 *ἐσχάρα μὲν κυρίως ὁ ἐπὶ τῆς γῆς βόθρος ἔνθα ἐναγίζουσι τοῖς κάτω ἐρχομένοις, βωμὸς δὲ ἐν ᾧ θύουσι τοῖς ἐπουρανίοις θεοῖς.*

[2] Porph. *de antr. nymph.* 3 *τοῖς μὲν Ὀλυμπίοις θεοῖς ναούς τε καὶ ἕδη καὶ βωμοὺς ἱδρύσαντο, χθονίοις δὲ καὶ ἥρωσιν ἐσχάρας, ὑποχθονίοις δὲ βόθρους καὶ μέγαρα.* The *megara* will be discussed later (p. 125).

[3] Aesch. *Eum.* 106.

[4] Eustath. ad *Il.* I. 459 § 134.

[5] Eustath. § 1057, 37.

uplifts his hands to pray. For the like reason the victim for the dead was black and that for the Olympians frequently white; that for the dead sacrificed at the setting of the sun, that for the Ouranians at the dawn[1]. Upon certain holocausts, as has already been seen, the sun might not look.

The ritual of the *ἐναγισμοί* is then of *purgation by placation of the spirits of the underworld.* The extreme need of primitive man for placation is from the stain of bloodshed; purgation from this stain is at first only obtained by the offering of the blood of the murderer himself, then by the blood of a surrogate victim applied to him.

It is, I think, probable that at the back of many a mythological legend that seems to us to contain what we call 'human sacrifice' there lies, not the slaying of a victim for the pleasure of a Moloch-like god, but simply the appeasement of an angry ghost. So long as primitive man preserves the custom of the blood-feud, so long will he credit his dead kinsman with passions like his own.

In this connection it is interesting to note some further details of the ritual terminology of *ἐναγισμοί* as contrasted with that of the service of the Olympians.

The sacrifice burnt that the Olympians may eat of it is *θῦμα*, the thing burned to smoke; the sacrificial victim slain to be eaten by the worshipper is *ἱερεῖον*, the holy thing; the victim slain for placation and purification is by correct authors called by another name, it is a *σφάγιον*, a thing slaughtered. The word explains itself: it is not the sacrifice burnt, not the sacred thing killed and carved for a meal, but simply the victim hacked and hewn to pieces. Such a victim was not even necessarily skinned. Of what use to carefully flay a thing doomed to utter destruction? In the *Electra* of Euripides[2] the old man describes such a *σφάγιον*:

> 'I saw upon the pyre with its black fleece
> A sheep, the victim, and fresh blood outpoured.'

It is interesting to note in this connection that the word *σφάγιον* is always used of human victims, and of such animals as

[1] Schol. ad Apoll. Rhod. I. 587 *τοῖς μὲν οὖν κατοιχομένοις ὡς περὶ ἡλίου δυσμὰς ἐναγίζουσι τοῖς δὲ οὐρανίδαις ὑπὸ τὴν ἕω, ἀνατέλλοντος τοῦ ἡλίου.*

[2] Eur. *El.* 514.

were in use as surrogates. The term is applied to all the famous maiden-sacrifices of mythology. Ion[1] asks Creousa:

'And did thy father sacrifice thy sisters?'

And Creousa with greater ritual precision makes answer:

'He dared to slay them as *sphagia* for the land.'

As a *σφάγιον* Polyxena[2] is slain on the tomb of Achilles; she dies as an atonement, a propitiation, as 'medicine of salvation.'

The normal and most frequent use of *σφάγια* was, as in the case of *ἐναγισμοί* in general, for purification by placation. In stress of great emergency, of pestilence, of famine, and throughout historical times at the moment before a battle, *σφάγια* were regularly offered. They seem to have been carried round or through the person or object to be purified. Athenaeus[3] records an instructive instance. The inhabitants of Kynaetho, a village in Arcadia, neglected the civilizing influences of dancing and feasting, and became so savage and impious that they never met except for the purpose of quarrelling. They perpetrated at one time a great massacre, and after this, whenever their emissaries came to any other of the Arcadian cities, the citizens by public proclamation bade them depart, and the Mantineans after their departure made a purification of the city, 'leading the slaughtered victims round the whole circuit of the district.'

As purifications the use of *σφάγια* needs no further comment. It is less obvious at first why *σφάγια* were always employed in the taking of oaths. The expression *τέμνειν σφάγια* is the equivalent of the familiar *τέμνειν ὅρκια*. In the *Suppliants* of Euripides[4] Athene says to Theseus:

'Hearken whereinto thou must cut the *sphagia*.'

She then bids him write the oaths in the hollow of a tripod-cauldron and afterwards cut the throats of the victims into the cauldron, thus clearly identifying the oaths and the blood.

[1] Eur. *Ion* 277

ΙΩ. *πατὴρ Ἐρεχθεὺς σὰς ἔθυσε συγγόνους;*
ΚΡ. *ἔτλη πρὸ γαίας σφάγια παρθένους κτανεῖν.*

[2] Eur. *Hec.* 121 *τύμβῳ σφάγιον.*

[3] Athen. xiv. 22, p. 626 *καθαρμὸν τῆς πόλεως ἐποιήσαντο σφάγια περιάγοντες κύκλῳ τῆς χώρας ἁπάσης.*

[4] Eur. *Supp.* 1296 *ἐν ᾧ δὲ τέμνειν σφάγια χρή σ' ἄκουέ μου.*

In the ordinary ritual of the taking of oaths, the oath-taker actually stood upon the pieces of the slaughtered animal. Pausanias[1], on the road between Sparta and Arcadia, came to a place called 'Horse's Tomb.' There Tyndareus sacrificed a horse and made Helen's suitors take an oath, causing them to stand on the cut-up pieces of the horse,—having made them take the oath, he buried the horse. At Stenyclerum[2] in Messenia was another monument, called 'Boar's Monument,' where it was said Herakles had given an oath to the sons of Neleus on the cut pieces of a boar. Nor is the custom of swearing on the cut pieces recorded only by mythology. In the Bouleuterion at Elis was an image of Zeus, 'of all others,' says Pausanias[3], 'best fitted to strike terror into evildoers.' Its surname was Horkios, He of the Oath. Near this image the athletes, their fathers, brothers, and trainers had to swear on the cut pieces of a boar that they would be guilty of no foul play as regarded the Olympian games. Pausanias regrets that he 'forgot to ask what they did with the boar after the oath had been taken by the athletes.' He adds, 'With the men of old days the rule was as regards a sacrificial animal on which an oath had been taken that it should be no more accounted as eatable for men. Homer,' he says, 'shows this clearly, for the boar on the cut pieces of which Agamemnon swore that Briseis had not been partner of his bed is represented as being cast by the herald into the sea:

> "He spake and with the pitiless bronze he cut
> The boar's throat, and the boar Talthybios whirled,
> And in the great wash of the hoary sea
> He cast it to the fish for food[4]."

This in ancient days was their custom about such matters.'

The custom of standing on the fragments of the victim points clearly to the identification of oath-taker and sacrifice. The victim

[1] P. III. 20. 9. [2] P. IV. 15. 8.

[3] P. v. 24. 10 *τοῖς γε ἀρχαιοτέροις ἐπὶ ἱερείῳ ἦν καθεστηκὸς ἐφ' ᾧ τις ὅρκιον ἐποιήσατο μηδὲ ἐδώδιμον εἶναι τοῦτ' ἔτι ἀνθρώπῳ*. Strictly speaking Pausanias ought to have written *ἐπὶ σφαγίῳ*, but his meaning is sufficiently clear. *τόμια* are actually *σφάγια*, not *ἱερεῖα*. Eustathius, in discussing the sacrifice of Odysseus to the ghosts in the Nekuia, makes the following statement: *ὅτι Ὁμήρου εἰπόντος ἱερήια τὰ ἐν Ἄιδου σφάγια ἐπὶ χοῇ νεκρῶν φασὶν οἱ παλαιοὶ οὐκ ὀρθῶς εἰρῆσθαι τοῦτο, ἐπὶ γὰρ νεκρῶν τόμιά φασι καὶ ἔντομα, ἐπὶ δὲ θεῶν ἱερεῖα*. Pausanias in the passage cited above (III. 20. 9) uses *θύειν* where *σφαγιάζεσθαι* would be more correct. He makes a sort of climax of confusion when, in describing the ritual of the hero Amphiaraos, he says (I. 34. 5): *ἐστὶ δὲ καθάρσιον τῷ θεῷ θύειν*, when he should have said *τῷ ἥρωι σφαγιάζεσθαι*.

[4] *Il.* XIX. 265.

was hewn in bits; so if the oath-taker perjure himself will he be hewn in bits: the victim is not eaten but made away with, utterly destroyed, *devoted*; a like fate awaits the oath-breaker: the oath becomes in deadly earnest a form of self-imprecation.

Still less obvious is it why sacrifices to the winds should uniformly have taken the form of *σφάγια* rather than *ἱερεῖα*. At first sight the winds would appear to be if anything Ouranian powers of the upper air, yet it seems that sacrifices to the winds were buried, not burnt.

What astonished Pausanias[1] more than anything else he saw at Methana in Troezen was a ceremony for averting the winds. 'A wind called Lips, which rushes down from the Saronic gulf, dries up the tender shoots of the vine. When the squall is upon them two men take a cock, which must have all its feathers white, tear it in two, and run round the vines in opposite directions, each of them carrying one half of the cock. When they come back to the place they start from they bury the cock there. This is the device they have invented for counteracting Lips. I myself,' he adds, 'have seen the people keeping off hail by sacrifices and incantations.' The Methanian cock is a typical *σφάγιον*: it is carried round for purification, the evil influences of the wind are somehow caught by it, in rather proleptic fashion, and then buried away. It is really of the order of pharmakos ceremonies, to be considered later, rather than a sacrifice proper. For a *σφάγιον* we should expect the cock to be black, but on the principle of sympathetic magic it is in this case white. The normal sacrifice to a wind was a black animal. When in the *Frogs*[2] a storm is brewing between Aeschylus and Euripides, and threatens to burst, Dionysos calls out:

> 'Bring out a ewe, boys, bring a black-fleeced ewe,
> Here's a typhoon that's just about to burst.'

Winds were underworld gods, but when propitious they had a strong and natural tendency to become Ouranian, and the white sacrifices with intent to compel their beneficence would help this out. They are an exact parallel to the black and white Eumenides already noted. Virgil[3] says:

> 'To Storm a black sheep, white to the favouring West.'

[1] P. II. 34. 3. [2] Ar. *Ran.* 817. [3] Virg. *Aen.* III. 120.

Equally instructive is the account given by Pausanias[1] of the ceremonies performed at Titane to soothe the winds, though with his customary vagueness Pausanias describes them by the word *θύειν* when they are really *ἐναγισμοί*. They are performed on one *night* in each year, and Pausanias adds, the priest also 'does secret ceremonies into four pits,' soothing the fury of the winds, and he chants over them, as they say, Medea's charms. Each of the four winds dwelt, it is clear, as a chthonic power, in a pit; his sacrifice was after the fashion of heroes and ghosts. It is possible, indeed probable, that the pits were in connection with the tomb of some hero or heroine. The sacrifice of Iphigeneia was *παυσάνεμος*[2], with power to stay the winds; that of Polyxena at the tomb of Achilles had the like virtue. Be that as it may, it will be seen when we come to demonology that the winds were regarded as ghosts, as breaths: as such their cult was necessarily chthonic.

Another of their functions *σφάγια* share with the ordinary animal-sacrifices, the *ἱερεῖα*. Like the *ἱερεῖα* they could be used for purposes of divination. Used as they were for purification in any great emergency, mere economy may have suggested that they should be further utilized for oracular purposes. The greater solemnity of *σφάγια* would lend to the omens taken from them a specially portentous virtue[3]. It is amusing to find that even Porphyry[4], averse though he is to human sacrifice, still seems to feel a dim possibility that for mantic purposes human entrails may have special virtue. 'But it will be urged,' he says, as though stating a possible and reasonable argument, 'that the future may be more clearly divined from the vitals of a man.'

Precise authors who know about ritual always distinguish between the omens taken from ordinary animal sacrifice and those from *σφάγια*. Thus Xenophon[5] in the *Anabasis* says, 'The sacrifices (*ἱερεῖα*) are propitious to us, the omens favourable, the *σφάγια* most propitious.' The practice of using *σφάγια* for omens

[1] P. II. 12. 1.

[2] Aesch. *Agam.* 214.

[3] The full and somewhat revolting details as to how omens were taken from *σφάγια* do not concern us here; they are given in full by the scholiast on Eur. *Phoenissae* 1255; see P. Stengel, *Hermes*, 1899, XXXIV. p. 642.

[4] Porph. *de Abst.* II. 51.

[5] Xen. *Anab.* VI. 5. 21.

before a battle would seem to have been uniform. When women, says Eteocles[1], are wailing and making a commotion, it is the part of men

> 'To slay the victims, take therefrom the omens
> Before the gods, at the onset of the foe.'

It is probably to this oracular function of *σφάγια* that we owe the very frequent use of the middle *σφαγιάζεσθαι*, as in the parallel case of *θύειν*, the sacrifice by fire. For *θύειν* and *θύεσθαι* the distinction is familiar, and expressly stated by Ammonius[2]: 'of those who simply sacrifice (active) the victims the word *θύουσι* is used, of those who take omens from the entrails *θύονται*.' The active is of the nature of thanksgiving, the middle partakes of prayer and impulsion. In the case of *σφάγια* the active is very rarely in use, and naturally, for the sacrifice of *σφάγια* has in it no element of thanksgiving[3].

The ritual then of *σφάγια* and of *ἐναγισμοί*, of slaughter and of purification, is based on the fear of ghosts, of ghosts and their action on living men, whether as evil winds, or for dread portents, or for vengeance on the broken oath, or, first and foremost, for the guilt of shed blood. Its essence is of *ἀποτροπή*, *aversion*.

Nowhere perhaps is this instinct of aversion so clearly seen, seen in a form where the instinct has not yet chilled and crystallized into definite ritual, as in the account of the murder of Absyrtos by Jason and Medea as given by Apollonius Rhodius[4]. The murder was by a treacherous ambuscade set for Absyrtos at the threshold

[1] Aesch. *Sept.* 230

> ἀνδρῶν τάδ' ἐστὶ σφάγια καὶ χρηστήρια
> θεοῖσιν ἔρδειν πολεμίων πειρωμένων.

[2] Ammon. p. 72 Valck. *θύουσι μὲν γὰρ οἱ σφάζοντες τὰ ἱερεῖα, θύονται δὲ οἳ διὰ τῶν σπλάγχνων μαντεύονται.*

[3] The question of *σφάγια* has been very fully discussed by Dr Paul Stengel in four papers as follows: '*Σφάγια*,' *Hermes*, 1886, XXI. p. 307; 'Miscellen,' XXV. p. 321; 'Prophezeiung aus der *Σφάγια*,' XXXI. p. 479 and XXXIV. p. 642. To this must be added papers by the same author on *ἐντέμνειν ἔντομα* in the *Zeitschrift für Gymnasial-Wesen*, 1880, p. 743, and in the *Jahrbuch für Philologie*, 1882, p. 322, and 1883, p. 375, and on the winds, *Hermes*, 1900, p. 626. I owe much in the matter of references to Dr Stengel's full collection of sources, but his conclusions as stated in 'Die Sakralaltertümer' (Iwan Müller's *Handbuch der kl. Altertumswissenschaft*, Band v. Abt. 3) seem to me to be vitiated by the assumption that ceremonies of purification are late and foreign importations.

[4] Apoll. Rhod. IV. 470, trans. by Mr Gilbert Murray.

of the temple of Artemis; Jason smites him like a bull for sacrifice, while Medea stands by.

> 'So by that portal old kneeling he fell,
> And while the last of life yet sobbed and passed,
> Craving, clasped both hands to the wound, to hold
> The dark blood back. But the blood reached, and sprang,
> And, where the veilèd woman shuddered from him,
> Lay red on the white robe and the white veil.
> Then swift a sidelong eye, a pitiless eye,
> The Erinys all subduing, that knoweth Sin,
> Awoke, and saw what manner of deed was there.
> And Aeson's son smote from that sacrifice
> Red ravine, and three times ravined with his mouth
> Amid the blood, and three times from him spewed
> That horror of sin; as men that slay by guile
> Use, to make still the raging of the dead.'

Apollonius tries to make a ritual of the awful instinct of physical fear. The body is mangled that the angry ghost may be maimed, the blood actually licked up that the murderer may spit it forth and rid himself of the fell pollution. Only then can the corpse be safely buried[1]. But it is too late, for Absyrtos has put the blood upon Medea.

Clytaemnestra, when she murdered Agamemnon, followed the same horrid practice of 'aversion.' Sophocles[2] makes Electra say:

> 'She lopped his limbs as though he were a foe
> And for libations wiped upon his head
> The blood stains.'

By the time of Apollonius the Erinys is no longer the actual ghost but a separate spirit of vengeance, and even the primitive ritual of *aversion* is explained as a sort of tendance; the lopped limbs are ἐξάργματα, first beginnings, a sort of hideous sacrifice to the murdered man rather than mainly the means of maiming

[1] Since the above was written my attention has been called to Dr J. G. Frazer's paper 'On certain Burial Customs as illustrations of the primitive theory of the soul' (*Journal of Anthropological Institute*, vol. xv. 1885—6). After a detailed examination of the burial rites and customs of the Greeks and many other peoples Dr Frazer reaches the following memorable and to me most welcome conclusion: 'In general I think we may lay down the rule that wherever we find so-called purification by fire or water from pollution contracted by contact with the dead we may assume with much probability that the original intention was to place a physical barrier of fire or water between the living and the dead, and that the conceptions of pollution and purification are merely the fictions of a later age invented to explain the purpose of a ceremony of which the original intention was forgotten.'

[2] Soph. *El.* 445.

him[1]. But the scholiast[2] on the *Electra* clearly explains the gist of the ceremonial. He says these things were done 'as taking away the force of the dead so that later they may suffer nothing fearful from them.'

It may perhaps be felt that such instances are purely mythological, and that fear of the ghost had wholly waned in historical times. The horrid practice of mutilation no doubt fell into abeyance, but the fear of the ghost and the sense that purification from guilt could only be obtained by direct appeal to the ghost itself lived on.

The case of Pausanias gives curious evidence as to the procedure of an educated murderer of the fifth century B.C. Pausanias[3] the traveller tells how his namesake sought protection from the Goddess of the Brazen House, but failed because he was defiled by blood. This pollution he tried by every possible means to expiate: he had recourse to purifications of all kinds, he made supplication to Zeus Phyxios, a being obviously akin to Meilichios—and he resorted to the Psychagogi, the Ghost-Compellers of Phigalia. They seem to have failed, for Plutarch[4] tells us he sent to Italy for experts, and they, after they had done sacrifice, *wrenched the ghost out of the sanctuary.*

The historical case of Pausanias is exactly parallel to that of the mythological Orestes. Man expects that the dead man will behave as he would behave were he yet living—pursue him for vengeance; the ghost is an actual, almost physical reality. It needed a Euripides to see that this ghost was a purely subjective horror, a disordered conscience. He makes Menelaos ask the mad Orestes[5]:

> 'What dost thou suffer? What disease undoes thee?'

and Orestes makes answer:

> 'Conscience, for I am conscious of fell deeds.'

[1] The details described by Suidas s.v. *ἐμασχαλίσθη* have a somewhat apocryphal air and are probably due to etymology.

[2] Schol. ad Soph. *El.* 445.

[3] P. III. 17. 7.

[4] Plut. *de ser. num. vind.* XVII. *μεταπεμφθέντες οἱ ψυχαγωγοὶ καὶ θύσαντες ἀπεσπάσαντο τοῦ ἱεροῦ τὸ εἴδωλον.*

[5] Eur. *Or.* 395

ΜΕ. *τί χρῆμα πάσχεις; τίς σ' ἀπόλλυσιν νόσος;*
ΟΡ. *ἡ ξύνεσις, ὅτι σύνοιδα δείν' εἰργασμένος.*

Anthropomorphism is usually regarded as a humane trait in Greek religion; it is noted as a thing distinguishing their cultus from the animal worship of less civilized nations. But anthropomorphism, as is clearly seen in ghost-worship, looks both ways. To be human is not necessarily to be humane. Man is cruel and implacable, and he makes the ghost after his own image. Man is also foolish and easily tricked, so he plays tricks upon the vengeful ghost, cheating him of his real meed of the murderer's or kinsman's blood. Hence the surrogate victims, hence the frequent substitution stories. Another element enters in. The gods, and specially the ghost-gods, are conservative; man gets in advance of the gods he has made, and is ashamed of the rites he once performed with complete confidence in their rightness. Then he tries by a cheat to reconcile his new view and his old custom. Religion, which once inspired the best in him, lags behind, expressing the worst.

Suidas[1] tells a story which curiously expresses this state of transition, this cheating of the god to save the conscience of the worshipper. The Greeks had a proverb, Ἔμβαρός εἰμι, 'I am Embaros,' which they used, according to Suidas, of a 'sharp man with his wits about him,' and, according to one of the collectors of proverbs, of those who 'gave a false impression, i.e. were out of their minds.' The origin of the proverb was as follows: There was a sanctuary of Artemis at Munychia. A bear came into it and was killed by the Athenians. A famine followed, and the god gave an oracle that the famine should cease if some one would sacrifice his daughter to the goddess. Embaros was the only man who promised to do it, on condition that he and his family should have the priesthood for life. He disguised his daughter and hid her in the sanctuary, and 'dressed a goat in a garment and sacrificed it as his daughter.' The story is manifestly aetiological, based on a ritual with a hereditary priesthood, and the sacrifice of a surrogate goat dressed as a woman.

It is probable, though not certain, that behind the figure of the Olympian Artemis, of the goddess who was kindly to lions' cubs and 'suckling whelps,' there lay the cult of some vindictive ghost or heroine who cried for human blood. In moments of great peril

[1] Suidas s.v. Ἔμβαρός εἰμι, *Paroimiograph.* I. 402, App. Cent. and Eustath. ad *Il.* II. 732 § 331.

this belief in the vindictiveness of ghosts, a belief kept in check by reason in the day-time, might surge up in a man's mind and haunt his dreams by night. Plutarch[1] tells an instructive story about a dream that came to Pelopidas before the battle of Leuctra. Near the field of battle was a field where were the tombs of the daughters of Scedasos, a local hero. The maidens, who were obviously local nymphs, were called from the place Leuctrides. The night before the battle, as Pelopidas was sleeping in his tent, he had a vision which 'caused him no small disturbance.' He thought he saw the maidens crying at their tombs and cursing the Spartans, and he saw Scedasos their father bidding him sacrifice to his daughters a maiden with auburn hair if he wished to overcome his enemies on the morrow. Being a humane as well as a pious man, the order seemed to him a strange and lawless one, but none the less he told the soothsayers and the generals about it. Some of them thought that it ought not to be neglected, and brought forward as precedents the ancient instances of Menoiceus, son of Creon, and Macaria, daughter of Herakles, and, in more recent times, the case of Pherecydes the philosopher, who was put to death by the Spartans and whose skin was preserved (no doubt as 'medicine') by their kings in accordance with an oracle; also the case of Leonidas, who sacrificed himself for Greece; and, lastly, the human victims sacrificed to Dionysos Omestes before the battle of Salamis, all which cases had the sanction of success. Moreover, they pointed out, Agesilaus, when he was about to set sail from Aulis itself, had the same vision as Agamemnon, and disregarding it through misplaced tenderness, came to grief in consequence. The more advanced section of the army used the argument of the fatherhood of God and the superior nature of the supreme deities; such sacrifices were only fit for Typhons and Giants and inferior and impotent demons. Pelopidas, while they were discussing the question in the abstract, only got more and more uncomfortable, when on a sudden a she-colt got loose from the herd and ran through the camp; the laymen present only admired her shining red coat, her proud paces and shrill neighing, but Theocritus the soothsayer saw the thing in his heart, and cried aloud to Pelopidas, 'Happy man, here is the sacred victim, wait for no

[1] Plut. *Vit. Pelop.* xxi.

other maiden, use the one the god has given thee.' And they took the colt and led her to the tombs of the maidens, and prayed and wreathed her head and cut her throat and rejoiced and published the vision of Pelopidas and the sacrifice to the army. Whether Plutarch's story is matter of fact or not is of little moment; it was felt to be *probable*, or else it would never have been narrated.

I have purposely dwelt on the dark side of ἐναγισμοί, of the service of the placation of ghosts, because in the vengeance of the ghost exacted for bloodshed lies the kernel of the doctrine of purification. But since man's whole activity is not bounded by revenge, ghosts have other and simpler needs than that of vengeance. The service of the underworld is not all *aversion*, there is also some element of *tendance*.

In the vase-painting in fig. 9, a design from a rather late

Fig. 9.

red-figured krater in the Bibliothèque Nationale[1] in Paris, we have a representation of a familiar scene, the raising of the ghost of

[1] *Cat.* 422.

Teiresias by Odysseus, as described in the *Nekuia*. Vase-paintings of this date tend to be rather illustrations than independent conceptions, but they sometimes serve the purpose of vivid presentation. Odysseus[1] has dug the trench, he has poured the drink-offering of mead and sweet wine and water, and sprinkled the white meal, and he has slain the sheep; the head and feet of one of them, seemingly a black ram, are visible above the trench. He has sat him down sword in hand to keep off the throng of lesser ghosts, and he and his comrades wait the up-rising of Teiresias. Out of the very trench is seen emerging the bald ghost-like head of the seer. This is a clear case, not of deprecation but of invocation. Teiresias by the strength of the black blood returns to life. There is a clear reminiscence of the ghost-raising[2] that went on at many a hero's tomb, for, as will later be seen in the discussion of hero-worship, every hero was apt to be credited with mantic powers. The victims slain are in a sense, as Homer calls them, *ἱερήια*; they are sacrificed and eaten, but eaten by a ghost. As such they have been accompanied by offerings that could only be intended for drink-offerings, not the *ἀπόνιμμα*, the offscourings, but libations of mead and wine and pure water. Here again the ghost is made in the image of man: the Homeric hero drinks wine in his life and demands it after his death. The service of the dead is here very near akin to that of the Olympians; it is no grim atonement, but at worst a bloody banquet, at best a human feast, too human, too universal to need detailed elucidation. It is a ritual founded on a belief deep-rooted and long-lived; with the Greeks it was alive in Lucian's[3] days. Charon asks Hermes why men dig a trench, and burn expensive feasts, and pour wine and honey into a trench. Hermes answers that he cannot think what good it can do to those in Hades, but 'anyhow people believe that the dead are summoned up from below to the feast, and that they flutter round the smoke and fat and drink the honey draught from the trench.' Here the ghosts invade the late and popular burnt sacrifice of the Olympians, but the principle is the same.

[1] *Od.* XI. 23 ff.

[2] For the ceremonials of ghost-raising, see Dr W. G. Headlam, *Classical Review*, 1902, p. 52.

[3] Luc. *Char.* 22.

The Anthesteria was a festival of ghosts, overlaid by a festival of Dionysos[1], and so far the *riddance* of ghosts by means of placation has been shown to be an important element in ancient sacrifice and in the ancient notion of purification. But placation of ghosts does not exhaust the content even of ancient sacrifice: another element will appear in the festival of early summer that has next to be considered, the *Thargelia*.

[1] According to Prof. Ridgeway's recent theory (*J.H.S.* xx. 115) the drama of Dionysos took its rise from mimetic dances at the tombs of local heroes and save for the one element of the Satyric play was not Dionysiac. The festival of the Anthesteria with its Pot-Contests would therefore present an easy occasion of fusion; see my *Primitive Athens*, p. 99. Independently of Prof. Ridgeway, Dr M. Nilsson suggests the same origin for tragedy; see his paper on 'Totenklage und Tragödie' (from *Comment. philologae in hon. Joh. Paulson Göteborg*, 1905) resumed in the *Archiv f. Religionswissenschaft*, 1906, p. 286.

CHAPTER III.

HARVEST FESTIVALS.

The Thargelia, Kallynteria, Plynteria.

'Λοιδορούμενοι εὐλογοῦμεν, διωκόμενοι ἀνεχόμεθα, βλασφημούμενοι παρακαλοῦμεν· ὡς περικαθάρματα τοῦ κόσμου ἐγενήθημεν πάντων περίψημα.'

Spring-time, it has been seen in the last chapter, is the season for *purification* by means of the *placation of ghosts.* But spring-time is not the only anxious time for primitive man. As the year wears on, a season approaches of even more critical import, when purification was even more imperatively needed, the season of harvest; in the earliest days the gathering in of such wild fruits as nature herself provides, in later times the reaping and garnering of the various kinds of cereals.

In the North with our colder climate we associate harvest with autumn; our harvest festivals fall at the end of September. September was to the Greek the month of the grape harvest, the vintage, but his grain harvest fell in ancient days as now in the month Thargelion, the latter part of May and the beginning of June. This month is marked to the Greeks by three festivals, the Thargelia, which gave its name to the month, the Kallynteria, and the Plynteria. No festival has been more frequently discussed than the Thargelia, and on no festival has comparative anthropology thrown more light. The full gist of the ceremony has never, I think, been clearly set forth, owing to the simple fact that the Thargelia has usually been considered alone, not in connection with the two other festivals[1]. In the present chapter I shall consider first that element in the festival to which it and the month owe their names, i.e. the first-fruits; second, the ceremony of the Pharmakos, which has made the festival famous; third the connection with the Kallynteria and Plynteria and the light thrown on both by the Roman festival of the Vestalia. Finally from the consideration of the gist of these harvest festivals it will be possible to add some further elements to our conception of Greek religious thought, and especially of the Greek notion of sacrifice.

THARGELION AND THARGELIA.

About the meaning[2] of the word Thargelia there is happily not the slightest doubt. Athenaeus[3] quotes a statement made by Krates, a writer of about the middle of the 2nd century B.C., in his book on the Attic dialect as follows: 'The *thargelos* is the first loaf made after the carrying home of the harvest.' Now a loaf of bread is *not* a very primitive affair, but happily Hesychius[4] records an earlier or at least more rudimentary form of nourishment: 'Thargelos,' he says, 'is a pot full of seeds.' From Athenaeus[5] again we learn that the cake called *thargelos* was sometimes also called *thalusios*. The Thalusia, the festival of the first-fruits of Demeter, is familiar to us from the lovely picture in the Seventh Idyll of Theocritus[6]. The friends meet Lycidas the goatherd and say to him:

'The road on which our feet are set it is a harvest way,
For to fair-robed Demeter our comrades bring to-day
The first-fruits of their harvesting. She on the threshing place
Great store of barley grain outpoured, for guerdon of her grace.'

[1] A. Mommsen (*Feste der Stadt Athen*, p. 486) discusses the Thargelia, Kallynteria and Plynteria in immediate succession, but without a hint of the connection of the two last with the first; for the non-Attic Thargelia see Dr M. P. Nilsson's *Griechische Feste*, which has appeared since the publication of my first edition.

[2] Vaniček (s.v. p. 310) derives Θαργήλια, which appears also in the form Ταργήλια, from a root *ταργ* meaning 'hot' and 'dry' and connects it with *τρυγ* in *τρύσκω*, *τρυγάω* etc. All these analogous forms have the same meaning, i.e. 'ripened by the sun,' 'ready for harvesting.'

[3] Athen. III. 52, p. 115 *θάργηλον καλεῖσθαι τὸν ἐκ τῆς συγκομιδῆς πρῶτον γενόμενον ἄρτον.*

[4] Hesych. s.v. *θάργηλος χύτρα ἐστὶν ἀνάπλεως σπερμάτων.*

[5] loc. cit. supra.

[6] Theocr. *Id.* VII. 31 *ἁ δ' ὁδὸς ἅδε Θαλυσίας.*

Homer[1] tells how the plague of the Calydonian boar came to waste the land of the Aetolians, because Oineus their king forgot to celebrate the Thalusia, and Eustathius, commenting on the passage, says: 'The first-fruits are the *thalusia.*' He adds that some of the rhetoricians call the *thalusia* 'feasts of the Harvest-Home.'

It is then abundantly clear that the festival of the Thargelia is in the main a festival of the offering of first-fruits on the occasion of harvest, and the month Thargelion the month of harvest rites. Of one of these harvest rites, the carrying of the *Eiresione*[2], we have unusually full particulars.

In the *Knights* of Aristophanes[3], Cleon and the Sausage-Seller are clamouring at the door of Demos. Demos comes out and asks angrily:

> 'Who's bawling there? do let the door alone,
> You've torn my Eiresione all to bits.'

The scholiast explains. 'At the Pyanepsia and the Thargelia the Athenians hold a feast to Helios and the Horae, and the boys carry about branches twined with wool, from which they get the name of *Eiresiones,* and they hang them up before the doors.' It is very probable that the wool (εἶρος), taken perhaps from a sacred animal, gave its name to the Eiresione, but there were many other things besides wool hung on the branch. Our fullest account comes from the rhetorician Pausanias, who is quoted by Eustathius[4] in his commentary on the *Iliad.* Eustathius is explaining that the term ἀμφιθαλής means a child with both parents alive, and he adds by way of illustration that children of this sort were chosen by the ancients to deck out the Eiresione. He then quotes from the works of Pausanias the following account of the ceremony:

[1] Hom. *Il.* IX. 534

> ὃ οἱ οὔ τι θαλύσια γουνῷ ἀλωῆς
> Οἰνεὺς ῥέξ'.

Eustath. ad loc. θαλύσια δὲ αἱ ἀπαρχαί...τινὲς δὲ τῶν ῥητόρων καὶ συγκομιστήρια ταῦτα καλοῦσιν...ἔτι δὲ καὶ θαλύσιος ἄρτος ὁ ἐκ τῆς τῶν καρπῶν, φασί, συγκομιδῆς πρῶτος γινόμενος.

[2] The sources for the Eiresione are very fully given and discussed by Mannhardt. *Wald- und Feldkulte*, pp. 214—248; see Dr Frazer, *Golden Bough*, 2nd edition, vol. I. p. 190, for modern parallels.

[3] Ar. *Eq.* 729, schol. ad loc.

[4] Eustath. ad *Il.* XXII. 496, p. 1283

> ἦδον δὲ παῖδες
> εἰρεσιώνη σῦκα φέρει καὶ πίονας ἄρτους
> καὶ μέλιτος κοτύλην καὶ ἔλαιον ἐπικρήσασθαι
> καὶ κύλικα εὔζωρον ἵνα μεθύουσα καθεύδῃ.

'The Eiresione is a branch of olive twined with wool, and having hanging from it various fruits of the earth; a boy, both of whose parents are alive, carries it forth and places it in front of the doors of Apollo's sanctuary, at the feast of Pyanepsia.' He then goes on to an aetiological legend about Theseus, and finally records the words of the song sung by the children who carried or attended the Eiresione:

'Eiresione brings
All good things,
Figs and fat cakes to eat,
Soft oil and honey sweet,
And brimming wine-cup deep
That she may drink and sleep.'

The boy who actually carried the Eiresione must have both parents alive, because any contact with death even remote was unlucky; the ghost of either parent might be about. The song is of some interest because of the half-personification of Eiresione. The Maypole or harvest-sheaf is halfway to a harvest Maiden; it is thus, as will be seen later, that a goddess is made. A song is sung, a story told, and the very telling fixes the outline of personality. It is possible to worship long in spirit, but as soon as the story-telling, myth-making, instinct awakes you have anthropomorphism and theology.

What was hung on the Eiresione no doubt depended on the wealth of particular worshippers; we hear of white wool and purple wool, vessels of wine, figs, strings of acorns, cakes; nothing in the way of natural produce came amiss. The Eiresione once fixed over the door remained there, a charm against pestilence and famine, till the next year; then it was changed for a new one. The withered branch must have been a familiar sight at Athens. When in the *Plutus*[1] of Aristophanes the young rough is insulting the old woman and thrusting his torch into her withered face, she cries:

'For pity's sake don't bring your torch so near me,'

and Chremylus says:

'Yes, right she is, for if she caught a spark
She'd burn up like an old Eiresione.'

[1] Ar. *Plut.* 1054, schol. ad loc. *ταύτην δὲ τὴν εἰρεσιώνην πρὸ τῶν οἰκημάτων ἐτίθεντο οἱ 'Αθηναῖοι καὶ κατ' ἔτος αὐτὴν ἤλλαττον...ἕκαστος πρὸ τῶν θυρῶν ἔστησαν εἰρεσιῶνας εἰς ἀποτροπὴν τοῦ λοιμοῦ, καὶ διέμενεν εἰς ἐνιαυτόν. ἣν καὶ ξηρανθεῖσαν πάλιν κατ' ἔτος ἐποίει ἑτέραν χλοάζουσαν.*

The Eiresione, Pausanias says, was fastened before the door of the sanctuary of Apollo. Plutarch[1], in his rather clumsy aetiological account of the Oschophoria, connects the Eiresione with vows paid to Apollo by Theseus on his return from Crete to Athens. Harpocration[2] says 'The Thargelia was celebrated in the month of Thargelion, which is sacred to Apollo,' and the author of the *Etymologicon Magnum*[3] states 'The Thargelia, a festival at Athens. The name is given from the *thargelia*, and *thargelia* are all the fruits that spring from the earth. The festival is celebrated in the month Thargelion to Artemis and Apollo.' From Suidas[4] we learn that there was a musical contest at the Thargelia, and that the actors dedicated their prize tripods in the sanctuary of Apollo known as the Pythion.

All this makes it quite clear that at some time or other the festival of the Thargelia was connected with the Olympian Apollo, and more vaguely with his sister Artemis, but the connection is obviously loose and late. The Eiresione was fastened up not only over the door of the sanctuary of Apollo, but over the house-door of any and every Athenian. The house of Demos was no sanctuary of Apollo. Moreover, when the scholiast on Aristophanes[5] is commenting on the Eiresione, he says, to our surprise, that it was carried and hung at the Thargelia and Pyanepsia in honour, not of Apollo and Artemis, but of 'Helios and the Horae.' Porphyry[6] does not definitely name the Eiresione, but he is clearly alluding to it when he speaks of the procession that still took place at Athens in his own day to Helios and the Horae. It is evidence, he says, that in early days the gods desired in their service not the sacrifice of animals, but the offering of vegetable first-fruits. 'In this procession they carried wild herbs as well as ground pulse, acorns, barley, wheat, a cake of dried figs, cakes of wheat and barley flour, and a pot (χύτρος).'

It is abundantly clear that the Eiresione is simply a harvest-home, an offering of first-fruits that was primarily an end in itself,

[1] Plut. *Vit. Thes.* XVIII. The account of Plutarch is substantially the same as that of his contemporary Pausanias the rhetorician; both appear to draw from some common source, which may be Krates' *περὶ θυσιῶν*: see Mannhardt, *Wald- und Feldkulte*, p. 219.

[2] Harpocrat. s.v.

[3] *Etym. Mag.* s.v.

[4] Suidas s.v. Πύθιον.

[5] Schol. ad Ar. *Plut.* 1054.

[6] Porph. *de Abst.* II. 7. The text contains obscure words, e.g. *ἐλυσπόα* of which Nauck observes *loci medela nobis negata*, but those translated above seem certain.

but that could easily be affiliated to any dominant god. It will be remembered[1] that Oineus got into trouble because, when all the other gods had their feasts of hecatombs, he did not offer first-fruits to Artemis, great daughter of Zeus. Oineus, we may conjecture, was the faithful conservative worshipper of earlier gods; the Athenians were wiser in their generation; their ancient service of the primitive Helios and the Horae they somehow affiliated to that of the incoming Olympians.

It remains to ask more precisely what was the primitive significance of the offering of first-fruits. At first sight it may seem as if the question were superfluous. Surely we have here the simplest possible instance of the service of 'tendance' (*θεραπεία*), the primitive sacrifice that embodies the very essence of *do ut des*, a gift given to the god to 'smooth his face,' a gift that necessarily presupposes the existence of a god with a face to be smoothed.

Such seems to have been the view of Aristotle[2]. He says in characteristically Greek fashion, 'They hold sacrifices, and meetings in connection therewith, paying rites of worship to the gods while providing rest and recreation for themselves. For the most ancient sacrifices and meetings seem to be as it were offerings of first-fruits after the gathering in of the various harvests. For those were the times of year when the ancients were especially at leisure.' Aristotle clearly takes the view of sacrifice already discussed, that sacrifice is mainly an occasion for enjoyment and the result of leisure, but his remark as to its early connection with first-fruits goes deeper down than he himself knows. Regarded as a *θυσία*, a sacrifice, the offering of first-fruits presupposes, as we have said, a god or spirit to whom sacrifice is made, and a god of human passions. But it must not be forgotten that in this view we are making a very large assumption, i.e. that of the existence of some such god or spirit. It is instructive to note that among other primitive races ceremonies have been observed which apparently are not addressed to any god or spirit, and yet which seem to contain in them a possible germ of some idea akin to sacrifice.

1 *Iliad* loc. cit. supra.

2 Aristot. *Eth. Nic.* 1160 Θ. ix. 5 *θυσίας τε ποιοῦντες καὶ περὶ ταύτας συνόδους, τιμάς <τε> ἀπονέμοντες τοῖς θεοῖς καὶ αὑτοῖς ἀναπαύσεις πορίζοντες μεθ' ἡδονῆς. αἱ γὰρ ἀρχαῖαι θυσίαι καὶ σύνοδοι φαίνονται γίνεσθαι μετὰ τὰς τῶν καρπῶν συγκομιδὰς οἷον ἀπαρχαί. μάλιστα γὰρ ἐν τούτοις ἐσχόλαζον τοῖς καιροῖς.*

Such are the ceremonies of the Australian Arunta, observed and described in detail by Messrs Spencer and Gillen[1]. These ceremonies, consisting of lengthy and elaborate mummeries, are called *Intichiuma*, and their object seems to be to secure the increase of the animal or plant associated with a particular totem. The pantomimes enacted seem to be of the nature of sympathetic magic, and they are interspersed with chanted invitations to the particular plant or animal to be fertile. The point of special interest is that the ceremonies are closely connected with certain taboos on particular foods. Mr Lang[2] suggests that the removal of the taboo at the time of the *Intichiuma* may indicate that the necessary 'close time' is over. The imposition of the taboo is on this showing not due to any primary moral instinct in man, but simply a practical necessity if the plant or animal is not to become extinct. The removal of the taboo after a suitable lapse of time is, if man himself is not to become extinct, equally practical and necessary. This sort of taboo is in fact a kind of primitive 'game law.' Philochoros[3] gives an instance: 'At Athens,' he says, 'a prohibition was issued that no one should eat of unshorn lamb on the occasion of failure in the breed of sheep.' If at the end of the close time it was customary to eat a little of a plant or animal, the eating being accompanied by certain solemn ceremonials, the food itself would easily come to be regarded as specially sacred and as having sacramental virtue, and the further step would soon be taken of regarding it as consecrated to certain spirits or divinities. This *may* have been in part the origin of the offering of first-fruits.

The removal of a taboo is assuredly not the same thing as the worship of a god, but it is easy to see how the one might slide over into the other. A taboo is by common consent placed upon the harvest fruits till all are ripe: such harvest-fruits are *sacred*, forbidden, dangerous. Why? As soon as primitive man has fashioned for himself any sort of god in his own image, the answer is ready, 'The Lord thy God is a jealous God.' Primitive man is so instinctively anthropomorphic that it seems to me rash to assert

[1] Spencer and Gillen, *Native Tribes of Central Australia*, pp. 167 ff.

[2] A. Lang, *Religion and Magic*, p. 265.

[3] Philoch. ap. Athen. I. 16, p. 9 Φιλόχορος δὲ ἱστορεῖ καὶ κεκωλῦσθαι Ἀθήνησι ἀπέκτου ἀρνὸς μηδένα γεύεσθαι ἐπιλιπούσης ποτὲ τῆς τῶν ζῴων τούτων γενέσεως.

that the notion of taboo *precedes* that of sacrifice. The natives of Central Australia appear to have taboo without the notion of sacrifice, i.e. of any spirit to whom sacrifice is made; another race might have a primitive notion of a spirit to be placated without the notion of taboo; or the two might be inextricably blended and only our modern habit of pitiless analysis separate them.

Late writers on ritual, and it is only late that there are such writers, always explain taboo as consecration rather than prohibition. Festus[1] says 'they called the juice of the vine *sacrima* because they sacrificed (or consecrated) it to Liber with a view to the protection of the vineyards and the vessels and the wine itself, just as they sacrificed to Ceres a first harvest from the ears they had first reaped.' Here the 'sacramental' wine is clearly a sacrifice of the Olympian kind; but in the Pithoigia, already discussed, the more primitive notions of release from taboo and 'aversion' of evil influences clearly emerge. 'Libation of the new wine is poured out that the use of the magical thing (*φαρμάκου*) may become harmless and a means of safety[2].' In the Thargelia we have no definite information as to a solemn *eating* as well as offering of first-fruits, but this element will appear when we reach the great harvest festival commonly known as the Eleusinian Mysteries.

It remains to note some details as to the material of sacrifice. The general principle is clear and simple. The god fares as his worshipper. Porphyry[3], in discussing the various kinds of animals sacrificed, observes with much common sense, 'No Greek sacrifices a camel or an elephant to the gods, because Greece does not produce camels and elephants.'

It might not be necessary to state a fact so obvious but that writers on the subject of ritual seem haunted by the notion that certain animals are sacrificed to certain gods because they are in some mystical sense 'sacred to them,' and this notion has introduced much needless complexity. It is quite true that locally we find certain taboos on the sacrifice of certain animals, the cause of

[1] Fest. § 318 *sacrima* appellabant mustum quod Libero sacrificabant, pro vineis et vasis et ipso vino conservando, sicut praemetium de spicis quas primum messuissent sacrificabant Cereri.

[2] Plut. *Q. Symp.* III. 7. 1 *καὶ πάλαι γ' ὡς ἔοικεν εὔχοντο τοῦ οἴνου πρὶν ἢ πιεῖν ἀποσπένδοντες ἀβλαβῆ καὶ σωτήριον αὐτοῖς τοῦ φαρμάκου τὴν χρῆσιν γενέσθαι.*

[3] Porph. *de Abst.* I. 14.

which is unknown, but these taboos are local and by no means uniform. Moreover the animal 'sacred' to the particular god is by no means always the material of sacrifice; the owl, for reasons to be later discussed, is 'sacred' to Athene, but we hear of no sacrifice of owls. Broadly then, as noted before, the material of sacrifice is conditioned, not by the character of the god, but by the circumstances of the worshipper.

The principle that the god fares as his worshipper is however crossed by another, *he sometimes fares worse.* This was noticed by writers on ritual such as Porphyry[1] and Eustathius[2], and they explain it as a sort of survival of a golden age of simple manners, dear to the conservatism of the gods. This conservatism of the gods mirrors, of course, the natural and timid conservatism of their worshippers. They have begun by offering just what they eat themselves, and, from the fact that they have once offered it, they attach to this food special sanctity. They advance in civilization, and their own food becomes more delicate and complex, but they dare not make any change in the diet of their gods; they have learnt to bake and eat fermented bread themselves, but the gods are still nurtured on barley grains and porridge. Porphyry[3] reduces the successive stages of sacrifice to a regular system of progressive vegetarianism. First men plucked and offered grass, which was like the 'soft wool' of the earth; then the fruit of trees and their leaves, the acorn and the nut; then barley appeared first of the grains, and they offered simple barley-corns; then they broke and bruised grain and made it into cakes. In like fashion they made libations first of water, then of honey, the natural liquid prepared for us by bees, thirdly of oil, and last of all of wine; but after each advance the older service remained 'in memory of the ancient manner of life.' Last, through diverse influences of ignorance and fear, came 'the luxury of flesh and imported forms of diet[4].'

The incoming of the luxury of flesh diet was, it has already been noted, due not to ignorance and fear but to the inroad

[1] Porph. *de Abst.* II. 56. The treatise of Porphyry, so far as it relates to sacrifice, is mainly based on the previous treatise of Theophrastos.

[2] Eustath. ad *Il.* I. 449 § 132.

[3] Porph. *de Abst.* II. 20.

[4] Porph. loc. cit. *μετὰ δὲ τοὺς οὐλοχύτας αἱ θυσίαι καὶ ἡ ἐν αὐταῖς κρεωφαγία. διότι καὶ μετὰ τὴν τῶν ἀναγκαίων τροφῶν εὕρεσιν ἡ τῆς κρεωδαισίας πολυτέλεια καὶ τὸ τῆς τροφῆς ἐπείσακτον εὕρηται.*

of a flesh-eating Northern race whose splendid physical stature and strength Porphyry was little likely to appreciate. They were not wholly flesh-eaters; hence, as has been seen, they offered the sacrifice of the barley grains (*οὐλοχύται*), and offered these at a time when they were themselves eating some form of manufactured bread. The primitive character of the rite is, I think, marked by the ritual precedence. The *οὐλοχύται*, the sprinkling of grains, has usually been explained as the sprinkling of meal on the heads of the victims, as the equivalent of the *mola salsa* of the Romans; but Eustathius is probably right when, in commenting on the sacrifice of Nestor[1], he says, 'the sprinkled grains are in memory of the food of old times which consisted in grains, i.e. barley-corns.' 'Hence,' he adds, 'one of the ancient commentators explains the sprinkled grains as barley-corns.' That *οὐλοχύται* were nothing more nor less than the actual barley-corns is also shown by a passage from Strato[2]. A cook, who apparently from his use of archaic terminology is according to his master more like a male sphinx than a cook, calls for *οὐλοχύται*:

> 'Οὐλοχύται—why what on earth is that?'

And the answer is

> 'Just barley-corns.'

The first act in a Homeric sacrifice was uniformly prayer and the sprinkling of grain[3], and it is important to observe that Eustathius[4] expressly notes this as a previous sacrifice (*πρόθυμα*); the *οὐλοχύται* were, he says, a mixture of grain and salt poured on the altar before the sacrificial ceremony began. By the 'sacrificial ceremony' Eustathius means the slaying of the animal victim. It is important to note that the grain was poured *on the altar* and was therefore in itself a sacrifice, as it is sometimes stated that it was merely thrown on the head of the victim. The statement of Eustathius is confirmed by the account in Euripides[5]

[1] Eustath. ad *Od.* III. 440, 1476. 37 *ὡς καὶ οἱ οὐλοχύται τῆς παλαιᾶς τροφῆς ἀνεμίμνησκον τῆς τε τῶν οὐλῶν, ὅπερ ἐστὶ τῶν κριθῶν, διὸ καὶ τοὺς οὐλοχύτας τῶν τις παλαιῶν κριθὰς ἡρμήνευσεν.*

[2] Strato ap. Athen. IX. 29, p. 382.

[3] For a full discussion of *οὐλαί* and *οὐλοχύται* see Dr H. von Fritze, *Hermes* 1897, p. 236.

[4] Eustath. ad *Il.* I. 449 § 132, 23 *εἰσὶ δὲ οὐλοχύται...τὰ προθύματα...οἱ οὐλοχύται οὐλαὶ ἦσαν τουτέστι κριθαὶ μετὰ ἁλῶν ἃς ἐπέχεον τοῖς βωμοῖς πρὸ τῆς ἱερουργίας.*

[5] Eur. *El.* 804

> *λαβὼν δὲ προχύτας μητρὸς εὐνέτης σέθεν*
> *ἔβαλλε βωμούς, τοιάδ' ἐννέπων ἔπη.*

of the sacrifice made by Aegisthus to the Nymphs. Here, before the elaborate slaying of the bull, we have, just as in Homer, the sprinkling of the grain, and *it is sprinkled on the altar*. The Messenger tells Electra that when all was ready Aegisthus

'Took the grains for sprinkling and he cast them
Upon the altar and these words he spake.'

The sprinkling of *salted* meal (*mola salsa*) was, if we may believe Athenaeus[1], a later innovation. He tells us distinctly, quoting Athenion as his authority, that the use of salt for seasoning was a comparatively late discovery and therefore excluded from certain sacrifices to the gods.

'Whence even now. remembering days of old,
The entrails of their victims for the gods
They roast with fire and bring no salt thereto,
Because at first they knew no use for salt.
And even when they knew and loved its savour
They kept their fathers' sacred written precepts.'

The sacrifice of the animal victim never in Homer takes place without the 'previous sacrifice' of grain-sprinkling and prayer, but prayer and grain-sprinkling can take place, as in the prayer of Penelope[2], without the animal sacrifice. This looks as though the animal sacrifice were rather a supplementary later-added act than a necessary climax. Later, when animal sacrifice became common and even as a rule imperative, the real sacrificial intent of the preliminary grain-sprinkling would naturally become obscured and it would be brought into connection with animal sacrifice by the practice of sprinkling grain on the heads of the victims.

By Plutarch's[3] time the sprinkling of grain was regarded as something of an archaeological curiosity. He asks in his *Greek Questions* 'Who is he who is called among the Opuntians *kritho-logos*,' i.e. the 'barley collector'? The answer is 'Most of the Greeks make use of barley for their very ancient sacrifices when the citizens offer first-fruits. And the man who regulates these sacrifices and gets in these first-fruits is called *krithologos*.' He adds a curious detail illustrative of the two strata of worship, 'and they had two priests, one to supervise divine things, one for those of things demonic.' In like archaic fashion, when Pisthetairos[4]

[1] Athen. XIV. 81, p. 661.
[2] Hom. *Od.* IV. 761.
[3] Plut. *Q. Gr.* VI.
[4] Ar. *Av.* 622.

would inaugurate the blessed simplicity of bird-rule, he revives the ancient ritual of the sprinkling of barley-corns:

'O better than worship of Zeus Most High
Is the service of Birds that sing and fly.
They ask for no carven temple's state,
They clamour not for a golden gate.
The shrine they ask of a mortal's vow
Is leave to perch on an olive bough.
In the little thickets of ash and oak
They dwell anigh us. We humble folk
Never need fare to the far-off lands
Of Ammon or Delphi, but lift our hands
Under our vine and our fig-tree's shade.
For a slender grace let our prayer be said,
As we cast up our barley in little showers
And a little grace from the Birds is ours.'

The barley grain sprinkled is part of the ritual of the Olympians, but in the case of the two survivals to be next considered, the *pelanos* and the *nephalia*, their use was almost wholly confined to, and characteristic of, the lower stratum of worship, that of ghosts and sprites and underworld divinities.

After the sacrifice of the natural fruits of the earth, the *παγκαρπία*, comes the most primitive form of artificial food, i.e. the *pelanos*, a sort of porridge.

We speak of Bread and Wine as sacramental *elements*, but both are far removed from being elemental. Leavened bread, the Greek *ἄρτος*, is a product of advanced civilization, and with a true conservative ritual instinct the Roman Church prescribes to this day the use of the unleavened wafer. Athenaeus[1], citing the author of a play called the *Beggars*, tells us that when the Athenians set a meal in the Prytaneum for the Dioscuri they serve upon the tables cheese and barley-porridge (*φυστήν*) and chopped olives and leeks, making remembrance of their ancient mode of life. And Solon bids them supply to those who had free meals in the Prytaneum barley cake (*μάζαν*), but at feasts to place in addition loaves of bread (*ἄρτον*), and this in imitation of Homer. For Homer, when he brought the chiefs together to Agamemnon, says 'they stirred up meal.' The words 'they stirred up meal,' *φύρετο δ' ἄλφιτα*, do not occur in our text, but the author of the *Beggars* clearly refers to the ordinary Homeric meal, and takes us straight

[1] Athen. IV. 14, p. 137.

back to the real primitive meaning of *pelanos*. On the shield of Achilles[1] we have the picture of a harvest feast:

> 'The heralds dight the feast apart beneath a spreading oak,
> The ox they slew, and much white barley-meal the women folk
> Sprinkled, a supper for the thralls.'

The lord and his fellows feast on flesh-meat, the workmen have their supper of primitive porridge. So the Townley scholiast clearly understands the passage; he comments: *πάλυνον, ἔμασσον ἢ ἔφυρον*, 'they sprinkle, i.e. they knead or mix together.' It is noticeable that he employs the exact word, *ἔφυρον*, quoted by Athenaeus as in the text of Homer[2]. To explain the passage as 'sprinkle on the heads of the victims or on the roast flesh' is to miss the whole antithesis between master and man. Eustathius[3], that close observer of primitive fact, saw what was being done in Homer and doubtless still by the poor of his own days. He says 'to sprinkle barley-meal does not mean bread-making but a sort of paste in ordinary use among the ancients.' To any one who has watched the making of porridge, the shift of meaning from *παλύνειν*, to *sprinkle*, to *φύρειν* and *μάσσειν*, to stir and to knead, is natural and necessary. You first sprinkle the meal on the water, you then stir it, so far you have porridge; if you let it get thicker and thicker you must knead it and then you have oat-cake. It has of course frequently been noted that a *pelanos* may be either fluid or solid, and herein lies the explanation. When the *pelanos* is thick and subjected to fire, baked, it becomes a *pemma*, an ordinary cake. The Latin *libum*[4], a cake, is a strict parallel; it was primarily a thing out-poured, a *libation*, then a solid thing cooked and eaten.

A *pelanos* was then primarily the same as *alphita*, barley-meal.

[1] Hom. *Il.* XVIII. 560.

[2] The process of primitive bread-making is fully discussed by Prof. Benndorf (*Eranos Vindobensis*, p. 374), to whom I am indebted for the view here expressed. In Yorkshire within my own remembrance a rather repulsive mess of corn stewed in milk with currants was always eaten on Christmas Eve before the regular feast began. It was served as soup and called *frummety*.

[3] Eustath. ad *Il.* XVIII. 563 *τὸ δὲ παλύνειν ἄλφιτα οὐδὲ νῦν δηλοῖ ἀρτοποιΐαν ἀλλὰ τὸ ἐπίπασμα σύνηθες ὂν τοῖς παλαιοῖς*, and again in discussing the feast of Eumaeus (§ 1751, 33) *ὁ δ' ἄλφιτα λευκὰ ἐπάλυνεν, ὅ ἐστιν ἐπέπασε κατὰ ἔθος ἀρχαῖον τὸ ὕστερον ἀργῆσαν*.

[4] Varro *L.L.* v. 106 libum quod ut libaretur. The Latin *puls* and *polenta* are probably from the same root as *πέλανος*. Pliny (*N.H.* XVIII. 19) says it is clear that in ancient days *pulte non pane Romanos vixisse*. He adds that to his day primitive rites and those on birthdays are carried on with *pulse*.

The food of man was the food of the gods, but the word was early specialized off to ritual use. There is, I believe, no instance in which a *pelanos*, under that name, is eaten in daily life or indeed eaten at all save by Earth and underworld gods, their representative snakes and other Spirits of Aversion[1]. The comic poet Sannyrion[2] puts it thus:

'We gods do call it *pelanos*,
You pompous mortals barley-meal.'

To us the pomposity seems on the side of the gods.

As there was a time when leavened bread was not, and men ate porridge cooked or uncooked, so before the coming of the vine men drank a honey drink. And as the conservative gods, long after men ate fermented bread, were faithful to their porridge, so long after men drank wine they still offered to the gods who were there before the coming of the vine 'wineless libations,' nephalia[3].

The ritual of the underworld gods is in many respects identical with that of the ghosts out of which they are developed, but with this difference—ghosts are less conservative than fully developed gods; the habits and tastes of ghosts are more closely akin to those of the men who worship them. Quite early, it would appear, man offered to ghosts the wine he loved so well himself.

Atossa[4] brings for the ghost of Darius a *pelanos*, as was meet. She brings also all manner of 'soothing gifts' (μειλικτήρια), but she pours wine also:

'A holy heifer's milk, white, fair to drink,
Bright honey drops from flowers bee-distilled,
With draughts of water from a virgin fount,
And from the ancient vine its mother wild
An unmixed draught, this gladness; and fair fruit
Of gleaming olive ever blossoming
And woven flowers, children of mother earth.'

The dead fare as the living; wine is added to milk and honey

[1] Aesch. *Pers.* 204 ἀποτρόποισι δαίμοσι, and 523 γῇ τε καὶ φθιτοῖς δωρήματα.

[2] Sannyr. frg. 1 Koch.

[3] The sources for νηφάλια are well collected and discussed by Dr von Fritze, *De Libatione veterum Graecorum*, Berlin 1893, also by Stengel, *Hermes* XXII. p. 645, and 'Chthonische und Totenkult' in *Festschrift für Friedländer*, p. 418, and W. Barth, 'Bestattungsspende bei den Griechen,' *Neue Jahrbücher für klass. Altertüm.* 1900, p. 177. W. Barth draws distinctions between the cultus of the dead and that of chthonic divinities, which I think cannot be clearly made out.

[4] Aesch. *Pers.* 607.

and olive oil and water, but wine perhaps significantly as an innovation is never *named*. Atossa seems also consciously to insist over much on its being wild, primitive, ancient, and therefore permissible. We are reminded of the religious shifts to which the Romans were put by the introduction of wine into their daily life and thence into their ritual. Plutarch[1] in his *Roman Questions* says that 'when the women poured libations of wine to Bona Dea, they called it by the name of milk,' and Macrobius[2] adds 'that wine could not be brought in under its own name, but the wine was called milk and the vessel containing it a honey-jar.'

The ghosts of the dead admit and even welcome the addition of wine, but actual chthonic divinities are stricter. When Oedipus[3] comes to the precinct of the Semnae, the Chorus bid him make atonement, because, though unwittingly, he has violated the precinct. He asks the precise ritual to be observed. The answer, though it is thrice familiar, is so important for the understanding of chthonic ceremonies that it must be given in full:

'*Oed.* And with what rites, O strangers? teach me this.
Chor. First, fetch thou from an ever-flowing fount,
Borne in clean hands, an holy drink-offering.
Oed. And next, when I have brought the holy draught?
Chor. Bowls are there next, a cunning craftsman's work,
Crown thou their lips and handles at the brim.
Oed. With branches, woollen webs, or in what wise?
Chor. Of the ewe-lamb take thou the fresh-shorn wool.
Oed. So be it, and then to what last rite I pass?
Chor Pour thy drink offerings, facewards to the dawn.
Oed. With these same vessels do I pour the draught?
Chor. Yes, in three streams, the last pour wholly out.
Oed. And filled wherewith this last? teach me this also.
Chor. *Water and honey—bring no wine thereto.*
Oed. When the dark shadowed earth hath drunk of this?
Chor. Lay on it thrice nine sprays of olive tree
With both thine hands, and make thy prayer the while.
Oed. That prayer? vouchsafe to teach, for mighty is it.
Chor. Pray thou that, as they are called the Kindly Ones,
With kindly hearts they may receive and bless.
Be this thy prayer, thine own or his who prays
For thee. Whisper thy prayer nor lift thy voice,
Then go, look not behind, so all is well.'

The Kindly Ones, though their name is only adjectival, have

[1] Plut. *Q. R.* xx. *οἶνον δ' αὐτῇ σπένδουσι γάλα προσαγορεύουσαι.*
[2] Macr. I. 12. 25 quod vas in quo vinum inditum est mellarium nominetur et vinum lac nuncupetur.
[3] Soph. *Oed. Col.* 468.

crystallized into divinities; they are no longer ghosts, and none may tamper with their archaic ritual.

For the dread counterpart of the Eumenides, the Erinyes, there is the same wineless service, witness the reproach of Clytaemnestra. The Erinyes have deserted her, yet she has given them of the ritual they exact[1]:

> 'Full oft forsooth from me have ye licked up
> Wineless libations, sober balms of wrath.'

To offer wine was the last outrage done by the parvenu Apollo to ancient ritual, hence the bitter protest[2]:

> 'Thou hast bewildered the old walks of life,
> With wine the Ancient Goddesses undone.'

The wineless service of the Eumenides in the *Oedipus Coloneus* is of course no mere invention of the poet. At Titane near Sicyon Pausanias[3] came to a grove of evergreen oaks and a temple of the goddesses whom, he says, the Athenians call Semnae, but the Sicyonians Eumenides, and every year on one day they celebrate a festival in their honour, 'sacrificing sheep with young and a *libation of water and honey*.'

The scholiast in the *Oedipus Coloneus*[4] gives a list of the divinities to whom at Athens wineless sacrifices were made. He quotes as his authority Polemon. 'The Athenians were careful in these matters and scrupulously pious (ὅσιοι) in the things that pertain to the gods, and they made wineless sacrifices to Mnemosyne the Muse, to Eos, to Helios, to Selene, to the Nymphs, to Aphrodite Ourania.' The list is at first surprising. We associate *nephalia* with the Underworld powers, but here it is quite clear that, in primitive days, side by side with the Earth-gods were worshipped sky-gods, but in their own simple being as Dawn and Sun and Moon, not as full-blown human Olympians. Mnemosyne[5], it will later be seen, had a well of living water herself; she needed no wine. The Heavenly Aphrodite is more surprising, but her honey libation is further attested by Empedokles[6]. He

[1] Aesch. *Eum.* 104. [2] Aesch. *Eum.* 727.

[3] P. II. 11. 3. The relation between the Semnae and the Eumenides and the ritual of the Semnae, which is identical with that of the Eumenides, will be discussed later in Chapter v.

[4] Schol. ad *Oed. Col.* 100. [5] Porph. *de antr. Nymph.* 7.

[6] Emped. frg. ap. Porph. *de Abst.* II. 21.

tells of the days long ago when the god Ares was not, nor King Zeus, nor Kronos, nor Poseidon, but only

> 'Kypris the Queen
> Here they adored with pious images,
> With painted victims and with fragrant scents,
> With fume of frankincense and genuine myrrh.
> Honey of yellow bees upon the ground
> They for libation poured.'

But though here and there a very early 'Heavenly One' claimed the honey service, it was mostly the meed of the dead. Porphyry knew that honey was used to embalm the body of the dead because it prevented putrefaction, and this custom of honey burial is echoed in the myth of Glaukos and the honey-jar. The marvellous sweetness of honey lent itself to the notions of propitiation and placation—'sweets to the sweet' or rather, as it seemed to the practical primitive mind, 'sweets to the spirits to be sweetened,' the Meilichioi, ghosts and heroes to be appeased[1].

One more element in archaic ritual yet remains to be considered—the fireless sacrifice.

Fire, it has been seen, was used in the Homeric burnt sacrifice *for sublimation.* By fire, Eustathius[2] says in speaking of the burning of the dead among the northern nations, 'the divine element was borne on high as though in a chariot and mingled with the heavenly beings.' In like fashion we may suppose the burnt victim was freed from the grosser elements and in purified vaporous form ascended to the gods of the upper air. This is what Porphyry[3] means when he says that in burnt sacrifice we 'immortalize the dues of the heavenly gods by means of fire.' Fire again in the service of the underworld gods was used, it has further been seen, for utter destruction, for the holocaust. But in certain rituals established, it may be, before the discovery of fire, it was definitely prescribed that the sacrifice should be fireless. Diogenes Laertius[4] relates that according to tradition there was but one altar in Delos at which Pythagoras could worship, the 'Altar of Apollo the Sire,' which stood behind the great Altar of

[1] Some further points as to the Nephalia will be considered in relation to the Eleusinian ritual (p. 150), and the Orphic mysteries (Chapter x.).

[2] Eustath. ad *Il.* I. 52. For a full discussion of the purport of cremation see Prof. Ridgeway, *Early Age of Greece* I. p. 540.

[3] Porph. *de Abst.* II. 5.

[4] Diog. Laert. VIII. 13.

the Horns, because on this altar wheat and barley and cakes are the only offering laid and the sacrifice is without fire and there is no sacrificial victim—so Aristotle stated in his *Constitution of the Delians.* This altar was also known as the Altar of the Pious. The foundation of the great blood-stained Altar of the Horns may still be seen in Delos; the primitive Altar of the Sire has left no trace, but in some bygone time a voice, it would seem, had been heard on Mount Cynthus saying, 'Thou shalt not hurt nor destroy in all my Holy Mountain.'

What ancient worship of a 'Sire' Apollo had taken to himself in Delos we do not know, but in remote Arcadia a fireless sacrifice of a specially simple kind went on right down to the time of Pausanias[1] in honour of a home-grown goddess, Demeter. At Phigalia Pausanias visited the cave-sanctuary of the Black Demeter; indeed he says in his pious way it was chiefly for her sake that he went to Phigalia, and he adds 'I sacrificed no victim to the goddess, such being the custom of the people of the country. They bring instead as offerings the fruit of the vine and of other trees they cultivate, and honey-combs and wool which is still unwrought and full of the natural grease; these they lay on the altar which is set up in front of the cave, and having laid them there they pour on them olive oil. Such is the rite of sacrifice observed by private persons and once a year by the Phigalian people collectively.' Everything here prescribed is in its most natural form, grapes rather than wine, honey-comb rather than honey, unwrought wool not artificial fillets, and the service is fireless. It was a service to content even Pythagoras.

That there was between the early fireless sacrifice and the burnt sacrifice of the Olympian in some prehistoric time a rivalry and clashing of interests, is clear from the Rhodian tradition of the Heliadae. Pindar[2] tells how:

'Up to the hill they came,
  Yet in their hand
No seed of burning flame,
  And for the Rhodian land
With fireless rite
The grove upon the citadel they dight.'

And the scholiast commenting on the passage says: 'The Rhodians going up to the Acropolis to sacrifice to Athene, forgot

[1] P. VIII. 42. 5.

[2] Pind. *Ol.* VII. 47, schol. ad loc.

to take fire with them for their offerings (ἐναγίσμασι) and made a fireless sacrifice. Hence it came about that, as the Athenians were the first to sacrifice by fire, Athene thought it best to live with them.' Athene was always a prudent goddess, ready to swim with the tide; she was 'all for the father,' all for the Olympians, and she had her reward. Philostratos[1] tells the same story with something more of emphasis. He contrasts the Acropolis of Athens and the Acropolis of Rhodes: the Rhodians had only a fireless cheap service, the people of Athens provide the savour of burnt sacrifice and fragrant smoke; the goddess went to live with them because 'they were wiser in their generation (σοφωτέρους) and good at sacrificing.' From Diodorus[2] we learn that it was Cecrops who introduced the fire-sacrifice at Athens. On Cecrops were fathered many of the innovations of civilized life, among them marriage. He was halfway between the old and the new, half civilized man, half snake. He, Pausanias[3] significantly tells us, was the first to give to Zeus the name of the Highest. He too became all for the Olympian.

These forms of primitive sacrifice—the *pelanos*, the barley grains, the *nephalia*, the fireless rites—have been considered at some length because, though in part they went over to the Olympians, they remain broadly speaking and in their simplest forms characteristic of the lower stratum and of the worship of underworld spirits. Moreover it is these primitive rites which were, as will later be seen, taken up and mysticized by the religion of Orpheus.

It remains to consider the second and by far the most important element in the harvest festival of the Thargelia, the ceremony of the Pharmakos.

THE PHARMAKOS.

That the leading out of the *pharmakos* was a part of the festival of the Thargelia we know from Harpocration[4]. He says in commenting on the word: 'At Athens they led out two men to be purifications for the city; it was at the Thargelia, one was

[1] Philostrat. *Eik.* II. 27 § 852.
[2] Diod. v. 56.
[3] P. VIII. 2. 2.
[4] Harpocrat. s.v. φαρμακός.

for the men and the other for the women.' These men, these pharmakoi, whose function it was to purify the city, were, it will later be seen, in all probability put to death, but the expression used by Harpocration is noteworthy—they were led out. The gist of the ceremony is not death but expulsion; death, if it occurs, is incidental.

The ceremony of expulsion took place, it is again practically certain, on the 6th day of Thargelion, a day not lightly to be forgotten, for it was the birthday of Socrates. Diogenes Laertius[1] says in his life of Socrates: 'He was born on the 6th day of Thargelion, the day when the Athenians purify the city.' The pharmakos is not expressly named, but it will be seen in the sequel that the cleansing of the city by the expulsion of the pharmakos was regarded as *the* typical purification of the whole year. The etymology of the word will be best considered when the nature of the rites has been examined[2].

The ceremony of the pharmakos has been often discussed, but I think frequently and fundamentally misapprehended. It appears at first sight to involve what we in our modern terminology call 'Human Sacrifice.' To be told that this went on in civilized Athens in the 5th cent. B.C. shocks our preconceived notions of what an Athenian of that time would be likely to do or suffer. The result is that we are inclined to get out of the difficulty in one of two ways: either we try to relegate the ceremony of the pharmakos to the region of prehistoric tradition, or we so modify and mollify its main issues as to make it unmeaning.

The issue before us is a double one and must not be confused. We have to determine what the ceremonial of the pharmakos was, and next, did that ceremonial last on into historic times?

My own view is briefly this: that we have no positive evidence that it did last on into the 5th century B.C., but that, if the gist of the ceremonial is once fairly understood, there is no a priori difficulty about its continuance, and that, this a priori difficulty being removed, we shall accept an overwhelming probability. The evidence for the historical pharmakos is just as good as

[1] Diog. Laert. II. 4.

[2] Classical sources for the *pharmakos* are most fully enumerated by Mannhardt, *Myth. Forschungen*, pp. 123, 133. For primitive analogies see Frazer, *Golden Bough*, 2nd ed., vol. III. p. 93, from whom I have taken the instances adduced.

e.g. the evidence for the chewing of the buckthorn at the Anthesteria.

It should be noted at the outset that the pharmakos, i.e. the human scape-goat, though it seems to us a monstrous and horrible notion, was one so familiar to the Greek mind as to be in Attic literature practically proverbial. Aristophanes[1] wants to point the contrast between the old mint of sterling state officials and the new democratic coinage: he says, now-a-days we fill offices by

> 'Any chance man that we come across,
> Not fit in old days for a pharmakos,
> These we use
> And these we choose,
> The veriest scum, the mere refuse,'

and again in a fragment[2]:

> '*Your* kinsman! how and whence, you pharmakos,'

and in the *Knights*[3] Demos says to Agoracritos:

> 'I bid you take the seat
> In the Prytaneum where this pharmakos
> Was wont to sit.'

Pharmakos is in fact, like its equivalent 'offscouring' (*κάθαρμα*), a current form of utter abuse, disgust and contempt.

Moreover its ritual import was perfectly familiar. Lysias[4] in his speech against Andokides is explicit: 'We needs must hold that in avenging ourselves and ridding ourselves of Andokides we purify the city and perform apotropaic ceremonies, and solemnly expel a pharmakos and rid ourselves of a criminal; for of this sort the fellow is.'

For the fullest details of the horrid ceremony we are indebted to a very late author. Tzetzes[5] (A.D. 1150) in his *Thousand*

[1] Ar. *Ran.* 734. [2] Ar. frg. 532. [3] Ar. *Eq.* 1405.

[4] Lys. *c. Andok.* 108. 4: *νῦν οὖν χρὴ νομίζειν τιμωρουμένους καὶ ἀπαλλαττομένους Ἀνδοκίδου τὴν πόλιν καθαίρειν καὶ ἀποδιοπομπεῖσθαι καὶ φαρμακὸν ἀποπέμπειν καὶ ἀλιτηρίου ἀπαλλάττεσθαι, ὡς ἓν τούτων οὗτός ἐστι.*

[5] Fragments of Hipponax (6th cent. B.C.) incorporated by Tzetzes, *Hist.* 23. 726—756:

> *Τί τὸ κάθαρμα;*
> *ὁ φαρμακὸς τὸ κάθαρμα τοιοῦτον ἦν τὸ πάλαι.*
> *ἂν συμφορὰ κατέλαβε πόλιν θεομηνίᾳ,*
> *εἴτ' οὖν λιμὸς εἴτε λοιμὸς εἴτε καὶ βλάβος ἄλλο,*
> *τῶν πάντων ἀμορφότερον ἦγον ὡς πρὸς θυσίαν*
> *εἰς καθαρμὸν καὶ φάρμακον πόλεως τῆς νοσούσης.*
> *εἰς τόπον δὲ τὸν πρόσφορον στήσαντες τὴν θυσίαν*
> *τυρόν τε δόντες τῇ χειρὶ καὶ μάζαν καὶ ἰσχάδας,*
> *ἑπτάκις γὰρ ῥαπίσαντες ἐκεῖνον εἰς τὸ πέος*

Histories describes it as follows: 'The pharmakos was a purification of this sort of old. If a calamity overtook the city by the wrath of God, whether it were famine or pestilence or any other mischief, they led forth as though to a sacrifice the most unsightly of them all as a purification and a remedy to the suffering city. They set the sacrifice in the appointed place, and gave him cheese with their hands and a barley cake and figs, and seven times they smote him with leeks and wild figs and other wild plants. Finally they burnt him with fire with the wood of wild trees and scattered the ashes into the sea and to the winds, for a purification, as I said, of the suffering city. Just as, I think, Lycophron records it of the Locrian maidens, speaking somewhat after this manner, I do not remember the exact verse, "when, having consumed their limbs with fuel from fruitless trees, the flame of fire cast into the sea the ashes of the maidens that died on the hill of Traron."'

Tzetzes is not inventing the ceremonies, and in his awkward confused way he goes on to tell us his source—the iambic poet Hipponax. 'And Hipponax gives us the best complete account of the custom when he says, "*to purify the city and strike* (the pharmakos) *with branches*"; and in another place he says in his first iambic poem, "*striking him in the meadow and beating him with branches and with leeks like a pharmakos*"; and again in other places he says as follows: "*we must make of him a pharmakos*"; and he says, "*offering him figs and a barley cake and cheese such as pharmakoi eat*"; and "*they have long been waiting agape for them, holding branches in their hands as pharmakoi do*"; and some-

σκίλλαις, συκαῖς ἀγρίαις τε καὶ ἄλλοις τῶν ἀγρίων,
τέλος πυρὶ κατέκαιον ἐν ξύλοις τοῖς ἀγρίοις,
καὶ τὸν σποδὸν εἰς θάλασσαν ἔρραινον καὶ ἀνέμους
καὶ καθαρμὸν τῆς πόλεως ὡς ἔφην τῆς νοσούσης.

ὁ δὲ Ἱππῶναξ ἄριστα σύμπαν τὸ ἔθος λέγει
1 *πόλιν καθαίρειν καὶ κράδησι βάλλεσθαι (φαρμακόν),*
καὶ ἀλλαχοῦ δέ πού φησι πρώτῳ ἰάμβῳ γράφων
2 *βάλλοντες ἐν λειμῶνι καὶ ῥαπίζοντες*
κράδησι καὶ σκίλλησιν ὥσπερ φαρμακόν.
καὶ πάλιν ἄλλοις τόποις δὲ ταῦτά φησι κατ' ἔπος
3 *δεῖ δ' αὐτὸν ἐς φαρμακὸν ἐκποιήσασθαι.*
4 *κἄφη παρέξειν ἰσχάδας τε καὶ μᾶζαν*
καὶ τυρὸν οἷον ἐσθίουσι φαρμακοί.
5 *πάλαι γὰρ αὐτοὺς προσδέχοντα(ι) χάσκοντες*
κράδας ἔχοντες ὡς ἔχουσι φαρμακοί.
καὶ ἀλλαχοῦ δέ πού φησιν ἐν τῷ αὐτῷ ἰάμβῳ
6 *λιμῷ γένηται ξηρὸς ὡς ἐν τῷ θυμῷ*
φαρμακὸς ἀχθεὶς ἑπτάκις ῥαπισθείη.

where else he says in the same iambic poem, "*may he be parched with hunger, so that in (their) anger he may be led as pharmakos and beaten seven times.*"'

Tzetzes quotes for us six fragmentary statements from Hipponax, and the words of Hipponax correspond so closely in every detail with his own account that we are justified in supposing that his account of the end of the ceremonial, the burning and scattering of the ashes, is also borrowed; but the evidence of this from Hipponax he omits.

Hipponax makes his statements apparently, not from any abstract interest in ritual, but as part of an insult levelled at his enemy Boupalos. This is made almost certain by another fragment of Hipponax[1] in which he says, 'as they uttered imprecations against that abomination (*ἄγος*) Boupalos.' The fragments belong obviously to one or more iambic poems in which Hipponax expresses the hope that Boupalos will share the fate of a pharmakos, will be insulted, beaten, driven out of the city, and at last presumably put to death. Hipponax is *not* describing an actual historical ceremony, but to make his insults have any point he must have been alluding to a ritual that was, in the 6th century B.C., perfectly familiar to his hearers.

Some of the statements of Hipponax as to the details of the ritual are confirmed from other sources, and are given in these with certain slight variations which seem to show that Hipponax was not the only source of information.

Helladius[2] the Byzantine, quoted by Photius, says that 'it was the custom at Athens to lead in procession two pharmakoi with a view to purification; one for the men, one for the women. The pharmakos of the men had black figs round his neck, the other had white ones, and he says they were called *συβάκχοι*.' Helladius added that 'this purification was of the nature of an apotropaic ceremony to avert diseases, and that it took its rise from Androgeôs the Cretan, when at Athens the Athenians suffered abnormally from a pestilential disease, and the custom obtained of constantly purifying the city by pharmakoi.'

The man and woman and the black and white figs are variant details. Helladius is our sole authority for the curious name

[1] Hippon. frg. 11 (4) *ὡς οἱ μὲν ἄγεϊ Βουπάλῳ κατηρῶντο.*
[2] Hellad. ap. Phot. *Bibl.* c. 279, p. 534.

συβάκχοι: what this means is not certain[1]. The term may have meant 'pig-Bacchoi.' The Bacchoi, as will later be seen, were sacred and specially purified persons with magical powers, and the term may have been applied to mark analogous functions. Crete was the home of ceremonies of purification.

Harpocration, in the passage already quoted, confirms the view that there were two pharmakoi, but he says they were both men: one for the women, one for the men. The discrepancy is not serious. It would be quite easy if necessary to dress up a man as a woman, and even a string of white figs would be sufficient presentment of gender; *simulata pro veris* is a principle of wide acceptation in primitive ritual.

The beating of the pharmakoi was a point of cardinal importance. It was a ceremonial affair and done to the sound of the flute. Hesychius[2] says, 'The song of the branches is a measure that they play on the flute when the pharmakoi are expelled, they being beaten with branches and fig sprigs. The pharmakos was actually called "he of the branches."' It must have been a matter of very early observation that beating is expulsive. You beat a bush, a bird escapes; you beat a garment, the dust comes out; you beat a man, the evil, whatever it be, will surely emerge. We associate beating with moral stimulus, but the first notion is clearly expulsive.

Probably some notion of the application or instigation of good as well as the expulsion of evil early came in. This may be conjectured from the fact that rods made of special plants and trees were used, notably leeks and fig-trees. Plants with strong smells, and plants the eating of which is purgative, are naturally regarded as 'good medicine'; as expulsive of evil, and hence in a secondary way as promotive of good.

Pythagoras[3] taught that to have a leek hung up over a doorway was a good thing to prevent the entrance of evil, and Dioscorides[4] records the same belief. Lucian[5] makes Menippus

[1] Lewy, *Semitische Fremdwörter*, p. 256, suggests that *συβάκχοι* is from זְבָחִים *z'bāḥīm*, the plural of זֶבַח which occurs in Phenician. If so the form *συβάκχοι* would be due to popular etymology.

[2] Hesych. s.v. *κραδίης νόμος*.

[3] Plin. *N.H.* xx. 9. 39.

[4] Diosc. *de mat. med.* II. 202.

[5] Luc. *Nek.* 7 *ἐκάθηρέ τε με καὶ ἀπέμαξε καὶ περιήγνισε δᾳδίοις καὶ σκίλλῃ.*

relate how before he was allowed to consult the oracle of the dead he was 'purged and wiped clean and consecrated with leek and torches.'

The *locus classicus* on beating with leek is of course the beating of the god Pan by his Arcadian worshippers. Theocritus[1] makes Simichidas sing:

'Dear Pan, if this my prayer may granted be
Then never shall the boys of Arcady
Flog thee on back and flank with leeks that sting
When scanty meat is left for offering;
If not, thy skin with nails be flayed and torn
And amid nettles mayst thou couch till morn.'

And the scholiast remarks, 'they say that a festival was held in Arcadia in which the youths beat Pan with leeks when the officials sacrificed a small victim, and there was not enough to eat for the worshipper; or the Arcadians when they went out hunting if they had good sport paid honour to Pan; if the reverse they maltreated him with leeks because, being a mountain god, he had power over the produce of the chase.' The first explanation confuses cause with effect, the second is undoubtedly right. Pan is beaten because, as lord of the chase, he has failed to do his business.

It is sometimes said that Pan is beaten, and the pharmakoi beaten, in order to 'stimulate their powers of fertility.' In a sense this is ultimately true, but such a statement gives a false and misleading emphasis. The image and the pharmakoi are beaten partly to drive out evil influences, partly, it should not be forgotten, to relieve the feelings of the beaters. When the evil influences are beaten out, the god will undoubtedly do better next time, but it is only in this sense that the powers of fertility are stimulated. The pharmakos has no second chance. He is utterly impure, so that the more purifying influences, the more good medicine brought to bear upon him, the better; but he is doomed to death, not to reform. In the Lupercalia, already discussed (p. 51), the women are struck by the *februum* as a fertility charm, but even here the primary notion must have been the expulsion of evil influences.

The beating, like the pharmakos, became proverbial. Aristophanes[2] makes Aeacus ask how he is to torture the supposed Xanthias, and the real Xanthias makes answer:

'Oh, in the usual way, but when you beat him
Don't do it with a leek or a young onion.'

[1] Theocr. *Id.* VII. 104, schol. ad loc.

[2] Ar. *Ran.* 620.

Here undoubtedly the meaning is, 'don't let this be a merely ceremonial beating, a religious performance,' and the allusion gains in point by the fact that the supposed slave was a real god to be treated worse than a pharmakos. Lucian[1] says that the Muses, he is sure, would never deign to come near his vulgar book-buyer, and instead of giving him a crown of myrtle they will beat him with myrrh and mallow and *get rid of him*, so that he may not pollute their sacred fountains. Clearly here the vulgar book-buyer is a pharmakos.

We have then abundant evidence that the pharmakos was beaten; was he also put to death? Tzetzes, as has been seen, states that he was burnt with the wood of certain fruitless trees, and that his ashes were scattered to the sea and the winds. The scholiast on Aristophanes[2] also states expressly that by *δημόσιοι*, i.e. people fed and kept at the public expense, was meant 'those who were called pharmakoi, and these pharmakoi purified cities by their slaughter.' So far it need not have been inferred that he was speaking of Athens, but he goes on, 'for the Athenians maintained certain very ignoble and useless persons, and on the occasion of any calamity befalling the city, I mean a pestilence or anything of that sort, they sacrificed these persons with a view to purification from pollution and they called them purifications' (*καθάρματα*). Tzetzes said a pharmakos was excessively ungainly (*ἀμορφότερον*), the scholiast, worthless and useless.

The scholiast is of course a late and somewhat dubious authority, and did the fact of the death of the pharmakos rest on him and on Tzetzes alone, we might be inclined to question it. A better authority is preserved for us by Harpocration[3]; he says, 'Istros (*circ.* B.C. 230), in the first book of his Epiphanies of Apollo, says that Pharmakos is a proper name, and that Pharmakos stole sacred *phialae* belonging to Apollo, and was taken and stoned by the men with Achilles, and the ceremonies done at the Thargelia are mimetic representations of these things.' The aetiology of Istros

[1] Luc. *Indoct.* 1.

[2] Schol. ad Ar. *Eq.* 1136.

[3] Harpocrat. s.v. *φαρμακός· ὅτι δὲ ὄνομα κύριόν ἐστιν ὁ φαρμακός, ἱερὰς δὲ φιάλας τοῦ Ἀπόλλωνος κλέψας καὶ ἁλοὺς ὑπὸ τῶν περὶ τὸν Ἀχιλλέα κατελεύσθη, καὶ τὰ τοῖς Θαργηλίοις ἀγόμενα τούτων ἀπομιμήματά ἐστιν, Ἴστρος ἐν πρώτῳ τῶν Ἀπόλλωνος ἐπιφανειῶν εἴρηκεν.* On the mythological gist of this legend and its possible connection with the epic Thersites see H. Usener, "Der Stoff d. gr. Epos," *Sitzungsber. d. Phil. Hist. kl. d. k. Ak. d. Wissenschaften*, Band 137, 1898, Wien, p. 47.

is of course wrong, but it is quite clear that he believed the ceremonies of the Thargelia to include the stoning of a man to death.

That in primitive pharmakos-ceremonies the human pharmakos was actually put to death scarcely admits of doubt: that Istros believed this took place at the ceremony of the Thargelia in honour of Apollo may be *inferred* from his aetiology. There still remains in the minds of some a feeling that the Athens of the fifth century was too civilized a place to have suffered the actual death of human victims, and that periodically, as part of a public state ritual. This misgiving arises mainly, as was indicated at the outset, from a misunderstanding of the gist of the ceremony. Tzetzes, after the manner of his day, calls it a θυσία, a burnt sacrifice; but it was not really a sacrifice in our modern sense at all, though, as will later be shown, it was one of the diverse notions that went to the making of the ancient idea of sacrifice.

The pharmakos was not a sacrifice in the sense of an offering *made to appease an angry god.* It came to be associated with Apollo when he took over the Thargelia, but primarily it was not intended to please or to appease any spirit or god. It was, as ancient authors repeatedly insist, a καθαρμός, a purification. The essence of the ritual was not atonement, for there was no one to atone, but riddance, the artificial making of an ἄγος, a pollution, to get rid of all pollution. The notion, so foreign to our scientific habit of thought, so familiar to the ancients, was that evil of all kinds was a physical infection that could be caught and transferred; it was highly catching. Next, some logical savage saw that the notion could be utilized for artificial riddance. The Dyaks[1] sweep misfortunes out of their houses and put them into a toy-house made of bamboo; this they set adrift on a river. On the occasion of a recent outbreak of influenza in Pithuria 'a man had a small carriage made, after a plan of his own, for a pair of scapegoats which were harnessed to it and driven to a wood at some distance where they were let loose. From that hour the disease completely ceased in the town. The goats never returned; had they done so the disease must have come back with them.' It

[1] For these modern savage analogies and many others see Dr Frazer, *Golden Bough*, 2nd ed., vol. III. p. 93.

is needless for our purpose to accumulate instances of the countless varieties of scape-goats, carts, cocks, boats, that the ingenuity of primitive man has invented. The instance chosen shows as clearly as possible that, as the gist of the ceremony is magical riddance, it is essential that the scape-goat, whatever form he takes, *should never return*.

This necessity for utter destruction comes out very clearly in an account of the way the Egyptians treated their scape-goats. Plutarch[1] in his discourse on Isis and Osiris says, on the authority of Manetho, that in the dog-days they used to burn men alive whom they called Typhonians, and *their ashes they made away with by winnowing and scattering them.* The winnowing-fan in which the corn was tossed and by means of which the chaff was blown utterly away was to Clement of Alexandria[2] the symbol of utter ruin and destruction. In his protest against the ruinous force of convention among pagan people, he says finely: 'let us fly from convention, it strangles men, it turns them away from truth, it leads them afar from life; convention is a noose, a place of execution, a pit, a winnowing-fan; convention is ruin.'

The pharmakos is killed then, not because his death is a vicarious sacrifice, but because he is so infected and tabooed that his life is a practical impossibility. The uneducated, among whom his lot would necessarily be cast, regard him as an infected horror, an incarnate pollution; the educated who believe no such nonsense know that the kindest thing is to put an end to a life that is worse than death. Moreover nearly every civilized state to this day offers 'human sacrifice' in the shape of the criminals it executes. Why not combine religious tradition with a supposed judicial necessity? Civilized Athens had its barathron; why should civilized Athens shrink from annually utilizing two vicious and already condemned criminals to 'purify the city'?

The question of whether the pharmakos was actually put to death in civilized Athens is of course for our purpose a strictly subordinate one. It has only been discussed in detail because the answer that we return to it depends in great measure on how

[1] Plut. *de Is. et Os.* LXXIII. *ζῶντας ἀνθρώπους κατεπίμπρασαν ὡς Μανεθὼς ἱστόρηκε Τυφωνίους καλοῦντες καὶ τὴν τέφραν αὐτῶν λικμῶντες ἠφάνιζον καὶ διέσπειρον.*

[2] Clem. Al. *Protr.* XII. 118 *φύγωμεν οὖν τὴν συνήθειαν...ἄγχει τὸν ἄνθρωπον, τῆς ἀληθείας ἀποτρέπει, ἀπάγει τῆς ζωῆς, πάγις ἐστὶν βάραθρόν ἐστιν βόθρος ἐστὶ λίκνον ἐστίν, κακὸν ἡ συνήθεια.*

far we realize the primary gist of a pharmakos, i.e. the two notions of (*a*) the *physicalness*, the actuality of evil, and (*b*) the possibility of contagion and transfer.

Our whole modern conception of the scape-man is apt to be unduly influenced by the familiar instance of the Hebrew scape-goat. We remember how

> 'The scape-goat stood all skin and bone
> *While moral business, not his own,*
> *Was bound about his head.*'

And the pathos of the proceeding haunts our minds and prevents us from realizing the actuality and the practicality of the more primitive physical taboo. It is interesting to note that even in this moralized Hebrew conception, the scape-goat was not a sacrifice proper; its sending away was *preceded by sacrifice.* The priest 'made an atonement for the children of Israel for all their sins once a year,' and when the sacrifice of bullock and goat and the burning of incense, and the sprinkling of blood was over, then and not till then the live goat was presented to the Lord[1]. The Hebrew scriptures emphasize the fact that the burden laid upon the goat is not merely physical evil, not pestilence or famine, but rather the burden of moral guilt. 'And Aaron shall lay both his hands upon the head of the live goat and confess over him all the iniquities of the children of Israel and all their transgressions in all their sins, putting them upon the head of the goat, and shall send him away by the hand of a fit man into the wilderness. And the goat shall bear upon him all their iniquities into a land not inhabited.'

But so close is the connection of moral and physical that even here, where the evil laid upon the scape-goat is moral only, there is evident danger of infection: the goat is sent forth into a land not inhabited and it would be manifestly undesirable that he should return. At Athens we hear of no confession of sins, it is famine and pestilence from which a terror-stricken city seeks riddance.

This physical aspect of evil is still more clearly brought out in a ceremony performed annually at Chaeronea. Plutarch[2] himself, when he was archon, had to preside over the ritual and has

[1] Lev. xvi. 21, and for the Egyptian scape-animal see Herod. II. 39.
[2] Plut. *Q. Symp.* VI. 8.

left us the account. A household slave was taken and ceremonially beaten with rods of agnus castus—again a plant of cathartic quality—and driven out of doors to the words, 'Out with hunger, in with wealth and health.' The ceremony was called the 'expulsion of hunger,' and Plutarch speaks of it as an 'ancestral sacrifice.' It was performed by each householder for his own house, and by the archon for the common hearth of the city. When Plutarch was archon he tells us the ceremony was largely attended. The name of the 'ceremony' is instructive, it is *ἐξέλασις*, riddance, expulsion, not as the pharmakos was, *καθαρμός*, purification; both are called *θυσίαι*, sacrifices, only by concession to popular usage when every religious ceremony is regarded as of the nature of burnt sacrifice. The ceremony of the pharmakos was taken on by Apollo, but in the Chaeronea 'expulsion' there is no pretence that any god is worshipped; the performance remains frankly magical.

At Chaeronea the slave was merely beaten and expelled. At Delphi a pharmakos ceremony of still milder form took place in which the victim was merely a puppet.

In his 12th *Greek Question* Plutarch asks, 'What is Charila among the Delphians?' His answer is as follows: 'Concerning Charila they tell a story something on this wise. The Delphians were afflicted by a famine following after a drought. They came to the gates of the king's palace with their children and their wives to make supplication. And the king distributed grain and pulse to the noblest of them as there was not enough for all. And there came a little girl who had lost both her father and mother, and she made supplication. But he struck her with his shoe and threw the shoe into her face. Now she was poor and desolate but of noble spirit, and she went away and loosed her girdle and hanged herself. As the famine went on and pestilence was added thereto, the Pythia gave an oracle to the king that he must appease Charila, a maiden who had died by her own hand. After some difficulty they found out that this was the name of the girl who had been struck. So they performed a sacrifice which had in it some admixture of a purification, and this they still perform every nine years.'

The tale told of Charila is, of course, pure aetiology, to account for certain features in an established ritual. The expression

Plutarch uses, a 'sacrifice with admixture of purification' (*μεμιγμένην τινὰ καθαρμοῦ θυσίαν*), is interesting because it shows that though by his time almost every religious ceremony was called a *θυσία,* his mind is haunted by the feeling that the Charila ceremony was in reality a purification, a *καθαρμός*; he would have been nearer the truth had he said it was a 'purification containing in it a certain element of sacrifice.'

He then proceeds to give the actual ritual. 'The king is seated to preside over the pulse and the grain and he distributes it to all, both citizens and strangers: there is brought in an image of Charila as a little girl, and when they all receive the corn, the king strikes the image with his shoe and the leader of the Thyiades takes the image and conducts it to a certain cavernous place, and there fastening (a rope) round the neck of the image they bury it where they buried the strangled Charila.'

The festival Charila, festival of rejoicing and grace, is like the Thargelia, a festival of first-fruits containing the ceremony of the Pharmakos, only in effigy. Charila is beaten with a shoe: leather is to this day regarded as magically expulsive, though the modern surrogate is of white satin. On a curious vase in the National Museum at Athens[1], we have a representation of a wedding procession at which a man is in the act of throwing a shoe. It is still to-day regarded as desirable that bride and bridegroom should be hit, evil influences are thereby expelled, and the shower of fertilizing rice is made the more efficacious. The effigy of Charila is buried, not burnt, possibly a more primitive form of destruction. The origin of the ceremony is dated back to the time when the king was priest, but the actual celebrants are women.

A pharmakos ceremony that is known to have taken place at Marseilles adds some further instructive details. Servius, in commenting on the words *auri sacra fames*[2] 'accursed hunger of gold,' notes that *sacer* may mean accursed as well as holy, and he seems, rather vaguely, to realize that between these two meanings is the

[1] My attention was kindly drawn to this vase by M. Perdrizet, see *Ephemeris Arch.* 1905, pl. 6, 7, and E. Samter, *Hochzeitsbräuche* in *Neue Jahrbücher f. Kl. Altertum*, 1907, XIX. p. 131. Suidas (s.v. *εἴδωλον*) seems to refer to the Charila ceremony, *κελεύει ἡ Πυθία εἴδωλόν τι πεπλασμένον εἰς ὄψιν γυναικὸς μετέωρον ἐξαρτᾶν καὶ ἀνερρώσθη ἡ πόλις.* For this and the *oscilla* ceremonies and the analogy of Artemis *ἀπαγχομένη* (P. VIII. 23. 7) see Lobeck, *Aglaoph.* p. 175. The beating of the female slave in the temple of Leucothea (Plut. *Q. R.* XVI.) seems to have been based on a racial taboo, but a *φαρμακός* ceremony may underlie it.

[2] Serv. ad Verg. *Aen.* III. 75.

middle term 'devoted.' The use of the term, he says, is derived from a custom among the Gauls: 'Whenever the inhabitants of Marseilles suffer from a pestilence, one of the poorer class offers himself to be kept at the public expense and fed on specially pure foods. After this has been done he is decorated with sacred boughs and clad in holy garments, and led about through the whole city to the accompaniment of curses, in order that upon him may fall all the ills of the whole city, and thus he is cast headlong down.'

Here we have the curious added touch that the vehicle of impurity is purified. To our modern minds pure and impure stand at two opposite poles, and if we were arraying a scape-goat we certainly should not trouble about his preliminary purification. But the ancients, as Servius dimly feels, knew of a condition that combined the two, the condition that the savage describes as 'taboo.' For this condition the Latins used the word 'sacer,' the Greeks, as has already been seen, the word ἄγος. It is in such complex primitive notions as those of *sacer* and ἄγος, that our modern habit of clear analysis and differentiation causes us to miss the full and complex significance.

The leading out of the pharmakos is then a purely magical ceremony based on ignorance and fear; it is not a human sacrifice to Apollo or to any other divinity or even ghost, it is a ceremony of physical expulsion. It is satisfactory to find that the etymology[1] of the word confirms this view, φαρμακός means simply 'magic-man.' Its Lithuanian cognate is *burīn,* magic; in Latin it appears as *forma,* formula, magical spell; our *formulary* retains some vestige of its primitive connotation. Φάρμακον in Greek means healing drug, poison, and dye, but all, for better for worse, are magical. To express its meaning we need what our language has lost, a double-edged word like the savage 'medicine.' The pharmakos of the Thargelia shows us a state of things in which man does not either tend or avert god[2] or ghost, but seeks, by the

[1] For a full and very interesting discussion of the etymology and meaning of φαρμακός, see Osthoff, 'Allerhand Zauber etymologisch beleuchtet,' Bezzenberger, *Beiträge* XXIV. p. 109. As to the accentuation of the word φαρμακός Eustathius (1935. 15) notes that it was proparoxytone 'among the Ionians.'

[2] As to the god worshipped at the Thargelia it is probable that when godhead came to be formulated Demeter Chloe long preceded Apollo. Diogenes Laertius (II. 44) notes that on the sixth day of Thargelion when the Athenians purified the city, sacrifice was done to Demeter Chloe. Here as elsewhere Apollo took over the worship of an Earth-goddess.

'medicine' he himself makes, to do, on his own account, his spring or rather Whitsuntide 'thorough cleaning.' The ceremony of the pharmakos went in some sense to the making of the Greek and modern notion of sacrifice, but the word itself has other and perhaps more primitive connotations.

Tzetzes, looking back at the ceremony of the expulsion of the pharmakos, calls it a sacrifice (*θυσία*), but we need not imitate him in his confusion of ideas new and old. The rite of the Thargelia was a rite of expulsion, of riddance, which incidentally, as it were, involved loss of life to a human being. The result is, indeed, in both cases the same to the human being, but the two ceremonials of sacrifice and riddance express widely different conditions and sentiments in the mind of the worshipper.

It may indeed be doubted whether we have any certain evidence of 'human sacrifice' in our sense among the Greeks even of mythological days. A large number of cases which were by the tragedians regarded as such, resolve themselves into cases of the blood feud, cases such as those of Iphigeneia and Polyxena, when the object was really the placation of a ghost, not the service of an Olympian. Perhaps a still larger number are primarily not sacrifices, *θυσίαι*, but ceremonies of riddance and purification, *καθαρμοί*. The ultimate fact that lies behind such ceremonies is the use of a human pharmakos, and then later, when the real meaning was lost, all manner of aetiological myths are invented and some offended Olympian is introduced.

The case of the supposed 'human sacrifice' of Athamas is instructive, both as to its original content and as to the shifting sentiments with which it was regarded. When Xerxes came to Alos in Achaia his guides, Herodotus[1] tells us, anxious to give him all possible information as to local curiosities, told him the tradition about the sanctuary of Zeus Laphystios: 'The eldest of the race of Athamas is forbidden to enter the Prytaneion which is called by the Achaians the *Leïton*. If he enters he can only go out to be sacrificed.' It was further told how some, fearing this fate, had fled the country, and coming back and entering the Prytaneion were decked with fillets and led out in procession to be

[1] Herod. VII. 197.

sacrificed (ὡς θύεταί τε ἐξηγέοντο στέμμασι πᾶς πυκασθεὶς καὶ ὡς σὺν πομπῇ ἐξαχθείς). Here there is obvious confusion, as the man who left the country to avoid death would never have been so foolish as, immediately on his return, to enter the forbidden place. The point is clear: great stress is laid on the leading forth in procession—the descendant of the royal race was a scape-goat. Herodotus makes this quite clear. Athamas was sacrificed because the Achaeans *were making a purification of the land* (καθαρμὸν τῆς χώρης ποιευμένων Ἀχαιῶν). Herodotus gives as the cause of this primitive and perfectly intelligible custom various conflicting reasons which well reflect the various stages of opinion through which the thinking Greek passed. We have first the real reason—Athamas as a scape-goat. Then the public conscience is uneasy, and we have a legend that the 'sacrifice' is interrupted at the moment of consummation either by Herakles (according to Sophocles in the lost *Athamas*) or by Kytissoros. It is wrong to sacrifice; hence the sacrifice is interrupted, but it is wrong to interrupt sacrifice, so the descendants of Kytissoros are punished. Then, finally, it is felt that the sacrifice must go on, but it is a dreadful thing, an ἄγος, so a chance of escape is given to the victim. Finally in the same complex legend we have the substitution of a ram for the human victim Phrixos.

Sometimes incidentally we learn that other peoples adopted the device which may have satisfied the Athenians, i.e. needing a pharmakos they utilized a man already condemned by the state. Thus in the long list of 'human sacrifices' drawn up by Porphyry[1] in his indictment of human ignorance and fear he mentions that on the 6th day of the month Metageitnion a man was sacrificed to Kronos, a custom, he says, which was maintained for a long time unchanged. *A man who had been publicly condemned to death* was kept till the time of the festival of Kronia. When the festival came they brought him outside the gates before the image (ἕδους) of Aristobule, gave him wine to drink and slew him. The victim is already doomed, and it would seem intoxicated before he is sacrificed.

In noting the substitution of animal for human sacrifice, one curious point remains to be observed. The step seems to us momentous because to us human life is sacrosanct. But to the

[1] Porphyr. *de Abst.* II. 53—56.

primitive mind the gulf between animal and human is not so wide. The larger animals, and certain animals which for various reasons were specially venerated, were in early days also regarded as sacrosanct, and to slay them was murder, to be atoned for by purification.

This notion comes out very clearly in the ritual of the Murder of the Ox, the *Bouphonia*[1], or, as it was sometimes called, the Dipolia[2]. The Bouphonia by the time of Aristophanes[3] was a symbol of what was archaic and obsolete. After the Just Logos in the *Clouds* has described the austere old educational *régime* of ancient Athens, the Unjust Logos remarks:

> 'Bless me, that's quite the ancient lot Dipolia-like, chock-full
> Of crickets and Bouphonia too.'

And the scholiast comments, 'Dipolia, a festival at Athens, in which they sacrifice to Zeus Polieus, on the 14th day of Skirophorion. It is a mimetic representation of what happened about the cakes (πέλανοι) and the cows[4].' What happened was this: 'Barley mixed with wheat, or cakes made of them, was laid upon the bronze altar of Zeus Polieus, on the Acropolis. Oxen were driven round the altar, and the ox which went up to the altar and ate the offering on it was sacrificed. The axe and knife with which the beast was slain had been previously wetted with water, brought by maidens called "water-carriers." The weapons were then sharpened and handed to the butchers, one of whom felled the ox with the axe and another cut its throat with the knife. As

[1] My account of the Bouphonia is taken from Dr Frazer's summary, which is exactly based on the complex double account given by Porphyry from Theophrastos (Porphyr. *de Abst.* II. 29 seq.) and Aelian (*V.H.* VIII. 3). With Dr Frazer's exhaustive commentary (*Golden Bough*, 2nd ed. vol. II. p. 295) I am in substantial agreement, save that I do not see in the murdered ox the representative of the Corn Spirit. The Bouphonia as ox-*murder* was first correctly explained by Prof. Robertson Smith (*Religion of the Semites*, p. 286 ff.). I have discussed it previously in *Mythology and Monuments of Ancient Athens*, p. 421 ff.: see also Dr Paul Stengel, *Rhein. Mus.* 1897, p. 187. With Dr von Prott's view (*Rhein. Mus.* 1897, p. 187) that the sense of guilt in the sacrifice arises from the fact that the ox was the surrogate of a human victim I wholly disagree.

[2] It is possible that Dipolia is etymologically not the festival of Zeus Polieus but the festival of the Plough Curse, see p. 23.

[3] Ar. *Nub.* 984.

[4] The scholiast is (so far as I know) the only authority who gives the female form. It is possible that the sacrifice may have been primarily to an earth-goddess and hence the animals are female. The curious ceremonial of the *Chthonia* (P. II. 35. 3) was a similar butchery of cows in honour of Chthonia and presided over by old women who did the actual slaughter, and no *man* native or foreigner was allowed to see it.

soon as he had felled the ox, the former threw the axe from him and fled, and the man who had cut the beast's throat apparently imitated his example. Meantime the ox was skinned and all present partook of its flesh. Then the hide was stuffed with straw and sewed up, and next the stuffed animal was set on its feet and yoked to a plough as if it were ploughing. A trial then took place in an ancient law court, presided over by the king (as he was called), to determine who had murdered the ox. The maidens who had brought the water accused the men who had sharpened the axe and knife, the men who had sharpened the axe and knife blamed the men who had handed these implements to the butchers, the men who had handed the implements to the butchers blamed the butchers and the butchers blamed the axe and knife, which were accordingly found guilty and condemned and cast into the sea.'

The remarks of the Unjust Logos are amply justified. That a mummery so absurd, with all its leisurely House-that-Jack-built hocus-pocus, should be regularly carried on in the centre of civilized Athens was enough to make the most careless and the most conventional reflect on the nature and strength of religious conservatism. But the rite was once of real and solemn import, and, taken as such, the heart of a terror-stricken service of Aversion. The ox had to be killed, man imperatively demanded his feast of flesh meat, but it was a dreadful *ἄγος*, an abomination, to kill it, as bad as, perhaps worse than killing a man, and the ghost of the ox and the spirits of vengeance generally must at all costs be tricked or appeased. So great is the terror that no one device is enough. You pretend that the ox is not really dead, or at least that he has come to life: if that is not enough you pretend that he was himself an offender: he ate the sacred cakes, not by compulsion, but of his own free, wicked will. Last you pretend that you did not do it yourself, it was some one else. No, not some one else, but some-*thing* else. Finally that thing is got rid of; the *ἄγος*, the pollution, is thrown into the sea.

The important point for the moment is that the ox, though no surrogate for human sacrifice, is as good as human, is a man. His murdered ghost, or at least the pollution of his murder, cries for placation and purification. It is satisfactory to note that if you had to be purified yourself for murdering an ox, an ox, even a bronze ox, had to be purified for murdering you. Pausanias[1] was told the following story about a bronze ox, dedicated at Olympia by the Corcyreans. A little boy was sitting playing under the ox, and suddenly he lifted up his head and broke it against the bronze, and a few days after he died of the wounds. The Eleans consulted as to whether they should remove the ox out of the Altis, as being guilty of blood, but the Delphic oracle, always conservative in the matter of valuable property, ordained 'that they were to leave it and perform the same ceremonies as were customary among the Greeks in the case of involuntary homicide.'

To return to the Bouphonia, the confused notion that a thing must be done, and yet that its doing involves an ἄγος, a pollution, comes out in all the rituals known as Flight-ceremonies. The gist of them is very clear in the account given by Diodorus[2] of the ceremonies of embalming among the Egyptians. He tells us 'the man called He-who-slits-asunder (παρασχίστης) takes an Aethiopian stone, and, making a slit in the prescribed way, instantly makes off with a run, and they pursue him and pelt him with stones, and heap curses on him, *as though transferring the pollution of the thing on to him.*'

The *Flight-Ceremony* recorded by Plutarch[3] is specially instructive, and must be noted in detail, the more so as it, like the Bouphonia, is connected with rites of the threshing-floor. In his 12th *Greek Question*, Plutarch says that among the three great festivals celebrated every eighth year at Delphi was one called *Stepterion*[4], and in another discourse (*De defect. orac.* XIV.) he describes the rite practised, though he mixes it up with so much aetiological mythology that it is not very easy to disentangle the actual facts. This much is clear; every eighth year a hut (καλιάς) was set up about the threshing-floor at Delphi. This hut, Plutarch says, bore more resemblance to a kingly palace than to a snake's lair; we

[1] P. v. 27. 6.

[2] Diod. I. 91 καθαπερεὶ τὸ μύσος εἰς ἐκεῖνον τρεπόντων.

[3] Plut. *De defect. orac.* XIV., the text is in places corrupt.

[4] I have elsewhere (*J.H.S.* XIX. 1899, p. 223) stated that the word 'Stepterion' cannot to my thinking be translated 'Festival of Crowning.' This explanation rests only on Aelian (*Hist. An.* XII. 34), and purification (κάθαρσις, ἔκθυσις), not crowning, is the main gist of the ceremonies. The name Stepterion, is, I suspect, connected with the enigmatic στέφη and στέφειν as occurring in Aesch. *Choeph.* 94, Soph. *Ant.* 431, *Elec.* 52, 458, and means in some way purification, but see Nilsson, *Griechische Feste*, p. 151.

may therefore safely infer that it held a snake. A boy with both his parents alive was led up by a certain prescribed way[1] with lighted torches; fire was set to the hut, a table overturned, and the celebrants took flight without looking back through the gates of the precinct; afterwards the boy went off to Tempe, fasted, dined, and was brought back crowned with laurel in solemn procession. Plutarch never says that the boy killed the snake, but as the ceremony was supposed to be a mimetic representation of the slaying of the Python and the banishment of Apollo, this may be inferred. Plutarch is of course *more suo* shocked at the idea that Apollo could need purification, and at a loss to account decently for the curious ceremonial, but he makes one acute remark: 'finally the wanderings and the servitude of the boy and the purifications at Tempe raise a suspicion of some great pollution and deed of daring' (*μεγάλου τινὸς ἄγους καὶ τολμήματος ὑποψίαν ἔχουσι*). This hits the mark: a sacred snake has been slain; the slayer has incurred an *ἄγος*, from which he must be purified. The slaying is probably formal and sacrificial, for the boy is led to the hut with all due solemnity, and has been carefully selected for the purpose; but the *τόλμημα*, the outrage, the deed of daring, is an *ἄγος*, so he must take flight after its accomplishment. Sacred snake, or sacred ox, or human victim, the procedure is the same.

To resume. The outcome of our examination of the ceremony of the pharmakos is briefly this: the gist of the pharmakos rite is physical purification, *καθαρμός*, and this notion, sometimes alone, sometimes combined with the notion of the placation of a ghost, is the idea underlying among the Greeks the notion we are apt to call Human Sacrifice. To this must be added the fact that in a primitive state of civilization the line between human and animal 'sacrifice' is not sharply drawn.

KALLYNTERIA, PLYNTERIA.

Plutarch[2] tells us that it was on a day of ill-omen that Alcibiades returned to Athens: 'On the day of his return they were solemnizing the Plynteria to the Goddess. For on the sixth

[1] Other instances are given Ael. *Hist. An.* XII. 34, Philostr. *Im.* II. 24. 850. For analogous Roman Festivals see Regifugium and Poplifugia, Warde-Fowler, *Roman Festivals*, pp. 327 and 174. For the Stepterion and savage analogies see Dr Frazer, *Pausanias*, vol. III. p. 53.

[2] Plut. *Vit. Alc.* XXXIV.

day of the third part of Thargelion the Praxiergidae solemnize the rites that may not be disclosed: they take off the adornments of the image, and cover it up. Hence the Athenians account this day as most unlucky of all, and do no work on it. And it seemed as though the Goddess were receiving him in no friendly or kindly fashion, as she hid her face from him and seemed to banish him from her presence.' At the Plynteria, as at other 'unlucky' festivals, the sanctuaries, Pollux[1] tells us, were roped round. The object was in part to keep out the common herd, perhaps primarily to 'avert' evil influences.

Photius[2] discusses the two festivals, the Kallynteria and the Plynteria, together, placing the Kallynteria first; they have indeed practically always been bracketed in the minds of commentators as substantially identical in content. The Plynteria, it is usually stated, was the washing festival. The image of Pallas was taken in solemn procession down to the sea, stripped of its gear, veiled from the eyes of the vulgar, washed in sea-water, and brought back. At the Kallynteria it was re-dressed, re-decked, 'beautified.' This simple explanation of the sequence of rites presents only one trifling difficulty. Photius expressly tells us that the Kallynteria preceded the Plynteria; the Kallynteria took place on the 19th of the month Thargelion, and the Plynteria on the second day of the third decade, i.e. on the 28th[3]. It would be strange if the image was first 'beautified' and then washed. The explanation of the seeming incongruity is of course a simple one. The word *καλλύνειν* means not only 'to beautify' but to brush out, to sweep, 'to give a shine to.' The Greek for broom is *καλλύντριον*, also *καλ<λ>υντρόν* in Hesych. s.v. *σαρόν*; and *καλλύσματα*, if we may trust Hesychius[4], means sweepings (*σάρματα*). In a word the Kallynteria is a festival of what the Romans call *everruncatio*, the festival of 'those who do the sweeping.' They swept out the sacred places, made them as we say now-a-days 'beautifully clean,' and then, having done their sweeping first like good housewives, when the house was ready they washed the image and brought it back in new shining splendour.

It is evident that when we hear of sweeping out sanctuaries

[1] Poll. *On.* VIII. 141. [2] Phot. s.v. Καλλυντήρια.

[3] Plutarch and Photius cannot both be right, but it is unlikely that Photius would give the *sequence* incorrectly.

[4] Hesych. s.v. *σάρματα*.

and washing an image we have come to a religious stage in which there is a definite god worshipped, and that god is conceived of as anthropomorphic. There may have been rites of the Thargelia, including the Pharmakos, i.e. the ceremony of the expulsion of evil, before there were any Kallynteria or Plynteria. Be this as it may, the Kallynteria and Plynteria throw light on the purport of the pharmakos, and emphasize the fact that all the cleansing, whether of image, sanctuary or people, was but a preliminary to the bringing in of the first-fruits.

This connection between first-fruits and purification explains a feature in the Plynteria that would otherwise remain obscure. In the procession that took place at the Plynteria, probably, though not quite certainly, the procession in which the image was taken down to the sea, Hesychius[1] tells us they carried a cake or mass of dried figs, which went by the name of *Hegeteria*. Hesychius is at no loss to account for the strange name. Figs were the first cultivated fruit of which man partook; the cake of figs is called Hegeteria because it 'Led the Way' in the matter of diet!

We may perhaps be allowed to suggest a possible alternative. Spite of its long vowels, may not the fig-cake be connected with the root of *ἅγος* rather than with *ἄγω*? Figs were used in purification. Is not the Hegeteria the fig-cake of purification? A necklace of figs was hung about the neck of the pharmakos, and the statues of the gods had sometimes a like adornment. Primitive man is apt to get a little confused as to cause and effect. He performs a rite of purification to protect his first-fruits; he comes to think the offering of those first-fruits is in itself a rite of purification.

As usual when we come to consider the analogous Roman festival the meaning of the rites practised is more baldly obvious. Plutarch[2] in his *Roman Questions* asks, 'Why did not the Romans marry in the month of May?' and for once he hits upon the right answer: 'May it be that in this month they perform the greatest of purificatory ceremonies?' What these purificatory ceremonies, these *καθαρμοί*, were, he tells us explicitly: 'for at the present day they throw images from the bridge into the river, but in old times they used to throw human beings.' We must here separate

[1] Hesych. s.v. *ἡγητηρία· παρὰ ἡγήσασθαι οὖν τῆς τροφῆς κέκληται ἡγητηρία.*
[2] Plut. *Q.R.* LXXXVI.

sharply the fact stated by Plutarch, the actual ritual that took place in his own day, from his conjecture about the past. We *know* images, puppets, were thrown from the bridge, we may conjecture, as Plutarch did, that they were the surrogates of human sacrifice, but we must carefully bear in mind that this is pure conjecture. The *fact* Plutarch certifies in another of his *Questions*[1], and adds the name of the puppets. 'What,' he asks, 'is the reason that in the month of May they throw images of human beings from the wooden bridge into the river, calling them Argeioi?' Ovid[2] tells us a little more: 'Then (i.e. on May 15th) the Vestal is wont to throw from the oaken bridge the images of men of old times, made of rushes.' He adds that it was in obedience to an oracle: 'Ye nations, throw two bodies in sacrifice to the Ancient One who bears the sickle, bodies to be received by the Tuscan streams.' Ovid and Plutarch clearly both held that the *Argei* of rushes were surrogates. It seems possible, on the other hand, that the myth of human sacrifice may have arisen from a merely dramatic apotropaic rite. The one certain thing is that the *Argei*[3] *were* pharmakoi, were καθάρματα.

That the time of the Argei, and indeed the whole month till the Ides of June, was unlucky is abundantly proved by the conduct of the Flaminica. Plutarch[4] goes on to say that the Flaminica is wont to be gloomy (σκυθρωπάζειν) and not to wash nor to adorn herself. Ovid[5] adds details of this mourning; he tells us that he consulted the Flaminica Dialis as to the marriage of his daughter, and learnt that till the Ides of June there was no luck for brides and their husbands, 'for thus did the holy bride of the Dialis speak to me: "Until tranquil Tiber has borne to the sea in his tawny waters the cleansings from Ilian Vesta it is not lawful for me to comb my shorn locks with the boxwood, nor to pare my nails with iron, nor to touch my husband though he be priest of Jove....Be not in haste. Better will thy daughter marry when Vesta of the Fire shines with a cleansed hearth."'

The Roman Vestalia fell a little later than the Kallynteria and

[1] Plut. *Q.R.* XXXII.

[2] Ov. *Fasti* V. 621.

[3] The whole ceremony of the *Argei* has been fully discussed by Mr Warde-Fowler (*The Roman Festivals*, p. 111). Abundant primitive analogies have been collected by Mannhardt (*Baumkultus*, pp. 155, 411, 416, and *Antike Wald- und Feldkulte*, p. 276). For the etymology of *Argei* see Mr A. B. Cook, *Class. Rev.* XVII. 1903, p. 269.

[4] Plut. *Q.R.* LXXXVI.

[5] Ov. *Fasti* VI. 219—234.

Plynteria, but their content is the same. I borrow the account of the ritual of the Vestalia from Mr Warde-Fowler[1]. On June 7 the *penus*, or innermost sanctuary of Vesta, which was shut all the rest of the year and to which no man but the pontifex maximus had at any time right of entry, was thrown open to all matrons. During the seven following days they crowded to it barefoot. The object of this was perhaps to pray for a blessing on the household. On plain and old-fashioned ware offerings of food were carried into the temple: the Vestals themselves offered the sacred cakes made of the first ears of corn, plucked as we saw in the early days of May; bakers and millers kept holiday, all mills were garlanded and donkeys decorated with wreaths and cakes. On June 15 the temple (*aedes*) was swept and the refuse taken away and either thrown into the Tiber or deposited in some particular spot. Then the *dies nefasti* came to an end, and the 15th itself became *fastus* as soon as the last act of cleansing had been duly performed. *Quando stercus delatum fas*, 'When the rubbish has been carried away.'

Dr Frazer[2] has collected many savage parallels to the rites of the Vestalia. The most notable is the *busk* or festival of first-fruits among the Creek Indians of North America, held in July or August when the corn is ripe. Before the celebration of the *busk* no Indian would eat or even touch the new corn. In preparation for its rites they got new clothes and household utensils: old clothes, rubbish of all kinds, and the old corn that remained were carefully burnt. The village fires were put out and the ashes swept away, and in particular the hearth and altar of the temple were dug up and cleaned out. The public square was carefully swept out 'for fear of polluting the first-fruit offerings.' Before the sacramental eating of the new corn a strict fast was observed, and (for the precautions taken by the savage ritualist are searching and logical) a strong purgative was swallowed. With the new corn was solemnly dispensed the freshly-kindled fire, and the priest publicly announced that the new divine fire had purged away the sins of the past year. Such powerful 'medicine' was the new corn that some of the men rubbed their new corn between their hands, then on their faces and breasts.

[1] Warde-Fowler, *Roman Festivals*, p. 148.
[2] Frazer, *Golden Bough*, 2nd ed., vol. II. p. 329.

To resume. In the Anthesteria we have seen that sacrifice was in intent purification, and that this purification took the form of the placation of ghosts. In the Thargelia, purification is again the end and aim of sacrifice, but this purification, though it involves the taking of a human life, is of the nature of a merely magical cleansing to prepare for the incoming first-fruits.

We pass to the consideration of the autumn festival of sowing, the *Thesmophoria*.

NOTE. Since my account of the Thargelia was written Mr W. R. Paton has kindly sent me a letter he has published in the *Revue Archéologique* on *The Pharmakos and the Story of the Fall*. Mr Paton's view is that the object of the pharmakos ceremony was to promote the success of *caprification*. This theory throws quite new light on the ceremony and seems to me of the first importance. It explains the black and white figs, the male and female victims, and, to the full, the ritual beating. Further, it offers a rational and most welcome hypothesis as to the ritual origin of the myth of the 'Fall.'

CHAPTER IV.

THE WOMEN'S FESTIVALS.

THESMOPHORIA, ARREPHORIA, SKIROPHORIA, STENIA, HALOA.

'τὰ θεσμοφόρι' ἄγουσιν ὥσπερ καὶ πρὸ τοῦ.'

The Thesmophoria.

WITH the autumn festival of the Thesmophoria[1] we come to a class of rites of capital interest. They were practised by women only and were of immemorial antiquity. Although, for reasons explained at the outset, they are considered after the Anthesteria and Thargelia, their character was even more primitive, and, owing to the conservative character of women and the mixed contempt and superstition with which such rites were regarded by men, they were preserved in pristine purity down to late days. Unlike the Diasia, Anthesteria, Thargelia, they were left almost uncontaminated by Olympian usage, and—a point of supreme interest—under the influence of a new religious impulse, they issued at last in the most widely influential of all Greek ceremonials, the Eleusinian Mysteries.

To the primitive character and racial origin of these rites we have the witness of Herodotus[2], though unhappily piety sealed his lips as to details. He says, 'Concerning the feast of Demeter which the Greeks call Thesmophoria I must preserve an auspicious silence, excepting in so far as every one may speak of it. It was the daughters of Danaus who introduced this rite from

[1] The sources for the Thesmophoria are collected and discussed by Dr J. G. Frazer, *Encyclopaedia Britannica*, Art. Thesmophoria.

[2] II. 171. See also Frazer, *Pausanias*, vol. v. p. 29; Harrison and Verrall, *Myth. and Mon. Anc. Athens*, pp. xxxiv. and 102—105 and 482; A. Lang, *Homeric Hymns*, Introd. Essay and Hymn to Demeter, and Nilsson, *Griechische Feste*, p. 313.

Egypt and taught it to the Pelasgian women; but after the upset of the whole of Peloponnesos by the Dorians the rite died down completely, and it was only those of the Peloponnesians who were left, and the Arcadians who did not leave their seats who kept it up.' Herodotus oddly enough does not mention the Athenians, who were as stable and as untouched as the Arcadians, but his notice is invaluable as fixing the pre-Dorian character of the rites. Knowing that they were of immemorial antiquity, *more suo* he attributes them to the Egyptians, and as will later be seen (p. 128) there may be some element of probability in his supposition.

The Thesmophoria, like the Anthesteria, was a three days' festival. It was held from the 11th—13th of Pyanepsion (October —November); the first day, the 11th, was called both *Kathodos* and *Anodos*, Downgoing and Uprising, the second *Nesteia*, Fasting, and the third *Kalligeneia*, Fair-Born or Fair-Birth[1]. The meaning of the name Thesmophoria and the significance of the three several days will appear later: at present it is sufficient to note that the Thesmophoria collectively was a late autumn festival and certainly connected with sowing. Cornutus[2] says, 'they fast in honour of Demeter...when they celebrate her feast at the season of sowing.' Of a portion of the ritual of the Thesmophoria we have an unusually detailed account preserved to us by a scholiast on the *Hetairae* of Lucian; and as this portion is, for the understanding of the whole festival, of capital importance it must at the outset be examined in detail. In the dialogue of Lucian, Myrto is reproaching Pamphilos for deserting her; 'the girl,' says Myrto, 'you are going to marry is not good-looking; I saw her close at hand at the Thesmophoria with her mother.' The notice is important as it has been asserted that the Thesmophoria was a festival of married women only, which, in Lucian's time, was clearly not the case.

The scholiast[3] on the passage comments as follows, and ancient

[1] Schol. ad Aristoph. *Thesm.* 78. Photius, s.v. and Schol. ad Aristoph. *Thesm.* 585.

[2] Cornut. *de Theol.* 28.

[3] Lucian, *Dial. Meretr.* II. 1, first published and commented on by E. Rohde, *Rhein. Mus.* XXV. p. 549. As the text is not very easily accessible it is given below: θεσμοφόρια ἑορτὴ Ἑλλήνων μυστήρια περιέχουσα. τὰ δὲ αὐτὰ καὶ σκιρροφόρια καλεῖται. ἤγετο δὲ κατὰ τὸν μυθωδέστερον λόγον, ὅτι ἀνθολογοῦσα ἡρπάζετο ἡ Κόρη ὑπὸ τοῦ Πλούτωνος. τότε κατ' ἐκεῖνον τὸν τόπον Εὐβουλεύς τις συβώτης ἔνεμεν ὗς καὶ συγκατεπόθησαν τῷ χάσματι τῆς Κόρης. εἰς οὖν τιμὴν τοῦ Εὐβουλέως ῥίπτεσθαι τοὺς χοίρους εἰς τὰ χάσματα τῆς Δήμητρος καὶ τῆς Κόρης. τὰ δὲ σαπέντα τῶν ἐμβληθέντων

commentators have left us few commentaries more instructive: 'The Thesmophoria, a festival of the Greeks, including mysteries, and these are called also Skirrophoria. According to the more mythological explanation they are celebrated in that Kore when she was gathering flowers was carried off by Plouton. At the time a certain Eubouleus, a swineherd, was feeding his swine on the spot and they were swallowed down with her in the chasm of Kore. Hence in honour of Eubouleus the swine are thrown into the chasms of Demeter and Kore. Certain women who have purified themselves for three days[1] and who bear the name of "Drawers up" bring up the rotten portions of the swine that have been cast into the *megara*. And they descend into the inner sanctuaries and having brought up (the remains) they place them on the altars, and they hold that whoever takes of the remains and mixes it with his seed will have a good crop. And they say that in and about the chasms are snakes which consume the most part of what is thrown in; hence a rattling din is made when the women draw up the remains and when they replace the remains by those well-known (ἐκεῖνα) images, in order that the snakes which they hold to be the guardians of the sanctuaries may go away.

'The same rites are called Arretophoria (carrying of things unnamed) and are performed with the same intent concerning the growth of crops and of human offspring. In the case of the Arretophoria, too, sacred things that may not be named and that are made of cereal paste, are carried about, i.e. images of snakes and of the forms of men[2]. They employ also fir-cones on account

εἰς τὰ μέγαρα καταναφέρουσιν ἀντλήτριαι καλούμεναι γυναῖκες, καθαρεύσασαι τριῶν ἡμερῶν. καὶ καταβαίνουσιν εἰς τὰ ἄδυτα καὶ ἀνενέγκασαι ἐπιτιθέασιν ἐπὶ τῶν βωμῶν. ὧν νομίζουσι τὸν λαμβάνοντα καὶ τῷ σπόρῳ συγκαταβάλλοντα εὐφορίαν ἕξειν. λέγουσι δὲ καὶ δράκοντας κάτω εἶναι περὶ τὰ χάσματα, οὓς τὰ πολλὰ τῶν βληθέντων κατεσθίειν· διὸ καὶ κρότον γενέσθαι ὅταν ἀντλῶσιν αἱ γυναῖκες καὶ ὅταν ἀποτιθῶνται πάλιν τὰ πλάσματα ἐκεῖνα, ἵνα ἀναχωρήσωσιν οἱ δράκοντες οὓς νομίζουσι φρουροὺς τῶν ἀδύτων. τὰ δὲ αὐτὰ καὶ ἀρρητοφόρια καλεῖται, καὶ ἄγεται τὸν αὐτὸν λόγον ἔχοντα περὶ τῆς τῶν καρπῶν γενέσεως καὶ τῆς τῶν ἀνθρώπων σπορᾶς. ἀναφέρονται δὲ κἀνταῦθα ἄρρητα ἱερὰ ἐκ στέατος τοῦ σίτου κατεσκευασμένα, μιμήματα δρακόντων καὶ ἀνδρῶν σχημάτων. λαμβάνουσι δὲ κώνου θαλλοὺς διὰ τὸ πολύγονον τοῦ φυτοῦ. ἐμβάλλονται δὲ καὶ εἰς τὰ μέγαρα οὕτως καλούμενα ἄδυτα ἐκεῖνά τε καὶ χοῖροι ὡς ἤδη ἔφαμεν, καὶ αὐτοὶ διὰ τὸ πολύτοκον, εἰς σύνθημα τῆς γενέσεως τῶν καρπῶν καὶ τῶν ἀνθρώπων, ὡς χαριστήρια τῇ Δήμητρι ἐπειδὴ τὸν δημήτριον καρπὸν παρέχουσα ἐποίησεν ἥμερον τὸ τῶν ἀνθρώπων γένος. ὁ μὲν οὖν ἄνω τῆς ἑορτῆς λόγος ὁ μυθικός· ὁ δὲ προκείμενος φυσικός· Θεσμοφόρια καλεῖται καθότι θεσμοφόρος ἡ Δημήτηρ κατονομάζεται, τιθεῖσα νόμον ἤτοι θεσμὸν καθ' οὓς τὴν τροφὴν πορίζεσθαί τε καὶ κατεργάζεσθαι ἀνθρώπους δέον.

[1] The rites of purification included strict chastity, for the purport of which as a conservation of energy see Dr Frazer, *Golden Bough*, 2nd ed. II. p. 210.

[2] *μιμήματα...ἀνδρῶν σχημάτων*, i.e. *φάλλοι*. Cf. Septuagint, Is. iii. 17. The Arrephoroi are not as I previously (*Myth. and Mon. Ancient Athens*, p. xxxiv.)

of the fertility of the tree, and into the sanctuaries called *megara* these are cast and also, as we have already said, swine—the swine, too, on account of their prolific character—in token of the growth of fruits and human beings, as a thank-offering to Demeter, inasmuch as she, by providing the grain called by her name, civilized the human race. The interpretation then of the festival given above is mythological, but the one we give now is physical. The name Thesmophoria is given because Demeter bears the title Thesmophoros, since she laid down a law or Thesmos in accordance with which it was incumbent on men to obtain and provide by labour their nurture.'

The main outline of the ritual, in spite of certain obscurities in the scholiast's account, is clear. At some time not specified, but during the Thesmophoria, women, carefully purified for the purpose, let down pigs into clefts or chasms called *μέγαρα* or chambers. At some other time not precisely specified they descended into the *megara*, brought up the rotten flesh and placed it on certain altars, whence it was taken and mixed with seed to serve as a fertility charm. As the first day of the festival was called both *Kathodos* and *Anodos* it seems likely that the women went down and came up the same day, but as the flesh of the pigs was rotten some time must have elapsed. It is therefore conjectured that the flesh was left to rot for a whole year, and that the women on the first day took down the new pigs and brought up last year's pigs.

How long the pigs were left to rot does not affect the general content of the festival. It is of more importance to note that the flesh seems to have been regarded as in some sort the due of the powers of the earth as represented by the guardian snakes. The flesh was wanted by men as a fertility charm, but the snakes it was thought might demand part of it; they were scared away, but to compensate for what they did not get, surrogates made of cereal paste had to be taken down. These paste surrogates were in the form of things specially fertile. It is not quite clear whether the pine-cones etc. or only the pigs were let down at the Thesmo-

suggested *Hersephoroi*, Carriers of Young Things. Suidas, it may be noted, has the formally impossible word *ἀρρηνοφορεῖν*. It may have arisen from a paronomasia and seems to point in the same direction as the *μιμήματα ἀνδρῶν σχημάτων* of the scholiast. On the use of the *φάλλος* among agriculturalists as a prophylactic against the evil eye and *ἐν ταῖς τελεταῖς...σχέδον ἁπάσαις*, see Diod. IV. 6.

phoria as well as the Arrephoria, but as the scholiast is contending for the close analogy of both festivals this seems probable. It does not indeed much matter what the exact form of the *sacra* was: all were fertility charms.

The remarks of the scholiast about the double λόγος, i.e. the double *rationale* of the festival, are specially instructive. By his time, and indeed probably long before, educated people had ceased to believe that by burying a fertile animal or a fir-cone in the earth you could induce the earth to be fertile; they had advanced beyond the primitive logic of 'sympathetic magic.' But the Thesmophoria was still carried on by conservative womanhood:

'They keep the Thesmophoria as they always used to do.'

An origin less crude and revolting to common sense is required and promptly supplied by mythology[1]. Kore had been carried down into a cleft by Plouton: therefore in her memory the women went down and came up. Pigs had been swallowed down at the same time: therefore they took pigs with them. Such a mythological *rationale* was respectable if preposterous. The myth of the rape of Persephone of course really arose from the ritual, not the ritual from the myth. In the back of his mind the scholiast knows that the content of the ritual was 'physical,' the object the impulsion of nature. But even after he has given the true content his mind clouds over with modern associations. The festival, he says, is a 'thank-offering' to Demeter. But in the sympathetic magic of the Thesmophoria man attempts direct compulsion, he admits no mediator between himself and nature, and he thanks no god for what no god has done. A thank-offering is later even than a prayer, and prayer as yet is not. To mark the transition from rites of compulsion to rites of supplication and consequent thanksgiving is to read the whole religious history of primitive man.

Some details of the rites of the Thesmophoria remain to be noted. The Thesmophoria, though, thanks to Aristophanes, we know them best at Athens, were widespread throughout Greece. The ceremony of the pigs went on at Potniae in Boeotia. The passage in which Pausanias[2] describes it is most unfortunately

[1] The influence of mimetic ritual on the development of mythology will be considered later, p. 279.

[2] P. IX. 8. 1.

corrupt; but he adds one certain detail, that the pigs there used were new-born, sucking pigs (ὗς τῶν νεογνῶν). Among nations more savage than the Greeks a real Kore took the place of the Greek sucking pig or rather reinforced it. Among the Khonds, as Mr Andrew Lang[1] has pointed out, pigs and a woman are sacrificed that the land may be fertilized by their blood: the Pawnees of North America, down to the middle of the present century, sacrificed a girl obtained by preference from the alien tribe of the Sioux, but among the Greeks there is no evidence that the pigs were surrogates.

The *megara* themselves are of some importance; the name still survives in the modern Greek form Megara. *Megara* appear to have been natural clefts or chasms helped out later by art. As such they were at first the natural places for rites intended to compel the earth; later they became definite sanctuaries of earth divinities. In America, according to Mr Lang's account, Gypsies, Pawnees, and Shawnees bury the sacrifices they make to the Earth Goddess in the earth, in natural crevices or artificial crypts. In the sanctuary of Demeter, at Cnidos, Sir Charles Newton[2] found a crypt which had originally been circular and later had been compressed by earthquake. Among the contents were bones of pigs and other animals, and the marble pigs which now stand near the Demeter of Cnidos in the British Museum. It is of importance to note that Porphyry[3], in his *Cave of the Nymphs*, says, that for the Olympian gods are set up temples and images and altars (βωμούς), for the chthonic gods and heroes hearths (ἐσχάραι), for those below the earth (ὑποχθονίοις) there are trenches and *megara*. Philostratos[4], in his Life of Apollonius, says, 'The chthonic gods welcome trenches and ceremonies done in the hollow earth.'

Eustathius[5] says that *megara* are 'underground dwellings of the two goddesses,' i.e. Demeter and Persephone, and he adds that 'Aelian says the word is μάγαρον not μέγαρον and that it is the place in which the mystical sacred objects are placed.' Unless this suggestion is adopted the etymology of the word remains

[1] *Nineteenth Century*, April, 1887.
[2] Newton, C. T., *Discoveries at Halicarnassus*, vol. II. p. 383, and *Travels and Discoveries in the Levant*, II. p. 180.
[3] Porphyr. *de antro Nymph.* VI.
[4] VI. 11. 18.
[5] Eustath. § 1387.

obscure[1]. The word itself, meaning at first a cave-dwelling, lived on in the *megaron* of kings' palaces and the temples of Olympian gods, and the shift of meaning marks the transition from under to upper-world rites.

Art has left us no certain representation of the Thesmophoria; but in the charming little vase-painting from a lekythos in the National Museum at Athens[2], a woman is represented sacrificing a pig. He is obviously held over a trench and the

Fig. 10.

three planted torches indicate an underworld service. In her left hand the woman holds a basket, no doubt containing *sacra*. There seems a reminiscence of the rites of the Thesmophoria, though we cannot say that they are actually represented.

It is practically certain that the ceremonies of the burying and resurrection of the pigs took place on the first day of the Thesmophoria called variously the *Kathodos* and the *Anodos*. It is further probable from the name *Kalligeneia*, Fairborn, that on the third day took place the strewing of the rotten flesh on the fields. The second, intervening day, also called *μέση*, the middle day, was a solemn fast, *Nesteia*; probably on this day the magical *sacra* lay upon the altars where the women placed them. The

[1] Dr Frazer reminds me that Prof. Robertson Smith (*Religion of the Semites*, p. 183) derived *μέγαρον* from the Phoenician *maghar*, Hebrew *meghara* 'a cave.' The form *μάγαρον* adduced by Aelian, favours this view; cf. also Photius s.v. *μάγαρον· οὐ μέγαρον, εἰς ὃ τὰ μυστικὰ ἱερὰ κατατίθενται· οὕτως Μένανδρος.*

[2] Heydemann, *Griechische Vasenbilder*, Taf. II. 3. For a somewhat similar design cf. *Brit. Mus. Cat.* E 819.

strictness of this fast made it proverbial. On this day prisoners were released, the law courts were closed, the Boule could not meet[1]. Athenaeus mentions the fast when he is discussing different kinds of fish. One of the Cynics comes in and says: 'My friends too are keeping a fast as if this were the middle day of the Thesmophoria since we are feasting like *cestreis*'; the *cestreus* being non-carnivorous.

The women fasted sitting on the ground, and hence arose the aetiological myth that Demeter herself, the desolate mother, fasted sitting on the 'Smileless Stone.' Apollodorus[2], in recounting the sorrows of Demeter, says: 'and first she sat down on the stone that is called after her "Smileless" by the side of the "Well of Fair Dances."' The 'Well of Fair Dances' has come to light at Eleusis, and there, too, was found a curious monument[3] which shows how the Eleusinians made the goddess in

Fig. 11.

[1] Marcellinus on Hermog. in *Rhet. Graec.*, ed. Walz, IV. 462. Sopater, *ibid.* VIII. 67. Aristoph. *Thesm.* 80. Dr Frazer kindly suggests to me that the custom of releasing prisoners at the Thesmophoria may be explained as a precaution against the magical influence of knots, fetters, and the like in trammeling spiritual activities whether for good or evil, cf. *Golden Bough*, 2nd ed. I. p. 392 sqq.

[2] Apollod. I. 5. 1.

[3] *Ath. Mitt.* 1899, Taf. VIII. 1.

their own image. In fig. 11 we have a votive relief of the usual type, a procession of worshippers bearing offerings to a seated goddess. But the goddess is not seated goddess-fashion on a throne; she is the Earth mother, and she crouches as the fasting women crouched on her own earth.

A passage in which Plutarch speaks of the women fasting is of great importance for the understanding of the general gist of the festival. In the discourse on Isis and Osiris[1] he is struck by the general analogy of certain agricultural ceremonies in Egypt and Greece, and makes the following instructive remarks: 'How are we to deal with sacrifices of a gloomy, joyless and melancholy character, if it be not well either to omit traditional ceremonies, or to upset our views about the gods or confuse them by preposterous conjectures? And among the Greeks also many analogous things take place about the same time of the year as that in which the Egyptians perform their sacred ceremonies, e.g. at Athens *the women fast at the Thesmophoria seated on the ground*, and the Boeotians stir up the *megara* of *Achaia*, calling that festival grievous (ἐπαχθῆ), inasmuch as Demeter was in grief (ἐν ἄχει), on account of the descent of her daughter. And that month about the rising of the Pleiades is the month of sowing which the Egyptians call Athor, and the Athenians Pyanepsion (bean month), and the Boeotians Damatrion. And Theopompos relates that those who dwell towards the West account and call the Winter Kronos, and the Summer Aphrodite, and the Spring Persephone, and from Kronos and Aphrodite all things take their birth. And the Phrygians think that in the Winter the god is asleep, and that in the Summer he is awake, and they celebrate to him revels which in winter are Goings-to-sleep and in summer Wakings-up. And the Paphlagonians allege that in winter the god *is bound down* and imprisoned, and in spring aroused and set free again.'

Whatever be the meaning of the difficult *Achaia*[2] Plutarch has hit upon the truth. Common to all the peoples bordering

[1] Plut. *de Is. et Os.* LXIX.

[2] The most satisfactory etymology of the difficult title 'Αχαία is that suggested by Dr Lagercrantz. He connects 'Αχαία with ὀχή, nourishment. This would explain also the loaves called ἀχαῖναι mentioned by Athenaeus (III. 74, p. 109) on the authority of Semos as in use at the Delian Thesmophoria; see Dr Nilsson, *Griechische Feste*, 1906, p. 325.

on the Aegean and, had he known it, to many another primitive race, were ceremonies of which the gist was pantomime, the mimicking of nature's processes, in a word the ritual of sympathetic magic. The women fasted seated on the ground because the earth was desolate; they rose and revelled, they stirred the *megara* to mimic the impulse of spring. Then when they knew no longer why they did these things they made a goddess their prototype.

Plutarch[1] has made for himself in his own image his 'ideal' Greek gods, serene, cheerful, beneficent; but he is a close observer of facts, and he sees there are ceremonies—'sacrifices' (*θυσίαι*) in his late fashion he calls them—which are 'mournful,' 'gloomy,' 'smileless.' He must either blink the facts of acknowledged authorized ritual—this he cannot and will not do, for he is an honest man—or he must confuse and confound his conceptions of godhead. Caught on the horns of this dilemma he betakes himself to comparative anthropology and notes analogies among adjacent and more primitive peoples.

Of two other elements in the Thesmophoria we have brief notice from the lexicographers. Hesychius[2] says of the word *δίωγμα* (pursuit), 'a sacrifice at Athens, performed in secret by the women at the Thesmophoria. The same was later called *ἀποδίωγμα*.' From Suidas[3] we learn that it was also called *Χαλκιδικὸν δίωγμα*, the 'Chalcidian pursuit,' and Suidas of course gives a historical explanation. Only one thing is clear, that the ceremony must have belonged to the general class of 'pursuit' rituals which have already been discussed in relation to the Thargelia.

The remaining ceremony is known to us only from Hesychius[4]. He says, '*ζημία* (penalty), a sacrifice offered on account of the things done at the Thesmophoria.'

Of the Thesmophoria as celebrated at Eretria we are told two characteristic particulars. Plutarch, in his *Greek Questions*[5], asks, 'Why in the Thesmophoria do the Eretrian women cook their

[1] Plut. loc. cit. *πῶς οὖν χρηστέον ἐστὶ ταῖς σκυθρωπαῖς καὶ ἀγελάστοις καὶ πενθίμοις θυσίαις εἰ μήτε παραλιπεῖν τὰ νενομισμένα καλῶς ἔχει, μήτε φύρειν τὰς περὶ θεῶν δόξας καὶ συνταράττειν ὑποψίαις ἀτόποις;* On the 'sorrowful character of rites of sowing' see Dr Frazer, *Adonis Attis Osiris*, p. 232.

[2] Hesych. s.v. *δίωγμα*.

[3] Suid. s.v.

[4] Hesych. s.v. *ζημία· θυσία τις ἀποδιδομένη ὑπὲρ τῶν γενομένων ἐν Θεσμοφορίοις.* It is possible, I think, that *ζημία* may conceal some form connected with Damia.

[5] Plut. *Q.Gr.* XXXI.

meat not by fire but by the sun, and why do they not invoke Kalligeneia?' The solutions suggested by Plutarch for these difficulties are not happy. The use of the sun in place of fire is probably a primitive trait; in Greece to-day it is not difficult to cook a piece of meat to a palatable point on a stone by the rays of the burning midday sun, and in early days the practice was probably common enough; it might easily be retained in an archaic ritual. Kalligeneia also presents no serious difficulty, the word means 'fair-born' or 'fair-birth.' It may be conjectured that the reference was at first to the good crop produced by the rotten pigs' flesh. With the growth of anthropomorphism the 'good crop' would take shape as Korẹ the 'fair-born,' daughter of earth. Of such developments more will be said when we discuss (p. 276) the general question of 'the making of a goddess.' A conservative people such as the Eretrians seem to have been would be slow to adopt any such anthropomorphic development.

Another particular as regards the Thesmophoria generally is preserved for us by Aelian in his *History of Animals*[1]; speaking of the plant *Agnos* (the *Agnus castus*), he says, 'In the Thesmophoria the Attic women used to strew it on their couches and it (the *Agnos*) is accounted hostile to reptiles.' He goes on to say that the plant was primarily used to keep off snakes, to the attacks of which the women in their temporary booths would be specially exposed. Then as it was an actual preventive of one evil it became a magical purity charm. Hence its name.

The pollution of death, like marriage, was sufficient to exclude the women of the house from keeping the Thesmophoria. Athenaeus[2] tells us that Democritus of Abdera, wearied of his extreme old age, was minded to put an end to himself by refusing all food; but the women of his house implored him to live on till the Thesmophoria was over in order that they might be able to keep the festival; so he obligingly kept himself alive on a pot of honey.

An important and easily intelligible particular is noted by Isaeus[3] in his oration About the Estate of Pyrrhos. The question comes up, 'Was Pyrrhos lawfully married?' Isaeus asks, 'If he were married, would he not have been obliged, on behalf of his lawful wife, to feast the women at the Thesmophoria and to

[1] IX. 26. [2] Athen. II. 26, p. 46. [3] Is. *Pyrr. Hered.* 80.

perform all the other customary dues in his deme on behalf of his wife, his property being what it was?' This is one of the passages on which the theory has been based that the Thesmophoria was a rite performed by married women only. It really points the other way; a man when he married by thus obtaining exclusive rights over one woman violated the old matriarchal usages and may have had to make his peace with the community by paying the expenses of the Thesmophoria feast.

Before passing to the consideration of the etymology and precise meaning of the word Thesmophoria, the other women's festivals must be briefly noted, i.e. the Arrephoria or Arretophoria, the Skirophoria or Skira, and the Stenia.

ARREPHORIA, SKIROPHORIA, STENIA.

The scholiast on Lucian, as we have already seen, expressly notes that the Arretophoria and Skirophoria were of similar content with the Thesmophoria. Clement of Alexandria[1], a dispassionate witness, confirms this view. 'Do you wish,' he asks, 'that I should recount for you the Flower-gatherings of Pherephatta and the basket, and the rape by Aïdoneus, and the cleft of the earth, and the swine of Eubouleus, swallowed down with the goddesses, on which account in the Thesmophoria they cast down living swine in the *megara*? This piece of mythology the women in their festivals celebrate in diverse fashion in the city, dramatizing the rape of Pherephatta in diverse fashion in the Thesmophoria, the Skirophoria, the Arretophoria.'

The Arretophoria or Arrephoria was apparently the Thesmophoria of the unmarried girl. Its particular ritual is fairly well known to us from the account of Pausanias. Immediately after his examination of the temple of Athene Polias on the Athenian Acropolis, Pausanias[2] comes to the temple of Pandrosos, 'who alone of the sisters was blameless in regard to the trust committed to them': he then adds, 'what surprised me very much, but is not generally known, I will describe as it takes place. Two

[1] Clem. Al. *Protr.* II. 17, p. 14, δι' ἣν αἰτίαν ἐν τοῖς Θεσμοφορίοις μεγαρίζοντες* (μεγάροις ζῶντας, Lobeck) χοίρους ἐμβάλλουσιν. ταύτην τὴν μυθολογίαν αἱ γυναῖκες ποικίλως κατὰ πόλιν ἑορτάζουσιν Θεσμοφόρια, Σκιροφόρια, Ἀρρητοφόρια ποικίλως τὴν Φερεφάττης ἐκτραγῳδοῦσαι ἁρπαγήν.

[2] I. 27. 3.

maidens dwell not far from the temple of Polias: the Athenians call them Arrephoroi, they are lodged for a time with the goddess, but when the festival comes round they perform the following ceremony by night. They put on their heads the things which the priestess of Athena gives them to carry, but what it is she gives is known neither to her who gives nor to them who carry. Now there is in the city an enclosure not far from the sanctuary of Aphrodite, called Aphrodite in the Gardens, and there is a natural underground descent through it. Down this way the maidens go. Below they leave their burdens, and getting something else which is wrapped up, they bring it back. These maidens are then discharged and others brought to the Acropolis in their stead[1].'

From other sources some further details, for the most part insignificant, are known. The girls were of noble family, they were four in number and had to be between the ages of seven and eleven, and were chosen by the Archon Basileus. They wore white robes and gold ornaments. To two of their number was entrusted the task of beginning the weaving of the peplos of Athene. Special cakes called ἀνάστατοι were provided for them, but whether to eat or to carry as *sacra* does not appear. It is more important to note that the service of the Arrephoroi was not confined to Athene and Pandrosos[2]. There was an Errephoros (*sic*) to Demeter and Proserpine[3], and there were Hersephoroi (*sic*) of 'Earth with the title of Themis' and of 'Eileithyia in Agrae[4].' Probably any primitive woman goddess could have Arrephoria.

Much is obscure in the account of Pausanias; we do not know what the precinct was to which the maidens went, nor where it was. It is possible that Pausanias confused the later sanctuary of Aphrodite (in the gardens) with the earlier sanctuary of the goddess close to the entrance of the Acropolis. One thing, however, emerges clearly: the main gist of the ceremonial was the

[1] Trans. J. G. Frazer. Dr Frazer in his commentary on the passage, vol. II. p. 344, enumerates the other sources respecting the Arrephoroi; see also Harrison and Verrall, *Mythology and Monuments of Ancient Athens*, pp. xxxii. and 512.

[2] Dr Frazer draws my attention to the curiously analogous ritual practised at Lanuvium, in a grove near the temple of the Argive Hera, described by Aelian (*Hist. An.* XI. 16) and Propertius (IV. 8. 3 sqq.). Once a year sacred maidens descended with bandaged eyes into a serpent's cave and offered it a barley cake. If the serpent ate of the cake the people rejoiced, taking it to show that the girls were pure maidens and that the year's crops would be good:

Si fuerint castae, redeunt in colla parentum;
Clamantque agricolae Fertilis annus erit.

[3] *C.I.A.* III., No. 19.

[4] *C.I.A.* III., Nos. 318, 319.

carrying of unknown *sacra*. In this respect we are justified in holding with Clement that the Arrephoria (held in Skirophorion, June—July) was a parallel to the Thesmophoria.

It is possible, I think, to go a step further. A rite frequently throws light on the myth made to explain it. Occasionally the rite itself is elucidated by the myth to which it gave birth. The maidens who carried the sacred *cista* were too young to know its holy contents, but they might be curious, so a scare story was invented for their safeguarding, the story of the disobedient sisters who opened the chest, and in horror at the great snake they found there, threw themselves headlong from the Acropolis. The myth is prettily represented on an amphora in the British

Fig. 12.

Museum[1], reproduced in fig. 12. The sacred chest stands on rude piled stones that represent the rock of the Acropolis, the child rises up with outstretched hand, Athene looks on in dismay and anger, and the bad sisters hurry away. Erichthonios is here a human child with two great snakes for guardians, but what the sisters really found, what the maidens really carried, was a snake[2] and symbols like a snake. Snake and child to the primitive mind are not far asunder; the Greek peasant of to-day has his child quickly baptized, for till baptized he may at any moment disappear in the form of a snake. The natural form for a human hero to assume is, as will later be seen, a snake.

[1] *B. M. Cat.* E 418, see *Myth. and Mon. Anc. Athens*, p. xxxii.

[2] ἄρρητα ἱερὰ...μιμήματα δρακόντων καὶ ἀνδρῶν σχημάτων, see p. 122, note 2.

The little girl-Arrephoroi in ignorance, as became their age, carried the same *sacra* as the full-grown women in the Thesmophoria. The perfect seemliness and reverence of the rite is shown by the careful precautions taken. When goddesses began to take shape the *sacra* were regarded, not as mere magical charms, but as offerings as was meet to Ge, to Themis, to Aphrodite, to Eileithyia, but always the carrying was a reverent 'mystery.'

The Skira or Skirophoria[1] presents more difficulties. It was specially closely associated with the Thesmophoria of which it may have formed part. The chorus in the *Thesmophoriazusae* of Aristophanes[2] says, 'If any of us bear a good citizen to the state, a taxiarch or strategos, she ought to be rewarded by some honourable office, the presidency ought to be given her at the Stenia and the Skira and at any other of the feasts which we (women) celebrate.' The scholiast remarks, 'both were feasts of women; the Stenia took place before the two days of the Thesmophoria on the 7th of Pyanepsion, and the Skira, some say, are the sacred rites that took place on this feast (i.e. the Thesmophoria) to Demeter and Kore. But others say that sacrifice was made ἐπὶ Σκίρῳ to Athene.' On the other hand in an inscription, usually a most trustworthy authority, the two ceremonies are noted as separate though apparently analogous. In the inscription in question[3] which is of the 4th century B.C., certain regulations are enforced 'when the feast of the Thesmophoria takes place, and at the Plerosia, and at the Kalamaia and the Skira, and if there is any other day on which the women congregate by ancestral usage.'

The ancients themselves had raised the question whether the Skira were sacred to Athene or to Demeter and Kore. This question is not really relevant to our enquiry; Athene, as will be seen later, when the 'making of a goddess' is discussed, is simply ἡ Ἀθηναία κόρη, the κόρη, the *maiden of Athens*, and any festival of any Kore—any maiden—would early attach itself to her.

More important is the question, What does the word σκίρα mean? Two solutions are offered. The scholiast on Aris-

[1] For various views of the Skirophoria, see Robert, *Hermes* xx. 394; Rohde, *Kleine Schriften*, p. 371; A. Mommsen, *Philolog.* L. p. 123.

[2] Ar. *Thesmoph.* 834.

[3] *C.I.A.* II. p. 422, n. 573 b.

tophanes[1] says σκίρον means the same as σκιάδειον, umbrella, and the feast and the month took that name from the fact that at a festival of Demeter and Kore on the 12th of Skirophorion, the priest of Erechtheus carried a white umbrella. A white umbrella is a slender foundation for a festival, but the element of white points in the right direction. The scholiast on the *Wasps* of Aristophanes[2] commenting on σκîρον has a happier thought: he says a certain sort of white earth, like gypsum, is called σκιρράς, and Athene is called Σκιρράς inasmuch as she is daubed with white, from a similarity in the name.

The same notion of white earth appears in the notice of the *Etymologicon Magnum* on the month *Skirophorion*, 'the name of a month among the Athenians; it is so called from the fact that in it Theseus carried σκίραν by which is meant gypsum. For Theseus, coming from the Minotaur, made an Athene of gypsum, and carried it, and as he made it in this month it is called Skirophorion.'

But, it will be asked, supposing it be granted that Skira means things made of gypsum and Skirophoria the carrying of such things, what, in the name of common sense, has this to do with a festival of women analogous to the Thesmophoria? Dr A. Mommsen[3], who first emphasized this etymology, proposes that the white earth was used as manure; this, though possible and ingenious, seems scarcely satisfactory. I would suggest another connection. The scholiast on Lucian has told us that the surrogates deposited in the *megara* were shaped out of paste made of grain. Is it not possible that the Σκίρα were such surrogates made of gypsum alone or part gypsum, part flour-paste? That such a mixture was manufactured for food we learn from Pliny[4]. In discussing the preparation of *alica* from *zea* (spelt) he says, 'astonishing statement, it is mixed with chalk.' In the case of a coarse sort of *zea* from Africa, the mixture was made in the proportion of a quarter of gypsum to three of *zea*. If this suggestion be correct, the Skirophoria is simply a summer Thesmophoria.

If the Skirophoria must, all said, remain conjectural, the gist

[1] Ar. *Eccles.* 18.

[2] Ar. *Vesp.* 925.

[3] A. Mommsen, 'Die Attischen Skira-Gebräuche,' *Philolog.* L. p. 123.

[4] Plin. *N.H.* XVII. 29. 2.

of the Stenia is clear and was understood by the ancients themselves. Photius remarks on *Stenia*—'a festival at Athens in which the Anodos of Demeter is held to take place. At this festival, according to Euboulos, the women abuse each other by night.' Hesychius[1] explains in like fashion and adds: *στηνιῶσαι*, 'to use bad language,' 'to abuse.' According to him they not only abused each other but 'made scurrilous jests.' Such abuse, we know from Aristophanes[2], was a regular element of the licence of the Thesmophoria. The *Gephyrismoi*, the jokes at the bridge, of the Eleusinian Mysteries, will occur to every one: similar in content is the stone-throwing, the Lithobolia of Damia and Auxesia.

It is interesting to note that in the primitive festivals of the Romans, the same scurrility contests appear. At the ancient feast of the *Nonae Capratinae*, Plutarch[3] tells us, 'the women are feasted in the fields in booths made of fig-tree branches, and the servant-maids run about and play; afterwards they come to blows and throw stones at one another.' The servant-maids represent here as elsewhere a primitive subject population; they live during the festival in booths as the women did at the Thesmophoria. How precisely this fight and this scurrility serve the end proposed, the promotion of fertility, is not wholly clear, but the throwing of stones, the beating and fighting, all look like the expulsion of evil influences. The scurrilous and sometimes to our modern thinking unseemly gestures savour of sympathetic magic, an intent that comes out clearly in the festival of the Haloa, the discussion of which must be reserved to the end.

We come next to the all-absorbing question, What is the derivation, the real root-meaning of the term *Thesmophoria* and the title *Thesmophoros*? The orthodox explanation of the Thesmophoria is that it was the festival of Demeter Thesmophoros, the law-carrier or law-giver. With Demeter, it is said, came in agriculture, settled life, marriage and the beginnings of civilized law. This is the view held by the scholiast on Theocritus[4]. In commenting on various sacred plants, which promoted chastity,

[1] Hesych. s.v. [2] Ar. *Thesm.* 533. [3] Plut. *Vit. Rom.* sub fin.

[4] Schol. ad Theocr. *Id.* IV. 25 *τὰς νομίμους βίβλους καὶ ἱερὰς ὑπὲρ τῶν κορυφῶν αὐτῶν ἀνετίθεσαν καὶ ὡσανεὶ λιτανεύσουσαι ἀπήρχοντο εἰς* 'Ελευσῖνα.

he adds, 'It was a law among the Athenians that they should celebrate the Thesmophoria yearly, and the Thesmophoria is this: women who are virgins and have lived a holy life, on the day of the feast, place certain customary and holy books on their heads, and as though to perform a liturgy they go to Eleusis.'

The scholiast gives himself away by the mention of Eleusis. He confuses the two festivals in instructive fashion, and clearly is reconstructing a ritual out of a cultus epithet. Happily we know from the other and better informed scholiast[1] that the women carried at the Thesmophoria not books but pigs. How then came the pigs and other *sacra* to be Thesmoi? Dr Frazer proposes a solution. He suggests that the *sacra*, including the pigs, were called *θεσμοί*, because they were 'the things laid down.' The women were called Thesmophoroi because they carried 'the things laid down'; the goddess took her name from her ministrants.

This interpretation is a great advance on the derivation from Thesmophoros, Law-giver. Thesmophoros is scarcely the natural form for law-*giver*, which in ordinary Greek appears as Thesmothetes. Moreover the form Thesmophoros *must* be connected with actual *carrying* and must also be connected with what we know *was* carried at the Thesmophoria. But Thesmoi in Greek did certainly mean *laws*, and Demeter *Thesmophoros* was in common parlance supposed to be Law-giver. What we want is a derivation that will combine both factors, the notion of law as well as the carrying of pigs.

In the light of Dr Verrall's new explanation of Anthesteria (p. 48) such a derivation may be found. If the Anthesteria be the festival of the charming up, the magical revocation of souls, may not the Thesmophoria be the festival of the carrying of the *magical sacra*? To regard the *θεσμοί*, whether they are pigs or laws, as simply 'things laid down,' deriving them from the root *θε*, has always seemed to me somewhat frigid. The root *θεσ* is more vivid and has the blood of religion, or rather magic, in its veins. Although it came, when man entered into orderly and civilized relations with his god, to mean 'pray,' in earlier days it carried a wider connotation, and meant, I think, to perform any kind of magical ceremonies. Is not *θέσκελος* alive with magic?

[1] See supra, p. 121 sq.

The Curse and the Law.

But what has law, sober law, to do with magic? To primitive man, it seems, everything. Magic is for cursing or for blessing, and in primitive codes it would seem there was no commandment without cursing. The curse, the *ἀρά*, is of the essence of the law. The breaker of the law is laid under a ban. 'Honour thy father and thy mother' was the first commandment 'with promise.' Law in fact began at a time long before the schism of Church and State, or even of Religion and Morality. There was then no such thing as 'civil' law. Nay more, it began in the dim days when religion itself had not yet emerged from magic, in the days when, without invoking the wrath of a righteous divinity, you could yet 'put a curse' upon a man, bind him to do his duty by magic and spells.

Primitive man, who thought he could constrain the earth to be fertile by burying in it fertile objects, by 'sympathetic magic,' was sure to think he could in like fashion compel his fellow. Curse tablets deposited in graves and sanctuaries have come to light in thousands; but before man learnt to write his curse, to spell out the formulary *καταδῶ*, 'I bind you down,' he had a simpler and more certain plan. In a grave in Attica was found a little lead figure[1] which tells its own tale. It is too ugly for needless reproduction, but it takes us into the very heart of ancient malignant magic. The head of the figure has been wrenched off, both arms are tightly swathed behind the back, and the legs in like fashion; right through the centre of the body has been driven a great nail. Dr Wünsch[2], in publishing the figure, compares the story recorded of a certain St Theophilos[3] 'who had his feet and hands bound by magic.' The saint sought relief in vain, till he was told in a dream to go out fishing, and what the fishermen drew up would cure him of his malady. They let down the net and drew up a bronze figure, bound hand and foot and with a nail

[1] Sixteen similar figures with feet and hands tightly bound, and in some cases the arms pierced by nails, were recently found on the site of the ancient Palestrina, see *Egypt Exploration Fund Quarterly Statement*, p. 332.

[2] R. Wünsch, 'Eine antike Rachepuppe,' *Philolog.* LXI. 1902, p. 26.

[3] Migne, *Patrol. Gr.* LXXXVII. 50 *περὶ Θεοφίλου τοῦ ἀπὸ μαγείας συνδεθέντος τὰς χεῖρας καὶ τοὺς πόδας.*

driven through the hand: they drew out the nail and the saint immediately recovered.

The *locus classicus* on ancient magic and spells is of course the second Idyll of Theocritus[1], on Simaetha the magician. Part of her incantation may be quoted here because a poet's insight has divined the strange fierce loveliness that lurks in rites of ignorance and fear, rites stark and desperate and non-moral as the passion that prompts them.

Delphis has forsaken her, and in the moonlight by the sea Simaetha makes ready her magic gear:

'Lo! Now the barley smoulders in the flame.
  Thestylis, wretch! thy wits are woolgathering!
Am I a laughing-stock to thee, a Shame?
  Scatter the grain, I say, the while we sing,
  "The bones of Delphis I am scattering."
Bird[2], *magic Bird, draw the man home to me.*

Delphis sore troubled me. I, in my turn,
This laurel against Delphis will I burn.
  It crackles loud, and sudden down doth die,
  So may the bones of Delphis liquefy.
Wheel, magic Wheel, draw the man home to me.

Next do I burn this wax, God helping me,
So may the heart of Delphis melted be.
  This brazen wheel I whirl, so, as before
  Restless may he be whirled about my door.
Bird, magic Bird, draw the man home to me.

Next will I burn these husks. O Artemis,
  Hast power hell's adamant to shatter down
And every stubborn thing. Hark! Thestylis,
  Hecate's hounds are baying up the town,
  The goddess at the crossways. Clash the gong.

* * * * * * *

Lo, now the sea is still. The winds are still.
The ache within my heart is never still.'

The incantations of Simaetha are of course a private rite to an individual end. That the practice of such rites was very frequent long before the decadent days of Theocritus is clear from the fact that Plato[3] in the *Laws* regards it as just as necessary that his

[1] Theocr. *Id.* II. 18 ff.

[2] The bird ἴϋγξ, supposed to be the wry-neck *Iynx torquilla*, bound on a wheel was a frequent love-charm. It is like the Siren (p. 201) a bird-soul, an enchanted maiden with the power to lure souls. Such enchanters, half-human, half-bird, were also the Keledones, cf. Athen. VII. p. 290 E *αἳ κατὰ τὸν αὐτὸν τρόπον ταῖς Σειρῆσι τοὺς ἀκροωμένους ἐποίουν ἐπιλανθανομένους τῶν τροφῶν διὰ τὴν ἡδονὴν ἀφαναίνεσθαι.* In metaphorical language Siren and Iynx are equivalents, cf. Xen. *Mem.* III. 11. 18; and cf. Diog. Laert. VI. 2. 76 *τοιαύτη τις προσῆν ἴϋγξ Διογένους τοῖς λόγοις.* For ἴυγξ, the moon, see Prof. Bury, *J.H.S.* VII. 1886, p. 157.

[3] Plat. *Legg.* 933.

ideal state should make enactments against the man who tries to slay or injure another by magic, as against him who actually does definite physical damage. His discussion of the two kinds of evil-doing is curious and instructive, both as indicating the prevalence of sorcery in his days, and as expressing the rather dubious attitude of his own mind towards such practices. 'There are two kinds of poisoning in use among men, the nature of which forbids any clear distinction between them. There is the kind of which we have just now spoken, and which is the injury of one body by another in a natural and normal way, but the other kind injures by sorceries and incantations and magical bindings as they are called (*καταδέσεσι*), and this class induces the aggressors to injure others as much as is possible, and persuades the sufferers that they more than any other are liable to be damaged by this power of magic. Now it is not easy to know the whole truth about such matters, nor if one knows it is one likely to be able lightly to persuade others. When therefore men secretly suspect each other at the sight of, say, waxen images fixed either at their doors or at the crossways or at the tombs of their parents, it is no good telling them to make light of such things because they know nothing certain about them.' Evidently Plato is not quite certain as to whether there *is* something in witchcraft or not: a diviner or a prophet, he goes on to admit, may really know something about these secret arts. Anyhow, he is clear that they are deleterious and should be stamped out if possible, and accordingly, any one who injures another either by magical bindings (*καταδέσεσιν*) or by magical inductions (*ἐπαγωγαῖς*) or by incantations (*ἐπῳδαῖς*) or by another form of magic is to die.

The scholiast[1] on the Idyll of Theocritus just quoted knows that one at least of the magical practices of Simaetha was also part of public ritual:

'The goddess at the crossways. Clash the gong.'

Hecate is magically *induced*, yet her coming is feared. The clash of the bronze gong is apotropaic. The scholiast says that

[1] Schol. ad Theocr. *Id.* II. 10 *τὸν γὰρ χαλκὸν ἐπῆδον ἐν ταῖς ἐκλείψεσι τῆς σελήνης καὶ ἐν τοῖς κατοιχομένοις* ἐπειδὴ ἐνομίζετο καθαρὸς εἶναι καὶ ἀπελαστικὸς τῶν μιασμάτων. διόπερ πρὸς πᾶσαν ἀφοσίωσιν καὶ ἀποκάθαρσιν αὐτῷ ἐχρῶντο, ὥς φησι καὶ Ἀπολλόδωρος ἐν τῷ περὶ θεῶν....φησὶν Ἀπολλόδωρος Ἀθήνῃσι τὸν ἱεροφάντην τῆς Κόρης ἐπικαλουμένης, ἐπικρούειν τὸ καλούμενον ἠχεῖον. καὶ παρὰ Λάκωσι βασιλέως ἀποθανόντος εἰώθασι κρούειν λέβητα.* The reading *κατοιχομένοις* is doubtful; see Mr A. B. Cook, *J.H.S.* 1902, p. 14.

'they sound the bronze at eclipses of the moon...because it has power to purify and to drive off pollutions. Hence, as Apollodorus states in his treatise *Concerning the Gods*, bronze was used for all purposes of consecration and purgation.' Apollodorus also stated that 'at Athens, the Hierophant of her who had the title of Kore sounded what was called a gong.' It was also the custom 'to beat on a cauldron when the king of the Spartans died.' All the ceremonies noted, relating to eclipses, to Kore and to the death of the Spartan king, are on *public* occasions, and all are apotropaic, directed against ghosts and sprites. Metal in early days, when it is a novelty, is apt to be magical. The *din* (*κρότος*) made by the women when they took down the *sacra*, whether it was a clapping of hands or of metal, is of the same order. The snakes are feared as hostile demons. These apotropaic rites are not practised against the Olympians, against Zeus and Apollo, but against sprites and ghosts and the divinities of the underworld, against Kore and Hecate. These underworld beings were at first dreaded and exorcised; then as a gentler theology prevailed, men thought better of their gods, and ceased to exorcise them as demons, and erected them into a class of 'spiritual beings who preside over curses.' Pollux[1] has a brief notice of such divinities. He says 'those who resolve curses are called Protectors from evil spirits, Who-send-away, Averters, Loosers, Putters-to-flight; those who impose curses are called gods or goddesses of Vengeance, Gods of Appeal, Exactors.' The many adjectival titles are but so many descriptive names for the ghost that cries for vengeance.

The 'curse that binds,' the *κατάδεσμος*, throws light on another element that went to the making of the ancient notion of sacrifice. The formula[2] in cursing was sometimes *καταδῶ* 'I bind down,' but it was also sometimes *παραδίδωμι* 'I give over.' The person cursed or bound down was in some sense a gift or sacrifice to the gods of cursing, the underworld gods: the man stained by blood is 'consecrate' (*καθιερωμένος*) to the Erinyes. In the little sanctuary of Demeter at Cnidos[3] the curse takes even more religious

[1] Poll. *On.* v. 131 *περὶ δαιμόνων τῶν ἐπὶ τῶν ἀρῶν. οἱ δὲ δαίμονες, οἱ μὲν λύοντες τὰς ἀρὰς ἀλεξίκακοι λέγονται ἀποπομπαῖοι, ἀποτροπαῖοι, λύσιοι, φύξιοι, οἱ δὲ κυροῦντες ἀλιτήριοι, ἀλιτηριώδεῖς, προστρόπαιοι, παλαμναῖοι.*

[2] W. H. D. Rouse, *Greek Votive Offerings*, p. 339. Dr Rouse says that 'binding spells' *δέματα* 'are still the terror of the Greek bridegroom.'

[3] C. T. Newton, *Discoveries at Cnidus and Halicarnassus.*

form. He or she dedicates (*ἀνιεροῖ*), or offers as a votive offering (*ἀνατίθητι*, for *ἀνατίθησι*), and finally we have the familiar *ἀνάθεμα* of St Paul. Here the services of cursing, the rites of magic and the underworld are half way to the service of 'tendance,' the service of the Olympians, and we begin to understand why, in later writers, the pharmakos and other 'purifications' are spoken of as *θυσίαι*. It is one of those shifts so unhappily common to the religious mind. Man wants to gain his own ends, to gratify his own malign passion, but he would like to kill two birds with one stone, and as the gods are made in his own image, the feat presents no great difficulty. Later as he grows gentler himself, he learns to pray only 'good prayers,' *bonas preces*[1].

The curse (*ἀρά*) on its religious side developed into the vow[2] and the prayer (*εὐχή*), on its social side into the ordinance (*θεσμός*) and ultimately into the regular law (*νόμος*); hence the language of early legal formularies still maintains as necessary and integral the sanction of the curse. The formula is not 'do this' or 'do not do that,' but 'cursed be he who does this, or does not do that.'

One instance may be selected, the inscription characteristically known as 'the Dirae of Teos[3].' The whole is too long to be transcribed, a few lines must suffice.

'Whosoever maketh baneful drugs against the Teans, whether against individuals or the whole people:

'*May he perish, both he and his offspring.*

'Whosoever hinders corn from being brought into the land of the Teans, either by art or machination, whether by land or sea, and whosoever drives out what has been brought in:

'*May he perish, both he and his offspring.*'

So clause after clause comes the refrain of cursing, like the

[1] Cato, *de agr. cult.* 134. 3 bonas preces precor uti sies volens propitius mihi liberisque, etc.

[2] Suidas in explaining *ἐξάρασθαι* says *τὸ ἐκτελέσαι τὰς ἀράς, τοῦτ' ἔστι τὰς εὐχὰς ἃς ἐπὶ ταῖς ἱδρύσεσι τῶν ναῶν εἰώθασι ποιεῖσθαι.* It is worth noting that in M.H.D. *segen* is not only as in modern German *benedictio* but also *maledictio*, see Osthoff, 'Allerhand Zauber etymologisch beleuchtet,' Bezzenberger, *Beiträge* XXIV. p. 180.

[3] Röhl, *I.G.A.* 497. The whole subject of legal curses has been well discussed by Dr Ziebart, 'Der Fluch im Griechischen Recht' (*Hermes* XXX. p. 57) to whom I owe many references. Also by the same writer in his 'Neue Attische Fluchtafeln' (*Nachrichten der K. Ges. d. Wiss. zu Göttingen*, Phil.-Hist. Kl. 1889, pp. 105 and 135), and by R. Wünsch, 'Neue Fluchtafeln' (*Rhein. Mus.* 1900, I. p. 62, II. p. 232). Curse Inscriptions are collected in an Appendix to the *Corpus Inscriptionum Atticarum*, under the title *Defixionum Tabulae*.

tolling of a bell, and at last as though they could not have their fill, comes the curse on the magistrate who fails to curse:

'Whosoever of them that hold office doth not make this cursing, what time he presides over the contest at the Anthesteria and the Herakleia and the Dia, let him be bound by an overcurse (ἐν τῇ ἐπαρῇ ἔχεσθαι), and whoever either breaks the stelae on which the cursing is written, or cuts out the letters or makes them illegible:

'*May he perish, both he and his offspring.*'

It is interesting to find here that the curses were recited at the Anthesteria, a festival of ghosts, and the Herakleia, an obvious hero festival, and at the Dia—this last surely a festival of imprecation like the Diasia.

On the strength of these *Dirae* of Teos, recited at public and primitive festivals, it might not be rash to conjecture that at the Thesmophoria some form of θεσμοί or binding spells was recited as well as carried. This conjecture becomes almost a certainty when we examine an important inscription[1] found near Pergamos and dealing with the regulations for mourning in the city of Gambreion in Mysia. The mourning laws of the ancients bore harder on women than on men, a fact explicable not by the general lugubriousness of women, nor even by their supposed keener sense of convention, but by those early matriarchal conditions in which relationship naturally counted through the mother rather than the father. Women, the law in question enacts, are to wear dark garments; men if they 'did not wish to do this' might relax into white; the period of mourning is longer for women than for men. Next follows the important clause: 'the official who superintends the affairs of women, who has been chosen by the people at the purifications that take place *before the Thesmophoria*, is to invoke blessings on the men who abide by the law and the women who obey the law that they may happily enjoy the goods they possess, but on the men who do not obey and the women who do not abide therein he is to invoke the contrary, and such women are to be accounted impious, and it is not lawful for them to make any sacrifice to the gods for the space of ten years, and the steward is to write up this law on two

[1] Dittenberger, *Syll. Inscr.* 879.

stelae and set them up, the one *before the doors of the Thesmophorion*, the other before the temple of Artemis Lochia.'

From the *Thesmophoriazusae* of Aristophanes we learn almost nothing of the ritual of the Thesmophoria, save the fact that the feast was celebrated on the Pnyx[1]: but the fashion in which the woman-herald prays is worth noting; she begins by a real prayer[2]:

> 'I bid you pray to Gods and Goddesses
> That in Olympus and in Pytho dwell
> And Delos, and to all the other gods.'

But when she comes to what she really cares about, she breaks into the old habitual curse formularies:

> 'If any plots against the cause of Woman
> Or peace proposes to Euripides
> Or to the Medes, or plots a tyranny,
> Or if a female slave in her master's ear
> Tells tales, or male or female publican
> Scants the full measure of our legal pint—
> *Curse him that he may miserably perish,*
> *He and his house*,—but for the rest of you
> Pray that the gods may give you all good things.'

It is of interest to find that not only were official curses written up at the doors of a Thesmophorion, but, at Syracuse, an oath of special sanctity 'the great oath' was taken there. Plutarch[3] tells us that when Callippus was conspiring against his friend Dion, the wife and sister of Dion became suspicious. To allay their suspicions, Callippus offered to give any pledge of his sincerity they might desire. They demanded that he should take 'the great oath' (ὀμόσαι τὸν μέγαν ὅρκον). 'Now the great oath was after this wise. The man who gives this pledge has to go to *the temenos of the Thesmophoroi*, and after the performance of certain sacred ceremonies, he puts on him the purple robe of the goddess, and taking a burning torch he denies the charge on oath' (ἀπόμνυσι). It is clear that this 'great oath' was some form of imprecation on the oath-taker, who probably by putting on the robe, dedicated himself in case of perjury to the goddess of the underworld. That the goddess was Kore we know from the fact that Callippus eventually forswore himself in sacrilegious fashion by sacrificing his victim on the feast of the *Koreia*, 'the feast of the goddess by whom he had sworn.' The curse is the dedication

[1] *Mon. and Myth. Anc. Athens*, p. 104.
[2] Ar. *Thesm.* 331.
[3] Plut. *Vit. Dion.* 56.

or devotion of others; the oath, like its more concrete form the ordeal, is the dedication of the curser himself.

The connection between primitive law and agriculture seems to have been very close. The name of the earliest laws recorded—they are rather precepts than in our sense laws—the 'Ploughman's Curses' speaks for itself. Some of these Ploughman's Curses are recorded. We are told by one of the 'Writers of Proverbs[1]' that 'the Bouzyges at Athens, who performs the sacred ploughing, utters many other curses and also curses those who do not share water and fire as a means of subsistence and those who do not show the way to those who have lost it.' Other similar precepts, no doubt sanctioned by similar curses, have come down to us under the name of the Thrice-Plougher *Triptolemos*[2], the first lawgiver of the Athenians. He bade men 'honour their parents, rejoice the gods with the fruits of the earth and not injure animals.' Perhaps these were to the Greeks the first commandments 'with promise.'

Such are the primitive precepts that grow up in a community which agriculture has begun to bind together with the ties of civilized life. In the days before curses were graven in stone and perhaps for long after, it was well that when the people were gathered together for sowing or for harvest, these salutary curses should be recited. Amid the decay of so much that is robust and primitive, it is pleasant to remember that in the Commination Service of our own Anglican Church with its string of holy curses annually recited

'They keep the Thesmophoria as they always used to do.'

THE HALOA.

The consideration of the *Haloa* has been purposely reserved to the end for this reason. The rites of the Thesmophoria, Skirophoria and Arrephoria are carried on by women only, and when they come to be associated with divinities at all, they are regarded as 'sacred to' Demeter and Kore or to analogous women goddesses Ge,

[1] Paroimiogr. I. 388 ὁ γὰρ βουζύγης Ἀθήνησιν ὁ τὸν ἱερὸν ἄροτον ἐπιτελῶν ἄλλα τε πολλὰ ἀρᾶται καὶ τοῖς μὴ κοινωνοῦσι κατὰ τὸν βίον ὕδατος ἢ πυρὸς ἢ μὴ ὑποφαίνουσιν ὁδὸν πλανωμένοις.

[2] Porph. *de Abst.* IV. 22.

Aphrodite, Eileithyia and Athene. Moreover the *sacra* carried are cereal cakes and nephalia: but the rites of the *Haloa*, though indeed mainly conducted by women, and sacred in part to Demeter, contain a new element, that of wine, and are therefore in mythological days regarded as 'sacred to' not only Demeter but Dionysos.

On this point an important scholion[1] to Lucian is explicit. The Haloa is 'a feast at Athens containing mysteries of Demeter and Kore and Dionysos on the occasion of the cutting of the vines and the tasting of the wine made from them.' Eustathius[2] states the same fact. 'There is celebrated, according to Pausanias, a feast of Demeter and Dionysos called the Haloa.' He adds, in explaining the name, that at it they were wont to carry first-fruits from Athens to Eleusis and to sport upon the threshing-floors, and that at the feast there was a procession of Poseidon. At Eleusis, Poseidon was not yet specialized into a sea-god only; he was *Phytalmios*, god of plants, and as such, it will be later seen (p. 427), his worship was easily affiliated to that of Dionysos.

The affiliation of the worship of the corn-goddess to that of the wine-god is of the first importance. The coming of Dionysos brought a new spiritual impulse to the religion of Greece, an impulse the nature of which will later be considered in full, and it was to this new impulse that the Eleusinian mysteries owed, apart from political considerations which do not concern us, their ultimate dominance. Of these mysteries the Haloa is, I think, the primitive prototype.

As to the primitive gist of the Haloa, there is no shadow of doubt: the name speaks for itself. Harpocration[3] rightly explains the festival, 'the Haloa gets its name, according to Philochorus, from the fact that people hold sports at the *threshing-floors*, and he says it is celebrated in the month Poseideon.' The sports held were of course incidental to the business of threshing, but it was these sports that constituted the actual festival. To this day the

[1] Schol. ad Luc. *Dial. Meretr.* VII. 4 Ἑορτὴ Ἀθήνησι μυστήρια περιέχουσα Δήμητρος καὶ Κόρης καὶ Διονύσου ἐπὶ τῇ τομῇ τῶν ἀμπέλων καὶ τῇ γεύσει τοῦ ἀποκειμένου ἤδη οἴνου γινόμενα παρὰ Ἀθηναίοις.

[2] Eustath. ad *Il.* IX. 530, 772 Ἰστέον δὲ ὅτι ἐπὶ συγκομιδῇ καρπῶν ἐφ' ᾗ καὶ τὰ θαλύσια ἐθύετο ἑορτὴ ἤγετο Δήμητρος καὶ Διονύσου κατὰ Παυσανίαν, ἁλῷα καλουμένη διὰ τὸ ταῖς ἀπαρχαῖς καὶ μάλιστα ἐν Ἀθήναις ἀπὸ τῆς ἅλω τότε καταχρᾶσθαι φέροντας εἰς Ἐλευσῖνα ἢ ἐπεὶ καθὰ καὶ Ὅμηρος ἐμφαίνει ἐν ἅλωσιν ἔπαιζον κατὰ τὴν ἑορτὴν ἐν ᾗ καὶ Ποσειδῶνος ἦν πομπή.

[3] Harp. s.v. Ἁλῷα.

great round threshing-floor that is found in most Greek villages is the scene of the harvest festival. Near it a booth (*σκηνή*) is to this day erected, and in it the performers rest and eat and drink in the intervals of their pantomimic dancing.

The Haloa was celebrated in the month Poseideon (December—January), a fact as surprising as it is ultimately significant. What has a threshing festival to do with mid-winter, when all the grain should be safely housed in the barns? Normally, now as in ancient days, the threshing follows as soon as may be after the cutting of the corn; it is threshed and afterwards winnowed in the *open* threshing-floor, and mid-winter is no time even in Greece for an open-air operation.

The answer is simple. The shift of date is due to Dionysos. The rival festivals of Dionysos were in mid-winter. He possessed himself of the festivals of Demeter, took over her threshing-floor and compelled the anomaly of a winter threshing festival. The latest time that a real threshing festival could take place is Pyanepsion, but by Poseideon it is just possible to have an early *Pithoigia* and to revel with Dionysos. There could be no clearer witness to the might of the incoming god.

As to the nature of the Haloa we learn two important facts from Demosthenes. It was a festival in which the priestess, not the Hierophant, presented the offerings, a festival under the presidency of women; and these offerings were bloodless, no animal victim (*ἱερεῖον*) was allowed. Demosthenes[1] records how a Hierophant, Archias by name, 'was cursed because at the Haloa he offered on the *eschara* in the court of Eleusis burnt sacrifice of an animal victim brought by the courtezan Sinope.' His condemnation was on a double count, 'it was not lawful on that day to sacrifice an animal victim, and the sacrifice was not his business but that of the priestess.' The epheboi[2] offered bulls at Eleusis, and, it would appear, engaged in some sort of 'bull fight[3],' but this

[1] Dem. 59. 116 *κατηρήθη αὐτοῦ (τοῦ ἱεροφάντου) καὶ ὅτι Σινώπῃ τῇ ἑταίρᾳ Ἁλῴοις ἐπὶ τῆς ἐσχάρας τῆς ἐν τῇ αὐλῇ Ἐλευσῖνι προσαγούσῃ ἱερεῖον θύσειεν, οὐ νομίμου ὄντος ἐν ταύτῃ τῇ ἡμέρᾳ ἱερεῖα θύειν οὐδὲ ἐκείνου οὔσης τῆς θυσίας ἀλλὰ τῆς ἱερείας.*

[2] *C.I.A.* II. 1, n. 471 *ἤραντο δὲ καὶ τοὺς βοῦς το[ὺς] ἐν Ἐλευσῖνι τῇ θυσίᾳ καὶ τοῖς προηροσίοις καὶ τοὺς ἐν τοῖς ἄλλοις ἱεροῖς καὶ γυμνασίοις.* Cf. Dittenberger, *De Epheb.* p. 77.

[3] The nature of the contest is not clear. Artemidorus (I. 8) says: *ταύροις ἐν Ἰωνίᾳ παῖδες Ἐφεσίων ἀγωνίζονται καὶ ἐν Ἀττικῇ παρὰ ταῖς θεαῖς ἐν Ἐλευσῖνι Κοῦροι Ἀθηναῖοι περιτελλομένων ἐνιαυτῶν.*' See Lobeck, *Agl.* p. 206.

must have been in honour either of Dionysos or of Poseidon who preceded him: the *vehicle* of both these divinities was the bull. It was the boast of the archon at the Haloa that Demeter had given to men 'gentle foods.'

Our fullest details of the Haloa, as of the Thesmophoria, come to us from the newly discovered scholia on Lucian[1]. From the scholiast's account it is clear that by his day the festival was regarded as connected with Dionysos as much as, or possibly more than, with Demeter. He definitely states that it was instituted in memory of the death of Ikarios after his introduction of the vine into Attica. The women he says celebrated it alone, in order that they might have perfect freedom of speech. The sacred symbols of both sexes were handled, the priestesses secretly whispered into the ears of the women present words that might not be uttered aloud, and the women themselves uttered all manner of what seemed to him unseemly quips and jests. The *sacra* handled are, it is clear, the same as those of the Thesmophoria: that their use and exhibition were carefully guarded is also clear from the exclusion of the other sex. The climax of the festival, it appears, was a great banquet. 'Much wine was set out and the tables were full of all the foods that are yielded by land and sea, save only those that are prohibited in the mysteries, I mean the pomegranate and the apple and domestic fowls, and eggs and red sea-mullet and black-tail and crayfish and shark. The archons prepare the tables and leave the women inside and

[1] Luc. *Dial. Meretr.* VII. 4 '*τήμερον Ἁλῷά ἐστι, τί δὲ σοὶ δέδωκεν εἰς τὴν ἑορτήν;*' schol. ad loc. *Ἑορτὴ Ἀθήνησι μυστήρια περιέχουσα Δήμητρος καὶ Κόρης καὶ Διονύσου ἐπὶ τῇ τομῇ τῶν ἀμπέλων καὶ τῇ γεύσει τοῦ ἀποκειμένου ἤδη οἴνου γινόμενα παρὰ Ἀθηναίοις ἐν οἷς προτίθεται* (d. Subject fehlt im Cod.: zu ergänzen ist *πέμματά?*) *τινα αἰσχύναις ἀνδρείοις* (sic) *ἐοικότα, περὶ ὧν διηγοῦνται ὡς πρὸς σύνθημα τῆς τῶν ἀνθρώπων σπορᾶς γινομένων ὅτι ὁ Διόνυσος δοὺς τὸν οἶνον....* After recounting the death of Ikarios the scholiast continues, *ὑπόμνημα δὲ τοῦ πάθους ἡ τοιαύτη ἑορτή. ἐν ταύτῃ καὶ τελετή τις εἰσάγεται γυναικῶν ἐν Ἐλευσῖνι, καὶ παιδιαὶ λέγονται πολλαὶ καὶ σκώμματα, μόναι δὲ γυναῖκες εἰσπορευόμεναι ἐπ' ἀδείας ἔχουσιν ἃ βούλονται λέγειν. καὶ δὴ τὰ αἴσχιστα ἀλλήλαις λέγουσι τότε, αἱ δὲ ἱέρειαι λάθρα προσιοῦσαι ταῖς γυναιξὶ κλεψιγαμίας πρὸς τὸ οὖς ὡς ἀπόρρητόν τι συμβουλεύουσιν. ἀναφωνοῦσι δὲ πρὸς ἀλλήλας πᾶσαι αἱ γυναῖκες αἰσχρὰ καὶ ἄσεμνα, βαστάζουσαι εἴδη σωμάτων* (so die Hs.: der Sinn erfordert *σχημάτων* genitalium) *ἀπρεπῆ* (*ἀπρεπεῖ* die Hs.) *ἀνδρεῖά τε καὶ γυναικεῖα. ἐνταῦθα οἶνός τε πολὺς πρόκειται καὶ τράπεζαι πάντων τῶν τῆς γῆς καὶ θαλάσσης γέμουσαι βρωμάτων, πλὴν τῶν ἀπειρημένων ἐν τῷ μυστικῷ, ῥοιᾶς φημὶ καὶ μήλου καὶ ὀρνίθων κατοικιδίων, καὶ ᾠῶν, καὶ θαλασσίας τρίγλης ἐρυθίνου* (*ἐριθύνου* die Hs.), *μελανούρου, κωράβου* (? *καράβου*), *γαλαιοῦ* (*γαλεοῦ?*). *παρατιθέασι δὲ τὰς τραπέζας οἱ ἄρχοντες καὶ ἔνδον καταλιπόντες ταῖς γυναιξὶν, αὐτοὶ χωρίζονται ἔξω διαμένοντες, ἐπιδεικνύμενοι τοῖς ἐπιδημοῦσι πᾶσι τὰς ἡμέρους τροφὰς παρὰ αὐτῶν εὑρεθῆναι καὶ πᾶσι κοινωνηθῆναι τοῖς ἀνθρώποις παρ' αὐτῶν. πρόσκειται δὲ ταῖς τραπέζαις καὶ ἐκ πλακοῦντος κατεσκευασμένα ἀμφοτέρων γενῶν αἰδοῖα. ἀλῷα δὲ ἐκλήθη διὰ τὸν καρπὸν τοῦ Διονύσου· ἀλωαὶ γὰρ αἱ τῶν ἀμπέλων φυτεῖαι.*

themselves withdraw and remain outside, making a public statement to the visitors present that the "gentle foods" were discovered by them (i.e. the people of Eleusis) and by them shared with the rest of mankind. And there are upon the tables cakes shaped like the symbols of sex. And the name Haloa is given to the feast on account of the fruit of Dionysos—for the growths of the vine are called *Aloai*.'

The materials of the women's feast are interesting. The diet prescribed is of cereals and of fish and possibly fowl, but clearly not of flesh. As such it is characteristic of the old Pelasgian population before the coming of the flesh-eating Achaeans. Moreover—a second point of interest—it is hedged in with all manner of primitive taboos. The precise *reason* of the taboo on pomegranates, red mullet and the like, is lost beyond recall, but some of the particular taboos are important because they are strictly paralleled in the Eleusinian mysteries. That the pomegranate was 'taboo' at the Eleusinian mysteries is clear from the aetiological myth in the Homeric hymn to Demeter[1]. Hades consents to let Persephone return to the upper air.

> 'So spake he, and Persephone the prudent up did rise
> Glad in her heart and swift to go. But he in crafty wise
> Looked round and gave her stealthily a sweet pomegranate seed
> To eat, that not for all her days with Her of sable-weed,
> Demeter, should she tarry.'

The pomegranate was dead men's food, and once tasted drew Persephone back to the shades. Demeter admits it; she says[2] to Persephone:

> 'If thou hast tasted food below, thou canst not tarry here,
> Below the hollow earth must dwell the third part of the year.'

Porphyry[3] in his treatise on *Abstinence from Animal Food*, notes the reason and the rigour of the Eleusinian taboos. Demeter, he says, is a goddess of the lower world and they consecrate the cock to her. The word he uses, ἀφιέρωσαν, really means put under a *taboo*. We are apt to associate the cock with daylight and his early morning crowing, but the Greeks for some reason regarded the bird as chthonic. It is a cock, Socrates remembers, that he owes to Asklepios, and Asklepios, it will be seen when we come

[1] *Hom. Hym. ad Cer.* 370.
[2] *v.* 399.
[3] Porphyr. *de Abst.* IV. 16.

to the subject of hero-worship, was but a half-deified hero. The cock was laid under a taboo, reserved, and then came to be considered as a sacrifice. Porphyry goes on 'It is because of this that the mystics abstain from barndoor fowls. And at Eleusis public proclamation is made that men must abstain from barndoor fowls, from fish and from beans, and from the pomegranate and from apples, and to touch these defiles as much as to touch a woman in child-birth or a dead body.' The Eleusinian Mysteries were in their enactments the very counterpart of the Haloa.

The Eleusinian Mysteries.

The Eleusinian Mysteries[1] are usually treated as if they were a thing by themselves, a ceremony so significant, so august, as to stand apart from the rest of Greek Ritual. If my view be correct, they are primarily but the Eleusinian *Haloa*: all their ultimate splendour and spiritual as well as social prestige are due to two things, first the fact that Athens for political purposes made them her own, second that at some date we cannot exactly fix, they became affiliated to the mysteries of Dionysos. To Athens the mysteries owe their external magnificence, to Dionysos and Orpheus their deep inward content. The external magnificence, being non-religious, does not concern us; the deep inward content, the hope of immortality and the like are matters of cardinal import, but must stand over till a later chapter, after the incoming of Dionysos has been discussed. For the present what concerns us is, setting aside all vague statements and opinions as to the meaning and spiritual influence attributed by various authors, ancient and modern, to the mysteries, to examine the actual ritual facts of which evidence remains.

Mysteries were by no means confined to the religion of Demeter and Kore. There were mysteries of Hermes, of Iasion, of Ino, of Archemoros, of Agraulos, of Hecate. In general mysteries

[1] The sources for the Eleusinian Mysteries are collected in Lobeck's *Aglaophamus*. Reference to inscriptions discovered since Lobeck's days will be found in Daremberg and Saglio's *Dictionnaire des Antiquités*, s.v. The best general account in English is that by Prof. Ramsay in the *Encyclopaedia Britannica*, in French two articles reprinted from the *Mémoires de l'Académie des Inscriptions et Belles Lettres*, vol. XXXV. 2nd part 1895, and vol. XXXVII. 1900, entitled 'Recherches sur l'origine et la nature des Mystères d'Eleusis,' and 'Les Grands Mystères d'Eleusis, Personnel, Cérémonies,' and for certain details see H. G. Pringsheim, *Archäologische Beiträge zur Geschichte d. eleusinischen Kults*, 1905.

seem to occur more usually in relation to the cult of women divinities[1], of heroines and earth-goddesses; from the worship of the Olympians in Homer they are markedly absent. In general, by a mystery is meant *a rite in which certain sacra are exhibited, which cannot be safely seen by the worshipper till he has undergone certain purifications.*

The date of the mysteries at Eleusis is fortunately certain. The ceremonies began on the 13th of Boedromion, i.e. about the end of September, an appropriate date for any harvest festival which was to include the later fruits and notably the grape. Our evidence for this date is an imperial Roman inscription[2], but this inscription expressly states that its enactments are 'according to ancient usage.' 'The people has decided to order the Kosmeter of the Epheboi in accordance with ancient usage to send them to Eleusis on the 13th day of Boedromion, in their customary dress, for the procession that accompanies the *sacra*, in order that on the 14th they may escort them to the Eleusinion which is at the foot of the Acropolis. Also to order the Kosmeter of the Epheboi to conduct them on the 19th to Eleusis in the same dress, escorting the *sacra*.' The inscription is of great importance, as it is clear evidence that *sacra* were part of the regular ritual. What precisely these *sacra* were we do not know; presumably they were objects like those in use at the Thesmophoria. The going to and fro from Eleusis to Athens is purely political. The *sacra* were really resident at Eleusis, but Athens liked to think she brought them there. The Epheboi *escorted* the *sacra*, but, as was fitting, they were really in charge of, and actually carried by, *priestesses*[3].

On the 15th of Boedromion took place the *ἀγυρμός* or assembling of the candidates for initiation, and the proclamation by the Hierophant in the Stoa Poikile interdicting those whose hands were defiled and those whose lips spoke unintelligible words[4]. Some such interdiction, some 'fencing of the tables,' took

[1] The rites at Eleusis were *probably* at first confined to women. Dionysios of Halicarnassos (*Ant. Rom.* I. 331) says in speaking of the cult of Demeter in Arcadia, *ἱδρύσαντο δὲ καὶ Δήμητρος ἱερὸν καὶ τὰς θυσίας αὐτῇ διὰ γυναικῶν καὶ νηφαλίους ἔθυσαν ὡς Ἕλλησι νόμος ὧν οὐδὲν ὁ καθ' ἡμᾶς ἤλλαξε χρόνος.*

[2] *C.I.A.* III. 5.

[3] Inscr. *A. Mitth.* 1894 p. 163 *ὡς ἂν τὰ ἱερὰ φέρωσιν αἱ ἱέρειαι ἀσφαλέστατα.*

[4] The exact formulary is preserved by Theon of Smyrna, p. 22, *τὸ κήρυγμα τοῦτο κηρύττεται 'ὅστις τὰς χεῖρας μὴ καθαρός...ὅστις φωνὴν ἀσύνετος.'* Some authorities

place in all probability before all mysteries. It is this *prorrhesis* of course that is parodied by Aristophanes in the *Frogs*[1], who actually dares to put his burlesque into the mouth of the Hierophant himself.

The 16th of Boedromion saw the accomplishment of a rite of cardinal importance. The day was called in popular parlance 'ἅλαδε μύσται,' 'To the sea ye mystics,' from the cry that heralded the act of purification. Hesychius[2] in commenting on the expression says 'a certain day of the Mysteries at Athens.' Polyaenus[3] is precise as to the date. He says 'Chabrias won the sea-fight at Naxos on the 16th of Boedromion. He had felt that this was a good day for a battle, because it was one of the days of the Great Mysteries. The same thing happened with Themistocles against the Persians at Salamis. But Themistocles and his troops had the "Iacchos" for their call, while Chabrias and his troops had "To the sea ye mystics."' The victory of Chabrias was won, as we know from Plutarch[4], at the full moon, and at the full moon the Mysteries were celebrated.

The procession to the sea was called by the somewhat singular name ἔλασις, 'driving' or 'banishing[5],' and the word is instructive. The procession was not a mere procession, it was a driving out, a banishing. This primary sense seems to lurk in the Greek word πομπή[6], which in primitive days seems to have mainly meant a conducting out, a sending away of evil. The bathing in the sea was a purification, a conducting out, a banishing of evil, and each man took with him his own pharmakos, a young pig. The ἔλασις, the driving, may have been literally the driving of the pig, which, as the goal was some 6 miles distant, must have been a lengthy and troublesome business. Arrived at the sea, each man bathed with his pig—the pig of purification was itself purified. When in the days of Phocion[7] the Athenians were compelled to receive a

think that φωνὴν ἀσύνετος means speaking an unknown, barbarous tongue, others that it meant having some impediment of speech that prevented the due utterance of the sacred formularies. I think the former more probable.

[1] Ar. *Ran.* 354.

[2] Hesych. s.v.

[3] Polyaen. *Strat.* III. 11.

[4] Plut. *de glor. Ath.* VII.

[5] *C.I.A.* IV. 385 d, l. 20 ἐπεμελήθησαν δὲ καὶ τῆς ἅλαδε ἐλάσεως.

[6] Mr R. A. Neil suggested that the same root and idea may lurk in the unexplained *pontifex*, i.e. maker of πομπαί. The connection with *bridges* is late and fanciful.

[7] Plut. *Vit. Phoc.* XXVIII.

Macedonian garrison, terrible portents appeared. When the ribbons with which the mystic beds were wound came to be dyed, instead of taking a purple colour they came out of a sallow death-like hue, which was the more remarkable as when it was the ribbons belonging to private persons that were dyed, they came out all right. And more portentous still—'when a mystic was bathing his pig in the harbour called Kantharos, a sea-monster ate off the lower part of his body, by which the god made clear beforehand that they would be deprived of the lower parts of the city that lay near the sea, but keep the upper portion.'

The pig of purification was a ritual element, so important that when Eleusis was permitted (B.C. 350—327) to issue her autonomous coinage[1] it is the pig that she chooses as the sign and symbol of her mysteries. The bronze coin in fig. 13 shows the pig standing on the torch: in the *exergue* an ivy spray. The pig was the cheapest and commonest of sacrificial animals, one that each and every citizen could afford. Socrates in the *Republic*[2] says 'if people are to hear shameful and monstrous stories about the gods it should be only rarely and to a select few in a mystery, and they should have to sacrifice not a (mere) pig but some huge and unprocurable victim.'

FIG. 13.

Purification, it is clear, was an essential feature of the mysteries, and this brings us to the consideration of the meaning of the word mystery. The usual derivation of the word is from μύω, I close the apertures whether of eyes or mouth. The *mystes*, it is supposed, is the person vowed to secrecy who has not seen and will not speak of the things revealed. As such he is distinguished from the *epoptes* who has seen, but equally may not speak; the two words indicate successive grades of initiation. It will later be seen (p. 480) that in the Orphic Mysteries the word *mystes* is applied, without any reference to seeing or not seeing, to a person who has fulfilled the rite of eating the raw flesh of a bull. It will also be seen that in Crete, which is

[1] Head, *Hist. Num.* p. 328: on the reverse is Triptolemos in his winged car.
[2] Plat. *Rep.* II. 378 A.

probably the home of the mysteries, the mysteries were open to all, they were not mysterious. The derivation of mystery from *μύω*, though possible, is not satisfactory. I would suggest another and a simple origin.

The ancients themselves were not quite comfortable about the connection with *μύω*. They knew and felt that *mystery*, secrecy, was not the main gist of 'a mystery': the essence of it all primarily was purification in order that you might safely eat and handle certain *sacra*. There was no revelation, no secret to be kept, only a mysterious *taboo* to be prepared for and finally overcome. It might be a *taboo* on eating first-fruits, it might be a taboo on handling magical *sacra*. In the Thesmophoria, the women fast before they touch the *sacra*; in the Eleusinian mysteries you sacrifice a pig before you offer and partake of the first-fruits. The gist of it all is purification. Clement[1] says significantly, 'Not unreasonably among the Greeks in their mysteries do ceremonies of purification hold the initial place, as with barbarians the bath.' Merely as an insulting conjecture Clement[2] in his irresponsible abusive fashion throws out what I believe to be the real origin of the word *mystery*. 'I think,' he says, 'that these orgies and mysteries of yours ought to be derived, the one from the wrath (*ὀργή*) of Demeter against Zeus, the other from the pollution (*μύσος*) relating to Dionysos.' Of course Clement is formally quite incorrect, but he hits on what seems a possible origin of the word *mystery*, that it is the doing of what relates to a *μύσος*, a pollution, it is primarily a ceremony of purification. Lydus[3] makes the same suggestion, 'Mysteries,' he says, 'are from the separating away of a pollution (*μύσος*) as equivalent to sanctification.'

The bathing with the pig was not the only rite of purification in the mysteries, though it is the one of which we have most definite detail. From the aetiology[4] of the Homeric

[1] Clem. Al. *Strom.* v. 689 *οὐκ ἀπεικότως καὶ τῶν μυστηρίων τῶν παρ' Ἕλλησιν ἄρχει μὲν καθάρσια καθάπερ καὶ ἐν τοῖς βαρβάροις τὸ λουτρόν.*

[2] Clem. Al. *Protr.* II. *μυστήρια...ἀπὸ τοῦ συμβεβηκότος περὶ τὸν Διόνυσον μύσους.*

[3] Lyd. *de mens.* IV. 38 *Μυστήρια ἀπὸ τῆς στερήσεως τοῦ μύσους ἀντὶ τῆς ἁγιοσύνης.* In form *μύστης* might come from *μύω* (cf. *ἀμυστί*), but Mr Gilbert Murray draws my attention to some uses of *μυστήριον* which point rather to *μύσος*, e.g. Eur. *Suppl.* 470 *λύσαντα σεμνὰ στεμμάτων μυστήρια* and *El.* 87 *ἐκ θεοῦ μυστηρίων.*

[4] The aetiology of the Hymn and the various ceremonies that gave rise to it are well explained by Mr F. B. Jevons, *Introd. to History of Religion*, Appendix to Chapter XXIV.

Hymn to Demeter, we may conjecture that there were, at least for children, rites of purification by passing through fire, and ceremonies of a mock fight or stone-throwing (*λιθοβολία*, *βαλλητύς*). All have the same intent and need not here be examined in detail.

On the night of the 19—20th[1] the procession of purified mystics, carrying with them the image of Iacchos, left Athens for Eleusis, and after that we have no evidence of the exact order of the various rites of initiation. The exact order is indeed of little importance. Instead we have recorded what is of immeasurably more importance, the precise formularies in which the mystics avowed the rites in which they had taken part, rites which we are bound to suppose constituted the primitive ceremony of initiation.

Before these are examined it is necessary to state definitely what already has been implied, i.e. the fact that at the mysteries there was an offering of first-fruits; the mysteries were in fact the *Thargelia* of Eleusis. An inscription[2] of the 5th century B.C. found at Eleusis is our best evidence. 'Let the Hierophant and the Torch-bearer command that at the mysteries the Hellenes should offer first-fruits of their crops in accordance with ancestral usage......To those who do these things there shall be many good things, both good and abundant crops, whoever of them do not injure the Athenians, nor the city of Athens, nor the two goddesses.' The order of precedence is amusing and characteristic. Here we have indeed a commandment with promise.

The 'token' or formulary by which the mystic made confession is preserved for us by Clement[3] as follows: '*I fasted, I drank the kykeon, I took from the chest, (having tasted?) I put back into the basket and from the basket into the chest.*' The statement involves, in the main, two acts besides the preliminary fast, i.e. the drinking of the *kykeon* and the handling of certain unnamed *sacra*.

[1] I omit altogether the ceremonies of the 17th—18th, the *Epidauria*, as they were manifestly a later accretion; the worship of the Epidaurian Asklepios was formally inaugurated at Athens (see p. 344) in 421 B.C.

[2] Dittenberger, *Syllog. Inscript.* 13.

[3] Clem. Al. *Protr.* II. 18 ἔστι τὸ σύνθημα Ἐλευσινίων Ἐνήστευσα, ἔπιον τὸν κυκεῶνα, ἔλαβον ἐκ κίστης, ἐργασάμενος (? ἐγγευσάμενος) ἀπεθέμην εἰς κάλαθον καὶ ἐκ καλάθου εἰς κίστην. Since the above was written, Dr Dieterich (*Eine Mithras-Liturgie*, p. 125) has shown good reason for supposing that ἐργασάμενος is a euphemism for rites analogous to the ἱερὸς γάμος: see p. 535.

It is significant of the whole attitude of Greek religion that the confession is not a confession of dogma or even faith, but an avowal of ritual acts performed. This is the measure of the gulf between ancient and modern. The Greeks in their greater wisdom saw that uniformity in ritual was desirable and possible; they left a man practically free in the only sphere where freedom is of real importance, i.e. in the matter of thought. So long as you fasted, drank the *kykeon*, handled the *sacra*, no one asked what were your opinions or your sentiments in the performance of those acts; you were left to find in every sacrament the only thing you could find—what you brought. Our own creed is mainly a *Credo*, an utterance of dogma, formulated by the few for the many, but it has traces of the more ancient conception of *Confiteor*, the avowal of ritual acts performed. *Credo in unam sanctam catholicam et apostolicam ecclesiam* is immediately followed by *Confiteor unum baptismum*, though the instinct of dogma surges up again in the final words *in remissionem peccatorum*.

The preliminary fast before the eating of sacred things is common to most primitive peoples; it is the simplest negative form of purification: among the more logical savages it is often accompanied by the taking of a powerful emetic. The *kykeon* requires a word of explanation. The first-fruits at Eleusis were presented in the form of a *pelanos*[1]. The nature of a *pelanos* has already been discussed, and the fact noted that the word *pelanos* was used only of the half-fluid mixture offered to the gods. Its equivalent for mortals was called *alphita* or sometimes *kykeon*. Eustathius in commenting on the drink prepared by Hekamede for Nestor, a drink made of barley and cheese and pale honey and onion and Pramnian wine, says that the word *kykeon* meant something between meat and drink, but inclining to be like a sort of soup that you could sup. Such a drink it was that in the Homeric Hymn Metaneira prepared for Demeter, only with no wine, for Demeter, as an underworld goddess 'might not drink red wine': and such a wineless drink, made in all probability from the *pelanos* and only differing from it in name, was set before the mystae.

Some ceremony like the drinking of the *kykeon* is represented in the vase-painting[2] in fig. 14. Two worshippers, a man and a

[1] *C.I.A.* vol. IV. p. 203, ll. 68 and 72.
[2] *Annali dell' Inst.* 1865, Tav. d' agg. F. Naples, Heydemann, *Cat.* 3358.

woman, are seated side by side; before them a table piled with food, beneath it a basket of loaves. They are inscribed *Mysta* (Μυστα). A priest holding in the left hand twigs and standing by a little shrine, offers to them a cylix containing some form of drink. The presence of the little shrine has made some commentators see in the priest an itinerant quack priest (ἀγύρτης), but it

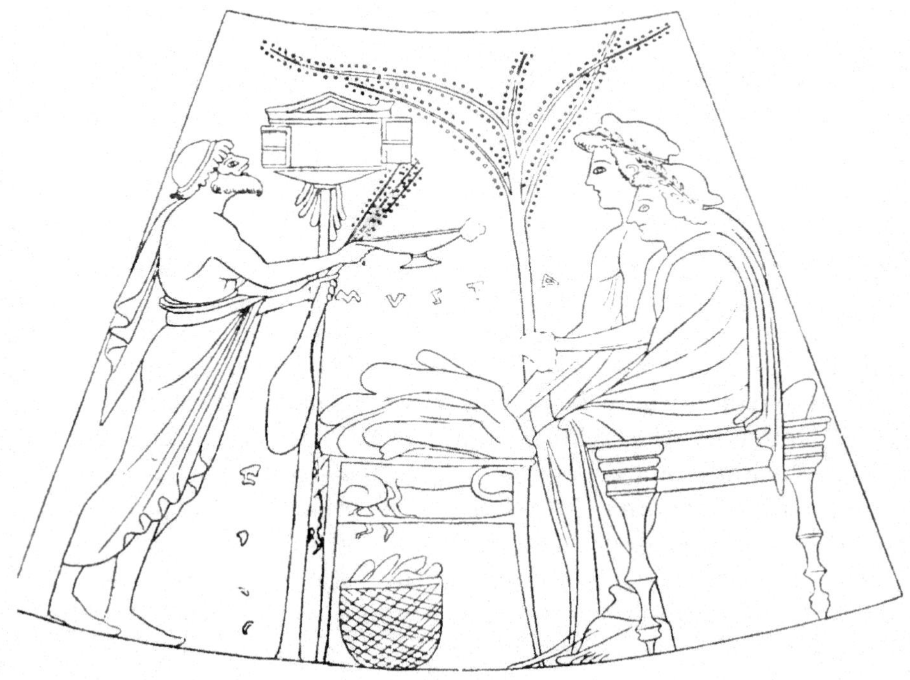

Fig. 14.

is quite possible that shrines of this kind containing *sacra* were carried at the Eleusinian mysteries. Anyhow the scene depicted is analogous.

Of the actual *sacra* which the initiated had to take from the chest, place in the basket, and replace in the chest, we know nothing. The *sacra* of the Thesmophoria are known, those of the Dionysiac mysteries were of trivial character, a ball, a mirror, a cone, and the like: there is no reason to suppose that the *sacra* of the Eleusinian mysteries were of any greater intrinsic significance.

Clement[1] in a passage preceding that already quoted gives the Eleusinian 'tokens,' with slightly different wording and with two additional clauses: he says 'the symbols of this initiation are, I ate from the timbrel, I drank from the cymbal, I carried the *kernos*, I passed beneath the *pastos*.' The scholiast[2] on Plato's *Gorgias* makes a similar statement. He says 'at the lesser mysteries many disgraceful things were done, and these words were said by those who were being initiated: I ate from the timbrel, I drank from the cymbal, I carried the *kernos*'; he further adds by way of explanation 'the *kernos* is the *liknon* or *ptuon*,' i.e. it is some form of winnowing fan.

There has been much and, I think, needless controversy as to whether this form of the tokens belongs to the mysteries at Eleusis or not. From the words that precede Clement's statement, a mention of Attis, Kybele and the Korybants, it is quite clear that he has in his mind the mysteries of the Great Mother of Asia Minor, but from his mentioning Demeter also, it is also clear that he does not exactly distinguish between the two. The mention of the 'tokens' by the scholiast on Plato is expressly made with reference to the Lesser Mysteries, and these, it will later (Chap. x.) be seen, are related especially to Kore and Dionysos. The whole confusion rests on the simple mythological fact that Demeter and Cybele were but local forms of the Great Mother worshipped under diverse names all over Greece. Wherever she was worshipped she had mysteries, the timbrel and the cymbal came to be characteristic of the wilder Asiatic Mother, but the Mother at Eleusis also clashed the brazen cymbals. In her 'tokens' however her mystics ate from the *cista* and the basket, but the distinction is a slight one.

The question of the *kernos* is of some interest. The scholiast states that the *kernos* was a winnowing fan, and the winnowing fan we shall later see (p. 548) was, at least in Alexandrine days,

[1] Clem. Al. *Protr.* I. 2. 13 Δηοῦς μυστήρια καὶ (leg. αἱ) Διὸς πρὸς μητέρα Δήμητρα ἀφροδίσιαι συμπλοκαὶ καὶ μῆνις τῆς Δηοῦς καὶ Διὸς ἱκετηρίαι. ταῦτα τελίσκουσιν οἱ Φρύγες Ἄττιδι καὶ Κυβέλῃ καὶ Κορύβασι,—τὰ σύμβολα τῆς μυήσεως ταύτης Ἐκ τυμπάνου ἔφαγον, ἐκ κυμβάλου ἔπιον, ἐκερνοφόρησα, ὑπὸ τὸν παστὸν ὑπέδυνον.

[2] Schol. ad Plat. *Gorg.* p. 123 ἐν οἷς (τοῖς σμικροῖς μυστηρίοις) πολλὰ μὲν ἐπράττετο αἰσχρά, ἐλέγετο δὲ πρὸς τῶν μυουμένων ταῦτα· ἐκ τυμπάνου ἔφαγον, ἐκ κυμβάλου ἔπιον, ἐκερνοφόρησα (κέρνος δὲ τὸ λίκνον ἤγουν τὸ πτύον ἐστίν), ὑπὸ τὸν παστὸν ὑπέδυνον καὶ τὰ ἑξῆς. The concluding formulary, which does not occur in the Eleusinian confession, will be explained later (Chap. x.).

used in the mysteries of Eleusis. It was a simple agricultural instrument taken over and mysticized by the religion of Dionysos. From Athenaeus[1] however we learn of another kind of *kernos.* In his discussion of the various kinds of cups and their uses he says: '*Kernos*, a vessel made of earthenware, having in it many little cups fastened to it, in which are white poppies, wheat, barley, pulse, vetch, ochroi, lentils; and he who carries it after the fashion of the carrier of the *liknon*, tastes of these things, as Ammonius relates in his third book On Altars and Sacrifices.' A second and rather fuller notice of the *kernos* is given by Athenaeus[2] a little later in discussing the *kotylos.* 'Polemon in his treatise "On the Dian Fleece" says, "And after this he performs the rite and takes it from the chamber and distributes it to those who have borne the *kernos* aloft."' Then follows an amplified list of the contents of the *kernos.* The additions are italicized: '*sage*, white poppies, wheat, barley, pulse, vetch, ochroi, lentils, *beans*, *spelt*, *oats*, *a cake*, *honey*, *oil*, *wine*, *milk*, *sheep's wool unwashed*.'

The list of the *παγκαρπία*, the offering of all fruits and natural products, is in some respects a primitive one: the unwashed wool reminds us of the simple offering made by Pausanias at the cave of Demeter at Phigalia; but there are late additions, the manufactured olive oil and wine. Demeter in early days would assuredly never have accepted wine. Vessels exactly corresponding to the description given by Athenaeus have been found in considerable numbers in Melos and Crete and, of later date, in the precinct at Eleusis, both vessels meant for use and others obviously votive. In the accounts[3] of the officials at Eleusis for the year 408—7 B.C. there is mention of a vessel called *κέρχνος*, which in all probability is identical with the *kernos* of Athenaeus. The shape and purport of the vessel are clearly seen in the early specimen from Melos[4] in

[1] Athen. XI. 52, p. 476.

[2] Athen. XI. 56, p. 478 *ὅσοι ἄνω τὸ κέρνος περιενηνοχότες. τοῦτο δ' ἐστὶν ἀγγεῖον κεραμεοῦν ἔχον ἐν αὐτῷ πολλοὺς κοτυλίσκους κεκολλημένους· ἔνεισι δ' αὐτοῖς ὅρμινοι, μήκωνες λευκοί, πυροί, κριθαί, πισοί, λάθυροι, ὦχροι, φακοί, κύαμοι, ζειαί, βρόμος, παλάθιον, μέλι, ἔλαιον, οἶνος, γάλα, ὄιον ἔριον ἄπλυτον. ὁ δὲ τοῦτο βαστάσας οἷον λικνοφορήσας τούτων γεύεται.* I have translated the difficult *ἄνω* by *aloft* taking it as referring to the carrying on the head, but see 'Kerchnos,' O. Rubensohn, *A. Mitt.* 1898, XXIII. p. 270, to whom I am indebted for many references. The *Kernophoria* is well shown in the Ninnion pinax on p. 559.

[3] 'Εφήμερις 'Αρχ. 1898, p. 61 *χρυσοῖ κέρχνοι* Γ.

[4] British Museum, *Annual of British School at Athens*, vol. III. p. 57, Pl. IV. As Professor Bosanquet pointed out to me it is likely that the Kernos at Eleusis was borrowed from the Cretan mysteries.

fig. 15. Such a vessel might well be called a *separator*; each of the little *kotyliskoi* attached would contain a sample of the various

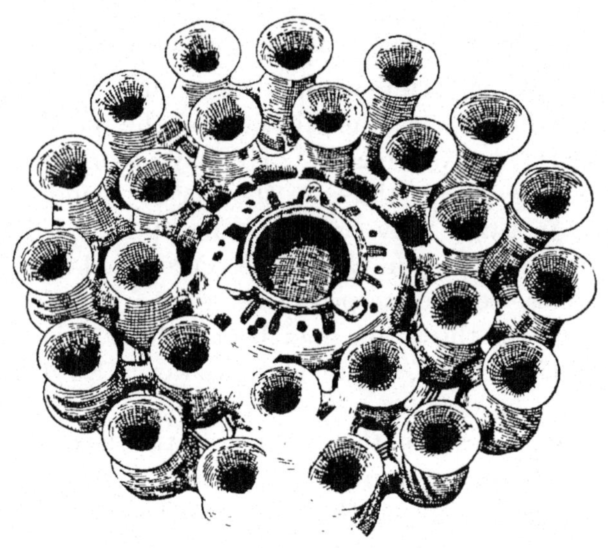

FIG. 15.

grains and products. It is easy to see how the scholiast might explain it as a *liknon*. The *liknon* was an implement for winnowing, *separating* grain from chaff, the *kernos* a vessel in which various sorts of grain could be kept separate. The *Kernophoria* was nothing but a late and elaborate form of the offering of first-fruits. In the simple primaeval form of the Mysteries as certified by the tokens, we have but two elements, the presentation and tasting of first-fruits and the handling of *sacra*. All later accretions will be discussed in the chapter on Orphic Mysteries.

In discussing the Anthesteria (p. 42) mention has already been made of a rite which, according to Athenaeus[1], took place on the final day of the Mysteries. On this day, which took its name from the rite, two vessels called *plemochoae* were emptied, one towards the east, the other towards the west, and at the moment of outpouring a mystic formulary was pronounced. Athenaeus explains that a *plemochoè* was an earthenware vessel 'shaped like a top but standing secure on its basis': it seems to have been a vessel in

[1] Athen. XI. 93, p. 496.

general use for the service of the underworld, for he quotes a play called *Peirithous* in which one of the characters said:

> 'That these *plemochoai* with well-omened words
> We may pour down into the chthonian chasm.'

What the mystic formulary was we cannot certainly say, but it is tempting to connect the libation of the *plemochoè* with a formulary recorded by Proclos[1]. He says 'In the Eleusinian Mysteries, looking up to the sky they cried aloud "Rain," and looking down to earth they cried "Be fruitful."' The simplicity of the solemn little prayer cannot be reproduced in English. It was a fitting close to rites so primitive.

Last of all, over those who had been initiated were uttered, if we may trust Hesychius[2], the mysterious words Κὸγξ ὄμπαξ.

It remains to resume the results of the last four chapters. It has been seen in examining four of the great public festivals of Athens, the Diasia, the Anthesteria, the Thargelia, the Thesmophoria, that neither their names, nor primarily their ritual, were concerned with the worship of the Olympian gods to whom the festivals were ostensibly dedicated. When the nature of that ritual was examined, it was seen to consist not in sacrifice like that paid to the Olympians, which was of the nature of *tendance* and might be embodied in the formula *do ut des*, but rather of ceremonies of *aversion* based on ignorance and fear. Its formula was *do ut abeas*. In the Anthesteria the ceremonies known as ἐναγισμοί were seen to be purifications (καθαρμοί), and by purifications were meant placations of Keres, of ghosts and sprites. In the Thargelia the ceremony of the pharmakos was seen to be also a purification, but in the sense not of the placation or riddance of ghosts and sprites but of a magical cleansing from physical evil. In the Thesmophoria the ceremony with the pigs was preceded by ceremonies of purification, and was in itself of magical intent. Moreover the element of cursing and *devotion* was seen to lie at the root of the later notion of *consecration*. To these three festivals, taken from the three seasons of the

[1] Procl. ad Plat. *Tim.* p. 293 ἐν τοῖς Ἐλευσινίοις εἰς μὲν τὸν οὐρανὸν ἀναβλέποντες ἐβόων 'ὕε,' καταβλέψαντες δὲ εἰς τὴν γῆν 'κύε.'

[2] Hesych. s.v. Κὸγξ ὄμπαξ· ἐπιφώνημα τετελεσμένοις. Mr F. M. Cornford suggests that the original form may have been Κόγξον πάξ, 'Sound the conch enough.' See also Lobeck, *Aglaoph.* 775.

agricultural year, has now been added the rite of the Eleusinian Mysteries, the gist of which has been shown to be purification as preliminary to the handling of magical *sacra* and to the partaking of first-fruits.

The only just way of understanding the religious notions of a particular race is to examine the terminology of the language of that race. Our modern notion of ancient religion is largely summed up by the word 'sacrifice.' We are too apt to ask 'what was the nature of sacrifice among the Greeks?' If we follow the lead of their language instead of imposing our language on them, it is abundantly clear that sacrifice, with all our modern connotations of vicarious expiation and of mystical communion, they had not. All the ancient ceremonies, so far considered, point to a thought simpler and nowise less beautiful or less deeply religious, and that thought is *purification*. Purification practically unknown to Olympian worship is the keynote of the lower stratum.

It is all important that this should be clearly and emphatically stated at this point in order that the sequel may be intelligible. When the new impulse connected with the names of Dionysos and Orpheus entered Greece, it left aside the great and popular Olympian system embodied in the formula *do ut des*, and, by a true instinct, fastened on an element which, if in some respects it was lower, was truer to fact and had in it higher possibilities, a religion that recognised evil, though mainly in physical form, and that sought for purification.

The essence of that new religion was, as will later be shown, the belief that man could become god: the new ritual feature it introduced, a feature wholly lacking in the old uneaten 'sacrifices,' was mystical communion by the eating of the body of the god. But, because man was mortal, there was mortality to be purged away; and hence, although with a new faith and hope, men reverted to the old ritual of purification.

So much by anticipation; but before we come to the study of the new impulse it is necessary to leave ritual and turn to theology, which is in fact mythology: the rites have been considered, and now in the next three chapters something must be said of the beings worshipped,—at first in vague shifting outlines as ghosts and sprites,—later crystallized into clear shapes as goddesses and gods.

CHAPTER V.

THE DEMONOLOGY OF GHOSTS AND SPRITES AND BOGEYS.

'ὦ μεγάλαυχοι καὶ φθερσιγενεῖς
Κῆρες Ἐρινύες.'

In the preceding chapters the nature of Greek ritual has been discussed. The main conclusion that has emerged is that this ritual in its earlier phases was mainly characterized by a tendency to what the Greeks called *ἀποτροπή*, i.e. the turning away, the *aversion* of evil. This tendency was however rarely quite untouched by an impulse more akin to our modern notion of worship, the impulse to *θεραπεία*, i.e. the induction, the fostering of good influences.

Incidentally we have of course gathered something of the nature of the objects of worship. When the ritual was not an attempt at the direct impulsion of nature, we have had brief uncertain glimpses of sprites and ghosts and underworld divinities. It now remains to trace with more precision these vague theological or demonological or mythological outlines, to determine the character of the beings worshipped and something of the order of their development.

In theology facts are harder to seek, truth more difficult to formulate than in ritual. Ritual, i.e. what men *did*, is either known or not known; what they meant by what they did—the connecting link between ritual and theology—can sometimes be certainly known, more often precariously inferred. Still more hazardous is the attempt to determine how man thought of the objects or beings to whom his ritual was addressed, in a word what was his theology, or, if we prefer the term, his mythology.

At the outset one preliminary caution is imperative. Our

minds are imbued with current classical mythology, our imagination peopled with the vivid personalities, the clear-cut outlines of the Olympian gods; it is only by a somewhat severe mental effort that we realize the fact essential to our study that *there were no gods at all*, that what we have to investigate is not so many actual facts and existences but only conceptions of the human mind, shifting and changing colour with every human mind that conceived them. Art which makes the image, literature which crystallizes attributes and functions, arrest and fix this shifting kaleidoscope; but, until the coming of art and literature and to some extent after, the formulary of theology is 'all things are in flux' (*πάντα ῥεῖ*).

Further, not only are we dealing solely with conceptions of the human mind, but often with conceptions of a mind that conceived things in a fashion alien to our own. There is no greater bar to that realizing of mythology[1] which is the first condition of its being understood, than our modern habit of clear analytic thought. The very terms we use are sharpened to an over nice discrimination. The first necessity is that by an effort of the sympathetic imagination we should think back the 'many' we have so sharply and strenuously divided, into the haze of the primitive 'one.'

Nor must we regard this haze of the early morning as a deleterious mental fog, as a sign of disorder, weakness, oscillation. It is not confusion or even synthesis; rather it is as it were a protoplasmic fulness and forcefulness not yet articulate into the diverse forms of its ultimate births. It may even happen, as in the case of the Olympian divinities, that articulation and discrimination sound the note of approaching decadence. As Maeterlinck[2] beautifully puts it, *la clarté parfaite n'est-elle pas d'ordinaire le signe de la lassitude des idées?*

There is a practical reason why it is necessary to bear in mind this primary fusion, though not confusion, of ideas. Theology, after articulating the one into the many and diverse, after a course of exclusive and determined discrimination, after differentiating a number of departmental gods and spirits, usually monotheizes, i.e. resumes the many into the one. Hence, as will be constantly seen, *mutatis mutandis*, a late philosophizing author is often of

[1] My position in this matter was stated long ago in an article in the *Journal of Hellenic Studies*, xx. 1899, pp. 211, 244.

[2] *Sagesse et Destinée*, p. 76.

great use in illustrating a primitive conception: the multiform divinity of an Orphic Hymn is nearer to the primitive mind than the clear-cut outlines of Homer's Olympians.

In our preliminary examination of Athenian festivals we found underlying the Diasia the worship of a snake, underlying the Anthesteria the revocation of souls. In the case of the Thesmophoria we found magical ceremonies for the promotion of fertility addressed as it would seem directly to the earth itself: in the Thargelia we had ceremonies of purification not primarily addressed to any one. In the Diasia and Anthesteria only was there clear evidence of some sort of definite being or beings as the object of worship. The meaning of snake-worship will come up for discussion later (p. 325), for the present we must confine ourselves to the theology or demonology of the beings worshipped in the Anthesteria, the Keres, sprites, or ghosts, and the theological shapes into which they are developed and discriminated.

The Ker as Ghost and Sprite.

That the Keres dealt with in the Anthesteria—'worshipped' is of course too modern a word—were primarily ghosts, admits, in the face of the evidence previously adduced (pp. 43, 44), of no doubt. That in the fifth century B.C. they were thought of as little winged sprites the vase-painting in fig. 7 clearly shows, and to it might be added the evidence of countless other Athenian white lekythi where the *eidolon* or ghost is shown fluttering about the grave. But to the ancients *Keres* was a word of far larger and vaguer connotation than our modern *ghosts*, and we must grasp this wider connotation if we would understand the later developments of the term.

Something of their nature has already appeared in the apotropaic precautions of the Anthesteria. Pitch was smeared on the doors to catch them, cathartic buckthorn was chewed to eject them; they were dreaded as sources of evil; they were, if not exactly evil spirits, certainly spirits that brought evil: else why these precautions? Plato has this in his mind when he says[1] 'There are

[1] *Legg.* XI. p. 937 D τοῖς πλείστοις αὐτῶν οἷον Κῆρες ἐπιπεφύκασιν, αἳ καταμιαίνουσί τε καὶ καταρρυπαίνουσιν αὐτά.

many fair things in the life of mortals, but in most of them there are as it were adherent Keres which pollute and disfigure them.' Here we have not merely a philosophical notion, that there is a soul of evil in things good, but the reminiscence surely of an actual popular faith, i.e. the belief that Keres, like a sort of personified bacilli, engendered corruption and pollution[1]. To such influences all things mortal are exposed. Conon[2] in telling the story of the miraculous head of Orpheus (p. 467) says that when it was found by the fisherman 'it was still singing, nor had it suffered any change from the sea nor any other of the outrages that human Keres inflict on the dead, but it was still blooming and bleeding with fresh blood.' Conon is of course a late writer, and full of borrowed poetical phrases, but the expression human Keres (*ἀνθρώπιναι κῆρες*) is not equivalent to the Destiny of man, it means rather sources of corruption inherent in man.

In fig. 7 we have seen a representation of the harmless Keres, the souls fluttering out of the grave-pithos. Fortunately ancient art has also left us a representation of a baleful Ker. The picture in fig. 16 is from a pelike[3] found at Thisbe and now in the Berlin Museum[4]. Herakles, known by his lion skin and quiver, swings his rudely hewn club (*κλάδος*) against a tiny winged figure with shrivelled body and distorted ugly face. We might have been at a loss to give a name to his feeble though repulsive

FIG. 16.

[1] I am indebted for this and many important references to the article on Keres by Dr Otto Crusius in Roscher's *Lexicon* (Bd. II. 1148). Dr Crusius' admirable exposition of the nature of the Keres suffers only from one defect, that he feels himself obliged to begin it with the comparatively late literary conceptions of Homer.

[2] Conon, *Narr.* XLV.

[3] Published and explained as Herakles *κηραμύντης* by Professor Furtwängler, *Jahrb. d. Inst.* 1895, p. 37.

[4] Berlin, *Inv.* 3317.

antagonist but for an Orphic Hymn to Herakles[1] which ends with the prayer:

> 'Come, blessed hero, come and bring allayments
> Of all diseases. Brandishing thy club,
> Drive forth the baleful fates; with poisoned shafts
> Banish the noisome Keres far away.'

The primitive Greek leapt by his religious imagination to a forecast of the truth that it has taken science centuries to establish, i.e. the fact that disease is caused by little live things, germs—bacilli we call them, he used the word Keres. A fragment of the early comic poet Sophron[2] speaks of Herakles throttling Hepiales. Hepiales must be the demon of nightmare, well known to us from other sources and under various confused names as Ephialtes, Epiales, Hepialos. The *Etymologicon Magnum*[3] explains 'Hepialos' as a shivering fever and 'a daimon that comes upon those that are asleep.' It has been proposed to regard the little winged figure which Herakles is clearly taking by the throat as Hepiales[4], demon of nightmare, rather than as a Ker. The question can scarcely be decided, but the doubt is as instructive as any certainty. Hepiales is a disease caused by a Ker; i.e. it is a special form of Ker, the nightmare bacillus. Blindness also was caused by a Ker, as was madness; hence the expression 'casting a black Ker on their eyes[5].' Blindness and madness, blindness of body and spirit[6] are scarcely distinguished, as in the blindness of Oedipus; both come of the Keres-Erinyes.

To the primitive mind all diseases are caused by, or rather *are*, bad spirits. Porphyry[7] tells us that blisters are caused by evil

[1] *Orph. Hymn.* xii.

> ἔλθε μάκαρ, νούσων θελκτήρια πάντα κομίζων·
> ἐξέλασον δὲ κακὰς ἄτας, κλάδον ἐν χερὶ πάλλων,
> πτηνοῖς τ' ἰοβόλοις κῆρας χαλεπὰς ἀπόπεμπε.

[2] Ahrens, No. 99 b, Ἡρακλῆς Ἡπιάλητα πνίγων.

[3] s.v. ῥιγοπύρετον.

[4] Roscher, *Lexicon* s.v. Nosoi p. 459, see also Roscher, Ephialtes, *Abhandl. d. K. Sächs. Ges.* Phil.-Hist. Kl. xx. 1900.

[5] Eur. *Phoen.* 950 μέλαιναν κῆρ' ἐπ' ὄμμασιν βαλών.

[6] Since I wrote the above much light has been thrown on the genesis of this primitive demonology by Mr F. M. Cornford in his *Thucydides Mythistoricus*, Chapter xiii.

[7] Wolff. Porphyr. *De philos. ex orac. haur.* p. 149 = Eusebius *Praep. Ev.* 4. 23. 3 καὶ γὰρ μάλιστα ταῖς ποιαῖς τροφαῖς χαίρουσι, σιτουμένων γὰρ ἡμῶν προσίασι καὶ προσιζάνουσι τῷ σώματι. καὶ διὰ τοῦτο αἱ ἁγνεῖαι, οὐ διὰ τοὺς θεοὺς προσηγουμένως ἀλλ' ἵν' οὗτοι ἀποστῶσι· μάλιστα δ' αἵματι χαίρουσι καὶ ταῖς ἀκαθαρσίαις καὶ ἀπολαύουσι τούτων, εἰσδύνοντες τοῖς χρωμένοις. The word προσηγουμένως does not so far as I know occur elsewhere, it seems from the context to mean 'inductively,' with a view to *induce* rather than expel.

spirits which come at us when we eat certain food and settle on our bodies. He goes to the very heart of ancient religious 'aversion' when he adds that it is on account of this that purifications are practised, *not in order that we may induce the presence of the gods, but that these wretched things may keep off.* He might have added, it is on account of these bad spirits that we fast; indeed ἁγνεία, the word he uses, means abstinence as well as purity. Eating is highly dangerous because you have your mouth open and a Ker may get in. If a Ker should get in when you are about to partake of specially holy food there will naturally be difficulties. So argues the savage. Porphyry being a vegetarian says that these bad spirits specially delight in blood and impurities generally and they 'creep into people who make use of such things.' If you kept about you holy plants with strong scents and purging properties, like rue and buckthorn, you might keep the Keres away, or, if they got in, might speedily and safely eject them.

The physical character of the Keres, their connection with 'the lusts of the flesh,' comes out very clearly in a quaint moralising poem preserved by Stobaeus and attributed to Linos. It deals with the dangers of Keres and the necessity for meeting them by 'purification.' Its ascetic tone and its attribution to Linos probably point to Orphic origin. It runs as follows[1]:

'Hearken to these my sayings, zealously lend me your hearing
To the simple truth about all things. Drive far away the disastrous
Keres, they who destroy the herd of the vulgar and fetter
All things around with curses manifold. Many and dreadful
Shapes do they take to deceive. But keep them far from thy spirit,
Ever watchful in mind. This is the purification
That shall rightly and truly purge thee to sanctification
(If but in truth thou hatest the baleful race of the Keres),
And most of all thy belly, the giver of all things shameful,
For desire is her charioteer and she drives with the driving of madness.'

It is commonly said that diseases are 'personified' by the Greeks. This is to invert the real order of primitive thought. It is not that a disease is realized as a power and then turned

[1] Stob. v. 22. *Λίνου.*
κῆρας ἀπωσάμενος πολυπήμονας αἵ τε βεβήλων
ὄχλον ἀνιστῶσαι ἄταις περὶ πάντα πεδῶσι
παντοίαις μορφῶν χαλεπῶν ἀπατήματ' ἔχουσαι
τὰς μὲν ἀπὸ ψυχῆς εἴργειν φυλακαῖσι νόοιο.
οὗτος γάρ σε καθαρμὸς ὄντως δικαίως †ὁσιεύσει†,
εἴ κεν ἀληθείῃ μισέεις ὀλοὸν γένος αὐτῶν,
νηδὺν μὲν πρώτιστ' αἰσχρῶν δώτειραν ἁπάντων
ἣν ἐπιθυμία ἡνιοχεῖ μαργοῖσι χαλινοῖς.

into a person, it is that primitive man seems unable to conceive of any force except as resulting from some person or being or sprite, something a little like himself. Such is the state of mind of the modern Greek peasant who writes *Χολέρα* with a capital letter. Hunger, pestilence, madness, nightmare have each a sprite behind them: *are* all sprites.

Of course, as Hesiod[1] knew, there were ancient golden days when these sprites were not let loose, when they were shut up safe in a *pithos* or large jar and

> 'Of old the tribes of mortal men on earth
> Lived without ills, aloof from grievous toil
> And catching plagues which Keres gave to men[2].'

But alas!

> 'The woman with her hands took the great lid
> From off the jar and scattered them, and thus
> Devised sad cares for mortals. Hope alone
> Remained therein, safe held beneath the rim,
> Nor flitted forth, for she thrust to the lid[3].'

Who the woman was and why she opened the jar will be considered later (p. 283); for the moment we have only to note what manner of things came out of it. The account is strange and significant. She shut the jar too late:

> 'For other myriad evils wandered forth
> To man, the earth was full, and full the sea.
> Diseases, that all round by day and night
> Bring ills to mortals, hovered, self-impelled,
> Silent, for Zeus the Counsellor their voice
> Had taken away[4].'

Proclus understands that these silent ghostly insidious things *are* Keres, though he partly modernizes them. He says in commenting on the passage, 'Hesiod gives them (i.e. the diseases) bodily form making them approach without sound, showing that even of these things spirits are the guardians, sending invisibly

[1] Hes. *Erg.* 90

> *πρὶν μὲν γὰρ ζώεσκον ἐπὶ χθονὶ φῦλ' ἀνθρώπων*
> *νόσφιν ἄτερ τε κακῶν καὶ ἄτερ χαλεποῖο πόνοιο*
> *νούσων τ' ἀργαλέων αἵτ' ἀνδράσι κῆρας ἔδωκαν.*

[2] I prefer to read: *ἅστ' ἀνδράσι κῆρες ἔδωκαν*, i.e. 'grievous diseases which Keres gave to men,' but I have translated the text as it stands, since possibly Hesiod, though he clearly knew of a connection between *νόσοι* and *κῆρες*, may have inverted cause and effect. I have already discussed the passage in the *Journal of Hellenic Studies*, xx. 1900, p. 104.

[3] Hes. *Erg.* 94. For Hope as an evil Ker, see Mr F. M. Cornford, *Thucydides Mythistoricus*, p. 224.

[4] Hes. *Erg.* 102. Procl. ad 102 *ἐσωματοποίησε δὲ αὐτὰς προσιούσας ἀφώνους ποιήσας ἐνδεικνύμενος ὅτι καὶ τούτων ἔφοροι δαίμονές εἰσιν· οἵτινες δρῶσιν ἀφανῶς ἐπιπέμποντες τὰς νόσους τὰς ὑπὸ τὴν Εἱμαρμένην τεταγμένας καὶ τὰς ἐν τῷ πίθῳ κῆρας διασπείροντες.*

the diseases decreed by fate and scattering the Keres in the jar.' After the manner of his day he thinks the Keres were presided over by spirits, that they were diseases sent by spirits, but primitive man believes the Keres *are* the spirits, *are* the diseases. Hesiod himself was probably not quite conscious that the jar or pithos was the great grave-jar of the Earth-mother Pandora (p. 286), and that the Keres were ghosts. 'Earth,' says Hesiod, 'was full and full the sea.' This crowd of Keres close-packed is oddly emphasized in a fragment by an anonymous poet[1]:

'Such is our mortal state, ill upon ill,
And round about us Keres crowding still;
No chink of opening
Is left for entering.'

This notion of the swarm of unknown unseen evils hovering about men haunts the lyric poets, lending a certain primitive reality to their vague mournful pessimism. Simonides of Amorgos[2] seems to echo Hesiod when he says 'hope feeds all men'—but hope is all in vain because of the imminent demon host that work for man's undoing, disease and death and war and shipwreck and suicide.

'No ill is lacking, Keres thousand-fold
Mortals attend, woes and calamities
That none may scape.'

Here and elsewhere to translate 'Keres' by fates is to make a premature abstraction. The Keres are still physical actual things not impersonations. So when Aeschylus[3] puts into the mouth of his Danaid women the prayer

'Nor may diseases, noisome swarm,
Settle upon our heads, to harm
Our citizens,'

the 'noisome swarm' is no mere 'poetical' figure but the reflection of a real primitive conviction of live pests.

The little fluttering insect-like diseases are naturally spoken of

[1] Frg. ap. Plut. *Consol. ad Apoll.* XXVI. *Τί οὖν; ἆρά γ' ἡμεῖς τοῦτο διὰ τοῦ λόγου μαθεῖν οὐ δυνάμεθα, οὐδ' ἐπιλογίσασθαι; ὅτι πλείη μὲν γαῖα κακῶν πλείη δὲ θάλασσα καὶ τοιάδε θνητοῖσι κακὰ κακῶν ἀμφί τε κῆρες εἰλεῦνται, κενεὴ δ' εἴσδυσις οὐδ' αἰθέρι.* Bergk (*Frg. adesp.* 2 B) points out that Plutarch's second quotation is an elegiac couplet, and for the MS. *αἰθέρι* reads *'Αΐδεω*. This gives no satisfactory sense. Mr Gilbert Murray reads *ἀθέρι* a conjecture made certain by a passage in the dialogue 'Theophrastos' (p. 399 E) by Aeneas of Gaza, *πλήρης δὲ καὶ ἡ γῆ καὶ ἡ θάλασσα καὶ τὰ ὑπὸ γῆν πάντα· καὶ ὡς ἔφη τις τῶν παρ' ἡμῖν σοφῶν κενὸν οὐδὲν οὐδ' ὅσον ἀθέρα καὶ τρίχα βαλεῖν.*

[2] Simon. Amorg. I. 20.

[3] Aesch. *Suppl.* 684.

for the most part in the plural, but in the *Philoctetes* of Sophocles[1] the festering sore of the hero is called 'an ancient Ker'; here again the usage is primitive rather than poetical. Viewing the Keres 'as little inherent physical pests,' we are not surprised to learn from Theognis[2] that

> 'For hapless man wine doth two Keres hold—
> Limb-slacking Thirst, Drunkenness overbold.'

Nor is it man alone who is beset by these evil sprites. In that storehouse of ancient superstition, the Orphic *Lithica*[3], we hear of Keres who attack the fields. Against them the best remedy is the Lychnis stone, which was also good to keep off a hailstorm.

> 'Lychnis, from pelting hail be thou our shield,
> Keep off the Keres who attack each field.'

And Theophrastus[4] tells us that each locality has its own Keres dangerous to plants, some coming from the ground, some from the air, some from both. Fire, also, it would seem, might be infested by Keres. A commentator on Philo says that it is important that no profane fire, i.e. such as is in ordinary use, should touch an altar because it may be contaminated by myriads of Keres[5]. Instructive too is the statement of Stesichorus[6], who according to tradition 'called the Keres by the name Telchines.' Eustathius in quoting the statement of Stesichorus adds as explanatory of Keres *τὰς σκοτώσεις*: the word *σκοτώσεις* is late and probably a gloss, it means darkening, killing, eclipse physical and spiritual. Leaving the gloss aside, the association of Keres with Telchines is of capital interest and takes us straight back into the world of ancient magic. The Telchines were the typical magicians of antiquity, and Strabo[7] tells us that one of their magic arts was

[1] Soph. *Phil.* 4.

[2] Theog. 837.

[3] Orph. *Lith.* 268 *Λύχνι, σὺ δ' ἐκ πεδίου ῥόθιόν τ' ἀπόεργε χάλαζαν*
ἡμετέρου καὶ κῆρας ὅσαι στιχόωσιν ἐπ' ἀγρούς.

[4] Theophr. *De caus. pl.* 5. 10. 4 *ἕκαστοι τῶν τόπων ἰδίας ἔχει κῆρας, οἱ μὲν ἐκ τοῦ ἐδάφους οἱ δ' ἐκ τοῦ ἀέρος οἱ δ' ἐξ ἀμφοῖν.*

[5] *ὅπως μὴ προσάψαιτο τοῦ βωμοῦ διὰ τὸ μυρίας ἴσως ἀναμεμάχθαι κῆρας.* This reference to Budaeus's commentary on Philo *Vita Mosis* I borrow from the Thesaurus of Stephanos. In connection with fire and fire-places the belief in Keres is not dead to-day. An Irish servant of mine who failed to light a fire firmly declined to make a second attempt on the ground that she knew 'there was a little fairy in the grate.' The Ker in this case was, as often in antiquity, a malign draught.

[6] Frg. ap. Eustath. 772. 3.

[7] XIV. 2. 652.

to 'besprinkle animals and plants with the water of Styx and sulphur mixed with it, with a view to destroy them.'

Thus the Keres, from being merely bad influences inherent and almost automatic, became exalted and personified into actual magicians. Eustathius in the passage where he quotes Stesichorus allows us to see how this happened. He is commenting on the ancient tribe of the Kouretes: these Kouretes, he says, were Cretan and also called Thelgines (*sic*), and they were sorcerers and magicians. 'Of these there were two sorts: one sort craftsmen and skilled in handiwork, the other sort pernicious to all good things; these last were of fierce nature and were fabled to be the origins of squalls of wind, and they had a cup in which they used to brew magic potions from roots. They (i.e. the former sort) invented statuary and discovered metals, and they were amphibious and of strange varieties of shape, some were like demons, some like men, some like fishes, some like serpents; and the story went that some had no hands, some no feet, and some had webs between their fingers like geese. And they say that they were blue-eyed and black-tailed.' Finally comes the significant statement that *they perished struck down by the thunder of Zeus or by the arrows of Apollo.* The old order is slain by the new. To the imagination of the conqueror the conquered are at once barbarians and magicians, monstrous and magical, hated and feared, craftsmen and medicine men, demons, beings endowed like the spirits they worship, in a word Keres-Telchines[1]. When we find the good, fruitful, beneficent side of the Keres effaced and ignored we must always remember this fact that we see them through the medium of a conquering civilization[2].

The Keres of Old Age and Death.

By fair means or foul, by such ritual procedures as have already been noted, by the chewing of buckthorn, the sounding of brass,

[1] Professor Ridgeway, *Early Age of Greece*, I. p. 177.

[2] As evidence of the evil reputation of Keres Mr Gilbert Murray calls my attention to the pun in Eur. *Tro.* 424 which seems to have escaped the attention of commentators:

τί ποτ' ἔχουσι τοὔνομα;
κήρυκες, ἓν ἀπέχθημα πάγκοινον βροτοῖς.

'What name have they? A *Ker*ish name.' Hermes as κῆρυξ invokes and revokes κῆρες with his κηρυκεῖον, see pp. 26 and 43.

the making of comic figures, most of the Keres could be kept at bay; but there were two who waited relentless, who might not be averted, and these were Old Age and Death. It is the thought that these two Keres are waiting that with the lyric poets most of all overshadows the brightness of life. Theognis[1] prays to Zeus:

'Keep far the evil Keres, me defend
From Old Age wasting, and from Death the end.'

These haunting Keres of disease, disaster, old age and death Mimnermus[2] can never forget:

'We blossom like the leaves that come in spring,
What time the sun begins to flame and glow,
And in the brief span of youth's gladdening
Nor good nor evil from the gods we know,
But always at the goal black Keres stand
Holding, one grievous Age, one Death within her hand.

And all the fruit of youth wastes, as the Sun
Wastes and is spent in sunbeams, and to die
Not live is best, for evils many a one
Are born within the soul. And Poverty
Has wasted one man's house with niggard care,
And one has lost his children. Desolate
Of this his earthly longing, he must fare
To Hades. And another for his fate
Has sickness sore that eats his soul. No man
Is there but Zeus hath cursed with many a ban.'

Here is the same dismal primitive faith, or rather fear. All things are beset by Keres, and Keres are all evil. The verses of Mimnermus are of interest at this point because they show the emergence of the two most dreaded Keres, Old Age and Death, from the swarm of minor ills. Poverty, disease and desolation are no longer definitely figured as Keres.

The vase-painter shows this fact in a cruder form. On a red-figured amphora (fig. 17) in the Louvre[3] Herakles is represented lifting his club to slay a shrivelled ugly little figure leaning on a stick—the figure obviously is an old man. Fortunately it is inscribed *γῆρας*. It is not an old man, but Old Age itself, the dreaded Ker. The representation is a close parallel to Herakles slaying the Ker in fig. 16. The Ker of Old Age has no wings: these the vase-painter rightly felt were inappropriate. It is in fact a Ker developed one step further into an impersonation. The vase may be safely dated as belonging to about the middle of the 5th century B.C. It is analogous in style, as in subject,

[1] Theog. 707.
[2] Mimnermus, 2.
[3] Pottier, *Cat.* 343. P. Hartung, *Philologos*, L. (N. F. IV. 2) Taf. I.

to an amphora[1] in the British Museum bearing the love-name Charmides.

Gradually the meanings of Ker became narrowed down to one, to the great evil, death and the fate of death, but always with a

FIG. 17.

flitting remembrance that there were Keres of all mortal things. This is the usage most familiar to us, because it is Homeric. Homer's phraseology is rarely primitive—often fossilized—and the regularly recurring 'Ker of death[2]' (*κὴρ θανάτοιο*) is heir to a long ancestry. In Homer we catch the word Ker at a moment of transition; it is half death, half death-spirit. Odysseus[3] says

'Death and the Ker avoiding, we escape,'

where the two words death and Ker are all but equivalents: they are both death and the sprite of death, or as we might say

[1] *Cat.* E 290. Cecil Smith, *J.H.S.* 1883, Pl. XXX. p. 96.
[2] *Od.* XI. 398 *Τίς νύ σε κὴρ ἐδάμασσε τανηλεγέος θανάτοιο.*
[3] *Od.* XII. 158 *Ἤ κεν ἀλευάμενοι θάνατον καὶ κῆρα φύγωμεν.*

now-a-days death and the angel of death. Homer's conception so dominates our minds that the custom has obtained of uniformly translating 'Ker' by fate, a custom that has led to much confusion of thought.

Two things with respect to Homer's usage must be borne in mind. First, his use of the word Ker is, as might be expected, far more abstract and literary than the usage we have already noted. It is impossible to say that Homer has in his mind anything of the nature of a tiny winged bacillus. Second, in Homer Ker is almost always defined and limited by the genitive *θανάτοιο,* and this looks as though, behind the expression, there lay the half-conscious knowledge that there were Keres of other things than death. Ker itself is *not* death, but the two have become well-nigh inseparable.

Some notion of the double nature, good and bad, of Keres seems to survive in the expression two-fold Keres (*διχθάδιαι* Κῆρες). Achilles[1] says:

> 'My goddess-mother silver-footed Thetis
> Hath said that Keres two-fold bear me on
> To the term of death.'

It is true that both the Keres are carrying him deathward, but there is strongly present the idea of the diversity of fates. The English language has in such cases absolutely no equivalent for Ker, because it has no word weighted with the like associations.

In one passage only in the *Iliad*[2], i.e. the description of the shield of Achilles, does a Ker actually appear in person, on the battlefield:

> 'And in the thick of battle there was Strife
> And Clamour, and there too the baleful Ker.
> She grasped one man alive, with bleeding wound,
> Another still unwounded, and one dead
> She by his feet dragged through the throng. And red
> Her raiment on her shoulders with men's blood.'

A work of art, it must be remembered, is being described, and the feeling is more Hesiodic than Homeric. The Ker is in this case not a fate but a horrible she-demon of slaughter.

[1] *Il.* IX. 410.

[2] *Il.* XVIII. 535.

THE KER AS HARPY AND WIND-DEMON.

In Homer the Keres are no doubt mainly death-spirits, but they have another function, they actually *carry off* the souls to Hades. Odysseus says[1]:

> 'Howbeit him Death-Keres carried off
> To Hades' house.'

It is impossible here to translate Keres by 'fates,' the word is too abstract: the Keres are *πρόσπολοι*, angels, messengers, death-demons, souls that carry off souls.

The idea that underlies this constantly recurring formulary, *κῆρες ἔβαν θανάτοιο φέρουσαι*, emerges clearly when we come to consider those analogous apparitions, the Harpies. The Harpies betray their nature clearly in their name, in its uncontracted form ''Αρεπυία,' which appears on the vase-painting in fig. 18; they are the Snatchers, winged women-demons, hurrying along like the storm wind and carrying all things to destruction. The vase-painting in fig. 18 from a large black-figured vessel in the Berlin

FIG. 18.

Museum[2] is specially instructive because, though the winged demons are inscribed as Harpies, the scene of which they form

[1] *Od.* XIV. 207.

[2] *Cat.* 1682, *Arch. Zeit.* 1882, Pl. 9.

part, i.e. the slaying of Medusa, clearly shows that they are Gorgons; so near akin, so shifting and intermingled are the two conceptions. On another vase (fig. 19), also in the Berlin Museum[1],

Fig. 19.

we see an actual Gorgon with the typical Gorgon's head and protruding tongue performing the function of a Harpy, i.e. of a Snatcher. We say 'an actual Gorgon,' but it is not a Gorgon of the usual form but a bird-woman with a Gorgon's head. The bird-woman is currently and rightly associated with the Siren, a creature to be discussed later (p. 197), a creature malign though seductive in Homer, but gradually softened by the Athenian imagination into a sorrowful death angel.

Fig. 20.

The tender bird-women of the so-called 'Harpy tomb' from Lycia (fig. 20), now in the British Museum, perform the functions of a Harpy, but very gently. They are at least near akin to the sorrowing Sirens on Athenian tombs. We can scarcely call them

[1] *Cat.* 2157, *Jahrbuch d. Arch. Inst.* I. p. 210.

by the harsh name of the 'Snatchers.' And yet, standing as it did in Lycia, this 'Harpy tomb' may be the outcome of the same stratum of mythological conceptions as the familiar story of the daughters of the Lycian Pandareos. Penelope[1] in her desolation cries aloud:

'Would that the storm might snatch me adown its dusky way
And cast me forth where Ocean is outpour'd with ebbing spray,
As when Pandareos' daughters the storm winds bore away,'

and then, harking back, she tells the ancient Lycian story of the fair nurture of the princesses, and how Aphrodite went to high Olympus to plan for them a goodly marriage. But whom the gods love die young:

'Meantime the Harpies snatched away the maids, and gave them o'er
To the hateful ones, the Erinyes, to serve them evermore[2].'

Early death was figured by the primitive Greek as a snatching away by evil death-demons, storm-ghosts. These snatchers he called Harpies, the modern Greek calls them Nereids. In Homer's lines we seem to catch the winds as snatchers, half-way to their full impersonation as Harpies. To give them a capital letter is to crystallize their personality prematurely. Even when they become fully persons, their name carried to the Greek its adjectival sense now partly lost to us.

Another function of the Harpies links them very closely with the Keres, and shows in odd and instructive fashion the animistic habit of ancient thought. The Harpies not only snatch away souls to death but they give life, bringing things to birth. A Harpy was the mother by Zephyros of the horses of Achilles[3]. Both parents are in a sense winds, only the Harpy wind halts between horse and woman. By winds as Vergil tells us mares became pregnant[4].

[1] *Od.* xx. 66

ἢ ἔπειτά μ' ἀναρπάξασα θύελλα
οἴχοιτο προφέρουσα κατ' ἠερόεντα κέλευθα
ἐν προχοῇς δὲ βάλοι ἀψορρόου Ὠκεανοῖο,
ὡς δ' ὅτε Πανδαρέου κούρας ἀνέλοντο θύελλαι.

[2] *Od.* xx. 77

τόφρα δὲ τὰς κούρας ἅρπυιαι ἀνηρείψαντο
καί ῥ' ἔδοσαν στυγερῇσιν ἐρινύσιν ἀμφιπολεύειν.

[3] *Iliad* XVI. 150.

[4] *Georg.* III. 274

saepe sine ullis
conjugiis vento gravidae, mirabile dictu.

As such a Harpy, half horse, half Gorgon-woman, Medusa is represented on a curious Boeotian vase (fig. 21) of very archaic

Fig. 21.

style now in the Louvre[1]. The representation is instructive, it shows how in art as in literature the types of Gorgon and Harpy were for a time in flux; a particular artist could please his own fancy. The horse Medusa was apparently not a success, for she did not survive.

It is easy enough to see how winds were conceived of as Snatchers, death-demons, but why should they impregnate, give life? It is not, I think, by a mere figure of speech that breezes (*πνοιαί*) are spoken of as 'life-begetting' (*ζωογόνοι*) and 'soul-rearing' (*ψυχοτρόφοι*). It is not because they are in our sense life-giving and refreshing as well as destructive: the truth lies deeper down. Only life can give life, only a soul gives birth to a soul; the winds *are* souls as well as breaths (*πνεύματα*). Here as so often we get at the real truth through an ancient Athenian cultus practice. When an Athenian was about to be married he prayed and sacrificed, Suidas tells us, to the Tritopatores. The statement is quoted from Phanodemus who wrote a book on *Attic Matters*[2].

[1] *Bull. de Corr. Hell.* xxii. 1898, Pl. v.

[2] Suidas s.v. Tritopatores. *Φανόδημος δὲ ἐν ἕκτῳ φησὶν ὅτι μόνοι Ἀθηναῖοι θύουσί τε καὶ εὔχονται αὐτοῖς ὑπὲρ γενέσεως παίδων ὅταν γαμεῖν μέλλωσιν. ἐν δὲ τῷ Ὀρφέως Φυσικῷ......ὀνομάζεσθαι τοὺς Τριτοπάτορας Ἀμαλκείδην καὶ Πρωτοκλέα καὶ Πρωτοκλέοντα θυρωροὺς καὶ φύλακας εἶναι τῶν ἀνέμων* ut supra *Δήμων ἐν τῇ Ἀτθίδι φησὶν ἀνέμους εἶναι τοὺς Τριτοπάτορας· Φιλόχορος δὲ τοὺς Τριτοπάτρεις πάντων γεγονέναι πρώτους. τὴν μὲν γὰρ γῆν καὶ τὸν ἥλιον, φησίν......γονεῖς αὐτῶν ἠπίσταντο οἱ τότε ἄνθρωποι τοὺς δὲ ἐκ τούτων τρίτους πατέρας.*

Suidas tells us also who the Tritopatores were. They were, as we might guess from their name, fathers in the third degree, forefathers, ancestors, ghosts, and Dêmon in his *Atthis* said they were winds. To the winds, it has already been seen (p. 67), are offered such expiatory sacrifices (*σφάγια*) as are due to the spirits of the underworld. The idea that the Tritopatores were winds as well as ghosts was never lost. To Photius and Suidas they are 'lords of the winds' and the Orphics make them 'gate-keepers and guardians of the winds.' From ghosts of dead men, Hippocrates[1] tells us, came nurture and growth and seeds, and the author of the *Geoponica*[2] says that winds give life not only to plants but to all things. It was natural enough that the winds should be divided into demons beneficent and maleficent, as it depends where you live whether a wind from a particular quarter will do you good or ill.

In the black-figured vase-painting in fig. 22, found at Naukratis and now in the British Museum[3], a local nymph is depicted: only

FIG. 22.

the lower part of her figure is left us, drapery, the ends of her long

[1] Hipp. Περὶ ἐνυπν. II. p. 14 *ἀπὸ γὰρ τῶν ἀποθανόντων αἱ τροφαὶ καὶ αὐξήσεις καὶ σπέρματα.*

[2] *Geop.* IX. 3 *οὐ τὰ φιτὰ μόνον ἀλλὰ καὶ πάντα ζωογονοῦσι.*

[3] *Cat.* B 4.

hair and her feet, but she must be the nymph Cyrene beloved of Apollo, for close to her and probably held in her hand is a great branch of the silphium plant. To the right of her, approaching to minister or to worship, are winged genii. It is the very image of *θεραπεία*, tendance, ministration, fostering care, worship, all in one. The genii tend the nymph who *is* the land itself, her and her products. The figures to the right are bearded: they can scarcely be other than the spirits of the North wind, the Boreadae, the cool healthful wind that comes over the sea to sun-burnt Africa. If these be Boreadae, the opposing figures, beardless and therefore almost certainly female, are Harpies, demons of the South wind, to Africa the wind coming across the desert and bringing heat and blight and pestilence[1].

It might be bold to assert so much, but for the existence of another representation on a situla from Daphnae (fig. 23), also, happily for comparison, in the British Museum[2]. On the one side, not figured here, is a winged bearded figure ending in a snake, probably Boreas: such a snake-tailed Boreas was seen by Pausanias[3] on the chest of Cypselus in the act of seizing Oreithyia. There is nothing harsh in the snake tail for Boreas, for the winds, as has already been noted (p. 68), were regarded as earth-born. Behind Boreas is a plant in blossom rising from the ground, a symbol of the vegetation nourished by the North wind. On the reverse (fig. 24) is a winged figure closely like the left hand genii of the Cyrene cylix, and this figure drives in front of it destructive creatures, a locust, the pest of the South, two birds of prey attacking a hare, and a third that is obviously a vulture. The two representations taken together justify us in regarding the left hand genii as destructive. Taking these two representations together with a third vase-painting, the celebrated Phineus cylix[4], we are further justified in calling these destructive wind-demons Harpies. On this vase[5] the Boreadae, Zetes and Kalais, show their true antagonism. The Harpies have

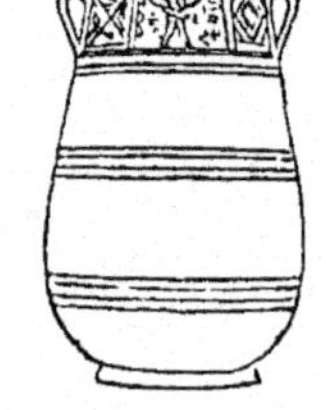

Fig. 23.

[1] The full interpretation of the Cyrene vase is due to Mr Cecil Smith, *Journal of Hellenic Studies*, p. 103, 'Harpies in Greek Art.' The vase is reproduced and discussed, but only with partial success, by Dr Studniczka in his *Kyrene*, p. 18.

[2] *Cat.* B 104.

[3] P. v. 19. 1 *Βορέας ἐστὶν ἡρπακὼς Ὠρείθυιαν, οὐραὶ δὲ ὄφεων ἀντὶ ποδῶν εἰσὶν αὐτῷ.*

[4] Würzburg, no. 354.

[5] Reproduced later, fig. 46.

fouled the food of Phineus like the pestilential winds they were, and the clean clear sons of the North wind give chase. It is

Fig. 24.

seldom that ancient art has preserved for us so clear a picture of the duality of things.

On black-figured vase-paintings little winged figures occur not unfrequently to which it is by no means easy to give a name. In

Fig. 25.

fig. 25 we have such a representation[1]—Europa seated on the bull passes in rapid flight over the sea, which is indicated by fishes and

[1] Cecil Smith, *J.H.S.* XIII. p. 112, fig. 2.

dolphins. In front of her flies a vulture-like bird, behind comes a winged figure holding two wreaths. Is she Nike, bringing good success to the lover? is she a favouring wind speeding the flight? I incline to think the vase-painter did not clearly discriminate. She is a sort of good Ker, a fostering favouring influence. In all these cases of early genii it is important to bear in mind that the sharp distinction between moral and physical influence, so natural to the modern mind, is not yet established.

We return to the Keres from which the wind demons sprang.

The Ker as Fate.

One Homeric instance of the use of Ker remains to be examined. When Achilles[1] had the fourth time chased Hector round the walls of Troy, Zeus was wearied and

> 'Hung up his golden scales and in them set
> Twain Keres, fates of death that lays men low.'

This weighing of Keres, this 'Kerostasia,' is a weighing of death fates, but it is interesting to find that it reappears under another name, i.e. the 'Psychostasia,' the weighing of souls. We know from Plutarch[2] that Aeschylus wrote a play with this title. The subject was the weighing of the souls or lives not of Hector and Achilles, but Achilles and Memnon. This is certain because, Plutarch says, he placed at either side of the scales the mothers Thetis and Eos praying for their sons. Pollux[3] adds that Zeus and his attendants were suspended from a crane. In the scene of the Kerostasia as given by Quintus Smyrnaeus[4], a scene which probably goes back to the earlier tradition of 'Arctinos,' it is noticeable that Memnon the loser has a swarthy Ker while Achilles the winner has a bright cheerful one, a fact which seems to anticipate the white and black Erinyes.

The scene of the Psychostasia or Kerostasia, as it is variously called, appears on several vase-paintings, one of which from the

[1] *Il.* XXII. 208. [2] Plut. *Moral.* p. 17 a. [3] Poll. *Onomast.* IV. 130.

[4] *Post-Hom.* II. 509

> *δοιαὶ ἄρ' ἀμφοτέροισι θεῶν ἑκάτερθε παρέσταν*
> Κῆρες· *ἐρεμναίη μὲν ἔβη ποτὶ Μέμνονος ἦτορ*
> *φαιδρὴ δ' ἀμφ' Ἀχιλῆα δαΐφρονα.*

Mr T. R. Glover, in the chapter on Quintus Smyrnaeus in his *Life and Letters in the Fourth Century*, points out that the Keres in the poem of Quintus have developed a supremacy unknown to Homer, they are *ἄφυκτοι*—even the gods cannot check them. They are by-forms of Aisa and Moira.

British Museum[1] is reproduced in fig. 26. Hermes holds the scales, in either scale is the Ker or *eidolon* of one of the combatants; the lekythos is black-figured, and is our earliest source for the Kerostasia. The Keres or ψυχαί are represented as miniature men, it is the *lives* rather than the fates that are weighed. So the notion shifts.

Fig. 26.

In Hesiod, as has already been noted (p. 169), the Keres are more primitive and actual, they are in a sense fates, but they are also little winged spirits. But Hesiod is Homer-ridden, so we get the 'black Ker,' own sister to Thanatos and hateful Moros (Doom) and Sleep and the tribes of Dreams[2]. We get also[3] the dawnings of an Erinys, of an *avenging* fate, though the lines look like an interpolation:

> 'Night bore
> The Avengers and the Keres pitiless.'

Hesiod goes on to give the names usually associated with the Fates, Klotho, Lachesis, Atropos, and says they

> 'To mortals at their birth
> Give good and evil both.'

Whether interpolated or not the passage is significant both because it gives to the Keres the functions Homer allotted to the Erinyes, and also because with a reminiscence of earlier thought it makes them the source of good and of evil. It is probably this last idea that is at the back of the curious Hesiodic epithet Κηριτρεφής, which occurs in the *Works and Days*[4]:

> 'Then, when the dog-star comes and shines by day
> For a brief space over the heads of men
> Ker-nourished.'

[1] *Cat.* B 639; Murray, *Hist. of Greek Sculpture*, vol. II. p. 28. Dr Murray cites this vase as an instance of primitive perspective. Hermes, depicted in an impossible position, actually between the two advancing combatants, is thought of as in the background.

[2] Hes. *Theog.* 211.

[3] *Theog.* 217 ff.

[4] Hes. *Erg.* 416. The only other passage in which this difficult word occurs is in one of the oracles collected in the συναγωγή of Mnaseas (3rd cent. B.C.) and preserved for us by the scholiast on the *Phoenissae* of Euripides (ad *v.* 638,

'Men nourished for death' assuredly is not the meaning; the idea seems to be that each man has a Ker within him, a thing that nourishes him, keeps him alive, a sort of fate as it were on which his life depends. The epithet might come to signify something like *mortal*, subject to, depending on fate. If this be the meaning it looks back to an early stage of things when the Ker had not been specialized down to death and was not wholly 'black,' when it was more a man's luck than his fate, a sort of embryo Genius.

Κηριτρεφής, Ker-nourished, would then be the antithesis of Κηρίφατος 'slain by Keres,' which Hesychius[1] explains as those who died of disease; and would look back to a primitive doubleness of functions when the Keres were demons of all work. In vague and fitful fashion they begin where the Semnae magnificently end, as Moirae with control over all human weal and woe.

> 'These for their guerdon hold dominion
> O'er all things mortal[2].'

In such returning cycles runs the wheel of theology.

But the black side of things is always, it would seem, most impressive to primitive man. Given that the Ker was a fate of death, almost a personified death, it was fitting and natural that it should be tricked out with ever increasing horrors. Hesiod, or the writer of the *Shield*, with his rude peasant imagination was ready for the task. The Keres of Pandora's jar are purely primitive, and quite natural, not thought out at all: the Keres of the *Shield* are a literary effort and much too horrid to be frightening. Behind the crowd of old men praying with uplifted hands for their fighting children stood

> 'The blue-black Keres, grinding their white teeth,
> Glaring and grim, bloody, insatiable;
> They strive round those that fall, greedy to drink
> Black blood, and whomsoever first they found
> Low lying with fresh wounds, about his flesh
> A Ker would lay long claws, and his soul pass
> To Hades and chill gloom of Tartarus[3].'

Müller *F.H.G.* 3, p. 157) where Kadmos is told to go on 'till he comes to the herds of the Ker-nourished Pelagon' (κηριτρεφέος Πελάγοντος). Here it looks as if the epithet indicated prosperity, the man nourished and favoured and cherished by the Keres, see Roscher, *Lexicon*, s.v. Kadmos, p. 834, and s.v. Keres, p. 1139, but it is possible that, as suggested to me by Mr Cornford, the word may have been coined by Hesiod in bitter parody of the Homeric Διοτρεφής. The notion of the evil wasting action of Keres comes out in the word κηραίνω, as in Eur. *Hipp.* 223 τί ποτ', ὦ τέκνον, τάδε κηραίνεις, and more physically in Aesch. *Supp.* 999 θῆρες δὲ κηραίνουσι.

[1] Hesych. s.v. ὅσοι νόσῳ τεθνήκασιν.

[2] Aesch. *Eum.* 930.

[3] Hes. *Scut.* 249.

Pausanias[1] in his description of the chest of Cypselus tells of the figure of a Ker which is thoroughly Hesiodic in character. The scene is the combat between Eteokles and Polyneikes; Polyneikes has fallen on his knees and Eteokles is rushing at him. 'Behind Polyneikes is a woman-figure with teeth, as cruel as a wild beast's, and her finger-nails are hooked. An inscription near her says that she is a Ker, as though Polyneikes were carried off by Fate, and as though the end of Eteokles were in accordance with justice.' Pausanias regards the word Ker as the equivalent of Fate, but we must not impose a conception so abstract on the primitive artist who decorated the chest.

We are very far from the little fluttering ghosts, the winged bacilli, but there is a touch of kinship with those other ghosts who in the Nekuia draw nigh to drink the black blood (p. 75), and—a forecast of the Erinyes—the 'blue-black[2]' Keres are near akin to the horrid Hades demon painted by Polygnotus on the walls of the Lesche at Delphi. Pausanias[3] says, 'Above the figures I have mentioned (i.e. the sacrilegious man, etc.) is Eurynomos; the guides of Delphi say that Eurynomos is one of the demons in Hades, and that he gnaws the flesh of the dead bodies, leaving only the bones. Homer's poem about Odysseus, and those called the *Minyas* and the *Nostoi*, though they all make mention of Hades and its terrors, know no demon Eurynomos. I will therefore say this much, I will describe what sort of a person Eurynomos is and in what fashion he appears in the painting. The colour is blue-black (*κυανοῦ τὴν χρόαν μεταξύ ἐστι καὶ μέλανος*) like the colour of the flies that settle on meat; he is showing his teeth and is seated on the skin of a vulture.' The Keres of the *Shield* are human vultures; Eurynomos is the sarcophagus incarnate, the great carnivorous vulture of the underworld, the flesh-eater grotesquely translated to a world of shadows. He rightly sits upon a vulture's skin. Such figures, Pausanias truly observes, are foreign to the urbane Epic. But rude primitive man, when

[1] P. v. 19. 6 *τοῦ Πολυνείκους δὲ ὄπισθεν ἕστηκεν ὀδόντας τε ἔχουσα οὐδὲν ἡμερωτέρους θηρίου καὶ οἱ καὶ τῶν χειρῶν εἰσὶν ἐπικαμπεῖς οἱ ὄνυχες· ἐπίγραμμα δὲ ἐπ' αὐτῇ εἶναί φησι Κῆρα, ὡς τὸν μὲν ὑπὸ τοῦ Πεπρωμένου τὸν Πολυνείκην ἀπαχθέντα, 'Ετεοκλεῖ δὲ γενομένης καὶ σὺν τῷ δικαίῳ τῆς τελευτῆς.*

[2] Blue-black, *κυάνεος*, remained the traditional colour of the underworld, as in the *Alcestis* of Euripides (*v.* 262):

ὑπ' ὀφρύσι κυαναυγέσι
βλέπων πτερωτός—†αἴδας†.

[3] P. x. 28. 4.

he sees a skeleton, asks who ate the flesh; the answer is 'a Ker.' We are in the region of mere rude bogeydom, the land of Gorgo, Empusa, Lamia and Sphinx, and, strange though it may seem, of Siren.

To examine severally each of these bogey forms would lead too far afield, but the development of the types of Gorgon, Siren and Sphinx both in art and literature is so instructive that at the risk of digression each of these forms must be examined somewhat in detail.

The Ker as Gorgon.

The Gorgons are to the modern mind three sisters of whom one, most evil of the three, Medusa, was slain by Perseus, and her lovely terrible face had power to turn men into stone.

The triple form is not primitive, it is merely an instance of a general tendency, to be discussed later—a tendency which makes of each woman-goddess a trinity, which has given us the Horae, the Charites, the Semnae, and a host of other triple groups. It is immediately obvious that the triple Gorgons are not really three but one + two. The two unslain sisters are mere superfluous appendages due to convention; the real Gorgon is Medusa. It is equally apparent that in her essence Medusa is a head and nothing more; her potency only begins when her head is severed, and that potency resides in the head; she is in a word a mask with a body later appended. The primitive Greek knew that there was in his ritual a horrid thing called a Gorgoneion, a grinning mask with glaring eyes and protruding beast-like tusks and pendent tongue. How did this Gorgoneion come to be? A hero had slain a beast called the Gorgon, and this was its head. Though many other associations gathered round it, the basis of the Gorgoneion is a cultus object, a ritual mask misunderstood. The ritual object comes first; then the monster is begotten to account for it; then the hero is supplied to account for the slaying of the monster.

Ritual masks are part of the appliances of most primitive cults. They are the natural agents of a religion of fear and 'riddance.' Most anthropological museums[1] contain specimens

[1] Admirable specimens of savage dancing-masks with Medusa-like tongue and tusks are exhibited in the Berlin Museum für Völkerkunde.

of 'Gorgoneia' still in use among savages, Gorgoneia which are veritable Medusa heads in every detail, glaring eyes, pendent tongue, protruding tusks. The function of such masks is permanently to 'make an ugly face,' *at* you if you are doing wrong, breaking your word, robbing your neighbour, meeting him in battle; *for* you if you are doing right.

Scattered notices show us that masks and faces were part of the apparatus of a religion of terror among the Greeks. There was, we learn from the lexicographers[1], a goddess Praxidike, Exactress of Vengeance, whose images were heads only, and her sacrifices the like. By the time of Pausanias[2] this head or mask goddess had, like the Erinys, taken on a multiple, probably a triple form. At Haliartos in Boeotia he saw in the open air 'a sanctuary of the goddesses whom they call Praxidikae. Here the Haliartans swear, but the oath is not one that they take lightly.' In like manner at ancient Pheneus, there was a thing called the Petroma[3] which contained a mask of Demeter with the surname of Kidaria: by this Petroma most of the people of Pheneus swore on the most important matters. If the mask like its covering were of stone, such a stone-mask may well have helped out the legend of Medusa. The mask enclosed in the Petroma was the vehicle of the goddess: the priest put it on when he performed the ceremony of smiting the Underground Folk with rods.

The use of masks in regular ritual was probably a rare survival, and would persist only in remote regions, but the common people were slow to lose their faith in the apotropaic virtue of an 'ugly face.' Fire was a natural terror to primitive man and all operations of baking beset by possible Keres. Therefore on his ovens he thought it well to set a Gorgon mask. In fig. 27, a portable oven now in the museum at Athens[4], the mask is outside guarding the entrance. In fig. 28 the upper part of a similar oven is shown, and inside, where the fire flames up, are set three masks. These ovens are not very early, but they are essentially primitive. The face need not be of the type we call a Gorgon. In fig. 29 we have a Satyr type, bearded, with stark upstanding ears and hair, the

[1] Hesych. s.v., Photius s.v.

[2] P. VIII. 15. 3, see Dr Frazer ad loc.

[3] P. VIII. 15. 3.

[4] For these ovens see Conze, 'Griechische Kohlenbecken,' *Jahrbuch d. Inst.*, 1890, Taf. I. and II., and Furtwängler, *op. cit.* 1891, p. 110.

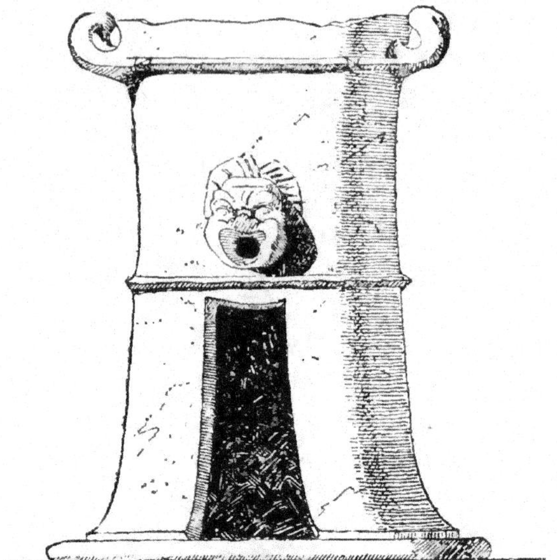

Fig. 27.

Fig. 28.

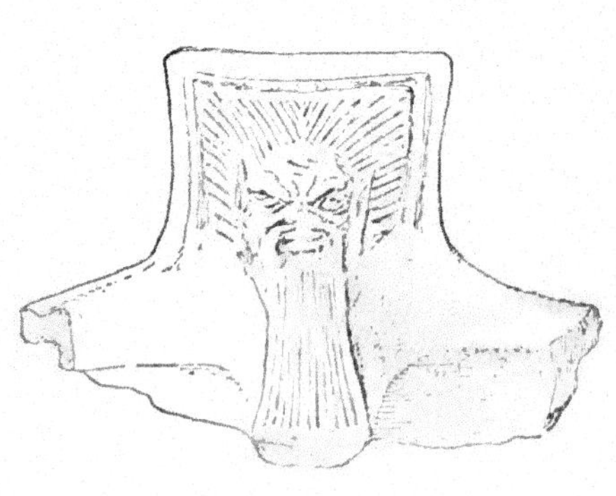

Fig. 29.

Fig. 30.

image of fright set to frighten the frightful. It might be the picture of Phobos himself. In fig. 30 we have neither Gorgon nor Satyr but that typical bogey of the workshop, the Cyclops. He wears the typical workman's cap, and to either side are set the thunderbolts it is his business to forge. The craftsman is regarded as an uncanny bogey himself, cunning over-much, often deformed, and so he is good to frighten other bogeys. The Cyclops was a terror even in high Olympus. Callimachus[1] in his charming way tells how

'Even the little goddesses are in a dreadful fright;
If one of them will not be good, up in Olympos' height,
Her mother calls a Cyclops, and there is sore disgrace,
And Hermes goes and gets a coal, and blacks his dreadful face,
And down the chimney comes. She runs straight to her mother's lap,
And shuts her eyes tight in her hands for fear of dire mishap.'

This fear of the bogey that beset the potter, and indeed beset every action, even the simplest, of human life, is very well shown in the Hymn[2] 'The Oven, or the Potters,' which shows clearly the order of beings against which the 'ugly face' was efficacious:

'If you but pay me my hire, potters, I sing to command.
Hither, come hither, Athene, bless with a fostering hand
Furnace and potters and pots, let the making and baking go well;
Fair shall they stand in the streets and the market, and quick shall
they sell,
Great be the gain. But if at your peril you cheat me my price,
Tricksters by birth, then straight to the furnace I call in a trice
Mischievous imps one and all, Crusher and Crasher by name,
Smasher and Half-bake and Him-who-burns-with-Unquenchable-Flame,
They shall scorch up the house and the furnace, ruin it, bring it to nought.
Wail shall the potters and snort shall the furnace, as horses do snort.'

How real was the belief in these evil sprites and in the power to avert them by magic and apotropaic figures is seen on a fragment of early Corinthian pottery[3] now in the Berlin Museum reproduced in fig. 31. Here is the great oven and here is the potter hard at work, but he is afraid in his heart, afraid of the Crusher and the Smasher and the rest. He has done what he can; a great owl is perched on the oven to protect it, and in front he has put a little ugly comic man, a charm to keep off evil spirits: he might have put a Satyr-head[4] or a Gorgoneion; he often did put both; it is all

[1] Callim. *Hym. ad Dian.* 67, and see *Myths of the Odyssey*, p. 26.
[2] Hom. *Epigr.* XIV. Κάμινος ἢ Κεραμεῖς.
[3] Pernice, *Festschrift für Benndorf*, p. 75. The inscriptions are not yet satisfactorily explained.
[4] A satyr-mask on an oven is figured in my *Greek Vase-paintings*, p. 9, fig. 1.

the same. Pollux[1] tells us it was the custom to put such comic figures (γελοῖα) before bronze-foundries; they could be either hung up or modelled on the furnace, and their object was 'the aversion of ill-will' (ἐπὶ φθόνου ἀποτροπῇ). These little images were

Fig. 31.

also called βασκάνια or by the unlearned προβασκάνια, charms against the evil eye; and if we may trust the scholiast on Aristophanes[2] they formed part of the furniture of most people's chimney corners at Athens. Of such βασκάνια the Gorgon mask was one and perhaps the most common shape.

In literature the Gorgon first meets us as a Gorgoneion, and this Gorgoneion is an underworld bogey. Odysseus[3] in Hades would fain have held further converse with dead heroes, but

'Ere that might be, the ghosts thronged round in myriads manifold,
Weird was the magic din they made, a pale-green fear gat hold
Of me, lest for my daring Persephone the dread
From Hades should send up an awful monster's grizzly head.'

[1] Poll. *On.* vii. 108.

[2] Schol. ad Ar. *Nub.* 436.

[3] *Od.* xi. 633

ἐμὲ δὲ χλωρὸν δέος ᾕρει
μή μοι γοργείην κεφαλὴν δεινοῖο πελώρου
ἐξ Ἀΐδεος πέμψειεν ἀγαυὴ Περσεφόνεια.

I have translated γοργείην 'grizzly,' not 'Gorgon,' advisedly. Homer does not commit himself to a definite Gorgon. Mr Neil on Aristoph. *Eq.* 1181 says 'Γοργολόφα means merely "fierce-plumed."' *The* Gorgon was made out of the terror, not the terror out of *the* Gorgon.

Homer is quite non-committal as to who and what the awful monster is; all that is clear is that the head only is feared as an *ἀποτρόπαιον*, a bogey to keep you off. Whether he knew of an actual monster called a Gorgon is uncertain. The nameless horror may be the head of either man or beast, or monster compounded of both.

In this connection it is instructive to note that, though the human Medusa-head on the whole obtained, the head of any beast is good as a protective charm. Prof. Ridgeway[1] has conclusively shown that the Gorgoneion on the aegis of Athene is but the head of the slain beast whose skin was the raiment of the primitive goddess; the head is worn on the breast, and serves to protect the wearer and to frighten his foe; it is a primitive half-magical shield. The natural head is later tricked out into an artificial bogey.

We are familiar with the Gorgoneion on shields, with the Gorgoneion on tombs, and as an amulet on vases. On the basis[2]

FIG. 32.

[1] *J.H.S.* XX. 1900, p. xliv. On an *askos* in the British Museum (*Cat.* G 80) decorated with a stamped relief, a Gorgon's head is figured with horns and animal ears. The head stands above, but separated from, a fantastic body.

[2] Th. Homolle, *Bull. de Corr. Hell.* XII. 1888, p. 464.

in fig. 32 the Gorgoneion is set to guard a statue of which two delicate feet remain. On two sides of the triangular statue we have the Gorgon head; on the third, serving a like protective purpose, a ram's head. The statue, dedicated in the precinct of Apollo at Delos, probably represents the god himself, but we need seek for no artificial connection between Gorgon, rams and Apollo; Gorgoneion and ram alike are merely prophylactic. The basis has a further interest in that the inscription[1] dates the Gorgon-type represented with some precision. The form of the letters shows it to have been the work and the dedication of a Naxian artist of the early part of the 6th century.

On a Rhodian plate[2] in the British Museum in fig. 33 the

FIG. 33.

[1] *ϝι[φ]ικαρτίδης | μ'ανέθεκε | ho | Νάhσιος*, see M. Homolle, *op. cit.*
[2] *J.H.S.* 1885, Pl. LIX. *Brit. Mus. Cat.*

Gorgoneion has been furnished with a body tricked out with wings, but the mask-head is still dominant. The figure is conceived in the typical heraldic fashion of the Mistress of Wild Things (*πότνια θηρῶν*); she is in fact the ugly bogey-, Erinys-side of the Great Mother; she is a potent goddess, not as in later days a monster to be slain by heroes. The highest divinities of the religion of fear and riddance became the harmful bogeys of the cult of 'service.' The Olympians in their turn became Christian devils.

Aeschylus[1] in instructive fashion places side by side the two sets of three sisters, the Gorgons and the Graiae. They are but two by-forms of each other. Prometheus foretells to Io her long wandering in the bogey land of Nowhere:

> 'Pass onward o'er the sounding sea, till thou
> Dost touch Kisthene's dreadful plains, wherein
> The Phorkides do dwell, the ancient maids,
> Three, shaped like swans, having one eye for all,
> One tooth—whom never doth the rising sun
> Glad with his beams, nor yet the moon by night—
> Near them their sisters three, the Gorgons, winged,
> With snakes for hair—hated of mortal man—
> None may behold and bear their breathing blight.'

The daughters of Phorkys, whom Hesiod[2] calls Grey Ones or Old Ones, Graiae, are fair of face though two-thirds blind and one-toothed; but the emphasis on the one tooth and the one eye shows that in tooth and eye resided their potency, and that in this they were own sisters to the Gorgons.

The Graiae appear, so far as I know, only once in vase-paintings, on the cover of a pyxis in the Central Museum at Athens[3], reproduced in fig. 34. They are sea-maidens, as the dolphins show; old Phorkys their father is seated near them, and Poseidon and Athene are present in regular Athenian fashion. Hermes has brought Perseus, and Perseus waits his chance to get the one eye as it is passed from hand to hand. The eye is clearly seen in the hand outstretched above Perseus; one blind sister hands it to the other. The third holds in her hand the fanged tooth. The vase-painter will not have the Graiae old and loathsome, they are lovely maidens; he remembers that they were white-haired from their youth.

[1] Aesch. *Prom. Vinct.* 793

[2] Hes. *Theog.* 270.

[3] *Cat.* 1956; *Ath. Mitt.* 1886, Taf. x. 270.

The account given by Aeschylus of the Gorgons helps to explain their nature:

'None may behold, and bear their breathing blight[1].'

They slay by a malign effluence, and this effluence, tradition said, came from their eyes. Athenaeus[2] quotes Alexander the

Fig. 34.

Myndian as his authority for the statement that there actually existed creatures who could by their eyes turn men to stone.

[1] Aesch. *Prom. Vinct.* 800 ἃς θνητὸς οὐδεὶς εἰσιδὼν ἕξει πνοάς. The line is usually rendered 'no mortal may behold them and live,' but, in the light of the account of Athenaeus, it is clear that the *πνοαί* are the intolerable exhalations, not the breath of life.

[2] Athen. v. 64 p. 221 κτείνει τὸν ὑπ' αὐτῆς θεωρηθέντα, οὐ τῷ πνεύματι ἀλλὰ τῇ γιγνομένῃ ἀπὸ τῆς τῶν ὀμμάτων φύσεως φορᾷ καὶ νεκρὸν ποιεῖ. The same account is given by Aelian, *Hist. An.* VII. 5, and Eustathius § 1704 in commenting on *Od.* XI. 633.

Some say the beast which the Libyans called Gorgon was like a wild sheep, others like a calf; it had a mane hanging over its eyes so heavy that it could only shake it aside with difficulty; it killed whomever it looked at, not by its breath but by a destructive exhalation from its eyes.

What the beast was and how the story arose cannot be decided, but it is clear that the Gorgon was regarded as a sort of incarnate Evil Eye. The monster was tricked out with cruel tusks and snakes, but it slew by the eye, it *fascinated*.

The Evil Eye itself is not frequent on monuments; the Gorgoneion as a more complete and more elaborately decorative horror attained a wider popularity. But the prophylactic Eye, the eye set to stare back the Evil Eye, is common on vases, on shields and on the prows of ships (see fig. 37). The curious design in fig. 35 is from a Roman mosaic dug up on the Caelian

FIG. 35.

hill[1]. It served as the pavement in an entrance hall to a Basilica built by a certain Hilarius, a dealer in pearls (*margaritarius*) and head of a college of Dendrophoroi, sacred to the Mother of

[1] Visconti, *Bull. de Comm. Arch.* 1890, Tav. I. and II. p. 24. A relief with similar design exists on the back of a Corinthian marble in the British Museum: its apotropaic functions are fully discussed by Prof. Michaelis, *J.H.S.* VI. 1885, p. 312.

the Gods. The inscription prays that 'God may be propitious to those who enter here and to the Basilica of Hilarius,' and to make divine favour more secure, a picture is added to show the complete overthrow of the evil eye. Very complete is its destruction. Four-footed beasts, birds and reptiles attack it, it is bored through with a lance, and as a final prophylactic on the eye-brow is perched Athene's little holy owl. Hilarius prayed to a kindly god, but deep down in his heart was the old savage fear[1].

The Gorgon is more monstrous, more savage, than any other of the Ker-forms. The Gorgoneion figures little in poetry though much in art. It is an underworld bogey but not human enough to be a ghost, it lacks wholly the gentle side of the Keres, and would scarcely have been discussed here, but that the art-type of the Gorgon lent, as will be seen, some of its traits to the Erinys, and notably the deathly distillation by which they slay:

> 'From out their eyes they ooze a loathly rheum[2].'

The Ker as Siren[3].

The Sirens are to the modern mind mermaids, sometimes all human, sometimes fish-tailed, evil sometimes, but beautiful always. Milton invokes Sabrina from the waves by

> '...the songs of Sirens sweet,
> By dead Parthenope's dear tomb,
> And fair Ligeia's golden comb
> Wherewith she sits on diamond rocks
> Sleeking her soft alluring locks.'

Homer by the magic of his song lifted them once and for all out of the region of mere bogeydom, and yet a careful exami-

[1] For the evil eye in Greece see O. Jahn, *Berichte d. k. sächs. Ges. d. Wissenschaften*, Wien, 1855, and P. Perdrizet, *Bull. de Corr. Hell.* 1900, p. 292, and for modern survivals, Tuchmann, *Melusine*, 1885.

[2] Aesch. *Eum.* 54 ἐκ δ' ὀμμάτων λείβουσι δυσφιλῆ δία. Following Dr Verrall, I keep the MS. reading.

[3] Since this section was written Dr G. Weicker's treatise *Der Seelenvogel* has appeared. As the substance of his argument as to the soul-origin of the Sirens had been previously published in a dissertation *De Sirenibus Quaestiones Selectae* (Leipzig, 1895) he had long anticipated my view and I welcome this confirmation of a theory at which I had independently arrived, a theory which indeed must occur to everyone who examines the art-form of the Sirens. I regret that his work was known to me too late for me to utilize the vast stores of evidence he has accumulated.

nation, especially of their art form, clearly reveals traces of rude origin.

Circe's warning to Odysseus runs thus[1]:

'First to the Sirens shalt thou sail, who all men do beguile.
Whoso unwitting draws anigh, by magic of their wile,
They lure him with their singing, nor doth he reach his home
Nor see his dear wife and his babes, ajoy that he is come.
For they, the Sirens, lull him with murmur of sweet sound
Crouching within the meadow: about them is a mound
Of men that rot in death, their skin wasting the bones around.'

Odysseus and his comrades, so forewarned, set sail[2]:

'Then straightway sailed the goodly ship and swift the Sirens' isle
Did reach, for that a friendly gale was blowing all the while.
Forthwith the gale fell dead, and calm held all the heaving deep
In stillness, for some god had lulled the billows to their sleep.'

The song of the Sirens is heard[3]:

'Hither, far-famed Odysseus, come hither, thou the boast
Of all Achaean men, beach thou thy bark upon our coast,
And hearken to our singing, for never but did stay
A hero in his black ship and listened to the lay
Of our sweet lips; full many a thing he knew and sailed away.
For we know all things whatsoe'er in Troy's wide land had birth
And we know all things that shall be upon the fruitful earth.'

It is strange and beautiful that Homer should make the Sirens appeal to the spirit, not to the flesh. To primitive man, Greek or Semite, the desire to know—to be as the gods—was the fatal desire.

Homer takes his Sirens as already familiar; he clearly draws from popular tradition. There is no word as to their form, no hint of parentage: he does not mean them to be mysterious, but by a fortunate chance he leaves them shrouded in mystery, the mystery of the hidden spell of the sea, with the haze of the noontide about them and the meshes of sweet music for their unseen toils,—knowing all things, yet for ever unknown. It is this mystery of the Sirens that has appealed to modern poetry and almost wholly obscured their simple primitive significance.

'Their words are no more heard aright
Through lapse of many ages, and no man
Can any more across the waters wan
Behold these singing women of the sea.'

Four points in the story of Homer must be clearly noted. The

[1] *Od.* XII. 39. [2] *Od.* XII. 166. [3] *Od.* XII. 184.

Sirens, though they sing to mariners, are *not* sea-maidens; they dwell on an island in a flowery meadow. They are mantic creatures like the Sphinx with whom they have much in common, knowing both the past and the future. Their song takes effect at midday, in a windless calm. The end of that song is death. It is only from the warning of Circe that we know of the heap of bones, corrupt in death—horror is kept in the background, seduction to the fore.

It is to art we must turn to know the real nature of the Sirens. Ancient art, like ancient literature, knows nothing of the fish-tailed mermaid. Uniformly the art-form of the Siren is that of the bird-woman. The proportion of bird to woman varies, but the bird element is constant. It is interesting to note that, though the bird-woman is gradually ousted in modern art by the fish-tailed mermaid, the bird element survives in mediaeval times[1]. In the *Hortus Deliciarum* of the Abbess Herrad (circ. A.D. 1160), the Sirens appear as draped women with the clawed feet of birds; with their human hands they are playing on lyres.

The bird form of the Sirens was a problem even to the ancients. Ovid[2] asks:

> 'Whence came these feathers and these feet of birds?
> Your faces are the faces of fair maids.'

Ovid's aetiology is of course beside the mark. The answer to his pertinent question is quite simple. The Sirens belong to the same order of bogey beings as the Sphinx and the Harpy; the monstrous form expresses the monstrous nature; they are birds of prey but with power to lure by their song. In the Harpy-form the ravening snatching nature is emphasized and developed, in the Sphinx the mantic power of all uncanny beings, in the Siren the seduction of song. The Sphinx, though mainly a prophetess, keeps Harpy elements; she snatches away the youths of Thebes: she is but

[1] Mediaeval Sirens are more fully discussed in my *Myths of the Odyssey*, p. 172.
[2] *Met.* v. 552

> vobis Acheloides unde
> pluma pedesque avium, cum virginis ora geratis?

Apollonius Rhodius also believes that the bird form was a metamorphosis. *Argon.* iv. 898

> τότε δ' ἄλλο μὲν οἰωνοῖσιν
> ἄλλο δὲ παρθενικῇς ἐναλίγκιαι ἔσκον ἰδέσθαι.

'a man-seizing Ker[1].' The Siren too, though mainly a seductive singer, is at heart a Harpy, a bird of prey.

This comes out very clearly in representations on vase-paintings. A black-figured aryballos[2] of Corinthian style (fig. 36), now in the Boston Museum of Fine Arts, is our earliest artistic source for the

FIG. 36.

Siren myth. Odysseus, bound to the mast, has come close up to the island: on the island are perched 'Sirens twain.' Above the ship hover two great black birds of prey in act to pounce on the mariners. These birds cannot be merely decorative: they in a sense duplicate the Sirens. The vase-painter knows the Sirens are singing demons sitting on an island; the text of Homer was not in his hands to examine the account word by word, but the Homeric story haunts his memory. He knows too that in popular belief the Sirens are demons of prey; hence the great birds. To the right of the Sirens on the island crouches a third figure; she is all human, not a third Siren. She probably, indeed all but certainly, represents the mother of the Sirens, Chthon, the Earth. Euripides[3] makes his Helen in her anguish call on the

> 'Winged maidens, virgins, daughters of the Earth,
> The Sirens,'

to join their sorrowful song to hers. The parentage is significant. The Sirens are not of the sea, not even of the land, but demons of the underworld; they are in fact a by-form of Keres, souls.

The notion of the soul as a human-faced bird is familiar in Egyptian, but rare in Greek, art. The only certain instance is,

[1] Aesch. *Sept.* 776. The nature of the Sphinx as a mantic earth-demon will be discussed in detail later (p. 207).

[2] Published and discussed by H. Bulle, *Strena Helbigiana*, p. 31. Recently acquired for the Boston Museum, see *Twenty-sixth Annual Report of Boston Museum of Fine Arts*, Dec. 31, 1901, p. 35.

[3] Eur. *Hel.* 167.

so far as I know, the vase in the British Museum[1] on which is represented the death of Procris. Above Procris falling in death hovers a winged bird-woman. She is clearly, I think, the soul of Procris. To conceive of the soul as a bird escaping from the mouth is a fancy so natural and beautiful that it has arisen among many peoples. In Celtic mythology[2] Maildun, the Irish Odysseus, comes to an island with trees on it in clusters on which were perched many birds. The aged man of the island tells him, 'These are the souls of my children and of all my descendants, both men and women, who are sent to this little island to abide with me according as they die in Erin.' Sailors to this day believe that sea-mews are the souls of their drowned comrades. Antoninus Liberalis[3] tells how, when Ktesulla because of her father's broken oath died in child-bed, 'they carried her body out to be buried, and from the bier a dove flew forth and the body of Ktesulla disappeared.'

The persistent anthropomorphism of the Greeks stripped the bird-soul of all but its wings. The human winged *eidolon* prevailed in art: the bird-woman became a death-demon, a soul sent to fetch a soul, a Ker that lures a soul, a Siren.

Later in date and somewhat different in conception is the scene on a red-figured stamnos in the British Museum[4] (fig. 37). The artist's desire for a balanced design has made him draw two islands, on each of which a Siren is perched. Over the head of one is inscribed Ἱμε(ρ)οπα 'lovely-voiced.' A third Siren flies or rather falls headlong down on to the ship. The drawing of the eye of this third Siren should be noted. The eye is indicated by two strokes only, without the pupil. This is the regular method of representing the sightless eye, i.e. the eye in death or sleep or blindness. The third Siren is dying; she has hurled herself from the rock in despair at the fortitude of Odysseus. This is clearly

[1] *Cat.* E 477. The vase is a *kelebe* of late style with columnar handles. In previously discussing this design (*Myths of the Odyssey*, p. 158, pl. 40 and *Myth. and Mon. Ancient Athens*, p. lxix, fig. 14) I felt uncertain whether the bird-woman were Harpy, Siren, or Soul. I am now convinced that a soul is intended, and that the bird form was probably borrowed from Egypt: see *Book of the Dead*, Vignette XCI.

[2] See *Myths of the Odyssey*, p. 180.

[3] Anton. Lib. I. I owe this reference to Prof. Sam. Wide, *A. Mitt.* XXVI. 1901, 2, p. 155. At the miracle plays it was a custom to let a bird fly when a person died—a crow for the impenitent thief and a white dove for the penitent one. See Mr Hugh Stewart, *Boethius*, p. 187.

[4] *B.M. Cat.* E 440. *Monimenti dell' Inst.* vol. I. pl. 8.

what the artist wishes to say, but he may have been haunted by an artistic tradition of the pouncing bird of prey. He also has adopted the number three, which by his time was canonical for the Sirens. By making the third Siren fly headlong between the two others he has neatly turned a difficulty in composition. On

FIG. 37.

the reverse of this vase are three Love-gods, who fall to be discussed later (Chap. XII.). Connections between the subject matter of the obverse and reverse of vases are somewhat precarious, but it is likely, as the three Love-gods are flying over the sea, that the vase-painter intended to emphasize the seduction of love in his Sirens.

The clearest light on the lower nature of the Sirens is thrown by the design in fig. 38 from a Hellenistic relief[1]. The monument is of course a late one, later by at least two centuries than the vase-paintings, but it reflects a primitive stage of thought and one moreover wholly free from the influence of Homer. The scene is a rural one. In the right-hand corner is a herm, in front of it an altar, near at hand a tree on which hangs a votive

[1] Published by Schreiber, *Hellenistische Reliefbilder*, Taf. LXI.: where the relief is now is not known. Fully discussed by Dr Otto Crusius, 'Die Epiphanie der Sirene,' *Philologos* (N.F. IV.), p. 93. Dr Crusius rightly observes that the relief has been misunderstood. It represents rather an ἔφοδος than a σύμπλεγμα, and the recumbent figure is a mortal man not a Silen.

syrinx. Some peasant or possibly a wayfarer has fallen asleep. Down upon him has pounced a winged and bird-footed woman. It is the very image of obsession, of nightmare, of a haunting midday dream. The woman can be none other than an evil Siren. Had the scene been represented by an earlier artist, he would have made her ugly because evil; but by Hellenistic times the Sirens were beautiful women, all human but for wings and sometimes bird-feet.

Fig. 38.

The terrors of the midday sleep were well known to the Greeks in their sun-smitten land; nightmare to them was also daymare. Such a visitation, coupled possibly with occasional cases of sunstroke, was of course the obsession of a demon[1]. Even a troubled tormenting illicit dream was the work of a Siren. In sleep the will and the reason are becalmed and the passions unchained. That the midday nightmare went to the making of the Siren is clear from the windless calm and the heat of the sun in Homer. The horrid end, the wasting death, the sterile enchantment, the loss of wife and babes, all look the same way. Homer, with perhaps some blend of the Northern mermaid in his mind, sets his Sirens by the sea, thereby cleansing their uncleanness; but later tradition kept certain horrid primitive elements when it made of the Siren a hetaira disallowing the lawful gifts of Aphrodite.

There remains another aspect of the Sirens. They appear frequently as monuments, sometimes as actual mourners, on tombs. Here all the erotic element has disappeared; they are substantially

[1] Pliny cites Dinon as authority for a like superstition in India. *Nat. Hist.* x. 49 (*F.H.G.* II. p. 90): Nec Sirenes impetraverunt fidem adfirmet licet Dinon Clitarchi celebrati auctoris pater in India esse mulcerique earum cantu quos gravatos somno lacerent. And cf. Aelian *H.A.* XVIII. 22, 23. Siren in the Septuagint is the word used of the desert bogey that our translation renders 'dragon,' Job xxx. 30 'I am brother to the dragon and companion to owls,' and again Micah i. 8 'I will make a wailing like the dragon and a mourning as the owls'; but the rendering Siren is probably due to a confusion between the plurals of תַּן* jackal and תַּנִּין sea-monster.

Death-Keres, Harpies, though to begin with they imaged the soul itself. The bird-woman of the Harpy tomb, the gentle angel of death, has been already noted (p.177). The Siren on a black-figured lekythos in the British Museum[1] (fig. 39) is purely monumental.

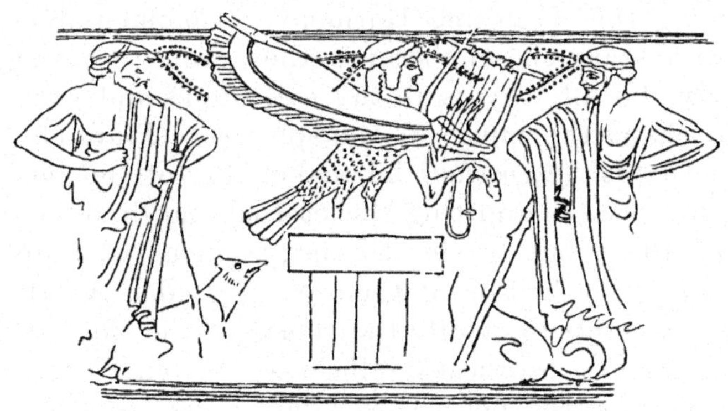

FIG. 39.

She stands on the grave stele playing her great lyre, while two bearded men with their dogs seem to listen intent. She is grave and beautiful with no touch of seduction. Probably at first the Siren was placed on tombs as a sort of charm, a *προβασκάνιον*, a soul to keep off souls. It has already been shown, in dealing with apotropaic ritual (p. 196), that the charm itself is used as counter-charm. So the dreaded Death-Ker is set itself to guard the tomb. Other associations would gather round. The Siren was a singer, she would chant the funeral dirge ; this dirge might be the praises of the dead. The epitaph that Erinna[2] wrote for her girl-friend Baukis begins

'Pillars and Sirens mine and mournful urn.'

On later funeral monuments Sirens appear for the most part as mourners, tearing their hair and lamenting. Their apotropaic function was wholly forgotten. Where an apotropaic monster is wanted we find an owl or a sphinx.

Even on funeral monuments the notion of the Siren as either soul or Death-Angel is more and more obscured by her potency as sweet singer. Once, however, when she appears in philosophy, there is at least a haunting remembrance that she is a soul who

[1] *B.M. Cat.* B 651. J. E. Harrison, *Myths of the Odyssey*, Pl. 39.
[2] Erinna, frg. 5 Στᾶλαι καὶ Σειρῆνες ἐμαὶ καὶ πένθιμε κρωσσέ.

sings to souls. In the cosmography with which he ends the *Republic*, Plato[1] thus writes: 'The spindle turns on the knees of Ananke, and on the upper surface of each sphere is perched a Siren, who goes round with them hymning a single tone. The eight together form one Harmony.' Commentators explain that the Sirens are chosen because they are sweet singers, but then, if music be all, why is it the evil Sirens and not the good Muses who chant the music of the spheres? Plutarch[2] felt the difficulty. In his *Symposiacs* he makes one of the guests say: 'Plato is absurd in committing the eternal and divine revolutions not to the Muses but to the Sirens; demons who are by no means either benevolent or in themselves good.' Another guest, Ammonius, attempts to justify the choice of the Sirens by giving to them in Homer a mystical significance. 'Even Homer,' he says, 'means by their music not a power dangerous and destructive to man, but rather a power that inspires in the souls that go from Hence Thither, and wander about after death, a love for things heavenly and divine and a forgetfulness of things mortal, and thereby holds them enchanted by singing. Even here,' he goes on to say, 'a dim murmur of that music reaches us, rousing reminiscence.'

It is not to be for a moment supposed that Homer's Sirens had really any such mystical content. But, given that they have the bird-form of souls, that they 'know all things,' are sweet singers and dwellers in Hades, and they lie ready to the hand of the mystic. Proclus[3] in his commentary on the *Republic* says, with perhaps more truth than he is conscious of, 'the Sirens are a kind of souls living the life of the spirit.' His interpretation is not merely fanciful; it is a blend of primitive tradition with mystical philosophy.

The Sirens are further helped to their high station on the spheres by the Orphic belief that purified souls went to the stars, nay even *became* stars. In the *Peace* of Aristophanes[4] the servant asks Trygaeus,

> 'It is true then, what they say, that in the air
> A man becomes a star, when he comes to die?'

[1] Plat. *Rep.* 617 B.   [2] Plut. *Symp.* IX. 14. 6.

[3] Procl. ad Plat. *Rep.* loc. cit. ψυχαί τινες νοερῶς ζῶσαι.

[4] Ar. *Pax*, 832. For this Orphic doctrine see Rohde, *Psyche*, II. p. 123[4], Dieterich, *Nekuia*, pp. 104 ff.

To the poet the soul is a bird in its longing to be free:

'Could I take me to some cavern for mine hiding,
On the hill-tops, where the sun scarce hath trod,
Or a cloud make the place of mine abiding,
As a bird among the bird-droves of God[1].'

And that upward flight to heavenly places is as the flying of a Siren:

'With golden wings begirt my body flies,
Sirens have lent me their swift winged feet,
Upborne to uttermost ether I shall meet
And mix with heavenly Zeus beyond the skies[2].'

But, though Plato and the poets and the mystics exalt the Siren, 'half-angel and half-bird,' to cosmic functions, yet, to the popular mind, they are mainly things, if not wholly evil, yet fearful and to be shunned. This is seen in the myth of their contest with the Muses[3]. Here they are the spirits of forbidden intoxication; as such on vases they join the motley crew of Centaurs and Satyrs who revel with Dionysos. They stand, it would seem, to the ancient as to the modern, for the impulses in life as yet unmoralized, imperious longings, ecstasies, whether of love or art or philosophy, magical voices calling to a man from his 'Land of Heart's Desire' and to which if he hearken it may be he will return home no more—voices too, which, whether a man sail by or stay to hearken, still sing on.

The Siren bird-woman transformed for ever by the genius of Homer into the sweet-voiced demon of seduction may seem remote from the Ker of which she is but a specialized form. A curious design[4] on a black-figured cylix in the Louvre (fig. 40) shows how close was the real connection. The scene is a banquet: five men are reclining on couches, two of them separated by a huge *deinos*, a wine-vessel, from which a boy has drawn wine in an oinochoe. Over two of the men are hovering winged figures, each holding a crown and a spray; over two others hover bird-women, each also holding a crown and a spray. What are we to call these ministrant figures, what would the vase-painter himself have called them? Are the human winged figures Love-gods, are the bird-women Sirens? For lack of context it is hard to say with certainty.

[1] Eur. *Hipp.* 732. [2] Eur. frg. 911. [3] *Myths of the Odyssey*, p. 166.
[4] *Bull. de Corr. Hell.* 1898, p. 238, fig. 6.

Thus much is clear, both kinds of figures are favouring genii of the feast, and for our purpose this is all-important: the bird-women, be they Sirens or not, and the winged human figures, be they Love-gods or merely Keres, *perform the same function.* The

Fig. 40.

development of the Love-god, Eros, from the Ker will be discussed later (Chap. XII.); for the present it is best to regard these bird-women and winged sprites as both of the order of Keres, as yet unspecialized in function.

The Ker as Sphinx.

Two special features characterize the Sphinx: she was a Harpy carrying off men to destruction, an incarnate plague; she was the soothsayer with the evil habit of asking riddles as well as answering them. Both functions, though seemingly alien, were characteristic of underworld bogeys; the myth-making mind put them together and wove out of the two the tale of the unanswered riddle and the consequent deathly pest.

On the vase-painting in fig. 41 from a cylix[1] in the Museo Gregoriano of the Vatican, we have a charming representation of the riddle-answering Oedipus, whose name is written *Oidipodes*,

[1] *Mus. Greg.* No. 186. Hartwig, *Meisterschalen*, Taf. LXXIII.

sitting meditating in front of the oracle. The Sphinx on her column is half monument, half personality; she is a very human monster, she has her lion-body, but she is a lovely attentive maiden. From her lips come the letters *και τρι*, which may mean *and three* or *and three* (*-footed*). In the field is a delicate decorative spray, which, occurring as it does on vases with a certain individuality of drawing, seems to be, as it were, the signature of a particular master[1].

FIG. 41.

The Sphinx in fig. 41 is all oracular, but occasionally, on vases of the same date, she appears in her other function as the 'man-snatching Ker.' She leaves her pedestal and carries off a Theban youth. The 5th century vase-painter with his determined euphemism, even when he depicts her carrying off her prey, makes her do it with a certain Attic gentleness, more like a death-Siren than

[1] Dr Hartwig, *op. cit.*, has collected and discussed these vases and gives to the artist the name 'Meister mit dem Ranke.'

a Harpy. Aeschylus[1] in the *Seven against Thebes* describes her as the monster she is; the Sphinx on the shield of Parthenopaeus is a horrid bogey, the 'reproach of the state,' 'eater of raw-flesh,' with hungry jaws, bringing ill-luck to him who bears her on his ensign.

In the curious vase-painting in fig. 42, a design from a late Lower Italy krater[2] in the museum at Naples, the Sphinx is wholly

Fig. 42.

oracular, and this time she must answer the riddle, not ask it. The Sphinx is seated on a rocky mound, near which stands erect a snake. The snake is not, I think, without meaning; it is the oracular beast of the earth-oracle. The Silenus who has come to consult the oracle holds in his hand a bird. The scene would be hopelessly enigmatic but for one of the fables that are current under the name of Aesop[3], which precisely describes the situation. 'A certain bad man made an agreement with some one to prove that the Delphic oracle was false, and when the appointed day came, he took a sparrow in his hand and covered it with his garment and came to the sanctuary, and standing in front of the oracle, asked whether the thing in his hand was alive or dead, and

[1] Aesch. *Sept. c. Theb.* 539.

[2] Heydemann, *Cat.* No. 2846. *Museo Borbonico* xii. 9. Discussed and explained by Dr Otto Crusius, *Festschrift für Overbeck*, p. 102. Dr Crusius holds that the snake is merely a 'Füllfigur.'

[3] Aesop. *Fab.* 55.

he meant if the oracle said it was dead, to show the sparrow alive, but if the oracle said it was alive, to strangle it first and then show it. But the god knew his wicked plan, and said to him, "Have done, for it depends on you whether what you hold is dead or living." The story shows plainly that the divinity is not lightly to be tempted.'

The story, taken in conjunction with the vase-painting it explains, shows clearly another thing. The Sphinx was mainly a local Theban bogey, but she became the symbol of oracular divinity. At Delphi there was an earth-oracle guarded by a snake, and in honour of that earth-oracle the Naxians upreared their colossal Sphinx[1] and set it in the precinct of Gaia. As time went on, the savage 'man-snatching' aspect of the Sphinx faded, remembered only in the local legend, while her oracular aspect grew: but the local legend is here as always the more instructive.

The next representation of the Sphinx (fig. 43), from the fragment of an oinochoe in the Berlin Museum[2], is specially suggestive. The monster is inscribed, not with the name we know her by, 'Sphinx,' but as 'Kassmia,' the Kadmean One, the bogey of Kadmos. The bearded monster with wings and claws and dog-like head has lost her orthodox lion-body, and lent it perhaps to Oedipus who stands in front of her. The scene is of course pure comedy, and shows how near to the Greek mind were the horrible and the grotesque, the thing feared and the thing scoffed at. The Kassmia, the bogey of Kadmos, may have brought her lion-body with Kadmos from the East, but the supposition, though very possible, is not necessary. Cithaeron was

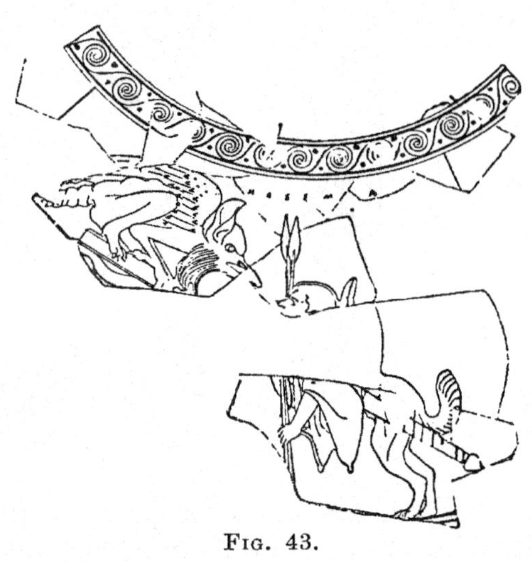

FIG. 43.

[1] Discovered in the excavations at Delphi, see Homolle, *Fouilles de Delphes*, 1902, T. II. pl. XIV.

[2] Berlin, *Inv.* 3186. *Jahrbuch d. Inst.* 1891, Anzeiger, p. 119, fig. 17.

traditionally lion-haunted[1]. The Sphinx may have borrowed some of her traits and part of her body from a real lion haunting a real local tomb.

It is worth noting in this connection that Hesiod[2] calls the monster not Sphinx but Phix:

> 'By stress of Orthios, she, Echidna, bare
> Disastrous Phix, a bane to Kadmos' folk.'

The scholiast remarks that 'Mount Phikion where she dwelt was called after her,' but the reverse is probably true. Phix was the local bogey of Phikion. The rocky mountain which rises to the S.-E. corner of Lake Copais is still locally known as Phaga[3]. By a slight and easy modification Phix became Sphix or Sphinx, the 'throttler,' an excellent name for a destructive bogey.

The last representation of the Sphinx, in fig. 44, brings us to her characteristic as tomb-haunter. The design is from a krater[4]

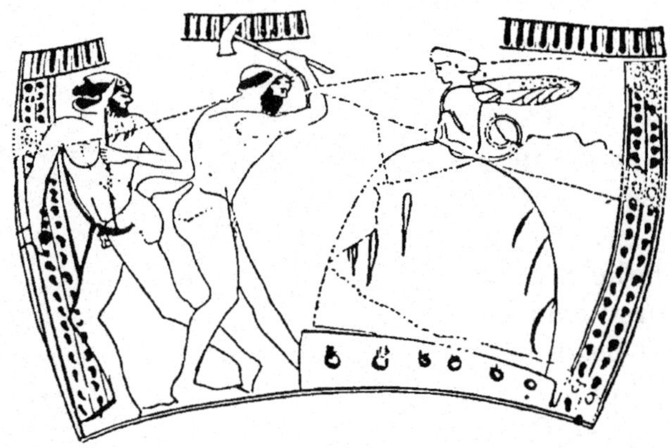

Fig. 44.

in the Vagnonville Collection of the Museo Greco Etrusco at Florence. The Sphinx is seated on a tomb-mound (χῶμα γῆς) of the regular sepulchral type. That the mound is sepulchral is certain from the artificial stone basis pierced with holes[5] on which it stands. Two lawless Satyrs attack the mound with

[1] P. I. 41. 4.
[2] Hes. *Theog.* 326 and *Scut. Her.* 33, and see Plat. *Crat.* 414 D.
[3] Dr Frazer ad P. IX. 26. 2.
[4] Milani, *Museo Topografico*, p. 69. 'Delphika,' *J.H.S.* 1899, p. 235.
[5] The purpose of these holes, which occur frequently in representations of tomb-mounds on Athenian lekythoi, is not, so far as I know, made out.

picks. The Sphinx is a tomb-haunting bogey, a Ker, but ultimately she fades into a decorative tomb monument, with always perhaps some prophylactic intent. In this, as in her mantic aspect, she is own cousin to the Ker-Siren, but with the Sphinx the mantic side predominates. The Sphinx, unlike the Siren, never developed into a trinity, though when she became decorative she is doubled for heraldic purposes.

It is time to resume the various shifting notions that cluster round the term Ker, perhaps the most untranslateable of all Greek words. Ghost, bacillus, disease, death-angel, death-fate, fate, bogey, magician have all gone to the making of it. So shifting and various is the notion that it is hard to say what is primary, what developed, but deep down in the lowest stratum lie the two kindred conceptions of ghost and bacillus. It is only by a severe effort of the imagination that we can think ourselves back into an adequate mental confusion to realize all the connotations of Ker.

When the lexicographers came to define the word they had no easy task. Their struggles—they are honest men, if not too intelligent—are instructive. Happily they make no attempt at real formulation, but jot things down as they come. Hesychius, after his preliminary statement '*κηρ* (neuter, with circumflex accent) the soul, (oxytone, feminine) death-bringing fate, death,' gives us suggestive particulars: *κῆρας· ἀκαθαρσίας, μολύσματα, βλάβας*, where we see the unclean bacilli; *κηρόν· λεπτὸν νοσηρόν*, which reminds us of the evil skinny Ker of the vase-painting (fig. 16); *κηριοῦσθαι· ἐκπλήττεσθαι*, where the bogey Ker is manifest; *κηριωθῆναι· ὑπὸ σκοτοδινοῦ ληφθῆναι*, where the whirlwind seems indicated, though it may be the dizziness of death. Kerukainae were the female correlatives of Kerykes, 'women whose business it was to collect things polluted' and carry them off to the sea[1]. Most curious and primitive of all, we are told[2] that *κήρυκες* itself means not only messengers, ministers, a priestly race descended from Hermes, but 'they call the insects that impregnate the wild fig *κήρυκας*.' Here are bacilli indeed, but for life not for death.

[1] Suidas s.v. *καὶ κηρυκαίνας ἐκάλουν Ἀλεξανδρεῖς γυναῖκας, αἵτινες εἰς τὰς αὐλὰς παριοῦσαι καὶ τὰς συνοικίας ἐφ' ᾧτε συναγείρειν τὰ μιάσματα καὶ ἀποφέρειν εἰς θάλασσαν ἅπερ ἐκάλουν φυλάκια.*

[2] Hesych. s.v. *καὶ τοὺς ἐρινάζοντας τοὺς ἐρίνους κήρυκας λέγουσι.*

The Ker as Erinys.

It has been already indicated that a Ker is sometimes an avenger, but this aspect of the word has been advisedly reserved because it takes us straight to the idea of the Erinys.

Pausanias[1], *à propos* of the grave of Koroibos at Megara, tells us a story in which a Ker figures plainly as an Erinys, with a touch of the Sphinx and of the death-Siren. Psamathe, daughter of Krotopos, King of Argos, had a child by Apollo, which, fearing her father's anger, she exposed. The child was found and killed by the sheep-dogs of Krotopos. Apollo sent Poine (Penalty or Vengeance) on the city of the Argives. Poine, they say, snatched children from their mothers until Koroibos, to please the Argives, slew her. After he had slain her, there came a second pestilence upon them and lasted on. Koroibos had to go to Delphi to expiate his sin; he was ordered to build a temple of Apollo wherever the tripod he brought from Delphi should fall. He built of course the town of Tripodisci. The grave of Koroibos at Megara was surmounted by the most ancient Greek stone images Pausanias had ever seen, a figure of Koroibos slaying Poine. There were elegiac verses carved on it recounting the tale of Psamathe and Koroibos. Now Pausanias mentions no Ker, only Poine; but the Anthologists[2] have preserved for us verses which, if not actually those carved on the grave, at all events refer to it, and in them occur the notable words:

> 'I am the Ker, slain by Koroibos, I dwell on his tomb,
> Here at my feet, on account of the tripod, he lies for his doom.'

Poine is clearly the avenging ghost of the child of Psamathe causing a pest which snatched babes from their mothers, and Poine the ghost-pest is a Ker and practically a Ker-Erinys.

The simple truth emerges so clearly as to be almost self-evident, yet is constantly ignored, that primarily the Keres-Erinyes are just what the words say, the 'Keres Angry-ones.' There is no reason to doubt the truth of what Pausanias[3] tells us, that the

[1] P. I. 43. 7.

[2] *Anthol. Pal.* VII. 154

> Εἰμὶ δὲ Κὴρ τυμβοῦχος, ὁ δὲ κτείνας με Κόροιβος
> κεῖται δ' ὧδ' ὑπ' ἐμοῖς ποσσὶ διὰ τρίποδα.

[3] P. VIII. 25. 4 ὅτι τῷ θυμῷ χρῆσθαι καλοῦσιν ἐρινύειν οἱ Ἀρκάδες.

Arcadians and, with the Arcadians, probably the rest of the primitive Greeks, called 'being in a rage' ἐρινύειν. Demeter at Thelpusa had two surnames and even two statues. When she was wroth they called her *Erinys*[1] on account of her wrath, when she relented and bathed they called her *Lousia*. Pausanias gives as literary authority for the surname Erinys, Antimachus who wrote (4th cent. B.C.) of the expedition of the Argives against Thebes.

The Erinyes, on this showing, are one form of the countless host of divine beings whose names are simply adjectival epithets, not names proper. Such others are the Eumenides the Kindly Ones, the Potniae the Awful Ones, the Maniae the Madnesses, the Praxidikae the Vengeful Ones. With a certain delicate shyness, founded possibly on a very practical fear, primitive man will not address his gods by a personal name; he decently shrouds them in class epithets. There are people living now, Celts for the most part, who shrink from the personal attack of a proper name, and call their friends, in true primitive fashion, the Old One, the Kind One, the Blackest One, and the like.

It is apparent that, given these adjectival names, the gods are as many as the moods of the worshipper, i.e. as his thoughts about his gods. If he is kind, they are Kindly Ones; when he feels vengeful, they are Vengeful Ones.

The question arises, why did the angry aspect of the Keres, i.e. the Erinyes, attain to a development so paramount, so self-sufficing, that already in Homer they are distinct from the Keres, with functions, if not forms, clearly defined, beyond possibility of confusion. It is precisely these functions that have defined them. A Ker, as has been seen, is for good and for evil, is active for plants, for animals, as for men: a Ker when angry is Erinys: a Ker is never so angry as when he has been killed. The idea of Erinys as distinct from Ker is developed *out of a human relation intensely felt.* The Erinys primarily is the Ker of a human being unrighteously slain. Erinys is not death; it is the outraged soul of the dead man crying for vengeance; it is the Ker as Poine. In discussing the Keres it has been abundantly shown that ghost

[1] The explanation of Erinyes as 'angry ones' is confirmed by modern philology. F. Froehde, Bezzenberger. *Beiträge*, xx. p. 188, derives the word Erinys from ἐ-ρυσ-νος, Lith. *rustas*, angry.

is a word too narrow: Keres denote a wider animism. With Erinys the case is otherwise: the Erinyes are primarily human ghosts, but all human ghosts are not Erinyes, only those ghosts that are angry, and that for a special reason, usually because they have been murdered. Other cases of angry ghosts are covered by the black Ker. It is the vengeful inhumanity of the Erinyes, arising as it does from their humanity, which marks them out from the Keres.

That the Erinyes are primarily the vengeful souls of murdered men can and will in the sequel be plainly shown, but it would be idle to deny that already in Homer they have passed out of this stage and are personified almost beyond recognition. They are no longer souls; they are the avengers of souls. Thus in Homer, in the prayer of Althaea, Erinys[1], though summoned to avenge the death of Althaea's brethren, is clearly not the ghost of either of them; she is one, they are two; she is female, they are male. Althaea prays:

> 'And her the Erinys blood-haunting[2]
> Heard out of Erebos' depths, she of the soul without pity.'

There is nothing that so speedily blurs and effaces the real origin of things as this insistent Greek habit of impersonation. We were able to track the Keres back to something like their origin just because they never really got personified. In this respect poets are the worst of mythological offenders. By their intense realization they lose all touch with the confusions of actuality. The Erinyes summoned by Althaea were really ghosts of the murdered brothers, but Homer separates them off into avengers.

[1] *Il.* IX. 571
τῆς δ' ἠεροφοῖτις 'Ερινὺς
ἔκλυεν ἐξ 'Ερέβεσφιν ἀμείλιχον ἦτορ ἔχουσα.

[2] On the epithet ἠεροφοῖτις 'blood-haunting,' usually translated 'walking in darkness,' Roscher (*Myth. Lex.* s.v.) has based a whole mistaken theory of the nature of the Erinyes as 'storm-clouds.' The Townley scholion (*ad loc.*) offers an alternative reading of the epithet more consonant with the nature of the Erinys: οἱ δὲ εἰαροπῶτις, ἐγκειμένου τοῦ εἴαρ ὅπερ ἐστὶ κατὰ Σαλαμινίους αἷμα. On this showing the Erinyes would be not those who 'walked in darkness' but those who sucked the blood, a view certainly consonant with the picture of the Erinyes presented by Aeschylus: ἀπὸ ζῶντος ῥοφεῖν ἐρυθρὸν ἐκ μελέων πέλανον (*Eum.* 264). The termination -πωτις instead of -φοιτις gives of course a simple and satisfactory meaning; but, accepting ἠερο- as representing the Cyprian form εἴαρ 'blood,' it is perhaps possible to retain -φοιτις and explain the epithet as 'blood-haunting.' Another alternative is suggested by Fick, i.e. that the primitive form is ἠαρο-ποῖτις 'blutrachend,' ποῖτις being akin to ποινή, cf. Apollo Poitios (see A. Fick, 'Götternamen,' in Bezzenberger. *Beiträge*, xx. p. 179).

In other Homeric Erinyes there is often not even a *fond* of possible ghosts. Phoenix transgresses against his father Amyntor[1] and Amyntor for his unnatural offence invokes against him the 'hateful Erinyes': they are no ancestral ghosts, they are merely avengers of the moral law, vaguer equivalents of 'Underworld Zeus and dread Persephone.' Ares[2] offends his mother Aphrodite, who is certainly *not* dead and has no ghost, and the wounds inflicted on him by Athene appease the 'Erinys of his mother.' In a word, in Homer, as has frequently been pointed out, the Erinyes are avengers of offences against blood-relations on the mother's and father's side, of all offences against moral, and finally even natural law.

The familiar case of Xanthus, the horse of Achilles[3], marks the furthest pole of complete abstraction. Xanthus warns Achilles that, for all their fleetness, his horses bear him to his death, and

> 'When he thus had spoken
> The Erinyes stayed his voice.'

The intervention of the Erinyes here is usually explained by a reference to the saying of Heracleitus[4] that 'the sun could not go out of his course without the Erinyes, ministers of justice, finding him out.' I doubt if the philosophy of Heracleitus supplies the true explanation. The horse speaks as the mouthpiece of the fates, the Erinyes; they tell of what fate (*μοῖρα*) will accomplish; nay more, *as fates* they, reluctant but obedient, carry him to his death. When Xanthus has uttered the mandate of fate, the Fates close his mouth, not because he transgresses their law, but because he has uttered it to the full.

Be that as it may, the view stated by Heracleitus is of capital importance. It shows that to a philosopher writing at the end of the 6th century B.C. the Erinyes were embodiments of law, ministers of Justice. Of course a philosopher is as little to be taken as reflecting popular faith as a poet, indeed far less; but even a philosopher cannot, save on pain of becoming unintelligible, use words apart from popular associations. Heracleitus was indeed drunk with the thought of law, of Fate, of unchanging 'moral

[1] *Il.* IX. 454.

[2] *Il.* XXI. 412.

[3] *Il.* XIX. 418 *ὡς ἄρα φωνήσαντος ἐρινύες ἔσχεθον αὐδήν.*

[4] Plut. *de Ex.* 11 *ἥλιος γὰρ οὐχ ὑπερβήσεται μέτρα* (*φησὶν ὁ Ἡράκλειτος*) *εἰ δὲ μὴ Ἐριννύες μιν, Δίκης ἐπίκουροι, ἐξευρήσουσιν.*

retribution,' with the eternal sequence of his endless flux; his Erinyes are cosmic beyond the imagination of Homer, but still the fact remains that he uses them as embodiments of the vengeance that attends transgression. By his time they are not Keres, not souls, still less bacilli, not even avengers of tribal blood, but in the widest sense ministers of Justice[1] (Δίκης ἐπίκουροι).

The Erinyes of Aeschylus.

Heracleitus has pushed abstraction to its highest pitch. When we come to Aeschylus we find, as would be expected, a conception of the Erinyes that is at once narrower and more vitalized, more objective, more primitive. In the *Septem*[2] the conception is narrower, more primitive than in Homer; the Erinys is in fact an angry ghost. This is stated with the utmost precision.

> 'Alas, thou Fate—grievous, dire to be borne,
> And Oedipus' holy Shade,
> Black Erinys, verily, mighty art thou,'

chant the chorus again and again. Fate is close at hand and nigh akin, but the real identity and apposition is between the shade, the ghost of Oedipus, and the black Erinys.

Here and in the *Prometheus Bound*[3] Aeschylus is fully conscious that it is the actual ghost, not a mere abstract vengeance that haunts and pursues. Io is stung by the oestrus[4] because she is a cow-maiden, but the real terror that maddens her is that most terrifying of all ancient ghosts, the phantom of earth-born Argus.

> 'Woe, Woe!
> Again the gadfly stings me as I go.
> The earth-born neatherd Argos hundred-eyed,
> Earth, wilt thou never hide?

[1] The conception of Dike was largely due to Orphic influence, see p. 506.

[2] *v.* 988

> ἰὼ μοῖρα βαρυδότειρα μογερὰ
> πότνιά τ' Οἰδίπου σκιὰ
> μέλαιν' Ἐρινύς, ἦ μεγασθενής τις εἶ.

[3] Aesch. *Prom. Vinct.* 566.

[4] The gadfly is purely incidental to Io in her primitive form as cow. Oistros is an incarnation of the distraction caused by the ghost. On a vase-painting representing the slaying of her children by Medea, Oistros (inscribed) is represented as a figure in a chariot drawn by snakes, and near at hand is 'the ghost of Aietes' (inscribed) who sent it. (*Arch. Zeit.* 1847, T. 3.)

O horror! he is coming, coming nigh,
Dead, with his wandering eye.
Uprising from the dead
He drives me famished
Along the shingled main,

His phantom pipe drones with a sleepy strain.
Ye gods, what have I done to cry in vain,
Fainting and frenzied with sting-driven pain?'

But when we come to the Oresteia, the Erinyes are envisaged from a different angle. The shift is due partly to the data of the plot, the primitive saga out of which it is constructed, partly to a definite moral purpose in the mind of the tragedian.

The primitive material of the trilogy was the story of the house of Atreus in which the motive is the blood-curse working from generation to generation, working within the narrow limits of one family and culminating in the Erinys of a slain mother. At the back of the Orestes and Clytaemnestra story lay the primaeval thought so clearly expressed by Plato in the *Laws*[1]. 'If a man,' says the Athenian, 'kill a freeman even unintentionally, let him undergo certain purifications, but let him not disregard a certain ancient tale of bygone days as follows: "He who has died by a violent death, if he has lived the life of a freeman, when he is newly dead, is angry with the doer of the deed, and being himself full of fear and panic on account of the violence he has suffered and seeing his murderer going about in his accustomed haunts, he feels terror, and being himself disordered[2] communicates the same feeling with all possible force, aided by recollection, to the guilty man—both to himself and to his deeds."' Here the actual ghost is the direct source of the disorder and works like a sort of bacillus of madness. It is not the guilty conscience of the murderer, but a sort of onset of the consciousness of the murdered.

[1] Plat. *Legg.* IX. 865.

[2] Mr F. M. Cornford draws my attention to a similar and even cruder English superstition. Sir Kenelm Digby, in his *Observations on the Religio Medici* (5th ed. p. 128), maintains as against Sir Thomas Browne who says that apparitions are devils, that those that appear in cemeteries and charnel-houses are the souls of the dead which have 'a byas and a languishing' towards their bodies, and that the body of a murdered man bleeds when the murderer approaches ('which is frequently seen in England') because the soul, desiring revenge, and being unable to speak, 'must endeavour to cause a motion in the subtilest or most fluid parts (and consequently the most moveable ones) of it. This can be nothing but the blood, which then being violently moved, must needs gush out at those places where it findeth issues.'

Its action is local, and hence the injunction that the murderer must leave the land. How fully Aeschylus was conscious of this almost physical aspect of crime as the action of the disordered ghost on the living comes out with terrible vividness in the *Choephori*[1]:

> 'The black bolt from below comes from the slain
> Of kin who cry for vengeance, and from them
> Madness and empty terror in the night
> Comes haunting, troubling.'

It is 'the slain of kin' who cries for vengeance. As Pausanias[2] says of the same house, 'the pollution of Pelops and the avenging ghost of Myrtilos dogged their steps.' 'Fate,' says Polybius[3], 'placed by his (Philip's) side Erinyes and Poinae and Pointers-to-Vengeance (*προστροπαίους*).' Here clearly all the words are synonymous. Apollo threatens the slayer of his mother with

> 'Yet other onsets of Erinys sent
> Of kindred blood the dire accomplishment,
> Visible visions that he needs must mark,
> Aye, though he twitch his eyebrows in the dark[4].'

To cause these 'onsets,' these *προσβολαί*, or, as they are sometimes called, *ἔφοδοι*, was, Hippocrates[5] tells us, one of the regular functions of dead men.

Behind the notion of these accesses of fright, these nocturnal apparitions caused by ghosts, there is in the mind of Aeschylus the still more primitive notion that the shed blood not only 'brings these apparitions to effect,' but is itself a source of physical infection. Here we seem to get down to a stratum of thought perhaps even more primitive than that of the bacillus-like Keres. The Chorus in the *Choephori* sings[6]:

> 'Earth that feeds him hath drunk of the gore,
> Blood calling for vengeance flows never more,
> But stiffens, and pierces its way
> Through the murderer, breeding diseases that none may allay.'

[1] Aesch. *Choeph.* 285.

[2] P. II. 18. 2 *τὸ μίασμα τὸ Πέλοπος καὶ ὁ Μυρτίλου προστρόπαιος ἠκολούθησε.*

[3] XXIII. 10. 2.

[4] *Choeph.* 282. In the interpretation of this passage I follow Dr Verrall, *Choephori*, ad *v.* 286.

[5] Hippocr. *περὶ ἱερῆς νούσου*, p. 123, 20 *ὁπόσα δὲ δείματα νυκτὸς παρίσταται καὶ φόβοι καὶ παράνοιαι καὶ ἀναπηδήσεις ἐκ κλινῆς Ἑκάτης φασὶν εἶναι ἐπιβουλὰς καὶ ἡρῴων ἐφόδους.*

[6] Aesch. *Choeph.* 64. The same idea comes out in the *Electra* of Euripides (*v.* 318).

The blood poisons the earth, and thereby poisons the murderer fed by earth. As Dr Verrall (ad loc.) points out, it is the old doctrine of the sentence of Cain, 'And now art thou cursed from the earth, which hath opened her mouth to receive thy brother's blood from thy hand; when thou tillest the ground, it shall not henceforth yield unto thee her strength.'

In the crudest and most practical form, this notion of the physical infection of the earth comes out in the story of Alcmaeon. Pausanias[1] tells us that when Alcmaeon had slain his mother Eriphyle, he came to Psophis in Arcadia, but there his disease nowise abated. He then went to Delphi, and the Pythia taught him that the only land where the avenger of Eriphyle could not dog him was the newest land which the sea had laid bare subsequently to the pollution of his mother's blood, and he found out the deposit of the river Achelous and dwelt there. There, by the new and unpolluted land he might be nourished and live. Apollodorus[2] misses the point: he brings Alcmaeon to Thesprotia and purifies him, but by the *waters* of Achelous.

The case of Alcmaeon does not stand alone. It has a curious parallel in the fate that befell Bellerophon, a fate that, I think, has not hitherto been rightly understood.

In Homer[3] the end of Bellerophon is mysterious. After the episode with Sthenoboea, he goes to Lycia, is royally entertained, marries the king's daughter, rules over a fair domain, begets three goodly children, and then, suddenly, without warning, without manifest cause, he comes to be

> 'Hated of all the gods. And in the Aleïan plain apart
> He strayed, shunning men's foot-prints, consuming his own heart.'

Homer, with a poet's instinct for the romantic and mysterious, asks no questions; Pindar[4] with his Olympian prejudice saw in the downfall of Bellerophon the proper meed of 'insolence.' Bellerophon's heart was 'aflutter for things far-off,' he had vainly longed for

> 'The converse of high Zeus.'

[1] P. VIII. 24. 8 and 9 *καὶ αὐτὸν ἡ Πυθία διδάσκει τὸν Ἐριφύλης ἀλάστορα ἐς ταύτην οἱ μόνην χώραν οὐ συνακολουθήσειν ἥτις ἐστὶ νεωτάτη, καὶ ἡ θάλασσα τοῦ μητρῴου μιάσματος ἀνέφηνεν ὕστερον αὐτήν. καὶ ὁ μὲν ἐξευρὼν τοῦ Ἀχελῴου τὴν πρόσχωσιν ἐνταῦθα ᾤκησε.*

[2] Apollod. III. 7. 5.

[3] *Il.* VI. 200.

[4] Pind. *Isth.* V. 66.

But the mythographers knew the real reason of the madness and the wandering, knew of the old sin against the old order. Apollodorus[1] says: 'Bellerophon, son of Glaukos, son of Sisyphos, having slain unwittingly his brother Deliades, or, as some say, Peiren, and others Alkimenes, came to Proetus and was purified.' On Bellerophon lay the *taboo* of blood guilt. He came to Proetus, but, the sequel shows, was *not* purified. In those old days he could not be. Proetus sent him on to the king of Lycia, and the king of Lycia drove him yet further to the only land where he *could* dwell, the Aleïan or Cilician plain[2]. This Aleïan plain was, like the mouth of the Acheloüs, *new land*, an alluvial deposit slowly recovered from the sea, ultimately in Strabo's time most fertile, but in Bellerophon's days a desolate salt-marsh. The madness of Bellerophon—for in Homer he is obviously mad—is the madness of Orestes, of the man blood-stained, Erinys-haunted; but the story of Bellerophon, like that of Alcmaeon, looks back to days even before the Erinys was formulated as a personality, to days when Earth herself was polluted, poisoned by shed blood.

Aeschylus then in the *Oresteia* is dealing with a primitive story and realizes to the uttermost its primaeval savagery. But he has chosen it for a moral purpose, nay more, when he comes to the Eumenides, with an actual topical intent. He desires first and foremost by the reconciliation of old and new to justify the ways of God to men, and next to show that in his own Athenian law-court of the Areopagus, those ways find their fullest practical human expression. That court, he somehow contrived to believe, or at least saw fit to assert, was founded on a fact of tremendous moral significance, the conversion of the Erinyes into Semnae. The conception of the Erinyes comes to Aeschylus from Homer almost full-fledged; his mythological data, unlike his plots, were 'slices from the great feasts of Homer,' and this in a very strict sense, for, owing no doubt partly to the primitive legend selected, he has had to narrow somewhat the Homeric conception of the Erinyes and make of them not avengers in general, but avengers of tribal blood. Moreover he has emphasized their legal character.

[1] Apollod. II. 2. 3.

[2] For this information as to the character of the Aleian plain, which suggested the view in the text, I am indebted to the kindness of Prof. Ramsay.

It is noteworthy that when Athene formally asks the Erinyes who and what they are[1], their answer is not 'Erinyes' but

> 'Curses our name in haunts below the earth.'

And when Athene further asks their function and prerogatives (τιμαί) the answer is:

> 'Man-slaying men we drive from out their homes[2].'

The essence of primitive law resided, as has already (p. 142) been seen, in the curse, the imprecation. Here the idea is not that of a cosmic Fate but of a definite and tangible curse, the curse of blood-guilt. It is scarcely possible to doubt that in emphasizing the curse aspect of the Erinyes, Aeschylus had in his mind some floating reminiscence of a traditional connection between the Arae and the Areopagus. He is going to make the Erinyes turn into Semnae, the local Athenian goddesses invoked upon the Areopagus: the conception of the Erinyes as Arae makes as it were a convenient bridge. The notion of the Erinyes as goddesses of Cursing is of course definitely present in Homer, but it is the notion of the curse of the broken oath rather than the curse of blood-guilt. In the great oath of Agamemnon[3] he, as became an Achaean, prays first to Zeus, but also to Earth and to the Sun and to the Erinyes who

> 'Beneath the earth
> Take vengeance upon mortals, whosoe'er
> Forswears himself.'

Hesiod[4], borrowing from Melampus, tells us that

> 'On the fifth day, they say, the Erinyes tend
> Oath at his birth whom Eris bore, a woe
> To any mortal who forswears himself.'

Aeschylus narrows the Homeric and Hesiodic conception of the Erinyes to the exigencies of the particular legend he treats; they are for him almost uniformly the personified Curses that attend the shedding of kindred blood, though now and again he rises to the cosmic conception of Heracleitus, as when the chorus in the *Eumenides* exclaim[5]

> 'O Justice, O ye thrones
> Of the Erinyes,'

[1] Aesch. *Eum.* 417. [2] *Ib.* 421. [3] *Il.* XIX. 258.
[4] Hes. *Erg.* 803. [5] Aesch. *Eum.* 511.

and chant the doom that awaits the transgressor in general; but the circumstances of the plot compel a speedy return within narrower limits.

The Tragic Erinyes.

The Erinyes in Homer are terrors unseen: Homer who lends to his Olympians such clear human outlines has no embodied shape for these underworld Angry Ones; he knows full well what they do, but not how they look. But Aeschylus can indulge in no epic vagueness. He has to bring his Erinyes in flesh and blood actually on the stage; he must make up his mind what and who they are. Fortunately at this point we are not left with a mere uncertain stage tradition or the statements of late scholiasts and lexicographers. From Aeschylus himself we know with unusual precision how his Erinyes appeared on the stage. The priestess has seen within the temple horrible things; she staggers back in terror to give—for her horror-stricken state—a description remarkably explicit. The exact order of her words is important[1]:

'Fronting the man I saw a wondrous band
Of women, sleeping on the seats. But no!
No women these, but Gorgons—yet methinks
I may not liken them to Gorgon-shapes.
Once on a time I saw those pictured things
That snatch at Phineus' feast, but these, but these
Are wingless—black, foul utterly. They snore,
Breathing out noisome breath. From out their eyes
They ooze a loathly rheum.'

The whole manner of the passage arrests attention at once. Why is Aeschylus so unusually precise and explicit? Why does he make the priestess midway in her terror give this little archaeological lecture on the art-types of Gorgons and Harpies? The reason is a simple one; the Erinyes *as Erinyes* appear for the first time in actual definite shape. Up to the time when Aeschylus brought them on the stage, no one, if he had been asked what an Erinys was like, could have given any definite answer: they were unseen horrors which art up to that time had never crystallized into set form. The priestess is literally correct when she says[2]:

'This race of visitants ne'er have I seen.'

[1] Aesch. *Eum.* 46 ff.

[2] *v.* 57.

Aeschylus had behind him, to draw from, a great wealth of bogey types; he had black Keres, such as those on the shield of Herakles; he had Gorgons, he had Harpies, but he had no ready-made shape for his Erinyes, only the Homeric horror of formlessness. What will he do? What he *did* do is clearly set forth by the priestess. When she first, in the gloom of the adyton, catches sight of the sleeping shapes, she thinks they are women, they have something human about them; but no, they are too horrible for women, they must be Gorgons. She looks a little closer. No, on second thoughts, they are not Gorgons; they have not the familiar Gorgon mask; there is something else she has seen in a picture, Harpies, 'those that snatch at Phineus' feast.' Can they be Harpies? No, again, Harpies have wings, and these are wingless. Here precisely came in the innovation of Aeschylus; he takes the Harpy-type, loathsome and foul, and rids them of their wings. It was a master-touch[1], shifting the Erinyes from the region of grotesque impossible bogeydom to a lower and more loathsome, because wholly human, horror.

The 'Gorgon shapes,' which indeed amount almost to Gorgon *masks*—so characteristic is the ugly face with tusks and protruding tongue—have been already fully discussed (p. 187), but for clearness' sake another illustration, which can be securely dated as before the time of Aeschylus, may be added here. The design in fig. 45 is from a black-figured *olpe* in the British Museum[2]. It is signed by the potter Amasis (Ἄμασίς μ' ἐποίησεν), and dates about the turn of the 6th and 5th centuries B.C. The scene depicted is the slaying of the Gorgon Medusa by Perseus. Medusa is represented with the typical ugly face, protruding tusks and tongue. On her lower lip is a fringe of hair; four snakes rise from her head. She wears a short purple chiton, over which is a stippled skin with two snakes knotted at the waist. She has high huntress-boots and two pairs of wings, one outspread the other recurved. The essential feature of the Gorgon in Greek art is the hideous mask-like head; but she has usually, though not always, snakes somewhere about her, in her hair or her hands or about her waist. The wings,

[1] A master-touch from the point of view of Aeschylus, who is all for the new order. It is however impossible to avoid a regret that he stooped to the cheap expedient of blackening the Erinyes as representatives of the old. He thereby half alienates our sympathies. See 'Delphika,' *J.H.S.* XIX. 1899, p. 251.

[2] *Cat.* B 471. *Vorlegeblätter* 1889, Taf. II. 1 *a*.

also a frequent though not uniform appendage, are sometimes two, sometimes four. In common with the Harpy, to whom she is so

Fig. 45.

near akin, she has the bent knee that indicates a striding pace. That Harpy and Gorgon are not clearly distinguished is evident from the vase-painting already discussed (p. 176, fig. 18), in which the Gorgon sisters of Medusa are inscribed in the dual, 'Harpies' ('Αρεπυία).

Broadly speaking the Gorgon is marked off from the Harpy by the mask-face. The Harpy is a less monstrous form of Gorgon, but at worst there was not much to choose between them. We

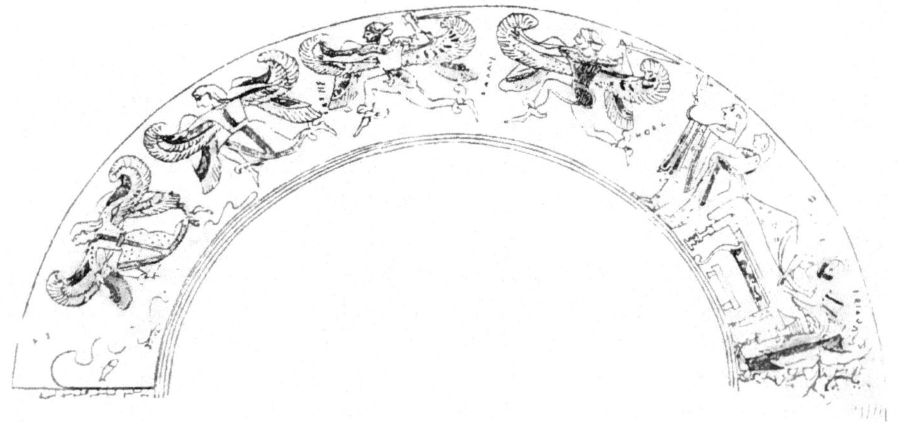

Fig. 46.

sympathize with the hesitation of the priestess, when we compare the Medusa-Gorgon of the Amasis vase (fig. 45) with the undoubted Harpies of the famous Würzburg[1] cylix (fig. 46). Here we have depicted the very scene remembered by the priestess, 'those pictured things that snatch at Phineus' feast.' The vase is in a disastrous condition, and the inscriptions present many difficulties as well as uncertainties, but happily those that are legible and certain are sufficient to place the subject of the scene beyond a doubt. It would indeed be clear enough without the added evidence of inscriptions. Phineus to the right reclines at the banquet, attended by women of his family, whose names present difficulties and need not here be discussed. The Harpies[2] ('Αρε...), pestilential unclean winds as they are, have fouled the feast. But for the last time they are chased away by the two sons of Boreas, Zetes and Kalais, sword in hand. The sons of the clean clear North Wind drive away the unclean demons. All the winds, clean and unclean, are figured alike, with four wings each; but the Boreadae are of course male, the women Harpies are draped.

Before returning to the tragic Erinyes, another vase must be

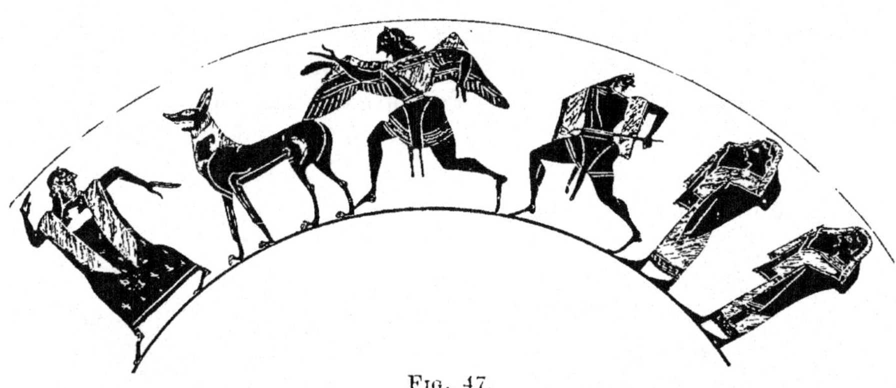

FIG. 47.

discussed. The design, from an early black-figured cylix in the Louvre[3], is reproduced in fig. 47. The centre of interest is clearly

[1] Würzburg, *Inv.* 354.

[2] The Phineus cylix is published in phototype by Carl Sittl, 'Die Phineus Schale, und ähnliche Vasen,' Programm xxv., forming part of the *Jahresbericht des Wagnerischen Kunst-Instituts der Kgl. Universität Würzburg*, 1892. The account there given of the difficult inscriptions is inadequate and must be supplemented by reference to Dr Böhlau's corrections in his paper on 'Die Ionischen Augenschalen,' *A. Mitt.* 1898 (XXIII.) pp. 54, 77; see also Furtwängler-Reinhold, Pl. 41.

[3] Pottier, *Cat. A.* 478, pl. 17. 1. The vase is further discussed by Mr Barnett, *Hermes*, 'Miscellen,' 1898, p. 639. Mr Barnett sees in the winged figure Iris, an interpretation with which I cannot agree.

the large dog, a creature of supernatural size, almost the height of a man. To the left of him a bearded man is hastening away; he looks back, apparently in surprise or consternation. Immediately behind the dog comes a winged figure, also in haste, and manifestly interested in the dog. Behind her is Hermes, and behind him, as quiet spectators, two women figures. There is only one possible explanation of the general gist of the scene. It is the story of the golden dog of Minos stolen from Crete by Pandareos, king of Lycia, and by him from fear of Zeus deposited with Tantalos. The scholiast on the *Odyssey*[1] tells the story in commenting on the lines 'As when the daughter of Pandareos the bright brown nightingale' as follows. 'There is a legend about the above-mentioned Pandareos, that he stole the golden dog of Zeus in Crete, a life-like work of Hephaistos, from the precinct of Zeus, and having stolen it he deposited it with Tantalos. And when Zeus demanded the stolen thing by the mouth of Hermes Tantalos swore that he had it not. But Zeus when he had got the dog again, Hermes having secretly taken it away, buried Tantalos under Sipylos.' Another scholiast[2] gives a different version, in which judgment fell on the daughters of Pandareos. 'Merope and Kleothera (daughters of Pandareos) were brought up by Aphrodite; but when Pandareos, having received the dog stolen from Crete in trust for Tantalos, denied that he ever took it, Merope and Kleothera were snatched away by the Harpies and given to the Erinyes.'

In the light of this version the vase-painting is clear. The moment chosen is the coming of Hermes to claim the dog. It is no use Pandareos denying he had it, for there it is, larger than life. The vase-painter had to put the dog in, to make the story manifest. The two women spectators are the daughters of Pandareos, Merope and Kleothera. Who is the winged figure? Archaeologists variously name her Iris, a Harpy, an Erinys. Iris I unhesitatingly reject. Between a Harpy and an Erinys the choice is harder, and the doubt is instructive. Taking into consideration the Lycian character of the story, and the not unimportant fact that the design of the reverse represents a Lycian myth also, Bellerophon and the Chimaera, I think we

[1] Schol. ad *Od.* τ 518 and P. x. 30. 2. Pind. Schol. *Ol.* I. 90.
[2] Schol. Ambros. B. ad τ 518.

may safely say that the figure is a Harpy, but it is a Harpy performing the functions of an Erinys, avenging the theft, avenging the broken oath, come also to fetch the two maidens whom she will give to be handmaids to the hateful Erinyes—so near akin, so fluctuating are the two conceptions.

The fact then that Aeschylus brought them on the stage and his finer poetical conception of horror compelled the complete and human formulation of the Erinyes; before his time they have no definite art-type. The Erinyes of Aeschylus are near akin to Gorgons, but they lack the Gorgon mask; nearer still to Harpies, but wingless. It is curious and interesting to note that at the close of the *Choephori*[1], where they do not appear on the stage, where they are visible only to the imagination of the mad Orestes, he sees them like the shapes he knows—

> 'These are like Gorgon shapes
> Black-robed, with tangled tentacles entwined
> Of frequent snakes.'

Aeschylus felt the imaginative gain of the purely human form,

FIG. 48.

but his fellow artist the vase-painter will not lightly forego the joy of drawing great curved wings. In vases that are immediately

[1] Aesch. *Choeph.* 1048. The noisome exudation from the eyes noted by Aeschylus (*Eum.* 54) has already been shown (p. 195) to be characteristically Gorgon.

post-Aeschylean the wingless type tends to prevail, though not wholly; later it lapses and the great fantastic wings reappear. On the red-figured vase-painting[1] in fig. 48—the earliest of the series and dating somewhere towards the end of the 5th century—we have the scene of the purification of Orestes. He is seated close to the omphalos—sword in hand. Above his head Apollo holds the pig of purification, in his left hand the laurel; to the right is Artemis as huntress with spears; to the left are the sleeping wingless Erinyes; the ghost of Clytaemnestra beckons to them to wake. From the ground rises another Erinys, a veritable earth demon. The euphemism of the vase-painter makes the Erinyes not only wingless but beautiful, as fair to see as Clytaemnestra.

The next picture[2] (fig. 49) is later in style, but far more

Fig. 49.

closely under dramatic influence. We have the very opening scene of the *Eumenides*. The inner shrine of the temple, a small

[1] *Monimenti dell' Inst.* iv. pl. 18. Baumeister, p. 1314. The vase, an *oxybaphon*, is now in the Louvre.

[2] Hermitage, *Cat.* i. 349. Stephani, *Compte Rendu*, 1863, pl. vi. 5.

Ionic naos, the omphalos, and the supplicant Orestes, with no Apollo to purify; the frightened priestess holding the symbol of her office, the great temple key with its sacred fillet. All about the shrine are lying the Erinyes, wingless and loathly; the scanty dishevelled hair and pouting barbarous lips are best seen in the rightmost Erinys, whose face is drawn profile-wise.

In the third representation[1] from a krater formerly in the Hope Collection (fig. 50) the style is late and florid, and the vase-painter

FIG. 50.

has shaken himself quite free from dramatic influence. Orestes crouches in an impossible pose on the great elaborately decorated omphalos; Apollo is there with his filleted laurel staff. The place of Artemis is taken by Athene, her foot resting on what seems to be an urn for voting. To the left is an Erinys, in huntress garb, with huge snake and high curved wings; but the vase-painter is indifferent and looks for variety: a second Erinys, who leans over the tripod, is well furnished with snakes, but has no wings.

[1] Millin, *Peintures des vases grecs*, II. 68. Baumeister, fig. 1315, p. 1118.

In the last and latest of the series, a kalpis in the Berlin Museum[1] (fig. 51), the Erinys is a mere angel of vengeance; her wings are no longer fantastic, she is no huntress, but a matronly, heavily draped figure; she holds a scourge in her hand, she is more Poine than Erinys, only about her is still curled a huge snake.

Fig. 51.

Aeschylus then, we may safely assert, first gave to the Erinyes outward and visible shape, first differentiated them from Keres, Gorgons, or Harpies. In this connection it is worth noting that the Erinyes or Poinae were not infrequently referred to in classical literature as though they were almost the exclusive property of the stage. Aeschines[2], in his oration against Timarchus, exhorts the Athenians not to imagine 'that impious men *as in the tragedies* are pursued and chastised by Poinae with blazing torches.' Plutarch[3] in his life of Dion tells how, when the conspiracy of Callippus was on foot against him, Dion had a 'monstrous and portentous vision.' As he was meditating alone one evening he heard a sudden noise and saw, for it was still light, a woman of gigantic size, 'in form and raiment exactly like a tragic Erinys.' She was sweeping the house with a sort of broom.

On Lower Italy vases the Erinyes as Poinae frequently appear

[1] *Jahrbuch d. Inst.* 1890, Anzeiger, p. 90.
[2] Aeschin. *c. Tim.* 80.
[3] Plut. *Vit. Dion.* c. 55.

(Chap. XI.). They are sometimes winged, sometimes unwinged. From the august ministers of the vengeance of the dead they have sunk to be the mere pitiless tormentors of hell. They lash on Sisyphos to his ceaseless task, they bind Peirithoös, they fasten Ixion to his wheel. But it is curious to note that, though the notion of pursuit is almost lost, they still wear the huntress garb, the short skirt and high boots. It is needless to follow the downward course of the Erinys in detail, a course accelerated by Orphic eschatology, but we may note the last stage of degradation in Plutarch's treatise 'On those who are punished by the Deity late[1].' The criminals whom Justice (Dike)—the Orphic divinity of purification rather than vengeance—rejects as altogether incurable are pursued by an Erinys, 'the third and most savage of the ministrants of Adrasteia.' She drives them down into a place which Plutarch very properly describes as 'not to be seen, not to be spoken of.' The Erinyes are from beginning to end of the old order, implacable, vindictive; they know nothing of Orphic penance and purgatory; as 'angels of torment[2]' they go to people a Christian Hell.

THE ERINYS AS SNAKE.

We return to Aeschylus. His intent was to humanize the Erinyes that thereby they might be the more inhuman. The more horrible the shape of these impersonations of the old order the greater the miracle of their conversion into the gentle Semnae, and yet the easier, for so early as we know them the Semnae are goddesses, human as well as humane.

In his persistent humanizing of the Erinyes Aeschylus suffers one lapse, the more significant because probably unconscious. When Clytaemnestra would rouse the Erinyes from their slumber, she cries[3],

> 'Travail and Sleep, chartered conspirators,
> Have spent the fell rage of the *dragoness*.'

It is of course possible to say that she uses the word 'dragoness' (δράκαινα) 'poetically,' for a monster in general,

[1] Plut. *de ser. num. vind.* XXII.
[2] ἄγγελοι βασανισταί in the Apocalypse of Peter; see Dieterich, *Nekuia*, p. 61.
[3] Aesch. *Eum.* 126.

possibly a human monster; but the question is forced upon us, why is this particular monster selected? why does she say 'dragoness' and not rather 'hound of hell'? In the next lines[1] comes the splendid simile of the dog hunting in dreams, and it would surely have been more 'poetical' to keep the figure intact. But language and associations sometimes break through the best regulated conceptions, and deep, very deep in the Greek mind lay the notion that the Erinys, the offended ghost, was a snake. The notion of the earth demon, the ghost as snake, will be considered when hero-worship is dealt with (p. 325). For the present it can only be noted in Aeschylus as an outcrop of a lower stratum of thought, a stratum in which the Erinys was not yet an abstracted or even humanized minister of vengeance, but simply an angry ghost in snake form.

The use of the singular number, 'dragoness,' is, in itself, significant. The Erinyes as ministers of vengeance are indefinitely multiplied, but the old ghost-Erinys is one, not many; she is the ghost of the murdered mother. Clytaemnestra herself is the real 'dragoness,' though she does not know it, and by a curious unconscious reminiscence the Erinyes sleep till she, the true Erinys, rouses them.

The mention by Aeschylus of the 'dragoness' does not stand alone. To Euripides also the Erinys is a snake. In the *Iphigeneia in Tauris*[2] the mad Orestes cries to Pylades,

> 'Dost see her, her the Hades-snake who gapes
> To slay me, with dread vipers, open-mouthed?'

Here it can hardly be said that the conception is borrowed from Aeschylus, for assuredly the stage Erinyes of Aeschylus, as he consciously conceived them, were in no wise snakes. Moreover the 'Hades-snake' confuses the effect of the 'dread vipers' that follow. In his *Orestes* also[3] Euripides makes the Erinyes 'maidens with the forms of snakes,' where it is straining language, and quite needlessly, to say that the word δρακοντώδεις means 'having snakes in their hands or hair.'

Art too has these harkings back to the primitive snake form. The design in fig. 52 is from a black-figured amphora in

[1] v. 131.
[2] Eur. *Iph. in T.* 286.
[3] Eur. *Or.* 256.

the Vatican Museum[1], dating about the turn of the 6th and 5th centuries B.C. We have the usual striding flying type, the four wings, the huntress boots—a type of which, as has been shown, it is hard to say whether it represents Gorgon or Harpy. There is no context to decide. One thing is clear. The vase-painter is afraid that we shall miss his meaning, shall not understand that this winged thing striding through the air is an earth demon, so he paints below, moving *pari passu*, a great snake. The winged demon *is* also a snake[2].

FIG. 52.

[1] Passerius, *Pict. Etrusc.* III. 297. *J.H.S.* vol. XIX. 1899, p. 219. This representation does not stand alone. Among the fragments of vase-paintings found in the excavations on the Acropolis, and as yet unpublished, is one of considerably earlier style than the design in fig. 52, and with a representation exactly similar in all essentials. The winged feet and part of the drapery of the figure remain, and below is a large snake with open mouth. Found as it was in the 'pre-Persian' débris, this fragment cannot be later and is probably much earlier than 480 B.C.

[2] This striding flying pose with the bent knee has been used by some archaeologists to explain the epithet καμψίπους. But bending or turning the *knee* is not bending or turning the foot. It is possible that in this epithet applied (Aesch. *Sept.* 791) to the Erinys we have merely an expression of the instinct to create an uncouth deformed bogey. M. Paul Perdrizet (*Mélusine*, vol. IX. 1898, p. 99, 'Les pieds ou les genoux à rebours') makes the interesting suggestion that the καμψίπους Ἐρινύς may be an Erinys with feet turned the reverse way, a horrid distorted cripple. This peculiar form of deformity was not unknown among the ancients, as witness the statuettes cited as examples by M. Perdrizet, a bronze in the British Museum (*Cat. Walters*, no. 216) and a terracotta in the National Museum at Athens (*Cat.* 7877: Stackelberg, *Gräber der Hellenen*, pl. LXXIII. 475). I do not feel confident of the rightness of this interpretation for two reasons, firstly, καμψίπους seems scarcely to be the right epithet for a striking distortion which would rather be στρεβλόπους or some such word, and secondly, constant stress is laid on the *swiftness* of the Erinys which would be inconsistent with a crippling deformity. On the other hand, figures with their feet reversed *may* have suggested the inevitable back-coming of the Erinys. Mr F. M. Cornford suggests to me that καμψίπους is the humanized equivalent of γαμψῶνυξ, an interpretation proffered by Blomfield but rejected in favour of *pernix*. The suggestion seems to me to carry fresh conviction now that the Erinys is seen to be in her original essence and in her art-form near akin to Harpy, Sphinx and Bird-woman. Sophocles (*Oed. Tyr.* 1199) calls the Sphinx γαμψῶνυξ. In fig. 43 she is claw-footed; the Harpy to the right in fig. 18 has crooked claws for hands. Aeschylus may be using an epithet that originally meant 'clutch-foot' in some new sense as 'plying the foot,' i.e. swift, or as 'back-returning.'

Most clearly of all the identity of ghost and snake comes out in the vase-painting in fig. 53 from an archaic vase of the type known as 'prothesis' vases, in the Museum at Athens[1]. They are a class used in funeral ceremonies and decorated with funeral subjects. Two mourners stand by a grave tumulus, itself surmounted by a funeral vase. Within the tumulus the vase-painter depicts what he believes to be there. Winged eidola, ghosts, and a great snake, also a ghost. Snake and eidolon are but two ways of saying the same thing. The little fluttering figures here represented are merely harmless Keres, not angry vindictive Erinyes, but when the Erinys developes into an avenger she yet remembers that she is a snake-ghost.

Fig. 53.

The Gorgon, too, has her snakes. To the primitive Greek mind every bogey was earth-born. In the design in fig. 54[2]

Fig. 54.

we have the slaying of the Gorgon Medusa. The inscriptions are not clearly legible, but the scene is evident. Perseus attended by Athene and one of the nymphs, who gave him the kibisis and

[1] *A. Mitt.* xvi. p. 379. *J.H.S.* xix. 1899, p. 219, fig. 4.
[2] Vienna Museum. Masner, *Cat.* 221. *Annali dell' Inst.* 1866, Tav. d' agg. R. 2.

helmet and winged sandals, is about to slay Medusa. Medusa is of the usual Gorgon type, but she holds in her hand a huge snake, the double of herself.

But the crowning evidence as to the snake-form of the Erinys is literary, Clytaemnestra's dream in the *Choephori*. Clytaemnestra dreams that she gives birth to and suckles a snake[1]. Dr Verrall (ad loc.) has pointed out that the snake is here the regular symbol of things subterranean and especially of the grave, and he conjectures that the snake may have been presented to the eyes of the audience by 'the visible tomb of Agamemnon which would presumably be marked as a tomb in the usual way.' I would go a step further. The snake is more than the symbol of the dead; it is, I believe, the actual vehicle of the Erinys. The Erinys is in this case not the ghost of the dead Agamemnon, but the dead Agamemnon's son Orestes. The symbol proper to the ghost-Erinys is transferred to the living avenger. Orestes states this clearly[2]:

> 'Myself in serpent's shape
> Will slay her.'

And this, not merely because he is deadly as a snake, but because he *is* the snake, i.e. the Erinys.

Again, when Clytaemnestra cries for mercy, Orestes answers[3]:

> 'Nay, for my father's fate *hisses* thy doom.'

The snake-Erinys in the *Eumenides*, and here again in the *Choephori*, remains of course merely an incidental survival, important mainly as marking the road Aeschylus has left far behind. It is an almost unconscious survival of a tradition that conceived of the Erinyes as actually ghosts, not merely as the ministers of ghostly vengeance.

Before we leave the snake-Erinys, one more vase-painting must be cited, which brings this conception very vividly before us. The design in fig. 55 is from an early black-figured amphora of the class known as 'Tyrrhenian,' formerly in the Bourguignon collection at Naples[4]. The figure of a woman just murdered lies prostrate over

[1] Aesch. *Choeph.* 527 and 531. [2] *v.* 549.

[3] *v.* 927

πατρὸς γὰρ αἶσα τόνδε συρίζει μόρον,

accepting Dr Verrall's reading συρίζει.

[4] *Jahrbuch d. Inst.* 1893, p. 93, pl. I. The vase is there interpreted as the slaying of Polyxena, but I agree with Dr Thiersch (*Tyrrhenische Amphoren*, p. 56) that the scene represented is the slaying of Eriphyle by Alcmaeon. In connection with the omphalos-tomb of the vase-painting it is worth noting that at Phlius near the house of divination of Amphiaraos there was an omphalos. See P. II. 13. 7.

an omphalos-shaped tomb. The warrior who has slain her escapes with drawn sword to the right. But too late. Straight out of the tomb, almost indeed out of the body of the woman, rises a huge snake, mouthing at the murderer. The intent is clear; it is

Fig. 55.

the snake-Erinys rising in visible vengeance. The murderer is probably Alcmaeon, who has just slain his mother Eriphyle. His story, already discussed (p. 220), is as it were the double of that of Orestes. The interpretation as Alcmaeon is not quite certain. It does not however affect the general sense of the scene, i.e. a murderer pursued by the instant vengeance of a snake-Erinys.

Before passing to the shift from Erinyes to Semnae it may be well to note that another tragedian—priest as well as poet—held to the more primitive view, realized definitely that the Erinyes, the avengers, were merely angry implacable Keres. To Sophocles in the *Oedipus Tyrannus*[1] Apollo is the minister, not, as in the *Eumenides*, of reconciliation, but of vengeance. He has taken over the functions of the Erinyes. With the lightning and fire of his father Zeus he leaps full-armed upon the guilty man;

[1] Soph. *Oed. Tyr.* 469. The attitude of Sophocles towards the Orestes myth, and the fashion in which he ignores the conflict between Apollo and the Erinyes, cannot be discussed here. It has been ably treated by Miss Janet Case in the *Classical Review*, May 1902, p. 195.

but even Apollo cannot dispense with the ancient avengers. With him

> 'Dread and unerring
> Follow the Keres.'

The Keres here are certainly regarded as a kind of Fate, but to translate the word 'Fates' is to precipitate unduly the meaning. The word calls up in the poet's mind[1], not only the notion of ministers of vengeance, but also the reminiscence of ghostly fluttering things. He says of the guilty man:

> 'Fierce as a bull is he,
> Homeless, with desolate foot he seeks to flee
> The dooms of Gaia's central mound.
> In vain, they live and flit ever around.'

Again, in the *Electra* of Euripides[2], though the Erinyes are fully personified as dog-faced goddesses, yet they are also Keres.

> 'They hunt you like dread Keres, goddesses
> Dog-faced, in circling madness.'

Here the word Keres seems to be used because Moirae is of too beneficent and omnipotent association; Keres keeps the touch of personal ghostly vengeance.

To resume: the Erinyes are attributive epithets of ghosts, formless in Homer, but gradually developed by literature, and especially by the genius of Aeschylus, into actual impersonations. In accordance with this merely attributive origin it is not strange that quâ Erinyes their cult is practically non-existent. In only one instance do we hear of a definite place of worship for the Erinyes *as such*. Herodotus[3] tells us that at Sparta the children of the clan of the Aegidae 'did not survive.' Accordingly in obedience to an oracle the Aegidae 'made a sanctuary to the Erinyes of Laios and Oedipus.'

Here the Erinyes are plainly offended ancestral ghosts, destructive to the offspring of their descendants, and demanding to be appeased. In so far as they are ghosts, the ghosts of murdered or outraged men, the Erinyes were of course everywhere propitiated, but rarely under their 'Angry' name. That the natural prudence of euphemism forbade. As abstract ministers of vengeance we have no evidence of their worship. Clytaemnestra[4]

[1] *v.* 475.
[2] Eur. *El.* 1252.
[3] Herod. IV. 149.
[4] Aesch. *Eum.* 106.

indeed recounts in detail her dread service to the Erinyes, but when closely examined it is found to be merely the regular ritual of the dead and of underworld divinities; it has all the accustomed marks, the 'wineless libations' and the 'nephalia for propitiation, the banquets by night' offered on the low brazier (*ἐσχάρα*) characteristic of underworld sacrifice (p. 62). The hour was one, she adds, 'shared by none of the gods.' What she means is none of the gods of the upper air, the Olympians proper: it was an hour shared by every underworld divinity. Aeschylus has in a word transferred the regular ritual of ghosts to his partially abstracted ministers of vengeance, and has thereby left unconscious witness to their real origin.

The 'Semnai Theai.'

To these Erinyes, adjectival, cultless, ill-defined, the Venerable Goddesses (*σεμναὶ θεαί*) present a striking contrast. If the Erinyes owe such substance and personality as they have mainly to poets, to Homer first, later to Aeschylus and the other tragedians, with the Semnae it is quite otherwise. Their names are of course adjectival—almost all primitive cultus names are—but from the first, as we know them, they are personal and local. The Erinyes range over earth and sea, the Semnae are seated quietly and steadfastly at Athens. They are the objects of a strictly local cult, never emerging to Pan-Hellenic importance. But for the fact that Aeschylus was an Athenian we should scarcely have realized their existence; they would have remained obscure local figures like the Ablabiae and the Praxidikae.

In this connection it is of cardinal importance that, though we are apt to speak of them as the Semnae, the Venerable Ones, this is not their cultus title, not the fashion in which they were actually addressed at Athens. They are uniformly spoken of, not as the Venerable Ones, but as the Venerable Goddesses[1] (*αἱ σεμναὶ θεαί*). The distinction is important. It marks the fact that the Semnae from the first moment they come into our view have

[1] Pausanias (I. 31. 2) mentions one other place in Attica where the Semnae are worshipped under this name. At Phlya in one and the same sanctuary there were altars of Demeter Anesidora, of Zeus Ktesios, of Athene Tithrone, of Kore Protogone and of goddesses called Venerable (*Σεμνῶν ὀνομαζομένων θεῶν*).

attained a complete anthropomorphism, have passed from ghosts to goddesses[1]; they are clearly defined personalities with a definite cultus; they are primitive forms, in fact *the* primitive forms, of earth goddesses, of such conceptions as culminated finally in the great figures of Demeter and Kore. Other such figures are, for Athens the two Thesmophoroi, who are indeed but developments, other aspects, of the Semnae; for Eleusis the 'two goddesses,' τὼ θεώ, known to us by inscriptions and reliefs; for Aegina Damia and Auxesia; and for the rest of Greece many another local form, dual or triune, which need not now be enumerated. The process of this gradual anthropomorphism, this passage from sprite and ghost and demon to full-fledged divinity will be fully traced when we come to the 'making of a goddess' (p. 257). For the present it can only be noted that the term 'goddesses' sharply differentiates the Semnae from the Erinyes, who, save for sporadic literary mention, never attained any such rank. Euripides[2] does indeed make Orestes call the Erinyes 'dread goddesses,' but Aeschylus[3] is explicit: 'their adornment (κόσμος) was neither human nor divine.' It must be distinctly understood that, as the Semnae are goddesses, they are dealt with at this point only by anticipation, to elucidate the transformation effected by Aeschylus.

What we certainly know of the Semnae, as distinct from kindred figures such as the Eumenides, is not very much, but such as it is, is significant. We know the site of their sanctuary, something of the aspect of their images, something also of their functions and of the nature of their ritual. We know in fact enough, as will be shown, to feel sure that like the Erinyes they were underworld potencies, ghosts who had become goddesses. The origin of the two conceptions is the same, but their development widely different, and moreover we catch it arrested at a different stage.

It is obvious from the play of the *Eumenides* that the worship of the Semnae at Athens was of hoary antiquity. It is true that Diogenes Laertius[4] states (on the authority of the augur Lobon)

[1] The best evidence of this is the language, always ceremonial, of oaths taken in the law courts, where we may be sure the Semnae are invoked by their official title, e.g. Deinarchus *c. Dem.* 47. Μαρτύρομαι τὰς σεμνὰς θεάς, ὦ ἄνδρες Ἀθηναῖοι. But so far as I am aware the Semnae are never alluded to merely as Semnae.

[2] Eur. *Or.* 259.

[3] Aesch. *Eum.* 55.

[4] Diog. Laert. I. x. 6. See Demoulin, *Épiménide de Crète*, p. 110.

that the sanctuary of the Semnae at Athens was founded by Epimenides. The scene of the operations of Epimenides was undoubtedly the Areopagos, but, as the purification of Athens took place in the 46th Olympiad, the statement that he founded the sanctuary must be apocryphal. Very likely he may have revived and restored the cult. Diogenes says that he took a number of black and white sheep and led them up to the Areopagos and thence let them go whither they would, and he commanded those who followed them to sacrifice each of them wherever the sheep happened to lie down, and so the plague would be stayed. Whence even now, adds Diogenes, you may find in the Athenian demes nameless altars in memory of this atonement. Some such altar as this was still to be seen at or near the Areopagos when St Paul preached there, and such an altar may have become associated with the Semnae, who like many other underworld beings were Nameless Ones.

The site of the worship of the Semnae was undoubtedly some sort of cave or natural chasm amplified artificially into a sanctuary. Such caves, clefts or chasms are, as has already been shown (p. 125), the proper haunts of underworld beings; they are also usually, though not uniformly, primitive. Of the sanctuary and the cultus images Pausanias[1] speaks as follows. After describing the Areopagos and the two unwrought stones called 'Transgression' (ὕβρις) and 'Pitilessness' (ἀναιδεία) on which accused and accuser stood, he says 'And near is a sanctuary (ἱερόν) of the goddesses whom the Athenians call Semnae, but Hesiod in the *Theogony* calls Erinyes. Aeschylus represents them with snakes in their hair, but in their images there is nothing frightful, nor in the other images of the underworld gods that are set up. There is a Pluto also and a Hermes and an image of Ge. And there those who have been acquitted in a suit before the Areopagos sacrifice. And others besides sacrifice, both strangers and citizens, and within the enclosure there is the tomb of Oedipus.'

Pausanias by his reference to Aeschylus betrays at once the source of his identification of the Semnae with the Erinyes. The statement cannot be taken as evidence that prior to Aeschylus any such identification was current. After the time of Aeschylus,

[1] P. I. 28. 6.

classical writers, except when they are quoting ritual formularies, begin to accept the fusion and use the names Erinyes, Eumenides, and Semnae as interchangeable terms. A like laxity unhappily obtains among modern commentators.

The statement of Pausanias, that about the cultus images of the Semnae there was nothing frightful, is important, as showing how foreign to the Semnae was the terror-haunted conception of the tragic Erinys. Aeschylus might fuse the Erinyes and the Semnae at will, but the cultus images of the Semnae take on no attribute of the Erinyes. About these cultus images we learn something more from the scholiast on Aeschines[1]. Commenting on the Semnae he says 'These were three in number and were called Venerable Goddesses, or Eumenides, or Erinyes. Two of them were made of lychnites stone by Scopas the Parian, but the middle one by Kalamis.' Here again we must of course discount the statement as regards the triple appellation, at least for a date preceding Aeschylus. The number of the statues is noticeable. At the time when the scholiast or his informant[2] wrote the images were unquestionably three. The origin and significance of the female trinities will be considered later (p. 286). For the present it is sufficient to note that the trinity was probably a later stage of development than the duality. From the notice of the scholiast we cannot be certain that the images were *originally* three; nay more, it looks as if there was some reminiscence of a duality. Moreover the scholiast on the *Oedipus Coloneus*[3] expressly states that according to Phylarchus the images of the Semnae at Athens were two in number. He adds that according to Polemon they were three. That the number three ultimately prevailed is highly probable, indeed practically certain. The scholiast on Aeschines goes on to say 'the court of the Areopagos adjudged murder cases

[1] Schol. ad Aeschin. *c. Timarch.* I. 188 c '*ταῖς σεμναῖς θεαῖς.*' *Τρεῖς ἦσαν αὗται αἱ λεγόμεναι σεμναὶ θεαὶ ἢ Εὐμενίδες ἢ 'Ερινννύες, ὧν τὰς μὲν δύο τὰς ἑκατέρωθεν Σκόπας ὁ Πάριος πεποίηκεν ἐκ τῆς λιχνίτου λίθου τὴν δὲ μέσην Κάλαμις. οἱ δὲ 'Αρεοπαγῖται τρεῖς που τοῦ μηνὸς ἡμέρας τὰς φονικὰς δίκας ἐδίκαζον ἑκάστῃ τῶν θεῶν μίαν ἡμέραν ἀπονέμοντες. ἦν δὲ τὰ πεμπόμενα αὐταῖς ἱερὰ πόπανα καὶ γάλα ἐν ἄγγεσι κεραμείοις. φασὶ μέντοι αὐτὰς Γῆς εἶναι καὶ Σκότους, οἱ δὲ Σκότους καὶ Εὐωνύμης ἣν καὶ Γῆν ὀνομάζεσθαι, κληθῆναι δὲ Εὐμενίδας ἐπιηρέστερον* [de conj.: *ἐπίηρα* Vat. *ἐπὶ 'Ορέστου* cett.] *πρῶτον καλουμένας.*

[2] Dr Wellmann (*de Istro* 14) has shown that in all probability the information of the scholiast is borrowed from the treatise of Polemon quoted by Clement of Alexandria in his *Protrepticus*, p. 41.

[3] Schol. ad *Oed. Col.* 39 '*ἔμφοβοι θεαί.*' *Φύλαρχός φησι δύο αὐτὰς εἶναι τά τε ἀγάλματα 'Αθήνησι δύο, Πολέμων δὲ τρεῖς αὐτάς φησι.*

on three days in each month, assigning one day to each goddess.' The three days were probably a primitive institution, three being a number sacred to the dead, and these three days may have helped the development of the threefold form of the Semnae. Later in considering the Charites and other kindred shapes (p. 286) it will be shown that many different strands went to the weaving of a trinity. The strictly definite number of the Semnae, be it two or three, is in marked contrast to the indefinite 'wondrous throng' (*θαυμαστὸς λόχος*) of the Aeschylean Erinyes. The contrast may have been softened, if in the concluding scene the chorus of Erinyes filed away in groups of three.

The sanctuary of the Semnae was, in the narrower sense of the word 'sanctuary,' a refuge for suppliants. This is, of course, a trait that it has in common with many other precincts. Thucydides[1] tells how in the conspiracy of Kylon some of the conspirators sat down at the altars of the Venerable Goddesses, and were put to death at the entrance. A monument, the Kyloneion, was put up close to the Nine Gates to expiate the pollution. Plutarch[2], in his account of this same conspiracy, adds a curious primitive touch: the conspirators connected themselves with the image of 'the goddess' by a thread, believing thereby they would remain immune; the thread broke of its own accord when they reached the Semnae: this was taken as an omen of rejection and they were put to death. Aristophanes twice alludes to the precinct of the Semnae as a place of sanctuary. In the *Knights*[3], he makes the outraged triremes say

'If this is what the Athenians like, we must needs set sail forthwith
And sit us down in the Theseion or in the Semnae's shrine.'

In the *Thesmophoriazusae*[4], when Mnesilochus is about to make off in a fright, Euripides asks

'You villain, where are you off to?'

and the answer is

'To the shrine of the Semnae.'

It is noticeable that in both these cases the name given to the goddesses of sanctuary is Semnae, not Erinyes or Eumenides.

[1] Thucyd. I. 126. [2] Plut. *Vit. Sol.* XII.

[3] Ar. *Eq.* 1312

ἢν δ' ἀρέσκῃ ταῦτ' Ἀθηναίοις καθῆσθαί μοι δοκεῖ
ἐς τὸ Θησεῖον πλεούσας ἢ 'πὶ τῶν σεμνῶν θεῶν.

[4] Ar. *Thesm.* 224

ΕΥΡ. *οὗτος σὺ ποῖ θεῖς;*
ΜΝ. *ἐς τὸ τῶν σεμνῶν θεῶν.*

The confusion of the three was never local, only literary, and by the time of Aristophanes it has not yet begun.

Euripides[1] is our solitary authority for the fact that the sanctuary was also oracular. At the close of the *Electra* he makes the Dioscuri, in a speech not untinged by irony, prophesy that Orestes, pursued by the Erinyes, will come to Athens and be acquitted by the equal vote, and that in consequence the baffled Erinyes will descend in dudgeon into a subterránean cleft hard by the Areopagos:

> 'A mantic shrine,
> Sacred, adored of mortals.'

Oracular functions were ascribed to most, if not all, underworld divinities, so that it is quite probable that the description of the Dioscuri is correct.

The sanctuary of the Semnae was open to suppliants and to those who sought oracular counsel, but to one unfortunate class of the community, happily a small one, it was rigidly closed. These were the people known as 'second-fated' or 'later-doomed.' Hesychius[2], in explaining the term 'second-fated' (δευτερόποτμος), says 'he is called by some "later-doomed." So a man is termed when the accustomed rites have been performed as though he were dead, and later on he reappears alive; and Polemon says that to such it was forbidden to enter the sanctuary of the Venerable Goddesses. The term is also used of a man who is reported to have died abroad and then comes home, and again of a man who passes a second time through the folds of a woman's garment, as was the custom among the Athenians in a case of second birth.'

This curious statement is fortunately explained to us in instructive detail by Plutarch in the answer to his 5th *Roman Question*. He there says 'Those who have had a funeral and sepulture as though they were dead are accounted by the Greeks as not pure, and they will not associate with them, nor will they permit them to approach sanctuaries. And they say that a certain Aristinus, who believed in this superstition, sent to Delphi to enquire of the god and to ask release from the disabilities this custom imposed on him, and the Pythian made answer:

> "Whatsoe'er is accomplished by woman that travails in childbed,
> That in thy turn having done, sacrifice thou to the gods."

[1] Eur. *El.* 1270.

[2] Hesych. s.v. δευτερόποτμος.

And Aristinus being a good and wise man gave himself up, like a new-born child, to the women to wash and swaddle and suckle, and all the others who were called "later-doomed" did the like.' 'But,' adds Plutarch, and doubtless most justly, 'some say that these things were done with respect to the "later-doomed" before Aristinus did them, and the custom was an ancient one.'

Plutarch says the exclusion was from all sacred rites. In this he is probably mistaken. Anyhow in the case of the Semnae, and of all underworld divinities, the significance is clear. If a man comes back to life after burial rites, the reason to the primitive mind is that there is something wrong with him; he is rejected by the powers below and unfit to mingle with his fellows in the world above; he is highly taboo. Despised of the gods, he is naturally rejected of his fellow men. The only chance for him is to be born again.

When we come to the ritual of the Semnae every detail confirms the view that they are underworld beings. From Aeschylus himself[1] we know that *σφάγια*, animal sacrifices consumed but not eaten, were offered to them. Athene bids the Erinyes, after they have turned Semnae,

> 'pass below the earth
> With these your sacred sphagia.'

The underworld nature of *sphagia*—the word has no English equivalent—has been fully discussed (p. 63). In careful writers, as has been seen, it is never interchangeable with *ἱερεῖα*, victims sacrificed and eaten.

The scholiast on Sophocles[2] speaks of the holocaust of a black sheep to the Eumenides, whom he identifies with the Semnae; but, as he expressly states that this sacrifice took place in the Peloponnese, we cannot safely attribute it to the local Semnae of Athens. It is probable that *σφάγια* formed part of the regular sacrifice mentioned by Pausanias as offered to the Semnae by the acquitted; *σφάγια* belong, as has already been shown, to the class of expiatory offerings. It was on *σφάγια*, which were also called *τόμια*, that

[1] Aesch. *Eum.* 1006

> ἴτε καὶ σφαγίων τῶνδ' ὑπὸ σεμνῶν
> κατὰ γῆς σύμεναι.

[2] Schol. ad Soph. *Oed. Col.* 42 'τὰς πάνθ' ὁρώσας Εὐμενίδας'......Τότε γὰρ πρῶτον Εὐμενίδας κληθῆναι εὐμενεῖς κριθέντι νικᾶν παρ' Ἀθηναίοις καὶ ὁλοκαυτῆσαι αὐταῖς ὄϊν μέλαιναν ἐν Καρνείᾳ [the reading Καρνείᾳ is doubtful] τῆς Πελοποννήσου. Φιλήμων δὲ ὁ κωμικὸς ἑτέρας φησὶ τὰς σεμνὰς θεὰς τῶν Εὐμενίδων.

oaths were taken (p. 64) in the law courts, oaths the extraordinary solemnity of which Demosthenes[1] emphasizes. A man so swearing stood on the fragments of victims officially and solemnly slain, and devoted himself and his household to destruction in case of perjury. By standing on the slain fragments he identifies himself proleptically with them. We have no explicit statement that the divinities by whom these awful oaths on the *τόμια* had to be taken were the Semnae, but as the Semnae were the underworld divinities resident on the Areopagos, and as they were frequently invoked with the local heroes, and as sacrifice was done to them by the acquitted, it seems highly probable. If they were the goddesses of oaths, this is another link with the Erinyes, the avengers of oaths. It is notable that in an ordinary imprecation in the law-courts they take precedence of Athene herself. Thus Demosthenes[2] says, 'I call to witness the Venerable Goddesses, and the place they inhabit, and the heroes of the soil, and Athene of the city, and the other gods who have the city and the land in their dominion.'

We learn from Philo[3] that no slave was allowed to take part in the processions of the Semnae. This in a worship of special antiquity and solemnity is natural enough. But it is strange to hear from Polemon[4] that there was the same taboo on all the Eupatrids. Strange at first sight, but easily explicable. The Semnae are women divinities, and in this taboo on the Eupatrids there seems to lurk a survival of matriarchal conditions. Aeschylus in the *Eumenides* is not concerned, save incidentally, to emphasize the issue between matriarchy and patriarchy, between kinship through the mother and through the father, but it lies at the back of the legend he has chosen for his plot. The stories of Orestes and Clytaemnestra, of Alcmaeon and Eriphyle, are deep-rooted in matriarchy—both look back to the days when the only relationship that could be proved, and that therefore was worth troubling about, was that through the mother; and hence special

[1] Dem. *c. Aristocr.* p. 642.

[2] Dem. *c. Dein.* 47.

[3] Philo *de praest. liber* p. 886 B διό μοι δοκοῦσιν οἱ τῶν Ἑλλήνων ὀξυδερκέστατοι Ἀθηναῖοι τὴν ἐπὶ ταῖς σεμναῖς θεαῖς πομπὴν ὅταν στέλλωσι δοῦλον μηδένα προσλαμβάνειν.

[4] Schol. ad Soph. *Oed. Col.* 489 'ἄπυστα φωνῶν.' τοῦτο ἀπὸ τῆς δρωμένης θυσίας ταῖς Εὐμενίσι· μετὰ γὰρ ἡσυχίας τὰ ἱερὰ δρῶσι καὶ διὰ τοῦτο οἱ μὲν ἀπὸ Ἡσύχου θύουσιν αὐταῖς καθάπερ Πολέμων ἐν τοῖς πρὸς Ἐρατοσθένην φησὶν οὕτω, τὸ δὲ τῶν Εὐπατριδῶν γένος οὐ μετέχει τῆς θυσίας ταύτης. εἶτα ἑξῆς· τῆς δὲ πομπῆς ταύτης Ἡσυχίδαι ὃ δὴ γένος ἐστὶ περὶ τὰς Σεμνὰς θεὰς καὶ τὴν ἡγεμονίαν ἔχει. καὶ προθύονται πρὸ τῆς θυσίας κριὸν Ἡσύχῳ ἱερόν, ἥρω τοῦτον οὕτω καλοῦντες διὰ τὴν εὐφημίαν· οὗ τὸ ἱερὸν παρὰ τὸ Κυλώνειον ἐκτὸς τῶν ἐννέα πυλῶν.

vengeance attends the slayer of the mother. In the light of this it is easy to understand why in the worship of the Semnae the family of Eupatrids—those well-born through their fathers—had no part. For them Apollo Patrôos was the fitter divinity. The family of the Eupatrids had their own rites of expiation, ancestral rites significantly called *πάτρια*, paternal. These rites as described by Dorotheos have been already discussed (p. 60).

The name of the family that held the priesthood of the Semnae is also recorded: they were the Hesychidae whom Hesychius[1] describes as 'a family of well-born people at Athens.' Polemon is again our authority for connecting these 'Silent Ones' with the cult of the Semnae. He is quoted by the scholiast already cited (p. 246 note). In commenting on the expression 'uttering words inaudible' the scholiast says 'This is from the sacrifice performed to the Eumenides. For they enact the sacred rites in silence, and on account of this the descendants of Hesychos (the Silent One) sacrifice to them, as Polemon says in his writings about Eratosthenes, thus: "the family of the Eupatrids has no share in this sacrifice"; and then further, "in this procession the Hesychidae, which is the family that has to do with the Venerable Goddesses, take the lead." And before the sacrifice they make a preliminary sacrifice of a ram to Hesychos...giving him this name because of the ritual silence observed. His sanctuary is by the Kyloneion outside the Nine Gates.'

Though these remarks of the scholiast are prompted by the cult of the Eumenides at Colonos, it is quite clear that Polemon is speaking of the Semnae at Athens. He states three important facts. The cult of the Semnae was in the hands of a clan descended from a hero called aetiologically 'the Silent One.' Sacrifice to the goddesses was regularly preceded by the sacrifice of a ram to the eponymous hero. That hero had a sanctuary of his own outside the Nine Gates of the old Pelasgic fortification, and near the historic monument of Kylon. The name 'Silent One' is possibly a mere cultus epithet, used to preserve safely the anonymity of the hero; heroes, as will later (p. 339) be seen, are dangerous persons to mention. On the other hand Hesychos may have been the actual name of a real hero, and after his death it may have seemed charged with religious significance. This seems quite possible, the more so as the name was adopted by the whole family. The

[1] Hesych. s.v. *γένος Ἀθήνησιν ἰθαγενῶν*.

female form Hesychia was a proper name in the days of Nikias, and it is curious to find that even then an omen could be drawn from it. Plutarch[1] recounts that when the Athenians were taking omens before the Syracusan expedition an oracle ordered them to fetch a priestess of Athene from Clazomenae. They found, when they got her, that her name was Hesychia; and this seemed 'a divine indication that they should remain quiet.'

The scholiast speaks of Hesychidae, male members of the family of Hesychos, but if we may trust Callimachus[2] it was the women of the family who brought burnt-offerings; and these offerings were, as we should expect, wineless libations and honey-sweet cakes. The name of the priestesses was according to Callimachus *λήτειραι*, and it is no doubt from this source that Hesychius[3] gets his gloss, 'Leteirai, priestesses of the Semnae.'

The Semnae were women divinities served by priestesses, and it is noticeable that Athene, who was 'all for the father,' promises to the Erinyes that, if they become Semnae, they shall have worshippers, both men and women[4]. But when the procession to the cave is actually formed, in strict accordance no doubt with the traditional ritual of the place, it is women attendants who bring the ancient image,

> 'A goodly band,
> Maidens and wives and throng of ancient dames[5].'

It can scarcely be doubted that among these ancient dames were members of the clan of Hesychids.

Aeschylus[6] has left us other notes of underworld significance in the ritual of the Semnae. When the procession is forming for the cave Athene speaks:

> 'Do on your festal garments crimson-dyed
> For meed of honour, bid the torches flame—
> So henceforth these our visitants shall bless
> Our land and folk with shining of their grace.'

[1] Plut. *Vit. Nik.* XIII.

[2] Callim. frg. (Schneider, II. 123)

> *Νηφάλι' αἱ καὶ τῇσιν ἀεὶ μελιηδέας ὄμπνας*
> *λήτειραι καίειν ἔλλαχον Ἡσυχίδες.*

[3] Hesych. s.v. *Λήτειραι· ἱέρειαι τῶν σεμνῶν θεῶν.*

[4] Aesch. *Eum.* 856.

[5] *v.* 1026.

[6] Aesch. *Eum.* 1028

> *φοινικοβάπτοις ἐνδυτοῖς ἐσθήμασιν*
> *τιμᾶτε καὶ τὸ φέγγος ὁρμάσθω πυρός,*
> *ὅπως ἂν εὔφρων ἥδ' ὁμιλία χθονὸς*
> *τὸ λοιπὸν εὐάνδροισι συμφοραῖς πρέπῃ.*

The construction of *τιμᾶτε* is uncertain, there being no expressed grammatical object; but the two ritual factors, the torches and crimson garments, are certain.

Athene proffers for guerdon to the Semnae the ritual that as underworld goddesses was already theirs, torches and crimson raiment.

In connection with the torches it cannot be forgotten that some, though possibly not all, the sittings of the court of the Areopagos took place by night, doubtless in honour of the underworld goddesses who presided. In Lucian's time, at least, these sittings were almost proverbial. He says of a man perceiving with difficulty[1], 'unless he chance to be stone-blind or like the Council of the Areopagos which gives its hearing by night': and again in the *Hermotimus*[2] 'he is doing it like the Areopagites who give judgment in darkness.' To these sittings in the night-time it may be that Athene refers when she says[3]

> 'This court I set, untouched of gain, revered,
> Alert, a wakeful guard o'er those who sleep.'

The garments of crimson or purple dye point to a ritual of placation and the service of the underworld. This is clearly shown in the details given by Plutarch[4] of the rites of placation performed annually for those who fell in the battle of Plataea. 'On the 16th day of the month Maimakterion the archon of Plataea, who on other days may not touch iron nor wear any garment that is not white, puts on a crimson chiton and taking a hydria and girded with a sword goes to the sepulchres. There with water from the spring he washes the stelae and anoints them with myrrh; he slays a black bull, prays to Zeus and Hermes Chthonios, and invokes to the banquet and the bloodshed the heroes who died for Greece.'

The crimson-purple is blood colour[5], hence it is ordained for the service of the dead. It has already been noted (p. 144) that Dion[6] when he took the great oath in the Thesmophorion identified himself with Kore of the underworld by putting on her crimson robe and holding a burning torch. Purple, Pliny[7] tells us, was employed when gods had to be appeased.

[1] Luc. *de domo* 18.
[2] Luc. *Hermot.* 806.
[3] Aesch. *Eum.* 706.
[4] Plut. *Vit. Aristid.* xxi.
[5] Cf. *αἵματι φοινόν* (*Il.* xvi. 159). *φοινός, φοῖνιξ* and *φόνος* are not far asunder: cf. also the tragic use of *αἷμα* for corpse. For purple in the ritual of the dead, see Diels, *Sibyllinische Blätter*, p. 69 note. Since the above was written Dr Headlam has conclusively shown that the crimson worn by the Semnae marks them as *μέτοικοι*, see his 'Last Scene of the Eumenides,' *J.H.S.* xxvi. 1906, p. 268.
[6] Plut. *Vit. Dion.* lvi. *περιβάλλεται τὴν πορφυρίδα τῆς θεοῦ καὶ λαβὼν δᾷδα καιομένην ἀπόμνυσι.*
[7] Plin. *N. H.* ix. 60 purpura dis advocatur placandis.

The purple robes, the torches, the night-time, above all the *σφάγια*, point to a dread underworld ritual, a ritual that shows clearly that the darker side of the Venerable Ones was not far remote from the Erinyes. But Aeschylus, whose whole mind is bent on a doctrine of mercy, naturally emphasizes the brighter side of their functions and worship. Athene[1] herself knows that they are underworld goddesses, that they must have low-lying altars and underground dwellings; only so seated will they ever feel really at home. She remembers even that for their feast they must have the wineless sacrifice that drives them mad[2]; but she bids them leave this madness, and they for their part promise that the earth, their kingdom as vengeful ghosts, shall cease to drink the black blood of citizens. Henceforth they will be content with the white side of their service[3].

> 'From this great land, thine is the sacrifice
> Of first-fruits offered for accomplishment
> Of marriage and for children[4].'

Again Athene offers what was theirs from the beginning. Underworld goddesses presided over marriage: in later days, as Plutarch[5] tells us, it was the priestess of Demeter; earlier we can scarcely doubt it was the Semnae. Here they stand in sharp contrast to the Erinyes, who are all black. Who would have bidden an Erinys to a marriage feast? as well bid Eris who, in form (fig. 56) and function as perhaps in name, was but another Erinys, Eris

FIG. 56.

> 'The Abominable, who uninvited came
> And cast the golden fruit upon the board.'

[1] Aesch. *Eum.* 804. The significance of the ἐσχάρα as distinguished from the βωμός has been already discussed (p. 61).
[2] Aesch. *Eum.* 860.
[3] Aesch. *Eum.* 980.
[4] *v.* 834.
[5] Plut. *Conj. Praec.* Proem. μετὰ τὸν πάτριον θεσμὸν ὃν ὑμῖν ἡ τῆς Δήμητρος ἱέρεια συνειργνυμένοις ἐφήρμοσεν.

The Erinyes transformed to Semnae ask Athene what spells they shall chant over the land. She makes answer[1]:

'Whatever charms wait on fair Victory
From earth, from dropping dew and from high heaven,
The wealth of winds that blow to hail the land
Sunlit, and fruits of earth and teeming flocks
Untouched of time, safety for human seed.'

The chorus accept these functions of health and life, and chant their promised guerdon[2].

'No wind to wither trees shall blow,
By our grace it shall be so;
Nor that nor shrivelling heat
On budding plants shall beat
With parching drouth
To waste their growth,
Nor any plague of dismal blight come creeping;
But teeming, doubled flocks the earth
In her season shall bring forth,
And evermore a wealthy race
Pay reverence for this our grace
Of spirits that have the rich earth in their keeping.'

We are reminded that Ploutos himself, the Wealth of the underworld, had, according to Pausanias[3], a statue in the precinct of the Venerable Goddesses. Moreover it is impossible to hear the words 'no wind to wither trees shall blow' without recalling the altar of the Wind-stillers (*Εὐδάνεμοι*), which stood somewhere on the western slope of the Areopagos. Arrian[4], speaking of the statues of Harmodios and Aristogeiton, says 'they stand at Athens in the Cerameicus where we go up to the citadel, just opposite the Metrôon not far from the altar of the Wind-stillers. Whoever has been initiated in the Eleusinia knows the altar of the Wind-stillers which stands on the ground.' A low-lying altar doubtless, an eschara, for, as has already been shown (p. 65), the winds were to primitive thinking ghosts or caused by ghosts and worshipped with underworld sacrifices. Hesychius[5] tells us that there was at Corinth a family called the Wind-calmers. The Areopagos was a

[1] Aesch. *Eum.* 903.
[2] Aesch. *Eum.* 938. The translation offered only attempts to render the general sense of this difficult passage, a sense sufficiently clear for the immediate purpose. No satisfactory explanation has yet been offered of the enigmatic *τὸ μὴ περᾶν ὅρον τόπων*, see Dr Verrall, ad loc.
[3] P. I. 28. 6.
[4] Arrian, *Anab.* III. 16. 8.
[5] Hesych. s.v. Ἀνεμοκοῖται.

wind-swept hill. It was thence, according to a form of the legend recorded by Plato[1], that Boreas caught up Oreithyia.

The Semnae claim as their special 'grace[2]' control over the winds. As goddesses who bring the blessings of marriage and of fertile breezes, they are but good fructifying Keres like the Tritopatores already discussed (p. 179); the Erinyes are blighting poisonous Keres, who Harpy-like foul the food by which men live.

The Erinyes, in the play of Aeschylus, are transformed into Semnae, into the local goddesses of Athens. Of this there is no shadow of doubt. They accept the citizenship of Pallas[3], and they are actually hailed as Semnae[4]. Aeschylus it is true never definitely states that they entered the cleft of the Areopagos, but Euripides, manifestly borrowing from him, is as has been seen explicit.

Such a conversion may have been gratifying to the patriotism of an Athenian audience, but Athenian though he is, it is not the glorification of a local cult that inspires Aeschylus; it is the reconciliation of the old order of vengeance with the new law of mercy. It is significant in this connection that Aeschylus, or some one who took his meaning, gave to the play the title, not as we should expect of *Semnae,* but of *Eumenides.* The moral of the play is thereby emphasized.

It is, to say the least, curious that a play called traditionally, if not by the author, the '*Eumenides*' should contain no single mention of the Eumenides by this name. Harpocration[5], commenting on the word Eumenides, says 'Aeschylus *in the Eumenides,* recounting what happened about the trial of Orestes, says that Athene, having mollified the Erinyes so that they did not deal harshly with Orestes, called them Eumenides.' Aeschylus says no such thing. The text of the play contains no mention of the Eumenides, though in the hypothesis prefixed to the text occur

[1] Plat. *Phaedr.* p. 229. The legend no doubt took its rise in the Areopagos, where the king's daughter was flower-gathering, or fetching water from the Enneakrounos just outside the city gate. It was transplanted later with many another legend and cult to the banks of the Ilissus, outside the enlarged city.

[2] Aesch. *Eum.* 939.

[3] Aesch. *Eum.* 916 δέξομαι Πάλλαδος ξυνοικίαν.

[4] *v.* 1041 δεῦρ' ἴτε, σεμναί.

[5] Harpocrat. s.v. Εὐμενίδες...Αἰσχύλος ἐν Εὐμενίσιν εἰπὼν τὰ περὶ τὴν κρίσιν τὴν Ὀρέστου φησὶν ὡς ἡ Ἀθηνᾶ πραΰνασα τὰς Ἐρινύας ὥστε μὴ χαλεπῶς ἔχειν πρὸς τὸν Ὀρέστην Εὐμενίδας ὠνόμασεν, εἰσὶ δὲ Ἀληκτώ, Μέγαιρα, Τισιφόνη.

the following words: 'Having prevailed by the counsel of Athene, he (Orestes) went to Argos, and when he had mollified the Erinyes he addressed them as Eumenides[1].' Harpocration attributes to Athene in the play what the hypothesis notes as done by Orestes in the sequel at Argos. By his use of the word 'mollified' (*πραΰνασα*) he betrays, I think, the source of his information. It must always be remembered that the Orestes legend was native to Argos and at Argos the local cult was of Eumenides not Semnae.

The Eumenides.

The worship of divinities bearing the name of Eumenides, though unknown at Athens[2], was wider-spread than that of the Semnae, which is found nowhere outside Attica. It was possibly for this reason that Aeschylus or later tradition gave this name to the play. The Semnae were familiar figures at Athens, and, spite of many underworld analogies, the shift from Erinyes to Semnae must have been a difficult one. A great deal is borne for the glory of the gods, but there must have been among the audience men conservative and hard-headed who would be likely to maintain that, all said and done, the Erinyes were not, could not be, Semnae. If asked to believe that the Erinyes became Eumenides, they would feel and probably say: that is a matter for Colonos, for Argos, for Sekyon to consider; it affects no Athenian's faith or practice. At Colonos it is certain that goddesses were worshipped who bore the name of Eumenides, goddesses of function and ritual precisely identical with the Semnae, but addressed by a different cultus epithet. We have the express statement of Sophocles[3], who, as a priest himself and a conservative, was not likely to

[1] Aesch. *Eum.* hypoth....ῇς βουλῇ νικήσας κατῆλθεν εἰς Ἄργος, τὰς δὲ Ἐρινύας πραΰνας προσηγόρευσεν Εὐμενίδας. To suit the statement of Harpocration, πραΰνας has been altered to πραΰνασα.

[2] There is no evidence that can be relied on to show that before Aeschylus wrote his play the Semnae ever bore the title of Eumenides. Pausanias indeed (VII. 25. 1) quotes an oracle from Dodona ostensibly belonging to the mythical days of Apheidas, in which the title Eumenides is given to the goddesses of the Areopagos,

> φράζεο δ' Ἄρειόν τε πάγον, βωμούς τε θυώδεις
> Εὐμενίδων κτλ.

And this oracle, he says, the Greek called to mind when the Peloponnesians came against Athens in the time of Codrus. The passage stands alone, and oracle-mongering was rife at all times.

[3] Soph. *Oed. Col.* 41.

tamper with ritual titles. He makes Oedipus ask the stranger who they are whose dread name he is to invoke. The answer is explicit:

> 'Eumenides all-seeing here the folk
> Would call them: other names please otherwhere.'

Sophocles no doubt shows the influence of Aeschylus in his 'other names please otherwhere.' He realizes that Eumenides and Semnae are 'one form of diverse names[1].' This truth it was the mission of the reconciling monotheist always to preach, but he would scarcely dare to tamper with the familiar titles of a local cult. In fact by this very statement, that elsewhere the goddesses bore other names, he makes the local appellation certain. He may indeed have brought Oedipus to Colonos rather than to the Areopagos, where he had also a grave, just because the local attributive title of the goddesses at Colonos suited the gentle moral of his play.

Again when Oedipus asks to be taught to pray aright, the Chorus lay emphasis on the title Eumenides.

> 'That, as we call them Kindly, from kind hearts
> They may receive the suppliant[2].'

So strong is the exclusiveness of local cults that, had the title of Eumenides occurred only at Colonos, neither Aeschylus nor tradition would perhaps have ventured to assume it for the Semnae. But from Pausanias we learn of sanctuaries of the Eumenides at Titane[3] near Sekyon, at Cerynaea[4] in Achaia, and in Arcadia near Megalopolis[5]. The sanctuary between Sekyon and Titane consisted of a grove and a temple. Pausanias expressly says these belonged to the goddesses whom the Athenians called Semnae and the Sikyonians Eumenides. The festival in their honour was a yearly one, and has already been discussed (p. 56). Tradition said that the sanctuary at Cerynaea was founded by Orestes, and that 'if any one stained by blood or any other pollution, or impious, entered the sanctuary wishing to see it, he straightway went out of his wits by the terrors he

[1] Aesch. *Prom. Vinct.* 209

> *Θέμις*
> *καὶ Γαῖα πολλῶν ὀνομάτων μορφὴ μία.*

[2] *Oed. Col.* 486

> *ὥς σφας καλοῦμεν Εὐμενίδας, ἐξ εὐμενῶν*
> *στέρνων δέχεσθαι τὸν ἱκέτην.*

[3] P. I. 11. 4. [4] P. VII. 25. 7. [5] P. VIII. 34. 2.

beheld. The images in it were made of wood[1]...and they were not large.' The ritual of the sanctuary at Megalopolis, with its black and white sides, addressed severally to the goddesses as Madnesses (Maniae) and Kindly Ones (Eumenides), has already been noted (p. 56). To the Madnesses Orestes sacrifices, it will be remembered, with underworld rites to avert their wrath; to the Kindly Ones when healed, and after the same fashion as to the gods; the clearest possible instance of two stages of development in ritual and theology, of *ἀποτροπή* side by side with *θεραπεία*.

To these four instances of the cult of the Eumenides a fifth may safely be added, the sanctuary at or near Argos. Of any such sanctuary we have no literary record, but we have what is of even greater value—monumental evidence. Three votive reliefs dedicated to the Eumenides have been found at the little church of Hag. Johannes, about half-an-hour to the east of the modern village of Argos[2]. They are still preserved in the local museum of the Demarchy. The material of all three is the hard local limestone, and they must have been set up in a local sanctuary. The sanctuary of Titane was nearly twenty miles away, too far to admit of any theory of transportation. All three are inscribed, and in each the dedicator is a woman. The relief reproduced in fig. 57 was found built into the outside of the Church of Hag. Johannes. It is clearly inscribed *Εὐμενίσιν εὐχάν*, a vow or prayer to the Eumenides. The beginning of the inscription is lost, but enough remains, . . *η* Λ . . *εία*, to show that a woman dedicated

Fig. 57.

[1] At this point unhappily a lacuna occurs.

[2] *A. Mitt.* IV. 1879, pl. IX. p. 176.

it, and that she was probably an Argive. It is a woman's offering, but she likes to have her husband carved upon it and she lets him walk first. Perhaps he went with her to the sanctuary and offered sacrifice of honey and water and flowers and a ewe great with young[1].

> 'The first-fruits offered for accomplishment
> Of marriage and for children.'

About the figures of the Eumenides at Argos, as of the Semnae at Athens, 'there is nothing frightful.' These are not the short-girt huntress women of the vases, nor yet the loathly black horrors of tragedy; they are gentle, staid, matronly figures, bearing in their left hands, for tokens of fertility, flowers or fruit, and in their right, snakes[2] as the symbols, not of terror and torture, but merely of that source of wealth, the underworld; but for the snakes, which lend a touch of austerity, they would be Charites (p. 297). From the inscriptions these reliefs are certainly known to be later than Aeschylus, but because a poet writes a great play at Athens the local stonemason does not alter the type of the votive offerings he supplies. Why should he frighten pious women and perhaps lose his custom? The Erinys of tragedy took strong hold of literature, but even at Athens there was a sceptic to whom the great conversion scene was merely absurd. If we may trust Suidas[3], the comic poet Philemon held to it that 'the Semnae were quite other than the Eumenides,' and we may be sure that the humour of the situation attempted would lose nothing in his hands. Great though the influence of Aeschylus over the educated undoubtedly was, it was powerless to alter traditional types in art; equally powerless we may be sure to abate or alter one jot or one tittle of hieratic ceremonial. The Erinyes remained Erinyes, and in popular bogey form went, as has been seen (p. 232), to people with horrors a Christian hell. Man was not ready yet to worship only the Kindly Ones. For generations, nay centuries, he must bear the hard yoke of *ἀποτροπή* before he might offer to gods remade in his own image the free-will offering of a kindly *θεραπεία*.

[1] The regular ritual offerings at Titane, see P. I. 11. 4 and Aesch. *Eum.* 834.

[2] The archaic marble statuette found at Olympia and representing a woman with polos on her head and a snake in each hand may very possibly be one of three Eumenides. See *Olympia*, vol. III. p. 27.

[3] Suidas s.v. *Εὐμενίδες· Φιλήμων δὲ ὁ κωμικὸς ἑτέρας φησὶ τὰς Σεμνὰς θεὰς τῶν Εὐμενίδων.*

CHAPTER VI.

THE MAKING OF A GODDESS.

'ΟΥ ΓΆΡ ΓΗ͂ ΓΥΝΑΙ͂ΚΑ ΜΕΜΊΜΗΤΑΙ ΚΥΉϹΕΙ ΚΑῚ ΓΕΝΝΉϹΕΙ ἈΛΛᾺ ΓΥΝῊ ΓΗ͂Ν.'

In the last chapter we have traced the development from Keres to Erinyes, and have seen that, on the whole, this development was a downward course. The Erinyes are in a sense more civilized than the Keres; they are beings more articulate, more clearly outlined and concerned with issues moral rather than physical; but the career they start as angry souls they end as Poinae, ministers of vindictive torment; there is in them no element of hope, no kindly impulse towards purification, they end where they began as irreconcileable demons rather than friendly gods.

We have further marked the attempt of Aeschylus to turn the vindictive demons of the old religion into the gentler divinities of the new, and we have seen that, for all his genius, the attempt failed wholly. The Erinyes never, save here and there to a puzzled antiquarian, became really Semnae; the popular instinct of their utter distinctness remained sound. We have now to note that, where the genius of a poet fails, the slow-moving widespread instinct of a people may prevail; ghosts are not wholly angry, and the gentler form of ghost may and does become a god.

The line between a spirit (*δαίμων*) and a regular god (*θεός*) is drawn with no marked precision. The difference is best realized by remembering the old principle that man makes all the objects of his worship in his own image. Before he has himself clearly realized his own humanity—the line that marks him off from other animals, he makes his divinities sometimes wholly animal, sometimes of mixed, monstrous shapes. His animal-shaped gods the Greek quickly outgrew: something will be said of them when we come to the religion of the Bull-Dionysos. Mixed monstrous shapes long haunted his imagination; bird-woman-souls, Gorgon-bogeys, Sphinxes, Harpies and the like were, as has been seen, the fitting vehicles of a religion that was mainly of vague fear. But as man became more conscious of his humanity and *pari passu* grew more *humane*, a more complete anthropomorphism steadily prevailed, and in the figures of wholly human gods man mirrored his gentler affections, his advance in the ordered relations of life.

Xenophanes[1], writing in the 6th century B.C., knew that God is 'without body, parts or passions,' but he knew also that, till man becomes wholly philosopher, his gods are doomed perennially to take and retake human shape. His thrice-familiar words still bear repetition:

'One God there is greatest of gods and mortals;
Not like to man is he in mind or body.
All of him sees, all of him thinks and hearkens.......
But mortal man made gods in his own image
Like to himself in vesture, voice and body.
Had they but hands, methinks, oxen and lions
And horses would have made them gods like-fashioned,
Horse-gods for horses, oxen-gods for oxen.'

We are apt to regard the advance to anthropomorphism as necessarily a clear religious gain. A gain it is in so far as a certain element of barbarity is softened or extruded, but with this gain comes loss, the loss of the element of formless, monstrous mystery. The ram-headed Knum of the Egyptians is to the mystic more religious than any of the beautiful divine humanities of the Greek. Anthropomorphism provides a store of lovely motives for art, but that spirit is scarcely religious which makes of Eros a boy trundling a hoop, of Apollo a youth aiming a stone at a lizard, of Nike a woman who stoops to tie her sandal. Xenophanes put his finger on the weak spot of anthropomorphism. He saw that it comprised and confined the god within the limitations of the worshipper. It is not every religion that advances as far as anthropomorphism, but the farthest of anthropomorphism is not very far.

[1] Xenoph. frg. 1, 2, 5 and 6.

Traces of animal form are among the recognized Greek gods few and scattered. Pausanias[1] heard at Phigaleia of a horse-headed Demeter, and again of a fish-bodied Eurynome[2] whom some called Artemis, but for the most part by the 6th and 5th centuries B.C. mixed forms, half animal, half human, belong to beings half-way between man and god, demons rather than full-fledged divinities and demons malignant rather than beneficent. Such are Boreas, Echidna, Typhon and the snake-tailed giants.

In the design from a black-figured cylix[3] in fig. 58 we have a curious and rare instance of beings of monstrous form, yet obviously

Fig. 58.

beneficent. The scene is a vineyard at the time of vintage. On the reverse (not figured here) we have the same vintage-setting, but goats, the destroyers of the vine, are nibbling at the vine-stems. On the obverse (fig. 58) we have snake-bodied nymphs rejoicing in the grape harvest. Two of them hold a basket of net or wicker in which the grapes will be gathered, a third holds a great cup for the vine-juice, a fourth plays on the double flutes.

[1] P. VIII. 42. 4. The material for the study of the non-human forms taken by Greek gods has been recently collected by Dr M. W. de Visser, *Die nicht-menschengestaltigen Götter der Griechen*, 1903.

[2] P. VIII. 41. 6.

[3] Munich. Published and discussed by Dr Böhlan, 'Schlangenleibige Nymphen,' *Philologos* LVII. N.F. XI. 1, and see 'Delphika,' *J.H.S.* XIX. 1899, p. 216, note 1.

Unhappily we can give no certain name to these kindly grape-gathering, flute-playing snake-nymphs. They are *δρακοντώδεις κόραι*, but assuredly they are not Erinyes and we dare not even call them Eumenides. Probably any Athenian child would have named them without a moment's hesitation, but we must be content to say that, in their essence, they are Charites, givers of grace and increase, and that their snake-bodies mark them not as malevolent, but as earth-daemons, genii of fertility. They are near akin to the local Athenian hero, the snake-tailed Cecrops, and we are tempted to conjecture that in art, though not in literature, he may have lent his snake-tail to the Agraulid nymphs, his daughters. Later it will be seen that earth-born goddesses, though they shed their snake-form, keep as their vehicle and attribute the snake they once were.

The Mother and the Maid.

The gods reflect not only man's human form but also his human relations. In the Homeric Olympus we see mirrored a family group of the ordinary patriarchal type, a type so familiar that it scarcely arrests attention. Zeus, Father of Gods and men, is supreme; Hera, though in constant and significant revolt, occupies the subordinate place of a wife; Poseidon is a younger brother, and the rest of the Olympians are grouped about Zeus and Hera in the relation of sons and daughters. These sons and daughters are quarrelsome among themselves and in constant insurrection against father and mother, but still they constitute a family, and a family subject, if reluctantly, to the final authority of a father.

But when we come to examine local cults we find that, if these mirror the civilization of the worshippers, this civilization is quite other than patriarchal. Hera, subject in the Homeric Olympus, reigns alone at Argos; Athene at Athens is no god's wife, she is affiliated in some loose fashion to Poseidon, but the relation is one of rivalry and ultimate conquest, nowise of subordination. At Eleusis two goddesses reign supreme, Demeter and Kore, the Mother and the Maid; neither Hades nor Triptolemos their nursling ever disputes their sway. At Delphi in historical days Apollo held the oracle, but Apollo, the priestess[1] knows, was preceded by a succession of women goddesses:

> 'First in my prayer before all other gods
> I call on Earth, primaeval prophetess.
> Next Themis on her mother's oracular seat
> Sat, so men say. Third by unforced consent
> Another Titan, daughter too of Earth,
> Phoebe. She gave it as a birthday gift
> To Phoebus, and giving called it by her name.'

Gaia the Earth was first, and elsewhere Aeschylus[2] tells us that Themis was but another name of Gaia. Prometheus says the future was foretold him by his mother:

> 'Themis she
> And Gaia, one in form with many names.'

In historical days in Greece, descent was for the most part traced through the father. These primitive goddesses reflect another condition of things, a relationship traced through the mother, the state of society known by the awkward term matriarchal[3], a state echoed in the lost *Catalogues of Women*, the *Eoiai* of Hesiod, and in the Boeotian heroines of the *Nekuia*. Our modern patriarchal society focusses its religious anthropomorphism on the relationship of the father and the son; the Roman Church with her wider humanity includes indeed the figure of the Mother who is both Mother and Maid, but she is still in some sense subordinate to the Father and the Son.

Of the many survivals of matriarchal notions in Greek mythology one salient instance may be noted. S. Augustine[4], telling the story of the rivalry between Athene and Poseidon, says that the contest was decided by the vote of the citizens, both men and women, for it was the custom then for women to take part in public affairs. The men voted for Poseidon, the women for Athene; the women exceeded the men by one and Athene prevailed. To appease the wrath of Poseidon the men inflicted on the women a triple punishment, 'they were to lose their vote, *their children were no longer to be called by their mother's name* and they

[1] Aesch. *Eum.* 1. [2] Aesch. *Prom. Vinct.* 209.

[3] The clearest and most scientific statement of the facts as to this difficult subject known to me is to be found in an article by Dr E. B. Tylor, 'The Matriarchal family system,' *Nineteenth Century*, July 1896.

[4] S. Augustine, *De civitat. Dei* 18. 9 ut nulla ulterius ferrent suffragia, ut nullus nascentium maternum nomen acciperet, ut ne quis eas Athenaeas vocaret.

themselves were no longer to be called after their goddess, Athenians.'

The myth is aetiological, and it mirrors surely some shift in the social organization of Athens. The citizens were summoned by Cecrops, and it is noticeable that with his name universal tradition associates the introduction of the patriarchal form of marriage. Athenaeus[1] quoting from Clearchos, the pupil of Aristotle, says, 'At Athens Cecrops was the first to join one woman to one man: before connections had taken place at random and marriages were in common—hence, as some think, Cecrops was called "Twy-formed" (διφυής), since before his day people did not know who their fathers were, on account of the number (of possible parents).' A society that had passed to patriarchy naturally misjudged the marriage-laws of matriarchy and regarded it as a mere state of promiscuity. Cecrops, tradition[2] said, was the first to call Zeus the Highest, and with the worship of Zeus the Father it is possible that he introduced the social conditions of patriarchy. Apollo, the son of Zeus, was worshipped at Athens as *Patroos*.

The primitive Greek was of course not conscious that he mirrored his own human relations in the figures of his gods, but, in the reflective days of Pythagoras, the analogy between human and divine was not left unnoted. The evidence he adduces as to the piety of women is perhaps the most illuminating comment on primitive theology ever made by ancient or modern. 'Women,' he[3] says, 'give to each successive stage of their life the same name as a god, they call the unmarried woman *Maiden* (Κόρη), the woman given in marriage to a man *Bride* (Νύμφη), her who has borne children *Mother* (Μήτηρ), and her who has borne children's children *Grandmother* (Μαῖα).' Invert the statement and we have the whole matriarchal theology in a nutshell. The matriarchal goddesses reflect the life of women, not women the life of the goddesses.

Of these various forms of the conditions of woman, woman as maiden, bride, mother and grandmother, the last, grandmother,

[1] Athen. XIII. 2 p. 555 and Tzetzes *Chil.* V. 19. 650. Other instances of the survival in Greek mythology of traces of matriarchal conditions are collected by Bachofen in his *Mutterrecht*, a book which, spite of the wildness of its theories, remains of value as the fullest existing collection of ancient facts.

[2] P. VIII. 2. 3.

[3] Diog. 8. 1. 10, and Iambl. *Vit. Pyth.* 3. 11.

comes little into prominence; it only lends a name to Maia, the mother of Hermes. Nymphs we have everywhere, but the two cardinal conditions are obviously to a primitive society Mother[1] and Maiden. When these conditions crystallized into the goddess forms of Demeter and Kore, they appear as Mother and *Daughter*, but primarily the conditions expressed are Mother and Maid, woman mature and woman before maturity, and of these two forms the Mother-form as more characteristic is, in early days, the more prominent; Kore *as daughter* rather than maiden is the product of mythology. When we come to the religion of Dionysos, it will be seen that the Mother-goddess has for her attribute of motherhood a son rather than a daughter.

THE EARTH-MOTHER AS KARPOPHOROS OR LADY OF THE WILD THINGS.

The Mother-goddess was almost necessarily envisaged as the Earth. The ancient Dove-priestesses at Dodona[2] were the first to chant the Litany:

> 'Zeus was, Zeus is, Zeus shall be, O great Zeus.
> Earth sends up fruits, so praise we Earth the Mother.'

The two lines have no necessary connection; it may be that their order is inverted and that long before the Dove-priestesses sang the praises of Zeus they had chanted their hymn to the Mother. It was fitting that women priestesses should sing to a woman goddess, to Ga who was also Ma. Mother-Earth bore not only fruits but the race of man. As the poet Asius[3] said:

> 'Divine Pelasgos on the wood-clad hills
> Black Earth brought forth, that mortal man might be.'

Pelasgos claimed no father, but he, the first father, had a mother. And here it must be noted that the local mother must necessarily have preceded Gaia the abstract and universal. Primi-

[1] The fundamental unity of all the Greek goddesses was, I think, first observed by Gerhard, *Ueber Metroon und Goetter-Mutter*, 1849, p. 103, but his illuminating suggestion has been obscured for half a century by systems, such as that of Preller and Max Müller, that see in ancient deities impersonations of natural phenomena.

[2] P. x. 12. 10

> Ζεὺς ἦν, Ζεὺς ἐστί, Ζεὺς ἔσσεται· ὦ μεγάλε Ζεῦ.
> Γᾶ καρποὺς ἀνίει, διὸ κλῄζετε ματέρα γαῖαν.

[3] P. VIII. 2. 4.

tive man does not tend to deal in abstractions. Each local hero claimed descent from a local earth-nymph or mother[1]. Salamis, Aegina and 'dear mother Ida' are not late geographical abstractions; each is a local mother, a real parent, and all are later merged in the great All-Mother Ge.

The Earth-Mother and each and every local nymph was mother not only of man but of all creatures that live; she is the 'Lady of the Wild Things' (πότνια θηρῶν). Art brings her figure very clearly before us. On an early stamped Boeotian amphora[2] in the National Museum at Athens (figs. 59 and 60) she is vividly presented. The Great Mother stands with uplifted hands exactly in the attitude of the still earlier figures recently discovered in the Mycenaean shrine at Cnossos. To either side of her is a lion, heraldically posed like the lions of the Gate at Mycenae; below her is a frieze of deer. The figure is supported or rather encircled by two women figures, one at either side. These seem to be part of a ring of encircling worshippers[3].

FIG. 59.

[1] The distinction has been acutely observed by Miss W. M. L. Hutchinson in discussing the earthborn parentage of Aeacus, see *Aeacus a Judge of the Underworld*, p. 6.

[2] 'Εφήμερις 'Αρχ. 1892, Pl. 9; for stamped Boeotian amphorae in general, see Mr A. de Ridder, *Bull. de Corr. Hell.* XXII. 1898, p. 440.

[3] Dr Wolters ('Εφ. 'Αρχ. 1892, p. 225) explains the figure of the Earth-Mother as Artemis Λεχώ. I entirely agree with Prof. S. Wide that her pose is not that of 'eine gebärende Frau': see S. Wide, 'Mykenische Götterbilder und Idole,' *A. Mitt.* XXVI. 1901, p. 253.

Fig. 60.

The design in fig. 61 from a painted Boeotian amphora[1], also in

Fig. 61.

the Museum at Athens, shows a similar and even more complete conception of the 'Lady of the Wild Things.' Her two lions still

[1] Ἐφ. Ἀρχ. 1892, Pl. 10. 1.

keep heraldic guard, above her outstretched arms are two birds[1], her gown is decorated with the figure of a great fish. We are reminded of the Eurynome of Phigalia with her fish-tailed body.

The interesting thing about these early representations, these and countless others, is that we can give the goddess no proper name. We call her rightly the Great Mother and the 'Lady of the Wild Things,' but farther we cannot go. She has been named Artemis and Cybele, but for neither name is there a particle of evidence.

The Great Mother is mother of the dead as well as the living. The design in fig. 62 is from the interior of a rock-hewn tomb

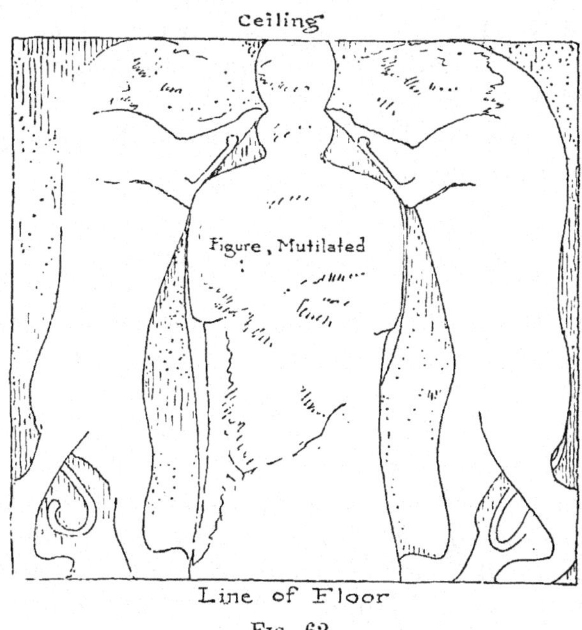

FIG. 62.

in Phrygia[2]. The great figure of the Mother and her lions occupies the whole height of the back wall of the tomb. 'All things,' as Cicero[3] says, 'go back to earth and rise out of the earth.'

[1] On the head of one of the idols in the recently discovered shrine at Cnossos, Mr Arthur Evans kindly tells me, is perched a dove, a forecast it may be of Aphrodite.

[2] See Prof. Ramsay, *J.H.S.* 1884, p. 245.

[3] Cic. *De Nat. Deor.* II. 26 et recidunt omnia in terras et oriuntur e terris.

'Dust we are, and unto dust we shall return,' and more tenderly Aeschylus[1]:

> 'Yea, summon Earth, who brings all things to life
> And rears and takes again into her womb.'

And so the Mother herself keeps ward in the *metro*polis of the dead, and therefore 'the Athenians of old called the dead "Demeter's people"[2].' On the festival day of the dead, the *Nekusia* at Athens, they sacrificed to Earth. To a people who practised inhumation, such ritual and such symbolism were almost inevitable. When the Earth-Mother developed into the Corn-Mother, such symbolism gained new life and force from the processes of agriculture. Cicero[3] records that in his day it was still the custom to sow the graves of the dead with corn: 'that which thou sowest is not quickened except it die[4].' Out of the symbolism of the corn sown the Greeks did *not* develope a doctrine of immortality, but, when that doctrine came to them from without, the symbolism of the seed lay ready to hand.

THE MOTHER AS KOUROTROPHOS.

Early art figures the Mother in quaint instructive fashion as *Kourotrophos*, the Child-Rearer. As such she appears in the design in fig. 63 taken from an early black-figured amphora of the 6th century B.C. in the British Museum[5]. This figure of the Mother is usually explained as Leto with the twins Apollo and Artemis, but such an interpretation is, I think, over-bold, and really misleading. The artist knows that there is a Mother-Goddess; one child would be sufficient as an attribute of motherhood, but in his quaint primitive fashion he wishes to emphasize her motherhood, he gives her all the children she can conveniently hold, one on each shoulder.

[1] Aesch. *Choeph.* 127.

[2] Plut. *de fac. in orb. lun.* 28 *καὶ τοὺς νεκροὺς Ἀθηναῖοι Δημητρείους ὠνόμαζον τὸ παλαιόν.*

[3] Cic. *Legg.* II. 22, and 25, 63.

[4] 1 Cor. xv. 36.

[5] *B. M. Cat.* B 213. Inghirami, *Vasi Fitt.* III. 300. Mr A. Lang, *Homeric Hymns*, plate facing p. 104, names the design 'Leto with her infants Apollo and Artemis.' The catalogue of the British Museum with just caution says 'Leto (?),' but adds that the children are 'probably Apollo and Artemis.' The figures to either side of the central 'Mother,' Dionysos and a Satyr, give no clue to the interpretation.

We have no right to name the children Apollo and Artemis, unless inscribed or marked as such by attributes. This is clear from the fact that, on a fragment of a vase found in the Acropolis excavations and unhappily still unpublished, we have a figure closely analogous, though later in style, to our Kourotrophos, bearing on her elbows two little naked imps *who are inscribed*: the one is *Himeros*, the other *E*(ros). The mother can in this case be none other than Aphrodite. The attribution is confirmed by another fragment[1] in which only half of the Mother-goddess is preserved and one child seated on her elbow; the child is not inscribed, but against the mother, in archaic letters, is written *Aphrodi*(te); near her as on our vase is standing Dionysos.

FIG. 63.

Pausanias[2], when examining the chest of Cypselos, saw a design on which was represented 'a woman carrying a white boy sleeping on her right arm; on the other arm she has a black boy who is like the one who is asleep; they both have their feet twisted (ἀμφοτέρους διεστραμμένους τοὺς πόδας); the inscriptions show that the boys are Death and Sleep, and that Night is the nurse of both.' He adds the rather surprising statement that it 'would have been easy to see who they were without the inscriptions.'

A woman with a child on each arm can then represent Aphrodite with Himeros and Eros; if one child is white and

[1] Mr G. C. Richards, *J.H.S.* XIII. 1892, p. 284, pl. XI.

[2] P. v. 18. 1. Dr Frazer translates the difficult word διεστραμμένους 'turned different ways'; the word seems usually to imply distortion, but in the case of Death and Sleep this seems inappropriate.

asleep and the other black, the group represents Night with Death and Sleep; if the group is to represent Leto and her twins, there must be something to mark the twins as Apollo and Artemis. On another amphora in the British Museum[1] there does exist just the necessary differentiation: the child on the left arm is naked, the child on the right though also painted black wears a short chiton. We are justified in supposing that the one is a boy the other a girl, and there is at least a high probability that the differentiation of sex points to Apollo and Artemis.

I have dwelt on this point because vase-paintings are here, as so often, highly instructive in the matter of the development and slow differentiation and articulation of theological types. At first all is vague and misty; there is, as it were, a blank formula, a mother-goddess characterized by twins. If we give her a name at all she is Kourotrophos. As her personality grows she differentiates, she is Aphrodite with Eros and Himeros, she is Night with Sleep and Death. When Apollo and Artemis came from the North they became *the* twins *par excellence*, and they are affiliated to the old religion; the Mother as Kourotrophos became Leto with Apollo and Artemis.

The like process goes on in literature, though it is less obviously manifest. At the opening of the Thesmophoria the Woman-Herald in Aristophanes[2] makes proclamation as follows:

> 'Keep solemn silence. Keep solemn silence. Pray to the two Thesmophoroi, to Demeter, and to Kore, and to Plouton, and to Kalligeneia, and to Kourotrophos, and to Hermes, and the Charites.'

Discussion from the time of the scholiast onwards has raged as to who Kourotrophos is—is she Hestia, is she Ge? The simple truth is never faced that she is *Kourotrophos*, an attribute become a personality. Her personality, it is true, faded before the dominant personality of the Mother of Eleusis, but her presence in the ancient ritual-formulary speaks clearly for her original actuality. Once she had faded, all the other more successful goddesses, Ge, Artemis, Hekate, Leto, Demeter, Aphrodite, even Athene, contend for her name as their epithet. There is no controversy so idle and apparently so prolific as that which seeks to find in these ancient

[1] *B. M. Cat.* B 168.

[2] Ar. *Thesm.* 295 and schol. ad loc. The words τῇ Γῇ have been interpolated after Κουροτρόφῳ but without MS. authority.

inchoate personalities, such as Kourotrophos and Kalligeneia, the epithets of the Olympians they so long predated.

The figure of the Mother as Kourotrophos lent itself easily to later abstractions. Themis is one of the earliest, and she attains a real personality; her sisters Eunomia and Dike are scarcely flesh and blood, they are beautiful stately shadows. The 'making of a goddess' is always a mystery, the outcome of manifold causes of which we have lost count. At the close of the 5th century B.C. at the end of the weary, fatal Peloponnesian war, Eirene, Peace, almost attained godhead, and godhead as the Mother. Cephisodotos, father of Praxiteles, made for the market-place at Athens a statue of her carrying the child Ploutos, the Athenians built her an altar and did sacrifice to her. Aristophanes brings her on the stage, but it is all too late and in vain, she remains an abstraction as lifeless as Theoria or Opora, and finds no place among the humanities of Olympus.

FIG. 64.

Tyche, Fortune, another late abstraction of the Mother, though she is scarcely more human than Eirene, obtained a wide popularity. Pausanias[1] saw at Thebes a sanctuary of Tyche; he remarks after naming the artists, 'it was a clever plan of them to put Ploutos in the arms of Tyche as his mother or nurse, and Cephisodotos was no less clever; he made for the Athenians the image of Eirene holding Ploutos.'

These abstractions, Tyche, Ananke and the like, were popular with the Orphics. Their very lack of personality favoured a growing philosophic monotheism. The design in fig. 64 is carved in low relief on one of the columns of the Hall of the Mystae of

[1] P. IX. 16. 2.

Dionysos, recently excavated at Melos[1]. Tyche holds a child—presumably the local Ploutos of Melos—in her arms. Above her is inscribed, 'May Agathe Tyche of Melos be gracious to Alexandros, the founder of the holy Mystae.' Tyche, Fortune, might be, to the uninitiated, the Patron, the Good Luck of any and every city, but to the mystic she had another and a deeper meaning; she, like the Agathos Daimon, was the inner Fate of his life and soul. In her house, as will later be seen (Chap. XI.), he lodged, observing rules of purity and abstinence before he was initiated into the underworld mysteries of Trophonios, before he drank of the waters of Lethe and Mnemosyne. It is one of the countless instances in which the Orphics went back behind the Olympian divinities and mysticized the earlier figures of the Mother or the Daughter.

Demeter and Kore.

So long as and wherever man lived for the most part by hunting, the figure of the 'Lady of the Wild Things' would content his imagination. But, when he became an agriculturist, the Mother-goddess must perforce be, not only Kourotrophos of all living things, but also the Corn-mother, Demeter.

The derivation of the name Demeter has been often discussed[2]. The most popular etymology is that which makes her Δαμήτηρ, Earth-mother, Δᾶ, which occurs in such interjections[3] as *φεῦ δᾶ*, *οἰοῖ δᾶ*, being regarded as the equivalent of Γᾶ. From the point of view of meaning this etymology is nowise satisfactory. Demeter is *not* the Earth-Mother, not the goddess of the earth in general, but of the fruits of the civilized, cultured earth, the *tilth*; not the 'Lady of the Wild Things,' but She-who-bears-fruits, *Karpophoros*. Mannhardt was the first to point out another etymology, more consonant with this notion. The author of the

[1] Mr R. C. Bosanquet, 'Excavations of the British School at Melos,' *J.H.S.* XVIII. 1898, p. 60, Fig. I, and Dr P. Wolters, 'Melische Kultstatuen,' *A. Mitt.* XV. 1890, p. 248.

[2] All the proposed etymologies, possible and impossible, are collected by Mannhardt, *Mythologische Forschungen*, p. 287. To his discussion must now be added Dr Kretschmer's view that Δᾶ like Μᾶ means mother and that the form Δαμάτηρ arose when Δᾶ had crystallized into a proper name. See *Festschrift der Wiener-Studien*, 1902, p. 291.

[3] Aesch. *Prom. Vinct.* 568.

Etymologicon Magnum[1], after stringing together a whole series of senseless conjectures, at last stumbles on what looks like the truth. 'Deo,' he says, 'may be derived from *τὰς δηάς*, for barley grains are called by the Cretans *δηαί*.' The Cretan word *δηαί* is near akin to the ordinary Greek *ζειά*, the word used for a coarse wheat or spelt; the fruitful field in Homer[2] bears the epithet *ζείδωρος*, 'spelt-yielding.' Demeter, it will later be seen (p. 564), probably came from Crete, and brought her name with her; she is the Earth, but only in this limited sense, as 'Grain-Mother.'

To the modern mind it is surprising to find the processes of agriculture conducted in the main by women, and mirroring themselves in the figures of women-goddesses. But in days when man was mainly concerned with hunting and fighting it was natural enough that agriculture and the ritual attendant on it should fall to the women. Moreover to this social necessity was added, and still is among many savage communities, a deep-seated element of superstition. 'Primitive man,' Mr Payne[3] observes, 'refuses to interfere in agriculture; he thinks it magically dependent for success on woman, and connected with child-bearing.' 'When the women plant maize,' said the Indian to Gumilla, 'the stalk produces two or three ears. Why? Because women know how to produce children. They only know how to plant corn to ensure its germinating. Then let them plant it, they know more than we know.' Such seems to have been the mind of the men of Athens who sent their wives and daughters to keep the Thesmophoria and work their charms and ensure fertility for crops and man.

It was mainly in connection with agriculture, it would seem, that the Earth-goddess developed her double form as Mother and Maid. The ancient 'Lady of the Wild Things' is both in one or perhaps not consciously either, but at Eleusis the two figures are clearly outlined; Demeter and Kore are two persons though one god. They take shape very charmingly in the design in fig. 65, from an early red-figured skyphos[4], found at Eleusis. To the left Demeter stands, holding in her left hand her sceptre, while with her right she gives the corn-ears to her nursling,

[1] *Etym. Mag.* s.v. Δηώ sub fin.: ἡ Δηώ, παρὰ τὰς δηάς· οὕτω γὰρ δηαὶ προσαγορεύονται ὑπὸ Κρητῶν αἱ κριθαί.

[2] Hom. *Il.* II. 528 ζείδωρος ἄρουρα.

[3] *History of the New World*, vol. II. p. 7.

[4] O. Rubensohn, 'Eleusinische Beiträge,' *A. Mitth.* 1899, pl. VII.

Triptolemos, who holds his 'crooked plough.' Behind is Kore, the maiden, with her simple chiton for dress, and her long flowing

Fig. 65.

hair, and the torches she holds as Queen of the underworld. Mother and Maid in this picture are clearly distinguished, but not infrequently, when both appear together, it is impossible to say which is which.

The relation of these early matriarchal, husbandless goddesses, whether Mother or Maid, to the male figures that accompany them is one altogether noble and womanly, though perhaps not what the modern mind holds to be feminine. It seems to halt somewhere half-way between Mother and Lover, with a touch of the patron saint. Aloof from achievement themselves, they choose a local hero for their own to inspire and protect. They ask of him, not that he should love or adore, but that he should do great deeds. Hera has Jason, Athene Perseus, Herakles and Theseus, Demeter and Kore Triptolemos. And as their glory is in the hero's high deeds, so their grace is his guerdon. With the coming of patriarchal conditions this high companionship ends. The women goddesses are sequestered to a servile domesticity, they become abject and amorous.

It is important to note that primarily the two forms of the Earth or Corn-goddess are not Mother and *Daughter*, but Mother and Maiden, Demeter and Kore. They are, in fact, merely the older and younger form of the same person; hence their easy confusion. The figures of the Mother and *Daughter* are mythological rather than theological, i.e. they arise from the story-telling instinct:

'Demeter of the beauteous hair, goddess divine, I sing,
She and the slender-ancled maid, her daughter, whom the king
Aidoneus seized, by Zeus' decree. He found her, as she played
Far from her mother's side, who reaps the corn with golden blade[1].'

The corn is reaped and the earth desolate in winter-time. Aetiology is ready with a human love-story. The maiden, the young fruit of the earth, was caught by a lover, kept for a season, and in the spring-time returns to her mother; the mother is comforted, and the earth blossoms again[2]:

'Thus she spake, and then did Demeter the garlanded yield
And straightway let spring up the fruit of the loamy field,
And all the breadth of the earth, with leaves and blossoming things
Was heavy. Then she went forth to the law-delivering kings
And taught them, Triptolemos first.'

Mythology might work its will, but primitive art never clearly distinguished between the Mother and the Maid, never lost hold of the truth that they were one goddess. On the Boeotian plate[3] in fig. 66 is figured the Corn-goddess, but whether as Mother or Maid it is difficult, I incline to think impossible, to decide. She is a great goddess, enthroned and heavily draped, wearing a high polos on her head. She holds ears of corn, a pomegranate, a torch; before her is an omphalos-like altar, on it what looks like a pomegranate—is she Demeter or Persephone? I incline to think she is both in one; the artist has not differentiated her.

[1] *Hom. Hymn. ad Cer.* 1.

[2] *Hom. Hymn. ad Cer.* 470. The elaborate aetiology of the whole Homeric Hymn to Demeter has been fully examined and explained by Mr F. B. Jevons in his *Introduction to the History of Religion*, ch. XXIII. and Appendix.

[3] Athens Nat. Mus. 484. Fig. 66 is reproduced from a photograph kindly sent me by Prof. Sam. Wide. For further particulars of this class of vases I must refer to Prof. Wide's article 'Eine lokale Gattung Boiotischer Gefässe,' *A. Mitt.* XXVI. 1901, p. 143. Prof. Wide makes the interesting suggestion that the bird in the field is a bird-soul and points out that merely decorative 'Füllfiguren' do not occur on this class of vases. This interpretation seems to me highly probable, but till further evidence emerges, I hesitate to adopt it as certain.

The dead, according to Plutarch's[1] statement, were called by the Athenians 'Demeter's people.' The ancient 'Lady of the Wild

Fig. 66.

Things,' with her guardian lions, keeps ward over the dead in the tombs of Asia Minor, and every grave became her sanctuary. But in Greece proper, and especially at Eleusis, where the Mother and the Maid take mythological, differentiated form as Demeter and her daughter Persephone, their individual functions tend more and more to specialize. Demeter becomes more and more agricultural, more and more the actual corn. As Plutarch[2] observes—with full consciousness of the anomalous blend of the human and the physical—a poet can say of the reapers:

> 'What time men shear to earth Demeter's limbs.'

The Mother takes the physical side, the Daughter the spiritual—the Mother is more and more of the upper air, the Daughter of the underworld.

Demeter as Thesmophoros has for her sphere more and more the things of this life, laws and civilized marriage; she grows more and more human and kindly, goes more and more

[1] Plut. *de fac. in orb. lun.* XXVIII.

[2] Plut. *de Is. et Osir.* LXVI. *ποιητὴς δέ τις ἐπὶ τῶν θεριζόντων 'Τῆμος ὅτ' αἰζηοὶ Δημήτερα κωλοτομεῦσιν.'*

over to the humane Olympians, till in the Homeric Hymn she, the Earth-Mother, is an actual denizen of Olympus. The Daughter, at first but the young form of the mother, is in maiden fashion sequestered, even a little *farouche*; she withdraws herself more and more to the kingdom of the spirit, the things below and beyond:

> 'She waits for each and other,
> She waits for all men born,
> Forgets the earth her mother,
> The life of fruits and corn.
> And spring and seed and swallow
> Take wing for her and follow
> Where summer song rings hollow
> And flowers are put to scorn.'

And in that kingdom aloof her figure waxes as the figure of the Mother wanes:

> 'O daughter of earth, my mother, her crown and blossom of birth,
> I am also I also thy brother, I go as I came unto earth.'

She passes to a place unknown of the Olympians, her kingdom is not of this world.

> 'Thou art more than the Gods, who number the days of our temporal breath,
> For these give labour and slumber, but thou, Proserpina, Death.'

All this is matter of late development. At first we have merely the figures of the Two Goddesses, the Two Thesmophoroi, the Two Despoinae. Demeter at Hermione is Chthonia, in Arcadia[1] she is at once Erinys and Lousia. But it is not surprising that, as will later be seen, a religion like Orphism, which concerned itself with the abnegation of this world and the life of the soul hereafter, laid hold rather of the figure of the underworld Kore, and left the prosperous, genial Corn-Mother to make her way alone into Olympus.

The Anodos of the Maiden Earth-goddesses.

In discussing the Boeotian plate (fig. 66), it has been seen that it is not easy always to distinguish in art the figures of the Mother and the Maid. A like difficulty attends the interpretation of the series of curious representations of the earth-goddess now to be considered (figs. 67—71).

[1] P. VIII. 25. 4—7.

We begin with the vase-painting in fig. 67, where happily an inscription makes the interpretation certain. The design is from a red-figured krater, now in the Albertinum Museum at Dresden[1]. To the right is a conventional earth-mound (χῶμα γῆς). In front

FIG. 67.

of it stands Hermes. He holds not his *kerykeion*, but a rude forked *rhabdos*. It was with the *rhabdos*, it will be remembered (p. 44), that he summoned the souls from the grave-*pithos*. Here, too, he is present as Psychagogos; he has come to summon an earth-spirit, nay more, *the* Earth-goddess herself. Out of the artificial mound, which symbolizes the earth itself, rises the figure of a woman. At first sight we might be inclined to call her Ge, the Earth-*Mother*, but the figure is slight and maidenly, and over her happily is written (Phe)rophatta. It is the Anodos of Kore—the coming of the goddess is greeted by an ecstatic dance of goat-

[1] *Jahrbuch d. Inst. Anz.* 1893, p. 166.

horned *Panes*. They are not Satyrs: these, as will later be seen (p. 379), are horse demons. By the early middle of the 5th century B.C., the date of this red-figured vase, the worship of the Arcadian Pan was well-established at Athens, and the goat-men, the Panes, became the fashionable and fitting attendants of the Earth-Maiden. The inscriptions above their heads can, unfortunately, not be read.

A vase of much later date (fig. 68) shows us substantially the

FIG. 68.

same scene. The design is from a red-figured krater[1] in the Berlin Antiquarium. The goddess again rises from an artificial mound decorated with sprays of foliage. The attendant figures are different. A goat-legged Pan leans eagerly over the mound, but Dionysos himself, with his thyrsos, sits quietly waiting the Anodos, and with him are his real attendants, the horse-tailed Satyrs. In the left-hand corner a little winged Love-god plays on the double flutes. The rising goddess is not inscribed, and she is

[1] Berl. *Cat.* 2646. *Mon. d. Inst.* XII. tav. IV. This vase with others of the same type is explained by Dr Robert, *Archäologische Mährchen*, p. 196, as the rising of a Spring-Nymph, but the inscribed Berlin vase was not known to him, see also 'Delphika,' *J.H.S.* XIX. 1899, p. 232.

best left unnamed. She is an Earth-goddess, but the presence of Dionysos makes us suspect that there is some reminiscence of Semele (p. 406). The presence of the Love-god points, as will be explained later (Chap. XII.), to the influence of Orphism.

More curious, more instructive, but harder completely to explain, is the design in fig. 69, from a black-figured lekythos in

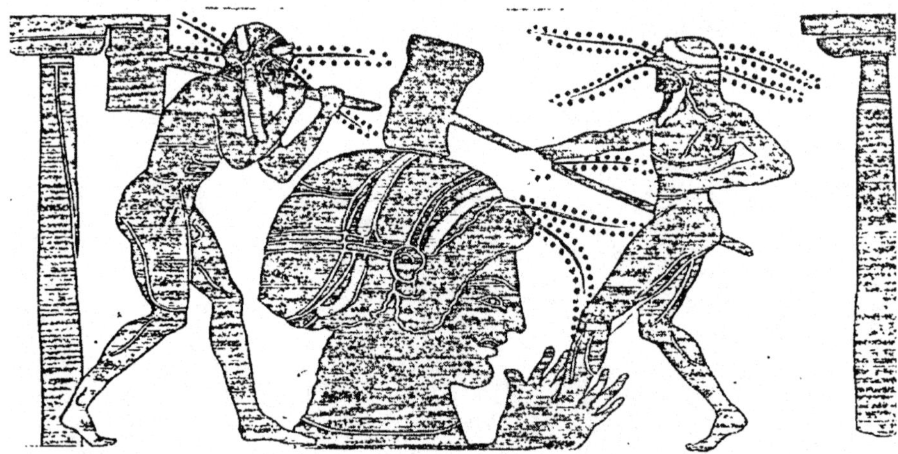

Fig. 69.

the Bibliothèque Nationale[1] at Paris. The colossal head and lifted hands of a woman are rising out of the earth. This time there is no artificial mound, the scene takes place in a temple or sanctuary, indicated by the two bounding columns. Two men, not Satyrs, are present, and this time not as idle spectators. Both are armed with great mallets or hammers, and one of them strikes the head of the rising woman.

Some possible light is thrown on this difficult vase by the consideration of two others. First we have two designs from the obverse and reverse of an amphora[2], shown together in fig. 70.

[1] *Cat.* 298. Milliet et Giraudon, Pl. LII. B, discussed by Prof. Furtwängler, *Jahrbuch d. Inst.* 1891, p. 113, and Prof. Gardner, *J.H.S.* XXI. 1901, p. 5, and J. E. Harrison, 'Delphika,' *J.H.S.* XIX. 1899, p. 232.

[2] Vasi dipinti del Museo Vivenzio designati di C. Angelini nel MDCCXCVI. Illustrato di G. Patroni 1900, Tav. XXIX. All the plates of this publication are of course reproduced from very old drawings and are quite untrustworthy as regards style. The vase under discussion is now lost, so that the original cannot be compared. Sig. Patroni thinks the drawing is authentic. I reproduce it partly because the subject is not wholly explicable, partly in the hope that by making it more widely known, I may lead to the rediscovery of the vase, which may be in some private collection.

On the obverse to the left we have a scene fairly familiar, a goddess rising from the ground, watched by a youth, who holds in his hand some sort of implement, either a pick or a hammer.

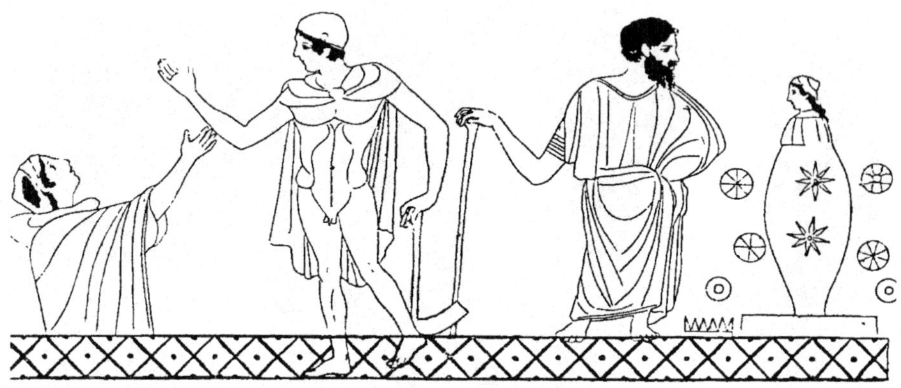

Fig. 70.

The meaning of the reverse design is conjectural. A man, short of stature and almost deformed in appearance, looks at a curious and problematic figure, half woman and half vase, set on a quadrangular basis. Before it, if the drawing be correct, is a spiked crown; round about, in the field, a number of rosettes. A design so problematic is not likely to be a forgery. Before its meaning is conjectured, another vase, whose interpretation is perfectly clear and certain, remains to be considered. Its meaning may serve to elucidate the others.

The design in fig. 71 is from a red-figured amphora[1] of the finest period, in the Ashmolean Museum at Oxford. At a first glance, when we see the splendid figure rising from the ground with outstretched arms, the man with the hammer and Hermes attendant, we think that we have the familiar scene of the rising of Kore or Ge. As such, had no inscriptions existed, the design would certainly have been interpreted. But, as it happens, each figure is carefully inscribed. To the left *Zeus*, next to him *Hermes*, next *Epimetheus*, and last, not Ge or Kore, but *Pandora*. Over Pandora, to greet her uprising, hovers a Love-god with a fillet in his outstretched hands.

[1] Prof. Percy Gardner, 'A new Pandora Vase,' *J.H.S.* XXI. 1901, Plate 1.

Pandora rises from the earth: she *is* the Earth, giver of all gifts. This is made doubly sure by another representation of her birth or rather her making. On the well-known *Bale*-cylix of the

FIG. 71.

British Museum[1] Pandora, half statue half woman, has just been modelled by Hephaistos, and Athene is in the act of decking her. Pandora she certainly is, but against her is written her other name (A)nesidora[2], 'she who sends up gifts.' Pandora is a form or title of the Earth-goddess in the Kore form, entirely humanized and vividly personified by mythology.

In the light of this substantial identity of Pandora and the Earth-Kore, it is possible perhaps to offer an explanation of the

[1] *Brit. Mus. Cat.* D 4. *White Athenian Vases*, Plate 19. *Myth. and Mon. of Anc. Athens*, p. 450, fig. 50.

[2] The worship of Ge as Anesidora at Phlya will be later discussed, Chap. XII.

problematic vase in fig. 70. Have we not on obverse and reverse a juxtaposition of the two scenes, the Rise of Kore, the Making of Pandora? On this showing the short deformed man would be Hephaistos, and Pandora, half woman half vase, may be conceived as issuing from her once famous *pithos*.

The *contaminatio* of the myths of the Making of Pandora and the Anodos of Kore may explain also another difficulty. In the making and moulding of Pandora, Hephaistos the craftsman uses his characteristic implement, the hammer[1]. This hammer he also uses to break open the head of Zeus, in representations of the birth of Athene (p. 365). On vases with the Anodos of Kore the Satyrs or *Panes* carry and use sometimes an ordinary pick, sometimes a hammer, like the hammer of Hephaistos. The pick is the natural implement for breaking clods of earth, the spade appears to have been unknown before the iron age—the hammers have always presented a difficulty. May they not have arisen in connection with the myth of the making of Pandora, and then, by confusion, passed to the Anodos of Kore?

Finally, returning to the difficult design in fig. 69, I would offer another suggestion. The fact that the scene takes place in a sanctuary seems to me to indicate that we have here a representation of some sort of mimetic ritual. The Anodos of Kore was, as has already been seen (p. 131), dramatized at certain festivals; exactly how we do not know. At the festival of the *Charila* (p. 107) a puppet dressed as a girl was brought out, beaten, and ultimately hanged in a chasm. Is it not possible that at some festival of the Earth-goddess there was a mimetic enactment of the Anodos, that the earth or some artificially-formed chasm was broken open by picks, and that a puppet or a real woman emerged. It is more likely, I think, that the vase-painter had some such scene in his mind than that the Satyrs with their picks or hammers represent the storm and lightning from heaven beating on the earth to subdue it and compel its fertility[2]. At Megara,

[1] A lost play of Sophocles was called Πανδώρα ἢ Σφυροκόποι. The σφῦρα though characteristic of Hephaistos the craftsman was used by agriculturists. Trygaeus in the *Pax* (*v.* 566) remembers that his σφῦρα waits at home glittering and ready, see *J.H.S.* xx. 1900, p. 107.

[2] Prof. Furtwängler, *Jahrbuch d. Inst.* 1891, pp. 117 and 124, 'Ein uraltes mythisches Symbol für die Blitze sind aber Hammer und Beil. Sie sind es...die mit mächtigen Gewittern den Kopf der grossen Mutter Erde schlagen und hämmern bis sie erwacht und erweicht.'

near the Prytaneion, Pausanias[1] saw 'a rock which was called Anaklethra[2], "Calling Up," because Demeter, if anyone like to believe it, when she was wandering in search of her daughter, called her up there.' He adds, 'the women of Megara to this day perform rites that are analogous to the legend told.' Unhappily he does not tell us what these rites were. Lucian devotes a half-serious treatise to discussing the scope and merits of pantomimic dancing, Xenophon[3] in his *Banquet* lets us see that educated guests after dinner preferred the acting of a myth to the tumbling of a dancing girl, but the actual *ritual* pantomime of the ancients is to us a sealed book. Of one thing we may be sure, that the 'things done' (δρώμενα) of ritual helped to intensify mythological impersonation as much as, or perhaps more than, the 'things spoken' (ἔπη) of the poet.

PANDORA.

To the primitive matriarchal Greek Pandora was then a real goddess, in form and name, of the Earth, and men did sacrifice to her. By the time of Aristophanes[4] she had become a misty figure, her ritual archaic—matter for the oracles of 'Bakis.' The prophet instructing Peisthetairos reads from his script:

'First to Pandora sacrifice a white-fleeced ram.'

The scholiast gives the correct and canonical interpretation 'to Pandora, the earth, because she bestows all things necessary for life.' By his time, and long before, explanation was necessary. Hipponax[5] knew of her; Athenaeus, in his discussion of cabbages, quotes from memory the mysterious lines:

'He grovelled, worshipping the seven-leaved cabbage
To which Pandora sacrificed a cake
At the Thargelia for a pharmakos.'

The passage, though obscure, is of interest because it connects Pandora the Earth-goddess with the Thargelia, the festival of the

[1] P. I. 43. 2...ἐοικότα δὲ τῷ λόγῳ δρῶσιν ἐς ἡμᾶς ἔτι αἱ Μεγαρέων γυναῖκες.

[2] The *Etymologicon Magnum* has the form Ἀνακληθρίς.

[3] Xen. *Symp.* VII. 5. I have elsewhere (*Myth. and Mon. of Anc. Athens*, p. cxvii) discussed the possible influence of such mimetic presentations on the fixed mythological types of vase-paintings. Dr Frazer (*Golden Bough*, 2nd ed. vol. III. p. 165) makes the interesting suggestion that in sacred dramas may be found a possible meeting-ground between Euhemerists and their opponents.

[4] Ar. *Av.* 971, schol. ad loc.

[5] Frg. Hippon. ap. Athen. IX. § 370.

first-fruits of the Earth. Effaced in popular ritual she emerges in private superstition. Philostratos[1], in his *Life of Apollonius*, tells how a certain man, in need of money to dower his daughter, 'sacrificed' to Earth for treasure, and Apollonius, to whom he confided his desire, said, 'Earth and I will help you,' and he prayed to Pandora, sought in a garden, and found the desired treasure.

Pandora is in ritual and matriarchal theology the earth as Kore, but in the patriarchal mythology of Hesiod her great figure is strangely changed and minished. She is no longer Earth-born, but the creature, the handiwork of Olympian Zeus. On a late, red-figured krater in the British Museum[2], obviously inspired by Hesiod, we have the scene of her birth. She no longer rises half-way from the ground, but stands stiff and erect in the midst of the Olympians. Zeus is there seated with sceptre and thunderbolt, Poseidon is there, Iris and Hermes and Ares and Hera, and Athene about to crown the new-born maiden. Earth is all but forgotten, and yet so haunting is tradition that, in a lower row, beneath the Olympians, a chorus of men, disguised as goat-horned Panes, still dance their welcome. It is a singular reminiscence, and, save as a survival, wholly irrelevant.

Hesiod loves the story of the Making of Pandora: he has shaped it to his own *bourgeois*, pessimistic ends; he tells it twice. Once in the *Theogony*[3], and here the new-born maiden has no name, she is just a 'beautiful evil,' a 'crafty snare' to mortals. But in the *Works and Days*[4] he dares to name her and yet with infinite skill to wrest her glory into shame:

'He spake, and they did the will of Zeus, son of Kronos, the Lord,
For straightway the Halting One, the Famous, at his word
Took clay and moulded an image, in form of a maiden fair,
And Athene, the gray-eyed goddess girt her and decked her hair.
And about her the Graces divine and our Lady Persuasion set
Bracelets of gold on her flesh; and about her others yet,
The Hours with their beautiful hair, twined wreaths of blossoms of spring,
While Pallas Athene still ordered her decking in everything.
Then put the Argus-slayer, the marshal of souls to their place,
Tricks and flattering words in her bosom and thievish ways.

[1] Philostr. *Vit. Apoll.* XXXIX. § 275.

[2] *Brit. Mus. Cat.* E 467. *J.H.S.* XI. pl. 11 and 12, p. 278, and Roscher, *Lex.* s.v. Pandora, fig. 2.

[3] Hes. *Theog.* 570, trans. Mr D. S. MacColl.

[4] Hes. *Op.* 69 ff.

> He wrought by the will of Zeus, the Loud-thundering giving her voice,
> Spokesman of gods that he is, and for name of her this was his choice,
> PANDORA, because in Olympus the gods joined together then
> And *all* of them gave her, a *gift*, a sorrow, to covetous men.'

Through all the magic of a poet, caught and enchanted himself by the vision of a lovely woman, there gleams the ugly malice of theological animus. Zeus the Father will have no great Earth-goddess, Mother and Maid in one, in his man-fashioned Olympus, but her figure *is* from the beginning, so he re-makes it; woman, who was the inspirer, becomes the temptress; she who made all things, gods and mortals alike, is become their plaything, their slave, dowered only with physical beauty, and with a slave's tricks and blandishments. To Zeus, the archpatriarchal *bourgeois*, the birth of the first woman is but a huge Olympian jest[1]:

> 'He spake and the Sire of men and of gods immortal laughed.'

Such myths are a necessary outcome of the shift from matriarchy to patriarchy, and the shift itself, spite of a seeming retrogression, is a necessary stage in a real advance. Matriarchy gave to women a false because a magical prestige. With patriarchy came inevitably the facing of a real fact, the fact of the greater natural weakness of women. Man the stronger, when he outgrew his belief in the magical potency of woman, proceeded by a pardonable practical logic to despise and enslave her as the weaker. The future held indeed a time when the non-natural, mystical truth came to be apprehended, that the stronger had a need, real and imperative, of the weaker. Physically nature had from the outset compelled a certain recognition of this truth, but that the physical was a sacrament of the spiritual was a hard saying, and its understanding was not granted to the Greek, save here and there where a flicker of the truth gleamed and went through the vision of philosopher or poet.

So the great figure of the Earth-goddess, Pandora, suffered eclipse: she sank to be a beautiful, curious woman; she opened her great grave-*pithos*[2], she that was Mother of Life; the Keres fluttered forth, bringing death and disease;—only Hope remained. Strangely enough, when the great figure of the Earth-Mother re-emerges, she re-emerges, it will later be seen, as Aphrodite.

[1] Hes. *Op.* 59. [2] For the origin of the *pithos* see *J.H.S.* xx. 1900, p. 99.

THE MAIDEN-TRINITIES.

So far we have seen that a goddess, to the primitive Greek, took twofold form, and this twofold form, shifting and easily interchangeable, is seen to resolve itself very simply into the two stages of a woman's life, as Maiden and Mother. But Greek religion has besides the twofold Mother and Maiden a number of *triple* forms, Women-Trinities, which at first sight are not so readily explicable. We find not only three Gorgons and three Graiae, but three Semnae, three Moirae, three Charites, three Horae, three Agraulids, and, as a multiple of three, nine Muses.

First it should be noted that the trinity-form is confined to the women goddesses. Greek religion had in Zeus and Apollo the figures of the father and the son, but of a male trinity we find no trace. Zeus and Apollo, incomers from the North, stand alone in this matter of relationship. We do not find the fatherhood of Poseidon emphasized, nor the sonship of Hermes; there is no wide and universal development of the father and the son as there was of the Mother and the Maiden. Dualities and trinities alike seem to be characteristic of the old matriarchal goddesses.

Evidence is not lacking that the trinity-form grew out of the duality. Plutarch[1] notes as one of the puzzling things at Delphi which required looking into, that two Moirae were worshipped there, whereas everywhere else three were canonical. It has already been seen (p. 242) that the number of the Semnae varied between two and three, and that, as three was the ultimate canonical number, we might fairly suppose the number two to have been the earlier. It is the same with the Charites. Pausanias[2] was told in Boeotia that Eteocles not only was 'the first who sacrificed to the Charites,' but, further, he 'instituted three Charites.' The names Eteocles gave to his three Charites the Boeotians did not remember. This is unfortunate, as Orchomenos was the most ancient seat of the worship of the Charites; their images there were natural stones that fell to Eteocles from heaven. Pausanias goes on to note that 'among the Lacedaemonians two Charites only were worshipped; their names were Kleta and Phaenna. The Athenians also from ancient days worshipped two Charites, by

[1] Plut. *de Ei ap. Delph.* II. 1. [2] P. IX. 35. 1.

name Auxo and Hegemone.' Later it appears they fell in with the prevailing fashion, for 'in front of the entrance to the Acropolis there were set up the images of three Charites.' The ancient Charites at Orchomenos, at Sparta, at Athens, were two, and it may be conjectured that they took form as the Mother and the Maid.

The three daughters of Cecrops[1] are by the time of Euripides 'maidens threefold'; the three daughters of Erechtheus[2], who are but their later doubles, are a 'triple yoke of maidens,' and yet—in the case of the daughters of Cecrops—there is ample evidence[3] that originally they were two, and these two probably a mother and a maid. Aglauros and Pandrosos are definite personalities; they had regular precincts and shrines, known in historical times, Aglauros on the north slope of the Acropolis[4], where the maidens danced, Pandrosos to the west of the Erechtheion[5]. But of a shrine, precinct, or sanctuary of Herse we have no notice. Ovid[6] probably felt the difficulty; he lodges Herse in a chamber midway between Aglauros and Pandrosos. The women of Athens swore by Aglauros and more rarely by Pandrosos[7]. Aglauros, by whom they swore most frequently, and who gave her name to the Agraulids, was probably the earlier and mother-form. Herse was no good even to swear by; she is the mere senseless etymological eponym of the festival of the Hersephoria, a third sister added to make up the canonical triad. The Hersephoria out of which she is made was not in her honour; it was celebrated to Athene, to Pandrosos, to Ge, to Themis, to Eileithyia.

The women-trinities rose out of dualities, but not every duality became a trinity. Plutarch[8], in discussing the origin of the nine Muses, notes that we have not three Demeters, or three Athenes, or three Artemises. He touches unconsciously on the reason why some dualities resisted the impulse to become trinities. Where personification had become complete, as in the case of Demeter and Kore, or of their doubles, Damia and Auxesia, no third figure could lightly be added. Where the divine pair were still in flux,

[1] Eur. *Ion* 496. [2] Eur. *Erech.* frg. v. 3.

[3] I have collected and discussed this evidence in 'Mythological Studies,' *J.H.S.* vol. XII. 1891, p. 350.

[4] P. I. 18. 2. [5] P. I. 26. 6. [6] Ov. *Met.* II. 739.

[7] Schol. ad Ar. *Thesm.* 533 κατὰ γὰρ τῆς Ἀγραύλου ὤμνυον κατὰ δὲ τῆς Πανδρόσου σπανιώτερον.

[8] Plut. *Quaest. Symp.* IX. 14. 2.

still called by merely adjectival titles that had not crystallized into proper names, a person more or less mattered little. Thus we have a trinity of Semnae, of Horae, of Moirae, but the Thesmophoroi, who *as* Thesmophoroi might have easily passed into a trinity, remain always, because of the clear outlines of Demeter and Kore, a duality.

When we ask what was the impulse to the formation of trinities, the answer is necessarily complex. Many strands seem to have gone to their weaving.

First, and perhaps foremost, in the ritual of the lower stratum, of the dead and of chthonic powers, three was, for some reason that escapes us, a sacred number[1]. The dead were thrice invoked; sacrifice was offered to them on the third day; the mourning in some parts of Greece lasted three days; the court of the Areopagus, watched over by deities of the underworld, sat, as has been seen (p. 242), on three days; at the three ways the threefold Hecate of the underworld was worshipped. It was easy and natural that threefold divinities should arise to keep ward over a ritual so constituted. When the powers of the underworld came to preside over agriculture, the transition from two to three seasons would tend in the same direction. For two seasons a duality was enough—the Mother for the fertile summer, the Maid for the sterile winter—but, when the seasons became three, a trinity was needed, or at least would be welcomed.

Last, the influence of art must not be forgotten. A central figure of the mother, with her one daughter, composes ill. Archaic art loved heraldic groupings, and for these two daughters were essential. Such compositions as that on the Boeotian amphora in fig. 59 might easily suggest a trinity[2].

Once the triple form established, it is noticeable that in Greek mythology the three figures are always regarded as *maiden* goddesses, not as mothers. They may have taken their rise in the

[1] For three in the cultus of the dead, see Diels, *Sibyllinische Blätter*, p. 40. For a discussion of trinities other than of maiden goddesses, see Usener, 'Dreiheit' (*Rhein. Mus.* LVIII. pp. 1—47).

[2] In this connection it may be worth noting that where the nature of the dual goddess prevents her taking a central place as in the case of Eileithyia she never merges into a trinity. There are often two Eileithyiai, e.g. one to either side of Zeus at the birth of Athene, but never three.

Mother and the Maid, but the Mother falls utterly away. The Charites, the Moirae, the Horae, are all essentially maidens. The reverse is the case in Roman religion; trinities of women goddesses of fertility occur frequently in very late Roman art, but they are Matres, Mothers[1]. Three Mothers are rather heavy, and do not dance well.

In the archaic votive relief[2] in fig. 72 we have the earliest sculptured representation of the maiden trinity extant. Had the relief been uninscribed, we should have been at a loss how to name the three austere figures. Two carry fruits, and one a wreath. They might be Charites or Eumenides, or merely nymphs. Most happily the sculptor has left no doubt. He has written against them Κόρας Σοτίας, 'Sotias (dedicated) the Korai' the 'Maidens.' Sotias has massed the three stately figures very closely together; he is reverently conscious that though they are three persons, yet they are but one goddess. He is half monotheist.

Fig. 72.

The same origin of the maiden trinity is clearly indicated in the relief[3] in fig. 73, found during the 'Enneakrounos' excavations in the precinct of Dionysos, at Athens. The main field of the relief is occupied by two figures of *Panes*, with attendant goats; between them an altar. The Panes are twofold, not because they are father and son, but because there were two caves of Pan, and the god is thought of as dwelling in each. After the battle of Marathon the worship of Pan was established in the ancient dancing-ground of the Agraulids; by the time of Euripides[4], Pan is thought of as host and they as guests:

[1] Roscher, *Lex.* s.v. Matres, Matronae.
[2] Fröhner, Coll. Tyszkiewisk, Pl. xvi.; *J.H.S.* xix. p. 218, fig. 3.
[3] *A. Mitt.* 1896, p. 266, Taf. viii.
[4] Eur. *Ion* 490, trans. Mr D. S. MacColl.

'O seats of Pan and rock hard by
To where the hollow Long Rocks lie,
Where before Pallas' temple-bound
Agraulos' daughters three go round
Upon their grassy dancing-ground
  To nimble reedy staves,
When thou, O Pan, art piping found
  Within thy shepherd caves.'

But Pan was a new-comer; the Agraulids were there from the beginning, as early as Cecrops, their snake-tailed father. Busy

FIG. 73.

though he is with Pan, the new-comer, the artist cannot, may not forget the triple maidens. He figures them in the upper frieze, and in quaint fashion he hints that though three they are one. In the left-hand corner he sets the image of a threefold goddess, a Hecate[1].

But, as time went on, the fact that the three were one is more

[1] For the development of the type of Hecate in conjunction with the Charites, see *Myth. and Mon. Anc. Athens*, p. 373.

and more forgotten. They become three single maidens, led by Hermes in the dance; by Hermes *Charidotes*, whose worship as the young male god of fertility, of flocks and herds, was so closely allied to that of the Charites.

There is no more frequent type of votive relief[1] than that of which an instance is given in fig. 74. The cave of Pan is the

Fig. 74.

scene, Pan himself is piping, and the three maidens, led by Hermes, dance. The cave, the artist knows, belonged in his days to Pan, but the ancient dwellers there, the Maidens, still bulk the largest. As a rule the reliefs are not inscribed, sometimes there is a dedication 'to the Nymphs.' The personality of the Agraulids has become shadowy, they are merely Maidens or Brides.

The ancient threefold goddesses, as all-powerful Charites, paled before the Olympians, faded away into mere dancing attendant maidens; but sometimes, in the myths told of these very Olympians, it is possible to trace the reflection of the older potencies. A very curious instance is to be found in the familiar

[1] In the Vienna Museum, found at Gallipoli, *Arch. Epigr. Mitt.* vol. I. Taf. 1. Prof. O. Benndorf, 'Die Chariten des Sokrates,' *Arch. Zeit.* 1869.

story[1] of the 'Judgment of Paris,' a story whose development and decay are so instructive that it must be examined in some detail.

THE 'JUDGMENT OF PARIS.'

The myth in its current form is sufficiently patriarchal to please the taste of Olympian Zeus himself, trivial and even vulgar enough to make material for an ancient Satyr-play or a modern *opera-bouffe*.

> 'Goddesses three to Ida came
> Immortal strife to settle there—
> Which was the fairest of the three,
> And which the prize of beauty should wear.'

The bone of contention is a golden apple thrown by Eris at the marriage of Peleus and Thetis among the assembled gods. On it was written, 'Let the fair one take it,' or, according to some

FIG. 75.

authorities, 'The apple for the fair one[2].' The three high goddesses betake them for judgment to the king's son, the shepherd Paris. The kernel of the myth is, according to this version, a *καλλιστεῖον*, a beauty-contest.

[1] The sources for the story are well collected in Roscher's *Lexicon*, s.v. Paris, but the author of the article seems to have no suspicion of the real substratum of the myth.

[2] Luc. *dial. deor.* 20 ἡ καλὴ λαβέτω. Tzetzes ad Lycophr. 93 τῇ καλῇ τὸ μῆλον.

On one ancient vase, and on one only of all the dozens that remain, is the Judgment so figured. The design in fig. 75 is from a late red-figured krater in the Bibliothèque Nationale[1]. Paris, dressed as a Phrygian, is seated in the centre. Hermes is telling of his mission. Grouped around, the three goddesses prepare for the beauty-contest in characteristic fashion. Hera needs no aid, she orders her veil and gazes well satisfied in a mirror; Aphrodite stretches out a lovely arm, and a Love-God fastens 'a bracelet of gold on her flesh'; and Athene, watched only by the great grave dog, goes to a little fountain shrine and, clean-hearted goddess as she is, lays aside her shield, tucks her gown about her, and has—a good wash. Our hearts are with Oenone when she cries:

> '"O Paris,
> Give it to Pallas!" but he heard me not,
> Or hearing would not hear me, woe is me!'

It is noteworthy that even in this representation, obviously of a beauty-contest, the apple is absent.

It is quite true that now and again one of the goddesses holds in her hand a fruit. An instance is given in the charming design in fig. 76, from a red-figured stamnos in the British Museum[2].

FIG. 76.

Fruit and flowers are held indifferently by one or all of the goddesses, and the reason will presently become clear. In the present case Hera holds a fruit, in fig. 80 the two last goddesses hold each a fruit. In fig. 76, against both Aphrodite and Hera, is inscribed Καλή, 'Beautiful,' and before the blinding beauty of the goddesses Paris veils his face. The inscription Χαρμίδης

[1] *Cat.* 422. Milliet et Giraudon, Pl. 104.
[2] *B. M. Cat.* E 289. *J.H.S.* VII. 1886, p. 9.

enables us to date the vase as belonging to the first half of the 5th cent. B.C.

Turning to black-figured vases, a good instance is given in fig. 77 from a patera[1] in the Museo Greco-Etrusco at Florence.

FIG. 77.

The three goddesses, bearing no apple and no attributes, the centre one only distinguished by the spots upon her cloak, follow Hermes into the presence of Paris. Paris starts away in manifest alarm. In the curious design[2] in fig. 78, Hermes actually seizes Paris by the wrist to compel his attendance. There is here clearly no question of voluptuous delight at the beauty of the goddesses. The three maiden figures are scrupulously alike; each carries a wreath. Discrimination would be a hard task. The figures are placed closely together, as in the representation of the Maidens in fig. 72.

[1] *J.H.S.* VII. 1888, p. 198, fig. 1.
[2] *J.H.S.* VII. 1888, p. 203.

Finally, in fig. 79, a design from a black-figured amphora[1], we have the type most frequent of all; Hermes leads the three

Fig. 78.

goddesses, but in the Judgment of Paris *no figure of Paris is present.* Without exaggeration it may be said that in three out of four representations of the 'Judgment' in black-figured vase-paintings the protagonist is absent. The scene takes the form of a simple procession, Hermes leading the three goddesses.

This curious fact has escaped the attention of no archaeologist who has examined the art types of the 'Judgment.' It has been variously explained. At a time when vase-paintings were supposed to have had literary sources, it was usual to attempt a literary explanation. Attention was called to the fact that Proklos[2], in his excerpts of the *Kypria*, noted that the goddesses, 'by command of Zeus were led to Ida by Hermes'; of this leading it was then supposed that the vase-paintings were 'illustrations.'

[1] *J.H.S.* VII. 1888, p. 282.

[2] Procl. *Excerpt.* αἳ πρὸς Ἀλέξανδρον ἐν Ἴδῃ κατὰ Διὸς προσταγὴν ὑφ' Ἑρμοῦ πρὸς τὴν κρίσιν ἄγονται. See Schneider, *Der troische Sagenkreis*, p. 99, and Welcker, *Ep. Kyklos*, II. 88.

Such methods of interpretation are now discredited; no one supposes that the illiterate vase-painter worked with the text of the *Kypria* before him. Art had its own traditions.

Another explanation, scarcely more happy, has been attempted. 'Archaic art,' we are told, 'loved processions.' Archaic art, concerned

FIG. 79.

to fill the space of a circular frieze surrounding a vase, did indeed 'love processions,' but not with a passion so fond and unreasonable, and it loved something else better, the lucid telling of a story. In depicting other myths, archaic art is not driven to express a story in the terms of an inappropriate procession; it is indeed largely governed by traditional form, but not to the extent of tolerating needless obscurity. The 'Judgment' is a situation essentially stationary, with Paris for centre; Hermes is subordinate.

We are so used to the procession form that it requires a certain effort of the imagination to conceive of the myth embodied otherwise. But, if we shake ourselves loose of preconceived notions, surely the natural lucid way of depicting the myth would be something after this fashion: Paris in the centre, facing the successful Aphrodite, to whom he speaks or hands the apple or a crown; behind him, to indicate neglect, the two defeated goddesses; Hermes anywhere, to indicate the mandate of the gods. Such a form does indeed appear later, when the vase-painter thought for himself and shook himself free of the dominant tradition. The procession form, as we have it, *was not made for the myth*, it was merely adapted and taken over, and instantly the suggestion occurs, 'Did not the myth itself in some sense rise out of the already existing art form, an art form in which Paris had no place, in which the golden apple was not?' That form was the ancient type of *Hermes leading the three Korai or Charites.* In the design in fig. 79, the centre figure Athene is differentiated by her tall helmet and her aegis. Athene is the first of the goddesses to be differentiated—and why? She was not victorious, but the vase-painter is an Athenian, and he is concerned for the glory of ἡ Ἀθηναία Κόρη, the Maiden of Athens.

In the design in fig. 80, from a black-figured amphora in the Berlin Museum[1], the three goddesses are all alike: the first holds

Fig. 80.

a flower, the two last fruits, all fitting emblems of the Charites. Hermes, their leader, carries a huge irrelevant sheep—irrelevant for the herald of the gods on his way to Ida, significant for the leader of the Charites, the god of the increase of flocks and herds. Does the picture represent a 'Judgment,' or Hermes and the Charites? Who knows? The doubt is here, as often, more instructive than certainty.

[1] *Berl. Cat.* 2154. Endt, *Beiträge zur Ionischen Vasenmalerei*, p. 29, figs. 11, 12 and 13.

From vases alone it would be sufficiently evident, I think, that the 'Judgment of Paris'[1] is really based on Hermes and the Charites, but literary evidence confirms the view. The Κρίσις, the Decision, of Paris is always as much a Choice as a Judgment; a Choice somewhat like that invented for Heracles by the philosopher Prodicus, though at once more spontaneous and more subtle than that rather obvious effort at edification. The particular decision is associated in legend with the name of a special hero, of one particular 'young man moving to and fro alone, in an empty hut in the firelight[2].' It is an anguish of hesitancy ending in a choice which precipitates the greatest tragedy of Greek legend. But before Paris was there the Choice was there. The exact elements of the Choice vary in different versions. Athene is sometimes Wisdom and sometimes War. But in general Hera is Royalty or Grandeur; Athene is Prowess; Aphrodite of course is Love. And what exactly has the 'young man' to decide? Which of the three is fairest? Or whose gifts he desires the most? It matters not at all, for both are different ways of saying the same thing. Late writers, Alexandrian and Roman, degrade the story into a beauty-contest between three thoroughly personal goddesses, vulgar in itself and complicated by bribery still more vulgar. But early versions scarcely distinguish the goddesses from the gifts they bring. There is no difference between them except the difference of their gifts. They are Charites, Gift-bringers. They are their own gifts. Or, as the Greek put it, their gifts are their *σημεῖα*, their tokens. And Hermes had led them long since, in varying forms, before the eyes of each and all of mankind. They might be conceived as undifferentiated, as mere Givers-of-Blessing in general. But it needed only a little reflection to see that *Χάρις* often wars against *Χάρις*, and that if one be chosen, others must be rejected[3].

As gift-givers the same three goddesses again appear in the

[1] The figure of Paris which does not here concern us came in with the popularity of the Homeric cycle, and the connection between the conflict of *σημεῖα* and the Trojan war may probably have been due to the author of the *Kypria*.

[2] Eur. *Andr.* 281.

[3] Since the above was written I see that Eustathius (§ 1665. 59) expressly states that Aphrodite strove *with the Charites*: *ἔνθα ἐρίσαι περὶ κάλλους τήν τε Ἀφροδίτην καὶ τὰς Χάριτας αἷς ὀνόματα Πασιθέη, Καλὴ καὶ Εὐφροσύνη, τὸν δὲ δικάσαντα κρῖναι καλὴν τὴν Καλήν, ἣν καὶ γῆμαι τὸν Ἥφαιστον.* He goes on to say that Kalè married Arachnos in Crete and that Arachnos *μιγέντα αὐχεῖν τῇ Ἀφροδίτῃ μιγῆναι.*

myth of the daughters of Pandareos, but this time they are not rivals; and with them comes a fourth, Artemis, whose presence is significant. Homer tells the story by the mouth of Penelope[1]:

'Their father and their mother dear died by the gods' high doom,
The maidens were left orphans alone within their home;
Fair Aphrodite gave them curds and honey of the bee
And lovely wine, and Hera made them very fair to see,
And wise beyond all women-folk. And holy Artemis
Made them to wax in stature, and Athene for their bliss
Taught them all glorious handiworks of woman's artifice.'

The maiden goddesses tend the maidens, but to Homer *the* Maiden above all others is Artemis, sister of Apollo, daughter of Zeus[2]. He puts the story into the mouth of Penelope as part of a prayer to Artemis.

But, owing to the influence of Homer and the civilization he represented, the figure of Artemis waxes more and more dominant, and this especially by contrast with the Kore of the lower stratum, Aphrodite. In the *Hippolytus* of Euripides they are set face to face in their eternal enmity. The conflict is for the poet an issue of two moral ideals, but the human drama is played out against the shadowy background of an ancient racial theomachy, the passion of the South against the cold purity of the North.

Belonging as she does to this later Northern stratum, the figure of Artemis lies properly outside our province, but to one of the ancient maiden trinity, to Athene, she lent much of her cold, clean strength. An epigram[3] to her honour in the *Anthology* is worth noting, because it shows, clearly and beautifully, how the maidenhood of the worshipper mirrors itself in the worship of a maiden, whether of the South or of the North:

'Maid of the Mere, Timaretè here brings,
  Before she weds, her cymbals, her dear ball
To thee a Maid, her maiden offerings,
  Her snood, her maiden dolls, their clothes and all.
Hold, Leto's Child, above Timaretè
Thine hand, and keep her virginal like thee.'

[1] Hom. *Od.* xx. 67.

[2] I follow Prof. Ridgeway (*J.H.S.* 1898, p. xxxiv) in holding that Artemis with her father Zeus and her brother Apollo are immigrants from the North, divinities of the Achaean stock. Hence their dominance in Homer.

[3] *Anthol. Palat.* VI. 280; the play on *κόρα* in the lines

τὰς τε κόρας, Λιμνᾶτι κόρᾳ, κόρα, ὡς ἐπιεικὲς
ἄνθετο καὶ τὰ κορᾶν ἐνδύματ' Ἀρτέμιδι

cannot be rendered in English.

It would be a lengthy though in some respects a profitable task to take each maiden form that the great matriarchal goddess assumed and examine it in turn, to enquire into the rise and development of each local Kore, of Dictynna, of Aphaia, of Callisto, of Hecate, of Bendis and the like. Instead it will be necessary to confine ourselves to the three great dominant Korai of the 'Judgment,' Hera, Athene and Aphrodite.

ATHENE.

The doubt has probably long lurked in the reader's mind, whether two of the three, Hera and Aphrodite, have any claim to the title 'maiden.' Happily in the case of Athene no such difficulty arises. She is *the* Parthenos, *the* maiden; her temple is the maiden-chamber, the Parthenon; natural motherhood she steadfastly refuses, she is the foster-mother of heroes after the old matriarchal fashion; Ge, the real mother, bears Erichthonios, and Athene nurtures him to manhood; she bears the like relationship to Herakles, she is the maiden of Herakles (*Ἡρακλέους κόρη*[1]).

Moreover it has been frequently observed that the early form of her name *Athenaia* is purely adjectival[2], she is the Athenian one, the Athenian Maid, Pallas, our Lady of Athens. Plato[3] in the *Laws* sees clearly that Athenaia is but the local Kore, the incarnation of Athens, though, after the fashion of his day, he inverts cause and effect; he makes the worshipper in the image of the worshipped. Speaking of the armed Athene, he says, 'and methinks our Kore and Mistress who dwells among us, joying her in the sport of dancing, was not minded to play with empty hands, but adorned her with her panoply, and thus accomplished her dance, and it is fitting that in this our youths and our maidens should imitate her.' It was she who imitated her youths and maidens, she who was the very incarnation of their life and being, dancing in armour as they danced, fighting when they fought, born of her father's head when they were reborn as the children of Reason and Light.

[1] Dilthey, *Arch. Zeit.* 1873.
[2] Pauly-Wissowa s.v. Athena, p. 1941, 50.
[3] Plat. *Legg.* 796 *ἡ δὲ αὖ που παρ' ἡμῖν Κόρη καὶ δέσποινα...ἃ δὴ πάντως μιμεῖσθαι πρέπον ἂν εἴη κόρους τε ἅμα καὶ κόρας.*

Athene's other name, Pallas, tells the same tale. If Athene is the Kore of the local clan of the Athenians, Pallas is the Kore of the clan of the Pallantidae, the foes of Athenian Theseus; later their male eponym was Pallas[1]:

> 'Pallas had for lot
> The southern land, rough Pallas, he who rears
> A brood of giants.'

The very name Pallas means, it would seem, like Kore, the maiden. Suidas in defining the word says, 'a great maiden, and it is an epithet of Athene.' More expressly Strabo[2], in discussing the cults of Egyptian Thebes, says, 'To Zeus, whom they worship above all other divinities, a maiden of peculiar beauty and illustrious family is dedicated; *such maidens the Greeks call Pallades.*' This local Pallas had for her dominion the ancient court of the Palladium; her image as Pallas, not as Athene, was carried in procession by the epheboi[3]; but with the subjection of her clan her figure waned, effaced by that of Athenaia. Pallas became a mere adjectival *praenomen* to Athene, as Phoebus to Apollo. It may be conjectured that this ancient image of Pallas was resident on the Areopagos, home of the ancient Semnae, a place probably of sacred association to a local clan long before the dominance of the Acropolis; it is by her name of Pallas that the Semnae[4] hail the goddess:

> 'I welcome Pallas' fellowship.'

In such a matter a poet might well have been instinctively, though unconsciously, true to fact.

To tell the story of the making of Athene is to trace the history of the city of Athens, to trace perhaps, in so far as they can be severed, its political rather than its religious development. At first the maiden of the elder stratum, she has to contend for supremacy with a god of that stratum, Poseidon. Poseidon, the late Mr R. A. Neil[5] has shown, was the god of the ancient aristocracy of Athens, an aristocracy based, as they claimed descent from

[1] Soph. frg. ap. Strabo § 392. That Pallas was the eponymous hero of the Pallantidae was first pointed out by Duncker, *Hist. of Greece*, vol. I. p. 113.

[2] Strab. XVII. 46 § 816 *παρθένος ἱερᾶται ἃς καλοῦσιν οἱ Ἕλληνες παλλάδας*: see A. Fick, *Indogerm. Beiträge* 1896.

[3] *C.I.A.* II. 470. 10 *συνεξήγαγον δὲ (οἱ ἔφηβοι) Παλλάδα μετὰ τῶν γεννητῶν καὶ πάλιν εἰσήγαγον μετὰ πάσης εὐκοσμίας.*

[4] Aesch. *Eum.* 916.

[5] *The Knights of Aristophanes*, p. 83.

Poseidon, on patriarchal conditions. The rising democracy not unnaturally revived the ancient figure of the Kore, but in reviving her they strangely altered her being and reft from her much of her beauty and reality. They made her a sexless thing, neither man nor woman; she is laden with attributes like the Parthenos of Pheidias, charged with intended significance, but to the end she remains manufactured, unreal, and never convinces us. She is, in fact, the Tyche, the Fortune of the city, and the real object of the worship of the citizens was not the goddess but the city herself, 'immortal mistress of a band of lovers[1]':

> 'The grace of the town that hath on it for crown
> But a head-band to wear
> Of violets one-hued with her hair,
> For the vales and the green high places of earth hold nothing so fair
> And the depths of the sea know no such birth of the manifold births they bear,'

a city,

> 'Based on a crystalline sea
> Of thought and its eternity.'

Nowhere is this artificiality, this unreality of Athene as distinct from Athens so keenly felt as in the famous myth of her birth from the brain of Zeus. A poet may see its splendour:

> 'Her life as the lightning was flashed from the light of her Father's head,'

but it remains a desperate theological expedient to rid an earth-born Kore of her matriarchal conditions. The Homeric Hymn[2] writer surrounds the Birth with all the apparatus of impressiveness, yet it never impresses; the goddess is manifestly to him Reason, Light and Liberty; she is born at the rising of the Sun:

> 'Hyperion's bright son stayed
> His galloping steeds for a space.'

The event is of cosmic import:

> 'High Olympus reeled
> At the wrath in the sea-grey eyes and Earth on every side
> Rang with a terrible cry, and the Deep was disquieted
> With a tumult of purple waves and outpouring of the tide
> Suddenly.

Fear takes hold of all the Immortals, and 'the Councillor Zeus is glad,' but the mortal reader remains cold. It is all an unreal,

[1] See Mr Gilbert Murray, *Ancient Greek Literature*, p. 178.
[2] *Hom. Hymn.* XXVIII., translated by Mr D. S. MacColl.

theatrical show, and through it all we feel and resent the theological intent. We cannot love a goddess who on principle forgets the Earth from which she sprang; always from the lips of the Lost Leader we hear the shameful denial[1]:

> 'There is no mother bore me for her child,
> I praise the Man in all things (save for marriage),
> Whole-hearted am I, strongly for the Father.'

Politics and literature turned the local Kore of Athens into a non-human, unreal abstraction. It is pleasant to find that the art of the simple conservative vase-painter remembered humbler beginnings. The design in fig. 81 is from a Corinthian alabastron in the Museum at Breslau[2]. In the centre of the design, Herakles is engaged in slaying a Hydra with an unusually large number of heads. Iolaos comes up from the right to engage some of the heads, the charioteer of Iolaos, Lapythos, waits in the chariot.

FIG. 81.

Throughout the design all the figures are carefully and legibly inscribed in early Corinthian letters, dating about the beginning of the 6th century B.C. 'Athena,' the Maiden of Herakles, has also come up (to the left) in her chariot to help her hero. Just behind her, perched on the goad, is a woman-headed bird. Had there been no inscription we should at once have named it a 'decorative Siren,' but against the woman-headed bird is clearly written Ϝοῦς. At first sight the inscription does not seem to help much, but happily the lexicographers enable us to explain the word[3]. The *Etymologicon Magnum* tells us that by πώυγγες

[1] Aesch. *Eum.* 736.

[2] Rossbach, *Griechische Antiken des arch. Museums in Breslau, Festgruss 40 d. Philologen* (Görlitz, 1889), Taf. I.

[3] The meaning of the woman-headed bird and of her name was first seen by Dr Maximilian Mayer, 'Mythhistorica,' *Hermes* XXVII. p. 483.

are meant *αἴθυιαι*, and that another form of the word was *βοῦγγες*. Hesychius merely states that the *πῶυξ* is 'a kind of bird,' and refers us to Aristotle[1] 'On Animals.' Our text of Aristotle gives the form *φῶυξ*. It seems clear that the Ϝοῦς of the Corinthian vase is a variant form of a name given to the Diver-bird.

The inscriptions prove the vase to be Corinthian, and Corinth is not far remote from Megara. Pausanias[2], in discussing the genealogies of Athenian kings, tells us that Pandion fled to Megara. There he fell sick and died, and by the sea in the territory of Megara is his tomb, on a cliff which is called the cliff of Athene Aithuia, i.e. Athene the Diver-bird. Bird myths haunt the family of Pandion: Procne, Philomela, Itys and Tereus[3] all turn into birds, and Tereus, the hoopoe, had a regular cult at his grave. There, they say, the hoopoe first appeared, and the story looks like a reminiscence of a bird soul seen haunting a grave. Lycophron knows of a maiden goddess, a Diver-bird; he makes Cassandra in her prophetic madness foresee the outrage of Ajax and her own empty prayers[4]:

'In vain shall I invoke the Diver-Maid.'

Returning, with this evidence in our minds, to the woman-headed bird in fig. 81, the conclusion seems inevitable that we have in her an early local form of Athene. The vase-painter had advanced to an anthropomorphic conception of the goddess, so he draws her in full human form as Athene, but he is haunted by the remembrance of the Megarian Diver, Aithuia, so he adds her figure, half as the double of Athene (hence the parallelism of attitude), half as attendant, and calls her Ϝοῦς. Athene on the Acropolis had another attendant bird, the little owl that still at evening haunts the sacred hill and hoots among the ruins of the Parthenon. Whatever bird was locally abundant and remarkable would naturally attach itself to the goddess, and be at first her vehicle and later her attribute: at seaside Megara the diver, at Athens the owl. The vase-painter remembers Athens as well as Megara, and adds for completeness a little owl.

[1] Ar. *Hist. Anim.* IX. 18, p. 617 *a* 9.

[2] P. I. 5. 3 and I. 41. 6; see Dr Frazer ad loc.

[3] P. I. 41. 9.

[4] Lyc. *Al.* 359. In connection with Lycophron's account it is curious to find that in the earliest known representation of the rape of Cassandra in vase-paintings (*J.H.S.* 1884, Pl. XL.) behind the figure of Athene stands a large human-headed bird, but this may be a mere coincidence.

The design in fig. 82 is from a black-figured lekythos in a private collection in Sicily[1]. The scene represents Cassandra

FIG. 82.

flying from Ajax and taking refuge at the xoanon of Athene. To the left stands old King Priam, in helpless anguish. The notable point about the scene is that Athene, who, statue though she be, is apparently about to move to the rescue, has sent as her advance guard her sacred animal, a great snake. The snake is clearly regarded as the vehicle of the wrath of the goddess. Just such a snake did Chryse, another local Kore, send out against the intruder Philoctetes[2], and the snake of Chryse, Sophocles expressly tells us, was the secret guardian of the open-air shrine. This 'house-guarding snake,' we may conjecture, was the earliest form of every earth-born Kore. At Athens, in the chryselephantine statue of Pheidias, it crouched beneath the shield, and tradition said it was the earth-born hero Erichthonios, fostered by the goddess. But almost certainly this guardian snake was primarily the guardian genius and fate of the city, before that genius or fate emerged to the status of godhead. When the Persians besieged the citadel, Herodotus[3] says, the guardian snake left the honey cake that was its monthly sacrificial food untouched, and, 'when

[1] O. Benndorf, *Griechische und Sicilische Vasenbilder*, pl. 51. 1.
[2] Soph. *Phil.* 1327.
[3] Herod. VIII. 41.

the priestess told this, the Athenians the more readily and eagerly forsook their city, inasmuch as it seemed that the goddess had abandoned the citadel.'

The design in fig. 83 is from a late red-figured lekythos in the National Museum at Athens[1]. The scene represented is a

Fig. 83.

reminiscence of the Judgment of Paris, but one goddess only is present, Athene, and by her side, equal in height and majesty, a great snake. The artist seems dimly conscious that the snake is somehow the double of Athene[2]. To the left is the figure of a woman, probably Helen; she seems to be imploring the little xoanon of Athene to be gracious. Eros is apparently drawing the attention of Paris away from Athene to Helen.

Athene, by the time she appears in art, has completely shed her animal form, has reduced the shapes she once wore of snake and bird to attributes, but occasionally in black-figured vase paintings she still appears with wings. On the obverse of the black-figured cup[3] in fig. 84 the artist gives her wings: but for her helmet we might have called her an Erinys. In the *Eumenides* of Aeschylus, a play in which Athene is specially concerned to

[1] Collignon et Couve, *Cat.* 1942. *Jahrbuch d. Inst.* Anzeiger, 1896, p. 36.

[2] Since the above was written Mr Evans has discovered at Cnossos the figure of a goddess with a snake in either hand and a snake or snakes coiled about her head. She may prove to be the prototype of Athene, of the Erinys and of many another form of Earth-goddess. See *Annual British School*, IX. 1903, p. 74, Fig. 54.

[3] Coll. Faina. *Röm. Mitt.* 1897, XII. pl. 12. Another instance of a winged Athene occurs on the fine vase published by Mr A. de Ridder, *Cat. Bibl. Nat.* No. 269, p. 173, fig. 23. Athene flies over the sea carrying the dead body of a hero. Here she performs the office of Eos or of a Death-Siren or Harpy.

slough off all traces of primitive origin, she lays suspicious emphasis on the fact that she *can fly without wings*[1]:

> 'With foot unwearied haste I without wings,
> Whirred onward by my aegis' swelling sail.'

FIG. 84.

On the reverse of the vase she is wingless: the artist has no clear conviction. The vase is instructive as showing how long the art type of a divinity might remain in flux.

APHRODITE.

The next of the three 'Maidens' to be considered is Aphrodite. A doubt perhaps arises as to her claim to bear the name. Kore she is in her eternal radiant youth: Kore as virgin she is not. She is rather *Nymphe* the Bride, but she is the Bride of the old order; she is never wife, never tolerates permanent patriarchal wedlock. In the lovely Homeric hymn it is clear that her will is for love, not marriage. Admitted to the patriarchal Olympus, an attempt

[1] Aesch. *Eum.* 407.

foolish and futile is made to attach her to one husband, the craftsman Hephaistos, and, significantly enough, her other name as his bride is Charis[1]. She is the Charis of physical beauty incarnate.

In Homer it is evident that she is a new-comer to Olympus, barely tolerated, an alien, and always thankful to escape. Like the other alien, Ares, she is fain to be back in her own home. Her Homeric titles, Kypris and Kythereia, show that originally and locally she is goddess of the island South, never really at home in the cold austere North, where Artemis loved to dwell. She has about her too much of the physical joy of life ever to find an abiding home far from the sunshine.

Another note of her late coming into Greece proper is that she is in Homer a departmental goddess, having for her sphere one human passion. The earlier forms of divinities are of larger import, they tend to be gods of all work. When the fusion of tribes and the influence of literature conjointly bring together a number of local divinities, perforce, if they are to hold together, they divide functions and attributes, i.e. become departmental. Poseidon, who locally was Phytalmios, is narrowed down to the god of one element; Hermes, who at home had dominion over flocks and herds and all life and growth, becomes merely a herald.

Some such process of narrowing of functions has, we may suspect, gone on in the shaping of the figure of Aphrodite. It would be rash to assert that she was primarily an earth-goddess, but certain traits in her cult and character show clearly that she had analogies with the 'Lady of the Wild Things.' Fertile animals belong to her, especially the dove and the goat, the dove probably from very early days. In the Mycenaean shrine recently discovered by Mr Arthur Evans, one of the figures of goddesses, a quaint early figure with cylindrical body and upraised hands, bears on her head a dove. Such a figure, dating more than a thousand years B.C., may be the prototype of Aphrodite. About the cylindrical bodies of other similar figures snakes are coiled, as though to mark an earth-goddess. In those early days differentiation was not sharply marked, and as yet we dare not give to these early divinities Olympian names.

At Pompeii the excavations have recently brought to light the

[1] *Il.* XVIII. 382.

charming relief in fig. 85[1], a relief which from its style must date about the turn of the 5th and 4th centuries B.C. A goddess is

FIG. 85.

seated Demeter-like upon the ground, and holds her sceptre as Queen. Worshippers approach, man and wife and children. The offerings they bring, a sheep and a dove, mark the goddess as Aphrodite.

The myth of her birth from the sea—a myth which probably took its rise in part from a popular and dubious etymology—seems, at first sight, to sever Aphrodite wholly from the company of the earth-born Korai. And yet, even here, when we come to examine the art-forms of the myth, it is at once manifest that the Sea-birth is but the Anodos adopted and adapted.

The design in fig. 86 is from a red-figured hydria[2] now in the museum of the Municipio at Genoa. It dates about the middle of the 5th century B.C. and is, so far as I know, the only instance of the birth of Aphrodite in a vase-painting. In the centre of the picture a goddess, clad only in a chiton, rises up from below, but whether from sea or land the vase-painter is apparently not concerned to express. Had he wished to utter his meaning more precisely nothing would have been easier than to represent

[1] From a photograph. The slab is now in the Museum at Naples.
[2] E. Petersen, *Röm. Mittheil.* 1899, pl. VII. p. 154.

the sea by the curved lines that in his day were the conventional indication of waves. But he is silent and I think

FIG. 86.

significantly. The goddess on the vase-painting is received by a slender winged Eros; she uplifts her hands to take the taenia with which he greets her. Eros is here grown to young manhood and his presence at once makes us think of Aphrodite; but we are bound to remember that on the Ashmolean amphora already discussed (fig. 71) it is the Anodos of Pandora, not of Aphrodite, that is greeted by the Love-god with a taenia. Moreover, it must also be remembered that on the Berlin krater (fig. 68) a Love-god greets the rising of an Earth-goddess, be she Ge or Kore or Semele[1].

So far then all that can safely be said is that on the Genoa hydria we have the Anodos of *a* goddess greeted by Eros. But to the right of the picture, behind the rising goddess, stands another figure, a woman, and she holds out a piece of drapery with which

[1] Some further instances of the rising of an Earth-goddess greeted by Erotes will be discussed in Chapter XII., and see p. 569.

she is about to clothe the rising goddess. This is a new element in the Anodos type and it is this element that inclines me, with certain reservations and qualifications, to call the goddess Aphrodite, though I am by no means sure that the vase-painter conceives her as *rising from the sea.*

On two occasions, according to ancient tradition, Aphrodite is received and decked by her women attendants, be they Charites or Horae, on her Birth from the Sea and after her sacred Bath in Paphos. Of the Bath we hear in the lay of Demodocus[1]. He tells how after the joy and terror of her marriage with Ares she uprose

> 'And fast away fled she,
> Aphrodite, lover-of-laughter, to Cyprus over the sea,
> To the pleasant shores of Paphos and the incensed altar-stone,
> Where the Graces washed her body, and shed sweet balm thereon,
> Ambrosial balm that shineth on the Gods that wax not old,
> And wrapped her in lovely raiment, a wonder to behold.'

Of the bedecking at the Birth we learn in a Homeric Hymn[2]:

> 'For the West Wind breathed to Cyprus and lifted her tenderly
> And bore her down the billow and the stream of the sounding sea
> In a cup of delicate foam. And the Hours in wreaths of gold
> Uprose in joy as she came, and laid on her fold on fold
> Fragrant raiment immortal, and a crown on the deathless head.'

The two events, the ritual Bath and the Sea-birth, are not I think clearly distinguished, and both have somehow their counterpart in the making and decking of Pandora. The ritual bath[3] Aphrodite shared with the two other Korai, Athene and Hera. Callimachus devotes a Hymn to the 'Bath of Pallas.' Pallas in her austerity, even when she contends for the prize of beauty, rejects the mirror and gold ornaments and mingled unguents; but, because she is maiden goddess, year by year she must renew her virginity by the bath in the river Inachus. The renewal of virginity is no fancy. Pausanias[4] saw at Nauplia a spring called Canathus and the Argives told him that every year Hera bathed in it and became a virgin. He adds significantly, 'this

[1] Hom. *Od.* VIII. 270.

[2] *Hom. Hymn* VI. 2, trans. by Mr Gilbert Murray.

[3] At Sekyon, though we are not expressly told of a bath of Aphrodite, she had a maiden-priestess who was called Loutrophoros, see P. II. 10. 4. The Orphic Hymn to Aphrodite (LV. 19) joins together the notions of bath and birth: *Αἰγύπτου κατέχεις ἱερῆς γονιμώδεα λουτρά.*

[4] P. II. 38. 2.

story is of the mysteries and is their explanation of a rite which they celebrate to Hera.' Virginity was to these ancients in their wisdom a grace not lost but perennially renewed, hence the immortal maidenhood of Aphrodite.

The artist of the Genoa hydria *probably* knew of the birth of Aphrodite from the sea, he *certainly* knew of her reception by Eros; but that he remembered also the ritual bath is, I think, clear from the fact that the scene is laid in a sanctuary, indicated in the vase-painter's fashion by the altar and sacred palm-tree standing to the right just below the handle. Probably the sanctuary at Paphos is intended.

The Genoa hydria is of great importance because it helps to the understanding of another monument, earlier and far more beautiful.

The design in fig. 87 is from a sculptured slab[1], one of three that served to decorate the so-called 'Ludovisi Throne' now in the Boncompagni collection in the Museo delle Terme at Rome. Again we have manifestly an Anodos, again the like uncertainty as to who the goddess is and whence she uprises. The two women who support her, and to whom in her uprising she clings, stand on a sloping bank of shingle. Between the edges of the banks is no indication of the sea, simply a straight line. Is the goddess rising from earth or sea or sacred river or ritual bath? Archaeologists offer, explanations apparently the most diverse, and it is this doubt and diversity that instruct. One sees in the design the Birth of Aphrodite from the Sea, another a ceremonial Bath at the lesser mysteries of Agrae, another the Anodos of Kore. No one, so far as I am aware, sees that the artist is haunted by, is as

[1] Reproduced from a photograph. The relief is published and fully discussed by Dr Petersen, *Röm. Mittheilungen*, 1892, Taf. II. p. 32. The relief with two other slabs manifestly belonging to the same structure came to light on a Sunday during the summer of 1887, during the absence of the official inspector, in the piece of ground formerly belonging to the Villa Ludovisi and now bounded by the Vie Boncompagni, Abbruzzi e Piemonte. It is said to have been found in an upright position, but as no other monuments came to light, though the ground was examined to a depth of 50 metres, the reliefs were probably not *in situ*. Dr Petersen thinks they formed the three sides of a throne of Aphrodite. They may, however, have formed part of the decoration of the mouth of a well. That they were in some way connected with Aphrodite is practically certain from the design on the two other reliefs (not figured here). These represent respectively a nude woman playing on the double flutes, who, from the analogy of similar representations on vase-paintings, is certainly a hetaira, and a woman draped and veiled bringing incense who is probably a bride. The various interpretations and restorations of the monument are given by Dr Helbig, *Führer Rom* II. p. 128, and *Antike Denkmäler d. K. Arch. Inst.* vol. II. Pl. 6 and 7, p. 3.

it were halting between, reminiscences of each and all. Or rather the Anodos, the Bath, the Birth are as yet undifferentiated. By their articulation and separation we have immeasurably lost.

FIG. 87.

One other point remains. On the Ludovisi relief we have no Eros. The relief is archaic. The straight folds of the drapery, the delicate over-long feet, the strong chin, the over-emphasis of the lovely breasts, all remind us vividly of red-figured vases of the severe style; they belong to the last bloom of archaism just before the perfect utterance of Pheidias. Pheidias[1] on the pedestal of the image of Zeus at Olympia sculptured 'Eros receiving Aphrodite as she rises from the sea and Peitho crowning Aphrodite.' Pheidias was much, perhaps over, inspired by Homeric tradition, hence a certain sense of literary chill in his conceptions. He forgets the ritual Bath, and remembers the mythological Birth. The artist of the Genoa hydria is very near to his tradition, but the drapery held by Peitho, the altar and the palm-tree, recall rather the Bath than the Birth. But the sculptor of the relief

[1] P. v. 11. 8.

embodies a tradition more theological, less mythological, than either Pheidias or the vase-painter. He is inspired by the Anodos[1] and the Bath, which was but one of its ritual humanized forms, and a form that we may venture to call matriarchal. What he is concerned to show is the birth and re-birth of Aphrodite, Aphrodite untouched of Eros, eternally virgin, central figure of a Trinity of Maidens and, as Ourania, She of the Heavens.

Aphrodite as island queen comes to have a birth from the sea, but a poet remembers that, though she is of the sea and of the air, she is of earth also:

'We have seen thee, O Love, thou art fair, thou art goodly, O Love,
Thy wings make light in the air as the wings of a dove;
Thy feet are as winds that divide the stream of the sea,
Earth is thy covering to hide thee, the garment of thee.'

Aphrodite the earth-born Kore is also sea-born, as became an island Queen, but more than any other goddess she becomes Ourania, the Heavenly One, and the vase-painter sets her sailing through heaven on her great swan[2]. She is the only goddess who in passing to the upper air yet kept life and reality. Artemis becomes unreal from sheer inhumanity; Athene, as we have seen, becomes a cold abstraction; Demeter, in Olympus, is but a lovely metaphor. As man advanced in knowledge and in control over nature, the mystery and the godhead of things natural faded into science. Only the mystery of life, and love that begets life, remained, intimately realized and utterly unexplained; hence Aphrodite keeps her godhead to the end. For a while, owing to special social conditions, and, as will be seen, owing to the impulse of Orphism, her figure is effaced by that of her son Eros, but effaced only to re-emerge with a new dignity as Mother rather than Maid. In the image of Venus Genetrix[3] we have the old radiance of Aphrodite, but sobered somehow, grave with the hauntings of earlier godheads, with shadows about her cast by

[1] Since the above was written I see that M. Joubin (*La Sculpture Grecque entre les guerres médiques et l'époque de Periclès*, p. 204) has anticipated me in using the Genoa vase as evidence to show that the uprising woman in the Ludovisi relief is Aphrodite. But unfortunately M. Joubin fails to see that Aphrodite is also Kore; he says, 'D'autres archéologues avaient identifié le personnage figuré à mi-corps avec Korè ou Ge; mais la découverte du vase de Gènes coupe court toutes ces interprétations.' This is to my mind to miss the real religious significance of the figure; but M. Joubin is, of course, mainly concerned with artistic criticism.

[2] Brit. Mus. *Cat.* D 2. The best reproduction of this beautiful vase is plate XV. of *White Athenian Vases in Brit. Mus.*

[3] Lucret. I. 1.

Ourania, by Harmonia, by Kourotrophos, by Eirene, by each and every various form of the ancient Mother of Earth and Heaven:

'Of Rome the Mother, of men and gods the pleasure,
Fostering Venus, under heaven's gliding signs
Thou the ship-bearing sea, fruit-bearing land
Still hauntest, since by thee each living thing
Takes life and birth and sees the light of the sun.

Thee, goddess, the winds fly from, thee the clouds
And thine approach; for thee the daedal earth
Sends up sweet flowers, the ocean levels smile,
And heaven shines with floods of light appeased.

Thou, since alone thou rulest all the world
Nor without thee can any living thing
Win to the shores of light and joy and love,
Goddess, bid thou throughout the seas and land
The works of furious war quieted cease.'

HERA.

The figure of Hera remains. At first sight she seems all wife, not maiden; she is the great typical bride, Hera Teleia, queen in Olympus by virtue of her marriage with Zeus; their Sacred Marriage is the prototype of all human wedlock. This is true for Homeric theology, but a moment's reflection on the facts of local cultus and myth shows that this marriage was not from the beginning. The Hera who in the ancient Argonautic legend is queen in Thessaly and patron of the hero Jason is of the old matriarchal type; it is she, Pelasgian Hera, not Zeus, who is really dominant; in fact Zeus is practically non-existent. In Olympia, where Zeus in historical days ruled if anywhere supreme, the ancient Heraion where Hera was worshipped alone long predates the temple of Zeus. At Argos the early votive terra-cottas[1] are of a woman goddess, and the very name of the sanctuary, the Heraion, marks her supremacy. At Samos, at the curious festival of the *Tonea*[2], it is the image of a woman goddess that is carried

[1] As long ago as 1857, H. D. Müller in his remarkable book *Mythologie der Griechischen Stämme*, pp. 249—255, saw that Zeus and Hera belonged to stocks racially distinct, and that in the compulsory marriage of Hera to Zeus is reflected the subjugation of a primitive race to Achaean invaders. In discussing the American excavations at Argos I followed his leading, see 'Primitive Hera-Worship,' *Cl. Review*, Dec. 1892, p. 474, and 1893, p. 44. The relation of Hera to Zeus has since been examined by Mr A. B. Cook with far wider learning than I could command, see *Cl. Review*, 1906, p. 365, and p. 416. For the connection of the name Ἥρα with ἥρως see the important evidence from inscriptions adduced by Dr Sam Wide in his 'Chthonische and Himmlische Götter,' *Archiv f. Religionswissenschaft*, 1907, p. 258.

[2] Athen. p. 672.

out of the town and bound among the bushes, and Strabo[1] tells us that in ancient days Samos was called Parthenia, the island of the Maiden. At Stymphalus, in remote Arcadia, Pausanias[2] says that Hera had three sanctuaries and three surnames: while yet a girl she was called Child, married to Zeus she was called Complete or Full-Grown (τελεία), separated from Zeus and returned to Stymphalus she was called Chera (Widow). Long before her connection with Zeus, the matriarchal goddess may well have reflected the three stages of a woman's life; Teleia, full-grown, does not necessarily imply patriarchal marriage.

Homer himself was dimly haunted by the memory of days when Hera was no wife, but Mistress in her own right. Otherwise, unless the poet was the lowest of low comedians, what means her ceaseless turbulence and the unending unseemly strife between the Father of Gods and Men and the woman he cannot even beat into submission? What her urgent insistent tyranny over Herakles whom Zeus loves yet cannot protect? Is the tyrannous mistress really made by the Greek housewife even of Homeric days in her own image? The answer is clear: Hera has been forcibly married, but she is never really wife, and a wife's submission she leaves to the shadowy double of Zeus, who echoed his nature and (significant fact) took his name, she who was the real Achaean patriarchal double—Dione[3].

Once fairly married, Zeus and Hera became Sharers of one Altar (ὁμοβώμιοι), and against the conjunction the older women divinities are but too often powerless. In the designs[4] in figs. 88 and 89 we have a curious instance of the ruthless fashion in which the Olympian pair extrude the objects of an ancient local cult. In fig. 88 we have a votive relief to the Nymphs of the familiar type: three maiden figures linked together. That the figures are Nymphs is certain, for above is the inscription, 'To the Mistress Nymphs (Κυρίαις Νύμφαις).' The relief, one of a large

[1] Strab. § 637.

[2] P. VIII. 22. 2. The sources for the cult of Hera are well collected by Mr Farnell in his *Cults of the Greek States*, p. 211, but with Mr Farnell's main thesis 'that her association with Zeus is a primitive factor in the Greek worship of Hera' I am still as he then notes (p. 199) completely at issue.

[3] Again acutely observed by H. D. Müller, *Mythologie d. Gr. Stämme*, pp. 254, 255, where the identity of Dione and Juno is noted.

[4] These reliefs are now in the Museum at Sofia: there were discovered in all ninety-two of the same type. *Bull. de Corr. Hell.* XXI. 1897, p. 130, fig. 12; p. 138, fig. 17.

series found together at Orochák and now in the local Museum

Fig. 88.

at Sofia, is of late Roman style. The design in fig. 89 shows a theological shift. The two dominant Olympians, of large

Fig. 89.

stature to mark their supremacy, occupy the forefront; they hold each an expectant *phiale* for libations; to them only is sacrifice to be made. It is they who hold the sceptres. Humbly in the background, minished and all but effaced, are the three ancient Maidens. The local peasant is conservative[1], and we may hope they too had their meed of offering.

The intrusion of Zeus[2] and Hera on the local cultus of the Nymphs brings to mind a story preserved by Diogenes Laertius[3] in his Life of Epimenides. Theopompus in his 'Wonderful Things' told how when Epimenides was preparing the sanctuary of the Nymphs a voice was heard from heaven saying, 'Epimenides, not of the Nymphs, but of Zeus.' Perhaps Epimenides went further than the orthodox Olympian religion could tolerate in the matter of the revival of ancient cults. To him, as has been already seen (p. 241), was credited the founding of the sanctuary of the

FIG. 90.

Semnae; he introduced ceremonies of purification brought from Crete, and wholly alien to Olympian ritual. It was time for Zeus to reassert himself.

[1] The survival of the type of the 'Three Sisters' in mediaeval days has been well traced by Miss Eckenstein, *Woman under Monasticism*, p. 40 ff.

[2] After the above was written Mr A. B. Cook with great kindness and generosity allowed me to read in proof his article on 'Zeus, Jupiter and the Oak,' since published in the *Classical Review*, 1903 and 1904. Mr Cook believes that the worship of Zeus was indigenous in Greece and that Zeus, Poseidon and Hades are three forms of one primaeval god. His contention is supported by an immense mass of evidence. I am at present unconvinced, but space forbids my entering on the controversy here.

[3] Diog. Laert. *Vit. Epim.* XI.

The conflict of theological conceptions is very clearly seen in the design in fig. 90, from a votive relief[1] found at Eleusis and now in the National Museum at Athens. The general type of the design, which belongs to the class known in English as 'Funeral Banquets,' will be discussed more in detail later, when we come to hero-worship. For the present it is enough to note that on the left side of the relief we have the two Goddesses of Eleusis, the old matriarchal couple, seated side by side as equals, on the right a patriarchal couple, man and wife, the man reclining at the banquet and holding a great *rhyton*, the wife submissively seated by his side. In naming them it is safest at present not to go beyond what is written. The artist has inscribed over their heads the non-committal words, 'To the God,' and 'To the Goddess.'

It was not only the Olympian Father Zeus who victoriously took over to himself the cult of the Earth-Mother and the Earth-Maidens. Even more marked is the triumph of the Olympian Son, Apollo[2]. The design in fig. 91 is from a rather late red-

Fig. 91.

figured amphora in the Naples Museum[3]. A wayfarer, possibly Orestes, has come to Delphi to consult the god; he finds him seated on the very omphalos itself, holding the laurel and the lyre

[1] 'Εφ. 'Αρχ. 1866, pl. 3. The 'patriarchal couple' are, I incline to think, rightly explained by Dr Svoronos (*Journal d'Archéol. et Num.* 1901, p. 503) as Asklepios and Hygieia, but as for my purpose it is not necessary to name them, and as the evidence is too detailed to be resumed here, I prefer not to go beyond the inscription.

[2] I follow Prof. Ridgeway in holding that Apollo belongs to the immigrant Achaean stock, see p. 31, note 1.

[3] Heydemann, *Cat.* 108. Raoul Rochette, *Mon. Inéd.* pl. 37.

in his hands. So Hermes found him in the prologue to the *Ion* of Euripides[1]:

> 'To Delphi, where
> Phoebus, on earth's mid navel o'er the world
> Enthronèd, weaveth in eternal song
> The sooth of all that is or is to be.'

The vase-painter knows quite well that it is really a priestess who utters the oracles. Only a priestess can mount the sacred tripod, and he paints her so seated, the laurel wreath on her head and the sacred taenia in her hand, but he knows also that Apollo is by this time Lord of All.

In the *Eumenides* of Aeschylus, where the contest is between the old angry ghosts, the Erinyes envisaged as merely the spirits of the blood feud, and the mild and merciful god, our sympathies

FIG. 92.

are at least in part with the new-comer. But even here, so stately and yet so pitiful are the ancient goddesses that our hearts are sore for the outrage on their order. And on the vase-painting, when we remember that the omphalos is the very seat and symbol of the Earth-Mother[2], that hers was the oracle and hers the

[1] Eur. *Ion* 5.

[2] The evidence for this I have collected elsewhere, see 'Delphika,' B. The Omphalos, *J.H.S.* 1899, XIX. 225.

holy oracular snake that Apollo slew, the intrusion is hard to bear.

The triumph of the Olympian order is still more clearly presented in the design in fig. 92, from a votive relief[1] in the local Museum at Sparta. The centre of the design is occupied by the omphalos on a low basis. It looks very humble and obscure. At either side of it are perched new guardians, the great eagles of Olympian Zeus. The story[2] said that starting from either end of the world they met at Pytho, at the omphalos. The birds were variously said to be swans or eagles. Neither swans nor eagles have anything to do with the Earth-goddess; they are Ouranian eagles for Zeus or swans for Apollo, and, standing over the omphalos, they mark the dominion of the Father and the Son. But the artist has uttered his meaning still more emphatically. Towering over the omphalos is the great figure of Apollo with his lyre. He holds out a cup, and libation to him is poured by his sister Artemis. The Olympian victory is complete.

So far we have dealt with the *Making of a goddess*; we have seen one woman-form take various shapes as Mother and Maiden, as duality and trinity; we have seen these shapes crystallize into Olympian divinities as Athene, as Aphrodite, as Hera, and as it were resume themselves again into the great monotheistic figure of Venus Genetrix. We have noted evidence, very scattered and fragmentary, of earlier animal forms of the goddess as bird and snake. But it has been obvious enough that the weak point in the argument is just this transitional phase. The goddesses, when they first come into our ken, *are* goddesses, fully human and lovely in form, figures whose lineaments have been fixed and beautified by art, and of mythological rather than of ritual content. In a word links are wanting in the transition from ghost or snake or bogey to goddess. Two reasons may be suggested. The full development of the women divinities seems to have been earlier accomplished, the sublimation earlier complete, and hence the early phases of that development are more effaced; and next these goddess figures became more completely material for poetic treatment. In the *Making of a god* we catch in some figures the process at an earlier stage, and many missing links in the passage from ghost and snake to Olympian will thereby become manifest.

[1] *A. Mitt.* 1887, Taf. XII.

[2] Plut. *de defect. orac.* 1.

CHAPTER VII.

THE MAKING OF A GOD.

'ἰὼ θεοὶ νεώτεροι, παλαιοὺς νόμους
καθιππάσασθε.'

FREQUENTLY, in his wanderings through Greece, Pausanias came upon the sanctuaries of local heroines, and these sanctuaries are almost uniformly tombs at which went on the cultus of the dead. At Olympia[1] inside the Altis he noted the *Hippodameion* or sanctuary of Hippodameia, a large enclosure surrounded by a wall. Into this enclosure once a year women were permitted to enter to sacrifice to Hippodameia and do other rites in her honour. The tomb of Auge[2] was still to be seen at Pergamos, a mound of earth enclosed by a stone basement and on the top the figure of a naked woman. At Leuctra[3] in Laconia there was an actual *temple* (*ναός*) of Cassandra with an image; the people of the place called her Alexandra, 'Helper of Men.' At Sparta[4] Helen had a sanctuary, and in Rhodes she was worshipped as She of the Tree, 'Dendritis,' and to her as Dendritis, if we may trust Theocritus[5], maidens brought offerings. At her wedding they sing:

'O fair, O gracious maiden, the while we chant our lay,
A wedded wife art thou. But we, at dawning of the day,
Forth to the grassy mead will go, to our old racing place,
And gather wreaths of odorous flowers, and think upon thy face,
Again, again, Helen, on thee, as young lambs in the dew
Think of the milk that fed them and run back to mother ewe.
For thee the first of Maidens shall the lotus creeping low
Be culled to hang in garlands where the shadowy plane doth grow;
To thee where grows the shadowy plane the first oil shall be poured,
Drop by drop from a silver cruse, to hold thy name adored:
And letters on the bark be wrought, for him who goes to see,
A message graven Dorian-wise: "Kneel; I am Helen's tree."'

[1] P. VI. 20. 7.
[2] P. VIII. 4. 9.
[3] P. III. 26. 5.
[4] P. III. 15. 3.
[5] Theocr. *Id.* XVIII. 38.

Helen as local heroine had, it would seem, not only a sanctuary and a sacred tree but a very ancient image. The design in figs. 93 and 94 is from a lekythos[1] in the Louvre, of the kind usually known as 'proto-Corinthian.' Its style dates it as not later than the 7th century B.C., and it is our earliest extant monument of 'the rape of Helen.' The subject seems to have had a certain popularity in archaic art, as it occurred on the throne of Apollo at Amyclae[2]. In the centre of the design stands a woman-figure of more than natural size. Two men advance against her from the right; the foremost seizes her by the wrist. In his left hand he holds a sceptre. He is Theseus, and behind him comes Peirithoös, brandishing a great sword. To the left of Helen are her two brothers, the horsemen Kastor and Polydeukes. It is important to note that Helen is here more image than living woman. Dr Blinkenberg,

FIG. 93.

FIG. 94.

who rightly interprets the scene as the rape of Helen, says 'ses mains levées expriment la surprise et l'effroi,' but since the discovery of the early image of the Mycenaean goddess with uplifted hands[3] it will at once be seen that the gesture is hieratic rather than human. This early 7th century document suggests that 'the rape of Helen' was originally perhaps the rape of a xoanon from a sanctuary, rather than of a wife from her husband.

[1] *Inv. C.A.* 617. Published by M. L. Couve, *Revue Archéologique*, 1898, p. 213, figs. 1 and 2, and discussed by Dr Blinkenberg, 1898, p. 398.

[2] P. III. 18. 15.

[3] Dr S. Wide, 'Mykenische Götterbilder und Idole,' *A. Mitt.* 1901, p. 247, Pl. XII.

Be that as it may, the great dominant hieratic figure on the vase is more divine than human.

For Homer, poet of the immigrant Achaeans, Helen of the old order of daughters of the land is a mortal heroine, beautiful and sinful, yet in a sense divine. To the modern poet she is altogether goddess, for she is Beauty herself:

> 'O Light and Shadow of all things that be,
> O Beauty, wild with wreckage like the sea,
> Say, who shall win thee, thou without a name?
> O Helen, Helen, who shall die for thee?'

Hebe, another local heroine, has at Phlius[1] a sacred grove and a sanctuary, 'most holy from ancient days.' The goddess of the sanctuary was called by the earliest authorities of the place Ganymeda, but later Hebe. Her sanctuary was an asylum, and this was held to be her greatest honour that 'slaves who took refuge there were safe and prisoners released hung their fetters on the trees in her grove.' That a sanctuary should be an asylum is a frequent note of antiquity. When the immigrant conqueror reduces the whole land to subjection, he, probably from superstitious awe, leaves to the conquered their local sanctuary, the one place safe from his tyranny. Hebe-Ganymeda, female correlative of Ganymedes, is promoted to Olympus, but significantly she is admitted only as cupbearer and wife of Herakles. Olympus here as always mirrors human relations. Hera by marriage with Zeus is admitted to full patriarchal citizenship, her shadowy double Hebe is but her Maid of Honour.

As a rule then the local heroine remains merely the object of a local cult. Where she passed upward to the rank of a real divinity, the steps of transition are almost wholly lost. We feel inwardly sure that Hera and Aphrodite were once of mere local import, like Auge or Iphigeneia, but we lack definite evidence. In the case of Athene the local origin, it has been shown (p. 300), is fairly clear.

The reason why the local heroine failed to emerge to complete godhead is sometimes startlingly clear. Her development was checked midway by the intrusion of a full-blown goddess of the Olympian stock. Near to Cruni in Arcadia Pausanias[2] saw the

[1] P. II. 13. 3. For Hebe-Ganymeda-Dia and the shift of husbands between her and Hera see the valuable articles by Mr A. B. Cook, 'Who was the wife of Zeus?' *Class. Rev.* 1906, pp. 365 and 416.

[2] P. VIII. 35. 8.

grave of Callisto. It was a high mound on which grew trees, some of them fruit-bearing, some barren. 'On the top of the mound,' Pausanias adds, 'is a sanctuary of Artemis with the title Calliste.' Nothing could be clearer. Over the tomb of the old Bear-Maiden, Callisto, daughter of Lycaon, Artemis the Northerner, the Olympian, has superposed her cult, and to facilitate the shift she calls herself *Calliste,* the Fairest. Possibly here, as at Athens under the title of Brauronia, she kept up the ancient bear-service[1].

The passage from ghost to goddess is for the most part lost in the mists of time, but of the analogous process from ghost to god the steps are still in historical times clearly traceable. The reason is clear. The intrusion of the patriarchal system, the practice of tracing descent from the father instead of the mother, tended to check, if it was powerless wholly to stop, the worship of eponymous heroines. Conservatism compelled the worship of old established heroines, but no fresh canonizations took place. The ideal woman of Pericles was assuredly not the stuff of which goddesses were made. If we would note the actual process of the manufacture of divinity, it is to *hero*-worship we must turn[2].

THE HERO AS SNAKE.

The design in fig. 95 is from an archaic relief[3] of the sixth century B.C., now in the local Museum at Sparta. It forms one of a series of reliefs found near Sparta, all of which are cast approximately in the same type. A male and a female figure are seated side by side on a great throne-like chair. The female figure holds her veil, the male figure a large cantharus or two-handled cup, as if expecting libation. Worshippers of diminutive

[1] For the bear-service of Artemis and the bear dedicated to her, see *Myth. and Mon. Anc. Athens*, p. 403.

[2] The materials for the study of hero-worship are well collected in Roscher's *Lexicon*, s.v. Heroes, and for English readers there is an excellent survey in Mr W. H. D. Rouse's *Greek Votive Offerings*, c. I. In the pages that follow I confine myself for the most part to such aspects of hero-worship as affect my main argument, and to certain evidence from art which seems to me to have been neglected, or misunderstood. I must also note that, advisedly, I only deal with the 'Making of a God' in so far as the god developes out of the hero. The most important and far more difficult question of the relation between totemism and god-making, a problem for the solution of which Greek tradition provides but scanty material, I leave for the present untouched. It can only be decided by much wider anthropological investigation than is within my scope.

[3] *A. Mitt.* 1877, pl. XXII.

size approach with offerings—a cock and some object that may be a cake, an egg or a fruit. The reliefs are, for the most part, uninscribed, but on some of rather later date names are written

FIG. 95.

near the figure, and they are the names of mortals, e.g. 'Timocles[1].' It is clear that we have in these monuments representations of the dead, but the dead conceived of as half divine, as heroized—hence their large size compared with that of their worshipping descendants. They are κρείττονες, 'Better and Stronger Ones.'

The artist of the relief in fig. 95 is determined to make his meaning clear. Behind the chair, equal in height to the seated figures, is a great curled snake, but a snake strangely fashioned. From the edge of his lower lip hangs down a long beard; a

[1] For the 'Timocles' relief and for the whole class in general, see *Myth. and Mon. Anc. Athens*, p. 590, where I have discussed the influence of the typography of these hero-reliefs on Attic gravestones.

decoration denied by nature. The intention is clear; he is a *human* snake, the vehicle, the incarnation of the dead man's ghost. Snakes lurk about tombs, they are uncanny-looking beasts, and the Greeks are not the only people who have seen in a snake the vehicle of a ghost. M. Henri Jumod[1], in discussing the beliefs of the Barongas, notes that among this people the snake is regarded as the *chikonembo* or ghost of a dead man, usually of an ancestor. The snake, so regarded, is feared but not worshipped. A free-thinker among the Barongas, if bored by the too frequent re-appearance of the snake ancestor, will kill it, saying, 'Come now, we have had enough of you.'

Zeus Meilichios, it has been seen (p. 18), was worshipped as a snake. If we examine the great snake on his relief in fig. 1 (p. 18) it is seen to be also bearded. The beard in this case is not at the end of the lip, but a good deal further back.

The addition of the beard was no doubt mainly due to frank anthropomorphism; the snake is in a transition stage between animal and human, and human for the artist means divine. He gives the snake a beard to mark his anthropomorphic divinity, just as he gave to the bull river-god on coins a human head with horns. The further question arises, 'Was there anything in nature that might have acted as a possible suggestion of a beard?' An interesting answer to this question has been suggested to me by an eminent authority on snakes, Dr Hans Gadow, and to him I am indebted for the following scientific particulars.

The snake represented in fig. 1 (p. 18) Dr Gadow believes to be the species known as *Coelopeltis lacertina*. It occurs from Spain to Syria and specimens of 6 ft. long are not uncommon. The creature's head, according to Dr Gadow, is reproduced with admirable fidelity; the name *lacertina* is due to the lizard-like, instead of snake-like, depressed head. Moreover this species is really poisonous, but only to its proper prey, e.g. mice, rats, lizards, etc., while it is practically harmless to man, on account of the position of the poison fangs, which are far back in the mouth instead of near the front. This is a somewhat exceptional arrangement and probably well known to the ancients. In fact the *Coelopeltis lacertina* is a snake with poison that does not ordinarily strike. On occasion it could bite a man's hand, i.e. if it opened

[1] H. Jumod, *Les Barongas*, p. 396, and see 'Delphika,' *J.H.S.* XIX. 1899, p. 216.

its mouth *very* wide, as wide as a striking cobra. This position of the dropped jaw, according to Dr Gadow, is very noticeable and must have been observed by the ancients. The angle of the dropped jaw is just that of the beard on the snake in fig. 1 (p. 18). It seems possible and even highly probable that the dropped jaw, seen at a distance, might have suggested a beard, or that an artist representing an actual dropped jaw may have been copied by another who misinterpreted the jaw into a beard. In any case the scheme of the dropped jaw would be ready to hand and would help to soften the anomaly of the bearded snake[1].

In snake form the hero dwelt in his tomb, and to indicate this fact not uncommonly on vase-paintings we have a snake depicted on the very grave mound itself. The design in fig. 96, from a black-

FIG. 96.

figured lekythos[2] in the Museum at Naples, is a good instance. The funeral mound which occupies the centre of the design is, on the original vase, white, and on it is painted a black snake; the mound itself is surmounted by a black stele: whether the vase-painter regards his snake as painted actually *outside* the tomb or as representing the snake-hero actually resident *within*, is not

[1] Mr F. M. Cornford kindly points out to me that the *bearded* snake is not unknown to Greek literature. He is one of the many θαύματα that meet us in the life of Apollonius of Tyana, see Philostr. *Vit. Apoll.* III. 7 and 8. These snakes belong to the wonder land of India.

[2] Published and discussed, 'Delphika,' *J.H.S.* XIX. 1899, p. 229, figs. 9 and 10.

easy to determine. The figure of a man on the left of the tomb with uplifted sword points probably to the taking of an oath, it may be of vengeance.

In the curious design in fig. 97, from a kotylos also in the Naples Museum[1], we have again a funeral mound, again decorated

Fig. 97.

with a huge snake, this time represented with dropped jaw and beard. The tomb seems to have become a sort of mantic shrine. Two men are seated watching attentively the portent of the eagle and the snake. On the reverse of the vase, to the right, the tomb-mound is decorated with a stag, and the portent is an eagle devouring a hare.

Herodotus[2] notes that among the Libyan tribe of the Nasamones tombs were used for two purposes, for the taking of oaths and for dream oracles. 'In their oaths and in the art of divination they observe the following practice: they take oaths by those among them who are accounted to be most virtuous and excellent, by touching their tombs, and when they divine they regularly resort to the monuments of their ancestors, and having made supplication they go to sleep, and whatever vision they behold, of that they make use.' Herodotus like many travellers was more familiar, it would seem, with the customs of foreigners than with those of his own people. He notes the two customs as though they were alien curiosities, but the practice of swearing on a

[1] *Cat.* 2458. *J.H.S.* 1899, p. 227, figs. 7 and 8. I have here discussed and rejected a possible mythological interpretation.
[2] Herod. IV. 172.

tomb must have been familiar to the Greeks. The slave in the *Choephori* says to Electra[1]:

> 'Reverencing thy father's tomb like to an altar,
> Mine inmost thoughts I speak, doing thy hest.'

By the hero Sosipolis at Olympia[2] oaths were taken 'on the greatest occasions'—by Sosipolis who in true hero-fashion was wont to appear in snake-form. That these oaths were taken on his actual tomb we are not told, but the sanctuary of a snake-hero can scarcely in its origin have been other than his tomb. Almost every hero in Greece had his dream oracle. Later, as the hero was conceived of as in human rather than animal shape, the connection between hero and snake is loosened, and we get the halting, confused theology of Aeneas[3]:

> 'Doubtful if he should deem the gliding snake
> The genius of the place, or if it were
> His father's ministrant.'

In fig. 98 we have an altar to a hero found in Lesbos[4], not the old primitive grave mound which was the true original form, but a late decorative structure such as might have served an Olympian. It is inscribed in letters of Roman date, 'The people to Aristandros the hero, son of Cleotimos,' and that the service is to a hero is further emphasized by the snakes sculptured on the top round the hollow cup which served for libations. There are two snakes; it is no longer realized that the hero himself is a snake, but the snake reminiscence clings.

Fig. 98.

If the question be raised, 'why did the Greeks image the dead hero as a snake?' no very certain or satisfactory answer can be offered. Aelian[5] in his treatise on 'The Nature of Animals' says that the backbone of a dead man when the marrow has decayed turns into a snake. The chance, sudden apparition of a snake near a dead body may

[1] Aesch. *Choeph.* 105. [2] P. VI. 20. 3. [3] Verg. *Aen.* V. 95.
[4] A. Conze, *Reise in der Insel Lesbos*, Pl. IV. fig. 5, p. 11.
[5] Ael. *Hist. An.* I. 51.

have started the notion. Plutarch[1] tells how, when the body of Cleomenes was impaled, the people, seeing a great snake wind itself about his head, knew that he was 'more than mortal' (κρείττονος). Of course, by the time of Cleomenes, the snake was well established as the vehicle of a hero, but some such coincidence may very early have given rise to this association of ideas. Plutarch adds that 'the men of old time associated the snake most of all beasts with heroes.' They did this because, he says, philosophers had observed that 'when part of the moisture of the marrow is evaporated and it becomes of a thicker consistency it produces serpents.'

The snake was not the only vehicle. As has already been noted (p. 304), the spirit of the dead could take shape as a human-headed bird or even perhaps, if a bird happened to perch on a tomb, as a mere natural hoopoe or swallow. Between the bird-souls and the snake-souls there is this difference. So far as we know, the human-headed bird was purely a creature of mythology, whereas the bearded human snake was the object of a cult. Also the bird-soul, though sometimes male, tends, on the whole, to be a woman; the snake, even when not bearded, is usually the vehicle of a male ghost; as such he is the incarnation rather of the hero than the heroine. So close is the connection that it gave rise to the popular expression 'Speckled hero,' which arose, Photius[2] explains, because snakes which are speckled are called heroes. Of these snake-heroes and their cultus Homer knows absolutely nothing, but the belief in them is essentially primitive and recrudesces with other popular superstitions.

[1] Plut. *Vit. Cleom.* 39.

[2] Phot. s.v. ἥρως ποικίλος. After Christian days the notion started by the Olympian religion that the snake was bad was strengthened by association with the 'old serpent' of Semitic mythology. Mr R. C. Bosanquet kindly drew my attention to a curious survival of the belief that a bad soul takes the form of a snake in the account of the life and miracles of the fifth century saint, St Marcellus (*Boll. Acta Sanctorum* 1—3, vol. LXIII. of the whole series, pp. 259 and 267). It was related that a certain matron of noble family, but bad character, died and was buried with great pomp. 'Ergo ad consumendum ejus cadaver coepit serpens immanissimus frequentare, et, ut dicam clarius, mulieri, cujus membra bestia devorabat, ipse draco factus est sepultura.' St Marcellus subdued the snake by striking it thrice with his staff and putting his prayer-book on its head. To the present day among the Greeks an unbaptized child, who is not yet quite human (Χριστιανός), is sometimes spoken of as a snake-monster (δράκος) and is apt to disappear in snake form. For the δράκος see Abbott, *Macedonian Folklore*, p. 261.

THE CULTUS-TITLES.

The great snake, later worshipped as Zeus Meilichios, was, we have already seen (p. 21), not Zeus himself, but an underworld being addressed by the title Meilichios, gracious, kindly, easy to be intreated. It will now be evident that his snake form marks him as the vehicle or incarnation of a ghost, a local hero. He was only one of a large class of local divinities who were invoked not by proper names but by adjectival epithets, descriptive of their nature, epithets which gradually crystallized into cultus-titles. That these titles were really adjectival is shown sometimes by the actual word, e.g. *Meilichios*, which retains its adjectival sense, sometimes by the fact that it is taken on as a distinguishing epithet by an Olympian, e.g. Zeus-Amphiaraos. These cultus-titles mark an important stage in the making of a god and must be examined somewhat more in detail.

Herodotus[1] in discussing the origins of Greek theology makes the following significant statement: 'The Pelasgians formerly made all sorts of sacrifice to the gods and invoked them in prayer, as I know from what I heard in Dodona, but they gave to none of them either name or eponym, for such they had not yet heard: they addressed them as gods because they had set all things in order and ruled over all things. Then after a long lapse of time they learnt the names of the other gods which had come from Egypt and much later that of Dionysos. As time went on they inquired of the oracle at Dodona about these names, for the oracle there is held to be the most ancient of all the oracles in Greece and was at that time the only one. When therefore the Pelasgians inquired at Dodona whether they should adopt the names that came to them from the barbarians, the oracle ordained that they should use them. And from that time on they sacrificed to the gods making use of their names.'

If the gods were in these primitive days invoked in prayer, some sort of name, some mode of address they must have had. Is it not at least possible that the advance noted by Herodotus is the shift from mere cultus-title, appropriate to any

[1] Herod. II. 51 *θεοὺς ὅτι κόσμῳ θέντες*. Herodotus according to the fashion of his day derives *θεοί* from the root *θε*, to put in order.

and every divinity, to actual *proper* name which defined and crystallized the god addressed? Any and every hero or divinity might rightly be addressed as *Meilichios*, but a single individual personality is caught and crystallized in the proper name *Zeus*. When an epithet lost its adjectival meaning, as is the case with Amphiaraos, then and not till then did it denote an individual god. Apollo, Artemis, Zeus himself may have been adjectival to begin with, mere cultus epithets, but their meaning once lost they have become proper and personal.

It is significant that the shift is said to have taken place owing to an oracle at Dodona. There, accepting Prof. Ridgeway's[1] theory, was the first clash of Pelasgian and Achaean, there Zeus and his shadow-wife Dione displaced the ancient Earth-Mother with her dove-priestesses; there perhaps the Pelasgians with their 'nameless' gods, their heroes and heroines addressed by cultus epithets, met and mingled with the worshippers of Zeus the Father and Dione the wife, and learnt to fix the personalities of their formless shifting divinities, learnt the lesson not from the ancient civilized Egyptians but from the northern 'barbarians.'

The word *hero* itself is adjectival. A gloss in Hesychius[2] tells us that by hero was meant 'mighty,' 'strong,' 'noble,' 'venerable.' In Homer the hero is the strong man *alive*, mighty in battle; in cultus the hero is the strong man *after death*, dowered with a greater, because a ghostly, strength. The dead are, as already noted, *κρείττονες*, 'Better and Stronger Ones.' The avoidance of the actual proper name of a dead man is an instructive delicate decency and lives on to-day. The newly dead becomes, at least for a time, 'He' or 'She'; the actual name is felt too intimate. It is a part of the tendency in all primitive and shy souls, a tendency already noted (p. 214), to remove a little whatever is almost too close, to call your friend 'the kind one,' or 'the old one,' or 'the black one,' and never name his silent name. Of course the delicate instinct soon crystallizes into definite ritual prescription,

[1] Prof. Ridgeway, *Early Age of Greece*, vol. I. p. 339. Aristotle distinctly states that the region round Dodona was 'ancient Greece,' see Ar. *Meteor.* I. 12. 9 *αὕτη δὲ (ἡ Ἑλλὰς ἡ ἀρχαία) ἐστὶν ἡ περὶ τὴν Δωδώνην καὶ τὸν Ἀχελῷον...ᾤκουν γὰρ οἱ Σέλλοι ἐνταῦθα καὶ οἱ καλούμενοι τότε μὲν Γραικοὶ νῦν δὲ Ἕλληνες*, see Prof. Bury, *J.H.S.* XV. p. 217, and Pietschmer, *Einleitung*, p. 255.

[2] Hesych. s.v. *ἥρως· δυνατός, ἰσχυρός, γενναῖος, σεμνός.*

and gathers about it the practical cautious utilitarianism of *de mortuis nil nisi bene*.

It is often said that the Greeks were wont to address their heroized dead and underworld divinities by 'euphemistic' titles, Eumenides for Erinyes, χρηστέ, 'Good One,' when they meant 'Bad One.' Such is the ugly misunderstanding view of scholiasts and lexicographers. But a simpler, more human explanation lies to hand. The dead are, it is true, feared, but they are also loved, felt to be friendly, they have been *kin* on earth, below the earth they will be *kind*. But in primitive days it is only those who have been kin who will hereafter be kind; the ghosts of your enemies' kin will be *un*kind; if to them you apply kindly epithets it is by a desperate euphemism, or by a mere mechanical usage.

Of such euphemism Homer[1] has left us a curious example. Zeus would fain remind the assembled gods of the blindness and fatuity of mortal man:

> 'Then spake the Sire of Gods and Men, and of the Blameless One,
> Aigisthos, he bethought him, whom Agamemnon's son,
> Far-famed Orestes, slew.'

Aigisthos, traitor, seducer, murderer, craven, is 'the Blameless One.' The outraged morality of the reader is in instant protest. These Olympians, these gods 'who live at ease,' go too far.

The epithets in Homer are often worn very thin, but here, once the point is noted[2], it is manifest that ἀμύμων, 'the Blameless One,' is a title perfectly appropriate to Aigisthos *as a dead hero*. Whatever his life on the upper earth, he has joined the company of the κρείττονες, 'the Stronger and Better Ones.' The epithet ἀμύμων in Homer is applied to individual heroes, to a hero's tomb[3], to magical, half-mythical peoples like the Phaeacians and Aethiopians[4] who to the popular imagination are half canonized, to the magic island[5] of the god Helios, to the imaginary half-magical Good Old King[6]. It is used also of the 'convoy[7]' sent by the gods, which of course is magical in character; it is never, I believe, an epithet of the Olympians themselves. There

[1] Hom. *Od.* I. 29.

[2] I owe this explanation of ἀμύμων entirely to Mr Gilbert Murray. Since the publication of Dr Frazer's *Origin of the Kingship* it has become further clear that the magical power of the dead king was only a prolongation of his living prerogative.

[3] Hom. *Od.* XXIV. 80.

[4] *Il.* I. 423.

[5] *Od.* XII. 261.

[6] *Od.* XIX. 109.

[7] *Il.* VI. 171.

is about the word a touch of what is magical and demonic rather than actually divine.

Homer himself is ignorant of, or at least avoids all mention of, the dark superstitions of a primitive race; he knows nothing at least ostensibly of the worship of the dead, nothing of the cult at his tomb, nothing of his snake-shape; but Homer's epithets came to him already crystallized and came from the underlying stratum of religion which was based on the worship of the dead. And here comes in a curious complication. To Homer, though he calls him mechanically, or if we like 'euphemistically,' the 'Blameless One,' Aigisthos is really bad, though not perhaps so black as Aeschylus painted him. But was he bad in the eyes of those who first made the epithet? The story of Aigisthos is told *by the mouth of the conquerors.* Aigisthos is of the old order, of the primitive population, there before the coming of the family of Agamemnon. Thyestes, father of Aigisthos, had been banished[1] from his home; Aigisthos is reared as an alien and returns to claim his own. Clytaemnestra too was of the old order, a princess of the primitive dwellers in the land, regnant in her own right. Agamemnon leaves her, leaves her significantly in the charge of a bard[2], one of those bards pledged to sing the glory of the conquering Achaeans, and the end is inevitable: she reverts to the prince of the old stock, Aigisthos, to whom we may even imagine she was plighted before her marriage to Agamemnon. Menelaos in like fashion marries a princess of the land and his too are the sorrows of the king-consort. The tomb of Aigisthos was shown to Pausanias[3]. We hear of no cult; possibly under the force of hostile epic tradition it dwindled and died, but in old days we may be sure 'the Blameless One' had his meed of service at Argos, and the epithet itself remains as eternal witness.

Salmoneus to the Achaean mind was scarcely more 'Blameless' than Aigisthos and yet he too bears the epithet. In the Nekuia[4] Odysseus says:

> 'Then of the throng of women-folk first Tyro I did see,
> Child of Salmoneus, Blameless One, a noble sire he.'

[1] Aesch. *Choeph.* 1586. Prof. Ridgeway, *Early Age of Greece*, vol. I. p. 97, has pointed out that Agamemnon and Menelaos were new-comers, and that Helen was of the indigenous stock. I venture to suggest that Aigisthos and Clytaemnestra belong also to the 'Pelasgian' stratum.

[2] Hom. *Od.* III. 267.

[3] P. II. 16. 7.

[4] Hom. *Od.* XI. 235.

The case of Salmoneus is highly significant. He too belongs to the old order, as indeed do all the Aeolid figures connected with the group of dead heroines, and more, in his life he was in violent opposition to the new gods. To Hesiod[1] he is 'the Unjust One' (*ἄδικος*). He even dared to counterfeit the thunder and lightning of Zeus, and Zeus enraged slew him with a thunderbolt. He is the very mirror of the picture drawn by Vergil[2] of the insolent king:

> 'Through the Greek folk, midway in Elis town
> In triumph went he; for himself, mad man,
> Honours divine he claimed.'

To every worshipper of the new order his crime must have seemed heinous and blasphemous, but among his own people he was glorious before death and probably 'Blameless' after.

The case of Tityos, Son of Earth, presents a close parallel, though Tityos never bore the title of 'Blameless.' To the orthodox worshipper of the Olympians he was the vilest of criminals; as such Homer[3] knew him:

> 'For he laid hands on Leto, the famous bride of Zeus,
> What time she fared to Pytho through the glades of Panopeus.'

And for this his sin he lay in Hades tortured for ever. This is from the Olympian point of view very satisfactory and instructive, but when we turn to local tradition Tityos is envisaged from quite another point of view. Strabo[4], when he visited Panopeus, learnt that it was the fabled abode of Tityos. He reminds us that it was to the island of Euboea that, according to Homer[5], the Phaeacians conducted fair-haired Rhadamanthys that he might see Tityos, Son of Earth. We wonder for a moment why the just Rhadamanthys should care to visit the criminal. Homer leaves us in doubt, but Strabo makes the mystery clear. On Euboea, he says, they show a 'cave called Elarion from Elara who was mother to Tityos, and a hero-shrine of Tityos, and some kind of honours are mentioned which are paid to him.' One 'blameless'

[1] Hes. frg. ap. Schol. Pind. *Pyth.* IV. 253.

[2] Verg. *Aen.* VI. 585. Hygin. *Fab.* 61. For the whole subject of Salmoneus see Dr Frazer, *Lectures on the Early History of the Kingship*, pp. 197 and 204. It will later (Chap. XI.) be shown that the canonical Hades was peopled by these heroes of an early racial stratum.

[3] *Od.* XI. 576.

[4] Strab. IX. 3 § 423.

[5] *Od.* VII. 323.

hero visits another, that is all. Golden-haired Rhadamanthys found favour with the fair-haired Achaeans; but for Tityos, *the son of Earth*, there is no place in the Northern Elysium.

We may take it then that the 'euphemistic' epithets were applied at first in all simplicity and faith to heroes and underworld gods by the race that worshipped them. The devotees of the new Achaean religion naturally regarded the heroes and saints of the old as demons. Such was in later days the charitable view taken by the Christian fathers of the Olympian gods in their turn. All the activities that were uncongenial, all the black side of things, were carefully made over by the Olympians to the divinities they had superseded. Only here and there the unconscious use of a crystallized epithet like 'Blameless' lets out the real truth. The ritual prescription that heroes should be worshipped by night, their sacrifice consumed before dawn, no doubt helped the conviction that as they loved the night their deeds were evil. Their ritual too was archaic and not lacking in savage touches. At Daulis[1] Pausanias tells of the shrine of a hero-founder. It was evidently of great antiquity, for the people of the place were not agreed as to who the hero was; some said Phocos, some Xanthippos. Service was done to him every day, and when animal sacrifice was made the Phocians poured the blood of the victim through a hole into the grave; the flesh was consumed on the spot. Such plain-spoken ritual would go far to promote the notion that the hero was bloodthirsty.

Sometimes a ritual prescription marks clearly the antipathy between old and new, between the hero and the Olympian. Pausanias[2] describes in detail the elaborate ceremonial observed in sacrificing to Pelops at Olympia. The hero had a large *temenos* containing trees and statues and surrounded by a stone wall, and the entrance, as was fitting for a hero, was towards the west. Sacrifice was done into a pit and the victim was a black ram. Pausanias ends his account with the significant words: 'Whoever eats of the flesh of the victim sacrificed to Pelops, whether he be of Elis or a stranger, *may not enter the temple of Zeus.*' But we are glad to know from Pindar[3] that no spiteful

[1] P. x. 4. 10. [2] P. v. 13. 3.
[3] Pind. *Ol.* I. 90 schol. ad loc.

ritual prescription of the Olympian could dim the splendour of the local hero:

> 'In goodly streams of flowing blood outpoured
> Upon his tomb, beside Alpheios' ford,
>   Now hath he still his share;
> Frequent and full the throng that worship there.'

The scholiast comments on the passage: 'Some say that it was not (merely) a tomb but a sanctuary of Pelops and that the followers of Herakles sacrificed to him before Zeus.'

At yet another great pan hellenic centre there is the memory, though more faded, of the like superposition of cults. The scholiast on Pindar[1] says that the contest at Nemea was of the nature of funeral games (ἐπιτάφιος) and that it was in honour of Archemoros, but that later, after Herakles had slain the Nemean lion, he 'took the games in hand and put many things to rights and ordered them to be sacred to Zeus.'

More commonly there is between the Olympian and the hero all appearance of decent friendliness. A compromise is effected; the main ritual is in honour of the Olympian, but to the hero is offered a preliminary sacrifice. A good instance of this procedure is the worship of Apollo at Amyclae[2] superposed on that of the local hero Hyakinthos. The great bronze statue of Apollo stood on a splendid throne, the decorations of which Pausanias describes in detail. The image itself was rude and ancient, the lower part pillar-shaped, but for all that the god was a new-comer. 'The basis of the image was in form like an altar, and they say that Hyakinthos was buried in it, and at the festival of the Hyakinthia *before* the burnt sacrifice (θυσίας) to Apollo, they devote offerings (ἐναγίζουσιν) to Hyakinthos into this altar through a bronze door.'

Apollo and Hyakinthos established a *modus vivendi*. Apollo instituted his regular Olympian sacrifices (θυσίαι) and left to Hyakinthos his underworld offerings (ἐναγίσματα). But not every Olympian was so successful. Ritual is always tenacious. So too at Delphi, Apollo may seat himself on the omphalos, but he is still forced to utter his oracles through the mouth of the *priestess*

[1] Schol. ad hyp. *Nem.* Ὁ ἀγὼν (τῶν Νεμέων) ἐπιτάφιος ἐπὶ Ἀρχεμόρῳ...ὕστερον δὲ νικήσας Ἡρακλῆς...ἐπεμελήθη τοῦ ἀγῶνος τὰ πολλὰ ἀνορθωσάμενος καὶ Διὸς εἶναι ἱερὸν ἐνομοθέτησε.

[2] P. III. 19. 3.

of Gaia. Zeus, we have seen, arrogated to himself the title of Meilichios; he had the old snake reliefs dedicated to him, but he was powerless to change the ritual of the hero, and had to content himself, like an underworld god, with holocausts. All that he could do was to emphasize the untruth that he, not the hero, was Meilichios, Easy to be intreated.

All that could be effected by theological *animus* was done. It has been seen (p. 9) how in the fable of Babrius the hero-ancestor is positively forbidden to give good things, and meekly submits; and, long before Babrius, the blackening process had set in. The bird-chorus in Aristophanes[1] tells of the strange sights it has seen on earth:

> 'We know of an uncanny spot,
> Very dark, where the candles are not;
> There to feast with the heroes men go
> By day, but at evening, oh no!
> For the night time is risky you know.
> If the hero Orestes should meet with a mortal by night,
> He'd strip him and beat him and leave him an elegant sight.'

Orestes was of course a notable local thief, but the point of the joke is the ill-omened character of a hero. The scholiast says that 'heroes are irascible and truculent to those they meet and possess no power over what is beneficial.' He cites Menander as his authority, but adds on his own account that this explains the fact that 'those who go past hero-shrines keep silence.' So easy is it to read a bad meaning into a reverent custom. So possessed are scholiasts and lexicographers by the Olympian prejudice that, even when the word they explain is dead against a bad interpretation, they still maintain it. Hesychius[2], explaining *κρείττονας*, 'Better or Stronger Ones,' says 'they apply the title to heroes, and they seem to be a bad sort of persons; it is on this account that those who pass hero-shrines keep silence lest the heroes should do them some harm.' Among gods, as among mortals, one rule holds good: the king can do no wrong and the conquered no right.

[1] Ar. *Av.* 1482, schol. ad loc. Athenaeus (XI. 4, p. 461) gives the same account of the character of heroes: *χαλεποὺς γὰρ καὶ πλήκτας τοὺς ἥρωας νομίζουσι.*
[2] Hesych. s.v. *κρείττονας.*

ASKLEPIOS AND THE HEROES OF HEALING.

Heroes, like the ghosts from which they sprang, had of course their black angry side, but, setting aside the prejudice of an Olympianized literature, it is easy to see that in local cultus they would tend rather to beneficence. The ghost you worship and who by your worship is erected into a hero is your kinsman, and the ties of kinship are still strong in the world below. 'In almost all West African districts,' says Miss Mary Kingsley[1], 'is a class of spirits called "Well-disposed Ones" and this class is clearly differentiated from "Them," the generic term for non-human spirits. These "Well-disposed Ones" are ancestors and they do what they can to benefit their particular village or family fetish who is not a human spirit or ancestor.' So it was with the Greek; he was careful not to neglect or offend his local hero, but on the whole he relied on his benevolence:

> 'When a man dies we all begin to say
> The sainted one has passed away, he has "fallen asleep,"
> Blessed therein that he is vexed no more.
> And straight with funeral offerings we do sacrifice
> As to a god and pour libations, bidding
> Him send good things up here from down below[2].'

The cult of heroes had in it more of human 'tendance' than of demonic 'aversion.'

The hero had for his sphere of beneficence the whole circle of human activities. Like all primitive divinities he was of necessity a god-of-all-work; a primitive community cannot afford to departmentalize its gods. The local hero had to help his family to fight, to secure fertility for their crops and for themselves, act as oracle when the community was perplexed, be ready for any emergency that might arise, and even on occasion he must mend a broken jug. But most of all he was adored as a Healer. As a Healer he rises very nearly to the rank of an Olympian, but through the gentleness of his office he keeps a certain humanity that prevents complete deification. A typical instance of the Hero-Healer is the god Asklepios.

We conceive of Asklepios as he is figured in many a Greek and Graeco-Roman statue, a reverend bearded god, somewhat of

[1] *West African Studies*, p. 132.

[2] Ar. *Tagenist.* frg. 1.

the type of Zeus, but characterized by the staff on which he leans and about which is twined a snake. The snake, our hand-books tell us, is the 'symbol of the healing art,' and hence the attribute of Asklepios, god of medicine.

The design in fig. 99, from a votive relief[1] found in the Asklepieion and now in the National Museum at Athens, gives

FIG. 99.

cause for reflection. The god himself stands in his familiar attitude, waiting the family of worshippers who approach with offerings. A little happy honoured boy is allowed to lead the procession bringing a sheep to the altar. Behind the god is his attribute, a huge coiled snake, his head erect and level *with the god he is*. Take away the human Asklepios and the scene is yet complete, complete as on the Meilichios relief in fig. 2, the great hero snake and his worshippers.

[1] *Cat.* 1407, from a photograph. For permission to publish this relief and those in figs. 100, 103, 104, my grateful thanks are due to Mr Kabbadias, Ephor of Antiquities at Athens.

The relief in fig. 99 is under a foot in length, the offering probably of some poor man who clung to his old faith in the healing snake-hero. It forces us in its plain-spoken simplicity to face just the fact that the dedicator of the next relief[1] (fig. 100) is so anxious to conceal. The second relief is the

FIG. 100.

offering of a rich man, the figures are about half life-size; it was found in the same Asklepieion on the S. slope of the Acropolis. Asklepios no longer stands citizen-fashion leaning on his staff: he is seated in splendour, and beside him is coiled a very humble attributive snake. Behind are two figures, probably of a son and a daughter, and they all three occupy a separate chapel aloof from their human worshippers.

In token of his humble birth as the ghost of a mortal the snake always clings to Asklepios, but it is not the only evidence. An essential part of his healing ritual was always and everywhere the ἐγκοίμησις[2], the 'sleeping in' his sanctuary. The patient who came to be cured must sleep and in a dream the god either healed him or revealed the means of healing. It was the dream

[1] *Cat.* 1377, from a photograph.

[2] For the whole subject of ἐγκοίμησις see L. Deubner, *De Incubatione capitula duo.*

oracle sent by Earth herself[1] that Apollo the Olympian came to supersede. All the strange web of human chicanery that was woven round the dream cure it would here be irrelevant to examine: only the simple fact need be noted that the prescribed ritual of sleep was merely a survival of the old dream oracle of the hero. It was nowise peculiar to Asklepios. When men came to the beautiful little sanctuary of Amphiaraos[2] at Oropus they purified themselves, sacrificed a ram, and spreading the skin under them they went to sleep 'awaiting a revelation in a dream.'

The dream oracle remained always proper to the earth-born heroes; we hear of no one *sleeping* in the precinct of Zeus, or of Apollo, and the belief in the magic of sleep long outlasted the service of the Olympians. To-day year by year on the festival of the Panagia a throng of sick from the islands round about make their pilgrimage to Tenos, and the sick sleep in the Church and in the precinct and are healed, and in the morning is published the long list of miraculous cures (*θαύματα*). It is only the truth and the true gods that lived. The Panagia has taken to herself all that was real in ancient faith, in her are still incarnate the Mother and the Maid and Asklepios the Saviour. Like most primitive faiths the belief in the dream cure appealed to something very deep-down and real, however misunderstood and perverted, something in the secret bidding of nature that said, that always will say:

'Sleep Heart, a little free
From thoughts that kill.
Nothing now hard to thee
Or good or ill.
And when the shut eyes see
Sleep's mansions fill,
Night might bring that to be
Day never will.'

The worship of Asklepios, we know from the evidence of an inscription[3], was introduced at Athens about 421 B.C.: it was still no doubt something of a new excitement when Aristophanes wrote his *Plutus*. But Athens was not left till 421 B.C. without a Hero-Healer. Asklepios came to Athens as a full-blown god, came first from Thessaly, where he was the rival of Apollo, and

[1] Eur. *Iph. in T.* 1261.
[2] P. I. 34. 5.
[3] *A. Mitt.* 1893, p. 250. The introduction of the healer of Epidauros may have been connected with the great plague at Athens.

finally from his great sanctuary at Epidauros, and, when he came, we have definite evidence that his cult was superimposed on that of a more ancient hero. 'Affiliated' is perhaps the juster word, for when a hero from without took over the cult of an indigenous hero there is no clash of ritual as in the case of an Olympian, no conflict between *θυσίαι* and *ἐναγισμοί*; both heroes alike are content with the simple offering of the *pelanos*.

In the course of the 'Enneakrounos' excavations Dr Dörpfeld came upon a small sanctuary consisting of a precinct, an altar, and a well[1]. The precinct wall, the well and the conduit leading to it were clearly, from the style of their masonry, of the date of Peisistratos. Within and around the precinct were votive offerings that pointed to the worship of a god of healing, reliefs representing parts of the human body, breasts and the like, a man holding a huge leg marked with a varicose vein, reliefs of the usual 'Asklepios' type, and above all votive snakes. Had there been no inscriptions the precinct could have been at once claimed as 'sacred to Asklepios,' and we should have been left with the curious problems, 'Why had Asklepios two precincts, one on the south, one on the west of the Acropolis; and, if the god had already a shrine on the west slope in the days of Peisistratos, why did he trouble to make a triumphant entry into Athens on the south slope in 421 B.C.?'

Happily we are left in no such dilemma. On a stele found in the precinct we have the following inscription[2]: 'Mnesiptolemè on behalf of Dikaiophanes dedicated (this) to Asklepios Amynos.' If the inscription stood alone, we should probably decide that Asklepios was worshipped in the precinct *under the title of Amynos*, the Protector. Whatever the original meaning of the word Asklepios—and we may conjecture it was merely a cultus-title—it soon became a proper name, and could therefore easily be associated with an adjectival epithet.

A second inscription[3] happily makes it certain that Amynos was not merely an adjective, but an adjectival title of a person distinct from Asklepios. It runs as follows: 'Certain citizens

[1] A. Koerte, 'Bezirk eines Heilgottes,' *A. Mitt.* 1893, p. 237, and 1896, p. 311.

[2] Koerte, *op. cit.* Μνησιπτολέμη ὑπὲρ Δικαιοφάνους Ἀσκληπίῳ Ἀμύνῳ ἀνέθηκε.

[3] Koerte, *op. cit.* ἄνδρες δίκαιοι γε[γόν]ασι περὶ τὰ κοινὰ τῶν ὀργεώνων τοῦ Ἀμύνου καὶ τοῦ Ἀσκληπίου καὶ τοῦ Δεξίονος ἐπαινέσαι κτλ.

held it just to commemorate concerning the common weal of the members of the thiasos of Amynos and of Asklepios and of Dexion.' Here we have the names of three personalities manifestly separate and enumerated in significant order. We know Asklepios and most fortunately Dexion. The author of the *Etymologicon Magnum*[1], in explaining the word *Dexion*, says: 'The title was given by the Athenians to Sophocles after his death. They say that when Sophocles was dead the Athenians, wishing to give him added honours, built him a hero-shrine and named him Dexion, the Receiver, from his reception of Asklepios—for he received the god in his own house and set up an altar to him.' For the heroization of Sophocles we have earlier evidence than the *Etymologicon Magnum*. The historian Istros[2] (3rd cent. B.C.) is quoted as saying that the Athenians 'on account of the man's virtue passed a vote that yearly sacrifice should be made to him.'

It seems an extraordinary story, but, if we do not press too hard the words of the panegyrist, the explanation is natural enough. Sophocles was not exactly canonised 'because of his virtue.' He became a hero, officially, because he had officially received Asklepios, and the 'Receiver' of a god, like the 'Founder' of a town, had a right to ritual recognition. 'Dexion' is the Receiver of the god, and from the fact that the inscription with his name is set up in the little precinct on the west slope of the Acropolis we may be sure his worship went on there. It was in that little precinct, we may conjecture, that he served as priest. This conjecture is made almost certain by the fact that a later inscription[3] (1st cent. B.C.), with a dedication to Amynos and Asklepios, is dated by the priesthood of a 'Sophocles,' probably a descendant of the poet. Sophocles as a hero was not a success, probably he was too alive and human as a poet; he was in his own precinct completely submerged by the god he 'received.'

The theological history of the little precinct is quite clear. The inscription preserves the ritual order of precedence. The sanctuary began, not later than Peisistratos, as an Amyneion, shrine of a local hero worshipped under the title of Amynos, Protector. At some time, probably owing to the recent pestilence

[1] *Etym. Mag.* s.v. *Δεξίων*. It seems possible that by the *οἰκία* in which Sophocles received Asklepios is meant the Amyneion.

[2] Istr. frg. 51.

[3] Koerte, *op. cit.* *ἐπὶ ἱερέως Σοφοκλέους τοῦ Φιλώτου*.

which the local hero had failed to avert, it was thought well to affiliate a Healer-god who had attained enormous prestige in the Peloponnesus. The experiment was quietly and carefully tried in the little Amyneion before the foundation of the great Asklepieion on the south slope. It was a very simple matter. A sacred snake would be sent for[1] from Epidauros, to join the local snake of Amynos. Both were snakes, both were healers; the same offerings served for both, the votive limbs, the *pelanoi*. Sophocles the human Receiver, who had introduced Asklepios in due course, naturally enough dies, and a third healing hero is added to the list. Dexion fades, and Asklepios gradually effaces Amynos and takes his name as a ceremonial title.

Because Athens alone is really alive to us, because we know Sophocles as human poet, Asklepios as divine Healer, the case of Amynos, Asklepios, Sophocles seems specially vital and convincing. But we must take it only as one instance of the ladder from earth to heaven that had its lowest rungs planted in every village scattered over Greece—a ladder that reached sometimes, but not always or even often, up to high Olympus itself. Whether a local hero became a god depended on a multitude of chances and conditions, the clue to which is lost. If a local hero became famous beyond his own parish the Olympian religion made every effort to meet him half-way. Herakles was of the primitive Pelasgian[2] stock. His name, if the most recent etymology[3] be accepted, means only *the* young dear Hero—*the* Hero *par excellence*. No pains were spared to affiliate him. He is allowed the Olympian burnt sacrifice[4], he is passed through the folds of Hera's robe to make him her child by adoption[5], he is married in Olympus to Hebe, herself but newly translated, the vase-painter[6]

[1] Cf. P. VIII. 8. 4, II. 10. 3, III. 23. 7.

[2] Prof. Ridgeway, *The Early Age of Greece*, vol. I. p. 640.

[3] Usener, *Die Sinflutsagen*, p. 58, draws attention to the hypocoristic form Ἡρύκαλος, see Hesych. s.v. τὸν Ἡρακλέα Σώφρων ὑποκοριστικῶς, and supposes an old Greek diminutive καλος = Lat. *culus*, homunculus, Herculus. This nowise conflicts with his original connection with Hera, conclusively proved by Mr A. B. Cook, *Class. Rev.* 1906, p. 365. Rather it confirms it, for *Hera* as well as *Herakles* are in significance and in etymology akin to ἥρως. See Dr Sam Wide, 'Chthonische und himmlische Götter' in *Archiv f. Religionswissenschaft*, 1907, p. 262.

[4] See p. 12.

[5] Diod. Sic. IV. 40 τὴν Ἥραν ἀναβᾶσαν ἐπὶ κλίνην καὶ τὸν Ἡρακλέα προσλαβομένην πρὸς τὸ σῶμα διὰ τῶν ἐνδυμάτων ἀφεῖναι πρὸς τὴν γῆν μιμουμένην τὴν ἀληθινὴν γένεσιν· ὅπερ μέχρι τοῦ νῦν ποιεῖν τοὺς βαρβάρους ὅταν θετὸν υἱὸν ποιεῖσθαι βούλωνται.

[6] Rosch. *Lex.* s.v. Herakles, 'Apotheose,' p. 2239.

diligently paints his reception into Olympus, he is always elaborately entering, yet he is never really *in*, he is too much a man to wear at ease the livery of an Olympian, and literature, always over-Olympianized, makes him too often the laughing-stock of the stage.

Fig. 101.

More often it is the fate of a hero to become locally a divinity of healing, but never to emerge as a Panhellenic god. In the design in fig. 101 we have a good instance—from a vase[1] found in Boeotia and now in the National Museum at Athens. On the obverse a bearded man, wearing a wreath, reclines at a banquet. A table with cakes stands by his couch. An enormous coiled snake is about to drink from the wine-cup in his hand. On the reverse a woman-goddess holding a sceptre is seated, a girl brings offerings —an oinochoë, cakes, a lighted taper. Above are hung votive offerings—a hand, two legs, such as hang in the shrines of saints in Brittany and Italy to-day. An interpreter unversed in the complexity of hero-cults would at once name the god with the snake on the obverse Asklepios, the goddess with the votive-limbs on the reverse Hygieia; but to these names they have no sort of right. Found as the vase was in Boeotia, the vase-painter more probably intended Amphiaraos, or possibly Trophonios, and Agathe Tyche. All we can say is that they are a couple of healing divinities—hero and heroine divinized.

The vase is of late style, and the artist has forgotten that the snake is the hero; he makes him a sort of tame attributive pet, feeding out of the wine-cup. The snake is not bearded, but he has a touch of human unreality in that he is about to drink out of the wine-cup. These humanized snakes are fed with human food; their natural food would be a live bird or a rabbit. Dr Gadow kindly tells me that a snake will lap milk, but if he is to eat his sacrificial food, the *pelanos*, it must be made *exceedingly thin*; anything of the nature of a cake or even porridge he could not swallow. And yet the snake on the Acropolis had for his monthly

FIG. 102.

[1] Ἐφημερὶς Ἀρχ. 1890, Pl. VII.

due a 'honey cake,' and at Lebadeia[1] in the shrine of Trophonios, where it was a snake who gave oracles, the inhabitants of the country 'cast into his shrine flat cakes steeped in honey.'

Representations of the hero reclining at a feast occur very frequently on votive reliefs of a class shortly to be discussed. They appear very rarely on vases and only on those of late style. A good instance is the design in fig. 102 from a late red-figured krater in the Berlin Museum[2]. The attempt to give a name to the recumbent man is quite fruitless: the great snake marks him as a dead hero. The woman and boy can scarcely be said to be worshippers, though the boy brings cakes and fruit; it is rather the feast that went on in life figured as continuing after death.

It remains to examine some of the class of votive reliefs closely analogous to the vase-painting in fig. 102, reliefs usually known as 'Hero-Feasts' or 'Funeral Banquets.' They are monuments especially instructive for our purpose, because nowhere else is seen so clearly the transition from hero to god, and also the gradual superposition of the Olympians over local hero-cults.

THE 'HERO-FEASTS.'

Plato[3] in the *Laws* arranges the objects of divine worship in a regular sequence: first the Olympian gods together with those who keep the city; second the underworld gods whose share are things of unlucky omen; third the daemons whose worship is characterized as 'orgiastic'; fourth the heroes; fifth ancestral gods. He concludes the list with living parents to whom much honour should be offered. As early as Hesiod[4] theology attempted some differentiation between heroes and daemons; daemons being accounted divine in some higher sense. Of all this minute departmentalism ritual

[1] Schol. ad Ar. *Nub.* 508 *ἐν Λεβαδείᾳ ἱερὸν ἐστὶ Τροφωνίου ὅπου ὄφις ἦν ὁ μαντευόμενος ᾧ οἱ κατοικοῦντες πλακοῦντας ἔβαλλον μέλιτι δεδευομένους.* The 'pelanos' offered by the women in the fourth Mime of Herondas (*v.* 90) was a money commutation. See Dr Herzog's important paper 'Aus dem Asklepieion von Kos' in the *Archiv f. Religionswissenschaft*, 1907, p. 205.

[2] Berl. *Cat.* 3155. *Jahrb. d. Inst.* Anzeiger, 1890, p. 89.

[3] Plat. *Legg.* 717 A. The Olympian gods do not here concern us, but it may be worth noting that the gods who keep the state *τοὺς τὴν πόλιν ἔχοντας θεούς*, who are classed with the Olympians as of the first rank, seem to correspond with the *ἀστυνόμοι* and *ἀγοραῖοι* of Aeschylus (*Ag.* 90) who take rank with the *οὐράνιοι*. Some gods wherever found were Olympian, e.g. Zeus and Apollo; others though not Panhellenically recognised took rank as such locally, e.g. Demeter.

[4] Hes. *Erg.* 109.

knows nothing. The only recognised distinction is that burnt offerings are the meed of the Olympians, offerings *devoted* (*ἐναγισμοί*) of the chthonic gods. Between the chthonic gods and the whole class of dead men, heroes and daemons, the only distinction observed is, as already noted, that certain chthonic gods from sheer conservatism reject the service of wine, whereas it is apparently acceptable to dead men, to heroes and to daemons not fully divinized.

In like fashion votive reliefs of the type known as Hero-Feasts draw no distinction between hero and daemon, nor indeed do they clearly distinguish between ordinary dead man and hero. As a rule the 'Hero-Feasts' are depicted on reliefs set up in sanctuaries rather than graveyards, but they occur sometimes on actual tombstones[1] set up in actual cemeteries.

The 'Hero-Feast' is found broadcast over Attica, the Pelopon-

FIG. 103.

nese and the islands; there is scarcely a local museum that does not contain specimens. The design in fig. 103 is from a relief in

[1] There are several instances in the National Museum at Athens and 'Hero-Feasts' have been carved on sarcophagi which are still in the courtyard of the local museum at Paros.

the local museum at Samos[1]. Three heroes are lying at the banquet; one holds a large rhyton. A snake coiled about a tree is about to drink from it. Snake and tree mark a sanctuary, otherwise the scene is very homelike and *non*-hieratic. Of the inscription only two letters remain, and they tell nothing. The round shield and the horse's head and the dog tell us we have to do with actual heroes, but who they were it is impossible to say.

The relief in fig. 104 is also from Samos[2]. It is of the usual

Fig. 104.

type—the recumbent man, the seated woman, the boy about to draw wine. The field is full of characteristic tokens: for the man, the horse's head, the cuirass, helm, shield and greaves; for the woman, the work-basket of the shape so often occurring on

[1] *Inv.* 55, see Dr Wiegand, 'Antike Sculpturen in Samos,' *A. Mitt.* 1900, p. 176.
[2] *Inv.* 60.

Athenian grave-reliefs, and, it may be, the tame bird which stands on the casket pecking at a fruit. The snake is for both, for both are dead. The inscription at first surprises us; it is as follows: 'Lais daughter of Phoenix, heroine, hail.' There is no mention of the hero, but on examination of the stone it is seen that a previous inscription has been erased[1]. Some one cared more for Lais than for her husband, hence the palimpsest.

These two specimens from Samos have been selected out of countless others because in them it is quite certain that heroized mortals are represented. The earliest specimens of the 'Hero-Feast' discovered had no inscriptions, and though horse and snake were present an attempt was made to interpret them as sacred to Asklepios; the snake was 'the symbol of healing,' the horse that mysterious creature the 'horse of Hades[2].' The most ardent devotee of symbolic interpretation can scarcely make mythology out of the greaves and the work-basket.

Reliefs of the 'Hero-Feast' type are all of late date. The earliest one is doubtfully assigned to the end of the 5th century; the great majority are much later. The reason is not far to seek. In the fine period of Greek Art, the period to which we owe most of the grave-reliefs found at Athens, hero-worship is submerged. It is a time of rationalism, and the funeral monuments of that time tend to represent this life rather than the next. I have tried elsewhere to show that early Attic grave-reliefs are cast in the *type* of the Sparta hero-reliefs, but nowhere in Attic grave-reliefs of the 5th century do we find the dead heroized. But once the age of reason past, hero-worship re-emerged, and it would seem in greater force than before.

In the fine period of art hero-reliefs do exist, but not as funeral monuments. One of the earliest and finest[3] we possess is represented in fig. 105. It is not at all of the same type as the 'Hero-Feast,' and is figured here partly for its beauty and interest, partly to mark the contrast. A hero occupies the central place, leading his horse, followed by his hound. That he *is* a

[1] See Dr Wiegand, *op. cit.* p. 180.

[2] See Dr Verrall, 'Death and the Horse,' *J.H.S.*, XVIII. 1898, p. 1.

[3] Roscher, s.v. Heros, p. 2559, No. 5. A better reproduction in phototype has been published by Dr Chr. Blinkenberg, 'Et Attisk Votivrelief,' *Festskrift til J. L. Ussing*, Kopenhagen, 1900. I follow Dr Ussing's view (kindly translated for me by Dr Martin Nilsson).

hero we are sure, for in front of him is his low, omphalos-like altar, and to the left a worshipper approaches. Unhappily there

Fig. 105.

is no inscription, but yet we are tempted to give the hero a name.

Horse and horseman are set against a rocky background. The marble of which the relief is made is Pentelic, the style Attic, with many reminiscences of the Parthenon marbles. It is therefore not too bold to see in the rocky background a slope of the Acropolis. To the right above the hero is a seated figure, with only the lower part of the body draped. Zeus is so represented and Asklepios. Zeus has no shrine on the slopes of the Acropolis, nor is it probable he would be depicted on a relief of this date seated in casual fashion as a spectator. The figure is almost certainly Asklepios. Given that the figure is Asklepios, the narrative of Pausanias[1] supplies the clue to the remaining figures. 'Approaching the Acropolis by this road, next after the sanctuary of Asklepios is the temple of Themis, and in front of this temple is a mound upreared as a monument to Hippolytos.' Then Pausanias tells the story of Phaedra and Hippolytos; he does not actually mention the sanctuary of Aphrodite, but he says 'the old images were not there in my time, but those I saw were the work of no obscure artists.' Images of course presuppose a sanctuary, and such a sanctuary we now know from inscriptions

[1] P. I. 22. 1—3, see Dr Frazer ad loc., and *Myth. and Mon. Anc. Athens*, p. 328.

and votive offerings found on the spot to have existed, and that it was dedicated to Aphrodite Pandemos. The figures on the relief exactly correspond to the account of Pausanias. To the right, i.e. to the East, the figure of Asklepios; next Themis with her temple, clearly indicated by the two columns between which she stands; immediately in front of her Hippolytos with his sacred altar-mound. Above it Aphrodite, literally '*over* Hippolytos' (Ἱππολύτῳ δ' ἔπι). It is as Euripides[1] knew it:

> 'And Phaedra then, his father's Queen high born,
> Saw him, and as she saw her heart was torn
> With great love by the working of my will.
> And there, when he was gone, on Pallas' hill
> Deep in the rock, that Love no more might roam.
> She built a shrine and named it *Love-at-Home*.
> And the rock held it, but its face always
> Seeks Trozen o'er the seas.'

It is worth noting that the relief, now in the Torlonia Museum at Rome, was found not far from Aricia, where the hero Virbius, the Latin equivalent of Hippolytos, was worshipped.

It is possible that in the tragedy of the wrath of Aphrodite against the hero who worshipped Artemis, and in the title of the goddess 'over Hippolytos,' later misunderstood as 'because of,' 'for the sake of' Hippolytos, we have a reminiscence of a superposition of cults—that the actual contest was between a local hero and Aphrodite who had waxed to the glory of an Olympian. Such a view can however scarcely be deduced from the relief in question, which seems to present relations merely topographical and perfectly peaceful.

The design in fig. 106, from a relief in the Jacobsen[2] collection at Ny Carlsberg, Copenhagen, shows a clearer case of supersession. The design is not earlier than the 4th century B.C. and of the usual type of 'Hero-Feast'; we have the reclining man, seated wife, attendant cupbearer, and, to make the scene quite complete,

[1] Eur. *Hipp.* 26 ff., trans. Mr Gilbert Murray. For Aphrodite Endemos, *Love-at-Home*, see Dr Verrall, *Cl. Rev.*, Dec. 1901, p. 449. Dr Svoronos makes the interesting suggestion that the sanctuary founded by Phaedra may have been on the site later occupied by the temple of Nike Apteros, and that the Wingless Victory may have been a title rather of Aphrodite than of Athene. See *Journal International d'Archéologie*, 1901, p. 459.

[2] *Cat.* 95, published and fully discussed by Prof. Furtwängler, 'Ein sogenanntes Todtenmahlrelief mit Inschrift,' *Sitzungsberichte d. k. Bay. Ak. d. Wissenschaften*, Philos.-Philolog. Klasse 1897, p. 401.

three worshippers of smaller size. The procession of worshippers is a frequent, though not uniform, element in the reliefs representing 'Hero-Feasts.' When present they serve to show very clearly that the hero and his wife are objects of worship. As a

Fig. 106.

rule it is, we have seen, safest not to name the hero. In the cases so far where he or the heroine is inscribed, the name has been that of a mortal. In the present case the inscription has a surprise in store for us. Assuredly no one, without the inscriptions, would have ventured to conjecture the inscribed names. The inscription runs as follows:

'Aristomache, Theoris and Olympiodorus dedicated (it) to Zeus Epiteleios Philios, and to Philia the mother of the god, and to Tyche Agathe the wife of the god.'

Philia, the Friendly One, is mother not wife of Zeus Philios, 'Zeus the Friendly'; it is the old matriarchal relation of Mother and Son (p. 273). But the dedicators, related themselves no doubt after patriarchal fashion, seem to feel a need that Zeus Philios should be married; they give him not his natural shadow-wife Philia—she has been used up as mother—but Tyche Agathe,

'Good Fortune.' In the procession of worshippers there are two women with a man between them: probably they are his mother and wife and wish to see their relation to him mirrored in their dedication. But they are content with the traditional type of Hero-Feasts, possibly the only type that the conservative workman kept in stock in his workshop.

It is worth noting that this interesting relief came from a precinct of Asklepios in Munychia down at the Peiraeus, the same precinct which yielded the snake reliefs (figs. 1 and 2) dedicated to Meilichios. There were also found the relief in fig. 4, several reliefs adorned with snakes only, some reliefs representing Asklepios, and various ritual inscriptions. The precinct seems to have become a sort of melting-pot of gods and heroes. Tyche we know at Lebadeia as the wife of the Agathos Daimon, the Good or Rich Spirit, and it is curious to note that Zeus on the relief holds a cornucopia, symbol of plenty. His other title *Epiteleios* points the same way. Hesychius[1] tells us that the word *ἐπιτελείωσις* means the same as *αὔξησις*, 'increase,' and Plato[2] gives the name *ἐπιτελειώσεις*, 'accomplishments,' to family feasts held in thanksgiving for the birth *and welfare* of children.

It seems obvious that the precinct once belonged to a hero, worshipped under the form of a snake, and as Meilichios, god of the wealth of the underworld—a sort of Agathos Daimon or Good Spirit. He must have had two other titles—Epiteleios, the Accomplished, and Philios, the Friendly One. At some time or other Asklepios took over the shrine of Meilichios, Philios, Epiteleios, as he took over the shrine of Amynos, but Zeus also put in a claim and the two divided the honours of the place. The old snake-hero was forgotten, overshadowed by the Olympian and the great immigrant healer; but the Olympian does not wholly triumph. He cannot change the local ritual, and he must consent to a certain interchange of attributes.

This is quaintly shown in the two reliefs placed side by side in fig. 107[3]. The larger one to the left shows a seated god holding a cornucopia; beneath his chair is an eagle. In deference to this

[1] Hesych. s.v.

[2] Plat. *Legg.* VI. 784 D.

[3] Both reliefs are reproduced from photographs kindly given me by the German Archaeological Institute. The relief to Zeus Philios was found near the Hill of the Nymphs at Athens (*C.I.A.* II. 1330), that to the Agathos Daimon significantly at Thespiae (*C.I.A.* I. 1815).

characteristically Olympian bird we should expect the dedication to be to Zeus. We find it is to the 'Good Spirit[1].' In the smaller

FIG. 107.

relief a similar bird is perched below the chair, and a humble pig is the sacrifice, as it is to Zeus Meilichios; the inscription tells us that 'the Club-men dedicated it to Zeus Philios in the archonship of Hegesios.' The relief is dated by this archonship as set up in the year 324/3 B.C. The Friendly Zeus was the god of good fellowship and was of wide popularity[2]. To cheerful, hilarious souls it

[1] For identification of Zeus and Ἀγαθὸς δαίμων see Paus. 8. 36. 5 and Dr Martin Nilsson, *Griechische Feste*, p. 401.

[2] νὴ τὸν Φίλιον was a popular oath, cf. Ar. *Acharn.* 730. The omission of the proper name is significant.

was comforting to think that there was another Zeus, less remote, more of the cornucopia and less of the thunderbolt, and that he was ready to join a human feast. The diner-out needs and finds a god in his own image, and Zeus—Zeus with his title of Philios, accustomed as he was to Homeric banquets, was ready for the post. So the comic parasite reasons[1]:

'I wish to explain clearly
What a holy orthodox business this dining-out is—
An invention of the gods; the other arts
Were invented by men of talent, not by the gods.
But dining-out was invented by Zeus the Friendly,
By common consent the greatest of all the gods.
Now good old Zeus comes straight into people's houses
In his free and easy way, rich and poor alike.
Wherever he sees a comfortable couch set out
And by its side a table properly laid,
Down he sits to a regular dinner with courses,
Wine and dessert and all, and then off he goes
Straight back home, and he never pays his shot.'

The fooling is obviously based on ritual practice in the 'Hero-Feast' that developed into the Feasts of the Gods, the Theoxenia.

Our argument ends where it began—with Zeus Meilichios, an early chthonic stratum of worship, a later Olympian supersession. The two religions, alien in ritual, alien in significance, never more than mechanically fused[2]. We have also seen that the new religion was powerless to alter the old save in name; the Diasia becomes the festival of Zeus, the ritual is a holocaust offered to a snake; Apollo and Artemis take over the Thargelia, but it remains a savage ceremony of magical purification.

It might seem that we had reached the end. In reality, for religion in any deep and mystical sense, we have yet to watch the beginning; we have yet to see the coming of a god, who came from the North and yet was no Achaean, no Olympian, who belonging to the ancient stock revived the ancient ritual, the sacrifice that was in its inner content a sacrifice of purification, but revived it with a significance all his own, the god who took over the ritual of the Anthesteria, Dionysos.

[1] Diod. Sinop. frg. ap. Athen. VI. p. 239. Meineke, *F.C.G.* III. 543.

[2] For cases of fusion and transition see Dr Sam Wide's interesting paper 'Chthonische und himmlische Götter,' *Archiv f. Religionswissenschaft*, 1907, p. 257.

DIONYSOS ON HERO-RELIEFS.

The passing from the old to the new is very curiously and instructively shown in the two designs in figs. 108 and 109. The design in fig. 108 is from a relief found in the harbour of Peiraeus and now in the National Museum at Athens[1]. The material is Pentelic marble; in places the surface has suffered considerably from the corrosion of sea-water. The fine style of the relief dates it as probably belonging to the end of the 5th century B.C.

The general type of the relief is of course the same as that of the 'Hero-Feast[2].' A youth on a couch holds a rhyton, the

FIG. 108.

usual woman is seated at his feet, the usual procession stands to the left. But it is a 'Hero-Feast' with a difference. The group of 'worshippers' are not worshippers; they are talking among themselves, they hold not victims or other offerings, but the implements of the drama—a mask, a tambourine. This is

[1] *Cat.* 1500. Both designs in figs. 108 and 109 are reproduced from photographs.

[2] The most recent account of this much discussed relief is by Dr Studniczka, 'Ueber das Schauspielerrelief aus dem Peiraeus,' in *Mélanges Perrot*, p. 307. The relief was first published *A. Mittheilungen* 1882, Taf. 11, p. 389: see also *Hermes* 1887, p. 336. *A. Mitt.* 1888, p. 221. Reisch, *Weihgeschenke*, p. 23. *Jahrbuch d. Inst.* 1896, p. 104. *A. Mitt.* 1896, p. 362.

clearly seen in the case of the middle figure, a woman[1]. The 'worshippers' are tragic actors. This prepares us for the fact disclosed by the inscriptions beneath the figures of the youth and the attendant woman. Under the youth is written quite clearly *Dionysos*: under the woman was an inscription of which only two certain letters remain, the two last, *ια*. These inscriptions, it should clearly be noted, are later than the relief itself, probably not earlier than 300 B.C. The name of the woman attendant cannot certainly be made out: the most probable conjecture is (Paid)ia, Play, a natural enough name for a nymph attendant on Dionysos.

The name of the god is certain, and, though the inscription is an afterthought, it certainly voices the intention of the original artist. It is to the honour of Dionysos, not to that of a hero, that the actors with their masks assemble—to his *honour* rather than to his definite worship. But none the less there remains the significant fact that the god has taken over the art-type of the 'Hero-Feast.'

The second relief[2] in fig. 109 tells in slightly different and more elaborate form the same tale. The design is from a relief in the Museum at Naples, and is an instance of a type long known as the 'Ikarios reliefs.' Its style dates it as about the 2nd cent. B.C. It clearly presents a blend of the 'Hero-Feast' to the left and the triumphal entry of Dionysos, drunken, elderly, attended by a train of worshippers to the right. The immigrant god is received by the local hero. What local hero receives him we cannot say. Legend tells of such receptions by Ikarios, by Pegasos, by Amphictyon, by Semachos. The hero must remain unnamed; anyhow he plays to Dionysos the part played by Sophocles, he is *Dexion*, Receiver, Host. It is a Theoxenia, a feasting of the god. The 'Ikarios' reliefs are late, and, in the

[1] Dr Studniczka (op. cit. supra) has made a very close examination of the objects held, and attempts, I do not think successfully, to deduce therefrom the dramatic characters impersonated. The object held by the last figure to the left as well as his face is obliterated. It is sufficient for our purpose that it is clear from the middle figure they are *actors*.

[2] From a photograph. There are similar reliefs not quite so well preserved in the Louvre and in the British Museum (*Cat.* 176). A complete list of those extant is given by Hauser, *Die Neu-attischen Reliefs*, Anhang, p. 189. The earliest specimen, more nearly approaching the 'Hero-Relief,' and so marked by the presence of a snake, is published *Arch. Zeit.* 1882, Taf. XIV., and I have already discussed it, *Myth. and Mon. Anc. Athens*, p. xlv. fig. 7.

euphemistic manner of the time, the representation is all peace and harmony. The hero, be he who he may, receives in awe and reverence and gladness the incoming divine guest. But Herodotus tells another tale—a tale of the forcible wresting of the honours

Fig. 109.

of the hero to the glory of the god. In telling the early history of Sekyon under the tyrant Cleisthenes he[1] makes this notable statement: 'The inhabitants of Sekyon paid other honours to Adrastos and they celebrated his misfortunes by tragic choruses, for at that time they did not honour Dionysos, but honoured Adrastos. Now Cleisthenes *transferred these choruses* (from Adrastos) *to Dionysos*, but the rest of the sacrifice he gave to Melanippos.' It is a sudden glimpse into a very human state of affairs. To put down the cult of Adrastos, the hero of a family alien to his own, Cleisthenes introduced the worship of a Theban hero Melanippos. He dared not for some reason give the tragic choruses to Melanippos; rather than the local enemy should still have them he hands them over to a popular immigrant god, Dionysos.

The recumbent hero in the 'Hero-Feasts' is usually repre-

[1] Herod. v. 67. I owe this important reference to the article *Heros* in Roscher's *Lexicon*, p. 2492, but Dr Deneken calls no attention to its significance in relation to Dionysos.

sented as reclining at a feast and as drinking from a large wine-cup, attended by a cupbearer. It may be conjectured that this type, which does not appear till late in the 5th century, came in with the worship of Dionysos. The idea of future bliss as an 'eternal drunkenness came, it will later be seen (Chap. XI.), with the religion of Dionysos from the North. By anticipation we may note a curious fact. On the late Roman coins of the Bizuae[1], a Thracian tribe, the type of the Hero-Feast occurs. An instance is given in fig. 110. A hero is represented—of that we are sure from the cuirass suspended on the tree, from the horse and from the snake—but a hero, I would conjecture, conceived of as transfigured into the feasting god, Dionysos himself.

FIG. 110.

To the examination in detail of the cult of Dionysos we must now turn.

[1] *J.H.S.* v. p. 116. Prof. Percy Gardner explains the coin as belonging to Asklepios: my suggestion is made with the utmost diffidence as differing from so great an authority on numismatics.

CHAPTER VIII.

DIONYSOS.

‘ὦ μάκαρ ὅϲτιϲ εὐδαί-
μων τελετὰϲ θεῶν
εἰδὼϲ βιοτὰν ἁγιϲτεύει.’

So far the formula for Greek theology has been, ‘Man makes the gods in his own image.’ Mythological development has proceeded on lines perfectly normal, natural, intelligible. In so far as we understand humanity we can predicate divinity. The gods are found to be merely magnified men, on the whole perhaps better but with frequent lapses into worse, *quot homines tot sententiae, quot sententiae tot dei.*

As man grew more civilized, his image, mirrored in the gods, grew more beautiful and *pari passu* the worship he offered to these gods advanced from ‘aversion’ (*ἀποτροπή*) to ‘tendance’ (*θεραπεία*). But all along we have been conscious that something was lacking, that even these exquisite presentations of the Nymphs and the Graces, the Mother and the Daughter, are really rather human than divine, that their ritual, whether of ignorant and cruel ‘aversion’ or of genial ‘tendance,’ was scarcely in our sense religious. These perfect Olympians and even these gracious Earth-goddesses are not really Lords over man's life who made them, they are not even ghosts to beckon and threaten, they are lovely dreams, they are playthings of his happy childhood, and when full-grown he comes to face realities, from kindly sentiment he lets them lie unburied in the lumber-room of his life.

Just when Apollo, Artemis, Athene, nay even Zeus himself, were losing touch with life and reality, fading and dying of their own luminous perfection, there came into Greece a new religious impulse, an impulse really religious, the mysticism that is embodied for us in the two names Dionysos and Orpheus. The object of the chapters that follow is to try and seize, with as much precision as may be, the gist of this mysticism.

Dionysos is a difficult god to understand. In the end it is only the mystic who penetrates the secrets of mysticism. It is therefore to poets and philosophers that we must finally look for help, and even with this help each man is in the matter of mysticism peculiarly the measure of his own understanding. But this ultimate inevitable vagueness makes it the more imperative that the few certain truths that can be made out about the religion of Dionysos should be firmly established and plainly set forth.

Dionysos an immigrant Thracian.

First it is certain beyond question that Dionysos was a late-comer into Greek religion, an immigrant god, and that he came from that home of spiritual impulse, the North. These three propositions are so intimately connected that they may conveniently be dealt with together.

In the face of a steady and almost uniform ancient tradition that Dionysos came from without, it might scarcely be necessary to emphasize this point but for a recent modern heresy. Anthropologists have lately recognized[1], and rightly, that Dionysos is in one of his aspects a nature-god, a god who comes and goes with the seasons, who has like Demeter and Kore, like Adonis and Osiris, his Epiphanies and his Recessions. They have rashly concluded that these undoubted appearances and disappearances adequately account for the tradition of his immigration, that he is merely a new-comer year by year, not a foreigner; that he is welcomed every spring, every harvest, every vintage, exorcised, expelled and slain in the death of each succeeding winter. This error is beginning to filter into handbooks.

A moment's consideration shows that the actual legend points to the reverse conclusion. The god is first met with hostility, exorcised and expelled, then by the compulsion of his might and

[1] Mr A. G. Bather in an interesting article on 'The Problem of the Bacchae' (*J.H.S.* XIV. 1894, p. 263) concludes that the myths of the introduction of Dionysos 'do not find their origin in any introduction of the god from without, but in the yearly inbringing of the new statue.'

magic at last welcomed. Demeter and Kore are season-goddesses, yet we have no legend of their forcible entry. Comparative anthropology has done much for the understanding of Dionysos, but to tamper with the historical fact of his immigration is to darken counsel.

Ancient tradition must be examined, and first as to the lateness of his coming.

In Homer, Dionysos is not yet an Olympian. On the Parthenon frieze he takes his place among the seated gods. Somewhere between the dates of Homer and Pheidias his entry was effected. The same is true of the indigenous Demeter, so that this argument alone is inadequate, but the fact must be noted.

The earliest monument of art showing Dionysos as an actual denizen of Olympus is the curious design from an amphora[1] now in the Berlin Museum. The scene depicted is the birth of Athene

Fig. 111.

and all the divinities present are carefully and sometimes curiously inscribed. Zeus with his thunderbolt is seated on a splendid throne in the centre. Athene springs from his head. To the right are Demeter, Artemis, Aphrodite, and last of all Apollo. To the left Eileithyia, Hermes, Hephaestos, and last Dionysos holding his great wine cup.

From the style of the inscriptions the design can scarcely date later than the early part of the sixth century. The position and grouping of the different gods is noteworthy. Of course someone must stand on the outside, but Dionysos is markedly aloof from the main action. Hermes seems to come as messenger to the

[1] Berlin, *Cat.* 1704. *Mon. d. Inst.* 1873, vol. IX. Pl. LV. W. Helbig, *Annali* 1873, p. 106. The curious inscriptions do not here concern us.

furthest verge of Olympus to tell him the news. At the right, the other Northerner, Apollo, occupies the last place.

Moreover on vase-paintings substantially earlier than the Parthenon marbles the scene of his entry into Olympus is not infrequent. As we have no literary tradition of this entry, the evidence of vase-paintings is here of some importance. The design selected (fig. 112) is from a cylix signed by the potter Euxitheos[1] and can be securely dated as a work executed about the turn of the sixth and fifth centuries B.C. On the obverse is an

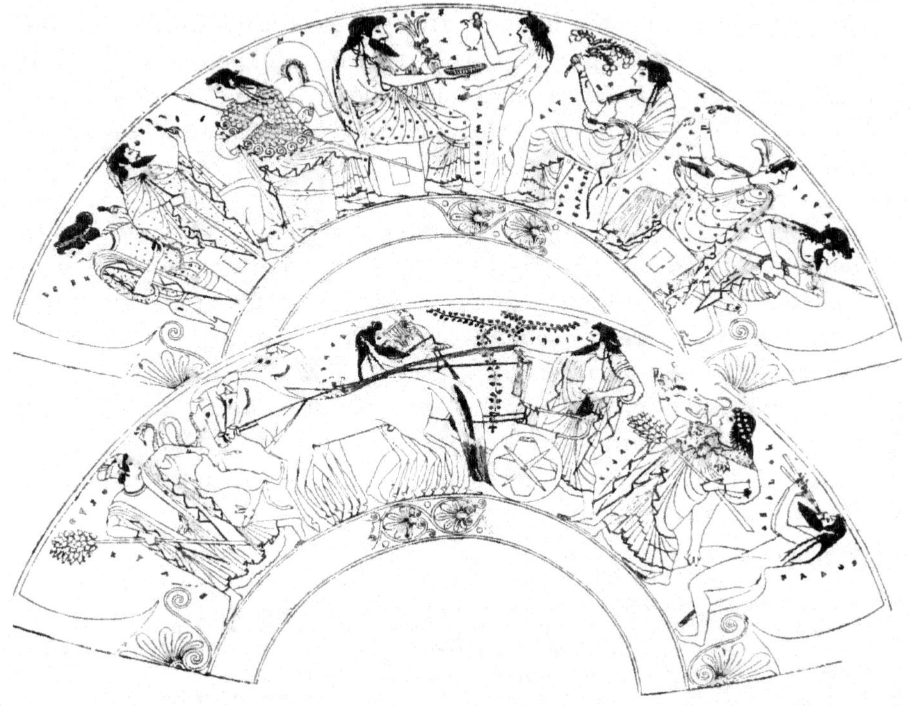

FIG. 112.

assembly of the Olympians all inscribed; Zeus himself with his thunderbolt and Ganymede about to fill his wine cup, Athene holding helmet and lance, Hermes with a flower, Hebe, Hestia with flower and a branch, Aphrodite with dove and flower, Ares with helmet and lance. We might not have named them right but for their inscriptions. Hera and Poseidon are absent, Demeter

[1] *Wiener Vorlegeblätter*, Serie D, Taf. 1 and 2. The vase is now in the Municipal Museum at Corneto.

not yét come. At this time the vase-painter is still free to make a certain choice, the twelve Olympians are not yet canonical. On the obverse the gods are seated waiting, and on the reverse the new god is coming in all his splendour in his chariot with vine and wine-cup in his hand. With him, characteristically, for he is never unaccompanied, come the Satyr Terpes playing on the lyre and the Maenad Thero with thyrsos and fawn and snake, and behind the chariot another Maenad Kalis with thyrsos and lion and a Satyr Terpon playing on the flute. At the close of the sixth century when Pratinas and Choirilos and Phrynichus were writing tragedies in his honour, the gates of that exclusive epic Olympus could no longer be closed against the people's god, and the potter knew it. But there had been a time of doubt and debate. We do not have these entries of Athene or Poseidon or even Hermes.

Homer is of course our first literary source and his main notice of Dionysos is so characteristic it must be quoted in full. The fact that the passage stands alone—elsewhere through all Homer Dionysos is of no real account—has led critics to suspect that it is of later and local origin[1]. Be that as it may, the story glistens like an alien jewel in a bedrock of monotonous fighting. Diomede meets Glaucus in battle, but so great is the hardihood of Glaucus that Diomede fears he is one of the immortals and makes pious, prudent pause:

'I, Diomedes, will not stand 'gainst heavenly Gods in war.
Not long in life was he of old who raised 'gainst gods his hand
Strong Lycoörgos, Dryas' son. Through Nysa's goodly land
He Dionysos' Nursing Nymphs did chase, till down in fear
They cast their wands upon the ground, so sore he smote them there,
That fell king with the ox-smiter. But Dionysos fled,
And plunged him 'neath the salt sea wave. Him sore discomfited
Fair Thetis to her bosom took. Great fear the god did seize.
With Lycoörgos they were wroth, those gods that dwell at ease,
And Kronos' son did make him blind, and he was not for long,
The immortal gods they hated him because he did them wrong.'

Homer is somewhat mysterious as to the end of Lycurgus—'Not long in life was he.' Sophocles[2] is more explicit, both as to his

[1] *Il.* VI. 129. Mr Gilbert Murray kindly draws my attention to the scholiast who states ad v. 131 that the Lycurgus story was told by Eumelos (of Corinth) in the *Europia*: τῆς ἱστορίας πολλοὶ ἐμνήσθησαν προηγουμένως δὲ ὁ τὴν Εὐρώπειαν πεποιηκὼς Εὔμηλος.

[2] Soph. *Ant.* 955.

nationality and his doom. He is a Thracian king, son of Dryas, and he was 'rock-entombed.' When Antigone is going to her death the chorus sing how in like fashion others had been forced to bend beneath the yoke of the gods, Danae, Lycurgus, the sons of Phineus, Oreithyia—three of them Thracians; and of Lycurgus they tell:

'He was bound by Dionysos, rock-entombed,
Dryas' son, Edonian king; swiftly bloomed
His dire wrath and drooped. So was he wrought
To know his blindness and what god he sought
With gibes mad-tongued. Yea and he set his hand
To stay the god-inspired band,
To quell his women and his joyous fire
And rouse the fluting Muses into ire.'

The loss of the Lycurgus trilogy of Aeschylus is hard to bear. One scene at least must have been something like a forecast of the *Bacchae* of Euripides. The dialogue between Lycurgus and the stranger-god captured and brought into his presence, is parodied by Aristophanes in the *Thesmophoriazusae* and the scholiast[1] tells us that the words:

'Whence doth the womanish creature come?'

occurred in the *Edonians*.

Neither Homer nor Sophocles knew anything of the murder of the children. Who first piled up this fresh horror we do not know. Vase-paintings of the rather late red-figured style (middle of the fifth century B.C.) are our first sources. The punishment of sin was to the primitive mind always incomplete unless the offender was cut off with his whole family root and branch, and the murder of the children may have been an echo of the story of the mad Heracles. It is finely conceived on a red-figured krater[2]. On the obverse is the mad Lycurgus with his children dead and dying. He swings a double axe (βουπλήξ). The 'ox-feller' of Homer is probably a double axe, not a goad. It is the typical weapon of the Thracian, and with it the Thracian women regularly on vases slay Orpheus (p. 462). Through the air down upon Lycurgus swoops a winged demon of madness, probably Lyssa herself, and smites at the king with her pointed goad. To the left, behind a hill, a Maenad smites her timbrel in token of the

[1] Ar. *Thesm.* 135, schol. ad loc.
[2] Naples. Heydemann, *Cat.* 3237. *Myth. and Mon. Anc. Athens*, pp. 260, 261, figs. 11 and 12.

presence of the god. On the reverse of the vase we have the peace of Dionysos who made all this madness. The god has sent his angel against Lycurgus, but no turmoil troubles him or his. About him his thiasos of Maenads and Satyrs seem to watch the scene, alert and interested but in perfect quiet.

The exact details of the fate of Lycurgus, varying as they do from author to author, are not of real importance. The essential thing, the factor which recurs in story after story, is the rage against the dominance of a new god, the blind mad fury, the swift helpless collapse at the touch of a real force. All this is no symbol of the coming of the spring or the gathering of the vintage. It is the mirrored image of a human experience, of the passionate vain beating of man against what is not man and is more and less than man.

The nature and essence of the new influence will be in part determined later. For the present the question that presses for solution is 'whence did it come?' 'where was the primitive seat of the worship of Dionysos?'

The testimony of historians, from Herodotus to Dion Cassius, is uniform, and confirms the witness of Homer and Sophocles. Herodotus[1] tells how Xerxes, when he marched through Thrace, compelled the sea tribes to furnish him with ships and those that dwelt inland to follow by land. Only one tribe, the Satrae, would suffer no compulsion, and then come the significant words: 'The Satrae were subject to no man so far as we know, but down to our own day they alone of all the Thracians are free, for they dwell on high mountains covered with woods of all kinds and snow-clad, and they are keenly warlike. These are the people that possess an oracle shrine of Dionysos and this oracle is on the topmost range of their mountains. And those among the Satrae who interpret the oracle are called Bessi; it is a priestess who utters the oracles as it is at Delphi, and the oracles are nothing more extraordinary than that.' Herodotus is not concerned with the religion of Dionysos; he does not even say that the religion of Dionysos spread southward into Greece, but he states the all-important fact that the Satrae were never conquered. They received no religion from without. Here among those splendid

[1] Herod. VII. 110.

unconquerable savages in their mountain fastnesses was the real home of the god.

Herodotus speaks of the Bessi as though they were a kind of priestly caste among the Satrae, but Strabo[1] knows of them as the wildest and fiercest of the many brigand tribes that dwelt on and around Mt. Haemus. All the tribes about Mt. Haemus were, he says, 'much addicted to brigandage, but the Bessi who possessed the greater part of Mt. Haemus were called brigands by brigands. They are the sort of people who live in huts in very miserable fashion, and they extend as far as Rhodope and the Paeonians.' He mentions the Bessi again[2] as a tribe living high up on the Hebrus at the furthest point where the river is navigable, and again emphasizes their tendency to brigandage.

The evil reputation of the Bessi lasted on till Christian days, till they bowed beneath the yoke of one gentler than Dionysos. Towards the end of the fourth century A.D. the good Bishop of Dacia, Niketas, carried the gospel to these mountain wolves and, if we may trust the congratulatory ode written to him by his friend Paulinus, he carried it not in vain. Paulinus celebrates the conversion of the Bessi as follows:

'Hard were their lands and hard those Bessi bold,
Cold were their snows, their hearts than snow more cold,
Sheep in the fold from roaming now they cease,
Thy fold of peace.

Untamed of war, ever did they refuse
To bow their heads to servitude's hard use,
'Neath the true yoke their necks obedient
Are gladly bent.

They who were wont with sweat and manual toil
To delve their sordid ore from out the soil
Now for their wealth with inward joy untold
Garner heaven's gold.

There where of old they prowled like savage beasts,
Now is the joyous rite of angel feasts.
The brigands' cave is now a hiding place
For men of grace[3].'

1 Strabo VII. § 318.

2 Strabo frg. VII.

3 Paulinus Nol. *carm. xxx. de reditu Niket. Episc. in Daciam.*

Nam simul terris animisque duri
et sua Bessi nive duriores
nunc oves facti duce te gregantur
pacis in aulam.
quasque cervices dare servituti
semper a bello indomiti negarant
nunc iugo veri domini subactas
sternere gaudent.

Thucydides[1] in his account of Thracian affairs is silent about the Bessi and his silence surprises us. It is probably accounted for by the fact that in his days the Odrysae had complete supremacy, a supremacy that seems to have lasted down to the days of Roman domination. The autochthonous tribes were necessarily obscured. He mentions however certain mountain peoples who had retained their autonomy against Sitalkes king of the Odrysae and calls them by the collective name Dioi. Among them were probably the Bessi, for we learn from Pliny[2] that the Bessi were known by many names, among them that of Dio-Bessi. It seems possible that to these *Dio*-Bessi the god may have owed one of his many names.

In the face of all this historical evidence, it is at first a little surprising to find that, in the *Bacchae* of Euripides, Dionysos is no Thracian. He is Theban born, and comes back to Thebes, after long triumphant wanderings not in Thrace but in Asia, through Lydia, Phrygia to uttermost Media and Arabia. On this point Euripides is explicit. In the prologue[3] Dionysos says:

'Far now behind me lies the golden land
Of Lydian and of Phrygian—far away
The wide, hot plains where Persian sun-beams play,
The Bactrian war-holds and the storm-oppressed
Clime of the Mede and Araby the blest,
And Asia all, that by the salt sea lies
In proud embattled cities, motley-wise
Of Hellene and Barbarian interwrought,
And now I come to Hellas, having taught
All the world else my dances and my rite
Of mysteries, to show me in man's sight
Manifest God.'

Dionysos is made to come from without, not as an immigrant

nunc magis dives pretio laboris
Bessus exultat, quod humi manuque
ante quaerebat, modo mente caeli
colligit aurum.
*   *   *   *   *   *
mos ubi quondam fuerat ferarum,
nunc ibi ritus viget angelorum
et latet justus quibus ipse latro
vixit in antris.

For this and many other valuable references about the Bessi, I am indebted to Dr Tomaschek's article 'Ueber Brumalia und Rosalia,' *Sitzungsber. d. K. Akad. d. Wissenschaften*, Phil.-Hist. Kl., Wien, 1868, p. 351.

[1] Thucyd. II. 96.

[2] Plin. *N.H.* IV. 18. 11. 10.

[3] Eur. *Bacch.* 13.

stranger but as an exile returned. Moreover, if historical tradition be true, he is made to come from the wrong place. He comes also attended by a train of barbarian women, Asiatic not Thracian. They chant their oriental origin[1]:

'From Asia, from the day-spring that uprises,
From Tmolus ever glorying we come,'

and again[2]:

'Hither, O fragrant of Tmolus the golden.'

Yet Euripides wrote the play in Macedonia and must have known perfectly well that these Macedonian rites that so impressed his imagination were from Thrace; that, as Plutarch tells us[3], 'The women called Klodones and Mimallones performed rites which were the same as those done by the Edonian women and the Thracian women about the Haemus.' He knows it perfectly well and when he is off his guard betrays his knowledge. In the epode of the third choric song[4] he makes Dionysos come to bless Pieria and in his coming cross the two Macedonian rivers, the Axios and Lydias:

'Blessed land of Pierie,
Dionysos loveth thee,
He will come to thee with dancing,
Come with joy and mystery,
With the Maenads at his hest
Winding, winding to the west;
Cross the flood of swiftly glancing
Axios in majesty,
Cross the Lydias, the giver
Of good gifts and waving green,
Cross that Father Stream of story
Through a land of steeds and glory
Rolling, bravest, fairest River
E'er of mortals seen.'

Euripides as poet can afford to contradict himself. He accepts popular tradition, too careless of it to attempt an irrelevant consistency. It matters nothing to him *whence* the god came[5]. The Theban birth-place, the home-coming were essential to the human

[1] Eur. *Bacch.* 65.
[2] *Ib.* 152.
[3] Plut. *Vit. Alex.* 2.
[4] Eur. *Bacch.* 565.
[5] To Euripides in the *Bacchae* Dionysos is the god of the grape. The vine probably came from Asia, though about this experts do not seem to be agreed, see Schrader, *Real-lexicon*; but Dionysos, as will later be shown, is earlier than the coming of the vine.

pathos of his story. But for that we should have missed the appeal to Dirce[1]:

'Achelous' roaming daughter,
Holy Dirce, virgin water,
Bathed he not of old in thee
The Babe of God, the Mystery?'

and again[2]:

'Why, O Blessed among Rivers,
Wilt thou fly me and deny me?
By his own joy I vow,
By the grape upon the bough,
Thou shalt seek him in the midnight, thou shalt love him even now.'

He came unto his own and his own received him not.

When we examine the evidence of art, we find that the simple vase-painter accepts the fact that Dionysos has become a Greek, and does not raise the question whence he came. In black and early red figured designs Dionysos is almost uniformly dressed as a Greek and attended by Greek Maenads. Later the artist becomes more learned and dresses Dionysos as a Thracian or occasionally as an Oriental. The vase-painting[3] in fig. 113, from a late aryballos

Fig. 113.

in the British Museum, has been usually interpreted as representing the Oriental triumph of Dionysos. Rightly so, I incline to think, because the figure on the camel is attended not only by Orientals but by Greek maidens playing on cymbals. Their free upward bearing contrasts strongly with the strange abject fantastic posturings of the Orientals. It must however be distinctly borne in mind that the figure on the camel carries no Dionysiac attributes and cannot be certainly said to be the god.

[1] Eur. *Bacch.* 519. [2] *Ib.* 530.
[3] *Brit. Mus. Cat.* E 695. *Mon. d. Inst.* 1833 tav. L.

The question remains—why did popular tradition, accepted by Euripides and embodied occasionally in vase-paintings, point to Asia rather than to the real home, Thrace? The answer in the main is given by Strabo[1] in his important account of the provenance of the orgiastic worships of Greece. Strabo is noting that Pindar, like Euripides, regards the rites of Dionysos as substantially the same with those performed by the Phrygians in honour of the Great Mother. 'Very similar to these are,' he adds, 'the rites called Kotytteia and Bendideia, celebrated among the Thracians. Nor is it at all unlikely that, as the Phrygians themselves are colonists from the Thracians, they brought their religious rites from thence.' In a fragment[2] of the lost seventh book he is still more explicit. He is mentioning the mountain Bernicos as formerly in possession of the Briges, and the Briges, he says, were 'a Thracian tribe of which some portion went across into Asia and were called by a modified name, Phrygians.'

The solution is simple and is indeed almost a geographical necessity. If the Thracians dwelling in the ranges of Rhodope and Haemus went south at all, they would inevitably split up into two branches. The one would move westward into Macedonia, across the Axios and Lydias into Thessaly and thence downwards to Phocis, Boeotia and Delphi[3]: the other eastward across the Bosporus or the Hellespont into Asia Minor. Greek colonists in Asia Minor would recognize in the orgiastic cults they found there elements akin to their own worship of Dionysos. Wise men are not slow to follow the star that leads to the east, and it was pleasanter to admit a debt to Asia Minor than to own kinship with the barbarous north. Similarity of names, e.g. Lydias and Lydia, may have helped out the illusion and most of all the Theban legend of the Phoenician Kadmos[4].

But mythology is too unconscious not to betray itself. Herodotus[5] says that the Thracians worship three gods only: Ares, Dionysos and Artemis. Between Ares and Dionysos there

[1] Strabo x. 3 § 470. [2] Strabo frg. 25.

[3] The evidence for Thracian settlements at Daulis, Trachis, Orchomenos, Thebes and Parnassos is fully given by Dr Weniger, 'Feralis Exercitus,' in *Archiv f. Religionswissenschaft*, 1907, p. 76.

[4] For the orientalism of the Theban character and legends, see Mr D. G. Hogarth, *Philip and Alexander*, p. 34.

[5] Herod. v. 7.

would seem to be but little in common, but in one current myth their kinship comes out all unconsciously. It is just these unconscious revelations that are in mythology of cardinal importance. The story is that known as 'the bonds of Hera' (Ἥρας δεσμοί). Hephaistos, to revenge himself for his downfall from heaven, sent to his mother Hera a golden throne with invisible bonds. The Olympians took counsel how they might free their queen. None but Hephaistos knew the secret of loosing. Ares[1] vowed he would bring Hephaistos by force. Hephaistos drove him off with firebrands. Force failed, but Hephaistos yielded to the seduction of Dionysos and was brought in drunken triumph back to Olympus. It was a good subject for broad comedy, and Epicharmus used it in his 'Revellers or Hephaistos.' It attained a rather singular popularity in art: the subject occurs on upwards of thirty vase-paintings black and red figured. Earlier than any literary source

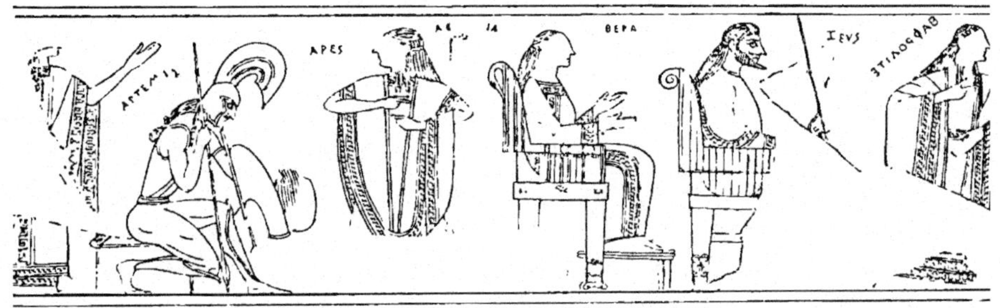

Fig. 114.

for the myth is unquestionably the famous François[2] vase (early sixth century B.C.) in the Museo Civico at Florence, where the scene is depicted in broad epic fashion and with some conscious

[1] Sappho, frg. 66.

[2] *Wiener Vorlegeblätter*, Serie II. Taf. iii., iv. An even earlier source is the Corinthian vase published by Dr Löschke, *A. Mitt.* 1894, p. 524, Taf. viii.

humour. All the figures are inscribed. Zeus is there and Hera, seated on the splendid, fatal throne. Dionysos leads the mule on which sits the drunken Hephaistos. Up they come into the very presence of Zeus with three attendant Silenoi carrying respectively a wine-skin, a flute, a woman. It is the regular revel rout. Behind the throne of Hera crouches Ares in deep dejection, on a sort of low stool of repentance, while Athene looks back at him with scorn. Why are Ares and Dionysos thus set in rivalry? Not merely because wine is mightier than war, but because the two, Ares and Dionysos, are Thracian rivals, with Hephaistos of Lemnos for a third. It is a bit of local mythology transplanted later to Olympus.

The diverse fates of these two Thracian gods are instructive. Ares was realized as a Thracian to the end. In Homer he is only half accepted in Olympus, he is known as a ruffian and a swashbuckler and like Aphrodite escapes[1] to his home as soon as he is released:

> 'Straightway forth sprang the twain;
> To savage Thrace went Ares, but Kypris with sweet smile
> Hied her to her fair altar place, in pleasant Paphos' isle.'

The newly admitted gods, such as Ares and Aphrodite, are never really at home in Olympus. Dionysos, as has already been seen (p. 365), has no place in the Homeric Olympus, but, once he does force an entry, his seat is far more stable. In the *Oedipus Tyrannos* Sophocles[2] realizes that Dionysos and Ares are the great Theban divinities, but Ares is of slaughter and death, Dionysos of gladness and life. He makes his chorus summon Dionysos to banish Ares his fellow divinity:

> 'O thou with golden mitre band,
> Named for our land,
> On thee in this our woe
> I call, thou ruddy Bacchus all aglow
> With wine and Bacchant song.
> Draw nigh, thou and thy Maenad throng,
> Drive from us with bright torch of blazing pine
> The god unhonoured 'mong the gods divine.'

Sophocles just hits the theological mark, Ares *is* a god but he is unhonoured of the orthodox gods, the Olympians.

[1] *Od.* VIII. 265.

[2] Soph. *Oed. Tyr.* 209.

Euripides[1] too lets out the kinship with Ares. He knows of

'Harmonia, daughter of the Lord of War,'

Harmonia, bride of Kadmos, mother of Semele, and though his Dionysos is at the outset all gentleness and magic, his kingdom scarcely of this world, Teiresias[2] knows that he is not only Teacher, Healer, Prophet, but

'of Ares' realm a part hath he.
When mortal armies mailèd and arrayed
Have in strange fear, or ever blade met blade,
Fled, maddened, 'tis this god hath palsied them,'

and though the panic he sends is from within not without, yet the mention is significant. Dionysos, for all his sweetness, is to the end militant, he came not to bring peace upon the earth but a sword, only in late authors his weapons are not those of Ares. On vase-paintings he is not unfrequently depicted doing on his actual armour, but Polyaenus[3], in the little treatise on mythological warriors with which he prefaces his *Strategika*, notes the secret armour of the god, the lance hidden in ivy, the fawn-skin and soft raiment for breastplate, the cymbals and drum for trumpet. To the end the god of the brigand Bessi was Lord of War.

Art tells the same tale, that the Thracian Dionysos succeeded where the equally Thracian Ares failed. Among the archaic seated gods on the frieze of the treasury of Cnidos recently discovered at Delphi[4] Ares has found a place, but a significant one, at the very end, on a seat by himself, as though naïvely to mark the difference. Even on the east frieze of the Parthenon, where all is softened down to a decent theological harmony, there is just a lingering, semi-conscious touch of the same prejudice. Ares is admitted indeed, but he is not quite at home among these easy aristocratic Olympians. He is grouped with no one, he leans his arm on no one's shoulder; even his pose is a little too consciously assured to be quite confident.

It is abundantly clear that the remote Asiatic origin of Dionysos is emphasized to hide a more immediate Thracian provenance. The Greeks knew the god was not home-grown,

[1] Eur. *Bacch.* 1356. [2] *Ib.* 302. [3] Polyaen. *Strat.* I. 1.
[4] This remarkable frieze is in the local museum at Delphi and is now reproduced in the official publication *Fouilles de Delphes*, Pls. vii.—xv.

but he was so great, so good, so all-conquering, that they were forced to accept him. But they could not bear the truth, that he came from their rough north-country kinsmen the Thracians. They need not have been ashamed of these Northerners, who were as well born as and more bravely bred than themselves. Even Herodotus[1] owns that 'the nation of the Thracians is the greatest among men, except at least the Indians.'

Once fairly uprooted from his native Thracian soil, it was easy to plant Dionysos anywhere and everywhere wherever went his worshippers. His homeless splendour grows and grows till by the time of Diodorus his birthplace is completely apocryphal. In Homer, as has been seen (p. 367), Nysa or as it is called Nyseïon, whether it be mountain or plain, is clearly in Thrace, home of Lycurgus son of Dryas. But already in Sophocles[2], in the beautiful fragment preserved by Strabo, wherever it may be, it is a place touched by magic, a silent land which

> 'The horned Iacchus loves for his dear nurse,
> Where no shrill voice doth sound of any bird.'

Euripides[3] never expressly states where he supposes Nysa to be, but the name comes to his lips coupled with the Korykian peaks on Parnassos and the leafy haunts of Olympus, so we may suppose he believed it to be northwards. As the horizon of the Greeks widened, Nysa is pushed further and further away to an ever more remote *Nowhere*. Diodorus[4] with much circumstance settles it in Libya on an almost inaccessible island surrounded by the river Triton. It mattered little so long as it was a far-off happy land.

Convinced as he was of this remote African Nysa and of the great Asiatic campaign of Dionysos, it is curious to note that even Diodorus cannot rid his mind of Thrace. He knows of course the story of the Thracian Lycurgus and mentions incidentally that it was in a place called Nysion that Lycurgus set upon the Maenads and slew them, he knows too of the connection between Dionysos and Orpheus[5] and never doubts but that Orpheus was a Thracian, a matter to be discussed later. Most significant of all, when he

[1] Herod. v. 3.
[2] Soph. frg. 782 ap. Strab. xv. 687.
[3] Eur. *Bacch.* 556.
[4] Diod. III. 4.
[5] *Ib.* 65.

is speaking[1] of the trieteric ceremonies instituted in memory of the Indian expedition, he automatically records that these were celebrated not only by Boeotians and the other Greeks but *by the Thracians*. Thrace is obscured by the glories of Phrygia, Lydia, Phoenicia, Arabia and Libya, but never wholly forgotten.

THE SATYRS.

Dionysos then, whatever his nature, is an immigrant god, a late comer, and he enters Greece from the north, from Thrace. He comes not unattended. With him are always his revel rout of Satyrs and of Maenads. This again marks him out from the rest of the Olympians; Poseidon, Athene, Apollo, Zeus himself has no such accompaniment. As man makes the gods in his own image, it may be well before we examine the nature and functions of Dionysos to observe the characteristics of his attendant worshippers, to determine who and what they are and whence they come.

The Satyrs first—they are (what else should they, could they be?) the *Satrae*[2]; and these Satrae-Satyrs have many traits in common with the more mythological Centaurs. The evidence of the coins of Macedonia is instructive. On the coins of Orreskii[3], a centaur, a horse-man, bears off a woman in his arms. At Lete close at hand, with a coinage closely resembling in style, fabric, weight the money of the Orreskii and other Pangaean tribes, the

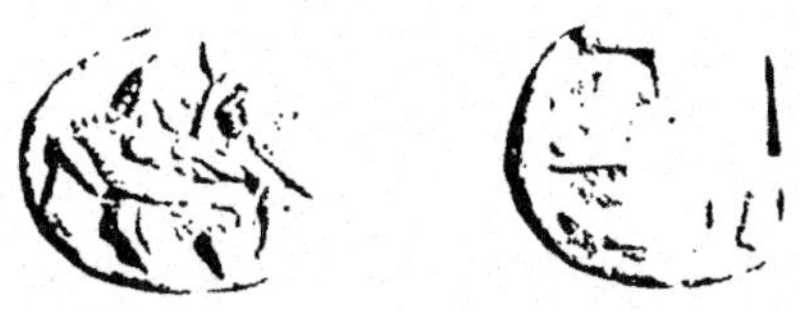

FIG. 115.

type is the same in *content*, though with an instructive difference of form—a naked Satyr or Seilenos with the hooves, ears and tail

[1] Diod. IV. 3.

[2] This was first, I believe, observed by Dr Head (*Hist. Num.* p. 176). In discussing the coinage of Lete in Macedonia he says: 'The coin types all refer to the orgiastic rites practised in the worship of the mountain Bacchus, which originated in the country of the Satrae or Satyrs' (Herod. VII. 111).

[3] Prof. Ridgeway (*Early Age of Greece*, vol. I. p. 343) identifies the Orreskii of the coins with the Orestae of Strabo (§ 434). He thinks the slight difference in form is due to a copyist's mistake of τ for κ.

of a horse seizes a woman round the waist. These coins are of the sixth century B.C. Passing to Thasos, a colony of the Thracians and like it rich in the coinage that came of gold mines, we find the same type. On a series of coins that range from *circ.* 500—411 B.C. we have again the Satyr or Seilenos bearing off the woman. An instance, for clearness' sake one of comparatively late date[1], is given in fig. 115.

This interchange of types, Satyr and Centaur, is evidence about which there can be no mistake. Satyr and Centaur, slightly diverse forms of the horse-man, are in essence one and the same. Nonnus[2] is right: 'the Centaurs are of the blood of the shaggy Satyrs.' It remains to ask—who are the Centaurs?

There are few mythological figures about which more pleasant baseless fancies have been woven; woven irresponsibly, because mythologists are slow to face solid historical fact; woven because, intoxicated by comparative philology, they refuse to seek for the origin of a myth in its historical birthplace. The Centaurs, it used to be said, are Vedic Gandharvas, cloud-demons. Mythology now-a-days has fallen from the clouds, and with it the Centaurs. They next became mountain torrents, the offspring of the cloud that settles on the mountain top. The Centaurs have possession of a wine-cask, the imprisoned forces of the earth's fertility are left in charge of the genius of the mountain. The cask is opened, this is the unlocking of the imprisoned forces at the approach of Herakles, the sun in spring, and this unlocking is the signal for the mad onset of the Centaurs, the wild rush of the torrents. Of the making of such mythology truly there is no end.

Homer[3] knew quite well who the opponents of Peirithoös were, not cloud-demons, not mountain torrents, but real wild *men* (φῆρες), as real as the foes they fought with. He tells of the heroes Dryas, father of Lycurgus, and Peirithoös and Kaineus:

> 'Mightiest were they, and with the mightiest fought,
> *With wild men mountain-haunting.*'

[1] Head, *Hist. Num.* p. 176.

[2] Nonnus, *Dionys.* XIII. 43
καὶ λασίων Σατύρων Κενταυρίδος αἷμα γενέθλης.

[3] *Il.* I. 262
κάρτιστοι μὲν ἔσαν καὶ καρτίστοις ἐμάχοντο
φηρσὶν ὀρεσκῴοισι.

No one has, so far as we know, reduced the mighty Peirithoös, Dryas and Lycurgus to mountain torrents or sun myths. Why are their mighty foes to be less human?

Again in the Catalogue of the Ships[1] we are told how Peirithoös

> 'Took vengeance on the shaggy mountain-men,
> Drave them from Pelion to the Aithikes far.'

In the name of common sense, did Peirithoös expel a storm-cloud or a mountain torrent and force it to leave Pelion and settle elsewhere? The vengeance of Peirithoös is simply the expulsion of one wild tribe by another.

In these passages from the *Iliad* the foes of Peirithoös are simply a tribe of wild men, Pheres. In the *Odyssey*, Homer[2] calls these same foes by the name Kentauri, and implies that they are *non*-human. Speaking of the peril of 'honey-sweet wine' he says:

> 'Thence 'gan the feud 'twixt Centaurs and mankind.'

For the right understanding of this later non-humanity of the Centaurs the development of their art type is of paramount importance.

We are apt to think of the Centaurs exclusively somewhat as they appear on the metopes of the Parthenon, i.e. as splendid horses with the head and trunk of a man. By the middle of the fifth century B.C. in knightly horse-loving Athens the horse form had got the upper hand. In archaic representations the reverse is the case. The Centaurs are in art what they are in reality, *men* with men's legs and feet, but they are shaggy mountain men with some of the qualities and habits of beasts; so to indicate this in a horse-loving country they have the hind-quarters of a horse awkwardly tacked on to their human bodies.

A good example is the vase-painting in fig. 116 from an early black-figured lekythos in the Boston Museum of Fine Arts. Vases of this style cannot be dated later than the beginning of the sixth century B.C. and may be somewhat earlier[3]. The scene

[1] *Il.* II. 711

> ὅτε φῆρας ἐτίσατο λαχνήεντας
> τοὺς δ' ἐκ Πηλίου ὦσε καὶ Αἰθίκεσσι πέλασσεν.

[2] *Od.* XXI. 303 ἐξ οὗ Κενταύροισι καὶ ἀνδράσι νεῖκος ἐτύχθη.

[3] Boston, *Inv.* No. 6508. *American Journal of Archaeology*, 1900, pl. VI. p. 441. The vase belongs to the class usually called 'proto-Corinthian.' Mr J. C. Hoppin prefers to call it 'Argive.'

represented is the fight of Herakles with the Centaurs. To the left is a Centaur holding in his right hand a branch, the primitive

FIG. 116.

weapon of a primitive combatant. He is figured as a complete man with a horse-trunk appended. In the original drawing the horse-trunk is made more obviously an extra appendage from the fact that the human body is painted red and the horse-trunk black. Herakles too is a fighter with rude weapons; he carries his club, which in this case is plainly what its Greek name indicates, a rough hewn trunk or branch or possibly root of a tree. The remainder of the design is not so clear and does not affect the present argument. The man with the sword to the right is probably Iolaos. The object surmounted by the eagles I am quite unable to explain.

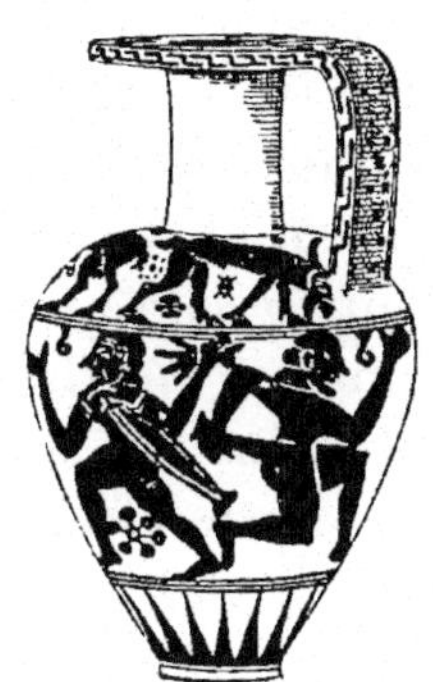

FIG. 117.

The next stage in the development of the Centaur is seen in the archaic gem from the British Museum[1] in fig. 118. Here the noticeable point is that the Centaur, though he has still the body of a man, is beginning to be more of a horse. He has hoofs for feet. He is behaving just like the Satyr on the coin in fig. 115, or the aggressor on the François vase (fig. 114), he is carrying off a

FIG. 118.

[1] *J.H.S.* vol. I. p. 130, fig. 1, published and discussed with other art representations by Mr Sidney Colvin.

woman. It is the last step in the transition to the Centaur of the Parthenon, i.e. the horse with head and trunk of a man. Between Satyr and Centaur the sole difference is this: the Centaur, primarily a wild man, became more and more of a horse, the Satyr resisted the temptation and remained to the end what he was at the beginning, a wild man, with horse adjuncts of ears, tail and occasionally hoofs. Greek art, as has been already seen in discussing the Gorgon, was liberal in its experiments with monster forms, the horse Medusa failed (p. 179), the horse Centaur prevailed[1].

The Parthenon type of the Centaur, the type in which the horse-form is predominant, obtains later in red-figured vase-paintings for all Centaurs save one, the virtuous Cheiron. Cheiron always keeps his human feet and legs and often wears a decent cloak to mark his gentle civilized citizenship. Pausanias[2] when examining the chest of Kypselos at Olympia, a monument dedicated in the seventh century B.C., noted this peculiarity: 'And the Centaur has not all his feet like a horse, but the front feet are the feet of a man.' Pindar[3] does definitely in the case of Cheiron identify φήρ and Κένταυρος, but art kept for Cheiron the more primitive and human type to emphasize his humanity, for he is the trainer of heroes, the utterer of wise saws, the teacher of all gentle arts of music and medicine, he has the kind heart of a man.

The charming little design in fig. 119 is from an oinochoë in

FIG. 119.

[1] It is, it would seem, a mere chance that we have not what might be called a 'fish Centaur.' On an early black-figured vase (*R. Mitt.* II. 1887, Taf. viii.) we have a series of men represented as completely human, not with the body ending in fish tails, but with an extra fish tail added to the complete human body. These are the natural monster-forms of a people dwelling on the sea-coast.

[2] P. v. 19. 9.

[3] Pind. *Pyth.* III. 5.

the British Museum[1]. Though the technique is black-figured the delicate soft style is archaistic rather than archaic and the vase is probably not older than the middle of the fifth century B.C. The good Cheiron is a quaint blend of horse and middle-aged citizen. The tree branch he still carries looks back to the primitive habits he has left far behind, and the little tree in front marks the woodland home. But there is nothing shaggy about his neat decorous figure. Even the dog who used to go hunting with him is now alert to give a courteous welcome to the guest. A father is bringing his child, a little miniature copy of himself, to be reared in the school of Cheiron. Father and son are probably Peleus and Achilles, but the child might be Jason or even Asklepios. It is the good Centaur only who concerns us. How has he of the mountains, fierce and untameable, come to keep a preparatory school for young heroes? The answer to this question is interesting and instructive.

Prof. Ridgeway[2] has shown that in the mythology of the Centaurs we have a reflection of the attitude of mind of the conquerors to the conquered. This attitude is, all the world over, a double one. The conquerors are apt to regard the conquered with mixed feelings, mainly, it is true, with hatred and aversion, but in part with reluctant awe. 'The conquerors respect the conquered as wizards, familiar with the spirits of the land, and employ them for sorcery, sometimes even when relations are peaceable employ them as foster-fathers for their sons, yet they impute to them every evil and bestial characteristic and believe them to take the form of wild beasts. The conquered for their part take refuge in mountain fastnesses and make reprisals in the characteristic fashion of Satyrs and Centaurs by carrying off the women of their conquerors.'

Nonnus is again right, it was jealousy that gave to the Satyrs their horns, their manes, tusks and tails, but not, as Nonnus supposed, the jealousy of Hera, but of primitive conquering man who gives to whatever is hurtful to himself the ugly form that utters and relieves his hate[3]. It should not be hard for us to

[1] *Brit. Mus. Cat.* B 620. *J.H.S.* vol. I. pl. ii. p. 132.

[2] *Early Age of Greece*, vol. I. p. 177.

[3] An analogous case to the Satyrs and Centaurs has already been noted (p. 172), i.e. the Keres, regarded as Telchines, and of monstrous forms; and still more clear is the case of the Kyklopes (p. 190), barbarous monsters yet builders and craftsmen.

realize this impulse: our own devil, with horns and tail and hoofs, died hard and recently.

Most instructive of all as to the real nature of the Centaurs and their close analogy to the Satrai-Satyroi is the story of the opening of the wine cask. Pindar[1] tells how

> 'Then when the wild men knew
> The scent of honeyed wine that tames men's souls,
> Straight from the board they thrust the white milk-bowls
> With hurrying hands, and of their own will flew
> To the horns of silver wrought,
> And drank and were distraught.'

Storm-clouds and mountain torrents, nay even four-footed beasts do not get drunk; the perfume of wine is for the subduing of man alone. The wild things (φῆρες) are all human, 'they thrust with their hands.'

The scene is a favourite one on vases. One of the earliest representations is given in fig. 120 from a skyphos in the Louvre[2]. It dates about the beginning of the sixth century B.C. The scene is the cave of the Centaur Pholos. The great pithos or

FIG. 120.

wine jar is open. Pholos himself has a large wine-cup in his hand. Pholos is sober still, he is a sort of Cheiron, but not so the rest. They are mad with drink and are hustling and fighting in wild confusion. Herakles comes out and tries to restore order. Wine has come for the first time to a primitive population unused to so strong an intoxicant. The result is the same all over the world. A like notion comes out in the popular myth of the wedding feast of Peirithoös; the Centaurs taste wine and fall to fighting and in Satyr fashion seek to ravish the bride. These stories are of paramount importance because they point the analogy between two sets of primitive worshippers of Dionysos, the Centaurs and the Satrai-Satyroi.

[1] Pind. frg. 44.
[2] *J.H.S.* I. Pl. ii.

To these Satrai-Satyroi we must now return. It is now sufficiently clear that, whatever they became to a later imagination, to Homer and Pindar and the vase-painters these horsemen, these attendants of Dionysos, were not fairies, not 'spirits of vegetation,' though from such they may have borrowed many traits, but the representatives of an actual primitive population. They owe their monstrous form, their tails, their horses' ears and hoofs, not to any desire to express 'powers of fertilization' but to the malign imagination of their conquerors. They are not incarnations of a horse-god Dionysos[1]—such a being never existed—they are simply Satrai. It is not of course denied that they ultimately *became* mythological, that is indeed indicated by the gradual change of form. As a rule the Greek imagination tends to anthropomorphism, but here we have a reverse case. By lapse of time and gradual oblivion of the historical facts of conquest, what was originally a primitive man developes in the case of the Centaurs into a mythological horse-demon.

The Satyrs undergo no such change, they remain substantially human. The element of horse varies but is never predominant.

FIG. 121.

The form in which there is most horse is well shown in fig. 121. This picture is from the reverse of the cylix in the Würzburg Museum[2], on which is depicted the feast of Phineus already

[1] The animal form assumed by Dionysos was (as will later be shown, p. 431) that of a bull. Had his own worshippers invented the monstrous Satyrs, they would probably have chosen the bull shape. With the horse, Dionysos, unlike his attendants, has no affinities.

[2] Würzburg, No. 354. *Mon. d. Inst.* x. 8 a. *Myth. and Mon. Ancient Athens*, p. lxxix.

discussed (p. 226). The fact is worth noting that both representations come from a Thracian cycle of mythology. Phineus is a Thracian hero, Dionysos a Thracian god. Dionysos stands in a chariot to which are yoked a lion and a stag. By his side is a woman, probably a goddess, but whether Ariadne or Semele cannot certainly be determined, nor for the present argument does it matter. The god has stopped to water his steeds at a fountain. Satyrs attend him, one is drawing water from the well basin, another clambers on the lion's back. Some maidens have bathed at the fountain, and are resting under a palm tree, one is just struggling back into her clothes. Two prying Satyrs look on with evil in their hearts. They are wild men with shaggy bodies, rough hair, horses' ears and tails, and they have the somewhat exceptional addition of hoofs; the human part of them is closely analogous to the shaggy Centaurs of fig. 120.

The Satyrs are not pleasant to contemplate; they are ugly in form and degraded in habits, and but for a recent theory[1] it might not be needful to emphasize so strongly their nature and functions. This theory, which has gained wide and speedy popularity, maintains that the familiar horse-men of black and red figured vases are not Satyrs at all. The Satyrs, we are told, are goat-men, the horse-men of the vases are Seilenoi. This theory, if true, would cut at the root of our whole argument. To deny the identity of the horse-men with the Satyrs is to deny their identity with the Satrai, i.e. with the primitive population who worshipped Dionysos.

Why then, with the evidence of countless vase-paintings to support us, may we not call the horse-men who accompany Dionysos Satyrs? Because, we are told, *tragedy* is the *goat-song*, the goat-song gave rise to the Satyric drama, hence the Satyrs must be *goat*-demons, hence they cannot be *horse*-demons, hence the *horse*-demons of vases cannot be Satyrs, hence another name must be found for them. On the François-vase (fig. 114) the horse-demons are inscribed Seilenoi, hence let the name Seilenoi be adopted for all *horse*-demons. Be it observed that the whole complex structure rests on the philological assumption that *tragedy* means the goat-song. What *tragedy* really does or

[1] The literature of this controversy is fully given and discussed by Dr K. Wernicke, 'Bockschöre und Satyrdrama,' *Hermes* XXXII. 1897, p. 29.

at least *may* mean will be considered later (p. 420); for the present the point is only raised because I hold to the view now discredited[1] that the familiar throng of idle disreputable vicious *horse*-men who constantly on vases attend Dionysos, who drink and sport and play and harry women, are none other than Hesiod's[2]

> 'race
> Of worthless idle Satyrs.'

That they are also called Seilenoi I do not for a moment deny. In different lands their names were diverse.

The Maenads.

It is refreshing to turn from the dissolute crew of Satyrs to the women-attendants of Dionysos, the Maenads. These Maenads are as real, as actual as the Satyrs; in fact more so, for no poet or painter ever attempted to give them horses' ears and tails. And yet, so persistent is the dislike to commonplace fact, that we are repeatedly told that the Maenads are purely mythological creations and that the Maenad orgies never appear historically in Greece.

It would be a mistake to regard the Maenads as the mere female correlatives of the Satyrs. The Satyrs, it has been seen, are representations of a primitive subject people, but the Maenads do not represent merely the women of the same race. Their name is the corruption of no tribal name, it represents a state of mind and body, it is almost a cultus-epithet. Maenad means of course simply 'mad woman,' and the Maenads are the women-worshippers of Dionysos of whatever race, possessed, maddened or, as the ancients would say, inspired by his spirit.

Maenad is only one, though perhaps the most common, of the many names applied to these worshipping women. In Macedonia Plutarch[3] tells us they were called Mimallones and Klodones, in Greece, Bacchae, Bassarides, Thyiades, Potniades and the like.

[1] Since the above was written I see with great pleasure that Dr Emil Reisch in his article 'Zur Vorgeschichte der attischen Tragödie' (*Festschrift Theodor Gomperz* 1902, p. 459) reasserts the old view that the horse-demons of the vases are Satyrs.

[2] Hes. frg. CXXIX.

[3] Plut. *Vit. Alex.* 2. For many references as to the Maenads I am indebted to the articles by Dr A. Rapp, 'Die Maenade in gr. Cultus in der Kunst und Poesie,' *Rhein. Mus.* 1872, pp. 1 and 562, and for references to the Thyiades to Dr Weniger's *Das Collegium der Thyiaden*.

Some of the titles crystallized into something like proper names, others remained consciously adjectival. At bottom they all express the same idea, women possessed by the spirit of Dionysos.

Plutarch in his charming discourse on Superstition[1] tells how when the dithyrambic poet Timotheos was chanting a hymn to Artemis he addressed the daughter of Zeus thus:

'Maenad, Thyiad, Phoibad, Lyssad.'

The titles may be Englished as Mad One, Rushing One, Inspired One, Raging One. Cinesias the lyric poet, whose own songs were doubtless couched in language less orgiastic, got up and said: 'I wish you may have such a daughter of your own.' The story is instructive on two counts. It shows first that Maenad and Thyiad were at the date of Timotheos so adjectival, so little crystallized into proper names, that they could be applied not merely to the worshippers of Dionysos, but to any orgiastic divinity, and second the passage is clear evidence that educated people, towards the close of the fifth century B.C., were beginning to be at issue with their own theological conceptions. Cultus practices however, and still more cultus epithets, lay far behind educated opinion. It is fortunately possible to prove that the epithet Thyiad certainly and the epithets Phoibad and Maenad probably, were applied to actually existing historical women. The epithet Lyssad, which means 'raging mad,' was not likely to prevail out of poetry. The chorus in the *Bacchae*[2] call themselves 'swift hounds of raging Madness,' but the title was not one that would appeal to respectable matrons.

We begin with the Thyiades. It is at Delphi that we learn most of their nature and worship, Delphi where high on Parnassos Dionysos held his orgies. Thus much even Aeschylus, though he is 'all for Apollo,' cannot deny. To this he makes the priestess[3] in her ceremonial recitation of local powers bear almost reluctant witness:

'You too I salute,
Ye nymphs about Korykia's caverned rock,
Kindly to birds, haunt of divinities.
And Bromios, I forget not, holds the place,
Since first to war he led his Bacchanals,
And scattered Pentheus, like a riven hare.'

[1] Plut. *de Superstit.* x.
Μαινάδα Θυιάδα Φοιβάδα Λυσσάδα.

[2] Eur. *Bacch.* 977.

[3] Aesch. *Eum.* 22.

Aeschylus[1], intent on monotheism, would fain know only the two divinities who were really one, i.e. Zeus and

'Loxias utterer of his father's will,'

the Father and the Son, these and the line of ancient Earth-divinities to whom they were heirs. But religious tradition knew of another immigrant, Dionysos, and Aeschylus cannot wholly ignore him. On the pediments of the great temple were sculptured at one end, Pausanias[2] tells us, Apollo, Artemis, Leto and the Muses, and at the other 'the setting of the sun and Dionysos with his Thyiad women.' The ritual year at Delphi was divided, as will later be seen, between Apollo and Dionysos.

The vase-painting in fig. 122 from a krater in the Hermitage Museum at St Petersburg[3] is a brief epitome of the religious

FIG. 122.

history of Delphi, marking its three strata. In the foreground is the omphalos of Gaia covered with fillets:

'First in my prayer before all other gods
I call on Earth, primaeval prophetess[4],'

Gaia, of whom her successors Themis and Phoebe are but by-forms. Higher up in the picture are other divinities superimposed on this primitive Earth-worship. Apollo and Dionysos clasp hands while about them is a company of Maenads and Satyrs. It is

[1] Aesch. *Eum.* 19.
[2] P. x. 19. 3.
[3] Hermitage, *Cat.* 1807.
[4] Aesch. *Eum.* 1.

perhaps not quite certain which is regarded as the first comer, but the balance is in favour of Dionysos as the sanctuary is already peopled with his worshippers. His dress has about it something of Oriental splendour as compared with the Hellenic simplicity of Apollo. Each carries his characteristic wand, Apollo a branch of bay, Dionysos a thyrsos.

In this vase-painting, which dates about the beginning of the fourth century B.C., all is peace and harmony and clasped hands. The Delphic priesthood were past masters in the art of glossing over awkward passages in the history of theology. Apollo had to fight with the ancient mantic serpent of Gaia and slay it before he could take possession, and we may be very sure that at one time or another there was a struggle between the followers of Apollo and the followers of Dionysos. Over this past which was not for edification a decent veil was drawn[1].

A religion which conquered Delphi practically conquered the whole Greek world. It was probably at Delphi, no less than at Athens, that the work of reforming, modifying, adapting the rude Thracian worship was effected, a process necessary to commend the new cult to the favour of civilized Greece. If then we can establish the historical actuality of the Thyiads at Delphi we need not hesitate to believe that they, or their counterparts, existed in the worship of Dionysos elsewhere.

Pausanias[2] when he was at Panopeus was puzzled to know why Homer spoke of the 'fair dancing grounds' of the place. The reason he says was explained to him by the women whom the Athenians call Thyiades. He adds, that there may be no mistake, 'these Thyiads are Attic women who go every other year with the Delphian women to Parnassos and there hold orgies in honour of Dionysos. On their way they stopped to dance at Panopeus, hence Homer's epithet.' Of course this college of sacred women, these Thyiades, were provided with an eponymous ancestress, Thyia. She *is* mythological. Pausanias[3] says in discussing the origin of Delphi that 'some would have it that there was a man called

[1] See Dr Verrall, *Euripides the Rationalist*, p. 223. The same theological euphemism is observable in the Hymn to Dionysos recently discovered at Delphi and which will be discussed later (p. 416). Here there is a manifest attempt to fuse the worship of Apollo and Dionysos. Dionysos even adopts the characteristic Apolline title of Paean.

[2] P. x. 4. 2.

[3] P. x. 6. 2.

Castalius, an aboriginal, who had a daughter Thyia, and that she was the first priestess of Dionysos and held orgies in honour of the god, and they say that afterwards all women who were mad in honour of Dionysos have been called Thyiades after her' (*ὅσαι τῷ Διονύσῳ μαίνονται Θυιάδας καλεῖσθαί φασιν ὑπὸ ἀνθρώπων*). If 'those who are mad in honour of Dionysos' are not substantially Maenads, it is hard to say what they are. It is fortunate that Pausanias saw and spoke to these women or else his statement[1] that they raved upon the topmost peaks of Parnassos in honour of Dionysos and Apollo would have been explained away as mere mythology.

Plutarch was a priest in his own Chaeronea and intimately acquainted with the ritual of Delphi, and a great friend of his, Klea, was president (*ἀρχηγός*) of the Thyiades at Delphi[2]. He mentions them more than once. In writing to Favorinus[3] on 'the First Principle of Cold' he argues that cold has its own special and proper qualities, density, stability, rigidity, and gives as an instance the cold of a winter's night out on Parnassos. 'You have heard yourself at Delphi how the people who went up Parnassos to bring help to the Thyiades were overtaken by a violent gale with snow, and their coats were frozen as hard as wood, so that when they were stretched out they crumbled and fell to bits.' The crumbling coats sound apocryphal, but the Thyiades out in the cold are quite real. You do not face a mountain snow-storm to succour the mythological 'spirits of the spring.'

It may have been from his friend Klea that Plutarch learnt the pleasant story of the Thyiades and the women of Phocis, which he records in his treatise on the 'Virtues of Women[4].' 'When the tyrants of Phocis had taken Delphi and undertook against them what was known as the Sacred War, the women who attended Dionysos whom they call Thyiades being distraught wandered out

[1] P. x. 32. 7.

[2] *De Is. et Os.* 35. Herodotus (VII. 178) mentions an altar of the winds at Delphi in a place called Thyia, the temenos of the heroine, who may herself have been a raging wind. The same precinct, we know from an inscription found at Delphi, was called Thyiai. See E. Bourguet, *Mélanges Perrot*, p. 25, and for the wind and storm aspect of Thyia see Dr Weniger's interesting discussion in 'Feralis Exercitus,' *Archiv f. Religionswissenschaft*, 1907, pp. 70 and 81. He rightly lays stress on the connection between Thyia and *θύελλα* and *Ὠρείθυια* mountain-wind, bride of Boreas the *tramontana*.

[3] Plut. *de prin. frig.* XVIII.

[4] Plut. *de mul. virt.* XIII.

of their way and came without knowing it to Amphissa. And being very weary and not yet having come to their right mind they flung themselves down in the agora and fell asleep anyhow where they lay. And the women of Amphissa were afraid lest, as their city had made an alliance with the Phocians and the place was full of the soldiery of the tyrants, the Thyiades might suffer some harm. And they left their houses and ran to the agora and made a ring in silence round them and stood there without disturbing them as they slept, and when they woke up they severally tended them and brought them food and finally got leave from their husbands to set them on their way in safety as far as the mountains.' These Thyiades are the historical counterparts of the Maenads of countless vases and bas-reliefs, the same mad revelry, the same utter exhaustion and prostrate sleep. They are the same too as the Bacchant Women of Euripides[1] on the slopes of Cithaeron:

> 'There, beneath the trees
> Sleeping they lay, like wild things flung at ease
> In the forest, one half sinking on a bed
> Of deep pine greenery, one with careless head
> Amid the fallen oak-leaves.'

In the reverence shown by the women of Amphissa we see that though the Thyiades were real women they were something more than real.

This brings us to another of the cultus titles enumerated by Timotheos, 'Phoibad.' Phoibas is the female correlative of Phoebus, a title we are apt to associate exclusively with Apollo. Apollo, Liddell and Scott say, was called Phoebus because of the purity and radiant beauty of youth. The epithet has more to do with purity than with radiant beauty; if with beauty at all it is 'the beauty of holiness.' Plutarch in discussing this title of Apollo makes the following interesting statement[2]: 'The ancients, it seems to me, called everything that was pure and sanctified *phoebic* as the Thessalians still, I believe, say of their priests when they are living in seclusion apart on certain prescribed days that they are living phoebically.' The meaning of this passage, which is practically untranslateable, is clear. The root of the word

[1] Eur. *Bacch.* 683.

[2] Plut. *de Ei apud Delph.* xx. 1 Φοῖβον δὲ δή που τὸ καθαρὸν καὶ ἁγνὸν οἱ παλαιοὶ πᾶν ὠνόμαζον ὡς ἔτι Θεσσαλοὶ τοὺς ἱερέας ἐν ταῖς ἀποφράσιν ἡμέραις αὐτοὺς ἐφ' ἑαυτῶν ἔξω διατρίβοντας οἶμαι φοιβονομεῖσθαι, see *J.H.S.* xix. p. 241.

Phoebus meant 'in a condition of ceremonial purity, holy in a ritual sense,' and as such specially inspired by and under the protection of the god, under a taboo. Apollo probably took over his title of Phoebus from the old order of women divinities to whom he succeeded. Third in order of succession after Gaia and Themis[1]:

> 'Another Titaness, daughter of Earth,
> Phoebe, possessed it, and for birthday gift
> To Phoebus gave it, and he took her name.'

Apollo, we may be sure, did not get his birthday gift without substantial concessions. He took the name of the ancient Phoebe, daughter of earth, nay more he was forced, woman-hater as he always was, to utter his oracles through the mouth of a raving woman-priestess, a Phoibas. Herodotus in the passage already quoted (p. 369) justly observed that in the remote land of the Bessi as at Delphi oracular utterance was by the mouth of a priestess. Kassandra was another of these women-prophetesses of Gaia. She prophesied at the altar-omphalos of Thymbrae, a shrine Apollo took over as he took Delphi[2]. Her frenzy against Apollo is more than the bitterness of maiden betrayed; it is the wrath of the prophetess of the old order discredited, despoiled by the new; she breaks her wand and rends her fillets and cries[3]:

> 'Lo now the seer the seeress hath undone.'

The priestess at Delphi, though in intent a Phoibas, was called the Pythia, but the official name of the priestess Kassandra was, we know, Phoibas[4]:

> 'The Phoibas whom the Phrygians call Kassandra,'

and the title, 'she who is ceremonially pure,' lends a bitter irony to Hecuba's words of shame.

The word Phoibades is never, so far as I know, actually applied to definite Bacchantes, though I believe its use at Delphi to be due to Dionysiac influence, but another epithet *Potniades* points

[1] Aesch. *Eum.* 6.

[2] On a curious 'Tyrrhenian' amphora (Gerhard, *Auserlesene Vasenbilder* 220), the scene of the slaying of Troilos is represented. This took place according to tradition in the Thymbraean sanctuary. The sanctuary is indicated by a regular omphalos covered by a fillet and against it is inscribed βωμός.

[3] Aesch. *Ag.* 1275.

[4] Eur. *Hec.* 827

ἡ Φοιβὰς ἣν καλοῦσι Κασσάνδραν Φρύγες.

the same way. In the *Bacchae*[1], when the messenger returns from Cithaeron, he says to Pentheus:

> 'I have seen the wild white women there, O king,
> Whose fleet limbs darted arrow-like but now
> From Thebes away, and come to tell thee how
> They work strange deeds.'

The 'wild white women' are in a hieratic state of holy madness, hence their miraculous magnetic powers. Photius[2] has a curious note on the verb with which 'Potniades' is connected. He says its normal use was to express a state in which a woman 'suffered something and entreated a goddess' and 'if any one used the word of a man he was inaccurate.' By 'suffering something' he can only mean that she was possessed by the goddess (ἔνθεος or κάτοχος), and he may have the Maenads and kindred worshippers in his mind. Madness could be caused by the Mother of the gods or by Dionysos, in fact by any orgiastic divinity.

It may possibly be objected that Maenads are not the same as either Thyiades or Phoibades. My point is that they *are*. The substantial basis of the conception is the actual women-worshippers of the god; out of these were later created his mythical attendants. Such is the natural order of mythological genesis. Diodorus[3] like most modern mythologists inverts this natural sequence, and his inversion is instructive. In describing the triumphal return of Dionysos from India he says: 'And the Boeotians and the other Greeks and the Thracians in memory of the Indian expedition instituted the biennial sacrifices to Dionysos and they hold that at these intervals the god makes his epiphanies to mortals. Hence in many towns of Greece every alternate year Bacchanalian assemblies of women come together and it is customary for maidens to carry the thyrsos and to revel together to the honour and glory of the god, and the married women worship the god in organized bands and they revel, and in every way celebrate the presence of Dionysos *in imitation of the*

[1] Eur. *Bacch.* 664

> βάκχας ποτνιάδας εἰσιδών, αἳ τῆσδε γῆς
> οἴστροισι λευκὸν κῶλον ἐξηκόντισαν.

Mr Murray's translation preserves the twofold connotation of the word, purity and inspired madness.

[2] Phot. *Bibl.* v. 533b ὅτι τὸ ποτνιᾶσθαι κυριώτερον ἐπὶ γυναῖκας τάττεται φησιν ὅταν κακόν τι πάσχῃ καὶ θήλειαν ἱκετεύῃ θεόν. ποτνιώμενον δὲ ἄνδρα ἄν τις εἴπῃ ἁμαρτάνει.

[3] Diod. IV. 3.

Maenads who from of old, it was said, constantly attended the god.' Diodorus is an excellent instance of mistaken mythologizing. Mythology invents a reason for a fact, does not base a fact on a fancy.

It is not denied for a moment that the Maenads *became* mythical. When Sophocles sings[1]:

'Footless, sacred, shadowy thicket, where a myriad berries grow,
Where no heat of the sun may enter, neither wind of the winter blow,
Where the Reveller Dionysos with his nursing nymphs will go,'

we are not in this world, and his nursing nymphs are 'goddesses'; but they are goddesses fashioned here as always in the image of man who made them.

The difficulty and the discrepancy of opinion as to the reality of the Maenads are due mainly to a misunderstanding about words. Maenad is to us a proper name, a fixed and crystallized personality; so is Thyiad, but in the beginning it was not so. Maenad is the Mad One, Thyiad the Rushing Distraught One or something of that kind, anyhow an adjectival epithet. Mad One, Distraught One, Pure One are simply ways of describing a woman under the influence of a god, of Dionysos. Thyiad and Phoibad obtained as cultus names, Maenad tended to go over to mythology. Perhaps naturally so; when a people becomes highly civilized madness is apt not to seem, save to poets and philosophers, the divine thing it really is, so they tend to drop the mad epithet and the colourless Thyiad becomes more and more a proper name.

Still Maenad, as a name of actual priestly women, was not wholly lost. An inscription[2] of the date of Hadrian, found in Magnesia and now in the Tschinli Kiosk at Constantinople, gives curious evidence. This inscription recounts a little miracle-story. A plane tree was shattered by a storm, inside it was found an image of Dionysos[3]. Seers were promptly sent to Delphi to ask what was to be done. The answer was, as might be expected, the Magnesians had neglected to build 'fair wrought temples' to Dionysos; they must repair their fault. To do this properly they

[1] *Oed. Col.* 670, trans. by Mr D. S. MacColl.

[2] First published by Kondolleon, *Ath. Mitt.* xv. (1890) p. 330, discussed by E. Maass, *Hermes* xxvi. (1891) p. 178, and S. Reinach, *Rev. des Études grecques* iii. (1890) p. 349, and O. Kern, *Beiträge zur Geschichte der griechischen Philosophie und Religion*, Berlin 1895.

[3] ἀφείδρυμα Διονύσου.

must send to Thebes and thence obtain three Maenads of the family of Kadmean Ino[1]. These would give to the Magnesians orgies and right customs. They went to Thebes and brought back three 'Maenads' whose names are given, Kosko, Baubo and Thettale; and they came and founded three thiasoi or sacred guilds in three parts of the city. The inscription is of course late; Baubo[2] and Kosko are probably Orphic, but the main issue is clear: in the time of Hadrian at least three actual women of a particular family were called 'Maenads.'

We are so possessed by a set of conceptions based on Periclean Athens, by ideas of law and order and reason and limit, that we are apt to dismiss as 'mythological' whatever does not fit into our stereotyped picture. The husbands and brothers of the women of historical days would not, we are told, have allowed their women to rave upon the mountains; it is unthinkable taken in conjunction with the strict oriental seclusion of the Periclean woman. That any woman might at any moment assume the liberty of a Maenad is certainly unlikely, but much is borne even by husbands and brothers when sanctioned by religious tradition. The men even of Macedonia, where manners were doubtless ruder, did not *like* the practice of Bacchic orgies. Bacchus came emphatically not to bring peace. Plutarch[3] conjectures that these Bacchic orgies had much to do with the strained relations between the father and mother of Alexander the Great. A snake had been seen lying by the side of Olympias and Philip feared she was practising enchantments, or worse, that the snake was the vehicle of a god. Another and probably the right explanation of the presence of the snake was, as Plutarch tells us, that 'all the women of that country had been from ancient days under the dominion of Orphic rites and Dionysiac orgies, and that they were called Klodones and Mimallones because in many respects they imitated the Edonian and Thracian women round about Haemus, from whom the Greek word *θρησκεύειν* seems to come, a word which is applied to excessive and overdone ceremonials. Now Olympias was more

[1] *ὄφρα λάβητε*
Μαινάδας αἳ γενεῆς Εἰνοῦς ἀπὸ Καδμηείης.
αἳ δ' ὑμῖν δώσουσι καὶ ὄργια καὶ νόμιμ' ἐσθλά.

[2] For the very primitive significance of Baubo see Diels, *Arcana Cerealia* in Miscellania di Archeologia 1907.

[3] Plut. *Vit. Alex.* 2.

zealous than all the rest and carried out these rites of possession and ecstasy in very barbarous fashion and introduced huge tame serpents into the Bacchic assemblies, and these kept creeping out of the ivy and the mystic likna and twining themselves round the thyrsoi of the women and their garlands, and *frightening the men out of their senses.*'

However much the Macedonian men disliked these orgies, they were clearly too frightened to put a stop to them. The women were possessed, magical, and dangerous to handle. Scenes such

Fig. 123.

as those described by Plutarch as actually taking place in Macedonia are abundantly figured on vases. The beautiful raging Maenad in fig. 123 from the centre of a cylix with white ground at Munich[1] is a fine example. She wears the typical Maenad garb, the fawn-skin over her regular drapery; she carries the thyrsos, she carries in fact the whole gear (*σκευή*) of Dionysos. When Pentheus would counterfeit a Bacchant he is attired just so; he wears the long trailing chiton and over it the dappled fawn-skin, his hair flows loose, in his hand is the thyrsos. For snood (*μίτρα*) in her hair the Maenad has twined a great snake. Another Maenad[2] is shown in fig. 124. She is characterized only

FIG. 124.

by the two snakes she holds in her hand. But for her long full drapery she might be an Erinys.

The snakes emerging from the sacred cistae are illustrated by the class of coins[3] known as cistophoroi, a specimen of which

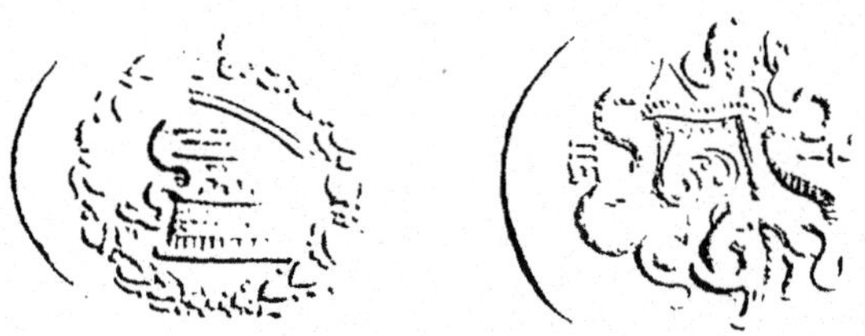

FIG. 125.

is reproduced in fig. 125. These coins, of which the type is uniform, originated, according to Dr Imhoof, in Ephesus a little

[1] Munich. Jahn, *Cat.* 382. *Greek Vase Paintings*, J. E. Harrison and D. S. MacColl, pl. xv. Baumeister, *Ab.* 928.
[2] *J.H.S.* xix. p. 220, fig. 6.
[3] Head, *Hist. Num.* p. 461, fig. 287.

before B.C. 200, and spread through all the dominions of Attalos the First. They illustrate a phase of Dionysos worship in Asia Minor closely akin to that of Macedonia.

Macedonia is not Athens, but the reforms of Epimenides allow us to divine that Athenian brothers and husbands also had their difficulties. Plutarch[1] again is our informant. Athens was beset by superstitious fears and strange appearances. They sent to Crete for Epimenides, a man beloved of the gods and skilled in the technicalities of religion, especially as regards enthusiastic and mystic rites. He and Solon made friends and the gist of his religious reforms was this: 'he simplified their religious rites, and made the ceremonies of mourning milder, introducing certain forms of sacrifice into their funeral solemnities and abolishing the cruel and barbarous elements to which the women were addicted. But most important of all, by lustrations and expiations and the foundings of worships he hallowed and consecrated the city and made it subserve justice and be more inclined to unity.' The passage is certainly not as explicit as could be wished, but the words used—*κατοργιάσας* and *καθοσιώσας*—and the fact that Epimenides was an expert in *ecstatic* rites, that they gave him the name of the new Koures, the special attention paid to the rites of women, though they are mentioned in relation to funerals, make it fairly clear that some of the barbarous excesses were connected with Bacchic orgies. This becomes more probable when we remember that many of Solon's own enactments were directed against the excesses of women. 'He regulated,' Plutarch[2] tells us, 'the outgoings of women, their funeral lamentations and their festivals, forbidding by law all disorder and excess.' Among these dreary regulations comes the characteristically modern touch that they are not to go out at night 'except in a carriage and with a light before them.' It was the going out at night that Pentheus could not bear[3]. When he would know what were the rites of Dionysos he asks the god:

> '*P.* How is this worship held, by night or day?
> *D.* Most oft by night, 'tis a majestic thing
> The Darkness.
> *P.* Ha, with women worshipping?
> 'Tis craft and rottenness.'

[1] Plut. *Vit. Sol.* XII. Epimenides is as it were a historical Orpheus. Coming from Crete, he, like Orpheus (p. 459), modified Dionysiac ritual.

[2] Plut. *Vit. Sol.* XXI.

[3] Eur. *Bacch.* 485.

Dionysos Liknites.

The Maenads then are the frenzied sanctified women who are devoted to the worship of Dionysos. But they are something more; they tend the god as well as suffer his inspiration. When first we catch sight of them in Homer (p. 367) they are his 'nurses' (*τίθηναι*). One of the lost plays of Aeschylus bore the title 'Rearer of Dionysos,' and Sophocles[1], here as so often inspired by Homer, makes his chorus sing:

> 'There the reveller Dionysos with his nursing nymphs doth go.'

In Homer and Aeschylus and Sophocles, though Dionysos has his goddess nurses, he is himself no nursling. A child no longer, he revels with them as coevals. Mythology has half forgotten the ritual from which it sprang. Fortunately Plutarch[2] has left us an account, inadequate but still significant, of the actual ritual of the Thyiades[3], and from it we learn that they worshipped and tended no full-grown god, but a baby in his cradle.

Plutarch is speaking of the identity of Osiris and Dionysos, both being embodiments according to him of the 'moist principle.' 'You, Klea,' he says, 'if any one, should know that Osiris is the same as Dionysos, you who are leader of the Thyiades at Delphi and were initiated by your father and mother into the rites of Osiris.' After pointing out various analogies, he adds: 'For the Egyptians, as has been said, point out tombs of Osiris in many places, and the Delphians hold that they possess the relics of Dionysos buried by the side of their oracular shrine; the Hosioi make a secret sacrifice in the sacred precinct of Apollo *when the Thyiades raise up Liknites.*' It will later (p. 482) be seen that Dionysos was represented in ritual as slain and dismembered; from this passage it is clear that there was some sort of resurrection of the god, a new birth as a little child. Liknites can be none other than the babe in the cradle. Hesychius in commenting on the word Liknites says: 'a title of Dionysos from the cradle in which they put children to sleep.' In primitive agricultural days,

[1] *Oed. Col.* 674, see p. 368.

[2] *De Isid. et Os.* XXXV. *καὶ θύουσιν οἱ Ὅσιοι θυσίαν ἀπόρρητον ἐν τῷ ἱερῷ τοῦ Ἀπόλλωνος ὅταν αἱ Θυιάδες ἐγείρωσι τὸν Λικνίτην.*

[3] The verb *θυίω* is used of the excited beating of the heart under strong emotion, e.g. Ap. Rhod. III. 754

> *πυκνὰ δέ οἱ κραδίη στηθέων ἔντοσθεν ἔθυιεν.*

the *liknon*, a shovel-shaped basket, served three purposes: it was a 'fan' with which to winnow grain, it was a basket to hold grain or fruit or sacred objects, it was a cradle for a baby. The various forms of *likna* and the beautiful mysticism that gathered round the cradle and the winnowing fan, will be considered when Orphic ceremonial is discussed (p. 517). For the present it is enough to note that the ceremony of raising or waking Liknites marks clearly the worship of a child-god.

The worship by women of Liknites, of the child in the cradle, reflects a primitive stage of society, a time when the main realized function of woman was motherhood and the more civilized, less elemental, function of wedded wife was scarcely adventured. It is at once a cardinal point and a primary note in the mythology of Dionysos that he is *the son of his mother*. The religion of the Mother and the Daughter is already familiar (p. 271); it reflected, as has been seen, primarily not so much the relations of mother and daughter as the two stages of woman's life, woman as maid, and woman as mother. If we are to have the relation of parent and child mirrored in mythology, assuredly the closest relation is not that even of mother and daughter but of mother and son. Father and son, Zeus and Apollo, reflect a still further advance in civilization.

Before leaving the Thyiades, it is important to note that they had a cult not only of Liknites, the child in the cradle, but of the mother who bore him, Semele, and this too at Delphi. Plutarch is again our authority. In his *Greek Questions*[1], he treats of the three great enneateric festivals of Delphi, the Stepterion, Heroïs and Charila. Of the Heroïs he says: 'Its inner meaning is for the most part mystical as is known to the Thyiades, but from the rites that are openly performed one may conjecture that it is a Return of Semele.' Plutarch's conjecture was undoubtedly right. The Heroïs was a resurrection festival, with rites of Return and Uprising, such as have been already (p. 277) fully discussed in relation to Demeter and Kore.

The relation of Dionysos to his father Zeus was slight and artificial. He is, as aforesaid, essentially the son of his mother,

[1] Plut. *Q. Gr.* XII. τῆς δὲ Ἡρωΐδος τὰ πλεῖστα μυστικὸν ἔχει λόγον ὃν ἴσασιν αἱ Θυιάδες, ἐκ δὲ τῶν δρωμένων φανερῶς Σεμέλης ἄν τις ἀναγωγὴν εἰκάσειε.

'child of Semele[1].' The meaning of the fatherhood of Zeus and the strange hieratic legend of the double birth will be discussed later: the question must first be asked 'Who is Semele?'

Dionysos Son of Semele.

Dionysos, we have seen, was a Thracian; if his mother can be shown to be Thracian too, each will confirm the other. The certain remains of the Phrygio-Thracian tongue are but scanty, happily however they suffice for the certain interpretation of the name Semele.

Prof. Ramsay in his Phrygian explorations[2] has brought to light a number of inscriptions from tombs which run after this fashion:

δη διως ζεμελω.
με ζεμελω κε δεος.
δεος κε ζεμ(ελω).
με ζεμελω.

These various permutations and combinations are followed by a curse formulary as follows: *ιος σεμουν κνουμανει κακουν αδδακει ετιττετικμενος ειτου*, which is Phrygian for ὃς *τούτῳ* (*τῷ*) *μνήματι κακὸν ἐπέθηκε ὑποκατάρατος ἔστω*, 'Cursed be he that does any damage to this tomb.' The inscriptions, which all date after the Christian era, belong to a time when the well-to-do classes spoke and wrote Greek, but, in the case of a curse, it was well to couch your inscription in a tongue understanded of the people. *με* and *δη* would appear to be affirmative curse particles; *με* has for cognates *μά*, *μήν* and possibly *μέν*, as well as the Latin *me* in *me Hercle*, *me Dius Fidius*. *δη* is cognate not only to the ordinary affirmative Greek *δή* but also to the *de* of the Latin oath *e-de-pol*. The divinities sworn by remain to be considered. *δη διως* can scarcely be other than *νὴ Δία*, 'by Zeus.' *ζεμελω* at once brings

[1] Eur. *Bacch.* 375 τὸν Βρόμιον
τὸν Σεμέλας.
v. 580 ὁ Σεμέλας,
ὁ Διὸς παῖς.
v. 278 ὁ Σεμέλης γόνος.

[2] Ramsay, *Journal of Asiatic Soc.* xv. 1883, pp. 120 ff., and Latischew, *Für vergleichende Sprachforschung*, vol. XXVIII. pp. 381 ff. The inscriptions are explained and discussed in relation to Semele by Dr Paul Kretschmer, 'Semele und Dionysos,' in *Aus der Anomia* (Berlin 1890), and to him I owe entirely the view adopted in the text.

Semele to mind. But who and what is Semele? Phrygian and Thracian are now admitted to belong to the Indo-European family of languages, and a conjoint consonantal characteristic of the two is that they replace the palatals *g* and *gh* (Greek γ and χ) by a spirant; this spirant the Greeks rendered indifferently by their nearest equivalents ζ and σ. The Phrygian ζεμελω is the Greek γῆ (earth) appearing in nasalized form as χαμαί, χθαμαλός, χθών, in Latin as *humus, humilis, homo,* in Sclavonic, to quote only a familiar and convincing instance, in Nova *Zembla*, 'new earth.' The Greek form γῆ looks remote but we have also its nasalized form Χαμύνη (Lit. *Zemyna*). At Elis Pausanias[1] saw, opposite the place where the umpires stood, an altar of white marble. On that altar sat the priestess of Demeter Chamyne, to behold the Olympic games. 'She of the Ground' was probably at Olympia long before the coming of Zeus.

Semele, mother of Dionysos, is the Earth. This the vase-painter knew well. In dealing with the Earth-Mother (p. 276) a number of vase-paintings have been considered, in which Kore, the

FIG. 126.

earth in her young form as maiden, has been seen represented as rising out of the actual earth she really is. To these as counterpart must now be added the curious vase-painting in fig. 126, now

[1] P. vi. 20. 9.

in the Hope collection at Deep-dene[1]. Out of the earth-mound rises a youthful figure, a male Kore; he holds a sceptre as king and is welcomed, or rather heralded, by a little winged Nike. His worshippers await him: a Maenad with thyrsos and tray of offerings to the right, a Satyr also with thyrsos to the left. The rising figure can be none other than the child of Semele, the earth-Dionysos himself. It is rash, I think, to give the rising god any special name, to call him Iacchos or Brimos; all we can be sure that the vase-painter meant was that the god is earth-born.

The same notion comes clearly out in the second design in fig. 127 from a kalpis in the British Museum[2]. Here the familiar type[3] of the birth of Erichthonios from the earth is taken over and adapted to the birth of Dionysos. The vase-painter thus in

FIG. 127.

instructive fashion assimilates the immigrant stranger to his own heroic mythology. Ge is rising from the earth; she presents, not Erichthonios, but another sacred child to a foster-mother, Athene. It is certainly probable that the child is Dionysos, not Erichthonios,

[1] I regret to be obliged to reproduce the publication of Tischbein (*Greek Vases* I. 39). As regards style it is obviously inadequate. The vase has been examined by Mr Cecil Smith (*Jahrbuch d. Inst.* 1891, p. 120, note 17) and the reproduction of Tischbein is pronounced by him to be as regards subject-matter substantially correct.

[2] B.M. *Cat.* vol. III. E 182, cf. C. Robert, *Archäologische Märchen* 161. Dr Robert explains the vase as the birth of Dionysos from the well-nymph Dirce, but vase-paintings offer no analogy to the representation of a well-nymph as a figure rising from the ground.

[3] Cf. *Myth. and Mon. Anc. Athens*, p. xxxix.

for the maiden who in such familiar fashion leans on the shoulder of Zeus is inscribed 'Wine-bloom,' Oinanthe. Zeus himself with his thunderbolt is a reminiscence of the thunder-smitten birth. On authentic representations of the birth of Erichthonios, Hephaistos, his putative father, is present, not Zeus. As in fig. 126 the new-born hero is welcomed by a winged Victory, who brings a taenia to crown him. It is clear that the vase-painter wants to make the new-born child as Athenian as possible, almost to substitute him for the autochthonous Erichthonios; he is welcomed and received not by Satyrs and Maenads, his own worshippers and kinsfolk, but by his new relations, Athene and Athenian Victory.

The third vase-painting in fig. 128 from a cylix in the Museum at Naples[1] is a much earlier piece of work. It dates about the

FIG. 128.

middle of the sixth century, and is free from any specifically Athenian influence. Out of the ground rise two great busts inscribed severally Διόνυσος (Dionysos) and Σεμέλη (Semele). Even without the inscriptions there could be no doubt as to Dionysos. The vase-painter in his primitive eager fashion makes assurance doubly sure. The god holds aloft with pardonable pride his characteristic high-handled wine-cup, the kantharos; behind him and Semele a great vine is growing, up one side of which a Satyr is clambering. Dionysos is not Liknites here; he

[1] Heydemann, *Cat. St Angelo Coll.* 172. Gerhard, *Ges. Abh.* Taf. LXVIII. The authenticity of the inscriptions has been questioned. I examined them recently in the Naples Museum and see no ground for suspicion.

is in the full bloom of his youth, not elderly though bearded, coeval with fair Semele.

At Thebes the legend of the birth of Dionysos took on a special form. He is not only son of Semele, of Earth[1], but son of Semele as Keraunia, Earth the thunder-smitten.

This aspect of Semele as Keraunia is familiar in classical literature. Sophocles[2] has 'thou and thy mother, she of the thunder.' To Euripides[3] in the *Hippolytus* Semele thunder-smitten is the stuff of which is made perhaps the most splendid poetry he ever wrote:

> 'O mouth of Dirce, O god-built wall
> That Dirce's wells run under;
> Ye know the Cyprian's fleet foot-fall,
> Ye saw the heavens round her flare
> When she lulled to her sleep that Mother fair
> Of Twy-born Bacchus and crowned her there
> The Bride of the bladed thunder:
> For her breath is on all that hath life, and she floats in the air
> Bee-like, death-like, a wonder.'

And this splendid poetry is based, it seems, not merely on mythology but on a local cult, a cult of thunder and a place thunder-smitten. The prologue[4] of the *Bacchae*, spoken by Dionysos, opens thus, with a description of the sanctuary of Semele:

> 'Behold god's son is come unto this land
> Of Thebes, even I, Dionysos, whom the brand
> Of heaven's hot splendour lit to life, when she
> Who bore me, Cadmus' daughter Semele,
> Died here. So, changed in shape from god to man,
> I walk again by Dirce's stream, and scan
> Ismenus' shore. There by the castle side
> I see her place, the Tomb of the Lightning's Bride,
> The wreck of smouldering chambers and the great
> Faint wreaths of fire undying, as the hate
> Dies not that Hera held for Semele.
> Ay Cadmus hath done well: in purity
> He keeps this place apart, inviolate
> His daughter's sanctuary, and I have set
> My green and clustered vines to robe it round.'

Nor again is this merely the effective scenic setting of a play.

[1] An inscription of the 5th century B.C. recently discovered shows that at Thebes there was an actual sanctuary of Earth. It runs as follows: *ἰαρὸν Γᾶς Μακαίρας Τελεσσφόρο*. The titles *μάκαιρα* and *τελεσφόρος* are applied to Ge in the Orphic Hymn (xxvi. 1 and 10). See *Bull. de Corr. Hell.* 1901, p. 363.

[2] Soph. *Ant.* 1139.

[3] Eur. *Hipp.* 555.

[4] Eur. *Bacch.* 1.

Any place that was struck by lightning was regarded as specially sacred[1]. If the place was the tomb of a local heroine there was a double sanctity. Such a tomb there unquestionably was at Thebes. Pausanias[2] asserts the fact though he does not state that he actually saw the tomb: 'There are also the ruins of the house of Lycus and Semele's monument.' Primarily of course the sanctity of a thunder-smitten place was more of the nature of a *taboo* than of consecration in our sense of the word. It would lend itself easily to a legend of judgment on a heroine or of a divine Epiphany. The figure of the great Earth-goddess Semele faded before the splendour of Zeus.

Possibly the cult of these thunder-smitten places may serve to answer a question asked by Plutarch[3]—'Who among the Boeotians are the Psoloeis (Smoky Ones) and who the Aioleiai?' Plutarch tells a confused story of the daughters of Minyas who went mad with desire for human flesh and slew the child of one of them. The dreadful deed was commemorated by a 'flight ceremony' that formed part of the Agrionia, in which the priest of Dionysos pursued with a sword the women of the clan in which the men were called Psoloeis and the women Aioleiai, and if he caught one, had leave to slay her. Zoilos, a priest in the time of Plutarch, actually availed himself of the permission. Bad luck followed. Zoilos sickened and died, and the priesthood ceased to be hereditary and became elective. The story is very obscure, but Lydus[4] in discussing thunderbolts says there are two kinds, the one is swift and rarefied (μανός) and fiery and is called ἀργής, the other is slow and smoky and is called ψολόεις. The family of the Smoky Ones *may* have been worshippers of the smoky kind of thunderbolt.

Be this as it may, the cult and mythology of Dionysos are haunted by reminiscences of lightning and sudden fiery apparitions that are probably not merely poetical but primitive. In the *Bacchae* not only is Dionysos fire-born and attended by the light of torches, but his Epiphany is marked by a manifest thunder-

[1] Such places were, if we may trust the *Etymologicon Magnum*, called ἐνηλύσια, which at least in popular etymology was believed to mean 'Places of Advent.' They are thus defined: ἐνηλύσια λέγεται εἰς ἃ κεραυνὸς εἰσβέβηκεν ἃ καὶ ἀνατίθεται Διὶ καταιβάτῃ καὶ λέγεται ἄδυτα καὶ ἄβατα.

[2] P. IX. 16. 7.

[3] Plut. *Q. Gr.* XXXVIII.

[4] Lydus, *de mens.* IV. 96.

storm, a storm that takes the shape of a resurgence of the flame on Semele's tomb. A voice is heard[1]:

'Unveil the Lightning's Eye, arouse
The fire that sleeps, against this house.'

And the chorus make answer:

'Ah saw ye, marked ye there the flame
From Semele's enhallowed sod
Awaken'd? Yea the Death that came
Ablaze from heaven of old—the same
Hot splendour of the shaft of God.'

And again on Cithaeron[2] there is not only the mysterious voice and the awful silence, but the manifestation of the pillar of fire:

'So spake he and there came
'Twixt earth and sky a pillar of high flame:
And silence took the air, and no leaf stirred
In all the forest dell. Thou hadst not heard
In that vast silence any wild thing's cry.'

The Epiphany by fire is of course common to many theologies; we have the Burning Bush and the Pentecostal tongues, but it is interesting to find that, in far-away Thrace, the favour of Dionysos was made manifest by a great light. The evidence comes from Aristotle[3]. He says: 'There is in the same place (i.e. in Krastonia near the district of the Bisaltae) a large and beautiful sanctuary of Dionysos, in which it is reported that at the time of the festival and the sacrifice, if the god intends to send a good season, *a great blaze of fire appears*, and this is seen by all those whose business is in the temenos; but if the god intends a barren season, the light does not make its appearance, but there is darkness on the place as on other nights.' It would be vain to ask what natural fact, whether of summer lightning or burning bush, caused the belief; the essential point is the primitive Epiphany by fire, an Epiphany not vengeful but beneficent.

Dionysos is then the son of an ancient Thracian Earth-goddess, Semele, and she is Keraunia, thunder-smitten, in some sense the bride, it would seem, of our old sky and thunder-god[4], a sort of Ouranos later effaced by the splendour of the Hellenic Zeus. If

[1] Eur. *Bacch.* 594.
[2] Eur. *Bacch.* 1082.
[3] Aristot. περὶ θαυμ. 122.
[4] See H. Usener, 'Keraunos,' *Rhein. Mus.* 1905, p. 1, and for Ζεὺς βροντῶν καὶ Ἀστράπτων see Kretschmer, *Einleitung in die Gesch. d. gr. Sprache*, p. 241.

some such old nature-god existed as is probable in the far background of primitive mythology, the affiliation of Zeus and Dionysos would be an easy matter.

In this connection it is interesting to note that not only Zeus himself was associated with the thunder and the lightning, but also the ancient 'Mother of the Gods.' Pindar[1], who all through the third Pythian has in his mind the sore sickness of Hieron, not only bethinks him of Cheiron the primitive Healer but also sings:

> 'I would pray to the Mother to loose her ban,
> The holy goddess, to whom and to Pan
> Before my gate, all night long,
> The maids do worship with dance and song.'

The scholiast tells us how it came that Pindar prayed to the Mother for healing. One day while Pindar was teaching a pupil on a mountain, possibly Cithaeron itself, 'there was heard a great noise, and a flame of lightning was seen descending, and Pindar saw that a stone image of the Mother had come down at their feet, and the oracle ordained that he should set up a shrine to the Mother.' The story is transparent—a thunderstorm, lightning and a fallen aerolite, the symbol of the Mother, surely of Keraunia. And the Mother, the scholiast further tells us, 'had power to purify from madness.' She had power to loose as well as to bind. In this she was like her son Dionysos. The magical power for purification of aerolites and indeed of almost any strange black stone is attested by many instances[2]. Orestes[3] was purified at Trozen from his madness, mother-sent, by a sacred stone. Most curious of all, Porphyry[4] tells us that Pythagoras when he was in Crete met one of the Idaean Dactyls, worshippers of the Mother, and was by him purified with a thunderbolt.

With a mother thunder-smitten, it was not hard for Dionysos to become adopted child of the Hellenic Zeus, God of the Thunderbolt. Theologians were ready with the myth of the double birth. Semele fell into partial discredit, obscured by the splendour of the Father. Matriarchy pales before the new

[1] Pind. *Pyth.* III. 77 and schol. ad loc.
[2] I have collected and discussed some instances of these in my article 'Delphika,' *J.H.S.* XIX. 1899, p. 238.
[3] P. VIII. 31. 4, and at Gythium, P. III. 22. 1.
[4] Porph. *Vit. Pyth.* XVII.

order of patriarchy, and from henceforth the name Dionysos[1], 'son of Zeus,' is supreme.

DIONYSOS SON OF ZEUS.

The fatherhood of Zeus is charmingly set forth by the lovely little vase-fragment in fig. 129 from a red-figured cylix[2], found in the excavations on the Acropolis and now in the National Museum at Athens. Zeus with his sceptre holds the infant Dithyramb and displays him proudly to the other Olympians. Semele is ignored, perhaps half forgotten. Dionysos in the new order is 'all for the father.'

FIG. 129.

The all-important question is forced upon us—why did Zeus adopt him? Dionysos is the child of the Earth-goddess, but why was this particular earth-child adopted? Why did his worship spread everywhere with irresistible might, overshadowing at the end even the cult of his adopted father? Kore too is daughter of Earth, she too in awkward fashion was half affiliated to Zeus, yet he never takes her in his arms and her cult though wide-spread has no militant missionary aspect.

Zeus holds the infant Dionysos in his arms, and Dionysos

[1] Dr Kretschmer, (*Aus der Anomia*, p. 23) has suggested that the second half of the name Dionysos (-νυσος) means 'son' or 'young man,' cf. *nŭrus*, νῠός, Sk. *snushas*, O.H.G. *schnur*. On the fragment of an early black-figured vase signed by Sophilos, three nymphs appear with the inscription Νυσαι which seems equivalent to κόραι or νύμφαι or παρθένοι (*A. Mitt.* XIV. Taf. i.). Kretschmer's derivation involves not only the difficulty as to quantity but also the loss of initial *s* before *n* in Thracian. Aristophanes seems to have vaguely felt or imagined some connection between the last half of the word and Nysa, the birthplace of the god, in his Νυσήιον Διὸς Διόνυσον (*Ran.* 215) echoed by Apollonius Rhodius in Διὸς Νυσήιον υἷα (*Arg.* IV. 1132). Dionysos then is practically either Διόσκουρος, a term of wide application, or possibly child of the tribe of Dioi (see p. 371). Dr Kretschmer further points out that the fluctuation in inscriptions between ι and ε (Δεόνυσος and Διόνυσος) is best accounted for by Thracian origin, as the Thracians appear to have had a vowel which was not exactly either, and was indifferently rendered in Greek by both. Probably then, though not certainly, Dionysos brought his name with him from the North. Kretschmer, *Einleitung*, p. 241.

[2] *Jahrbuch des Inst.* 1891, Taf. I. Sufficient fragments of the vase remain to show that the scene represented was the presentation of Dionysos to the Olympians.

holds in his the secret of his strength, the vine with its great bunch of grapes. But for that bunch of grapes Zeus would never have troubled to adopt him. To the popular mind Dionysos was always Lord of the Vine, as Athene was Lady of the Olive. It is by the guerdon of the grape that his Bacchants appeal to Dirce[1]:

'By his own joy I vow,
By the grape upon the bough.'

It is by his great gift of Wine to sorrowful man that his kingdom is established upon earth[2]:

'A god of Heaven is He,
And born in majesty,
Yet hath he mirth in the joy of the Earth
And he loveth constantly
Her who brings increase,
The Feeder of children, Peace.

No grudge hath He of the great,
No scorn of the mean estate,
But to all that liveth, his Wine he giveth,
Griefless, immaculate.
Only on them that spurn
Joy may his anger burn.'

It is the usual mythological inversion, he of the earth is translated to heaven that thence he may descend.

Dionysos as god of the grape is so familiar that the idea needs no emphasis. It is more important to note that the vine as the origin of his worship presents certain difficulties.

It has clearly been seen that Dionysos was a Northerner, a Thracian. Wine is not the characteristic drink of the North. Is it likely that wine, a drink characteristic to this day of the South, is the primitive essence of the worship of a god coming into Greece from the North?

The answer to this difficulty is an interesting one. The main distinguishing factor of the religion of Dionysos is always the cult of an intoxicant, but wine is not the only intoxicant, nor in the North the most primitive. Evidence is not wanting that the cult of the vine-god was superimposed on, affiliated to, in part developed out of, a cult that had for its essence the worship of an early and northern intoxicant, cereal not vinous.

To this conclusion I have been led by the consideration of the cultus titles of the god.

[1] Eur. *Bacch.* 535. [2] Eur. *Bacch.* 416.

BROMIOS. BRAITES. SABAZIOS.

Dionysos is a god of many names; he is Bacchos, Baccheus, Iacchos, Bassareus, Bromios, Euios, Sabazios, Zagreus, Thyoneus, Lenaios, Eleuthereus, and the list by no means exhausts his titles. A large number of these names are like Lenaios, 'He of the Wine-Press,' only descriptive titles; they never crystallize to the dignity of proper names. Some, like Iacchos and probably Bacchos itself, though they ultimately became proper names, were originally only cries. Iacchos was a song even down to the time of Aristophanes[1], and was probably, to begin with, a ritual shout or cry kept up long after its meaning was forgotten. Such cries from their vagueness, their aptness for repetition, are peculiarly exciting to the religious emotions. How many people attach any precise significance to the thrice repeated, stately and moving words that form the prooemium to our own Easter Hymn?

'Alleluia, Alleluia, Alleluia.'

They are a homage beyond articulate speech. Then, as now, these excited cries became sacred titles of the worshippers who used them: 'Evian women' (*εὔιοι γυναῖκες*) were the ancient and more reverent counterpart of our 'Hallelujah lasses.'

The various titles of the god are of course of considerable use in determining his nature, for they all express some phase of emotion in the worshipper, and it is of these phases that a god is compounded. Certain names seem to cling to certain places. Sabazios is Thracian and Phrygian, Zagreus Cretan, Bromios largely Theban, Iacchos Athenian. Some of the epithets have unquestionably shifted their meaning in the course of time. The Greeks were adepts at false etymology, and an excellent instance of this is a title of the first importance for our argument, *Bromios*.

The title Bromios has to our modern ears a poetical, somewhat mystical ring[2]. It never occurs in Homer, nor in Sophocles. Pindar and Aeschylus both use it, Euripides often. The poets, by their usage, clearly show that they connect the title with the

[1] Ar. *Ran.* 331.

[2] Preller (3rd ed. p. 665) goes so far as to say 'Βρόμιος scheint nur poetisches Beiwort zu sein.'

verb *βρέμω*, which means 'to make a confused sound.' Pindar in a dithyrambic fragment[1] says:

'We hymn thee Bromios and Him of the loud cry.'

The address it may be noted is to the Cadmean Dionysos.

Sometimes the association is definitely with thunder (*βροντή*). Thus in the second Olympian[2] we have:

'High in Olympus lives for evermore
She of the delicate hair,
Semele fair,
Who died by the thunder's roar.'

Here the title Bromios can scarcely have been remote from Pindar's mind, though he does not care to press the allusion. In the *Bacchae* there seems no consciousness of etymology. The titles Dionysos and Bromios come haphazard, but throughout the play Dionysos is in some degree a god of thunder as well as thunder-born, a god of mysterious voices, of strange, confused, orgiastic music, music which we know he brought with him from the North.

Strabo[3] has preserved for us two fragments from the lost *Edonians* of Aeschylus which deal with this music of orgy and madness. Aeschylus, he says, speaks in the *Edonians* of the goddess Kotys and the instruments of her worship, and immediately introduces the worshippers of Dionysos, thus:

'One on the fair-turned pipe fulfils
His song, with the warble of fingered trills
The soul to frenzy awakening.
From another the brazen cymbals ring.
The shawm blares out, but beneath is the moan
Of the bull-voiced mimes, unseen, unknown,
And in deep diapason the shuddering sound
Of drums, like thunder, beneath the ground.'

Of the 'bull-voiced mimes' we should have been glad to know more details, but the fragment, obscure as it is, leaves at least the impression of weird exciting ceremonial, and most of all of mysterious music.

All this must have helped to make of Bromios the god of

[1] Pind. frg. 45
τὸν Βρόμιον τὸν Ἐριβόαν τε καλέομεν.

[2] Pind. *Ol.* II. 27
ζώει μὲν ἐν Ὀλυμπίοις ἀποθανοῦσα βρόμῳ
κεραυνοῦ τανυέθειρα Σεμέλα.

[3] Strabo X. p. 470.

sounds and voices; yet it is probable, indeed almost certain, that the title had another origin, simpler, less poetical. We owe the clue to this primitive meaning to the Emperor Julian.

Julian in his northern campaign saw and no doubt tasted with compunction a wine, made not from the grape but from barley. After the fashion of his age he wrote an epigram[1] to this new, or rather very old, Dionysos. From the number of instructive puns it contains this epigram is almost untranslateable, but as its evidence is for our purpose of paramount importance it may be roughly Englished as follows:

To wine made of barley[2].

'Who and whence art thou, Dionyse? Now, by the Bacchus true
Whom well I know, the son of Zeus, say—"Who and what are you?"
He smells of nectar like a god, *you* smack of goats and spelt,
For lack of grapes from ears of grain your countryman the Celt
Made you. Your name's Demetrios, but never Dionyse,
Bromos, Oat-born, not Bromios, Fire-born from out the skies.'

The emperor makes three very fair puns, as follows: *βρόμος* oats, *βρόμιος* of the thunder; *πυρογενῆ* wheat-born, *πυριγενῆ* fire-born; *τράγος* goat and *τράγος* an inferior kind of wheat, spelt.

[1] *Anthol. Pal.* IX. 368

Εἰς οἶνον ἀπὸ κριθῆς.
Τίς πόθεν εἶς Διόνυσε; μὰ γὰρ τὸν ἀληθέα Βάκχον
οὔ σ' ἐπιγιγνώσκω· τὸν Διὸς οἶδα μόνον.
κεῖνος νέκταρ ὄδωδε, σὺ δὲ τράγον· ἦ ῥά σε Κελτοὶ
τῇ πενίῃ βοτρύων τεῦξαν ἀπ' ἀσταχύων.
τῷ σε χρὴ καλέειν Δημήτριον, οὐ Διόνυσον,
πυρογενῆ μᾶλλον καὶ βρόμον οὐ Βρόμιον.

The epigram is discussed and the play on *πυριγενῆ*, *πυρογενῆ*, *βρόμος* and *Βρόμιος* rightly observed by Hehn (*Kulturpflanzen*, 6th ed. p. 147), and to his book and Schrader's *Reallexicon* I am indebted for many references. Hehn misses the point of *τράγος* but it was noted long ago by Couring in the *Thesaurus* of Stephanos (2342 B) s.v. *τράγος*. He remarks apropos of the epigram: 'non hircum sed ex olyra et tritico confectum panem.' See also Dr W. Headlam, *Cl. Rev.* 1901, p. 23.

[2] Mr Francis Darwin kindly tells me that *τράγος* is said to be a kind of wheat known now as *triticum amylaeum*. It is akin to spelt, *triticum spelta*, the ancient *ζεία*. *βρόμος* is some form of oats, in modern Greek *βρώμη*. It is of interest to note that in the 4th century B.C. *βρόμος* was an important cereal accounted as more wholesome than barley. This is clear from the words of the physician Dieuches: *γίνεται δὲ ἄλφιτον καὶ ἀπὸ τοῦ βρόμου. φρύγεται δὲ σὺν τῷ ἀχύρῳ πᾶν. ἀποπήσσεταί τε καὶ τρίβεται καὶ ἐρύκεται καθάπερ καὶ τὸ κρίθινον ἄλφιτον. τοῦτο τὸ ἄλφιτον κρεῖττον καὶ ἀφυσώτερόν ἐστι τοῦ κριθίνου* (*xxi. veter. et clar. medic. Graec. var. opusc.* ed. F. de Matthaei, Mosquae 1808, p. 39; see Hehn, *Kulturpfl.* 7th ed. p. 553). By the time of Galen it seems to have fallen into comparative disuse, displaced probably by the richer cereals. He says (*de aliment. facult.* I. 14): *τροφὴ δ' ἐστὶν ὑποζυγίων οὐκ ἀνθρώπων, εἰ μή ποτε ἄρα λιμώττοντες ἐσχάτως ἀναγκασθεῖεν, ἐκ τούτου τοῦ σπέρματος*. The modern history of oats presents a close analogy. Displaced in the south by the richer wheat it remains the staple food of the northern Scot, and is the food of cattle only in the south.

The gist of the third pun will be considered more fully at a later stage of the argument. For the present it is sufficient to note that all three have the same substantial content, there *is* a Dionysos who is not of heaven but of earth. Julian propounds as an elegant jest the simple but illuminating mythological truth that the title Bromios points to a god born not of the lightning and thunder but of an intoxicant made from the cereal *βρόμος*. Bromios is Demetrios, son of Demeter the Corn-Mother, before he becomes god of the grape and son by adoption of Olympian Zeus.

Julian is not precise in his discrimination between the various edible grasses. His epigram is headed, 'To wine made of barley (*κριθῆς*)'; the god, he says, smacks of *spelt* (*τράγος*), he is *wheat-born* (*πυρογενῆ*) and he is of *oats* (*βρόμος*). It matters to Julian nothing, nor is it to our argument of first importance, of *what* particular cereal this new-old Dionysos is made. The point is that it is of some cereal, not of the grape. The god is thus seen to be son of Semele, Earth-goddess in her agricultural aspect as Demeter, Corn-Mother. We shall later (p. 517) see that he was worshipped with service of the winnowing-fan, and we shall further see that, when he-of-the-cereal-intoxicant became he-of-the-wine-of-grapes, the instrument that had been a winnowing-fan became a grape-basket.

The possibility of this simple origin of Bromios grows when we consider another epithet of the god. In the Paean to Dionysos recently discovered at Delphi[1] there occurs the title hitherto unexplained—Braites. The hymn opens thus with a string of cultus epithets:

> 'Come, O Dithyrambos, Bacchos, come,
> Euios, Thyrsos-Lord, Braites, come,
> Bromios, come, and coming with thee bring
> Holy hours of thine own holy spring.'

Nowhere else does the title Braites occur; but the hymn, as

[1] H. Weil, *Bull. de Corr. Hell.* XIX. p. 401

> [Δεῦρ' ἄνα Δ]ιθύραμβε, Βάκχ',
> ε[ὔϊε θυρσῆ]ρες, Βραϊ-
> τά, Βρόμι(ε), ἠρινα[ῖς ἱκοῦ
> ταῖσδ(ε)] ἱεραῖς ἐν ὥραις.

Dr Weil suggests 'faut-il le rattacher à ϝραίω = ῥαίω et l'expliquer "celui qui frappe et qui brise"?'

an actual ritual composition, inscribed and set up at Delphi, is an important source. Braites has been explained as the Breaker or Striker, but this is scarcely a happy epithet for the Spring-god. In the light of Bromios it may be suggested that the epithet is connected with the late Latin word *braisum*, which means 'grain prepared for the making of the beer *braisum*[1].' Braites would then like Bromios be an epithet derived from a cereal intoxicant.

An examination of the title Sabazios leads to results more certain and satisfactory. The name Sabazios has a more foreign sound than Dionysos, even than Bromios. Sabazios was never admitted even to the outskirts of Olympus. In the time of Demosthenes[2] his rites were regarded by the orthodox as foreign, outrageous, disreputable. One of the counts in the unmannerly attack of Demosthenes on Aeschines is that Aeschines had been instructed by his mother in mysteries and rites that were certainly those of Sabazios, that having performed various degrading ceremonials he 'led those admirable thiasoi about the streets, they being crowned with fennel and poplar, and gesticulated with great red snakes, waving them over his head and shouting Euoi Saboi.' The Saboi were the worshippers of Sabazios as the Bacchae of Bacchos. Of course Demosthenes is grossly unjust. The ceremonies of Sabazios could be closely paralleled by the perfectly orthodox ritual of Dionysos, but they passed under another name, were not completely canonical, and above all things were still realized as foreign. That pious men of good repute might quietly worship Sabazios is clear from the account of the 'Superstitious Man' in Theophrastos[3]. Against his moral character nothing can be urged, but that he was a little over-zealous, and 'whenever he chanced to see a red snake he would invoke Sabazios.'

Down to Christian days the snake was an important feature in the cult of Sabazios. Clement and Arnobius[4] both state that one of the 'tokens' of the mysteries of Sabazios was 'the god (gliding) through the bosom.' The snake was of course associated

[1] Ducange s.v. braisum: grana ad conficiendam braisum cerevisiam praeparata.
[2] Dem. *de Cor.* 313.
[3] Theophr. *Char.* LXXVII.
[4] Clem. Al. *Protr.* II. Arnob. *c. gent.* V. p. 170. For the curious votive hands twined round by snakes see Blinkenberg, 'Darstellungen d. Sabazios und Denkmäler seines Kultes' in his *Archäologische Studien*, pp. 66—128, Taf. II. and III.

also with Dionysos—he may have inherited it from the earlier god—but his more characteristic vehicle was the bull. Sabazios seems always to have been regarded as more primitive and savage than Dionysos. Diodorus[1], puzzled by the many forms of Dionysos, says: 'Some people fable that there was another Dionysos very much earlier in date than this one, for they allege that there was a Dionysos born of Zeus and Persephone, the one called by some Sabazios, whose birth and sacrifices and rites they instance as celebrated by night and in secret on account of shameless ceremonies attending them.' These last words probably refer to the mystic marriage of the god with the initiated (p. 534).

The symbolism of the snake has already (p. 325) been discussed. A god whose vehicle was the snake would find easy affiliation in Greece, where every dead hero was a snake.

Sabazios is left unsung by tragic poets, but the realism of comedy reflects the popular craze for semi-barbarian worship. The temper of Demosthenes was not, if Strabo[2] be right, characteristically Athenian. 'As in other matters,' Strabo says, 'the Athenians were always hospitable to foreign customs, so with the gods. They adopted many sacred customs from abroad and were ridiculed in comedies for doing so, and this especially as regards Phrygian and Thracian rites. Plato mentions the Bendidean, and Demosthenes the Phrygian, rites, in his accusation against Aeschines and his mother on the count that Aeschines joined his mother in her rites and went about in a thiasos and cried aloud Euoi Saboi and Hyes Attes, for these cries are of Sabazios and the Mother.'

It is then to comedy, to Aristophanes, that we owe most of our references to Sabazios, hints of his real character and his inner kinship with Dionysos. In an untranslateable pun in the *Birds*[3] he tells us that Sabazios is a Phrygian, and from the *Lysistrata*[4] we learn that his worship was orgiastic and much affected by women. The 'deputation man' exclaims:

> 'Has the wantonness of women then blazed up,
> Their tabourings, Sabazios all about,
> Their clamour for Adonis on the roofs?'

[1] Diod. IV. 4.
[2] Strab. x. 3 § 471.
[3] Ar. *Av.* 875
καὶ φρυγίλῳ Σαβαζίῳ καὶ στρουθῷ μεγάλῃ
μητρὶ θεῶν καὶ ἀνθρώπων.
[4] Ar. *Lys.* 388.

But most instructive of all is the mention of Sabazios in the opening of the *Wasps*[1]. The two slaves Sosias and Xanthias are watching over their master Bdelycleon. They know he is a dangerous monster and they ought to keep awake.

'*Xan.* I know, but I *do* want a little peace.
Sos. Well, chance it then. Some sweet and drowsy thing
Is falling drop by drop upon my eyes.
Xan. What? Are you clean mad or a Korybant?
Sos. No, a sleep holds me from Sabazios.
Xan. And I too herd the same Sabazios.
Just now a very Mede of a nodding sleep
Came down and made an onset on my eyes.'

Sabazios is here clearly not so much the god of ecstasy and orgy as of compelling irresistible sleep. And why? A late historian gives the simple answer.

Ammianus Marcellinus[2] tells us that, when the Emperor Valens was besieging Chalcedon, the besieged by way of insult shouted to him 'Sabaiarius.' He adds in explanation '*sabaia* is a drink of the poor in Illyria made of barley or corn turned into a liquor.' 'Sabaiarius' is then 'Beer-man,' beer-drinker or brewer. S. Jerome, himself a Dalmatian, says in his commentary on Isaiah[3] that 'there is a sort of drink made from grain and water, and in the provinces of Dalmatia and Pannonia it is called, in the local barbarian speech, *sabaium*.' To the wine-drinker the beer-drinker seemed a low fellow. Wine was in itself a rarer, finer beverage, probably at first more expensive. Even to-day in some parts of beer-drinking Germany to drink beer at the solemn midday dinner is almost a vulgarity. Sabazios, god of the cheap cereal drink, brings rather sleep than inspiration.

The testimony of Sabazios is now added to that of Bromios and Braites. Separately the conjectured etymology of each epithet might fall far short of conviction, but the cumulative force of the three together offers evidence that seems conclusive.

[1] Ar. *Vesp.* 5—12. The word *βουκολεῖς* (*v.* 6) points to the *βουκόλοι*, priests or attendants of the bull-Dionysos.

[2] Ammian. Marcell. 26. 8. 2: est autem sabaia ex ordeo vel frumento in liquorem conversis paupertinus in Illyrico potus. O. Schrader, *Reallexikon*, p. 89, points out that the derivation of Sabazios from *sabaia* is possible, if the view of Kretschmer (*Einleitung*, p. 195) be accepted that Sabazios represents an earlier *Savadios*; he compares the old Gallic divinity Braciaca 'God of Malt.' Mr A. B. Cook kindly drew my attention to the remark of De Vit in his edition of Forcellini's *Lexicon*, s.v. sabaia: 'unde etiam *zabaion* vulgo apud nostrates' (Venetos?).

[3] Hieron. *Com.* 7 *in Is.* cap. 19: quod genus est potionis ex frugibus aquaque confectum et vulgo in Dalmatiae Pannoniacque provinciis gentili barbaroque sermone appellatur *sabaium*.

A fourth link in the chain still remains. The emperor Julian's third pun τράγος, goat, and τράγος, spelt, has yet to be considered:

'*He* smells of nectar like a god, *you* smack of goats and spelt.'

The word τράγος is usually rendered 'goat,' and the meaning 'spelt' ignored. There is of course a reference to the time-honoured jest about the animal, but that the primary reference is to grain, not the goat, is clear from the words that immediately follow:

'For lack of grapes from ears of grain your countryman the Celt
Made you.'

In translating I have therefore used both the meanings; the formal pun is untranslateable.

It is an odd fact that the ancients seem to have called certain *wild* forms of fruits and cereals by names connecting them with the goat[1]. The reason is not clear, but the fact is well-established. The Latins called the wild fig *caprificus*; Pausanias expressly tells us that the Messenians gave to the wild fig-tree the name τράγος, goat. Vines, when they ran wild to foliage rather than fruit, were said τραγᾶν. I would conjecture that the inferior sort of spelt called τράγος, goat, owes its name to this unexplained linguistic habit. It is even possible that the beard with which spelt is furnished may have helped out the confusion. Tragedy I believe to be not the 'goat-song,' but the 'harvest-song' of the cereal τράγος, the form of spelt known as 'the goat.' When the god of the cereal, Bromios-Braites-Sabazios, became the god of the vine, the fusion and confusion of τραγῳδία, the spelt-song, with τρυγῳδία, the song of the winelees[2], was easy and indeed inevitable. The τραγῳδοί, the 'beanfeast-singers,' became τρυγῳδοί or 'must-singers.'

The difficulties in the way of the canonical etymology of *tragedy* are acknowledged to be great[3]. In discussing the Satyrs it has

[1] This was first observed by Grimm (*Geschichte d. d. Sprache*, p. 66), see Hehn, *Kulturpflanzen*, 7th edit. p. 550, but Hehn's explanation of the custom does not seem satisfactory. Our custom of calling inferior varieties of plants by *dog*-names, e.g. Dog-Rose, Dog-Violet, seems analogous.

[2] For the group of words denoting 'dregs' e.g. O.P. *dragios*, with which τρυγῳδία is connected, see Schrader, *Prehistoric Antiquities*, p. 322, and Hehn, *Kulturpflanzen*, p. 159.

[3] For the literature of this protracted controversy see U. v. Wilamowitz, Eur. *Her.* I. p. 32; A. Körte, *Jahrbuch d. Inst.* 1893, VIII. p. 61: Loschke, *A. Mitt.* XV.

already been shown that the primitive followers of Dionysos are mythologically conceived of not as *goat*-men, but as *horse*-men. The primitive '*goat*-song,' we are asked to believe, was sung by a chorus of *horse*-men. The case in fact stands thus. We are confronted on the one hand by the undoubted fact that on countless vase-paintings of the fifth and fourth centuries B.C. the attendants of Dionysos are *horse*-men, while *goat*-men attend the Earth-goddess (p. 277): on the other hand we have the *supposed* fact that tragedy is the *goat*-song. But this supposed fact is merely an etymological assumption. If another etymology be found for *tragedy*, the whole discrepancy disappears. Such an etymology is, I think, offered by τράγος 'spelt,' with the further advantage that it contains in itself a hint of how the goat misunderstanding arose.

A fragment of Aeschylus cited, but I think erroneously, as evidence of a goat chorus remains to be examined. In a lost tragedy[1] a Satyr on the stage sees for the first time fire just given to mortals, and he runs to kiss her as though she were a beautiful maiden. Prometheus warns him: if you do this

'You'll be a goat mourning his beard.'

The passage is used as evidence for the goat form and dress of the Satyric chorus. Surely such an inference is needless; the point of the jest is the morals and manners of the Satyr. To reconstruct a goat-chorus out of a casual joke is labour in vain.

We have then found four several titles, Bromios, Braites, Sabazios and tragedy, for which the supposition of a cereal drink affords a simple, satisfactory explanation. It remains to show that, though the words *bromos*, *braisum*, *sabaia* and *tragos* have become to us dim and almost forgotten in the lapse of time, a cereal drink such as they imply was widely in use in ancient days, and that among Northern nations.

The history of fermented drink in Europe seems to have been

1894, p. 518; K. Wernicke, *Hermes* 1897, p. 290; Bethe, *Proleg.* p. 48. My own view was first suggested in the *Classical Rev.* July 1902, p. 331.

[1] Aesch. frg. 190 ap. Plut. *Mor.* p. 86 τοῦ δὲ σατύρου τὸ πῦρ ὡς πρῶτον ὤφθη βουλομένου φιλῆσαι καὶ περιλαβεῖν ὁ Προμηθεύς

τράγος γένειον ἄρα πενθήσεις σύγε.

briefly this. Never, so far back as we can look into mythology, was miserable man without some rudimentary means of intoxication. Before he had advanced to agriculture he had a drink made of naturally fermented honey, the drink we now know as mead, which the Greeks called *μέθυ* or *μέθη*. The epithet 'sweet' which they constantly apply to wine surprises us, but as a characteristic of 'mead' it is natural enough. This mead made of honey appears in ancient legends. When Zeus would intoxicate Kronos he gave him not wine, Porphyry[1] says, for wine was not, but a honey-drink to darken his senses. Night says to Zeus:

> 'When prostrate 'neath the lofty oaks you see him
> Lie drunken with the work of murmuring bees,
> Then bind him,'

and again Plato[2] tells how when Poros falls asleep in the garden of Zeus he is drunk not with wine but with nectar, for wine was not yet. Nectar, the ancient drink of the gods, is mead made of honey; and men know this, for they offer to the primitive earth-god libations of honey (*μελίσπονδα*). The gods like their worshippers knew the joys of intoxication before the coming of the grape-Dionysos. Plutarch[3] says mead (*μέθυ*) was used as a libation before the appearance of the vine, and 'even now those of the barbarians who do not drink wine drink honey-drink' (*μελίτειον*). The *nephalia* are but intoxicants more primitive than wine.

Next in order came the drinks made of cereals fermented, the various forms of beer and crude malt spirit. These gave to the Thracian Dionysos his names Bromios, Braites, Sabazios, but they never seem to have found a real home in Greece. Mention of them occurs in classical writers, but they are always named as barbarian curiosities, as drinks in use in Thrace, Armenia, Egypt, but never like mead even in primitive times the national drink of Hellas. Isis in Egypt is addressed as not only Our Lady of Bread but also Our Lady of Beer[4], but Bromios when he comes to Greece forgets the oats from which he sprang.

The first beer was probably a very rude product, like the drink mentioned by Xenophon[5] as still in use among the Armenians of his day; the grain was pounded and allowed to ferment with the

[1] Porph. *de antr. nymph.* 7.
[2] Plat. *Symp.* p. 203.
[3] Plut. *Symp.* IV. 6.
[4] Brugsch, *Religion und Mythologie d. alten Egypter*, p. 647.
[5] Xen. *Anab.* IV. 5. 26 ἐνῆσαν δὲ καὶ αὐταὶ αἱ κριθαὶ ἰσοχειλεῖς.

grains still floating about in the drinking-cups. The Lithuanians in the Middle Ages are said to have made their beer over-night and drunk it next morning[1]. Beer of this primitive kind was best sucked up through a pipe. Archilochus[2] alludes to the practice.

The name given to the drink, *βρῦτον*, means simply something brewed or fermented. Aeschylus[3] in his *Lykurgos* makes some one, probably Lykurgos the Thracian, drink *βρῦτον*.

Athenaeus, in the passage in which he quotes Archilochus, cites quite a number of authorities about the making of these rude cereal drinks. According to Hellanicus in his *Origins*, *bruton* could be made also of roots. 'Some people,' he says, 'drink *bruton* made of roots as the Thracian drink is made of barley.' Hecataeus in his *Journey round Europe* notes that the Paeonians drank *bruton* made from barley and an admixture of millet and endive.

Another name for this drink made from grain was *zythos*. Diodorus[4] draws a lamentable picture of the straits to which the peoples of Gaul were put because 'from the excessive cold and intemperate character of the climate, the land could not bring forth either wine or oil. Bereft of these products the Gauls make of barley the drink that is called *zythos*; they likewise wash out their honeycombs with water and use the rinsings. They had only imported wine, but to this they were excessively addicted (*κάτοινοι*), they drank it intemperately and either fell asleep dead drunk or became stark mad.' Here we have the living historical prototype of the Centaurs, the uncivilized men who cannot support the taste of wine, the lamentable story of *imported* intoxicants told in all ages all the world over.

The number of primitive beers—*cervisia*, *korma*, *sabaia*, *zythos*

[1] Lasicius, *De Diis Sarmagitarum*, p. 44.

[2] Archil. frg. ap. Athen. x. 67 § 447. Bergk 32

ὥσπερ παρ᾽ αὐλῷ βρῦτον ἢ Θρῆιξ ἀνὴρ
ἢ Φρὺξ ἔβρυζε.

[3] Nauck, Aesch. frg. 124

κἀκ τῶνδ᾽ ἔπινε βρῦτον ἰσχναίνων χρόνῳ
καὶ σεμνοκόπτει τοῦτ᾽ ἐν ἀνδρείᾳ στέγῃ.

It is clear that someone drank something called *βρῦτον* but beyond that the meaning is obscure and Nauck throws no light. In my first edition I translated the passage wrongly.

In connection with *βρῦτον* Prof. Bury kindly draws my attention to the very interesting statement of Suidas, *βρούτιδες, γυναῖκες οὕτω καλούμεναι, οἱονεὶ Σίβυλλαι καὶ προφήτιδες.* These *βρούτιδες* were clearly inspired Maenads.

[4] Diod. v. 26.

—is countless and it would be unprofitable to discuss them in detail. All have this in common, and it is sufficient for our purpose, that they are spirituous drinks made of fermented grain, they appear with the introduction of agriculture, they tend to supersede mead, and are in turn superseded by wine. To put it mythologically the worship of Bromios, Braites and Sabazios pales before the Epiphany of Dionysos. Sabazios is almost wholly left behind, a foreigner never naturalized[1]. Bromios is transformed beyond recognition; to the old name is given a new meaning, a new etymology.

It is important to note that had there been only Sabazios, had Bromios never emerged from himself, both would probably have remained in Thracian obscurity. The Thracians never conquered Greece; there was, therefore, no historical reason why their god should impose himself. His dominance is unquestionably due to the introduction and rapid spread of the vine. Popular tradition enshrined as it usually does a real truth—the characteristic gift (χάρις) of Dionysos by which he won all hearts was wine, wine made not of barley but of the juice of the grape. A new, incoming plant attaches itself to the local divinity, whoever and whatever he be. The olive attached itself to Athene who was there before its coming, and by the olive the prestige of Athene was sensibly increased; but the olive, great glory though it was and though a Sophocles sang its praises, had never the divine omnipotence of the vine. Olive oil over all the countries of Southern Europe supplanted the other primitive grease, butter[2]. Butter is hard to keep fresh in hot countries, as every traveller finds to his cost in Italy and Greece to-day. But the supersession of butter by oil was a quiet, unnoticed advance, not a triumphant progress like the Coming of the Vine.

We are now at last in a position to say what was the characteristic essence of the worship of Dionysos. The fact however repugnant

[1] In the north as to-day the Beer-god retained his supremacy. It is interesting to note that the British saint, St Brigida, re-performed the miracle of Cana with the characteristically northern modification that she turned the water into excellent beer: *Christi autem ancilla videns quia tunc illico non poterat invenire cerevisiam, aquam ad balneum portatam benedixerit et in optimam cerevisiam conversa est a Deo et abundanter sitientibus propinata est. Acta SS. Febr.* I. Vita IV. S. Brigidae cap. IV. quoted by Hehn, *op. cit.* p. 149. In the Egyptian *Book of the Dead* (Chap. cx.) the desire of the soul is for cakes and *ale*.

[2] Hehn, *Kulturpflanzen*, 7th edit. p. 154.

must be fairly faced. This essence was intoxication. But by the very nature of primitive thought this essence was almost instantly transformed into something more, something deeper and higher than mere physical intoxication. It was intoxication thought of as possession. The savage tastes of some intoxicant for the first time, a great delight takes him, he feels literally a new strange life within him. How has it come about? The answer to him is simple. He is possessed by a god (ἔνθεος), not figuratively but literally and actually; there is a divine thing within him that is more than himself, he is mad, but with a divine madness. All intense sorrow or joy is to him obsession, possession. When in the *Hippolytus*[1] the chorus see Phaedra distraught with passion, instinctively they ask:

> 'Is this some spirit, O child of man,
> Doth Hecate hold thee perchance or Pan,
> Doth She of the Mountains work her ban
> Or the dread Corybantes bind thee?'

They utter not poetical imagery but a real belief.

To what beautiful imaginations, to what high spiritual vision this Bacchic cult of intoxication led will best be considered when we come to speak of Orpheus. For the present some other primitive elements in Dionysiac worship remain to be considered, elements essential to the understanding of his cult.

Dionysos the Tree-God (Dendrites).

Intoxication is of the essence of the god Dionysos, it is the element that marks him out from other gods, it is the secret of his missionary impulse; but to suppose that it exhausts his content would be a grave misunderstanding. There go to his making not only this distinctive element of intoxication but certain other primitive factors common to the gods of other peoples.

Thinking people even in antiquity, when the study of comparative mythology scarcely existed, were struck by analogies between Dionysos and other divinities. Plutarch, who thought much, if somewhat vaguely, on religious matters, was very sensible of this. In the enlightened and instructive parallel that he

[1] Eur. *Hipp.* 141.

draws[1] between Osiris and Dionysos, he sees that Dionysos like the gods of many other peoples is a god who in some sense embodies the life of nature that comes and goes with the seasons, dies and rises again with the fruits of the earth. In a passage full of insight he draws attention to the analogies of the diverse cults he had observed. 'The Phrygians think that the god is asleep in the winter, and is awake in summer, and at the one season they celebrate with Bacchic rites his goings to bed and at the other his risings up. And the Paphlagonians allege that in the winter he is bound down and imprisoned and in the spring he is stirred up and let loose.' The passage and others that will later be quoted are as it were a forecast of the whole comparative method.

The truth that Dionysos, like many another god, was a god of the impulse of life in nature was not only apprehended by the philosopher, it was also evidenced in cultus. This is seen very clearly in two popular phases of the worship of Dionysos, his worship as a *tree-god* and his worship as a *bull*.

The vine is a tree; but Dionysos is Dendrites, Tree-god, and a plant-god in a far wider sense. He is god of the fig-tree, Sykites; he is Kissos, god of the ivy; he is Anthios, god of all blossoming things; he is Phytalmios, god of growth. In this respect he differs scarcely at all from certain aspects of Poseidon, or from the young male god of Attica and the Peloponnese, Hermes. Probably this aspect of the god, at once milder and wider, was always acceptable in Southern Greece and made his affiliation with the indigenous Hermes an easy matter. This affiliation is clearly shown by the fact that in art Hermes and Dionysos appear, as they were worshipped in cultus, as herms; the symbol of both as gods of fertility is naturally the phallos. The young Dionysos, a maturer Liknites, is not distinguishable from Hermes.

On the beautiful cylix by Hieron[2] reproduced in fig. 130, perhaps the most exquisite thing that ancient ceramography has

[1] Plut. *de Is. et Osir.* LXIX. *Φρύγες δὲ τὸν θεὸν οἰόμενοι χειμῶνος καθεύδειν, θέρους δ' ἐγρηγορέναι, τότε μὲν κατευνασμούς, τότε δ' ἀνεγέρσεις βακχεύοντες αὐτῷ τελοῦσι. Παφλαγόνες δὲ καταδεῖσθαι καὶ καθείργνυσθαι χειμῶνος, ἦρος δὲ κινεῖσθαι καὶ ἀναλύεσθαι φάσκουσι.* The earlier portiou of this passage deals with the analogous cult of Demeter (p. 128) already discussed.

[2] Berlin, *Cat.* 2290. *Wiener Vorlegeblätter*, Serie A, Taf. VI.

left us, this affiliation is clearly shown. In the centre design Dionysos is all vine-god. He holds a great vine-branch in his left hand, in his right his own sceptre the thyrsos; his worshipper is a horse-Satyr piping on the double flutes. But on the exterior of

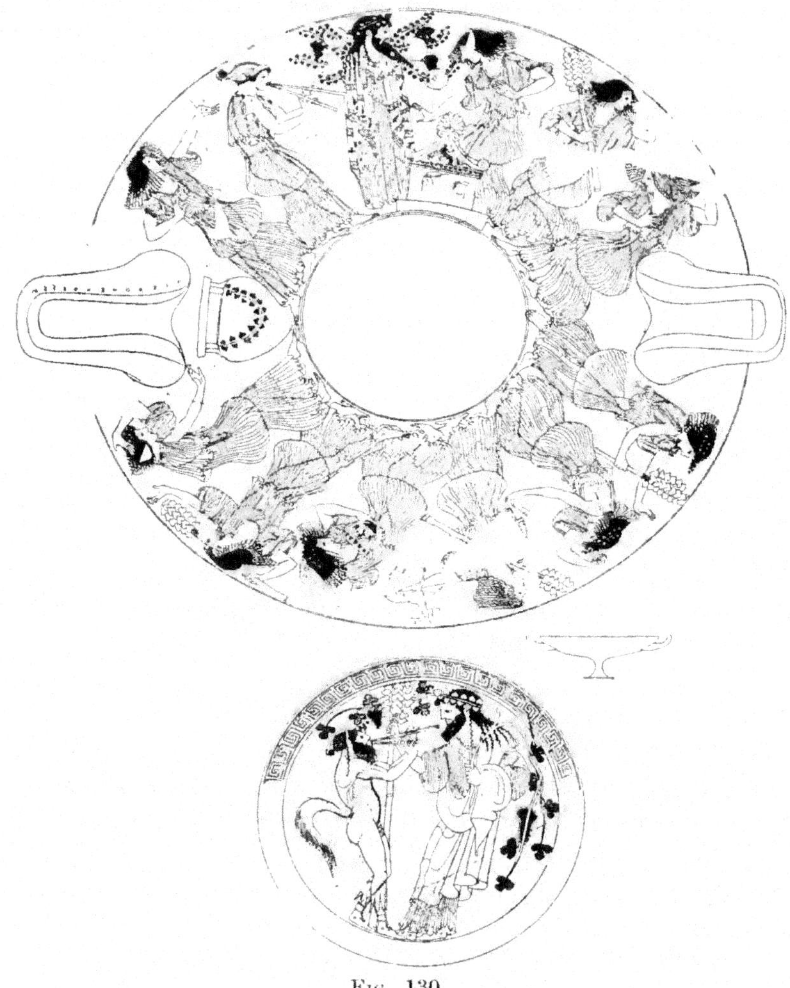

Fig. 130.

the cup, a scene of cultus rather than mythology, he is of wider import, he is Dendrites. The god round whom the lovely Maenads dance in circle is a rude pillar or plank draped with a splendid ritual garment. It is a primitive herm decorated with great bunches of grapes, but also with ivy sprigs and honeycombs and a necklace of dried figs, such as the Greek peasant now-a-days takes with him for food on a journey. He is god of all growing things, of every tree and plant and natural product, and only later exclusively of the vine. He takes to himself ivy and pine and honeycomb. The honey-drink he supersedes, yet honey is sacred to him. Only the olive he never takes, for Athene had it already. Ivy especially was sacred to him; his Maenads chewed ivy leaves[1] for inspiration, as the Delphic prophetess chewed the bay. Pliny[2] says: 'Even to this day ivy is used to decorate the thyrsos of the god and the helmets and shields used by the peoples of Thrace in their rites,' and this ritual ivy is remembered by Dionysos when he comes to Thebes[3]:

> 'I cry to Thebes to waken, set her hands
> To clasp my wand, mine ivied javelin,
> And round her shoulders hang my wild fawn-skin.'

Very primitive in form but wholly of the vine-god is the xoanon on a krater in the Campana collection of the Louvre[4]

FIG. 131.

[1] Plut. *Quaest. R.* CXII.
[2] Pliny *N.H.* XVI. 62.
[3] Eur. *Bacch.* 55.
[4] *Annali d. Inst.* 1862, Tav. d' agg. C.

(fig. 131). The image of the god is a column treated as a herm, and reminds us that Dionysos was called by the name Perikionios, He-about-the-pillar. The two representations in figs. 131 and 130 are characteristically different. The rude Satyrs have but one way of worshipping their god, they fall upon the wine-cup; the Maenads, worshipping the god of life, bend in ritual ecstasy to touch the earth, mother of life; the wine-jar in Hieron's vase is present as a symbol, but the Maenads revel aloof.

The worship of the tree-god was probably indigenous in Thrace long before the coming of the vine. We have evidence that it lingered on there down to Roman times. An inscription on a cippus recently discovered in a mosque at Eski Djoumi[1] and now in the museum at Saloniki affords curious evidence. The cippus marked the grave of a priestess of Dionysos. Her name is lost, but the word priestess (*ἱερεία*) is followed by two characteristically Bacchic epithets, *θύσα* and *εὐεία*. She is priestess of the thiasos of the 'Carriers of the Evergreen Oak' (*πρινοφόροι*), and she leaves to her guild certain property in vineyards. If they do not fulfil the conditions of the bequest, including the offering of a wreath of roses, the property is to go to another thiasos, that of the 'Carriers of the Oak' (*Δροιοφόροι*), and on the same conditions.

The tree-god was too simple for the philosopher. He wanted to abstract Dionysos, rid him of not only his anthropomorphic but his zoomorphic and phytomorphic shapes. Still he used the tree-god as a stepping-stone to his 'principle of moisture.' Plutarch[2] says the Greeks regard Dionysos as not merely lord and originator of wine, but of the whole principle of moisture. Of this, he adds, Pindar is in himself sufficient witness when he says:

'Of all the trees that are
He hath his flock, and feedeth root by root,
The Joy-god Dionysos, the pure star
That shines amid the gathering of the fruit.'

Plutarch is fond of this beautiful little bit of Pindar. He

[1] Perdrizet, *Bull. de Corr. Hell.* 1900, p. 322.

[2] Plut. *de Is. et Os.* XXXV. ὅτι δ' οὐ μόνον τοῦ οἴνου Διόνυσον ἀλλὰ καὶ πάσης ὑγρᾶς φύσεως Ἕλληνες ἡγοῦνται κύριον καὶ ἀρχηγὸν ἀρκεῖ Πίνδαρος μάρτυς εἶναι λέγων·
Δενδρέων δὲ νόμον Διόνυσος πολυγήθης αὐξάνοι
ἁγνὸν φέγγος ὀπώρας.

quotes it again in his *Symposiacs*[1]. A friend who is a farmer objects that Plutarch has shut out his calling from the worship of the Muses, whereas he had hoped that at least Thalia, goddess of increase, might be his to worship. Plutarch says the charge is not a just one, for farmers have Dendrites, He-of-the-Trees, and Anesidora, She-who-sends-up-gifts; and then he quotes his favourite passage. Pindar is of course no evidence for a Principle of Moisture. Neither poets nor primitive people use any such philosophical jargon; but all the world over primitive man did and still does welcome the coming and lament the going of the something or someone who makes the trees and plants to grow and beasts and man to bring forth. Later, though they are little the wiser as to what that something is, they will call it the 'Principle of Moisture,' or if they are poets Love or Life.

The 'Principle of Moisture' was in fashion among theologists long before Plutarch. In the *Bacchae* of Euripides the new wine of the religion of Dionysos has to be poured into some very old bottles. Teiresias in a typically orthodox fashion, characteristic of the timid and kindly priest all the world over, tries to water it down with weak rationalism. Dionysos, he urges, is not new at all, he is very old, as old and respectable as Demeter herself; she is the Principle of Dryness, he of Moisture, nothing could be more safe and satisfactory. He thus instructs honest Pentheus[2]:

'Two spirits there be,
Young prince, that in man's world are first of worth.
Demeter one is named. She is the Earth—
Call her what name thou wilt!—who feeds man's frame
With sustenance of things dry. And that which came
Her work to perfect, second, is the Power
From Semele born. He found the liquid shower
Hid in the grape[3].'

This is the rationalism not of the poet Euripides, but of the priest Teiresias. This is clear, for the poet in the next line breaks clean away from the tiresome Dryness and Moisture and is gone to the magic of sleep and the blood of the God outpoured.

[1] Plut. *Symp.* IX. 14. 4.

[2] Eur. *Bacch.* 274.

[3] The doctrine of Teiresias was wide-spread in Greece by the time of Diodorus. He says (IV. 3): *καθόλου δὲ μυθολογοῦσι τῶν θεῶν μεγίστης ἀποδοχῆς τυγχάνειν παρ' ἀνθρώποις τοὺς ταῖς εὐεργεσίαις ὑπερβαλομένους κατὰ τὴν εὕρεσιν τῶν ἀγαθῶν Διόνυσόν τε καὶ Δήμητρα, τὸν μὲν τοῦ προσηνεστάτου ποτοῦ γενόμενον εὑρέτην, τὴν δὲ τῆς ξηρᾶς τροφῆς τὴν κρατίστην παραδοῦσαν τῷ γένει τῶν ἀνθρώπων.*

Plutarch quotes Pindar as authority for the Principle of Moisture, and undoubtedly the sap of trees and plants sacred to Dionysos may have helped out the abstraction. But, had Plutarch known it, the notion is associated not so much with Dendrites, the Tree-God, as with a figure perhaps still more primitive, Dionysos the Bull.

Dionysos the Bull-God.

Dionysos Dendrites is easy to realize; he is but a step back from the familiar, canonical Vine-god. The Bull-god Dionysos is harder to accept because we have lost the primitive habit of thinking from which he sprang. The Greeks themselves suffered the like inconvenience. They rapidly advanced to so complete an anthropomorphism that in Periclean Athens the dogma of the Bull-incarnation was, we cannot doubt, a stumbling-block, a faith as far as possible put out of sight.

The particular animal in which a god is incarnate depends of course on the circumstances of the worshippers. If he is in a land lion-haunted his god will be apt to take shape as a lion; later the lion will be his attendant, his servitor. Lions attend the Mountain-Mother of Asia Minor, guard her as has been seen (p. 265) in heraldic fashion, draw her chariot, watch her throne[1]. In like manner Dionysos, son of Semele, who is but one form of the same Earth-Mother, has a chariot drawn by lions (fig. 121), and sometimes, though not so frequently as his Mother, an attendant lion.

In the vase-painting in fig. 132 from an amphora in the British Museum[2] Dionysos, with kantharos and great spreading vine, stands between two great prophylactic eyes. A little lion looks up at him, dog-like, adoring his master. On the reverse Hephaistos with his mallet carries the vine in token of the power of the god. The lion in this picture is losing his reality, because the lion has ceased to be a dominant terror in Greece. The god of a civilized, agricultural people must reincarnate himself in other animal shapes, in the Snake, in the Kid, most of all in the Bull. The Bull-god may have been too savage for Periclean

[1] *Myth. and Mon. Anc. Athens*, pp. 14—50.
[2] B.M. *Cat.* B 264. Gerhard, *Auserlesene Vasenbilder*, Taf. 38.

Athens, but Euripides must have found him in full force in Macedonia. To a people of goat-herds like the Arcadians the goat is the impersonation of life and generation; to a people of

Fig. 132.

cow-herds the bull is the more potent and splendid vehicle. In the *Bacchae* there are Snake-Epiphanies, Lion-Epiphanies, but first and foremost Bull-Epiphanies. At the mystery of the Birth[1]

'A Horned God was found
And a God with serpents crowned.'

In the supreme Orphic mystery, to be discussed later (p. 482), the worshipper before he became 'Bacchos' ate the raw flesh of a bull, and, probably in connection with this sacrament, the Bull form of the god crystallized into a mystery dogma. When Pentheus has imprisoned the 'Bacchos' he finds in the manger not the beautiful stranger but a raging bull; the hallucination was doubtless bred of ancient faith and ritual. Again when in the *Bacchae*[2] Dionysos

[1] Eur. *Bacch.* 99.

[2] Eur. *Bacch.* 918.

leads him forth enchanted to his doom on Cithaeron, Pentheus in his madness sees before him strange sights:

'Yea and mine eye
Is bright! Yon sun shines twofold in the sky,
Thebes twofold and the Wall of Seven Gates,
And is it a Wild Bull this, that walks and waits
Before me? There are horns upon thy brow!
What art thou, man or beast? For surely now
The Bull is on thee!'

and last when at the moment of their uttermost peril the Bacchants invoke their Lord to vengeance, the ancient incarnations loom in upon their maddened minds[1]:

'Appear, appear, whatso thy shape or name,
O Mountain Bull, Snake of the Hundred Heads,
Lion of the Burning Flame!
O God, Beast, Mystery, come!'

All this madness is based not only on a definite faith, but that faith is the utterance of a definite ritual. In discussing the name Bromios we have seen (p. 414) that in the ritual of Dionysos in Thrace there were 'bull-voiced mimes' who bellowed to the god. The scholiast[2] on Lycophron's *Alexandra* says that the 'women who worshipped Dionysos Laphystios wore horns themselves, in imitation of the god, for he is imagined to be bull-headed and is so represented in art.' Plutarch[3] gives more particulars. 'Many of the Greeks represent Dionysos in their images in the form of a bull, and the women of Elis in their prayers invoke the god to come to them with his bull-foot, and among the Argives there is a Dionysos with the title Bull-born. And they summon him by their trumpets out of the water, casting into the depths lambs to the Door-keeper; they hide their trumpets in their thyrsoi, as Socrates has told in his treatise on the Hosioi.' A bull-god is summoned and *he emerges from water*.

It will later (p. 495) be seen to what strange theological uses the Orphics put their bull and lion and snake-shaped Epiphanies; for the present it must be noted how near akin these were to the shapes that the Southern Greeks gave to their own indigenous

[1] Eur. *Bacch.* 1017
φανῆθι ταῦρος ἢ πολύκρανος ἰδεῖν
δράκων ἢ πυριφλέγων ὁρᾶσθαι λέων.

[2] Schol. ad Lyc. *Al.* 1237 κερατοφοροῦσι γὰρ καὶ αὗται κατὰ μίμησιν Διονύσου, ταυρόκρανος γὰρ φαντάζεται καὶ ζωγραφεῖται.

[3] Plut. *de Is. et Os.* XXXV.

gods. Zeus and Athene and even Poseidon had, by the fifth century B.C., become pure human shapes, but the ministrants of Poseidon at Cyzicus were down to the time of Athenaeus known as Bulls[1], and lower divinities like rivers still kept their bull shape, witness the pathetic story of Deianeira and Acheloüs[2]:

> 'A river was my lover, him I mean
> Great Acheloüs, and in threefold form
> Wooed me, and wooed again; a visible bull
> Sometimes, and sometimes a coiled gleaming snake,
> And sometimes partly man, a monstrous shape
> Bull-fronted, and adown his shaggy beard
> Fountains of clear spring water glistening flowed.'

In those old divine days a wooer might woo in a hundred shapes, and a maiden in like fashion might fly his wooing. It is again Sophocles[3] who tells us of the marriage of Pentheus:

> 'The wedlock of his wedding was untold,
> His wrestling with the maiden manifold.'

The red-figured vase-painting in fig. 133 looks almost like an illustration of the *Trachiniae*[4]. Here is the monster; but he is

FIG. 133.

man-fronted, his body that of a bull, and from his mouth flows the water of his own stream Acheloüs. Herakles is about to break off his mighty horn, the seat of his strength; Deianeira stands by unmoved. With odd insistence on his meaning the vase-painter

[1] Athen. p. 425 c. [2] Soph. *Trach.* 9. [3] Soph. frg. 548.
[4] *Archäologische Zeitung* XVI. (1883), Taf. 11. This vase is now in the Louvre.

draws in a horn parallel with the stream to show that the stream is itself a cornucopia of growth and riches. The vase-painting is many years earlier than the play of Sophocles.

I know of no instance where an actual bull-Dionysos is represented on a vase-painting, but in the design in fig. 134 from an

FIG. 134.

amphora[1] in the Würzburg Museum his close connection is indicated by the fact that he rides on a bull. From the kantharos in his hand he pours his gift of wine. This representation is of special interest because on the reverse of the same vase Poseidon holding his trident is represented riding on a white bull. This looks as though the vase-painter had in his mind some analogy between the two divinities of moisture and growth.

With the bull-Poseidon and the bull river-god at hand, the assimilation of the bull-shaped Dionysos would be an easy task, the more as he was god of sap and generation and life, as well as of wine. Water and wine were blended in theology as in daily life, and the Greeks of the South lent the element of water.

[1] Gerhard, *Auserlesene Vasenbilder*, Taf. 47.

Dionysos then by his tree-shape and his bull-shape is clearly shown to be not merely a spirit of intoxication, but rather *a primitive nature god laid hold of, informed by a spirit of intoxication.* Demeter and Kore are nature-goddesses, they have their uprisings and down-goings, but to the end they remain sedate and orderly. Dionysos is as it were the male correlative of Kore, but changed, transfigured by this new element of intoxication and orgy.

This double nature of the god finds expression in one of his titles, the cultus epithet of Dithyrambos, and it is only by keeping his double aspect clearly in mind that this difficult epithet can at all be understood.

Dithyrambos and the Dithyramb.

The title Dithyrambos given to Dionysos and the Dithyramb, the song sung in his honour, must be considered together; in fact this title like 'Iacchos' seems to have arisen out of the song.

The epithet Dithyrambos was always regarded by the Greeks themselves as indicating and describing the manner of the birth of the god. Disregarding the quantity of the vowel *i* in *Di* they believed it to be derived from Δῐ and *θύρα*, double door, and took it to mean 'he who entered life by a double door,' the womb of his mother and the thigh of his father. This was to them the cardinal 'mystery' of the birth. So much is clear from the birth-song of the chorus in the *Bacchae*[1]:

'Acheloüs' roaming daughter,
Holy Dirce, virgin water,
Bathed he not of old in thee
The Babe of God, the Mystery?
When from out the fire immortal
To himself his God did take him,
To his own flesh, and bespake him:
"Enter now life's second portal,
Motherless mystery; lo I break
Mine own body for thy sake,
Thou of the Two-fold Door, and seal thee
Mine, O Bromios"—thus he spake—
"And to this thy land reveal thee."'

Dithyrambos was 'he of the miraculous birth,' Liknites conceived mystically. The mistaken etymology need not make us distrust the substantial truth of the tradition.

[1] Eur. *Bacch.* 519.

As Dithyrambos is the Babe mystically born, so the Dithyramb was uniformly regarded as the Song of the Birth. Plato states this, though somewhat tentatively, in the *Laws*[1]. When discussing various kinds of music he says: 'Another form of song, the Birth of Dionysos called, I think, the dithyramb.'

It has already been seen that Dionysos as the principle of life and generation was figured as a bull, it is therefore no surprise to learn from Pindar[2] that the Dithyramb 'drives' the bull:

> 'Whence did appear the Charites who sing
> To Dionyse their king
> The dithyramb, the chant of Bull-driving?'

The Charites here halt half-way between ritual and poetry. They are half abstract rhythmical graces, half the Charites of an actual cult. The song of invocation to the Bull sung by the women of Elis has been already noted. It is the earliest Dithyramb preserved, and happily in his *Greek Questions* Plutarch[3] has left us a somewhat detailed account. He asks, 'Why do the women of Elis summon Dionysos in their hymns to be present with them with his bull-foot?' He goes on to give the exact words of the little ritual hymn:

> 'Hero, Dionysos, come
> To thy temple-home
> Here at Elis, worshipful
> We implore thee,
> With thy Charites adore thee,
> Rushing with thy bull-foot, come!
> Noble Bull, noble Bull.'

The fact that 'Hero' precedes 'Dionysos' in the invocation makes it tempting to conjecture that we have here a superposition of cults, that the women of Elis long before the coming of Dionysos worshipped a local hero in the form of a bull and that

[1] Plat. *Legg.* III. 700 B ἄλλο εἶδος ᾠδῆς Διονύσου γένεσις, οἶμαι, διθύραμβος λεγόμενος.

[2] Pind. *Ol.* XIII. 18

> ταὶ Διωνύσου πόθεν ἐξέφανεν
> σὺν βοηλάτᾳ χάριτες διθυράμβῳ;

[3] Plut. *Q. Gr.* XXXVI.

> Ἐλθεῖν ἥρω Διόνυσε
> Ἀλείων ἐς ναόν,
> ἁγνὸν σὺν χαρίτεσσιν
> ἐς ναὸν τῷ βοέῳ ποδὶ θύων.
> Ἄξιε ταῦρε, ἄξιε ταῦρε.

These women were also priestesses of Hera and as Dr Sam Wide, 'Chthonische und himmlische Götter' in *Archiv f. Religionswissenschaft*, x. 1907, p. 263, has I think conclusively shown, the two divinities worshipped were the Bull Ἥρως and the Cow Ἥρα.

Dionysos affiliated his cult; but another possibility is perhaps more probable, that Hero is in the hymn purely adjectival. It has already been shown that the word meant to begin with only 'strong' and then 'strong one.'

The mention of the Charites is important. They are the givers of increase (p. 298), who naturally attend the coming of the life-god; they seem here analogous to the nurses of Dionysos, the sober form of his Maenads. They attend alike his coming and his birth.

In the Delphic Paean (p. 416), where the birth of Dionysos in the spring is celebrated, the title Dithyrambos[1] is first and foremost, before Bacchos, Euios, Braites and Bromios:

'Come, O Dithyrambos, Bacchos, come,
Euios, Thrysos-Lord, Braites, come,
Bromios, come, and coming with thee bring
Holy hours of thine own holy spring.
  Evoe, Bacchos, hail, Paean, hail,
Whom in sacred Thebes the mother fair,
She, Thyone, once to Zeus did bear.
All the stars danced for joy. Mirth
Of mortals hailed thee, Bacchos, at thy birth.'

The new-born god is Dithyrambos, and he is born at the resurrection of earth in the spring-time.

The epithet Paean, belonging to Apollo, is here given to Dionysos. At the great festival of the finishing of the temple all is to be harmony and peace; theology attempts an edifying but impossible syncretism. Nothing in mythology is more certain than that the Paean and the Dithyramb were to begin with poles asunder, and it is by the contrast between them that we best understand not only the gist of the Dithyramb itself but the significance of the whole religion of Dionysos.

The contrast between Apollo and Dionysos, Paean and Dithyramb, has been sharply and instructively drawn by Plutarch,

[1] [Δεῦρ' ἄνα Δ]ιθύραμβε, Βάκχ',
ε[ὔιε θυρσῆ]ρες, Βραϊ-
τά, Βρόμι(ε), ἠρινα[ῖς ἱκοῦ
ταῖσδ(ε)] ἱεραῖς ἐν ὥραις.
Εὐοῖ ὦ ἰὸ [Βάκχ' ὦ ἰὲ Παιὰ]ν
[ὃ]ν Θήβαις ποτ' ἐν εὐίαις
Ζη[νὶ γείνατο] καλλίπαις Θυώνα.
πάντες δ' [ἀστέρες ἀγχ]όρευ-
σαν, πάντες δὲ βροτοὶ χ[άρη-
σαν σαῖς], Βάκχιε, γένναις.

I have followed throughout Dr H. Weil's version.

himself a priest at Delphi. The comparison instituted by Plutarch between the rites of Osiris and those of Dionysos has been already noted (p. 401). In the discourse about Isis and Osiris[1], it will be remembered, Plutarch says 'the affair about the Titans and the Night of Accomplishment accords with what are called in the rites of Osiris "Tearings to pieces," Resurrections, Regenerations. The same,' he adds, 'is true about rites of burying. The Egyptians show in many places burial chests of Osiris, and the Delphians also hold that the remains of Dionysos are deposited with them near to the place of the oracle, and the Consecrated Ones (ὅσιοι) perform a secret sacrifice in the sanctuary of Apollo what time the Thyiades awaken Liknites.' In a word, at Delphi there were rites closely analogous to those of Osiris and concerned with the tearing to pieces, the death and burial of the god Dionysos, and his resurrection and re-birth as a child[2].

In another discourse (*On the Ei at Delphi*) Plutarch[3] tells us that these ceremonials were concerned with the god as Dithyrambos, that the characteristic of the Dithyramb was that it sang of these mutations, these re-births, and that it was thereby marked off sharply from the Paean of Apollo. The passage is so instructive both as to the real nature of Dionysos and as reflecting the attitude of an educated Greek towards his religion that it must be quoted in full. Plutarch has been discussing and contrasting Dionysos and Apollo apropos of the worship of Dionysos at Delphi, a worship every detail of which he must certainly have known. Dionysos, he says, has just as much to do with Delphi as Apollo himself, a statement rather startling to modern ears. Then he begins to work out the contrast between the two gods after the philosophic fashion of his day. Apollo is the principle of simplicity, unity and purity, Dionysos of manifold change and metamorphosis. This is the esoteric doctrine known to experts, cloaked from the vulgar. Among these experts (σοφώτεροι) were probably, as will be seen later (p. 462), Orphic theologians. He goes on to tell how these esoteric doctrines were expressed in popular ritual. He of course inverts the natural order of development. He

[1] Plut. *de Is. et Os.* XXXV.

[2] For a curious and very interesting survival of the passion-play of Dionysos see R. M. Dawkins, 'The modern carnival in Thrace and the cult of Dionysos,' *J.H.S.* 1906, p. 191.

[3] Plut. *de Ei ap. Delph.* IX.

believes that the doctrine known only to the few gave rise to a ritual intended to express it in popular terms for the vulgar; whereas of course in reality the ritual existed first and was then by the experts made to bear a mystical meaning. Bearing this proviso in mind Plutarch's account is full of interest. 'These manifold changes that Dionysos suffers into winds and water and earth and stars and the births of plants and animals they enigmatically term "rending asunder" and "tearing limb from limb"; and they call the god Dionysos and Zagreus and Nyktelios and Isodaites, and tell of certain Destructions and Disappearances and Resurrections and New-Births which are fables and riddles, appertaining to the aforesaid metamorphoses. And to him (i.e. Dionysos) they sing *dithyrambic* measures full of sufferings and metamorphosis, which metamorphosis has in it an element of wandering and distraction. For "it is fitting," as Aeschylus says, that "the dithyramb of diverse utterance should accompany Dionysos as his counterpart, but the ordered Paean and the sober Muse should attend Apollo." And artists in sculpture represent Apollo as ever young and ageless, but Dionysos they represent as having many forms and shapes. In a word, they attribute to the one uniformity and order and an earnest simplicity, but to the other a certain incongruousness owing to a blend made up of sportiveness and excess and earnestness and madness. They invoke him thus:

"Euios, thou Dionysos, who by the flame of thy rite
Dost women to madness incite."'

Plutarch goes on to tell of the division of the ritual year at Delphi between Apollo and Dionysos. Apollo as incoming conqueror has taken the larger and the fairer portion.

'And since the time of the revolutions in these changes is not equal, but the one which they call Satiety is longer, and the other which they call Craving is shorter, they observe in this matter a due proportion. For the remainder of the year they use the Paean in their sacrificial ceremonies, but at the approach of winter they wake up the Dithyramb and make the Paean cease. For three months they invoke the one god (Dionysos) in place of the other (Apollo), as they hold that in respect to its duration the setting in order of the world is to its conflagration as three to one.'

Plutarch's use of technical terms, e.g. conflagration (ἐκπύρωσις), betrays that he is importing into his religious discussion philosophic speculations, and especially those of Heraclitus. Into these it is unnecessary to follow him; the important points that emerge for the present argument are that the Dithyramb was a ritual song sung in the winter season, probably at festivals connected with the winter solstice, of an orgiastic character and dealing with the god as an impersonation of natural forces, dealing with his sufferings, his death and resurrection, and as such contrasted with the sober simple Paean. In a word the Dithyramb, and with it the title Dithyrambos, resume the two factors that we have detected in the religion of Dionysos, the old spirit of life and generation, and the new spirit of intoxication.

It remains to enquire if any light can be thrown on the difficult etymology[1] of the word.

The popular etymology, that saw in Dithyrambos the god-of-the-double-door, is of course impossible. Dithyrambos, all philologists agree, cannot etymologically be separated from its cognate *thriambos*, which gave to the Latins their word *triumphus*. The word *thriambos* looks as if it were formed on the analogy of *iambos*. It may be that Suidas[2] among his many confused conjectures as to the meaning of the word throws out accidentally the right clue. He says 'they call the madness of poets *thriasis*.' May not *thriambos* mean the mad inspired orgiastic measure? The first syllable with its long *i* may possibly be referred to the root Δι already discussed under Diasia (p. 23). At a time when in etymology the length of syllables was wholly disregarded the Δι in Διός might help out the confusion, and last some brilliant theologian intent on edification thought of the double doors. Mythology has left us dim hints as to the functions of certain ancient maiden prophetesses at Delphi called Thriae. May they not have been the Mad Maidens who sang the mad song, the *thriambos*?

[1] The suggestion that follows as to the connection of the word Dithyramb with Thriae is only given tentatively. It is also possible that the word Dithyramb may be of foreign origin. Epiphanius (*Adv. Haeres.* vol. I. bk iii. p. 1093 D) tells of a goddess in Egypt, worshipped with orgiastic rites under the name Τίθραμβος. She was akin to Hecate (ἄλλοι δὲ τῇ Τιθράμβῳ Ἑκάτην ἑρμηνευομένην). Τίθραμβος may have come with other orgiastic elements from Crete to Thrace (see p. 459).

[2] Suidas s.v. λέγουσι γὰρ θρίασιν τὴν τῶν ποιητῶν μανίαν. Suidas also suggests connection with θρῖα fig-leaves, ἢ ἀπὸ τοῦ θρῖα, τὰ φύλλα τῆς συκῆς ἀνακειμένης τῷ Διονύσῳ. In view of Mr Paton's investigations, *Rev. Arch.* 1907, p. 51, this derivation spite of quantity seems possible.

Of the Thriae we are told by Philochoros[1] that they were nymphs of Parnassos, nurses of Apollo. Save for this mention we never hear that Apollo had any nurses, he was wholly the son of his father. Is it not more probable that they were nurses of Dionysos?

The account of these mysterious Thriae given in the Homeric Hymn[2] to Hermes is strange and suggestive. Hermes is made to tell how his first gift of prophecy came not from Zeus, but from three maiden prophetesses:

'For there are sisters born, called Thriae, maiden things,
Three are they and they joy them in glory of swift wings.
Upon their heads is sprinkled fine flour of barley white,
They dwell aloof in dwellings beneath Parnassos' height.
They taught me love of soothsaying, while I my herds did feed,
Being yet a boy. Of me and mine my father took no heed.
And thence they flitted, now this way, now that, upon the wing,
And of all things that were to be they uttered soothsaying.
What time they fed on honey fresh, food of the gods divine,
Then holy madness made their hearts to speak the truth incline,
But if from food of honeycomb they needs must keep aloof
Confused they buzz among themselves and speak no word of sooth.'

The Thriae are nurses like the Maenads, they rave in holy madness (*θυΐουσιν*) like the Thyiades, but their inspiration is not from Bacchos, the wine-god, not even from Bromios or Sabazios or Braites, the beer-gods; it is from a source, from an intoxicant yet more primitive, from honey. They are in a word 'Melissae[3],' honey-priestesses, inspired by a honey intoxicant; they are bees, their heads white with pollen; they hum and buzz, swarming confusedly. The honey service of ancient ritual has already been noted (p. 91), and the fact that not only the priestesses of Artemis at Ephesus were 'Bees,' but also those of Demeter, and, still more significant, the Delphic priestess herself was a Bee. The oracle of the Bessi (p. 369) was delivered by a priestess, and the analogy with Delphi is noted by Herodotus; may not the priestess of the Bessi have also been a Bee? The Delphic priestess in historical times chewed a laurel leaf, but when she was a Bee surely she must have sought her inspiration in the honeycomb.

[1] Philoch. frg. 125 ap. Zenob. *prov. cent.* v. 75, Φιλόχορός φησιν ὅτι νύμφαι κατεῖχον τὸν Παρνασσὸν τροφοὶ Ἀπόλλωνος τρεῖς καλούμεναι Θριαί, ἀφ' ὧν αἱ μαντικαὶ ψῆφοι θριαὶ καλοῦνται.

[2] *Hom. Hymn. ad Merc.* 551—563. I accept Hermann's reading Θριαί for Μοῖραι, cf. Gemoll ad loc.

[3] For Bee-goddesses and Bee-priestesses see Dr Neustadt's interesting monograph *De Iove Cretico*, III. *De Melissa dea.*

With all these divine associations about the bee, a creature wondrous enough in nature, it is not surprising that she was figured by art as a goddess and half human. In fig. 135 we have such a representation[1], a woman with high curled wings and a bee body from the waist downwards. The design is from a gold embossed plaque found at Camiros.

FIG. 135.

When Euripides would tell of the dread power of Aphrodite haunting with her doom all living things, Aphrodite who was heir to all the sacred traditions of the Earth-Mother, the image of the holy bee comes to his mind charged with mysterious associations half lost to us. He makes the chorus of maidens in the *Hippolytus* sing[2]:

> 'O mouth of Dirce, O god-built wall
> That Dirce's wells run under;
> Ye know the Cyprian's fleet foot-fall,
> Ye saw the heavens round her flare
> When she lulled to her sleep that Mother fair
> Of Twy-born Bacchus and crowned her there
> The Bride of the bladed thunder,
> For her breath is on all that hath life, and she floats in the air
> Bee-like, death-like, a wonder.'

The *thriambos*[3] was then, if this conjecture be correct, the song of the Thriae or honey-priestesses, a song from the beginning like the analogous Dithyramb confused, inspired, impassioned. The title Dithyrambos through its etymology and by its traditional use belonged to Dionysos, conceived of in his twofold aspect as the nature-god born anew each year, the god of plants and animals as well as of human life, and also as the spirit of intoxication. It remains to ask what was the significance of such a god to the Greeks who received him as an immigrant from the North. How far did they adopt and how far modify both elements in this strange and complex new worship?

[1] For a full account of 'the Bee in Greek Mythology' see Mr A. B. Cook, *J.H.S.* xv. 1895, p. 1.

[2] Eur. *Hipp.* 555.

[3] *θρίαμβος* translated by the Romans into the plain prose of 'triumph' seems to have remained to the Greeks a poetical word consecrated to poetical usage. Conon says indeed of Tereus in telling the story of Philomela: *τέμνει τὴν αὐτῆς γλῶσσαν δεδιὼς τὸν ἐκ λόγων θρίαμβον* (*Narrat.* XXXI.), but the story and the usage of the word seem borrowed from some poetical source. Sir Richard Jebb kindly drew my attention to the fact that in our earliest literary mention of the *thriambos* (Kratinos, Koch frg. 36) it is apparently sung by a female singer:

ὅτε σὺ τοὺς καλοὺς θριάμβους ἀναρύτουσ' ἀπηχθάνου.

First, what significance had Dionysos to the Greeks as a nature-god, in his animal and vegetable forms as bull and tree?

Long before the coming of Dionysos the Greeks had nature-gods: they had Demeter goddess of the corn, they had Poseidon Phytalmios god of the growth of plants, they had the Charites givers of all increase. But it should be distinctly noted that all these and many another nature-god had passed into a state of complete anthropomorphism. They represent human rather than merely physical relations, they have cut themselves as far as possible loose from plant and animal nature. Demeter is far more mother than corn. Hermes is the young man in his human splendour, and spite of his Herm-form and phallic worship has well nigh forgotten that he was once a spirit of generation in flocks and plants. Athene, like her mother the earth, had once for her vehicle a snake (p. 305), but she has waxed in glory till she comes to be a motherless splendour born of the brain of Zeus, an incarnate city of Athens. These magnificent Olympians have shed for ever the slough of animal shapes. Dionysos came to Greece at an earlier stage of his development when he was still half bull half tree, and this earlier stage was tolerated, even welcomed, by a people who had themselves outgrown it.

It is not hard to see how this came to be. Man when he worships a bull or a tree has not, even to himself, consciously emerged as human. He is still to his own thinking brother of plants and animals. As he advances he gains but also loses, and must sometimes retrace his steps. The Greeks of the sixth century B.C. may well have been a little weary of their anthropomorphic Olympians, tired of their own magnified reflection in the mirror of mythology, whether this image were distorted or halo-crowned. They had taken for their motto 'Know Thyself,' but at the fountain of self-knowledge no human soul has ever yet quenched its thirst. With Dionysos, god of trees and plants as well as human life, there came a 'return to nature,' a breaking of bonds and limitations and crystallizations, a desire for the life rather of the emotions than of the reason, a recrudescence it may be of animal passions. Nowhere is this return to nature more clearly seen than in the *Bacchae*[1] of Euripides. The Bacchants leave their human

[1] See Mr Gilbert Murray, *Euripides*, p. lxvii.

homes, their human work and ordered life, their looms and distaffs, and are back with the wild things upon the mountains. In token of this their hair flows loose, they clothe themselves with the skin of beasts, they are girt with snakes and crowned with ivy and wild briony, and leaving their human babes they suckle the young of wolves and deer[1]:

'And one a young fawn held, and one a wild
Wolf-cub, and fed them with white milk and smiled
In love, young mothers with a mother's breast,
And babes at home forgotten.'

Euripides, it may be, utters his own longing to be free from the tangle and stress of things human, but it is into the mouths of the chorus of Maenads that he puts the lovely song[2]:

'Will they ever come to me, ever again,
The long, long dances,
On through the dark till the dim stars wane?
Shall I feel the dew on my throat and the stream
Of wind in my hair? Shall our white feet gleam
In the dim expanses?
O feet of a Fawn to the greenwood fled,
Alone in the grass, and the loveliness;
Leap of the Hunted, no more in dread,
Beyond the snares and the deadly press.
Yet a voice still in the distance sounds,
A voice and a fear and a haste of hounds,
O wildly labouring, fiercely fleet,
Onward yet by river and glen—
Is it joy or terror ye storm-swift feet?—
To the dear lone lands untroubled of men,
Where no voice sounds, and amid the shadowy green
The little things of the woodland live unseen.'

Nor is it only that the Maenads escape from their humanity to worship on the mountain, they find there others, a strange congregation, that worship with them[3]:

'There
Through the appointed hour, they made their prayer
And worship of the Wand, with one accord
Of heart, and cry "Iacchos, Bromios, Lord,
God of God born!" And all the mountain felt
And worshipped with them; and the wild things knelt,
And ramped and gloried, and the wilderness
Was filled with moving voices and dim stress.'

This notion of a return to nature[4] is an element in the worship

[1] Eur. *Bacch.* 699. [2] *Ib.* 862. [3] *Ib.* 723.

[4] Nietzsche has drawn in this respect a contrast, beautiful and profoundly true, between the religion and art of Apollo and Dionysos. Apollo, careful to remain his splendid self, projects an image, a dream, and calls it *god*. It is illusion (*Schein*), its watchword is limitation (*Maass*), Know thyself, Nothing too much. Dionysos

of Dionysos so simple, so moving and in a sense so modern that we realize it without effort. It is harder to attain to anything like historical sympathy with the second element—that of intoxication.

It is not easy to deal with the worship of Dionysos without rousing in our own minds an instinctive protest. Intoxication to us now-a-days means not inspiration but excess and consequent degradation; its associations are with crime, with the slums, with hereditary disease, with every form of abuse that abases man, not to the level of the beasts but far beneath them.

In trying to understand how the Greeks felt towards Dionysos we must bear in mind one undoubted fact. The Greeks were not as a nation drunkards. Serious excess in drink is rare among southern nations, and the Greeks were no exception to the general rule. When they came in contact with northern nations like the Thracians, who drank deep and seriously, they were surprised and disgusted.

Of this we have ample evidence, much of it drawn from the discussion in the *Deipnosophistae* of Athenaeus[1] on Wine and Wine-cups. The general tone of the discourse, while it is strongly in favour of drinking, is averse to drunkenness. 'The men of old time were not wont to get drunk.' The reason given is characteristically Greek; they disliked the unbridled license that ensued. It was well said by the inventors of proverbs, 'Wine has no rudder.' Plato[2] in the sixth book of the *Laws* said it was unfitting for a man to drink to the point of drunkenness, except on the occasions of festivals of that god who was the giver of wine. An occasional and strictly defined license under the sanction of religion is widely different from a general habit of intemperance. In the first book of the *Laws*[3], in speaking of various foreign nations Northern and Oriental, e.g. Celts, Iberians, Thracians, Lydians and Persians, he says 'nations of that sort make a practice of drunkenness.'

The Greek habit of drinking was marked off from that of the Thracians by two customs, they drank their wine in small cups

breaks all bonds; his motto is the limitless Excess (*Uebermaass*), Ecstasy. *Das Individuum mit allen seinen Grenzen und Maassen ging hier in der Selbstvergessenheit der dionysischen Zustände unter, und vergass die apollinischen Satzungen* (Nietzsche, *Die Geburt der Tragödie*, p. 37).

[1] Ath. XI. 31 p. 427. [2] Plat. *Legg.* p. 775. [3] *Ib.* p. 637.

and they mixed it freely with water. One of the guests in Athenaeus remarks[1] that it is worth while enquiring whether the men of old times drank out of large cups. 'For,' he adds, 'Dicaearchus the Messenian, the disciple of Aristotle, in his discourse on Alcaeus says they used small cups and drank their wine mixed with much water.' He goes on to cite a treatise 'On Drunkenness' by Chamaeleon of Heracleia, in which Chamaeleon stated not only that the custom of using large cups was a recent one but that it was imported from the barbarians. Imported indeed but never really naturalized, for he goes on to say, 'They being devoid of culture rush eagerly to excess in wine and provide for themselves all manner of superfluous delicacies.' It is clear that in respect of wine and food as of everything else the Greek was in the main true to his motto 'Nothing too much.' Drunkenness was an offence in his eyes against taste as well as morals.

Large drinking cups were a northern barbarian characteristic[2]; they were made originally of the huge horns of the large breed of cattle common in the North, they were set in silver and gold, and later sometimes actually made of precious metals and called *rhyta*. Chamaeleon goes on to say, 'in the various regions of Greece neither in works of art nor in poems shall we find any trace of a large cup being made save in such as deal with heroes.' That to the dead hero was allowed even by the Orphics the guerdon of 'eternal drunkenness' will be seen later (Chap. XI.), but the living hero only drank of large cups of unmixed wine out of ceremonial courtesy to the Northerner. Xenophon in the seventh book of the *Anabasis* describes in detail the drinking festival given by the Thracian Seuthes. When the Greek general and his men came to Seuthes they embraced first and then *according to the Thracian custom* horns of wine were presented to them. In like manner the Macedonian Philip pledged his friends in a horn of wine. It was from silver horns that the Centaurs drank (p. 385). A flatterer and a demagogue might drink deep for his own base purposes. Of the arch-demagogue Alcibiades Plutarch[3] says: 'At Athens he scoffed and kept horses, at Sparta he went close-shaved and wore a short cloak and washed in cold

[1] Ath. XI. 4 p. 461. [2] Ath. XI. 51 p. 476.
[3] Plut. *De adul. et amic.* VII.

water, in Thrace he fought and drank.' War and drink, Ares and Dionysos, have been in all ages the chosen divinities of the Northerner. Diodorus[1] in speaking of ceremonial wine-drinking makes a characteristically Greek statement: 'They say that those who drink at banquets when unmixed wine is provided invoke the Good Genius, but when after the meal wine is given mixed with water they call on the name of Zeus the Saviour; for they hold that wine drunk unmixed produces forms of madness, but that when it is mixed with the rain of Zeus the joy of it and the delight remain, and the injurious element that causes madness and license is corrected.' The Good, or perhaps we ought to call him 'Wealthy,' Spirit is the very essence of the old wine-god of Thrace and Boeotia; the blending with the rain of Zeus is the taking of it over to the mildness and temperance of the Greek character.

Excess was rare among the southern Greeks, and, even when they exceeded, because they were a people of artists they euphemized. No one but a Greek could have conceived the lovely little vase-painting from an oinochoë in the Boston Museum

FIG. 136.

of Fine Arts[2] in fig. 136. A beautiful maiden is the centre of the scene. She is a worshipper of Dionysos. In her left hand is a tall thyrsos and she holds the cup of Dionysos, the

[1] Diod. IV. 3.

[2] *Boston Museum Annual Report*, 1901, p. 60, No. 20. P. Hartwig, *Strena Helbigiana*, p. 111.

kantharos, in her right. It is empty, and she seems to ask the Satyr who stands before her to refill it from his oinochoë. But he will not, she has had too much already. Over her beautiful head, slightly inclined as if in weariness, is inscribed—and who but a Greek would have dared to write it?—her name 'Kraipale.' Behind her comes a kindly sober friend bearing in her hand a hot drink, smoking still, to cure her sickness.

Perhaps because the extreme of drunkenness, its after degradation and squalid ugliness, was rare among the Greeks, they were better able to realize that in its milder forms it lent lovely motives for art. Wine by the release it brings from self-consciousness unslacks the limbs and gives to pose and gesture the new beauty of abandonment. Degas has dared to seize and fix for ever the beauty he saw in that tragedy of degradation—a woman of the people besotted by absinthe. The peeping moralist that lurks in most of us intrudes to utter truth beside the mark and say that she is wicked. To the Greek artist there was no such extreme issue between art and morality. To him, whether poet or vase-painter, to drink and fall asleep was if not a common at least a beautiful experience, one he painted on many a vase and sang in many a song. A festival without the grace and glory of wine would to him have been shorn of well nigh all its goodliness. On this it is needless to insist. To him peace and wine and sleep are playfellows loving and lovely[1]:

'Eyelids closed and lulled heart deep
In gentle, unforbidden sleep,
Street by street the city brims
With lovers' feasts and burns with lovers' hymns.'

Another point remains to be noted. Not only did the Greeks mix their Thracian wine with water, tempering the madness of the god, but they saw in Dionysos the god of spiritual as well as physical intoxication. It cannot be forgotten that the drama was early connected with the religion of Dionysos; his nurses are not only Maenads, they are Muses; from him and him only comes the beauty and magic of their song:

'Hail Child of Semele, only by thee
Can any singing sweet and gracious be.'

The contrast between sheer Thracian madness and the Athenian

[1] Bacchyl. *Paean*, Bergk 13, trans. by Mr D. S. MacColl.

notion of inspiration is very clearly seen in the two figures of Dionysos as represented on the two vase-paintings in fig. 137 and fig. 138, vase-paintings roughly contemporaneous, the first in the

FIG. 137.

style of Hieron, the second in that of Brygos. In fig. 137 from a red-figured stamnos[1] in the British Museum we have the Thracian Dionysos drunk with wine, a brutal though still splendid savage; he dances in ecstasy brandishing the fawn he has rent asunder in his madness. In the second picture[2] (fig. 138), a masterpiece of decorative composition, we have Dionysos as the Athenian cared to know him. The strange mad Satyrs are twisted and contorted to make exquisite patterns, they clash their frenzied crotala and wave great vine branches. But in the midst of the revel the god

[1] Brit. Mus. *Cat.* E 439, pl. xv. On the reverse a Satyr plays the flute to his master's dancing.

[2] Bibliothèque Nationale, *Cat.* 576. P. Hartwig, *Meisterschalen*, XXXIII. 1.

himself stands erect. He holds no kantharos, only a great lyre.

Fig. 138.

His head is thrown back in ecstasy; he is drunken, but with music, not with wine.

Again, with the Maenad worshippers there is the same transformation.

The delicate red-figured kotylos[1] in fig. 139 from the National Museum in Athens is like a little twofold text on the double aspect of the worship of Dionysos. On the obverse is a Maenad about to execute her old savage ritual of tearing a kid asunder. In a moment she will raise her bent head and chant[2]:

'O glad, glad on the Mountains
To swoon in the race outworn,
When the holy fawn-skin clings
And all else sweeps away,
To the joy of the quick red fountains,
The blood of the hill-goat torn,
The glory of wild-beast ravenings
Where the hill-top catches the day,
To the Phrygian, Lydian mountains
'Tis Bromios leads the way.'

[1] Athens, Nat. Mus. *Inv.* 3412. *Bull. de Corr. Hell.* XIX. 1895, p. 94.
[2] Eur. *Bacch.* 135.

On the reverse for counterpart is a sister Maenad. She dances

FIG. 139.

in gentle ecstasy, playing on her great timbrel. She is all for the service of the Muses, and she might sing[1]:

> 'But a better land is there
> Where Olympus cleaves the air,
> The high still dell, where the Muses dwell,
> Fairest of all things fair.
> O there is Grace, and there is the Heart's Desire,
> And peace to adore thee, thou Spirit of guiding Fire.'

There are some to whom by natural temperament the religion of Bromios, son of Semele, is and must always be a dead letter, if not a stumbling-block. Food is to such a troublesome necessity, wine a danger or a disgust. They dread all stimulus that comes from without, they would fain break the ties that link them with animals and plants. They do not feel in themselves and are at a loss to imagine for others the sacramental mystery of life and nutrition that is accomplished in us day by day, how in the faintness of fasting the whole nature of man, spirit as well as body, dies down, he cannot think, he cannot work, he cannot love; how in the breaking of bread, and still more in the drinking of wine, life spiritual as well as physical is renewed, thought is re-born, his equanimity, his magnanimity are restored, reason and morality

[1] Eur. *Bacch.* 409.

rule again. But to this sacramentalism of life most of us bear constant, if partly unconscious, witness. We will not eat with the man we hate, it is felt a sacrilege leaving a sickness in body and soul. The first breaking of bread and drinking of wine together is the seal of a new friendship; the last eaten in silence at parting is more than many words. The sacramental feast of bread and wine is spread for the newly married, for the newly dead.

Those to whom wine brings no inspiration, no moments of sudden illumination, of wider and deeper insight, of larger human charity and understanding, find it hard to realize what to others of other temperament is so natural, so elemental, so beautiful—the constant shift from physical to spiritual that is of the essence of the religion of Dionysos. But there are those also, and they are saintly souls, who know it all to the full, know the exhilaration of wine, know what it is to be drunken with the physical beauty of a flower or a sunset, with the sensuous imagery of words, with the strong wine of a new idea, with the magic of another's personality, yet having known, turn away with steadfast eyes, disallowing the madness not only of Bromios but of the Muses and of Aphrodite. Such have their inward ecstasy of the ascetic, but they revel with another Lord, and he is Orpheus.

CHAPTER IX.

ORPHEUS.

'πολλοὶ μὲν ναρθηκοφόροι, παῦροι δέ τε Βάκχοι.'

MYTHOLOGY has left us no tangle more intricate and assuredly no problem half so interesting as the relation between the ritual and mythology of Orpheus and Dionysos.

By the time of Herodotus[1] the followers of Orpheus and of Bacchus are regarded as substantially identical. In commenting on the taboo among the Egyptians against being buried in woollen garments he says: 'In this respect they agree with the rites which are called Bacchic and Orphic but are really Egyptian and Pythagorean.' The identification is of course a rough and ready one, an identification of race on the precarious basis of a similarity of rites, but one thing is clear to the mind of Herodotus—Orphic and Bacchic and Egyptian rites are either identical or closely analogous. The analogy between Orpheus and Bacchus passed by the time of Euripides into current language. Theseus[2] when he would taunt Hippolytus with his pseudo-asceticism says:

'Go revel thy Bacchic rites
With Orpheus for thy Lord,'

and Apollodorus[3] in his systematic account of the Muses states that Orpheus 'invented the mysteries of Dionysos.' The severance of the two figures by modern mythologists has often led to the misconception of both. The full significance, the higher spiritual developments of the religion of Dionysos are only understood

[1] Herod. II. 81 ὁμολογέουσι δὲ ταῦτα τοῖσι Ὀρφικοῖσι καλευμένοισι καὶ Βακχικοῖσι, ἐοῦσι δὲ Αἰγυπτίοισι καὶ Πυθαγορείοισι.

[2] Eur. *Hipp.* 954

Ὀρφέα τ' ἄνακτ' ἔχων
βάκχευε.

[3] Apollod. I. 3. 2, 3.

through the doctrine of Orpheus, and the doctrine of Orpheus apart from the religion of Dionysos is a dead letter.

And yet, clearly linked though they are, the most superficial survey reveals differences so striking as to amount to a spiritual antagonism. Orpheus reflects Dionysos, yet at almost every point seems to contradict him. The sober gentle musician, the precise almost pedantic theologist, is no mere echo, no reincarnation of the maddened, maddening wine-god. Diodorus expresses a truth that must have struck every thinker among the Greeks, that this real and close resemblance veiled an inner, intimate discrepancy. He says[1], in telling the story of Lycurgus, 'Charops, grandfather of Orpheus, gave help to the god, and Dionysos in gratitude instructed him in the orgies of his rites; Charops handed them down to his son Oiagros, and Oiagros to his son Orpheus.' Then follow the significant words: 'Orpheus, being a man gifted by nature and highly trained above all others, *made many modifications in the orgiastic rites*: hence they call the rites that took their rise from Dionysos, Orphic.' Diodorus seems to have put his finger on the secret of Orpheus. He comes later than Dionysos, he is a man not a god, and his work is to modify the rites of the god he worshipped.

It is necessary at the outset to emphasize the humanity of Orpheus. About his legend has gathered much that is miraculous, and a theory[2] has been started and supported with much learning and ability, a theory which sees in Orpheus an underworld god, the chthonic counterpart of Dionysos, and that derives his name from chthonic darkness (ὄρφνη). This is to my mind to misconceive the whole relation between the two.

Orpheus as Magical Musician.

Like the god he served, Orpheus is at one part of his career a Thracian, unlike him a magical musician. Dionysos, as has been seen (p. 451), played upon the lyre, but music was never of his essence.

In the matter of Thracian music we are happily on firm

[1] Diod. III. 65 πολλὰ μεταθεῖναι τῶν ἐν τοῖς ὀργίοις.

[2] E. Maass, *Orpheus*. To Dr Maass's learned book I owe much, but I am reluctantly compelled to differ from his main contention, that Orpheus is a god.

ground. The magical musician, whose figure to the modern mind has almost effaced the theologist, comes as would be expected from the home of music, the North. Conon[1] in his life of Orpheus says expressly, 'the stock of the Thracians and Macedonians is music-loving.' Strabo[2] too is explicit on this point. In the passage already quoted (p. 414), on the strange musical instruments used in the orgies of Dionysos, he says: 'Similar to these (i.e. the rites of Dionysos) are the Kotyttia and Bendideia practised among the Thracians, and with them also Orphic rites had their beginning.' A little further he goes on to say that the Thracian origin of the worship of the Muses is clear from the places sacred to their cult. 'For Pieria and Olympus and Pimplea and Leibethra were of old Thracian mountains and districts, but are now held by the Macedonians, and the Thracians who colonized Boeotia consecrated Helicon to the Muses and also the cave of the Nymphs called Leibethriades. And those who practised ancient music are said to have been Thracians, Orpheus and Musaeus and Thamyris, and the name Eumolpus comes from Thrace.'

The statement of Strabo is noticeable. As Diodorus places Orpheus two generations later than Dionysos, so the cult of the Muses with which Orpheus is associated seems chiefly to prevail in Lesbos and among the Cicones of Lower Thrace and Macedonia. We do not hear of Orpheus among the remote inland Bessi. This may point to a somewhat later date of development when the Thracians were moving southwards. That there were primitive and barbarous tribes living far north who practised music we know again from Strabo. He tells[3] of an Illyrian tribe, the Dardanii, who were wholly savage and lived in caves they dug under dung-heaps, but all the same they were very musical and played a great deal on pipes and stringed instruments. The practice of music alone does not even now-a-days necessarily mark a high level of culture, and the magic of Orpheus was, as will later be seen, much more than the making of sweet sounds.

Orpheus, unlike Dionysos, remained consistently a Northerner. We have no universal spread of his name, no fabulous birth stories everywhere, no mystic Nysa; he does not take whole nations by storm, he is always known to be an immigrant and is always of

[1] Conon, *Narr.* XLV. φιλόμουσον τὸ Θρᾳκῶν καὶ Μακεδόνων γένος.
[2] Strabo, X. 3 § 722.
[3] Strabo, VII. 7 § 315.

the few. At Thebes we hear of magical singers Zethus and Amphion, but not of Orpheus. In Asia he seems never to have prevailed; the orgies of Dionysos and the Mother remained in Asia in their primitive Thracian savagery. It is in Athens that he mainly re-emerges.

To the modern mind the music of Orpheus has become mainly fabulous, a magic constraint over the wild things of nature.

> 'Orpheus with his lute made trees
> And the mountain tops that freeze
> Bow themselves when he did sing.'

This notion of the fabulous music was already current in antiquity. The Maenads in the *Bacchae*[1] call to their Lord to come from Parnassos,

> 'Or where stern Olympus stands
> In the elm woods or the oaken,
> There where Orpheus harped of old,
> And the trees awoke and knew him,
> And the wild things gathered to him,
> As he sang among the broken
> Glens his music manifold,'

and again in the lovely song of the *Alcestis*[2], the chorus sing to Apollo who is but another Orpheus:

> 'And the spotted lynxes for joy of thy song
> Were as sheep in the fold, and a tawny throng
> Of lions trooped down from Othrys' lawn,
> And her light foot lifting, a dappled fawn
> Left the shade of the high-tressed pine,
> And danced for joy to that lyre of thine.'

In Pompeian wall-paintings and Graeco-Roman sarcophagi it is as magical musician, with power over all wild untamed things in nature, that Orpheus appears. This conception naturally passed into Christian art and it is interesting to watch the magical musician transformed gradually into the Good Shepherd. The bad wild beasts, the lions and lynxes, are weeded out one by one, and we are left, as in the wonderful Ravenna[3] mosaic, with only a congregation of mild patient sheep.

It is the more interesting to find that on black and red-figured vase-paintings, spite of this literary tradition, the power of the magical musician is quite differently conceived. Orpheus

[1] Eur. *Bacch.* 560. [2] Eur. *Alc.* 579.

[3] In the Church of S. Apollinare in Classe. See Kurth, *Mosaiken von der christlich. Era*, Taf. XXVII.

does not appear at all on black-figured vases—again a note of his late coming—and on red-figured vases never with the attendant wild beasts.

On a vase found at Gela and now in the Berlin Museum[1], reproduced in fig. 140, we have Orpheus as musician. He wears Greek dress and sits playing on his lyre with up-turned head, utterly aloof, absorbed. And round him are not wild beasts but

FIG. 140.

wild *men*, Thracians. They wear uniformly the characteristic Thracian dress, the fox-skin cap and the long embroidered cloak, of both of which Herodotus[2] makes mention as characteristic. The Thracians who joined the Persian expedition, he says, 'wore fox-skins on their heads and were clothed with various-coloured cloaks.' These wild Thracians in the vase-painting are all intent on the music; the one to the right looks suspicious of this new magic, the one immediately facing Orpheus is determined to enquire into it, the one just behind has gone under completely; his eyes are shut, his head falling, he is mesmerized, drunken but not with wine.

This beautiful picture brings to our minds very forcibly one

[1] Berlin Mus. *Cat.* 3172; *Progr. Winckelmannsfeste*, Berlin, No. 50, Taf. II.; Roscher, *Lexicon*, vol. III. p. 1179.
[2] Herod. VII. 75.

note of Orpheus, as contrasted with Dionysos, his extraordinary quiet. Orpheus never plays the flute 'that rouses to madness' nor clangs the deafening cymbals; he plays always on the quiet lyre, and he is never disturbed or distraught by his own music. He is the very mirror of that 'orderliness and grave earnestness' (τάξις καὶ σπουδή) which, as we have seen (p. 440), Plutarch took to be the note of Apollo. Small wonder that Apollo was imaged as Orpheus.

Orpheus, before the dawn of history, had made his home in Thrace. His music is all of the North, but after all, though mythology always emphasizes this music, it was not the whole secret of his influence. He was more priest than musician. Moreover, though Orpheus has certain Apolline touches, the two figures are not really the least like. About Apollo there is no atmosphere of mysticism, nothing mysterious and ineffable: he is all sweet reasonableness and lucidity. Orpheus came to Thrace and thence to Thessaly, but he may have come from the South. It will later be seen that his religion in its most primitive form is best studied in Crete. In Crete, and perhaps there only, is found that strange blend of Egyptian and primitive Pelasgian which found its expression in Orphic rites. Diodorus[1] says Orpheus went to Egypt to learn his ritual and theology, but in reality there was no need to leave his native island. From Crete by the old island route[2] he might pass northwards, leaving his mystic rites as he went at Paros, at Samos, at Samothrace, at Lesbos. At Maroneia among the Cicones he met the vine-god, among the Thracians he learnt his music. All this is by anticipation. That Crete was probably the home of Orphism will best be seen after examination of the mysteries of Orpheus (p. 564). For the present we must be content to examine his mythology.

The contrast between Orpheus and Dionysos is yet more vividly emphasized in the vase-painting[3] next to be considered (fig. 141), from a red-figured hydria of rather late style. Again Orpheus is the central figure, and again a Thracian in his long embroidered cloak and fox-skin cap is listening awe-struck. It is

[1] Diod. IV. 25.

[2] These wanderings by sea may perhaps be reflected in the voyage of the Argonauts.

[3] Roscher, *Lexicon*, vol. III. p. 1181, fig. 5. The vase was formerly in the Dutuit collection.

noticeable that in this and all red-figured vases of the fine period Orpheus is dressed as a Greek; he has been wholly assimilated, nothing in his dress marks him from Apollo. It is not till a very late date, and chiefly in Lower Italy, that the vase-painter shows himself an archaeologist and dresses Orpheus as a Thracian priest. Not only a Thracian but a Satyr looks and listens entranced.

FIG. 141.

But this time Orpheus will not work his magic will. He may tame the actual Thracian, he may tame the primitive population of Thrace mythologically conceived of as Satyrs, but the real worshipper of Dionysos is untameable as yet. Up from behind in hot haste comes a Maenad armed with a great club, and we foresee the pitiful end.

THE DEATH OF ORPHEUS.

The story of the slaying of Orpheus by the Thracian women, the Maenads, the Bassarids, is of cardinal importance. It was the subject of a lost play by Aeschylus, but vases of the severe red-figured style remain our earliest extant source. Manifold reasons, to suit the taste of various ages, were of course invented to account for the myth. Some said Orpheus was slain by Zeus because Prometheus-like he revealed mysteries to man. When love came into fashion he suffers for his supposed sin against the Love-God. Plato[1] made him be done to death by the Maenads, because, instead of dying for love of Eurydice, he went down alive into Hades. But serious tradition always connected his death somehow

[1] Plat. *Symp.* 179 c. Phanocles (ap. Stob. *serm.* LXIV.) makes Orpheus suffer for his introduction of paiderastia, the introduction of which is attributed by Aristotle (*Pol.* II. 10) to the *Cretan* Minos.

with the cult of Dionysos. According to one account he died the death of Dionysos himself. Proklos[1] in his commentary on Plato says: 'Orpheus, because he was the leader in the rites of Dionysos, is said to have suffered the like fate to his god.' It will later be shown in discussing Orphic mysteries (p. 483) that an important feature in Dionysiac religion was the rending and death of the god, and no doubt to the faithful it seemed matter of edification that Orpheus, the priest of his mysteries, should suffer the like passion.

But in the myth of the death by the hands of the Maenads there is another element, possibly with some historical kernel, the element of hostility between the two cults, the intimate and bitter hostility of things near akin. The Maenads tear Orpheus to pieces, not because he is an incarnation of their god, but because he despises them and they hate him. This seems to have been the form of the legend followed by Aeschylus. It is recorded for us by Eratosthenes[2]. 'He (Orpheus) did not honour Dionysos but accounted Helios the greatest of the gods, whom also he called Apollo. And rising up early in the morning he climbed the mountain called Pangaion and waited for the rising of the sun that he might first catch sight of it. Therefore Dionysos was enraged and sent against him his Bassarids, as Aeschylus the poet says. And they tore him to pieces and cast his limbs asunder. But the Muses gathered them together and buried them in the place called Leibethra.' Orpheus was a reformer, a protestant; there is always about him a touch of the reformer's priggishness; it is impossible not to sympathize a little with the determined looking Maenad who is coming up behind to put a stop to all this sun-watching and lyre-playing.

The devotion of Orpheus to Helios is noted also in the hypothesis to the Orphic *Lithika*[3]. Orpheus was on his way up a mountain to perform an annual sacrifice in company with

[1] Prokl. ad Plat. *Polit.* p. 398 Ὀρφεὺς ἅτε τῶν Διονύσου τελετῶν ἡγεμὼν γενόμενος τὰ ὅμοια παθεῖν λέγεται τῷ σφετέρῳ θεῷ.

[2] Eratosth. *Catast.* XXIV. Since the above was written M. Salomon Reinach's interesting paper 'La Mort d'Orphée' (*Rev. Arch.* 1902, p. 242) has appeared. He sees in Orpheus a fox-totem of the Bassarids. But the traits of Orpheus recorded by tradition seem to me exclusively human. I am more inclined to see in his dismemberment the echo of some tradition of 'secondary burial,' such as is known to have been practised in primitive Egypt and, significantly, in Crete, at Palaiokastro. See *J.H.S.* 1902, p. 386.

[3] Hypoth. ad *Orph. Lith.*

some friends, when he met Theiodamas. He tells Theiodamas the origin of the custom. When Orpheus was a child he was nearly killed by a snake and he took refuge in a neighbouring sanctuary of Helios. The father of Orpheus instituted the sacrifice and when his father left the country Orpheus kept it up. Theiodamas waits till the ceremony is over, and then follows the discourse on precious stones.

That there was a Thracian cult of the Sun-god later fused with that of Apollo is certain. Sophocles[1] in the *Tereus* made some one say:

> 'O Helios, name
> To Thracian horsemen dear, O eldest flame!'

Helios was a favourite of monotheism, as we learn from another fragment of Sophocles[2]:

> 'Helios, have pity on me,
> Thou whom the wise men call the sire of gods
> And father of all things.'

The 'wise men' here as in many other passages[3] may actually be Orphic teachers, anyhow they are specialists in theology. Helios, as all-father, has the air of late speculation, but such speculations are often only the revival in another and modified form of a primitive faith. By the time of Homer, Helios had sunk to a mere impersonation of natural fact, but he may originally have been a potent sky god akin to Keraunios and to Ouranos, who was himself effaced by Zeus. Orpheus was, as will later be seen, a teacher of monotheism, and it was quite in his manner to attempt the revival of an ancient and possibly purer faith.

Be this as it may, it is quite certain that ancient tradition made him the foe of Dionysos and the victim of the god's worshippers. His death at their hands is depicted on numerous vase-paintings of which a typical instance is given in fig. 142. The design is from a red-figured stamnos in the Museo Gregoriano of the Vatican[4]. The scheme is usually much the same; we have the onset of the Thracian women bearing clubs or double axes

[1] Soph. frg. 523.

[2] Soph. frg. 1017. The attribution to Sophocles is doubtful.

[3] Evidence of the use of οἱ σοφοί to indicate the Orphics has been collected by Dr J. Adam in his edition of the *Republic*, vol. II. p. 378.

[4] Museo Gregoriano, II. 60. 1; Roscher, *Lexicon*, III. p. 1187, fig. 12.

or great rocks for weapons. Usually they are on foot, but on the Vatican stamnos one Maenad appears mounted, Amazon fashion. Before this fierce onset the beautiful musician falls helpless, his only weapon of defence the innocent lyre. On a cylix[1] with white ground about the date of Euphronios, the Thracian Maenad who slays Orpheus is tattooed; on the upper part of her right arm is clearly marked a little stag. Popular aetiology connected this tattooing with the death of Orpheus. The husbands of the wicked women tattooed them as a punishment for their crime, and all husbands continued the practice down to the time of Plutarch. Plutarch[2] says he 'cannot praise them,' as long protracted punishment is 'the prerogative of the Deity.' Prof. Ridgeway[3] has shown that the practice of tattooing was in use among the primitive Pelasgian population but never adopted by the Achaeans.

FIG. 142.

The Maenads triumphed for a time.

> 'What could the Muse herself that Orpheus bore,
> The Muse herself for her enchanting son,
> Whom universal nature did lament,
> When by the rout that made the hideous roar
> His gory visage down the stream was sent,
> Down the swift Hebrus to the Lesbian shore?'

The dismal savage tale comes to a gentle close. The head of Orpheus, singing always, is found by the Muses, and buried in the sanctuary at Lesbos. Who are the Muses? Who but the Maenads repentant, clothed and in their right minds.

[1] *J.H.S.* 1888, pl. I. On another vase in the British Museum (*Cat.* E 301) a Maenad pursuing Orpheus is tattooed on the right arm and both insteps with a ladder-like pattern.

[2] Plut. *de ser. num. vind.* XII. *οὐδὲ γὰρ Θρᾷκας ἐπαινοῦμεν ὅτι στίζουσιν ἄχρι νῦν τιμωροῦντες Ὀρφεῖ τὰς αὐτῶν γυναῖκας*, and Phanocles ap. Stob. *Florileg.* p. 399 v. 13 says:

> *ποινὰς δ' Ὀρφῆϊ κταμένῳ στίζουσι γυναῖκας*
> *εἰς ἔτι νῦν κείνης εἵνεκεν ἀμπλακίης.*

[3] *Early Age of Greece*, vol. I. p. 398.

That Maenads and Muses, widely diverse though they seem to us, were not by classical writers sharply sundered is seen in the variant versions of the story of Lycurgus. Dionysos in Homer is attended by his nurses (τίθηναι) and these, as has already been shown (p. 401), are Maenads, but, when we come to Sophocles, these same nurses, these 'god-inspired' women, are not Maenads, but Muses. The chorus in the *Antigone*[1] sings of Lycurgus; how he

> 'Set his hand
> To stay the god-inspired woman-band,
> To quell his Women and his joyous fire,
> And rouse the fluting Muses into ire.'

Nor is it poetry only that bears witness. In the introduction to the eighth book of his *Symposiacs* Plutarch[2] is urging the importance of mingling improving conversation with the drinking of wine. 'It is a good custom,' he says, 'that our women have, who in the festival of the Agrionia seek for Dionysos as though he had run away, and then they give up seeking and say that *he has taken refuge with the Muses* and is lurking with them, and after some time when they have finished their feast they ask each other riddles and conundrums (αἰνίγματα καὶ γρίφους). And this mystery teaches us....' In some secret Bacchic ceremonial extant in the days of Plutarch and carried on by women only, Dionysos was supposed to be in the hands of his women attendants, but they were known as Muses not as Maenads. The shift of Maenad to Muse is like the change of Bacchic rites to Orphic; it is the informing of savage rites with the spirit of music, order and peace.

The Hero-shrine of Orpheus.

Tradition says that Orpheus was buried by the Muses, and fortunately of his burial-place we know some definite particulars. It is a general principle in mythology that the reputed death-place of a god or hero is of more significance than his birth-place, because, among a people like the Greeks, who practised hero-worship, it is about the death-place and the tomb that cultus is set up. The birth-place may have a mythical

[1] Soph. *Ant.* 962.

[2] Plut. *Symp.* VIII. Proem.

sanctity, but it is at the death-place that we can best study ritual practice.

Philostratos[1] in the *Heroicus* says: 'After the outrage of the women the head of Orpheus reached Lesbos and dwelt in a cleft of the island and gave oracles in the hollow earth.' It is clear that we have here some form of *Nekyomanteion*, oracle of the dead. Of such there were many scattered all over Greece; in fact, as has already been seen (p. 340), the tomb of almost any hero might become oracular. The oracular tomb of Orpheus became of wide repute. Inquirers, Philostratos[2] tells us, came to it even from far-off Babylon. It was from the shrine of Orpheus in Lesbos that in old days there came to Cyrus the brief, famous utterance: 'Mine, O Cyrus, are thine.'

Lucian[3] adds an important statement. In telling the story of the head and the lyre he says: 'The head they buried at the place where now they have a sanctuary of Bacchus. The lyre on the other hand was dedicated in a sanctuary of Apollo.' The statement carries conviction. It would have been so easy to bury head and lyre together. The truth probably was that the lyre was a later decorative addition to an old head-oracle story; the head was buried in the shrine of the god whose religion Orpheus reformed.

Antigonus[4] in his 'History of Wonderful Things' records a lovely tradition. He quotes as his authority Myrtilos, who wrote a treatise on Lesbian matters. Myrtilos said that, according to the local tradition, the tomb of the head of Orpheus was shown at Antissaia, and that the nightingales sang there more sweetly than elsewhere. In those wonder-loving days a bird had but to perch upon a tomb and her song became a miracle.

The oracle shrine of Orpheus is depicted for us on a somewhat late red-figured cylix of which the obverse[5] is reproduced in fig. 143. It is our earliest definite source for his cult. The head of Orpheus is prophesying with parted lips. We are reminded of

[1] Philostr. *Her.* v. § 704 *ἡ κεφαλὴ γὰρ μετὰ τὸ τῶν γυναικῶν ἔργον ἐς Λέσβον κατάσχουσα ῥῆγμα τῆς Λέσβου ᾤκισε καὶ ἐν κοίλῃ τῇ γῇ ἐχρησμῴδει.*

[2] Philostr. *Her.* v. § 704.

[3] Lucian *adv. indoct.* 11.

[4] Antig. *Hist. Mir.* v.

[5] Minervini, *Bull. Arch. Nap.* vol. VI. 1857, Tav. IV.; Roscher, *Lexicon*, III. p. 1178, fig. 3. The vase was last seen by Prof. Furtwängler in the Barone collection; where it now is I am unable to say. On the reverse of the vase (not figured here) a Muse is handing a lyre to a woman.

the vase-painting in fig. 9, where the head of Teiresias emerges bodily from the sacrificial trench near which Odysseus is seated. A youth has come to consult the oracle and holds in his hands a tablet and style. Whether he is putting down his own question

FIG. 143.

or the god's answer is uncertain. We know from Plutarch[1] that at the oracle shrine of another hero, Mopsos, questions were sometimes sent in on sealed tablets[2]. In the case cited by Plutarch a test question was set and the oracle proved equal to the occasion. The vase-painting calls to mind the lines in the *Alcestis* of Euripides where the chorus sings[3]:

'Though to high heaven I fly,
Borne on the Muses' wing,
Thinking great thoughts, yet do I find no thing
Stronger than stern Necessity.
No—not the spell
On Thracian tablets legible
That from the voice of Orpheus fell,
Nor those that Phoebus to Asklepios gave
That he might weary woe-worn mortals save.'

Orpheus on the vase-painting is a voice (γῆρυς) and nothing more. As to the tablets, if we may trust the scholiast on the passage, tablets accredited to Orpheus actually existed. He quotes Herakleitos[4] the philosopher as stating that Orpheus 'set

[1] Plut. *de defect. orac.* XLV.

[2] The scholiast on the *Plutus* of Aristophanes *v.* 39, commenting on the words ἔλακεν ἐκ στεμμάτων, says that persons who consulted an oracle made their inquiries of the god in writing. They wrote on a tablet (ἐν πυκτίῳ) placed in the shrine for that purpose and wreathing it with garlands gave it to the divining priest. But this information has an apocryphal air.

[3] Eur. *Alc.* 962.

[4] Schol. ad Eur. *Alc.* 968 ὁ δὲ φυσικὸς Ἡράκλειτος...γράφων οὕτως 'τὸ δὲ τοῦ Διονύσου κατεσκεύασται ἐπὶ τῆς Θρᾴκης ἐπὶ τοῦ καλουμένου Αἵμου, ὅπου δή τινας ἐν σανίσιν ἀναγραφὰς εἶναί φασιν.'

in order the religion of Dionysos in Thrace on Mount Haemus, where they say there are certain writings of his on tablets.' There is no reason to doubt the tradition, and it serves to emphasize the fact that Orpheus was an actual person, living, teaching, writing, writing perhaps in those old 'Pelasgian' characters which Linos used long before the coming of Phoenician letters, characters which it may be are those still undeciphered which have come to light in Crete[1].

Above the head of Orpheus in the vase-painting (fig. 143) stands Apollo. In his left hand he holds his prophetic staff of laurel, his right is outstretched, but whether to command or forbid is hard to say. A curious account of the oracle on Lesbos given by Philostratos[2] in his Life of Apollonius of Tyana informs us that the relations of Apollo and Orpheus were not entirely peaceable. Apollonius, says Philostratos, landed at Lesbos and visited the adyton of Orpheus. They say that in this place of old Orpheus was wont to take pleasure in prophecy until Apollo took the oversight himself. For inasmuch as men no longer resorted to Gryneion for oracles nor to Klaros nor to the place of the tripod of Apollo, but the head of Orpheus, recently come from Thrace, alone gave responses, the god came and stood over him as he uttered oracles and said: 'Cease from the things that are mine, for long enough have I borne with thee and thy singing.' Apollo will brook no rivalry even of his most faithful worshipper. The quaint story is evidence of the intolerance of a dominant and missionary cult.

Most circumstantial of all accounts of Orpheus is that given by Conon[3]. No one would of course accept as evidence *en bloc* the statements of Conon, concerned as he mainly is to compile a complete and interesting story. Certain of his statements however have an inherent probability which makes them of considerable

[1] According to Diodorus, Linos and Orpheus both used 'Pelasgic' letters, and in them Linos wrote the deeds of Dionysos. *τόνδ' οὖν Λίνον φασὶ τοῖς Πελασγικοῖς γράμμασι συνταξάμενον τὰς τοῦ πρώτου Διονύσου πράξεις καὶ τὰς ἄλλας μυθολογίας ἀπολιπεῖν ἐν τοῖς ὑπομνήμασιν. ὁμοίως δὲ τούτοις χρήσασθαι τοῖς Πελασγικοῖς γράμμασι τὸν Ὀρφέα.*

[2] Philostr. *Vit. Apoll.* XIV. 151. Dr Deubner (*de Incubat.* p. 11) notes that *ἐφίστασθαι* is the regular word used for sudden divine apparitions.

[3] Conon, *Narr.* XLV. The narrative concludes thus: *λαβόντες οὖν (τὴν κεφαλὴν) ὑπὸ σήματι μεγάλῳ θάπτουσι, τέμενος αὐτῷ περιείρξαντες, ὃ τέως μὲν ἡρῷον ἦν, ὕστερον δ' ἐξενίκησεν ἱερὸν εἶναι· θυσίαις τε γὰρ καὶ ὅσοις ἄλλοις θεοὶ τιμῶνται γεραίρεται· ἔστι δὲ γυναιξὶ παντελῶς ἄβατον.*

value. He devotes to Orpheus the whole of one of his narrations. He tells all the orthodox details, how Orpheus won the hearts of Thracians and Macedonians by his music, how he charmed rocks and trees and wild beasts and even the heart of Kore, queen of the underworld. Then he proceeds to the story of the death. Orpheus refused to reveal his mysteries to women, whom since the loss of his own wife he had hated *en masse*. The men of Thrace and Macedonia were wont to assemble in arms on certain fixed days, in a building at Leibethra of large size and well arranged for the purpose of the celebration of rites. When they went in to celebrate their orgiastic rites they laid down their arms before the entrance gate. The women watched their opportunity, seized the arms, slew the men and tore Orpheus to pieces, throwing his limbs into the sea. There was the usual pestilence in consequence and the oracular order that the head of Orpheus should be buried. After some search the head was found by a fisherman at the mouth of the river Meles. 'It was still singing nor had it suffered any change from the sea, nor any other of the outrages that the Keres which beset mortals inflict on the dead, but it was still blooming and even then after the long lapse of time it was bleeding with fresh blood.' Other stories of bleeding miraculous heads occur in antiquity. Aelian[1] records several and Phlegon[2] in his 'Wonders' tells of the miracle that happened at the battle against Antiochus in 191 A.D. A bleeding head gave an oracle in elegiac verse and very wisely ordained that the spectators were not to touch it but only to listen.

The details supplied by Conon are of course aetiological, but we seem to discern behind them some possible basis of historical fact, some outrage of the wild women of Thrace against a real immigrant prophet in whose reforms they saw contempt of their rites. The blood of some real martyr may have been the seed of the new Orphic church. How this came to be Conon at the end of his narrative explains: 'When the miraculous head, singing and bleeding, was found, they took it and buried it beneath a great monument and fenced it in with a sacred precinct, a precinct that no woman might ever enter.' The significant state-

[1] Ael. *V. H.* XII. 8.

[2] Phleg. *Mirab.* III. It is possible that the trait of the severed head was borrowed from the ritual of Adonis at Byblos. See C. Fries, *N. Jahrb. Kl. Alt.* VI. 1903, Heft 1.

ment is added that the tomb with its precinct was at first a *heroön*, but later it obtained as a *hieron*, and the proof was that it was honoured with burnt sacrifices (*θυσίαις*) and all the other meeds of the gods.

Conon has undoubtedly put his finger on the truth. Orpheus was a real man, a mighty singer, a prophet and a teacher, bringing with him a new religion, seeking to reform an old one. He was martyred and after his death his tomb became a mantic shrine. So long as it was merely a hero shrine the offerings were those proper to the dead (*ἐναγίσματα*), but an effort was made by the faithful to raise him to the rank of an upperworld Olympian. Locally burnt sacrifices, the meed of the Olympians of the upper air, were actually no doubt offered, but the cult of Orpheus *as a god* did not obtain. Translation to the Upper House of the Olympians was not always wholly promotion. What you gain as a personage you are apt to lose as a personality. Orpheus sacrificed divinity to retain his beautiful humanity. He is somewhere on the same plane with Herakles and Asklepios (p. 346), too human ever to be quite divine. But the escape was a narrow one. Probably if a greater than he, Apollo, had not 'taken the oversight,' the sequel would have been otherwise.

Conon writing in the time of Augustus believed Orpheus to have been a real man. So did Strabo[1]. In describing the Thermaean gulf he says that the city of Dium is not on the coast but about seven stadia distant and 'near the city of Dium is a village called Pimpleia where Orpheus lived.... Orpheus was of the tribe of the Cicones and was a man of magical power both as regards music and divination. He went about practising orgiastic rites and later, waxing self-confident, he obtained many followers and great influence. Some accepted him willingly, others, suspecting that he meditated violence and conspiracy, attacked and slew him.' He adds that 'in olden times prophets were wont to practise the art of music also.'

Still more completely human is the picture that Pausanias[2] draws of the life and work of Orpheus. In the monument to Orpheus that he saw on Mt Helicon the spell-bound beasts are listening to the music, and by the musician's side is the figure

[1] Strab. VII. frgs. 17, 18 and 19. [2] P. IX. 30. 12.

of *Telete*, 'Rite of Initiation.' Pausanias comments as follows: 'In my opinion Orpheus was a man who surpassed his predecessors in the beauty of his poems and attained to great power, because he was believed to have discovered rites of the gods and purifications for unholy deeds and remedies for diseases and means of averting divine wrath.' And again, at the close of his account of the various miraculous legends that had gathered about Orpheus he says: 'Whoever has concerned himself with poetry knows that all the hymns of Orpheus are short and that the number of them all is not great. The Lycomids[1] know them and chant them over their rites. In beauty they may rank as second to the hymns of Homer, but they have attained to even higher divine favour.'

Pausanias puts the relation between Homer and Orpheus in much the same fashion as Aristophanes[2], who makes Aeschylus recount the service of poets to the state:

'It was Orpheus revealed to us holy rites, our hands from bloodshed withholding;
Musaeos gave us our healing arts, oracular words unfolding;
And Hesiod showed us to till the earth and the seasons of fruits and ploughing;
But Homer the god-like taught good things, and this too had for his glory
That he sang of arms and battle array and deeds renowned in story.'

Homer sang of mortals, Orpheus of the gods; both are men, but of the two Orpheus is less fabulous. About both gather alien accretions, but the kernel remains human not divine.

Orpheus then halted half way on the ladder between earth and heaven, a ladder up which many mortals have gone and vanished into the remote unreality of complete godhead.

S. Augustine admirably hits the mark when he says[3]: 'After the same interval of time there came the poets, who also, since they wrote poems about the gods, are called theologians, Orpheus, Musaeus, Linus. But these theologians were not worshipped as gods, though in some fashion the kingdom of the godless is wont to set Orpheus as head over the rites of the underworld.'

The line indeed between hero and underworld god was, as has already been abundantly seen, but a shifting shadow. It is useless however to urge that because Orpheus had a local shrine and a cult he was therefore a god in the current acceptation of

[1] The worship of Eros by the Lycomids will be discussed later (p. 644).
[2] Ar. *Ran.* 1032.
[3] S. August. *de civit. dei*, XVIII. 14: Verum isti theologi non pro diis culti sunt quamvis Orpheum nescio quomodo inferiis sacris praeficere soleat civitas impiorum.

the term. Theseus had a shrine, so had Diomede, so had each and every canonical hero: locally they were potent for good and evil, but we do not call them gods. Athenaeus[1] marks the distinction. 'Apollo,' he says, 'the Greeks accounted the wisest and most musical of the gods, and Orpheus of the semi-gods.'

Once we are fairly awake to the fact that Orpheus was a real live man, not a faded god, we are struck by the human touches in his story, and most by a certain vividness of emotion, a reality and personality of like and dislike that attends him. He seems to have irritated and repelled some as much as he attracted others. Pausanias[2] tells how of old prizes were offered for hymns in honour of a god. Chrysothemis of Crete and Philammon and Thamyris come and compete like ordinary mortals, but Orpheus 'thought such great things of his rites and his own personal character that he would not compete at all.' Always about him there is this aloof air, this remoteness, not only of the self-sufficing artist, who is and must be always alone, but of the scrupulous moralist and reformer; yet withal and through all he is human, a man, who Socrates-like draws men and repels them, not by persuading their reason, still less by enflaming their passions, but by sheer magic of his personality. It is this mesmeric charm that makes it hard even now-a-days to think soberly of Orpheus.

Orpheus at Athens.

Orpheus, poet, seer, musician, theologist, was a man and a Thracian, and yet it is chiefly through his influence at Athens that we know him. The author of the *Rhesos* makes the Muse complain that it is Athene not Odysseus that is the cause of the tragedy that befell the Thracian prince. She thus appeals to the goddess[3]:

> 'And yet we Muses, we his kinsmen hold
> Thy land revered and there are wont to dwell,
> And Orpheus, he own cousin to the dead,
> Revealed to thee his secret mysteries.'

The tragedian reflects the double fact—the Thracian *provenance*, the naturalization in Athens.

Orpheus, we know, reorganized and reformed the rites of

[1] Athen. xiv. 32 p. 632. [2] P. x. 7. 2. [3] [Eur.] *Rhes.* 941.

Bacchus. How much he was himself reorganized and reformed we shall never fully know. The work of editing and popularizing Orpheus at Athens was accredited to Onomacritos, he who made the indiscreet interpolation in the oracles of Musaeus and was banished for it by the son of Peisistratos[1]. If Onomacritos interpolated oracles into the poems of Musaeus, why should he spare Orpheus? Tatian[2] writes that 'Orpheus was contemporary with Herakles,' another note that he is heroic rather than divine, and adds: 'They say that the poems that were circulated under the name of Orpheus were put together by Onomacritos the Athenian.' Clement[3] goes further. He says that these poems were actually by Onomacritos who lived in the 50th Olympiad in the reign of the Peisistratidae. The line in those days between writing poems of your own and editing those of other people was less sharply drawn than it is to-day. Onomacritos had every temptation to interpolate, for he himself wrote poems on the rites of Dionysos. Pausanias[4] in explaining the presence of the Titan Anytos at Lycosura says: 'Onomacritos took the name of the Titans from Homer and composed orgies for Dionysos and made the Titans the actual agents in the sufferings of Dionysos.'

Something then was done about 'Orpheus' in the time of the Peisistratidae as something was done about 'Homer,' some work of editing, compiling, revising. What form precisely this work took is uncertain. What is certain is that somehow Orphism, Orphic rites and Orphic poems had, before the classical period, come to Athens. The effect of this Orphic spirit was less obvious, less widespread, than that of Homer, but perhaps more intimate and vital. We know it because Euripides and Plato are deep-dyed in Orphism, we know it not only by the signs of actual influence, but by the frequently raised protest.

Orpheus, it has been established in the mouth of many witnesses, modified, ordered, 'rearranged' Bacchic rites. We naturally ask—was this all? Did this man whose name has come down to us through the ages, in whose saintly and ascetic

[1] Herod. VII. 6.

[2] Tat. *adv. Graec.* XLI. 271 τὰ ὑπ' αὐτοῦ ἐπιφερόμενά φασιν ὑπὸ 'Ονομακρίτου τοῦ 'Αθηναίου συντετάχθαι.

[3] Clem. Al. *Str.* I. 332 'Ονομάκριτος οὗ τὰ εἰς 'Ορφέα φερόμενα λέγεται εἶναι κατὰ τὴν τῶν Πεισιστρατιδῶν ἀρχὴν περὶ τὴν πεντηκοστὴν 'Ολυμπιάδα.

[4] P VIII. 37. 5.

figure the early Church saw the prototype of her Christ, effect nothing more vital than modification? Was his sole mission to bring order and decorum into an orgiastic and riotous ritual?

Such a notion is *a priori* as improbable as it is false to actual fact. Externally Orpheus differs from Dionysos, to put it plainly, in this. Dionysos is drunken, Orpheus is utterly sober. But this new spirit of gentle decorum is but the manifestation, the outward shining of a lambent flame within, the expression of a new spiritual faith which brought to man, at the moment he most needed it, the longing for purity and peace in this life, the hope of final fruition in the next.

Before proceeding to discuss in detail such records of actual Orphic rites as remain, this new principle must be made clear. Apart from it Orphic rites lose all their real sacramental significance and lapse into mere superstitions.

THE CARDINAL DOCTRINE OF ORPHISM.

The whole gist of the matter may thus be summed up. Orpheus took an ancient superstition, deep-rooted in the savage ritual of Dionysos, and lent to it a new spiritual significance. The old superstition and the new faith are both embodied in the little Orphic text that stands at the head of this chapter:

'Many are the wand-bearers, few are the Bacchoi.'

Can we be sure that this is really an Orphic text or was it merely a current proverb of any and every religion and morality? Plato[1] says: 'Those who instituted rites of initiation for us said of old in a parable that the man who came to Hades uninitiated lay in mud, but that those who had been purified and initiated and then came thither dwell with the gods. For those who are concerned with these rites say, They that bear the wand are many, the Bacchoi are few.' Plato does not commit himself to any statement as to who 'those who are concerned with these rites' were, but Olympiodorus commenting on the passage says: 'He (Plato) everywhere misuses the sayings of Orpheus and

[1] Plato, *Phaed.* p. 69 c εἰσὶ γὰρ δὴ φασὶν οἱ περὶ τὰς τελετὰς ναρθηκοφόροι μὲν πολλοί, Βάκχοι δέ τε παῦροι. Olympiod. ad loc. παρῳδεῖ πανταχοῦ τὰ τοῦ 'Ορφέως, διὸ καὶ στίχον αὐτοῦ φησί·

Πολλοὶ μὲν ναρθηκοφόροι, παῦροι δέ τε Βάκχοι.

ναρθηκοφόρους οὐ μὴν Βάκχους τοὺς πολιτικοὺς καλῶν Βάκχους δὲ τοὺς καθαρτικούς.

therefore quotes this verse of his, "Many are the wand-bearers, few are the Bacchoi," giving the name of wand-bearers and not Bacchoi to persons who engage in politics, but the name of Bacchoi to those who are purified.'

It has already been shown that the worshippers of Dionysos believed that they were possessed by the god. It was but a step further to pass to the conviction that they were actually identified with him, actually *became* him. This was a conviction shared by all orgiastic religions, and one doubtless that had its rise in the physical sensations of intoxication. Those who worshipped Sabazios became Saboi, those who worshipped Kubebe became Kubeboi, those who worshipped Bacchos Bacchoi; in Egypt the worshippers of Osiris after death became Osiris. The mere fact of intoxication would go far to promote such a faith, but there is little doubt that it was fostered, if not originated, by the pantomimic character of ancient ritual. It has been seen (p. 414) that in the Thracian rites 'bull-voiced mimes' took part, Lycophron (p. 433) tells that the women who worshipped the bull-Dionysos wore horns. It is a natural primitive instinct of worship to try by all manner of disguise to identify yourself more and more with the god who thrilled you.

Direct evidence of this pantomimic element in the worship of Dionysos is not wanting, though unhappily it is of late date. In the course of the excavations on the west slope of the Acropolis, Dr Dörpfeld laid bare a building known to be an 'Iobaccheion,' superimposed on an ancient triangular precinct of Dionysos, that of Dionysos in the Limnae. On this site was discovered an inscription[1] giving in great detail the rules of a thiasos of Iobacchoi in the time of Hadrian. Among a mass of regulations about elections, subscriptions, feast-days, funerals of members and the like, come enactments about a sacred pantomime in which the Iobacchoi took part. The divine persons

[1] Published by Dr Sam. Wide, *A. Mitt.* XIX. (1894), p. 248; discussed by Dr Ernst Maass, *Orpheus* (1895); see Dr Erwin Rohde, *Kleine Schriften*, p. 293.

Line 63 *οὐδενὶ δὲ ἐξέσται ἐν τῆι στιβάδι οὔτε ᾆσαι | οὔτε θορυβῆσαι οὔτε κροτῆσαι μετὰ δὲ | πάσης εὐκοσμίας καὶ ἡσυχίας τοὺς μερισ|μοὺς λέγειν καὶ ποιεῖν προστάσσοντος | τοῦ ἱερέως ἢ τοῦ ἀρχιβάκχου.*

Line 135 *εὔκοσμος δὲ κληρούσθω ἢ καθισ|τάσθω ὑπὸ τοῦ ἱερέως ἐπιφέρων τῶι ἀκοσ|μοῦντι ἢ θορυβοῦντι τὸν θύρσον τοῦ θε|οῦ ὧι δὲ ἂν παρατεθῆι ὁ θύρσος ἐπικρεί|ναντος τοῦ ἱερέως ἢ τοῦ ἀρχιβάκχου | ἐξερχέσθω τοῦ ἑστιατορείου. ἐὰν δὲ ἀ|πειθῆι αἱρέτωσαν αὐτὸν ἔξω τοῦ πυλῶ|νος οἱ κατασταθησόμενοι ὑπὸ τῶν | ἱερέων ἵπποι, καὶ ἔστω ὑπεύθυνος | τοῖς περὶ τῶν μαχομένων προστεί|μοις.*

to be represented were Dionysos, Kore, Palaemon, Aphrodite, Proteurhythmos, and the parts were distributed by lot.

The name Proteurhythmos, it will later (p. 655) be shown, marks the thiasos as Orphic, and thoroughly Orphic rather than Dionysiac are the regulations as to the peace and order to be observed. 'Within the place of sacrifice no one is to make a noise, or clap his hands, or sing, but each man is to say his part and do it in all quietness and order as the priest and the Archibacchos direct.' More significant still and more beautiful is the rule, that if any member is riotous an official appointed by the priest shall set against him who is disorderly or violent the thyrsos of the god. The member against whom the thyrsos is set up, must if the priest or the Archibacchos so decide leave the banquet hall. If he refuse, the 'Horses' appointed by the priest shall take him and set him outside the gates. The thyrsos of the god has become in truly Orphic fashion the sign not of revel and license, but of a worship fair and orderly.

We have noted the quiet and order of the representation because it is so characteristically Orphic, but the main point is that in the worship of Dionysos we have this element of direct impersonation which helped on the conviction that man could identify himself with his god. The term Bacchae is familiar, so familiar that we are apt to forget its full significance. But in the play of Euripides there are not only Bacchae, god-possessed women worshippers, but also a Bacchos, and about his significance there can be no mistake. He is the god himself incarnate as one of his own worshippers. The doctrines of possession and incarnation are complementary, god can become man, man can become god, but the Bacchic religion lays emphasis rather on the one aspect that man can become god. The Epiphany of the Bacchos, it may be noted, is after a fashion characteristically Orphic; the beautiful stranger is intensely quiet, and this magical quiet exasperates Pentheus just as Orpheus exasperated the Maenads. The real old Bromios breaks out in the Epiphany of fire and thunder, in the bull-god and the madness of the end.

The savage doctrine of divine possession, induced by intoxication and in part by mimetic ritual, was it would seem almost bound to develope a higher, more spiritual meaning. We have already seen (p. 452) that the madness of Dionysos included the madness of the Muses and Aphrodite, but, to make any real spiritual advance, there was needed it would seem a man of spiritual insight and saintly temperament, there was needed an Orpheus. The great step that Orpheus took was that, while he kept the old Bacchic faith that man might become a god, he altered the conception of what a god was, and he sought to obtain that godhead by wholly different means. The grace he sought was not physical intoxication but spiritual ecstasy, the means he adopted not drunkenness but abstinence and rites of purification.

All this is by anticipation, to clear the ground; it will be abundantly proved when Orphic rites and documents known to be Orphic are examined. Before passing to these it may be well to emphasize one point—the salient contrast that this new religious principle, this belief in the possibility of attaining divine life, presented to the orthodox Greek faith.

The old orthodox anthropomorphic religion of Greece made the gods in man's image, but, having made them, kept them aloof, distinct. It never stated in doctrine, it never implied in ritual, that man could become god. Nay more, against any such aspiration it raised again and again a passionate protest. To seek to become even *like* the gods was to the Greek the sin most certain to call down divine vengeance, it was 'Insolence.'

Pindar is full of the splendour and sweetness of earthly life, but full also of its insuperable limitation. He is instant in warning against the folly and insolence of any attempt to outpass it. To one he says[1], 'Strive not thou to become a god'; to another[2], 'The things of mortals best befit mortality.' It is this limitation, this constant protest against any real aspiration, that makes Pindar, for all his pious orthodoxy, profoundly barren of any vital religious impulse. Orphic though he was in certain tenets as to a future life, his innate temperamental materialism prevents his ever touching the secret of Orphism 'werde was du bist,' and he transforms the new faith into an other-worldliness. He is compounded of 'Know thyself' and 'Nothing too much.' 'In all things,' he says, 'take measure by thyself[3].' 'It behoveth to seek from the gods things meet for mortals, knowing the things

[1] Pind. *Ol.* v. 24. [2] *Isth.* IV. 14. [3] *Pyth.* II. 34.

that are at our feet and to what lot we are born. Desire not, thou soul of mine, life of the immortals, but drink thy fill of what thou hast and what thou canst[1].' In the name of religion it is all a desperate unfaith. We weary of this reiterated worldliness. It is not that he beats his wings against the bars; he loves too well his gilded cage. The gods are to him only a magnificent background to man's life. But sometimes, just because he is supremely a poet, he is ware of a sudden sheen of glory, an almost theatrical stage-effect lighting the puppet show. It catches his breath and ours. But straightway we are back to the old stock warnings against Tantalos, against Bellerophon, whose 'heart is aflutter for things far off[2].' Only one thing he remembers, perhaps again because he was a poet, that winged Pegasos 'dwelt for ever in the stables of the gods[3].'

The cardinal doctrine of Orphic religion was then the possibility of attaining divine life. It has been said by some that the great contribution of Dionysos to the religion of Greece was the hope of immortality it brought. Unquestionably the Orphics believed in a future life, but this belief was rather a corollary than of the essence of their faith. Immortality, immutability, is an attribute of the gods. As Sophocles says[4]:

> 'Only to gods in heaven
> Comes no old age nor death of anything,
> All else is turmoiled by our master Time.'

To become a god was therefore incidentally as it were to attain immortality. But one of the beautiful things in Orphic religion was that the end completely overshadowed the means. Their great concern was to become divine now. That could only be attained by perfect purity. They did not so much seek purity that they might become divinely immortal, they needed immortality that they might become divinely pure. The choral songs of the *Bacchae* are charged with the passionate longing after purity, in the whole play there is not one word, not one hint, of the hope of immortality. Consecration (ὁσιότης), perfect purity issuing in divinity, is, it will be seen, the keynote of Orphic faith, the goal of Orphic ritual.

[1] Pind. *Pyth.* III. 59. [2] *Isth.* VI. 36. [3] *Ol.* XIII. 92.
[4] Soph. *Oed. Col.* 607, trans. Mr Gilbert Murray.

CHAPTER X.

ORPHIC MYSTERIES.

'ἁγνὸν χρὴ νηοῖο θυώδεος ἐντὸς ἰόντα
ἔμμεναι· ἁγνείη δ' ἐστὶ φρονεῖν ὅσια.'

a. THE OMOPHAGIA.

THE most important literary document extant on Orphic ceremonial is a fragment of the *Cretans* of Euripides, preserved for us by Porphyry in his treatise on 'Abstinence from Animal Food'—a passage Porphyry says he had 'almost forgotten to mention.'

From an allusion in Aristophanes[1] to 'Cretan monodies and unhallowed marriages' it seems probable that the *Cretans* dealt with the hapless wedlock of Pasiphaë[2]. The fragment, Porphyry tells us, was spoken by the chorus of Cretan mystics who have come to the palace of Minos. It is possible they may have come to purify it from the recent pollution.

The mystics by the mouth of their leader make full and definite confession of the faith, or rather acknowledgement of the ritual acts, by which a man became a 'Bacchos,' and they add a statement of the nature of the life he was thereafter bound to lead. Though our source is a poetical one, we learn from it, perhaps to our surprise, that to become a 'Bacchos' it was necessary to do a good deal more than dance enthusiastically upon the mountains. The confession runs as follows[3]:

[1] Ar. *Ran.* 849; see Nauck ad loc.

[2] The new fragment of the *Cretans* (see Berliner Klassikertexte, 1907, p. 73, no. XVII.) makes this certain. It contains a speech by Pasiphaë reproaching Minos and attributing her disaster to the will of the gods. *v.* 38 seems an allusion to the practice of Omophagia.

[3] Eur. frg. 475 ap. Porph. *De Abst.* IV. 19, trans. Mr Gilbert Murray.

'Lord of Europa's Tyrian line,
Zeus-born, who holdest at thy feet
The hundred citadels of Crete,
I seek to thee from that dim shrine,

Roofed by the Quick and Carven Beam,
By Chalyb steel and wild bull's blood
In flawless joints of cypress wood
Made steadfast. There in one pure stream

My days have run, the servant I,
Initiate, of Idaean Jove;
Where midnight Zagreus roves, I rove;
I have endured his thunder-cry[1];

Fulfilled his red and bleeding feasts;
Held the Great Mother's mountain flame;
I am Set Free and named by name
A Bacchos of the Mailed Priests.

Robed in pure white I have borne me clean
From man's vile birth and coffined clay,
And exiled from my lips alway
Touch of all meat where Life hath been.'

This confession must be examined in detail.

The first avowal is:

'the servant I,
Initiate, of Idaean Jove[2].'

It is remarkable that the mystic, though he becomes a 'Bacchos,' avows himself as initiated to Idaean Zeus. But this Idaean Zeus is clearly the same as Zagreus, the mystery form of Dionysos. Zeus, the late comer (p. 318, n. 2), has taken over an earlier worship, the nature of which will become more evident after the ritual has been examined.

Zeus has in a sense supplanted Zagreus, but only by taking on his nature. An analogous case has already been discussed in dealing with Zeus Meilichios (p. 19). At a time when the whole tendency of theology, of philosophy and of poetry was towards monotheism these fusions were easy and frequent. Of such a monotheistic divinity, half Zeus, half Hades, wholly Ploutos, we are told in

[1] Mr Murray translates the MS. reading:

μύστης γενόμην
καὶ νυκτιπόλου Ζαγρέως βροντὰς
τάς τ' ὠμοφάγους δαῖτας τελέσας.

For βροντὰς Dr Diels would read βούτας, i.e. βουκόλος. (See Dieterich, *De Hymnis Orphicis*, p. 11, and cf. Eur. frg. 203.) This emendation seems to me probable, but as both MS. readings and all suggested emendations are uncertain I have based no argument on the word βροντάς.

[2] *v.* 10 Διὸς Ἰδαίου μύστης γενόμην.

another fragment of Euripides preserved by Clement of Alexandria[1]. His ritual is that of the earth-gods.

'Ruler of all, to thee I bring libation
And honey cake, by whatso appellation
Thou wouldst be called, or Hades, thou, or Zeus,
Fireless the sacrifice, all earth's produce
I offer. Take thou of its plentitude,
For thou amongst the Heavenly Ones art God,
Dost share Zeus' sceptre, and art ruling found
With Hades o'er the kingdoms underground.'

It has been conjectured that this fragment also is from the *Cretans*, but we have no certain evidence. Clement says in quoting the passage that 'Euripides, the philosopher of the stage, has divined as in a riddle that the Father and the Son are one God.' Another philosopher before Euripides had divined the same truth, and he was Orpheus, only he gave to his Father and Son the name of Bacchos, and, all important for our purpose, gave to the Son in particular the title of Zagreus.

In discussing the titles of Dionysos (p. 413), it has been seen that the names Bromios, Braites, Sabazios, were given to the god to mark him as a spirit of intoxication, of enthusiasm. The title Zagreus has been so far left unconsidered because it is especially an Orphic name. Zagreus is the god of the mysteries, and his full content can only be understood in relation to Orphic rites.

Zagreus is the mystery child guarded by the Kouretes, torn in pieces by the Titans. Our first mention of him is a line preserved to us from the lost epic the *Alcmaeonis*[2], which ran as follows:

'Holy Earth and Zagreus greatest of all gods.'

The name of Zagreus never occurs in Homer, and we are apt to think that epic writers were wholly untouched by mysticism. Had the *Alcmaeonis* not been lost, we might have had occasion to modify this view. It was an epic story the subject-matter of which was necessarily a great sin and its purification, and though primarily the legend of Alcmaeon was based, as has been seen, on a curiously physical conception of pollution (p. 220), it may easily have taken on Orphic developments. Zagreus appears little in literature; he is essentially a ritual figure, the centre of a

[1] Eur. frg. 904 ap. Clem. Al. *Strom.* v. p. 688.

[2] Ap. *Etym. Gud.* p. 227. The lexicographers explain the title as meaning mighty hunter, but in the ritual Zagreus is more hunted than hunter.

cult so primitive, so savage that a civilized literature instinctively passed him by, or at most figured him as a shadowy Hades.

But religion knew better. She knew that though Dionysos as Bromios, Braites, Sabazios, as god of intoxication, was much, Dionysos as Zagreus, as Nyktelios, as Isodaites[1], he of the night, he who is 'a meal shared by all' was more. The Orphics faced the most barbarous elements of their own faith and turned them not only quâ theology into a vague monotheism, but quâ ritual into a high sacrament of spiritual purification. This ritual, the main feature of which was 'the red and bleeding feast,' must now be examined.

The avowal of the first certain ritual act performed comes in the line where the mystic says

> 'I have......
> Fulfilled his red and bleeding feasts[2].'

The victim in Crete was a bull.

The shrine of Idaean Zeus, from which the mystics came, was cemented with bulls' blood[3]. Possibly this may mean that at its foundation a sacred bull was slain and his blood mixed with the mortar; anyhow it indicates connection with bull-worship. The characteristic mythical monster of Crete was the bull-headed Minotaur. Behind the legend of Pasiphaë, made monstrous by the misunderstanding of immigrant conquerors, it can scarcely be doubted that there lurks some sacred mystical ceremony of ritual wedlock (*ἱερὸς γάμος*) with a primitive bull-headed divinity. He need not have been imported from Thrace; zoomorphic nature-gods spring up everywhere. The bull-Dionysos of Thrace when he came to Crete found a monstrous god, own cousin to himself.

Such a monstrous god is depicted on the curious seal-impression found by Mr Arthur Evans[4] at Cnossos and reproduced in fig. 144. He is seated on a throne of camp-stool shape, and before him stands a human figure, probably a worshipper. That the monster is a god seems clear from the fact that he is seated; that he is a

[1] Plut. *de Ei*, IX. *Διόνυσον δὲ καὶ Ζαγρέα καὶ Νυκτέλιον καὶ Ἰσοδαίτην αὐτὸν ὀνομάζουσι.* Taking the three ritual titles in conjunction it seems almost certain that *Ἰσοδαίτης* refers to the *ὠμόφαγοι δαῖτες* of the Zagreus ritual shared alike by all mystics.

[2] *v.* 11 *τάς τ' ὠμοφάγους δαῖτας τελέσας.*

[3] Eur. frg. 476 *καὶ ταυροδέτῳ κόλλῃ κραθεῖσ'.*

[4] A. Evans, *Annual of British School at Athens*, vol. VII. p. 18, fig. 7 *a*.

bull-god is not so certain. The head is not drawn with sufficient exactness for us to be sure what beast is intended. He has certainly no horns, but the hoof and tail might be those of a bull. The seal-impressions found by Mr Hogarth[1] in such large numbers at Zakro show how widespread in Crete were these fantastic forms. The line between man and beast is a faint one. Mr Hogarth holds that the majority of these sealings have nothing to do with cults—they are the product, he thinks, of an art which has 'passed from monsters with a meaning to monsters of pure fancy.' He excepts however certain sealings where a Minotaur is represented[2], a monster with horned bull-head, pronounced bovine ears and tail, but apparently human trunk, arms and legs. Like the monster in fig. 144, this Minotaur is seated, but with his left leg crossed human-fashion over his right knee and with human hands extended.

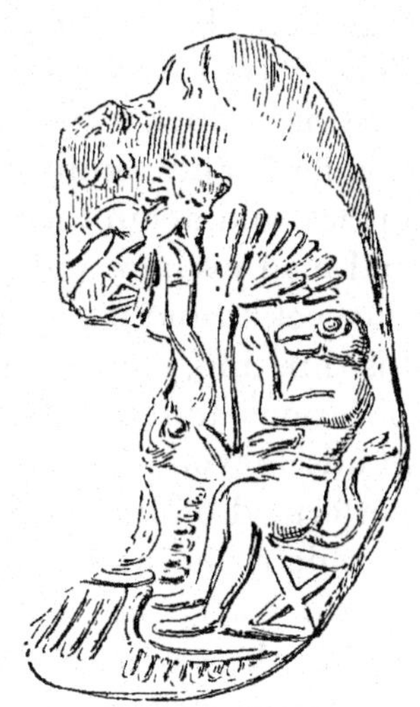

FIG. 144.

The traditional Minotaur took year by year his tale of human victims. Of the ritual of the bull-god in Crete, we know that it consisted in part of the tearing and eating of a bull, and behind is the dreadful suspicion of human sacrifice.

Part of the avowal of the Cretan mystic is that he has accomplished the *ὠμοφαγία*, the rite of 'the feast of raw flesh.' That a feast of raw flesh of some sort was traditionally held to be a part of Bacchic ceremonial, is clear from the words Euripides[3] put into the mouth of his Maenads:

> 'The joy of the red quick fountains,
> The blood of the hill-goat torn,'

where the expression in the original, *ὠμοφάγον χάριν* 'joy in eating raw flesh,' admits of no doubt.

An integral part of this terrible ritual was the tearing asunder of the slain beast, in order, no doubt, to get the flesh as raw as

[1] D. Hogarth, *J.H.S.* vol. XXII. 1902, p. 76 and plates VI—IX.
[2] *Op. cit.* nos. 17—18, and *Ann. B.S.A.* VII. fig. 45.
[3] See supr. p. 451.

might be, for the blood is the life. Plutarch[1], in his horrified protest against certain orgiastic rites, joins the two ritual acts together, the 'eatings of raw flesh' and the 'rendings asunder.' 'There are certain festivals,' he says, 'and sacrificial ceremonies as well as unlucky and gloomy days, in which take place eatings of raw flesh and rendings asunder, and fastings and beatings of the breast, and again disgraceful utterances in relation to holy things, and mad ravings and yells upraised with a loud din and tossing of the neck to and fro.' These ceremonies, he goes on to explain, are, to his thinking, not performed in honour of any *god*, but 'they are propitiations and appeasements performed with a view to the riddance of mischievous *demons*; such also, he says, were the human sacrifices performed of old.' Plutarch's words read like a commentary on the Orphic ritual under discussion: we have the fasting, we have the horrid feast; he sees the savage element of 'riddance,' but he misses the saving grace of enthusiasm and mystic significance.

If the sympathetic religious-minded Plutarch was horrified at a ritual so barbarous, it filled the Christian Fathers with unholy joy. Here was an indefeasible argument against paganism, and for once they compel our reluctant sympathy. 'I will not,' cries Clement[2], 'dance out your mysteries, as they say Alcibiades did, but I will strip them naked, and bring them out on to the open stage of life, in view of those who are the spectators at the drama of truth. The Bacchoi hold orgies in honour of a mad Dionysos, they celebrate a divine madness by the Eating of Raw Flesh, the final accomplishment of their rite is the distribution of the flesh of butchered victims, they are crowned with snakes, and shriek out the name of Eva, that Eve through whom sin came into the world, and the symbol of their Bacchic orgies is a consecrated serpent.' And again[3]: 'the mysteries of Dionysos are wholly inhuman; for while he was still a child and the Kouretes were dancing their armed

[1] Plut. *de defect. orac.* XIV.

[2] Clem. Al. *Protr.* II. 12 Διόνυσον μαινόλην ὀργιάζουσι Βάκχοι ὠμοφαγίᾳ τὴν ἱερομηνίαν (? ἱερομανίαν) ἄγοντες καὶ τελέσκουσι τὰς κρεανομίας τῶν φόνων ἀνεστεμμένοι τοῖς ὄφεσιν, ἐπολολύζοντες Εὐάν κτλ.; and again speaking of the analogous ceremonies of the Korybants Clement (*Protr.* II. 6) says: καὶ ταῦτ' ἔστι τὰ μυστήρια, συνελόντι φάναι, φόνοι καὶ τάφοι.

[3] Clem. Al. *Protr.* II. 17 τὰ γὰρ Διονύσου μυστήρια τέλεον ἀπάνθρωπα, ὃν εἰσέτι παῖδα ὄντα ἐνόπλῳ κινήσει περιχορευόντων Κουρήτων δόλῳ δὲ ὑποδύντων Τιτάνων ἀπατήσαντες παιδαριώδεσιν ἀθύρμασιν οὗτοι δὴ οἱ Τιτᾶνες διέσπασαν ἔτι νηπίαχον ὄντα ὡς ὁ τῆς τελετῆς ποιητὴς Ὀρφεύς φησιν ὁ Θρᾴκιος: and *Protr.* XII. 119 referring to the *Bacchae* he speaks of the Maenads as αἱ δύσαγνον κρεανομίαν μυόμεναι.

dance about him, the Titans stole upon him, deceived him with childish toys and tore him to pieces.'

Arnobius[1] pretends that the Bacchanalia are so horrible he must pass them by, and then goes on to revel in revolting detail over the rites 'which the Greeks call Feasts of Raw Flesh (*ὠμοφαγίαι*) in which with feigned frenzy and loss of a sane mind you twine snakes about you, and, to show yourselves full of the divinity and majesty of the god, you demolish with gory mouths the entrails of goats bleating for mercy.' The gentle vegetarian Porphyry[2] knows that in Chios, according to tradition, there had been a Dionysos called Omadius, the Raw One, and that the sacrifice he used to exact was the tearing of a man to pieces. Istros[3] stated that of old the Kouretes sacrificed children to Kronos. On Kronos all human sacrifice was apt to be fathered, but the mention of the Kouretes, coupled with the confession of the Cretan mystic, shows that the real divinity is Zagreus.

To these vague though consistent traditions of the eating and tearing of raw flesh, whether of man or goat or calf, in honour of some form of Dionysos, evidence more precise and definitely descriptive of Cretan ritual has been left us, again by a Christian Father, Firmicus Maternus[4]. The festival he describes was, like many others in honour of Dionysos, trieteric, i.e. celebrated each alternate year.

Firmicus in the fashion of his day gives first a long and purely aetiological narrative of the death of the son of a king of Crete, to appease whose wrath the ceremony, it was believed, was instituted. 'The Cretans commemorated the death of the boy by certain ceremonies, doing all things in regular order which the

[1] Arnob. v. 19 atque *vos plenos Dei numine ac majestate docentes* caprorum reclamantium viscera cruentatis oribus dissipatis: the words in italics show that Arnobius understood the real gist of the rite.

[2] Porphyr. *De Abst.* II. 55 *ἔθυον δὲ καὶ ἐν Χίῳ τῷ Ὠμαδίῳ Διονύσῳ ἄνθρωπον διασπῶντες καὶ ἐν Τενέδῳ ὥς φησιν Εὔελπις ὁ Καρύστιος.*

[3] Ap. Porphyr. *De Abst.* II. 56. Clement (*Protr.* III. 4) says, citing as his authority the *Nostoi* of Antikleides, that this human sacrifice was offered by the Lyctii, a Cretan tribe.

[4] Firmicus Maternus, *de err. profan. relig.* c. 6 Cretenses, ut furentis tyranni saevitiam mitigarent, festos funeris dies statuunt et annuum sacrum trieterica consecratione componunt, omnia per ordinem facientes, quae puer moriens aut fecit aut passus est. Vivum laniant dentibus taurum, crudeles epulas annuis commemorationibus excitantes et per secreta silvarum clamoribus dissonis ejulantes fingunt animi furentis insaniam ut illud facinus non per fraudem factum sed per insaniam crederetur.

boy did or suffered.' These ceremonies included an enactment of the scene of the child playing with the toys and surprised by the Titans, and perhaps originally the slaying and tearing to pieces of a real child, but in the festival as described by Firmicus a bull was surrogate. 'They tear in pieces a live bull with their teeth and by howling with discordant shouts through the secret places of the woods they simulate the madness of an enraged mind.'

Firmicus, by his obviously somewhat inaccurate statement, has gone far to discredit his own testimony. After the performance of a religious ceremony that involved the tearing of a *live* bull's flesh by human teeth[1] the surviving worshippers would be few. But, because of this exaggeration, we need not discredit the whole ritual of the bull-slaying, nor the tearing and eating of *raw*, though not actually living, flesh. The bull indeed comes in so awkwardly in the midst of the aetiological story of the child, that we may be practically sure this account of a bygone ritual is authentic.

Some light is thrown on the method, and much on the meaning, of the horrible feast by an account left us by S. Nilus[2], a hermit of Mt. Sinai in the 4th century, of the sacrifice of a camel among the Arabs of his time. S. Nilus seems to have spent some of his abundant leisure in the careful examination of the rites and customs of the heathen around, and it is much to be regretted that in his 'Narrations' he has not recorded more of his observations. The nomadic condition of the Arabs about Sinai impressed him much; he notes that they are without trade, arts or agriculture, and if other food failed them, fed on their camels and only cooked the flesh just enough to enable them to tear it with their teeth. They worshipped no god, either in spirit or through an image made by hands, but sacrificed to the morning star at its rising. They by preference sacrificed boys in the flower of their age and of special beauty, and slew them at dawn on a rude heap

[1] If any one finds the tearing of the bull with the teeth a hard saying, he may be reassured by the statement of Nonnus (*Dionys.* VI. 205) that the bull-shaped Dionysos was cut in little bits *by a knife*, which would greatly facilitate matters:

ἀμοιβαίῃ δὲ φονῆες
ταυροφυῆ Διόνυσον ἐμιστύλλοντο μαχαίρῃ.

[2] *Nili opera*, Narrat. III. 28, Migne, *Patrol.* LXXIX. I owe this reference to Nilus to Prof. Robertson Smith's *Religion of the Semites*, p. 320, but as the passage is of cardinal importance in relation to the account of Firmicus I have substituted a translation for his summary.

of piled-up stones. He pathetically observes that this practice of theirs caused him much anxiety; he was nervous lest they should take a fancy to a beautiful young boy convert he had with him and sacrifice 'his pure and lovely body to unclean demons.' But, he goes on, 'when the supply of boys was lacking, they took a camel of white colour and otherwise faultless, bent it down upon its knees, and went circling round it three times in a circuitous fashion. The leader of the song and of the procession to the star was either one of their chiefs or a priest of special honour. He, after the third circuit had been made, and before the worshippers had finished the song, while the last words were still on their lips, draws his sword and smites the neck of the camel and eagerly tastes of the blood. The rest of them in like fashion run up and with their knives some cut off a small bit of the hide with its hairs upon it, others hack at any chance bit of flesh they can get. Others go on to the entrails and inwards and leave no scrap of the victim uneaten that might be seen by the sun at its rising. They do not refrain even from the bones and marrow, but overcome by patience and perseverance the toughness of the resistance.'

The account of Nilus leaves no doubt as to the gist of the ceremony: the worshippers aim at devouring the victim before the life has left the still warm blood. Raw flesh, Prof. Robertson Smith points out, is called in Hebrew and Syriac 'living' flesh. Thus, in the most literal way, all those who shared in the ceremony absorbed into themselves part of the victim's life.

For *live* bull then we substitute *raw* bull, and the statement of Firmicus presents no difficulties. Savage economy demands that your *juju*, whatever it may be, should be as fresh as possible. Probably, at first, the bull may have been eaten just for the sake of absorbing its strength, without any notion of a divine sacrament.

The idea that by eating an animal you absorb its qualities is too obvious a piece of savage logic to need detailed illustration. That the uneducated and even the priestly Greek had not advanced beyond this stage of sympathetic magic is shown by a remark of Porphyry's[1]. He wants to prove that the soul is held to be affected or attracted even by corporeal substances of kindred nature, and of this belief he says we have abundant experience.

[1] Porphyr. *De Abst.* II. 48.

'At least,' he says, 'those who wish to take unto themselves the spirits of prophetic animals, swallow the most effective parts of them, such as the hearts of crows and moles and hawks, for so they possess themselves of a spirit present with them and prophesying like a god, one that enters into them themselves at the time of its entrance into the body.' If a mole's heart can make you see into dark things, great virtue may be expected from a piece of raw bull. It is not hard to see how this savage theory of communion would pass into a higher sacramentalism, into the faith that by partaking of an animal who was a divine vehicle[1] you could enter spiritually into the divine life that had physically entered you, and so be made one with the god. It was the mission of Orphism to effect these mystical transitions.

Because a goat was torn to pieces by Bacchants in Thrace, because a bull was, at some unknown date, eaten raw in Crete, we need not conclude that either of these practices regularly obtained in civilized Athens. The initiated bull-eater was certainly known of there, and the notion must have been fairly familiar, or it would not have pointed a joke for Aristophanes. In the audacious prorrhesis of the *Frogs*[2] the uninitiated are bidden to withdraw, and among them those

> 'Who never were trained by bull-eating Kratinos
> In mystical orgies poetic and vinous.'

The worship of Dionysos of the Raw Flesh must have fallen into abeyance in Periclean Athens; but though civilized man, as a rule, shrinks from raw meat, yet, given imminent peril to rouse the savage in man, even in civilized man the faith in Dionysos Omestes burns up afresh. Hence stories of human sacrifice on occasions of great danger rise up and are accepted as credible. Plutarch[3], narrating what happened before the battle of Salamis,

[1] One of the titles of Dionysos, i.e. Eiraphiotes, is as Mr R. A. Neil has pointed out the etymological equivalent of the Sanscrit *varsabha*, bull: see *Golden Bough*, 2nd edit. vol. II. p. 164.

[2] Ar. *Ran.* 355 μηδὲ Κρατίνου τοῦ ταυροφάγου γλώττης Βακχεῖ' ἐτελέσθη, trans. Rogers.

[3] Plut. *Vit. Them.* XIII. In this same way a legend grew up and was accredited by Neanthes, the Cyzicene historian, that when Epimenides was 'purifying Attica by human blood' a youth, Kratinos, offered himself as a willing sacrifice. But how apocryphal such stories may be is owned by Athenaeus himself (XIII. 78, p. 602), who adds after his narrative that he is aware that the whole story was said by Polemon to have been a fiction.

writes as follows: 'As Themistocles was performing the sacrifice for omens (σφαγιαζομένῳ) alongside of the admiral's trireme, there were brought to him three captives of remarkable beauty, attired in splendid raiment and gold ornaments; they were reputed to be the sons of Artaÿktes and Sandauke sister to Xerxes. When Euphrantides the soothsayer caught sight of them, and observed that at the same moment a bright flame blazed out from the burning victims, and at the same time a sneeze from the right gave a sign, he took Themistocles by the hand and bade consecrate and sacrifice all the youths to Dionysos Omestes, and so make his prayer, for thus both safety and victory would ensue to the Greeks. Themistocles was thunderstruck at the greatness and strangeness of the omen, it being such a thing as was wont to occur at great crises and difficult issues, but the people, who look for salvation rather by irrational than rational means, invoked the god with a loud shout together, and bringing up the prisoners to the altar imperatively demanded that the sacrifice should be accomplished as the seer had prescribed. These things are related by Phanias the Lesbian, a philosopher not unversed in historical matters.' Phanias lived in the 4th century B.C. Plutarch evidently thought him a respectable authority, but the fragments of his writings that we possess are all of the anecdotal type, and those which relate to Themistocles are evidently from a hostile source. His statement, therefore, cannot be taken to prove more than that a very recent human sacrifice was among the horrors conceivably possible to a Greek of the 4th century B.C., especially if the victim were a 'barbarian.'

The suspicion is inevitable that behind the primitive Cretan rites of bull-tearing and bull-eating there lay an orgy still more hideous, the sacrifice of a human child. A vase-painting in the British Museum[1], too revolting for needless reproduction here, represents a Thracian tearing with his teeth a slain child, while the god Dionysos, or rather perhaps we should say Zagreus, stands by approving. The vase is not adequate evidence that human children were slain and eaten, but it shows that the vase-painter of the 5th century B.C. believed such a practice was appropriate to the worship of a Thracian god.

[1] Published and discussed in relation to the myth of Zagreus by Mr Cecil Smith, *J.H.S.*, 1890, p. 343.

A very curious account of a sacrifice to Dionysos in Tenedos helps us to realize how the shift from human to animal sacrifice, from child to bull or calf, may have come about. Aelian[1] in his book on the Nature of Animals makes the following statement: 'The people of Tenedos in ancient days used to keep a cow with calf, the best they had, for Dionysos, and when she calved, why, they tended her like a woman in child-birth. But they sacrificed the new born calf, having put cothurni on its feet. Yes, and the man who struck it with the axe is pelted with stones in the holy rite and escapes to the sea.' The conclusion can scarcely be avoided that here we have a ritual remembrance of the time when a child was really sacrificed. A calf is substituted but it is humanized as far as possible, and the sacrificer, though he is bound to sacrifice, is guilty of an outrage[2]. Anyhow, that the calf was regarded as a child is clear; the line between human and merely animal is to primitive man a shifting shadow.

The mystic in his ritual confession clearly connects his feast of raw flesh with his service of Zagreus:

> 'Where midnight Zagreus roves, I rove;
> I have endured his thunder-cry;
> Fulfilled his red and bleeding feasts.'

It remains to consider more closely the import of the sacred legend of Zagreus.

That the legend as well as the rite was Cretan and was connected with Orpheus is expressly stated by Diodorus[3]. In his account of the various forms taken by the god Dionysos, he says 'they allege that the god (i.e. Zagreus) was born of Zeus and Persephone in Crete, and Orpheus in the mysteries represents him as torn in pieces by the Titans.'

When a people has outgrown in culture the stage of its own primitive rites, when they are ashamed or at least a little anxious and self-conscious about doing what yet they dare not leave undone, they instinctively resort to mythology, to what is their theology, and say the men of old time did it, or the gods suffered it. There is nothing like divine or very remote human precedent. Hence the

[1] Ael. *N.A.* XII. 34 λίθοις βάλλεται τῇ ὁσίᾳ. ὁσία is the regular word for a *mystic* rite, cf. *Hom. Hymn. ad Cer.* 211 ὁσίης ἐπέβη.
[2] See supra, p. 113.
[3] Diod. Sic. v. 75. 4.

complex myth of Zagreus. When precisely this myth was first formulated it is impossible to say; it comes to us in complete form only through late authors[1]. It was probably shaped and re-shaped to suit the spiritual needs of successive generations. The story as told by Clement and others is briefly this: the infant god variously called Dionysos and Zagreus was protected by the Kouretes or Korybantes who danced around him their armed dance. The Titans desiring to destroy him lured away the child by offering him toys, a cone, a rhombos, and the golden apples of the Hesperides, a mirror, a knuckle bone, a tuft of wool. The toys are variously enumerated[2]. Having lured him away they set on him, slew him and tore him limb from limb. Some authorities add that they cooked his limbs and ate them. Zeus hurled his thunderbolts upon them and sent them down to Tartaros. According to some authorities, Athene saved the child's heart, hiding it in a cista. A mock figure of gypsum was set up, the rescued heart placed in it and the child brought thereby to life again. The story was completed under the influence of Delphi by the further statement that the limbs of the dismembered god were collected and buried at Delphi in the sanctuary of Apollo.

The monstrous complex myth is obviously aetiological through and through, the kernel of the whole being the ritual fact that a sacrificial bull, or possibly a child, was torn to pieces and his flesh eaten. Who tore him to pieces? In actual fact his worshippers, but the myth-making mind always clamours for divine precedent. If there was any consistency in the mind of the primitive mythologist we should expect the answer to be 'holy men or gods,' as an example. Not at all. In a sense the worshipper believes the sacrificial bull to be divine, but, brought face to face with

[1] The scattered sources for the Zagreus myth are given in full in Abel's *Orphica* (pp. 230 ff.). They appear to be all based on a lost poem or poems attributed to Orpheus of which Clement in the passage already discussed (p. 483) quotes two lines: *ὡς ὁ τῆς τελετῆς ποιητὴς Ὀρφεύς φησιν ὁ Θρᾴκιος·*

κῶνος καὶ ῥόμβος καὶ παίγνια καμπεσίγυια
μῆλά τε χρύσεα καλὰ παρ᾽ Ἑσπερίδων λιγυφώνων,

and the scholiast on the passage observes (Dind. I. p. 433) *ὠμὰ γὰρ ἤσθιον κρέα οἱ μυόμενοι Διονύσῳ, δεῖγμα τοῦτο τελούμενοι τοῦ σπαραγμοῦ ὃν ὑπέστη Διόνυσος ὑπὸ Τιτάνων.*

[2] Among these sacred objects, which cannot be discussed in detail here, perhaps the most interesting was the rhombos or bull-roarer still in use among savage tribes, on the significance of which fresh light has recently been thrown by Dr Frazer in his paper 'On some ceremonies of the Central Australian Tribes.' Melbourne, 1900.

the notion of the dismemberment of a god, he recoils. It was primitive bad men who did this horrible deed. Why does he imitate them? This is the sort of question he never asks. It might interfere with the pious practice of ancestral custom, and custom is ever stronger than reason. So he goes on weaving his aetiological web. He eats the bull; so the bad Titans must have eaten the god. But, as they were bad, they must have been punished; on this point primitive theology is always inexorable. So they were slain by Zeus with his thunderbolts.

Other ritual details had of course to be worked in. The Kouretes, the armed Cretan priests, had a local war or mystery dance: they were explained as the protectors of the sacred child. Sacred objects were carried about in cistae; they were of a magical sanctity, fertility-charms and the like. Some ingenious person saw in them a new significance, and added thereby not a little to their prestige; they became the toys by which the Titans ensnared the sacred baby. It may naturally be asked why were the Titans fixed on as the aggressors? They were of course known to have fought against the Olympians in general, but in the story of the child Dionysos they appear somewhat as bolts from the blue. Their *name* even, it would seem, is aetiological, and behind it lies a curious ritual practice.

The *Dionysiaca* of Nonnus[1] is valuable as a source of ritual and constantly betrays Orphic influence. From it we learn in many passages[2] that it was the custom for the mystae to bedaub themselves with a sort of white clay or gypsum. This gypsum was so characteristic of mysteries that it is constantly qualified in Nonnus by the epithet 'mystic.' The technical terms for this ritual act of bedaubing with clay were 'to besmear' and 'to smear off' (*περιμάττειν* and *ἀπομάττειν*), and they are used as roughly

[1] Nonnus may have based his poem on the Βασσαρικά of Dionysius, to which it seems possible that the fragments recently discovered of an epic poem dealing with Bacchic subjects belong. These fragments contain a curious account of the slaying and eating of a human victim disguised as a stag. See Mr Kenyon in Herwerden's *Album Gratulatorium* and Dr Ludwich, 'Das Papyros-Fragment eines Dionysos-Epos' (*Berl. Philolog. Wochenschrift*, Jan. 3, 1903, p. 27).

[2] Nonn. *Dionys.* xxvii. 228

ἐλευκαίνοντο δὲ γύψῳ
μυστιπόλῳ

and see xxvii. 204, xxix. 274, xxxiv. 144, xlvii. 732. Cf. also the disguise of the Phocians described by Herodotus (viii. 27).

equivalent for 'to purify.' Harpocration[1] has an interesting note on the word 'smear off' (ἀπομάττων). 'Others use it in a more special sense, as for example when they speak of putting a coat of clay or pitch on those who are being initiated, as we say to take a cast of a statue in clay; for they used to besmear those who were being purified for initiation with clay and pitch. In this ceremony they were mimetically enacting the myth told by some persons, in which the Titans, when they mutilated Dionysos, wore a coating of gypsum in order not to be identified. The custom fell into disuse, but in later days they were plastered with gypsum out of convention (νομίμου χάριν).' Here we have the definite statement that in rites of initiation the worshippers were coated with gypsum. The 'some persons' who tell the story of Dionysos and the Titans are clearly Orphics. Originally, Harpocration says, the Titans were coated with gypsum that they might be disguised. Then the custom, by which he means the original object of the custom, became obsolete, but though the reason was lost the practice was kept up out of convention. They went on doing what they no longer understood.

Harpocration is probably right. Savages in all parts of the world, when about to perform their sacred mysteries, disguise themselves with all manner of religious war-paint. The motive is probably, like most human motives, mixed; they partly want to disguise themselves, perhaps from the influence of evil spirits, perhaps because they want to counterfeit some sort of bogey; mixed with this is the natural and universal instinct to 'dress up' on any specially sacred occasion, in order to impress outsiders. An element in what was at once a disguise and a decoration was coloured clay. Then having become sacred from its use on sacred occasions it became itself a sort of *medicine*, a means of purification and sanctification, as well as a ceremonial sign and token of initiation. Such performances went on not only in Crete but in civilized Athens. One of the counts brought by Demosthenes against Aeschines[2] was, it will be remembered (p. 417), 'that he purified the initiated and wiped them clean with mud and pitch' —*with*, be it noted, not *from*. Cleansing with mud does not seem to us a practical procedure, but we are back in the state of

[1] Harpocrat. s.v. ἀπομάττων.
[2] Dem. *de Coron.* § 259.

mind fully discussed in an earlier chapter (p. 39), when purification was not physical cleansing in our sense of the word, but a thing at once lower and higher, a magical riddance from *spiritual* evil, from evil spirits and influences. For this purpose clay and pitch were highly efficacious.

But what has all this to do with the Titans? Eustathius[1], commenting on the word Titan, lets us into the secret. 'We apply the word *titanos* in general to dust, in particular to what is called *asbestos,* which is the white fluffy substance in burnt stones. It is so called from the Titans in mythology, whom Zeus in the story smote with his thunderbolts and consumed to dust. For from them, the fine dust of stones which has got crumbled from excessive heat, so to speak Titanic heat, is called *titanic*, as though a Titanic penalty had been accomplished upon it. And the ancients call dust and gypsum *titanos.*'

This explanation is characteristically Eustathian. In his odd confused way the Archbishop, as so often, divines a real connection, but inverts and involves it. The simple truth is that the Titan myth is a 'sacred story' (*ἱερολογία*) invented to account for the ritual fact that Orphic worshippers, about to tear the sacred bull, daubed themselves with white clay, for which the Greek word was *tĭtănos*: they are Titans, but not as giants (Τῑτᾶνες), only as white-clay-men (*τῐτᾰνοι*). The Homeric Titans have probably no original etymological connection with the white-clay-men[2].

That this connection of meaning, this association of white-clay-men of the mysteries with primaeval giants, was late and fictitious is incidentally shown by the fact that it was fathered on Onomacritus. In the passage from Pausanias[3] already quoted (p. 472), we are told that Onomacritus *got the name of the Titans from Homer*, and composed 'orgies' for Dionysos, *and made the*

[1] Eustath. ad *Il.* II. 735 § 332 *τίτανον δὲ κυρίως τὴν κονίαν φαμέν, τὸ ἰδιωτικῶς λεγόμενον ἄσβεστον τὸ ἐν λίθοις κεκαυμένοις χνοῶδες λευκόν. ἐκλήθη δὲ οὕτως* (Τῖτανος, a town in Thessaly) *ἀπὸ τῶν μυθικῶν* Τιτάνων *οὓς ὁ τοῦ μύθου Ζεὺς κεραυνοῖς βαλὼν κατέφρυγε. δι' αὐτοὺς γὰρ καὶ τὸ ἐξ ἄγαν πολλῆς καύσεως καὶ ὡς οἷον εἰπεῖν τιτανώδους διατρυφθὲν ἐν λίθοις λεπτὸν τίτανος ὠνομάσθη, οἷα ποίνης τινὸς* Τιτανικῆς *γενομένης καὶ ἐν αὐτῷ. οἱ δὲ παλαιοί φασι τίτανος κόνις γύψος*, and see Eustath. 1676 where a child who sees snow for the first time is said to have mistaken it for *τίτανος*.

[2] Since writing the above I find that my explanation of the Titans has been anticipated by Dr Dieterich, *Rh. Mus.* 1893, p. 280. His high authority is a welcome confirmation of my view. See also Dr Ludwig Weniger, 'Feralis exercitus' in *Archiv f. Religionswissenschaft*, 1906, p. 242.

[3] P. VIII. 37. 5.

Titans the actual agents in the sufferings of Dionysos. He did not invent the white-clay worshippers, but he gave them a respectable orthodox though philologically improbable Homeric ancestry. What confusion and obscurity he thereby introduced is seen in the fact that a bad mythological precedent is invented for a good ritual act; all consistency was sacrificed for the sake of Homeric association.

But nothing, nothing, no savage rite, no learned mythological confusion, daunts the man bent on edification, the pious Orphic. The task of spiritualizing the white-clay-men, the dismembered bull, was a hard one, but the Orphic thinker was equal to it. He has not only taken part in an absurd and savage rite, he has brooded over the real problems of man and nature. There is evil in the universe, human evil to which as yet he does not give the name of sin, for he is not engaged with problems of free-will, but something evil, something that mixes with and mars the good of life, and he has long called it impurity. His old religion has taught him about ceremonial cleansings and has brought him, through conceptions like the Keres, very near to some crude notion of spiritual evil. The religion of Dionysos has forced him to take a momentous step. It has taught him not only what he knew before—that he can rid himself of impurity, but also that he can become a Bacchos, become divine. He seems darkly to see how it all came about, and how the old and the new work together. His forefathers, the Titans, though they were but 'dust and ashes,' dismembered and ate the god; they did evil, and good came of it; they had to be punished, slain with thunderbolts; but even in their ashes lived some spark of the divine; that is why he their descendant can himself become Bacchos. From these ashes he himself has sprung. It is only a little hope; there is all the element of dust and ashes from which he must cleanse himself; it will be very hard, but he goes back with fresh zeal to the ancient rite, to eat the bull-god afresh, renewing the divine within him.

Theology confirms his hope by yet another thought. Even the wicked Titans, before they ate Dionysos, had a heavenly ancestry; they were children of old Ouranos, the sky-god, as well as of Ge, the earth-mother. His master Orpheus worshipped the sun (p. 461). Can he not too, believing this, purify himself from his earthly nature and rise to be the 'child of starry heaven'? Perhaps it is not a very satisfactory theory of the origin of evil; but is the sacred legend of the serpent and the apple more illuminating? Anyhow it was the faith and hope the Orphic, as we shall later see (p. 570), carried with him to his grave.

There were other difficulties to perplex the devout enquirer. The god in the mysteries of Zagreus was a bull, but in the mysteries of Sabazios (p. 418) his vehicle was a snake, and these mysteries must also enshrine the truth. Was the father of the child a snake or a bull; was the 'horned child' a horned snake? It was all very difficult. He could not solve the difficulty; so he embodied it in a little dogmatic verse, and kept it by him as a test of reverent submission to divine mysteries:

'The Snake's Bull-Father—the Bull's Father-Snake[1].'

The snake, the bull, the snake-bull-child[2]—'not three Incomprehensibles, but one Incomprehensible.' On the altar of his Unknown God through all the ages man pathetically offers the holocaust of his reason.

The weak point of the Orphic was, of course, that he could not, would not, break with either ancient ritual or ancient mythology, could not trust the great new revelation which bade him become 'divine,' but must needs mysticize and reconcile archaic obsolete traditions. His strength was that in conduct he was steadfastly bent on purity of life. He could not turn upon the past and say, 'this daubing with white clay, this eating of raw bulls, is savage nonsense; give it up.' He could and did say, 'this daubing with white clay and eating of raw bulls is not in itself enough, it must be followed up by arduous endeavour after holiness.'

This is clear from the further confession of the Cretan chorus, to which we return. From the time that the neophyte is accepted

[1] *Ταῦρος δράκοντος καὶ δράκων ταύρου πατήρ*, frg. ap. Clem. Al. *Protr.* I. 2. 12. What was made of such a reverent mystic dogma by the unsavoury minds of Christian Fathers can be read by the curious.

[2] M. Salomon Reinach, who has done so much for the elucidation of Orphism, has shown that the Celts held in honour and depicted on their monuments a *horned snake*. Such a conception would keep up the confusion of bull and snake. He believes the original form of Zagreus to have been that of a horned snake. The point is an interesting one and is evidence of Northern elements in Orphic as well as Dionysiac conceptions, see *Rev. Arch.* 1899, vol. xxxv. p. 210, S. Reinach, 'Zagreus le serpent cornu.'

as such, i.e. performs the initiatory rites of purification and thereby becomes a *Mystes*, he leads a life of ceremonial purity (*ἁγνόν*). He accomplishes the rite of eating raw sacrificial flesh and also holds on high the torches to the Mountain Mother. These characteristic acts of the *Mystes*, are, I think, all preliminary stages to the final climax, the full fruition, when, cleansed and consecrated by the Kouretes, he is named by them a Bacchos, he is made one with the god.

Before we pass to the final act consummated by the Kouretes, the place of the Mountain Mother has to be considered. The mystic's second avowal is that he has

'Held the Great Mother's mountain flame[1].'

In the myth of Zagreus, coming to us as it does through late authors, the child is all-important, the mother only present by implication. Zeus the late comer has by that time ousted Dionysos in Crete. The mythology of Zeus, patriarchal as it is through and through, lays no stress on motherhood. Practically the Zeus of the later Hellenism has no mother. But the bull-divinity worshipped in Crete was wholly the son of his mother, and in Crete most happily the ancient figure of the mother has returned after long burial to the upper air. On a Cretan seal Mr Arthur Evans found the beast-headed monster whom men called Minotaur; on a Cretan seal also he found the figure of the Mountain Mother, found her at Cnossos, the place of the birth of the bull-child, Cnossos overshadowed by Ida where within the ancient cave the holy child was born and the 'mailed priests' danced at his birth.

The design in fig. 145 is from the clay impression of a signet ring found at the palace at Cnossos[2]. It is a veritable little

[1] *v.* 12 *μητρί τ' ὀρείᾳ δᾷδας ἀνασχών*. In the recently discovered fragment of Timotheos (*v.* 135) it is to the 'Mountain Mother' that the drowning sailor would pray:

εἰ δυνατὰ πρὸς μελαμπεταλο-
χίτωνα Ματρὸς οὐρεί-
ας δεσπόσυνα γόνατα πεσεῖν....

See Timotheos, *Die Perser*, Wilamowitz-Moellendorff, 1903.

[2] Published and discussed by the discoverer Mr Evans in the *Annual of the British School at Athens*, vol. VII. 1900—1901, p. 29, fig. 9. The enlargement ($\frac{3}{1}$) here reproduced from the *Annual* is based on a restoration, but a perfectly certain one. A series of clay fragments impressed by the same seal, but not from the same impression, were found in a deposit of burnt wood. The various fragments overlapped sufficiently for certain reconstruction. When I first saw a drawing of the seal I was inclined to think it was 'too good to be true,' but by Mr Evans' kindness

manual of primitive Cretan faith and ritual. On the very apex of her own great mountain stands the Mountain Mother. The Mycenaean women of Cnossos have made their goddess in their own image, clad her, wild thing though she was, in their own grotesque flounced skirt, and they give her for guardians her own fierce mountain-ranging lions, tamed into solemn heraldic

Fig. 145.

guardians. We know the lions well enough; they came to Mycenae to guard the great entrance-gate. Between them at Mycenae is a column, a thing so isolated and protected, that we long suspected it was no dead architectural thing but a true shrine of a divinity, and here on the Cretan seal the divinity has come to life. She stands with sceptre or lance extended, imperious, dominant. Behind her is her shrine of 'Mycenaean' type, with its odd columns and horns, these last surely appropriate enough to a cult whose central rite was the sacrifice of a bull; before her in rapt ecstasy of adoration stands her Mystes.

Pre-historic Crete has yielded, I venture to think will yield, no figure of a *dominant* male divinity, no Zeus; so far we have only a beast-headed monster and the Mountain Mother. The little seal impression is a standing monument of matriarchalism. In

I was allowed while at Crete to examine the original fragments and am satisfied that the reconstruction is correct. We owe the most important monument of Mycenaean religion to the highly trained eye and extraordinarily acute perception of the excavator.

Greece the figure of the Son was developed in later days, the relation of Mother and Son almost forgotten; child and parent were represented by the figures of the Mother and the Daughter. It matters very little what names we give the shifting pairs. In Thrace, in Asia Minor, in Crete, the primitive form is the Mother with the Son as the attribute of Motherhood; the later form the Son with the Mother as the attribute of Sonship. A further development is the Son with only a faded Mother in the background, Bacchos and Semele; next the Son is made the Son of his Father, Bacchos is Dionysos; finally he eclipses his Father and reigns omnipotent as Zeus-Hades. The Mother with the Son as attribute came back from Asia Minor to Greece when in Greece the Mother was but the appendage of the Son, and coming made sore confusion for mythology. But for prehistoric Crete, for the Cretan mystic of Euripides in the days of Minos, the ritual is of the Mother and the Son.

The 'mystic' holds aloft the torches of the mother. Fire as well as water is for cleansing. He is finally consecrated (ὁσιωθείς) by the Kouretes:

'I am Set Free and named by name
A Bacchos of the Mailed Priests[1].'

The Kouretes need not long detain us. They are the Cretan brothers of the Satyrs, the local Satyrs of Crete. Hesiod[2] knows of their kinship: from the same parent

'The goddesses, nymphs of the mountain, had their being,
And the race of the worthless do-nothing Satyrs,
And the divine Kouretes, lovers of sport and dancing.'

Hesiod's words are noteworthy and characteristic of his theological attitude. The Satyrs, we have seen (p. 379), are *Satrai*, primitive Dionysos-worshippers of Thrace and Thessaly. Seen through the hostile eyes of their conquerors they have suffered distortion and degradation in form as in content, they are horsemen, worthless, idle. The Kouretes have just the same beginning in actuality, but their mythological ending is different. They are

1 καὶ Κουρήτων
βάκχος ἐκλήθην ὁσιωθείς.
The word ὁσιωθείς is rendered 'Set Free' by Mr Murray in his translation for reasons explained later, p. 503.

2 Hes. frg. cxxix. ap. Strab. x. p. 323.

seen, not through the distorting medium of conquest, but with the halo of religion about their heads; they are divine (θεοί) and their dancing is sacred. It all depends on the point of view.

Strabo, in his important discussion of the Kouretes and kindred figures, knows that they are all ministers (πρόσπολοι) of orgiastic deities, of Rhea and of Dionysos; he knows also that Kouretes, Korybantes, Daktyloi, Telchines and the like represent primitive populations[1]. What bewilders him is the question which particular form originated the rest and where they all belong. Did Mother Rhea send her Korybants to Crete? how do the Kouretes come to be in Aetolia? Why are they sometimes servants of Rhea, sometimes of Dionysos? why are some of them magicians, some of them handicraftsmen, some of them mystical priests? In the light of Prof. Ridgeway's investigations, discussed in relation to the Satyrs (p. 384), much that puzzled Strabo is made easy to us.

The Kouretes then are, as their name betokens, the young male population considered as worshipping the young male god, the *Kouros*; they are 'mailed priests' because the young male population were naturally warriors. They danced their local war-dance over the new-born child, and, because in those early days the worship of the Mother and the Son was not yet sundered, they were attendants (πρόσπολοι) on the Mother also. They are in fact the male correlatives of the Maenads as Nurses (τίθηναι). The women-nurses were developed most fully, it seems, in Greece proper; the male attendants, in Asia Minor and the islands.

In the fusion and confusion of these various local titles given to primitive worshippers, this blend of Satyrs, Korybants, Daktyls, Telchines, so confusing in literature till its simple historical basis is grasped, one equation is for our purpose important—Kouretes =Titans. The Titans of ritual, it has been shown, are men be-daubed with white earth. The Titans of mythology are children of Earth, primitive giants rebellious against the new Olympian order. Diodorus[2] knows of a close connection between Titans and Kouretes and attempts the usual genealogical explanation. The Titans, he says, are, according to some, sons of one of the Kouretes and of a mother called Titaia; according to others of

[1] On the origin of the mythological conception of the Idaean Dactyls much light has been thrown by Kaibel in his 'Ἰδαῖοι Δακτύλοι' *Nachrichten d. k. Ges. d. Wiss. Phil.-hist. Kl.* 1901, p. 488.

[2] Diod. v. 66.

Ouranos and Ge. Titaia is mother Earth. The Cretans, he says, allege that the Titans were born in the age of the Kouretes and that the Titans settled themselves in the district of Cnossos 'where even now there are shown the site and foundations of a house of Rhea and a cypress grove dedicated from ancient days.' The Titans as Kouretes worshipped the Mother, and were the guardians of the Son, the infant Zagreus, to whom later monotheism gave the name of Zeus.

From the time that the neophyte enters the first stage of initiation, i.e. becomes a 'mystic' (*μύστης*), he leads a life of abstinence (*ἁγνόν*). But abstinence is not the end. Abstinence, the sacramental feast of raw flesh, the holding aloft of the Mother's torches, all these are but preliminary stages to the final climax, the full fruition when, cleansed and consecrated, he is made one with the god and the Kouretes name him 'Bacchos.'

The word *ἁγνόν*, i.e. 'pure,' in the negative sense, 'free from evil,' marks, I think, the initial stage—a stage akin to the old service of 'aversion' (*ἀποτροπή*). The word *ὁσιωθείς*, 'set free,' 'consecrated,' marks the final accomplishment and is a term of positive content. It is characteristic of orgiastic, 'enthusiastic' rites, those of the Mother and the Son, and requires some further elucidation.

THE HOSIOI AND HOSIA.

At Delphi there was an order of priests known as Hosioi. Plutarch is our only authority for their existence, but, for Delphic matters, we could have no better source. In his 9th *Greek Question* he asks[1] 'who is the Hosioter among the Delphians, and why do they call one of their months Bysios?' The second part of the question only so far concerns us as it marks a connection between the Hosioter and the month Bysios, which, Plutarch tells us, was at the 'beginning of spring,' the 'time of the blossoming of many plants.' On the 8th day of this month

[1] Plut. *Q. Gr.* IX. *Τίς ὁ παρὰ Δελφοῖς Ὁσιωτὴρ καὶ διὰ τί Βύσιον ἕνα τῶν μηνῶν καλοῦσιν; Ὁσιωτῆρα μὲν καλοῦσι τὸ θυόμενον ἱερεῖον, ὅταν Ὅσιος ἀποδειχθῇ, πέντε δέ εἰσιν ὅσιοι διὰ βίον καὶ τὰ πολλὰ μετὰ τῶν προφητῶν δρῶσιν οὗτοι καὶ συνιερουργοῦσιν, ἅτε γεγονέναι δοκοῦντες ἀπὸ Δευκαλίωνος.* Stephanos comments 'mendose ut videtur pro *τὸν θυόμενον*, accipiendo sc. *θυόμενον* active pro *θύοντα*...Recte autem habet *τὸ* si quidem *Ὁσιωτὴρ* (*ταῦρος*) est Hostia quae immolatur.'

fell the birthday of the god and in olden times 'on this day only did the oracle give answers.'

Plutarch's answer to his question is as follows: 'They call Hosioter the animal sacrificed when a Hosios is designated.' He does not say *how* the animal's fitness was shown, but from another passage[1] we learn that various tests were applied to the animals to be sacrificed, to see if they were 'pure, unblemished and uncorrupt both in body and soul.' As to the body Plutarch says it was not very difficult to find out. As to the soul the test for a bull was to offer him barley-meal, for a he-goat vetches; if the animal did not eat, it was pronounced unhealthy. A she-goat, being more sensitive, was tested by being sprinkled with cold water. These tests were carried on by the Hosioi and by the 'prophets' (*προφῆται*), these last being concerned with omens as to whether the god would give oracular answers. The animal, we note, became *Hosios* when he was pronounced unblemished and hence fit for sacrifice: the word *ὅσιος*, it appears, carried with it the double connotation of purity and consecration; it was used of a thing found blameless and then made over to, accepted by, the gods.

The animal thus consecrated was called Hosioter, which means 'He who consecrates.' We should expect such a name to be applied to the consecrating priest rather than the victim. If Plutarch's statement be correct, we can only explain Hosioter on the supposition that the sacrificial victim was regarded as an incarnation of the god. If the victim was a bull, as in Crete, and was regarded as divine, the title would present no difficulties.

That the Hosioter was not merely a priest is practically certain from the fact that there were, as already noted, priests who bore the cognate title of Hosioi. Of them we know, again from Plutarch, some further important particulars. They performed rites—as in the case of the testing of the victims—in conjunction with the 'prophets' or utterers of the oracle, but they were not identical with them. On one occasion, the priestess while prophesying had some sort of fit, and Plutarch[2] mentions that not only did all the seers run away but also the prophet and 'those of the Hosioi that were present.'

[1] Plut. *de Defect. Orac.* XLIX. οἱ γὰρ ἱερεῖς καὶ θύειν φασὶ τὸ ἱερεῖον κτλ.
[2] Plut. *de Defect. Orac.* LI.

In the answer to his 'Question' about the Hosioter, Plutarch states definitely that the Hosioi were five in number, were elected for life, and that they did many things and performed sacred sacrifices with the 'prophets.' Yet they were clearly not the same[1]. A suspicion of the real distinction dawns upon us when he adds that they were reputed to be descended from Deucalion. Deucalion marks Thessalian ancestry and Thessaly looks North. We begin to surmise that the Hosioi were priests of the immigrant cult of Dionysos. This surmise approaches certainty when we examine the actual ritual which the Hosioi performed.

It will be remembered[2] that when Plutarch is describing the ritual of the Bull Dionysos, he compares it, in the matter of 'tearings to pieces' and burials and new births, to that of Osiris. Osiris has his tombs in Egypt and 'the Delphians believe that the fragments of Dionysos are buried near their oracular shrine, and the Hosioi offer a secret sacrifice (*θυσίαν ἀπόρρητον*) in the sanctuary of Apollo at the time when the Thyiades wake up Liknites.' To clinch the argument Lycophron[3] tells us that Agamemnon before he sailed

> 'Secret lustrations to the Bull did make
> Beside the caves of him the God of Gain
> Delphinios,'

and that in return for this Bacchus Enorches overthrew Telephos, tangling his feet in a vine. The scholiast commenting on the 'secret lustrations' says, 'because the mysteries were celebrated to Dionysos in a corner.' It is, I think, clear that the mysteries of Liknites at Delphi, like those of Crete, included the sacrifice of a sacred bull, and that the bull at Delphi was called Hosioter, that, in a word, Hosioi and Hosioter are ritual terms specially linked with the primitive mysteries of Dionysos.

The word Hosios was then, it would seem, deep-rooted in the savage ritual of the Bull; but with its positive content, its notion of consecration, it lay ready to hand as a vehicle to express the

[1] Nikitsky, *Delphisch-Epigraphische Studien*, p. 145, points out that in inscriptions two hereditary families of priests are traceable; these he thinks may correspond with the *προφῆται* or utterers whom he holds to be Apolline and the *ὅσιοι* who are manifestly Dionysiac. His book is in Russian, and I only know it at second hand.

[2] Plut. *de Is. et Os.* xxxv. and see p. 439. Had the treatise by Socrates *περὶ Ὁσίων* which Plutarch refers to been preserved, we should have been informed.

[3] Lyc. *Al.* 207 and schol. ad loc. *ταῦρος δὲ ὁ Διόνυσος...ὅτι ἐν παραβύστῳ τὰ μυστήρια ἐτελεῖτο τῷ Διονύσῳ.*

new Orphic doctrine of identification with the divine. Its use was not confined to Dionysiac rites, though it seems very early to have been specialized in relation to them, probably because the Orphics always laid stress on *fas* rather than *nefas*. In ancient curse-formularies, belonging to the cult of Demeter[1] and underworld divinities, the words *ὅσια καὶ ἐλεύθερα*, 'consecrated and free,' are used in constant close conjunction and are practically all but equivalents. The offender, the person cursed, was either 'sold' or 'bound down' to the infernal powers; but the cursing worshipper prays that the things that are accursed, i.e. tabooed to the offender, may to him be *ὅσια καὶ ἐλεύθερα*, 'consecrated and free,' i.e. to him they are freed from the taboo. It is the dawning of the grace in use to-day 'Sanctify these creatures to our use and us to thy service'; it is the ritual forecast of a higher guerdon, 'Ye shall know the truth and the truth shall make you free.'

This primitive notion of release from *taboo*, which lay at the root of the Orphic and Christian notion of spiritual freedom, comes out very clearly in the use of the word *ἀφοσιοῦσθαι*. For this word we have no exact English equivalent, but it may be rendered as 'to purify by means of an expiatory offering.' Plato in the *Laws* describes the ceremonial to be performed in the case of a man who has intentionally murdered one near of kin. The regular officials are to put him to death, and this done 'let them strip him, and cast him outside the city into a place where three ways meet, appointed for the purpose, and on behalf of the city collectively let the authorities, each one severally, take a stone and cast it on the head of the dead man, and thereby purify (*ἀφοσιούτω*) the city.' The significance of this ritual is drastically explicit. The taint of the murder, the taboo of the blood-guilt, is on the whole city; the casting of the stones, on behalf of the city, *purifies it off* on to the criminal; it is literally conveyed from one to other by the stone. The guilty man is the *pharmakos*, and his fate is that of a *pharmakos*; 'this done let them carry him to the confines of the city, and cast him out unburied, as is ordained.' Dedication, *devotion* of the thing polluted, *ἀφοσίωσις*, is the means whereby man attains *ὁσίωσις*, consecration. The scholiast[2] on the

[1] C. T. Newton, *Discoveries at Cnidos*, p. 735, and Insc. 88, 83 etc.

[2] Plat. *Legg.* 873 B, schol. ad loc. *ἀφοσιούτω*] *καθαιρέτω, ὡς νῦν, ἢ ἀπαρχὰς προσαγέτω, ἢ τιμάτω, ἢ τὴν ἐπὶ θανάτῳ ἀποδιδότω τιμήν, ἢ πληροφορείτω.* I owe the reference to this interesting passage to Mr F. M. Cornford. I am not sure what the

passage has an interesting gloss on the word ἀφοσιούτω. 'It is used,' he says, 'as in this passage, to mean "to purify," or "to bring first-fruits," or "to give honour," or "to give a meed of honour on the occasion of death," or "to give fulfilment."' He feels dimly the shifts and developments of meaning. You can devote, 'make over' a *pharmakos*; you can devote, consecrate first-fruits, thereby releasing the rest from taboo; you can consecrate a meed of honour on the occasion of death.

In this connection it is interesting to note the well-known fact that in common Greek parlance ὅσιος is the actual opposite of ἱερός. Suidas[1] tells us that a ὅσιον χωρίον is 'a place on which you may tread, which is *not* sacred, into which you may go.' He quotes from the *Lysistrata* of Aristophanes, where a woman with child prays:

> 'O holy Eileithyia, keep back the birth
> Until I come unto a *place allowed.*'

He further notes the distinction often drawn by the orators between goods that are *sacred* (ἱερά) and those that are (in the Latin sense) *profane* (ὅσια). The contrast is in fact only fully intelligible when we go back to the primitive notions, under a taboo, released from a taboo. The notion 'released from a taboo' was sure to be taken up by a spiritual religion, a religion that aimed at expansion, liberation, enthusiasm rather than at check, negation, restraint. If we may trust Suidas, the word ὅσιοι was applied to those who 'were nurtured in piety, even if they were not priests.' The early Christians owed some of their noblest impulses to Orphism.

As we find ὅσιος contrasted with ἱερός, so also between the two kindred words καθαίρω and ὁσιόω a distinction may be observed. Both denote purification, but ὁσιόω marks a stage more final and complete. It is the word chosen to describe the state of those who are *fully* initiated. Plutarch[2] says that the souls of men pass, by a natural and divine order, from mortal men to heroes, from heroes to daemons, and finally, if they are completely purified and consecrated (καθαρθῶσι καὶ ὁσιωθῶσιν), as if

scholiast means by the post-classical word πληροφορέω; the passive means in the New Testament 'to have full assurance' of faith and the like. It may point to the final stage of initiation.

[1] Suidas, s.v. ὅσιος, ὅσιον χωρίον.

[2] Plut. *Vit. Rom.* 28.

by a rite of initiation they pass from daemons to the gods. Lucian[1] again in speaking of the final stage of initiation reserved for hierophants uses the word 'consecrated' (*ὡσιώθησαν*).

Plutarch[2] makes another interesting suggestion. In a wild attempt to glorify Osiris and make him the god of everything, he derives his name from the two adjectives *ὅσιος* and *ἱερός*, and incidentally lets fall this suggestive remark, 'the name of Osiris is so compounded because his significance is compounded of things in heaven and things in Hades. It was customary among the ancients to call the one *ὅσια* the other *ἱερά*.' The things of the underworld are *ὅσια*; of the upper sky, things Ouranian, *ἱερά*. Translated into ritual, this means that the old underworld rites already discussed, the rites of the primitive Pelasgian stratum of the population, were known as *ὅσια*, the new burnt sacrifices of the Ouranians or Olympians were *ἱερά*. Dionysos was of the old order: his rites were *ὅσια*, burial rites were *ὅσια*. It was the work of Orpheus to lift these rites from earth to heaven, but spiritualized, uplifted as they are, they remain in their essence primitive. It is because of this peculiar origin that there is always about *ὅσιος* something of an antique air; it has that 'imprint of the ancient,' that 'crust and patina' of archaism, which Iamblichus[3] says were characteristic of things Pythagorean, and which, enshrining as it does a new life and impulse, lends to Orphism a grace all its own.

Moreover, though *ὅσιος* is so 'free' that it verges on the profane, the secular, yet it is the freedom always of consecration, not desecration; it is the negation of the Law, but only by the Gospel. Hence, though this may seem paradoxical, it is concerned rather with the Duty towards God, than the Duty towards our Neighbour. Rising though it does out of form, it is so wholly aloof from formalism, that it tends to become the 'unwritten law.' Hence such constant oppositions as *οὐ θέμις οὐδ' ὅσιον*, 'allowed by neither human prescription nor divine law,' and again *οὐδ' ὅσιον οὐδὲ δίκαιον*, 'right neither in the eye of God nor of man.' Plato[4]

[1] Lucian, *Lexiphan*. 10.

[2] Plut. *de Is. et Os.* LXI. *ὁ Ὄσιρις ἐκ τοῦ ὁσίου καὶ ἱεροῦ τοὔνομα μεμιγμένον ἔσχηκε· κοινὸς γάρ ἐστι τῶν ἐν οὐρανῷ καὶ τῶν ἐν ᾅδου λόγος. ὧν τὰ μὲν ἱερὰ τὰ δὲ ὅσια τοῖς παλαιοῖς* <*ἔθος*?> *ἦν προσαγορεύειν*. It is practically certain that *τὰ μέν* refers to the first mentioned class, i.e. *τὰ ἐν οὐρανῷ*.

[3] Iambl. *Vit. Pythag*. 58, *χαρακτὴρ παλαιοτρόπος...ἀρχαιοτρόπου δὲ καὶ παλαιοῦ πίνου*.

[4] Plat. *Gorg*. p. 507 B.

says 'he who does what is proper in relation to man, would be said to do just things (δίκαια), he who does what is proper towards God, holy things (ὅσια).' Hence finally the spiritual illumination and advance of ὅσια πανουργήσασ'[1], breaking through human Justice for the Divine Right, the duty, sacred, sacrosanct, of rebellion.

The Greeks had their goddess Dike, she who divides and apportions things mortal, who according to Hesiod[2] was sister of the lovely human figures, Fair Order and Peace. But, because she was human, she carried the symbol of human justice, the sword. She lapses constantly into Vengeance. The Bacchants of Euripides[3] are fully initiated, consecrated as well as cleansed, yet in their hour of extreme need it is to this Goddess of Vengeance they cry for visible, physical retribution on the blasphemer Pentheus:

> 'Hither for doom and deed,
> Hither with lifted sword,
> Justice, Wrath of the Lord,
> Come in our visible need,
> Smite till the throat shall bleed,
> Smite till the heart shall bleed
> Him the tyrannous, lawless, godless, Echion's earth-born seed.'

Orpheus did all he could to raise the conception of Dike. We are expressly told that it was he who raised her to be the 'Assessor of Zeus.' Demosthenes[4] pleads with his fellow citizens to honour Fair Order (Εὐνομία), who loves just deeds and is the Saviour of cities and countries, and Justice (Dike), holy and unswerving, *whom Orpheus who instituted our most sacred mysteries declares to be seated by the throne of Zeus.* The dating of Orphic hymns is precarious, but it looks as though Demosthenes had in his mind the Orphic Hymn to Dike[5] or at least its prototype:

> 'I sing the all-seeing eye of Dike of fair form,
> Who sits upon the holy throne of Zeus
> The king, and on the life of mortals doth look down,
> And heavy broods her justice on the unjust.'

The Orphic could not rid himself of the notion of Vengeance. Dike as avenger finds a place, it will be seen later (p. 611), in the Orphic Hades. Hosia, the real Heavenly Justice, she who is Right and Sanctity and Freedom and Purity all in one, never

[1] Soph. *Ant.* 74.
[2] Hes. *Theog.* 901.
[3] Eur. *Bacch.* 991, ἴτω Δίκα φανερὸς ἴτω ξιφηφόρος.
[4] Dem. *c. Aristogeit.* XXV. 11.
[5] *Orph. Hymn.* LXII.

attained a vivid and constant personality; she is a goddess for the few, not the many; only Euripides[1] called her by her heavenly name and made his Bacchants sing to her a hymn:

'Thou Immaculate on high;
Thou Recording Purity;
Thou that stoopest, Golden Wing,
Earthward, manward, pitying,
Hearest thou this angry king?'

It was Euripides, and perhaps only Euripides, who made the goddess Hosia in the image of his own high desire, and, though the Orphic word and Orphic rites constantly pointed to a purity that was also freedom, to a sanctity that was by union with rather than submission to the divine, yet Orphism constantly renounced its birth-right, reverted as it were to the old savage notion of abstinence (*ἁγνεία*). After the ecstasy of

'I am Set Free and named by name
A Bacchos of the Mailed Priests,'

the end of the mystic's confession falls dull and sad and formal:

'Robed in pure white I have borne me clean
From man's vile birth and coffined clay,
And exiled from my lips alway
Touch of all meat where Life hath been[2].'

He that is free and holy (*ὁσιωθείς*) and divine, marks his divinity by a dreary formalism. He wears white garments, he flies from death and birth, from all physical contagion, his lips are pure from flesh-food, he fasts after as before the Divine Sacrament. He follows in fact all the rules of asceticism familiar to us as 'Pythagorean.'

Diogenes Laertius[3] in his life of Pythagoras gives a summary of these prescriptions, which show but too sadly and clearly the reversion to the negative purity of abstinence (*ἁγνεία*). 'Purifica-

[1] Eur. *Bacch.* 370, Ὁσία πότνα θεῶν. It is worth noting in connection with the Ὁσία of Euripides, that on tomb-inscriptions in Phrygia, and so far as at present known only there, dedications occur to a divinity bearing the titles ὅσιος καὶ δίκαιος. These inscriptions are of Roman date, and it is usual to refer them to Mithras worship, but, found as they are in Phrygia, the home of the Bacchants, it is possible, I think, that they may indicate an old tradition of Cybele worship. See Roscher, s.v. Hosios.

[2] πάλλευκα δ' ἔχων εἵματα φεύγω
γένεσίν τε βροτῶν καὶ νεκροθήκης
οὐ χριμπτόμενος, τήν τ' ἐμψύχων
βρῶσιν ἐδεστῶν πεφύλαγμαι.

[3] Diog. Laert. *Vit. Pyth.* 19 § 33.

tion, they say, is by means of cleansings and baths and aspersions, and because of this a man must keep himself from funerals and marriages and every kind of physical pollution, and abstain from all food that is dead or has been killed, and from mullet and from the fish melanurus, and from eggs, and from animals that lay eggs, and from beans, and from the other things that are forbidden by those who accomplish holy rites of initiation.' The savage origin of these fastings and taboos on certain foods has been discussed; they are deep-rooted in the ritual of *ἀποτροπή*, of aversion, which fears and seeks to evade the physical contamination of the Keres inherent in all things. Plato[1], in his inverted fashion, realizes that the Orphic life was a revival of things primitive. In speaking of the golden days before the altars of the gods were stained with blood, when men offered honey cakes and fruits of the earth, he says then it was not holy (*ὅσιον*) to eat or offer flesh-food, but men lived a sort of 'Orphic' life, as it is called.

Poets and philosophers, then as now, sated and hampered by the complexities and ugliness of luxury, looked back with longing eyes to the old beautiful gentle simplicity, the picture of which was still before their eyes in antique ritual, in the *ὅσια*, the rites of the underworld gods—those gods who in their beautiful conservatism kept their service cleaner and simpler than the lives of their worshippers. Sophocles[2] in the lost *Polyidos* tells of the sacrifice 'dear to these gods':

'Wool of the sheep was there, fruit of the vine,
Libations and the treasured store of grapes.
And manifold fruits were there, mingled with grain
And oil of olive, and fair curious combs
Of wax compacted by the yellow bee.'

Some of these gods, it has been seen, would not taste of the fruit of the vine: such were at Athens the Sun, the Moon, the Dawn, the Muses, the Nymphs, Mnemosyne and Ourania. To them the Athenians[3], who were careful in matters of religion (*ὅσιοι*), brought only sober offerings, *nephalia*; and such an offering we have seen was brought to Dionysos-Hades. Philochoros[4], to our great surprise, extends the list of wineless divinities to

[1] Plat. *Legg.* VI. p. 782.
[2] Soph. frg. 464, ap. Porphyr. *de Abst.* II. p. 134.
[3] Schol. ad Soph. *Oed. Col.* 100.
[4] Philoch. frg. 30, ap. Schol. ad Soph. *Oed. Col.* 99.

Dionysos. Plutarch[1] knows the custom of the wineless libation to Dionysos, and after the fashion of his day explains it as an ascetic protest. In his treatise on 'the Preservation of Health' he says, 'We often sacrifice *nephalia* to Dionysos, accustoming ourselves rightly not to desire unmixed wine.' The practice is manifestly a survival in ritual of the old days before Dionysos took possession of the vine, or rather the vine took possession of him.

Empedokles had taught men that 'to fast from evil' was a great and divine thing; it is not surprising that the 'wineless' rites became to those who lived the Orphic life the symbol, perhaps the sacrament, of their spiritual abstinence. Plutarch we know (p. 627) was suspected by his robuster friends of Orphism, and probably with good reason. In his dialogue on 'Freedom from Anger' he[2] makes one of the speakers, who is transparently himself, tell how he conquered his natural irritability. He set himself to observe certain days as sacred, on which he would not get angry, just as he might have abstained from getting drunk or taking any wine, and these 'angerless days' he offered to God as 'Nephalia' or 'Melisponda,' and then he tried a whole month, and then two, till he was cured. To a greater than Plutarch, a priest who was poet also, the wineless sacrifice of the Eumenides[3] is charged with sacramental meaning; the rage of the king is over, in his heart is meekness, in his hands olive, shorn wool, water and honey; so only may he enter their sanctuary, 'he sober and they wineless.'

In the confession of the Orphic there is no mention of wine, no avowal of having sacramentally drunk it, no resolve to abstain. The Bacchos, with whom the mystic is made one, is the ancient Bull-god, lord of the life of Nature, rather than Bromios, god of intoxication. Also it must not be forgotten that the mystic is a votary of the Mother as well as the Son, and though the Mother is caught and carried away in the later revels of the Son, she is never goddess of the vine. It is noteworthy that the later Orphics turned rather to the Mother than the Son; they revived the ancient rite of earth to earth burial, supplanted for a time by cremation, and the house of Pythagoras[4] was called by the people

[1] Plut. *de tuend. sanit.* XVII. [2] Plut. *de cohibend. ir.* XVI. sub fin.
[3] Soph. *Oed. Col.* 100, νήφων ἀοίνοις, and schol. ad loc.
[4] Diog. Laert. *Vit. Pythag.* xv., and see p. 91.

of Metapontum the 'temple of Demeter.' Pythagoras never insisted on 'total abstinence,' but he told his disciples that if they would drink plain water they would be clearer in head as well as healthier in body. In the ancient rites of the Mother, rites instituted before the coming of the grape, they found the needful divine precedent[1]:

> 'Then Metaneira brought her a cup of honey-sweet wine,
> But the goddess would not drink it, she shook her head for a sign,
> For red wine she might not taste, and she bade them bring her meal
> And water and mix it together, and mint that is soft to feel.
> Metaneira did her bidding and straight the posset she dight,
> And holy Deo took it and drank thereof for a rite.'

It is strange that Orpheus if he came from the North, the land of Homeric banquets, should have preached abstinence from flesh: if he was of Cretan origin the difficulty disappears. Perhaps also such abstinence is a necessary concomitant of a mysticism that asks for nothing short of divinity. The mystic Porphyry[2] says clearly that his treatise on 'Abstinence from Animal Food' is not meant for soldiers or for athletes; for these flesh food may be needful. He writes for those who would lay aside every weight and 'entering the stadium naked and unclothed would strive in the Olympic contest of the soul.' And a great modern mystic[3], looking more deeply and more humbly into the mystery of things natural, writes as follows:

'*Toute notre justice, toute notre morale, tous nos sentiments et toutes nos pensées dérivent en somme de trois ou quatre besoins primordiaux, dont le principal est celui de la nourriture. La moindre modification de l'un de ces besoins amènerait des changements considérables dans notre vie morale.*' Maeterlinck believes, as Pythagoras did, that those who abstain from flesh food '*ont senti leurs forces s'accroître, leur santé se rétablir ou s'affermir, leur esprit s'alléger et se purifier, comme au sortir d'une prison séculaire nauséabonde et misérable.*'

But the plain carnal man in ancient Athens would have none of this. What to him are *ὅσια*, things hallowed to the god, as compared with *νόμιμα*, things consecrated by his own usage? So

[1] *Hom. Hymn. ad Cer.* 205—210,
δεξαμένη δ' ὁσίης ἐπέβη πολυπότνια Δηώ.

[2] Porphyr. *de Abst.* II. 4 and I. 31.

[3] Maeterlinck, *Le Temple enseveli*, p. 188.

Demosthenes taunts Aeschines, because he cries aloud 'Bad have I fled, better have I found'; so Theseus[1], the bluff warrior, hates Hippolytos, not only, or perhaps not chiefly, because he believes him to be a sinner, but because he is an Orphic, righteous overmuch. All his rage of flesh and blood breaks out against the prig and the ascetic.

> 'Now is thy day! Now vaunt thee; thou so pure,
> No flesh of life may pass thy lips! Now lure
> Fools after thee; call Orpheus King and Lord,
> Make ecstasies and wonders! Thumb thine hoard
> Of ancient scrolls and ghostly mysteries.
> Now thou art caught and known. Shun men like these,
> I charge ye all! With solemn words they chase
> Their prey, and in their hearts plot foul disgrace.'

Happily there were in Athens also those who did not hate but simply laughed, laughed aloud genially and healthily at the outward absurdities of the thing, at all the mummery and hocus-pocus to which the lower sort of Orphic gave such solemn intent. Among these genial scoffers was Aristophanes.

There is no more kindly and delightful piece of fooling than the scene in the *Clouds*[2] in which he deliberately and in detail parodies the Orphic mysteries. The tension of Orphism is great; it is, like all mysticisms, a state of mind intrinsically and necessarily transient, and we can well imagine that, in his lighter moods, the most pious of Orphics might have been glad to join the general fun. In any case it helps us to realize vividly both the *mise-en-scène* of the mysteries themselves and the attitude of the popular mind towards them. Exactly what particular rite is selected for parody we do not know; probably some lesser mystery of purification, for there is no allusion to the supreme sacramental feast of bull's flesh nor to the idea that the neophyte is made one with the god.

The old unhappy father Strepsiades comes to the 'Thinking Shop' of Sokrates that he may learn to evade his creditors by dexterity of speech and new-fangled sophistries in general. A disciple opens the door with reluctance and warns Strepsiades that he cannot reveal these 'mysteries' to the chance comer. Strepsiades enters and sees a number of other disciples lost in

[1] Eur. *Hipp.* 952.

[2] Ar. *Nub.* 223 ff. That this scene is in intent a parody of Orphic ceremonial was first observed by Dr Dieterich, *Rh. Mus.* 1893, p. 275.

the contemplation of earth and heaven. He calls for Sokrates and is answered by a voice up in the air.

'*Sok.* Why dost thou call me, Creature of a Day?
Str. First tell me please, what are you doing up there?
Sok. I walk in air and contemplate the Sun.'

Here is the first Orphic touch. Sokrates instead of climbing a mountain has taken an easier way: he is suspended in a basket, and, Orpheus-like, reveres the Sun. The mysteries are not Eleusinian, not of the underworld. The comedian might and did dare to bring the Mystics of Kore and Iacchos in Hades on the stage, but a direct parody of the *actual* ceremony of initiation at Eleusis would scarcely have been tolerated by orthodox Athens. The Eleusinian rites had become by that time a state religion, politically and socially sacred (*νόμιμα*). The Orphics were Dissenters, and a parody of Orphic mysteries was an appeal at once to popular prejudice and popular humour. Sokrates explains that he is sitting aloft to avoid the intermixture of earthly elements in his contemplation; again we have a skit on the Orphic doctrine of the double nature of man, earthly and heavenly, and the need for purification from earthly Titanic admixture.

After some preliminary nonsense Strepsiades tells his need, and Sokrates descends and asks:

'Now, would you fain
Know clearly of divine affairs, their nature
When rightly apprehended?
Str. Yes, if I may.
Sok. And would you share the converse of the Clouds,
The spiritual beings we worship?
Str. Why, yes, rather.
Sok. Then take your seat upon this sacred—campstool.
Str. All right, I'm here.
Sok. And now, take you this wreath.
Str. A wreath—what for? Oh mercy, Sokrates,
Don't sacrifice me, I'm not Athamas!
Sok. No, no. I'm only doing just the things
We do at initiations.'

Strepsiades is of the old order; he knows nothing of these new 'spiritual beings' worshipped by Orphics and sophists. Something religious and uncomfortable is going to be done to him, and his thoughts instinctively revert to the old order. A wreath suggests a sacrificial victim, and the typical victim is Athamas (p. 61). Sokrates at once corrects him, and puts the audience on the right scent. It is not a common old-world sacrifice; it is an 'initiation' into a new-fangled rite, in which it would appear the mystic was crowned, probably by way of consecration to the gods. Strepsiades is not clear about the use of such things:

> '*Str.* Well, what good
> Shall I get out of it?
> *Sok.* Why, just this, you'll be
> A floury knave, uttering fine flowers of speech.
> Now just keep still.
> *Str.* By Jove, be sure you do it,
> Come flour me well, I'll be a flowery knave[1].'

If any doubt were possible as to the nature of the ceremonies parodied, the words translated 'flour' (*τρίμμα, παιπάλη*) to preserve the pun, settle the matter. The word *τρίμμα* means something rubbed, pounded, *κρόταλος* the noise made in rubbing and pounding; it might be rendered 'rattle.' *παιπάλη* is the fine flour or powder resulting from the process. Strepsiades is to become subtle in his arguments, a rattle in his speech. The words would have no sort of point but for the fact that Sokrates at the moment takes up two pieces of gypsum, pounds them together and bespatters Strepsiades till he is white all over like a Cretan mystic. The scholiast[2] is quite clear as to what was done on the stage. 'Sokrates while speaking rubs together two friable stones, and beating them against each other collects the splinters and pelts the old man with them, as they pelt the victims with grain.' He is quite right as to the thing done, quite wrong as to the ritual imitated. Strepsiades, as Sokrates said, is *not* being sacrificed; it is not the ritual of sacrifice that is mimicked, but of initiation.

The certainty that the scene is one of initiation, not sacrifice, is made more certain by the fact that Strepsiades is sitting all the while, not on an altar, but on a sort of truckle-bed or camp-stool (*σκίμπους*). We have no evidence of the use of a *σκίμπους* in mystic ritual, but it is clearly the comic equivalent of the seat or throne (*θρόνος*) used in Orphic rites. The candidate for initiation,

[1] Ar. *Nub.* 259,

> ΣΤ. *εἶτα δὴ τί κερδανῶ;*
> ΣΩ. *λέγειν γενήσει τρίμμα, κρόταλον, παιπάλη.*
> *ἀλλ' ἔχ' ἀτρεμί.*
> ΣΤ. *μὰ τὸν Δί' οὐ ψεύσει γέ με·*
> *καταπαττόμενος γὰρ παιπάλη γενήσομαι.*

[2] Schol. ad Ar. *Nub.* 260, *ταῦτα μὲν λέγων ὁ Σωκράτης λίθους περιτρίβων πωρίνους καὶ κρούων πρὸς ἀλλήλους συναγαγὼν τὰ ἀπὸ τούτων θραύσματα βάλλει τὸν πρεσβύτην αὐτοῖς καθάπερ τὰ ἱερεῖα ταῖς οὐλαῖς οἱ θύοντες.*

whether Eleusinian or Orphic, was always seated, and the ceremony was known as the 'seating' or enthronement. Dion Chrysostom[1] says those who perform initiation ceremonies are wont in the ceremony called 'the seating' to make the candidates sit down and to dance round them. It is to this ceremonial that Plato[2] alludes in the *Euthydemus*. 'You don't see, Kleinias, that the two strangers are doing what the officials in the rites of the Korybantes are wont to do, when they perform the ceremony of "seating" for the man who is about to be initiated.' Kleinias is undergoing instruction like the neophyte in the mysteries; he has to sit in silence while his instructors dance argumentatively round him, uttering what seem to him unmeaning words.

So far Strepsiades is a *mystic* in the first stage of initiation, i.e. he is being prepared and purified. All this ceremonial is preliminary to the next stage, that of full vision (ἐποπτεία). He is seated on the stool, he is covered with chalk, to one end only, and that is that he may behold clearly, may hold communion with, the heavenly gods. Sokrates, in regular ritual fashion, first proclaims the sacred silence, then makes preliminary prayer to the sophistic quasi-Orphic divinities of Atmosphere and Ether[3], and finally invokes the Holy Clouds in pseudo-solemn ritual fashion:

'*Sok.* Silence the aged man must keep, until our prayer be ended.
O Atmosphere unlimited, who keepst our earth suspended,
Bright Ether and ye Holy Clouds, who send the storm and thunder,
Arise, appear above his head, a Thinker waits in wonder.
Str. Wait, please, I must put on some things before the rain has drowned me,
I left at home my leather cap and macintosh, confound me.
Sok. Come, O come! Bring to this man full revelation.
Come, O come! Whether aloft ye hold your station
On Olympus' holy summits, smitten of storm and snow,
Or in the Father's gardens, Okeanos, down below,
Ye weave your sacred dance, or ye draw with your pitchers gold
Draughts from the fount of Nile, or if perchance ye hold
Maiotis mere in ward, or the steep Mimantian height,
Snow-capped, hearken, we pray, vouchsafe to accept our rite
And in our holy meed of sacrifice take delight.'

[1] Dio Chrysost. *Or.* XII. 387, εἰώθασιν ἐν τῷ καλουμένῳ θρονισμῷ καθίσαντες τοὺς μυουμένους οἱ τελοῦντες κύκλῳ περιχορεύειν.

[2] Plat. *Euthyd.* 277 D.

[3] Ether, air and whirlwind frequently appear in the Orphic fragments preserved to us, e.g. Damasc. *Quaest. de primis princ.* p. 147, καὶ γὰρ Ὀρφεύς·
ἔπειτα δ' ἔτευξε μέγας Χρόνος αἰθέρι δίῳ
ᾠεὸν ἀργύρεον,

The address is after the regular ritual pattern, which mentions, for safety's sake, any and every place where the divine beings are likely to wander. That such an invocation formed part of Orphic Dionysiac rites is not only a priori probable but certain from the Iacchos song in the *Frogs* (p. 540). In a word the 'full revelation,' the ἐποπτεία, of these and all mysteries, was only an intensification, a mysticizing, of the old Epiphany rites—the 'Appear, appear' of the Bacchants, the 'summoning' of the Bull-god by the women of Elis (p. 437). It was this Epiphany, outward and inward, that was the goal of all purification, of all consecration, not the enunciation or elucidation of arcane dogma, but the revelation, the fruition, of the god himself. To what extent these Epiphanies were actualized by pantomimic performances we do not know; that some form of mimetic representation was enacted seems probable from the scene that follows the Epiphany of the Clouds, when Strepsiades confused and amazed gropes in bewilderment, and bit by bit attains clear vision of the goddesses.

That the new divinities are *goddesses* is as near as Aristophanes dare go to a skit on Eleusinian rites; that they are goddesses of the powers of the air, not dread underworld divinities, saves him from all scandal as regards his Established Church. He guards himself still further by making his Clouds, in one of their lovely little songs, chant the piety of Athens, home of the mysteries.

The Clouds themselves were as safe as they were poetical. Even the Orphics did not actually *worship* clouds; but their theogony, their cosmogony, is, as will later (Chap. XII.) be seen, full of vague nature-impersonations, of air and ether and Erebos and Chaos, and the whirlpool of things unborn. No happier incarnation of all this, this and the vague confused cosmical philosophy it embodied, than the shifting wonder of mists and clouds.

The scene, though it goes on far too long, must have been exquisitely comic. With no stage directions probably half the trivial and absurd details have been lost, but we can imagine that the whole hocus-pocus of an Orphic mystery was carefully

and in the fragment of a hymn to the Sun preserved by Macrobius, *Sat.* I. 23. 22, Solem esse omnia et Orpheus testatur his versibus:

κέκλυθι τηλεπόρου δίνης ἑλικαυγέα κύκλον
οὐρανίαις στροφάλιγξι περίδρομον αἰὲν ἑλίσσων
ἀγλαὲ Ζεῦ Διόνυσε, πάτερ πόντου, πάτερ αἴης,
Ἥλιε παγγενέτωρ παναίολε χρυσεοφεγγές,

words which might have been sung by Sokrates in his basket.

mimicked. We can even imagine that Sokrates was dressed up as an initiating Silen, such a one as is depicted in the relief in fig. 147.

We can also imagine that in Athens it was hard to be an Orphic, a dissenter, a prig, a man overmuch concerned about his own soul. We have seen how against such eccentrics the advocate Demosthenes could appeal to the prejudices of a jury. We know that to Theophrastos[1] it was the characteristic of a 'superstitious man' that he went every month to the priest of the Orphic mysteries to participate in these rites, and we gather dimly that he did not always find sympathy at home; his wife was sometimes 'too busy' to go with him, and he had to take the nurse and children.

Plutarch[2], sympathetic as he is to some aspects of Orphism, yet, in his protest against superstition, says, 'these are the sort of things that make men atheists, the incantations, wavings and enchantments and magic, runnings round and tabourings, *unclean purifications*, filthy cleansings, barbarous and outrageous penances in sanctuaries, and bemirings.' And again[3], when he is describing the hapless plight of the man who thinks that affliction comes to him as a punishment for sin, 'It is useless to speak to him, to try and help him. He sits girt about with foul rags, and many a time he strips himself and rolls about naked in the mud; he accuses himself of sins of omission and commission, he has eaten something or drunk something or walked in some road the divinity forbade him.' This morbid habit of self-examination is a thoroughly Orphic trait. Pythagoras[4] advised his disciples to repeat these lines to themselves when they went home at night:

> 'What have I done amiss? what of right accomplished?
> What that I ought to have done have I omitted to do?'

'When he is at his best,' Plutarch goes on, 'and has only a slight attack of superstition on him he will sit at home, becensed and

[1] Theoph. *Char.* XXVIII.

[2] Plut. *de Superstit.* XII. *τῆς δεισιδαιμονίας ἔργα καὶ πάθη καταγέλαστα καὶ ῥήματα καὶ κινήματα καὶ γοητεῖαι καὶ μαγεῖαι καὶ περιδρομαὶ καὶ τυμπανισμοὶ καὶ ἀκάθαρτοι μὲν καθαρμοί, ῥυπαραὶ δὲ ἁγνεῖαι, βάρβαροι δὲ καὶ παράνομοι πρὸς ἱεροῖς κολασμοὶ καὶ προπηλακισμοί.*

[3] Plut. *de Superstit.* VII.

[4] Diog. Laert. *Vit. Pyth.* XIX.

bespattered, with a parcel of old women round him, hanging all sorts of odds and ends on him as though, as Bion says, he were a peg.' Such rites as those described by Plutarch were not late decadent inventions, though we hear of them mainly from late authors; they were primitive savageries revived with new spiritual meaning by the Orphics. Herakleitos[1] refers to them: 'polluted they are purified with blood, as though if a man stepped into mud he should be purified by mud.'

This is the shady side of Orphism, the way it had of attaching to itself ancient, obscure and even degraded rites, the more obscure the easier to mysticize. It was this shady side that Plato hated, against which he protested. In the *Republic*[2] he says 'seers and mendicant quacks besiege rich men's doors, exhibiting books by Musaeus and Orpheus......and in accordance with these they perform sacrifices, inducing not only individual persons but whole cities to believe that you can obtain freedom and purification from sins, while you are still alive, by sacrifices and performances that might please a child, and that there are things they call "rites," which will release us from suffering after we are dead, and that if we do not perform them, then there are fearful things in store for us.' The Orphics, alas, fell before the temptation, always assailing the theologist, to enforce his moral and religious precepts by the terrors of another world; there can be little doubt that the lower class of Orphic priest in some fashion sold indulgences. The fearful things with which the uninitiated were threatened, will be discussed when we come to the question of Orphic eschatology.

The Liknophoria.

The tearing of the bull is, however mysticized, a savage orgy; the purification by mud and clay can never have been pleasing. It is a relief to turn to another Orphic ceremonial of more genial content—the Liknophoria, the carrying of the *liknon*.

In discussing the worship of Dionysos Liknites at Delphi, a worship attended, it will be remembered, by a secret sacrifice per-

[1] Herakleit. frg. 130, Bywater, *καθαίρονται δὲ αἵματι μιαινόμενοι ὥσπερ ἂν εἴ τις ἐς πηλὸν ἐμβὰς πηλῷ ἀπονίζοιτο.*
[2] Plato, *Rep.* 364 B.

formed by priests who bore the specially Orphic name of Hosioi, Holy Ones, we have seen the *liknon* in use as a cradle for the infant god (p. 401). It will further be noted that Dionysos Liknites is, like the infant Ploutos in the cornucopia, only an anthropomorphic presentation of the new-born fruits of the earth, of the fruits whether of spring or autumn; he is a male form of Kore the earth-daughter. The ceremony of 'waking' him was primarily but a mimetic summons to the earth to bring forth her fruits in due season.

On the relief in fig. 146 in the Glyptothek at Munich[1] we see a shovel-shaped *liknon*, of a shape that might well serve

FIG. 146.

for a cradle; but it contains not a child, only grapes and leaves, and the phallic symbol of animal life. The relief, of Hellenistic date, represents a peasant going to market; he carries fruits and some animal slung on a stick over his shoulder, and he drives in front of him a cow with her calf tied on to her. He is

[1] Munich Glyptothek, No. 601. Schreiber, *Hell. Reliefbilder*, Taf. 80 A.

passing a sanctuary of Dionysos; a wine cup and torches and a thyrsos are seen to the left. Up above is a second little shrine with a Herm, whether of Hermes or Dionysos it is impossible to say. High in the middle of the main building is an elaborate erection, on the top of which is set up the sacred *liknon*.

We are at once reminded of a fragment of Sophocles[1]:

> 'Go on your road,
> All ye the folk of handicraft who pray
> To Ergane, your bright-eyed child of Zeus,
> With service of your posted winnow-corbs.'

The passage is of interest because it shows that the *liknon*, the harvest basket, though undoubtedly used in the cult of Dionysos, was nowise confined to him. Athene Ergane, goddess at first no doubt of 'works' in the Hesiodic sense, of tilth[2] rather than of

Fig. 147.

weaving and handicraft, was, as has been previously shown (p. 300), only another Kore, the local Earth-daughter of Athens. To her rather than to the work-fellow of Hephaistos, the *liknon* full of

[1] Soph. frg. 724, στατοῖς
λίκνοισι προστρέπεσθε.

[2] I have already discussed the *liknon* in connection with the fragment of Sophocles in the *Classical Review*, vol. VIII. p. 270. In the Thorwaldsen collection at Copenhagen there is a relief closely analogous to that in fig. 146. A *liknon* is erected on a column: above it appears a large goat's head, see Schreiber, *Reliefbilder*, Taf. CXI. 1.

fruits was a fit offering, and in solemn consecration it was set up, erected (στατόν), as on the relief. The word '*erected*' is used no doubt to mark the contrast with other ceremonies of the *carrying* of the *liknon* (Liknophoria).

This setting up of the *liknon* was too open and public a matter to be a mystery. It was a mere offering of first-fruits whether to Athene or Kore or Liknites. But in the service of Liknites there was an element of mystery, the birth of the divine child, and it is largely in connection with the cult of Dionysos that the *liknon* takes on mystic developments. It is an excellent instance of determined Orphic mysticizing.

In the relief[1] reproduced in fig. 147 we have what is manifestly a Dionysiac mystery. The neophyte is in the act of being veiled; he may not look at the *liknon*, with its fruit and sacred symbol, which will presently be placed upon his head. A satyr holds it in readiness, and behind the neophyte is a Maenad with her cymbal.

The veiling of the head marks the mysterious character of the ceremony. We see it again in the delicate piece of stucco-work from

FIG. 148.

the Farnesina palace reproduced in fig. 148, and now in the Museo

[1] Baumeister, *Denkmäler*, p. 449, fig. 496. Campana, *op. plast.* 45. An almost identical relief on a 'Campana' terracotta is in the Kestner Museum at Hanover.

delle Therme at Rome[1]. The scene is clearly one of initiation; the thyrsos carried by the boy with head closely veiled marks it as a mystery of Dionysos. A priest is unveiling an object on what seems to be an altar. Unfortunately the stucco is much damaged and what the object is cannot be certainly made out; it looks like a *liknon* in shape[2]. In any case the ceremony of veiling at a Dionysiac mystery is clear. Behind the officiating priestess is a cista, containing no doubt the further *sacra* of the rite. The scene takes place in a sanctuary, indicated by a column and a sacred tree.

The custom of veiling survives for us in the ritual veil of the bride and the widow, but we have almost emptied it of its solemn ancient content. The bride veils herself, it is usually supposed, out of modesty. It is therefore with some surprise we learn that in the primitive church bridegroom as well as bride was veiled. This custom, according to the Abbé Duchesne[3], obtained till quite recently in France and still obtains in the Armenian Church. At the actual moment of the ceremony, apparently as an integral part of it, the priest spreads over bride and groom together a long red veil, the *flammeum* of the Romans. In the Coptic ritual the veil is white, but is spread alike over man and woman.

The real symbolism of the veil, which indicates neither modesty nor chastity, comes out when we examine classical usage. The question was raised long ago by Plutarch[4] 'Why do men veil their heads when they worship the gods and uncover them when they wish to do honour to men?' Plutarch is better at asking questions than at answering them, but, among the various odd solutions he propounds, he gives one suggestive clue, viz. that the custom was analogous to those of the Pythagoreans. Pythagorean, as we have seen, spells Orphic revival of primitive usage.

The real reason of the custom comes out in the ceremonial known as the Sacred Spring (ver sacrum), which Festus[5] describes as follows: 'The Sacred Spring was a rite of dedication among the Italians. Under the pressure of extreme disasters

[1] Helbig, *Museo delle Therme*, no. 1122. Fig. 148 is drawn from a photograph.

[2] Since the above was written and the drawing in fig. 148 made, I have examined the original, and find that the obscure object *is a liknon*; the main outline and even the handle can be clearly made out.

[3] Duchesne, *Origines du culte chrétien*, p. 416.

[4] Plut. *Q. R.* x.

[5] Festus, p. 379.

they used to make a vow that they would sacrifice all animal things born to them in the spring next ensuing. But as it seemed to them a barbarous thing to slay innocent boys and girls, when they came to adult years they *veiled them* and drove them out beyond the boundaries of their state.' Whether the horrid practice of the 'Sacred Spring' is real or imaginary, does not for our purpose greatly matter. One thing is clear: the practice of veiling symbolized, was the equivalent of, *dedication*. The bride and bridegroom alike are veiled because they are dedicated in the mystery of marriage, consecrated, made over to the powers of life. The penitent is veiled because he dedicates himself as atonement for sin; the widow is made over to the powers of death, primarily no doubt as a substitute for her sacrifice, her 'devotio' of herself to the ghost of her dead husband. Alcestis[1] when she returns to the upper air is veiled and silent, and must so remain for the space of three days; she is consecrate to Hades:

> 'Thou mayst not hear sound of her spoken words
> Till she be disenhallowed from the gods
> Of the nether earth and see the third day's light.'

The old meaning of *devotion* to the gods survives now-a-days only in the beautiful ceremonial of the Roman Church, known in popular parlance as 'taking the veil,' and even here its dread significance has been softened down by the symbolism of a mystic marriage; the 'devotio' for life is blended with the 'devotio' for death[2].

In fig. 146 the *liknon* has been set up (στατόν), on high, in open evidence; it contains simply an offering of first-fruits with the added symbol of the phallos; it is sacred, but nowise mysterious. It forms in this particular monument a part of the worship of Dionysos, but it might belong, as already noted, equally well to any and every god or goddess of harvest to whom first-fruits were due. In figs. 147 and 148 the *liknon* has become part of a mystery cult; it is about to be put on the head of the worshipper: he is veiled and may not look upon it. What are the elements of mystery and how were they imported?

[1] Eur. *Alc.* 1144. The ritual word ἀφαγνίσηται, disenhallowed, marks the primitive meaning, getting rid of the pollution of the dead; it is a form of ἀποτροπή.

[2] For the whole subject see 'Le voile d'oblation,' S. Reinach, Acad. des Inscriptions, *C.R.* 1897, p. 644.

In discussing the religion of Dionysos it has been seen that, at Delphi, he was worshipped as Liknites. Hesychius[1] thus explains the title: 'Liknites, a name of Dionysos, from the cradle in which they put children to sleep.' The *liknon*, the shovel-shaped basket used for the carrying of fruits, served in primitive days another purpose, that of cradle for a child.

On the vase-painting[2] in fig. 149, from a red-figured cylix in the Museo Gregoriano of the Vatican, we see the wicker-work *liknon* in

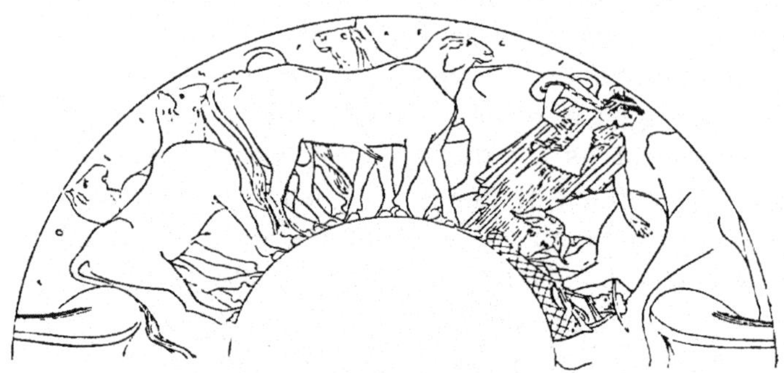

Fig. 149.

use as a cradle. The baby Hermes, wearing his broad petasos, sits up in his *liknon* looking at the oxen he has just stolen. One of them turns round surprised at the strange little object he sees, and gently snuffs the cradle. Maia, the mother of Hermes, comes up in consternation and holds out a protesting hand. It is the scene described in the Homeric hymn[3], though, as usual, the vase-painter is independent in matters of detail:

> 'Straightway did goodly Hermes back to his cradle hie,
> And round his shoulders pulled the clothes, as when a babe doth lie
> All snug and warm in swaddling bands. And—for he loved it well—
> Tight in his left hand held he his lyre of tortoise-shell.'

The Thyiades, as has been noted (p. 401), awakened the child Liknites. Of the actual ceremony of 'awakening' ancient art has left us no record; but on a sarcophagus in the Fitzwilliam Museum[4] at Cambridge (fig. 150) we have a scene depicted that

[1] Hesych. s.v. [2] Baumeister, *Denkmäler*, vol. I. p. 680, fig. 741.
[3] *Hom. Hymn. Merc.* 150.
[4] *Cat.* 31. Pashley, *Travels in Crete*, 1837, vol. I. p. 37. A very similar representation of Liknites carried by two Satyrs occurs on a sarcophagus in the Naples Museum. Dr Hans Graeven kindly pointed out to me a majolica plate in the Kestner Museum at Hanover on which oddly enough exactly the same scene occurs. Clearly it is a copy from an ancient sarcophagus. The only addition is that the group stands against the background of a mediaeval landscape.

looks like a reminiscence of some such ceremonial. On the front face of the sarcophagus is represented the triumphant procession of Bacchos; at one of the ends is the scene of the carrying of the infant god. The two men, one bearded, the other youthful, grasp the *liknon* by its convenient handles, and emerge hurriedly from behind a curtain slung between two trees. The curtain and the flaming torches point to a mystery scene enacted by night.

FIG. 150.

Nothing certain is known of the details of the ceremony, but it may be conjectured that at a given signal the birth of the sacred child was announced, and the attendants issued from behind a screen of some kind, bearing the child in a *liknon*.

The vase-painting in fig. 151 from a hydria in the Museum at Constantinople[1] offers a close analogy to Liknites, the child in the cradle, and throws instant light on his primitive significance. The vase is of somewhat late style, about the turn of the 5th and 4th centuries B.C., the drawing only indifferent, but the subject-matter all important. The scene is at Eleusis. Of that we are sure, because Triptolemos is present with his winged car and the corn-ears he is about to carry through the world. The side figures in the top row of vases of this class are always subordinate, usually difficult of interpretation. The figure in the left-hand corner is Aphrodite, by this time tediously omnipresent. The group to

[1] S. Reinach, *Revue Arch.* 1900, vol. XXXVI. p. 87. The vase has been more fully interpreted by Dr Svoronos, *Journal d'Archéologie et Numismatique*, 1901, p. 387.

the right cannot certainly be named, but the seated woman is known to be a priestess from the great temple-key she holds over her right shoulder. On the lower row the interpretation of the central group is certain. Ge rises from the ground, watched by

FIG. 151.

two goddesses; one to the right bears a gold lance; she is obviously Athene. The group to the left, of two women, one holding a torch, represents Kore and Demeter.

The scene represented is clearly the birth of a divine child at Eleusis. The birth of such a child[1] was, as will later be seen (p. 551), proclaimed by the hierophant at some moment during the celebration of the Mysteries: 'Brimo has borne a child Brimos,' but such a mystery would scarcely be represented openly on a vase-painting. A simpler name lies to hand. *The child rises out of a cornucopia, symbol of fertility.* He *is* the fruits of the earth. He is solemnly presented to Athene because Eleusis gave to Athens her corn and her mysteries. Art could speak no plainer. On vases representing Eleusinian scenes, e.g. the sending forth of Triptolemos, Plouton, who is none other than Ploutos, Wealth, is represented as an aged man, white-haired, carrying a cornucopia full of fruits[2]; but here we have the young Ploutos, the babe who *is* wealth itself. In like fashion the *liknon* is either

[1] The birth of Brimos is discussed later (p. 548).
[2] B. M. *Cat.* E 183. *Myth. and Mon. Ancient Athens*, p. liii, fig. 9.

a basket for fruits or a cradle for a child. It is all the same beautiful symbolism that refuses coldly to discriminate between the human and the natural, that sees in marriage the plough, in man the sower, in earth the mother, and in the fruits of the earth the new-born child.

When we realize that the *liknon* is, as it were, a cornucopia that for human fruit becomes a cradle, we naturally expect that, in its mystical sense, it will be a symbol of new birth, that Liknites will be connected with a doctrine of *palingenesia*, a sort of spiritual resurrection. The Orphics had their doctrine of *palingenesia*, but the symbolism of the *liknon* was to them mainly of purification, to which they added that of rebirth. The history of how this came to be is a curious and instructive chapter in the development of primitive mysticism.

The *locus classicus* on the *liknon* is the commentary of Servius on Virgil's[1] words in the first *Georgic*, where among the stock implements of Demeter he notes the *mystica vannus Iacchi*. So confused and confusing is the commentary that it has gone far to make the *liknon* or *vannus* mysterious.

Virgil first enumerates all the heavy agricultural implements: the ploughshare's heavy strength, the slow rolling waggons, the irksome weight of the mattock, and next he notes

'Slight wares entwined of wicker work that Celeus made for man,
Frames of arbutus wood compact, Iacchus' mystic fan.'

If we were left with Virgil only we should conclude that the fan *was a fan*, i.e. a thing with which to cause wind, to *ventilate*[2], and, as it was an instrument of Demeter, we should further

[1] Virg. *Georg.* I. 165,
Virgea praeterea Celei vilisque supellex,
Arbuteae crates, et mystica vannus Iacchi.
Serv. ad loc. Id est cribrum areale. *Mystica* autem *Iacchi* ideo ait quod Liberi Patris sacra ad purgationem animae pertinebant: et sic homines ejus Mysteriis purgabantur, sicut vannis frumenta purgantur. Hinc est quod dicitur Osiridis membra a Typhone dilaniata Isis cribro superposuisse: nam idem est Liber Pater in cujus Mysteriis *vannus* est: quia ut diximus animas purgat. Unde et Liber ab eo quod liberet dictus, quem Orpheus a gigantibus dicit esse discerptum. Nonnulli Liberum Patrem apud Graecos Λικνίτην dici adferunt; *vannus* autem apud eos λίκνον nuncupatur; ubi deinde positus esse dicitur postquam est utero matris editus. Alii mysticam sic accipiunt ut vannum vas vimineum latum dicant, in quod ipsi propter capacitatem congerere rustici primitias frugum soleant et Libero et Liberae sacrum facere. Inde *mystica*.

[2] Mr Andrew Lang (*Custom and Myth*, p. 36) conjectures that the 'use of the *mystica vannus Iacchi* was a mode of raising a sacred wind analogous to that employed by whirlers of the tundun or bull-roarer'; but with his accustomed frankness Mr Lang owns that like Servius he is 'only guessing.'

suppose that this fan was used for *ventilating*, for winnowing her corn. We should still be left with two unanswered questions: (1) 'why was a winnowing fan, a thing in constant use in every-day life, "mystic"?' and (2) 'how had the winnowing fan of the corn-goddess become the characteristic implement of the wine-god?' These two difficulties presented themselves to the mind of Servius, and he attempts to answer them after his kind. He does not fairly face the problem, but he tells us everything he can remember that anybody has said about or around the matter. His confused statement is so instructive it must be quoted in full:

'The mystic fan of Iacchus, that is the sieve (*cribrum*) of the threshing-floor. He calls it the mystic fan of Iacchus, because the rites of Father Liber had reference to the purification of the soul, and men were purified through his mysteries as grain is purified by fans. It is because of this that Isis is said to have placed the limbs of Osiris, when they had been torn to pieces by Typhon, on a sieve, for Father Liber is the same person, he in whose mysteries the fan plays a part, because as we said he purifies souls. Whence also he is called Liber, because he *liberates*, and it is he who, Orpheus said, was torn asunder by the Giants. Some add that Father Liber was called by the Greeks *Liknites*. Moreover the fan is called by them *liknon*, in which he is said to have been placed directly after he was born from his mother's womb. Others explain its being called "mystic" by saying that the fan is a large wicker vessel in which peasants, because it is of large size, are wont to heap their first-fruits and consecrate it to Liber and Libera. Hence it is called "mystic".'

If by 'mystic' is meant hopelessly and utterly unintelligible, the fan of Iacchos certainly justifies its name. Servius leaves us with a 'vannus' that is at once a sieve, a winnowing fan and a fruit basket, with mysterious contents that are at once a purified soul, an infant and a dismembered Dionysos, leaves us also with no clue to any possible common factor that might explain all three uses and their symbolism.

To solve the problems presented by Servius it is necessary briefly to examine the evidence of classical authors as to the process of winnowing and the shape of winnowing fans[1]. So far

[1] For the full discussion of this subject I may refer to papers, 'Mystica Vannus Iacchi,' I published in the *Journal of Hellenic Studies*, 1903, p. 292, 1904, p. 241, and *B.S.A.* x. 1903 and 1904, p. 144.

we have assumed that a winnowing fan is a basket, but when we turn to Homer we are confronted by an obvious difficulty.

It happens by an odd chance that we know something of the shape of the instrument for winnowing used in Homeric days. It was a thing so shaped that by a casual observer it could be mistaken for an oar. Teiresias[1] in Hades foretells to Odysseus what shall befall him after the slaying of the suitors: he is to go his way carrying with him a shapen oar, until he comes to a land where men have no knowledge of sea-things, and a sign shall be given to him where he is to abide. Teiresias thus instructs him:

> 'This token manifest I give, another wayfarer
> Shall meet thee and shall say, on thy stout shoulder thou dost bear
> A winnowing fan, that day in earth plant thou thy shapen oar
> And to Poseidon sacrifice a bull, a ram, a boar.'

The word used is not *liknon*; it is ἀθηρηλοιγός, chaff-destroyer, but none the less it is clear that the ancient instrument of winnowing was, roughly speaking, shaped like an oar[2]; confusion between the two was possible. Such an instrument might well be called a fan, and of some such shape must have been the primitive winnower. It is obviously quite a different thing from the *liknon* of the reliefs, the fruit basket. A thing shaped like an oar would not be easily carried on the head, nor would it suggest itself as a convenient cradle for a baby.

The way in which this primitive winnowing fan was used is clear from another Homeric passage[3]. In the fray of battle the Achaeans are white with falling dust, just as

> 'When in the holy threshing floors away the wind doth bear
> The chaff, when men are winnowing. She of the golden hair
> Demeter with the rushing winds the husk from out the grain
> Divideth, and the chaff-heaps whiten and grow amain.'

[1] Hom. *Od.* XI. 127,

> ὁππότε κεν δή τοι ξυμβλήμενος ἄλλος ὁδίτης
> φήῃ ἀθηρηλοιγὸν ἔχειν ἀνὰ φαιδίμῳ ὤμῳ
> καὶ τότε δὴ γαίῃ πήξας εὐῆρες ἐρετμὸν κτλ.

In the *Odysseus Acanthoplex* of Sophocles the winnowing fan was called by another of these descriptive epithets. Eustathius has preserved the line

> ὤμοις ἀθηρόβρωτον ὄργανον φέρων.

That it was understood to be simply the πτύον is clear from Porphyry (*De antr. nymph.* 35)...ὡς πτύον ἡγεῖσθαι εἶναι τὴν κώπην. Eustathius (§ 1675) pertinently observes πλάτη γὰρ θαλασσία τὸ ἐρετμὸν καὶ πλάτη χερσαία τὸ πτύον.

[2] Odysseus is figured on gems with a broad-bladed oar, see Inghirami, *Galleria Omerica* III., Harrison, *Myths of the Odyssey*, pl. 30.

[3] Hom. *Il.* v. 499.

The wind is the natural winnower, but man can help the wind by exposing the mixed chaff and grain. This he throws up on the winnowing fan against the wind, the wind blows away the chaff and the heavier grain falls to the ground. The best instrument with which to do this is naturally an oar-like pole, broadened at the end to serve as a shovel. Such an instrument was the *πτύον* or winnowing fan:

> 'As when from a broad winnowing fan, in a great threshing floor,
> The pulse and black-skinned beans leap out the whistling wind before
> Sped by the winnower's swinging, so the bitter arrow flew
> From Menelaos glancing far nor pierced his corslet through[1].'

Here the joint work of the wind and the human winnower is clearly shown.

A basket of the shape of an old-fashioned coal-scuttle could be used to scoop up the grain and toss it against the wind. It would not be so convenient as the oar-shaped winnowing fan, because the labourer would have to stoop to shovel up the grain, but it would hold more grain and would serve the second purpose of an ordinary basket and of a child's cradle. Primitive man is not averse to these economies.

The *liknon* and the *vannus* alike begin as winnowing fans and end as baskets for corn or fruit. The *liknon* of the Hellenistic reliefs and the *vannus* of Virgil are made of wicker-work; the fan of Homer shaped like an oar was made of sterner stuff, probably of wood. This may be gathered from a pathetic fragment of the *Proteus* of Aeschylus[2] where some one tells of

> 'The piteous dove who feeding beats and breaks
> Her hapless breast amid the winnowing fans.'

The winnowing fan is essentially and necessarily an instrument of Demeter. This Virgil knew, though he knew also that it had passed into the service of Iacchos. Theocritus[3] at the end of his harvest Idyll prays

[1] Hom. *Il.* XIII. 588,

> *ὡς δ' ὅτ' ἀπὸ πλατέος πτυόφιν μεγάλην κατ' ἀλωὴν*
> *θρώσκωσιν κύαμοι μελανόχροες ἢ ἐρέβινθοι*
> *πνοιῇ ὑπὸ λιγυρῇ καὶ λικμητῆρος ἐρωῇ.*

[2] Aesch. frg. 194, ap. Athen IX. p. 394.

[3] Theocr. *Id.* VII. 155,

> *ἇς ἐπὶ σωρῷ*
> *αὖθις ἐγὼ πάξαιμι μέγα πτύον.*

Cf. *πήξας εὐῆρες ἐρετμόν* of the oar of Odysseus. The scholiast on Theocritus says

'O once again may it be mine to plant
The great fan on her corn-heap, while she stands
Smiling, with sheaves and poppies in her hands.'

The 'great fan' here, as the word *πάξαιμι* 'fix' or 'plant' shows, must have been the oar-shaped fan, not the basket. The basket, the light thing of osier carried on the head, is mainly characteristic of Dionysos. An epigram in the *Anthology*[1] enumerates the various instruments of the worship of Bacchos, the rhombos, the fawn-skin, the cymbals, the thyrsos, and

'The timbrel lightly carried with its deep and muttering sound,
The liknon often borne aloft on hair with fillet bound.'

We have then, it is clear, two implements in use in ancient days for winnowing; distinct in shape and made of different materials. The 'chaff-consumer' of Homer, called also a *ptuon*, made of wood and later of iron, is an oar-shaped implement with a long handle; the *liknon* proper, the *vannus* of Virgil, is a shovel-shaped basket made of wicker work. The only factor common to the two is that they are both winnowers. There the resemblance ends. The *ptuon* remained a simple agricultural tool, the *liknon*, the winnow-*corb*, became 'mystic' because of its function as a purifier and because of its second use as a cradle for the mystery-babe. In it was carried the phallos, the symbol of life; hence it was reverently veiled. The confusion between the two is entirely caused by our modern terminology, which uses the word 'fan' to translate both *λίκνον*, 'winnow-corb,' and *πτύον*, 'winnow-fork' or 'shovel.' The religion of Dionysos, and with it the Orphic mysteries, adopted the *liknon*, the winnow-corb, and left the *ptuon*, the winnow-shovel, to Demeter.

The diverse shapes of the *liknon* have been discussed at length because they are of vital importance for the understanding of Orphic mysteries and Orphic mysticism. The shift from winnowing fan to fruit basket marks the transition from agriculture to vine culture, from Demeter to Bacchos, and the connecting link is Bromios. The vine-growers have no use for the winnowing fork

ὅταν δὲ λικμῶνται καὶ σωρεύωσι τὸν πυρὸν κατὰ μέσον πηγνύουσι τὸ πτύον καὶ τὴν θρινάκην κατέθεντο. For the modern representative of the *θρῖναξ* still used in Crete I may refer to my article in the *Hellenic Journal*, 1903, p. 303, fig. 9.

[1] *Anthol. Palat.* VI. 165.

but they were once grain-growers, and they keep the *liknon*-basket in their worship.

Moreover, and this is the most curious and conclusive evidence, though they have turned their winnowing fans into fruit-baskets, they by an instructive and half unconscious confusion take over from the winnowing fan its proper symbolism and apply it to the fruit-basket.

The winnowing fan symbolized purification; as the husk is separated from the grain so is evil winnowed away from good; it mattered little whether the separation was effected by an actual fan (*πτύον*) or by a sieve (*κόσκινον*)[1]. Plato[2], whose mind was charged with Orphism, knew that all purification is *discernment*, separation, from the outward cleansing of the body to that innermost purification which is 'the purging away by refutation of all prejudice and vain conceit within the soul.' We have kept among our sacraments the outward washing with water, but we have lost the lovely and more intimate symbolism of the *liknon*. Yet we still remember that 'His fan is in his hand and he will throughly purge his floor.'

The symbolism of the basket of first-fruits was quite other; it was the sign of plenty, of new life, of the birth of fruits and children. But the Orphic cannot forget purification; his fusion of new and old is at the back of all his confused mysticism that baffled Servius. The fan he knows symbolizes purification, but the basket is the cradle of the new-born Liknites. He sees in a flash how he can connect the two. Was not the child torn asunder? is it not that divine dismembered life by which all men are purged and consecrated and born anew? It even seems to him full of a wondrous significance that this divine dismembered life should be carried on the head, the seat of the divine reason, and he invents a story of a nymph, with an old Satyr name, Hippa[3], who carried the *liknon* on her head and symbolized the soul. Charged with all this symbolism we cannot wonder that the *liknon* as fan for winnowing, as sieve for sifting, as basket for first-fruits,

[1] *πτύον* according to Vaniček is from the root *pu*, meaning to cleanse, which in its various modifications gives us *πῦρ πνέω*. *κόσκινον* like *κεσκίον* is a reduplicated form of *sak*, *ska*, *ski* to separate. The symbolism of the sieve will be discussed later. In meaning it is identical with *cribrum*; both are 'separators.'

[2] Plat. *Soph.* 226 E, *πᾶσα ἡ τοιαύτη διάκρισις...λέγεται παρὰ πάντων καθαρμός τις.*

[3] Procl. in Plat. *Tim.* II. 124 C, D, and III. 208 D. According to Proclus, p. 171 F, Orpheus wrote a discourse on Hippa.

as cradle for a child, was, as Harpocration[1] tells, 'serviceable for every rite of initiation, for every sacrifice.'

The rite in which the *liknon* was used, and that a rite of supreme importance for the understanding of Orphic mysteries, has been reserved to the end—the rite of marriage.

On the engraved gem[2] in fig. 152, signed by the artist Tryphon, the scene represented is the marriage, or possibly the initiation

FIG. 152.

and marriage ceremonies in one, of Eros and Psyche. The subject is of course mythological, but none the less is it a transcript of actual usage. Eros and Psyche, *both* closely veiled, are led by a sacred fillet in the hand of the Eros who bears the nuptial torch. Another Eros to the right unveils a seat or couch. Over the veiled heads of bride and groom a third Eros holds the *liknon* full of fruits.

That the *liknon* was carried at marriage ceremonies is known also from literary sources. Plutarch[3] says it was the custom at

[1] Harpocrat. s.v. *τὸ λίκνον πρὸς πᾶσαν τελετὴν καὶ θυσίαν ἐπιτήδειον.*

[2] Müller-Wieseler, II. 54. The gem was formerly in the Marlborough Coll. It is published in phototype and discussed by Dr Furtwängler, *Ancient Gems*, pl. LVII. ii. p. 339. It is now in the Boston Museum of Fine Arts. The antiquity of both the artist's signature and the gem itself is accepted by Prof. Furtwängler, but has been questioned by many competent archaeologists. As I have not seen the original I am unable to express any certain conviction. For a full account of the controversy see *Boston Museum Annual Report*, XXIV. 1900, p. 88.

[3] Plutarch or the author of the 'Proverbial sayings of Alexander' (*Prov. Alex.* XVI. 1255), *νόμος ἦν Ἀθήνησι ἐν τοῖς γάμοις ἀμφιθαλῆ παῖδα λίκνον βαστάζοντα ἄρτων πλέων εἶτα ἐπιλέγειν Ἔφυγον κακὸν εὗρον ἄμεινον.*

Athens at marriages that a boy whose parents were both alive should carry a *liknon* full of loaves and then pronounce the words 'Bad have I fled, better have I found.' The fact that the boy must have both parents alive, i.e. that he should be uncontaminated by any contact however remote with the unlucky spirits and influences of the dead, shows clearly that here again the carrying of the *liknon* was a fertility charm, a charm to induce the birth of children and all natural wealth and increase. In a marriage rite the symbolism of Liknites, of fruit and child, could not be forgotten. The scholiast to Kallimachos[1] says 'in old days they were wont to lull babies to sleep in *likna* as an omen for wealth and fruits,' and Servius says, as already noted (p. 527), it was the custom to do this the moment the child was born.

But the *liknon* in the marriage rite became not merely a fertility charm but the symbol of spiritual grace. This is clear from the words of Suidas[2]. The boy, he says, carried branches of acanthus and acorns as well as loaves. If Suidas is right, these ruder natural products were only present as being earlier first-fruits before man made loaves of corn, but Suidas says he carried them and pronounced the formulary *signifying as in a riddle* the change to what is better, for the wreath of oak and acanthus signified what was bad. It was this mysticizing of everyday things that irritated the plain man, that seemed to him at once foolish and pretentious; this it was that raised Demosthenes to his angry protest: 'You bid your mystics,' he says to Aeschines[3], 'when you have daubed them with mud and purified them with clay, say "Bad have I fled, better have I found," pluming yourself that no one has ever before uttered such words, you,' he goes on, 'who are kistophoros and liknophoros.' Had not every plain man pronounced the words at his marriage and meant by them—increase of income and family?

The 'mystic fan of Iacchos' was used in marriage rites. This

[1] Schol. ad Kall. *Hymn. ad Jov.* 48, ἐν γὰρ λείκνοις τὸ παλαιὸν κατεκοίμιζον τὰ βρέφη πλοῦτον καὶ καρποὺς οἰωνιζόμενοι· λίκνον οὖν τὸ κόσκινον ἢ τὸ κούνιον ἐν ᾧ τὰ παιδία τιθέασιν. For similar modern customs see Mannhardt, *Mythologische Forschungen*, 'Kind und Korn,' p. 366. It is very interesting to find that in the 'Modern Carnival in Thrace' observed by Mr Dawkins (see p. 439, n. 2) the old nurse Babo carries the child in a λίκνι.

[2] Suidas, s.v. ἔφυγον κακόν, εὗρον ἄμεινον, and Hesych. s.v.

[3] Dem. *de Cor.* § 313.

brings us face to face with the question—did Orphic mysteries include a mystic marriage[1]? The Orphics worshipped, as has been seen (p. 498), both Mother and Son; they mysticized the birth of the Son; did they look back before the birth and mysticize the marriage of the Mother? On *a priori* grounds we should expect they did. A religion based on the belief of possible union with the divine had everything to gain from the symbolism of marriage. Happily we are not left to *a priori* speculation; we have positive evidence that Dionysiac mysteries contained a sacred marriage and that Orphics mysticized it.

The Sacred Marriage.

By a most unhappy chance our main evidence as to the Sacred Marriage of the mysteries comes to us from the Christian Fathers; their prejudiced imaginations see in its beautiful symbolism only the record of unbridled license. We may and must discredit their unclean interpretations, but we have no ground for doubting the substantial accuracy of their statements as to ritual procedure. They were preaching to men who had been initiated in the very mysteries they describe, and any mis-statement as to ritual would have discredited their teaching.

Clement[2] in his 'Exhortation' wishes to prove the abominable wickedness of Zeus and says that he became the husband of his daughter in the form of a snake. He adds: 'The token of the Sabazian mysteries is *the snake through the bosom*, and this snake gliding through the bosom of the initiated is the proof of the license of Zeus.' Arnobius[3] too holds that the ceremony of the snake is but a witness against Zeus. He adds the important detail that the snake was of gold. It was let down into the bosom and taken away from below. The *gold* snake is in itself evidence of the simple symbolic innocence of the rite.

[1] Strictly speaking a *ἱερὰ σύμμιξις*. These rites are probably of earlier origin than the patriarchal institution of monogamy.

[2] Clem. Al. *Protr.* 16, *Σαβαζίων γοῦν μυστηρίων σύμβολον τοῖς μυουμένοις ὁ διὰ κόλπου θεός. δράκων δέ ἐστιν οὗτος διελκόμενος τοῦ κόλπου τῶν τελουμένων ἔλεγχος ἀκρατίας Διός.* The meaning of *διὰ κόλπου* and with it *ὑπὸ κόλπου* is sufficiently evident from this passage. Any possible doubt is removed by the use of *ὑπὸ κόλπου* in Lucian's *Alexander*, c. 39.

[3] Arnob. *c. gent.* v. c. 21, ipsa novissime sacra et ritus initiationis ipsius quibus Sebadiis nomen est, testimonio esse potuerunt veritati, in quibus aureus coluber in sinum dimittitur consecratis et eximitur rursus ab inferioribus partibus.

The snake ceremony of Sabazios is of course the relic of a very primitive faith, of the time when the snake was the god. We are reminded of the story told of Philip of Macedon (p. 397) and his fear that Olympias was the bride of a divine snake. As civilization advanced the sacred marriage would take a purely human form.

Clement[1] again gives invaluable evidence. Happily he has preserved for us the symbols or *tokens* of initiation into the mysteries of the Great Mother in her Asiatic form as Cybele. 'The symbols,' he says, in his gross and ignorant blasphemy, 'will abundantly excite your laughter, though on account of the exposure you will not be in laughing condition: I have eaten from the timbrel, I have drunk from the cymbal, I have carried the kernos, I have gone down into the bridal chamber.' The first three *tokens* are, as has been already shown (p. 155), practically identical with the *tokens* of Eleusis and relate to the solemn partaking of first-fruits: the last is a manifest avowal of a Sacred Marriage. The word *παστός*[2] here used means bridal chamber or bridal bed. It is roughly the equivalent of *θάλαμος*, and like it had a hieratic as well as a secular use. The houses of the gods are built after the pattern of the dwellings of men.

It is curious and interesting to find that a *παστάς*, a bridal chamber, existed in the sanctuary of the Great Mother at Phlya. The anonymous author of the *Philosophoumena*[3] or 'Refutation of all Heresies' tells us the Bacchic rites of Orpheus 'were established and given to men at Phlya in Attica before the establishment of the Eleusinian rite of initiation.' These rites were those of her called the Great One. At Phlya there was a bridal chamber (*παστάς*) and on the chamber were paintings, existing to the

[1] Clem. Al. *Protr.* II. 15, *τὰ σύμβολα τῆς μυήσεως ταύτης ..ἐκ τυμπάνου ἔφαγον, ἐκ κυμβάλου ἔπιον· ἐκερνοφόρησα· ὑπὸ τὸν παστὸν ὑπέδυν. ταῦτα οὐχ ὕβρις τὰ σύμβολα, οὐ χλεύη τὰ μυστήρια;*

[2] The uses of the word *παστάς* are discussed by Sir Richard Jebb in commenting on *v.* 1207 of the *Antigone* of Sophocles, App. p. 263, where the suggestion is made that the *παστάς* was some interior portion or arrangement in the *θάλαμος*.

[3] *Philosophoumena*, ed. Cruice, v. 3, *τετέλεσται δὲ ταῦτα (τὰ βακχικὰ τοῦ Ὀρφέως)... πρὸ τῆς...ἐν Ἐλευσῖνι τελετῆς, ἐν Φλιοῦντι τῆς Ἀττικῆς, πρὸ γὰρ τῶν Ἐλευσινίων μυστηρίων ἐστὶ [τὰ] ἐν τῇ Φλιοῦντι τῆς λεγομένης Μεγάλης ὄργια. ἔστι δὲ παστὰς ἐν αὐτῇ, ἐπὶ δὲ τῆς παστάδος ἐγγέγραπται μέχρι σήμερον ἡ πάντων τῶν εἰρημένων λόγων ἰδέα. πολλὰ μὲν οὖν ἐστὶ τὰ ἐπὶ τῆς παστάδος ἐκείνης ἐγγεγραμμένα· περὶ ὧν καὶ Πλούταρχος ποιεῖται λόγους ἐν ταῖς πρὸς Ἐμπεδοκλέα δέκα βίβλοις.* Whether the *παστάς* is here bridal chamber or bridal bed it is impossible to decide; it may have been a sort of decorative baldacchino. That *παστός* meant sometimes bed, not chamber, is clear I think from the title *παστοφόρος* applied to Aphrodite.

author's own time, representing the whole semblance of what has been described. On the subject of the many representations Plutarch wrote in his ten books against Empedokles. Unhappily the treatise by Plutarch is lost and the author of the *Philosophoumena* only describes one painting, which will be discussed later (Chap. XII.) in relation to the theogony of Orpheus. At present it is important to note the one fact that in a primitive home of Orphism there was a sacred bridal chamber. In such a chamber must have been enacted a mimetic marriage.

Nor was it only at Phlya that a marriage chamber existed and a marriage ceremonial was enacted. At Athens itself was such a chamber, and our evidence for its existence is no less an authority than Aristotle[1]. In his discussion of the official residences of the various archons he notes that in past days the King Archon used to live in a place called the Boukolion near to the Prytaneion, 'And the proof of this is that to this day the union and marriage of the wife of the King Archon with Dionysos takes place there.'

In a place called the 'cattle shed' the Queen Archon was married to Dionysos. The conjecture lies near to hand that in bygone days there was a marriage to a sacred bull. We are reminded that the worshipper of Sabazios was said to 'herd' the god (p. 419). Be that as it may, at the festival of the Anthesteria the Queen Archon was 'given in marriage' to Dionysos, and from the author of the Speech against Neaira[2] we learn how dread and sacred was the rite.

The mother of Neaira, a base-born alien, had on behalf of the city performed the 'unspeakable sacrifice'; she had seen what none but an Athenian woman might see; she had entered where none but the Queen Archon might enter; she had heard what none might hear; she had administered the oath to her celebrants, fourteen in number, one for each of the altars of Dionysos, administered it on the sacred baskets before they touched the holy things. The oath was written on a stone stele set up by the

[1] Arist. *De Rep. Ath.* III. 5 (p. 118), *ἔτι καὶ νῦν γὰρ τῆς τοῦ βασιλέως γυναικὸς ἡ σύμμειξις ἐνταῦθα γίγνεται τῷ Διονύσῳ καὶ ὁ γάμος.* Rutherford and Hude bracket *καὶ ὁ γάμος.* I see no reason for this. By Aristotle's time the old matriarchal *σύμμειξις* was regarded as a regular patriarchal *γάμος.* The double expression marks a transitional attitude of mind.

[2] [Demosthenes], *in Neaer.* § 73. The sources for the ceremony in the Boukolion are fully given by Dr Martin Nilsson, *Studia de Dionysiis Atticis*, p. 156.

altar in the ancient sanctuary of Dionysos in the marshes, opened but once in the year at the festival of the marriage. It was set there in secret because it was too holy to be read by the many; the letters were dim with age; so the orator called for the sacred herald and bade him read it that the court might hear how 'holy and pure and ancient were its prescriptions.'

The Oath of the Celebrants.

'I fast[1] and am clean and abstinent from all things that make unclean and from intercourse with man and I celebrate the Theoinia and the Iobaccheia to Dionysos in accordance with ancestral usage and at the appointed times.'

Unhappily though we have the oath of purity we know nothing definite of either the Theoinia or the Iobaccheia[2]. Only this much is certain, a sacred marriage was enacted by a woman high-born and blameless, and that marriage was a mystery.

At Athens Dionysos is bridegroom, not new-born child. This is one of the shifts from Son to Father that constantly occur in Greek mythology. The Christian Fathers see in it evidence of incest, but the horrid supposition is wholly gratuitous. It has been shown in detail (p. 260) that the Mother and the Maid are two persons but one god, are but the young and the old form of a divinity always waxing and waning. It is the same with the Father and the Son; he is one but he reflects two stages of the same human life. We are perplexed because both Father and Son in the religion of Dionysos take on many names: Sabazios, Dionysos, Bacchos, Iacchos, Zagreus. Each reflects some special function, but each is apt to be both Father and Son. The Romans in their dull way, with little power for intense personification, leave the simple truth more manifest. Libera the Mother has a Son Liber, a *child*, but even with them the inevitable confusion arises, the *child* Liber grows up and becomes 'Father Liber.'

[1] *ἁγιστεύω καὶ εἰμὶ καθαρὰ καὶ ἁγνὴ ἀπό τε τῶν ἄλλων τῶν οὐ καθαρευόντων, καὶ ἀπ' ἀνδρὸς συνουσίας.*

[2] The club rules of the Iobacchoi, noted p. 474, do not deal with the mysteries of the cult.

Another bridal chamber in the cult of Dionysos remains to be noted, and one of special significance. On his way from Sekyon to Phlius Pausanias[1] came to a grove called Pyraea. In it there was a sanctuary of Demeter the Protectress and of Kore. 'Here the men celebrate a festival by themselves, and they give up the place called the Bridal Chamber (Νυμφῶνα) to the women for their festival. Of the images of Dionysos and Demeter and Kore in the Bridal Chamber the faces only are visible.' Here, as manifestly at Athens, the marriage service of Dionysos was accomplished by women; the men leave them alone with their god. If any one, Pentheus-like, charges these holy women with license, this plain primitive prescription refutes his impiety.

From the evidence of Aristotle and Pausanias we may be sure that the marriage rites, so grossly libelled by Christian Fathers, were not the products of their own imaginations. Their wilful misunderstanding is an ugly chapter in the history of human passion and prejudice. Now and again, when they seek an illustration for their own mysteries, they confess that the pagan mysteries of marriage were believed by the celebrants to be spiritual. Epiphanios[2] says 'some prepare a bridal chamber and perform a mystic rite accompanied by certain words used to the initiated, and they allege that it is a spiritual marriage'; and Firmicus[3] by a happy chance records the social formularies. 'Not only words,' he says, 'but even nuptial rites occur in their sacred mysteries, and the proof of this is the greeting in which the mystae hail those just initiated by the name of "brides":

"A light upon the shining sea—
The Bridegroom and his Bride."'

A mimetic marriage was, it is clear, an element in the rites of Dionysos and an element mysticized by the Orphics. Equally clear is it that in the ceremony of waking Liknites and in the story of Zagreus we have as another element the birth of a child. At present we have no evidence of definite connection between

[1] P. II. 11. 3.

[2] Epiph. *L. I. T.* III. p. 255, and Iren. I. 18, p. 89, *οἱ μὲν νυμφῶνα κατασκευάζουσι καὶ μυσταγωγίαν ἐπιτελοῦσι μετ' ἐπιρρήσεών τινων τοῖς τελουμένοις καὶ πνευματικὸν γάμον φάσκουσιν εἶναι.*

[3] Firmicus Mat. *de Ev. Pr. Relig.* p. 38 c, neque verba solum sed etiam ritus nuptialis sacris mysticis intercurrisse indicio est solemnis gratulatio qua mystae recens initiatos sponsarum nomine consalutabant—*χαῖρε νύμφιε, χαῖρε νέον φῶς.*

the two. At Athens in the Boukolion we have a marriage rite but no birth rite, at Delphi in the waking of Liknites we have a birth but no marriage[1]. When the mysteries at Eleusis are examined we find, as will shortly be seen, that the two rites—the marriage and the birth—were in close and manifest connection.

ORPHIC ELEMENTS IN ELEUSINIAN RITUAL.

The question may fairly be asked—are we entitled to use evidence drawn from Eleusinian mysteries to elucidate Orphic ceremonial? or in other words have we any clear evidence that the worship of Dionysos in the form known as 'Orphic' came to Eleusis and modified the simple rites of the Mother and the Maid?

These simple rites have been already examined. It has been shown from the plain evidence of the Eleusinian 'tokens' that the rites of Eleusis were primarily rites of a harvest festival, that the ceremonies consisted of elaborate purification and fasting, followed by the removal of the taboo on first-fruits, and the consequent partaking of the sacred *kykeon* and the handling of certain sacred objects. I have advisedly devoted no separate chapter to the Eleusinian Mysteries because all in them that was not a primitive harvest festival, all or nearly all their spiritual significance, was due to elements borrowed from the cult of Dionysos. We have now obtained some notion, fairly clear if fragmentary, of the contents of Orphic and Dionysiac rites; we have examined the Omophagia of Crete, the Liknophoria of Delphi and the Sacred Marriage of Athens and Phlya, and we are able to begin the enquiry as to whether and how far these rites are part of the ritual of Eleusis.

Before attempting to answer this question it may be well to resume briefly the literary evidence for the affiliation of Dionysos to the Eleusinian goddesses. The actual fact of his presence at Eleusis must be established before we consider the extent and nature of his influence on Eleusinian rites.

[1] In the 'Modern Carnival in Thrace' (*J.H.S.* 1906, p. 192) the various elements of the cult of Dionysos, the child in the basket, the marriage, the death, the resurrection, are all still loosely united in a folk-drama; see commentary by Mr Dawkins.

a. Iacchos at Eleusis.

Dionysos at Eleusis is known by the title of Iacchos. The *locus classicus* for Iacchos of the mysteries is of course the chorus of the Mystae in the *Frogs* of Aristophanes[1]:

CHORUS (*unseen*).
Iacchus, O Iacchus!
Iacchus, O Iacchus!

XANTHIAS.
That's it, sir. These are the Initiated
Rejoicing somewhere here, just as he told us.
Why, it's the old Iacchus hymn that used
To warm the cockles of Diagoras!

DIONYSUS.
Yes, it must be. However, we'd best sit
Quite still and listen, till we're sure of it.

CHORUS.
Thou that dwellest in the shadow
Of great glory here beside us,
Spirit, Spirit, we have hied us
To thy dancing in the meadow!
Come, Iacchus; let thy brow
Toss its fruited myrtle bough;
We are thine, O happy dancer; O our comrade, come and guide us!
Let the mystic measure beat:
Come in riot fiery fleet;
Free and holy all before thee,
While the Charites adore thee,
And thy Mystae wait the music of thy feet!

XANTHIAS.
O Virgin of Demeter, highly blest,
What an entrancing smell of roasted pig!

DIONYSUS.
Hush! hold your tongue! Perhaps they'll give you some.

CHORUS.
Spirit, Spirit, lift the shaken
Splendour of thy tossing torches!
All the meadow flashes, scorches:
Up, Iacchus, and awaken!
Come, thou star that bringest light
To the darkness of our rite,
Till thine old men dance as young men, dance with every thought forsaken
Of the dulness and the fear
Left by many a circling year:
Let thy red light guide the dances
Where thy banded youth advances
To be joyous by the blossoms of the mere!

The lovely hymn to Iacchos, as choragos of the mystae of

[1] Ar. *Ran.* 324.

Demeter, is speedily followed by a second hymn[1] to the goddess herself—the Fruit-bearer:

> One hymn to the Maiden; now raise ye another
> To the Queen of the Fruits of the Earth.
> To Demeter the Corn-giver, Goddess and Mother,
> Make worship in musical mirth.

The blend of the smell of roast pork and the odour of mystic torches, of buffoonery, and ecstasy, is the perfect image of the fusion of old and new.

In the ritual hymn of Delphi, already noted (p. 416), Dionysos, who in the prooemium is addressed by his titles as god of a cereal drink, as Bromios and Braites, is when he leaves Parnassos and comes to Eleusis hailed by his new name Iacchos[2]:

> 'With thy wine cup waving high,
> With thy maddening revelry,
> To Eleusis' flowery vale
> Comest thou—Bacchos, Paean, hail!
> Thither thronging all the race
> Come, of Hellas, seeking grace
> Of thy nine-year revelation,
> And they called thee by thy name,
> Loved Iacchos, he who came
> To bring salvation,
> And disclose
> His sure haven from all mortal woes.'

Sophocles[3] in the *Antigone* invokes the god of many names for the cleansing of sin-stricken Thebes, but being an Athenian he remembers the god of the mysteries of Eleusis:

> 'Thou of the Many Names, delight and wonder
> Of the Theban bride, Child of the pealing thunder,
> Thou who dost rule over Italia's pride
> And at Eleusis in Deo's bosom wide
> Dwellest, Deo, she the mother of all,
> Bacchos, Bacchos, on thee we call.'

Bacchos at Thebes, but, when the poet remembers the noc-

[1] Ar. *Ran.* 382.

[2] The text as emended by Dr Weil runs as follows, see *Bull. de Corr. Hell.* xix.

> [Οἰνοθα]λὲς δὲ χειρὶ πάλ-
> λών δ[έπ]ας ἐνθέοις [σὺν οἴσ-]
> τροις ἔμολες μυχοὺς ['Ελε]υ-
> σῖνος ἀν[θεμοεί]δεις
> Εὐοἱ ὦ ἰὸ Βάκχ' ὦ ἰ[ὲ Παι]άν·
> [ἔθνος ἔνθ'] ἅπαν Ἑλλάδος
> γᾶς ἀ[μφ(ὶ) ἐ]ννναέταις [φίλιον] ἐπ[όπ]ταις
> ὀργίων ὀσ[ίων Ἴα]κ-
> χον [κλείει σ]ὲ βροτοῖς πόνων
> ὦξ[ας] δ' ὅρ]μον [ἄλυπον].

[3] Soph. *Ant.* 1115, τὸν ταμίαν Ἴακχον. The title ταμίας points, I think, to the rites dispensed, 'steward of the mysteries.'

turnal rites of the mysteries, the name Iacchos comes irresistibly back:

> 'Thou who dost lead the choir
> Of stars aflame with fire,
> Of nightly voices King,
> Of Zeus offspring,
> Appear, O Lord, with thine attendant maids
> The Thyiades,
> Who mad and dancing through the long night chant
> Their hymn to thee, Iacchos, Celebrant.'

For Iacchos at the Eleusinian mysteries we are not left to the evidence of poetry alone. Herodotus[1] tells how, when Attica was being laid waste by Xerxes, Dicaeus, an exile, happened to be with Demaratos, a Lacedaemonian, in the Thriasian plain. They saw a great cloud of dust coming from Eleusis, so great that it seemed to be caused by thirty thousand men. They were wondering at the cloud, and they suddenly heard a sound, and the sound seemed to Dicaeus to be 'the mystic Iacchos.' Demaratos did not know about the sacred rites at Eleusis, and he asked what it might be that they heard. Dicaeus, who took the sound to be of ill omen to the Persians, explained it as follows: 'The Athenians celebrate this festival every year to the Mother and the Maiden, and any Athenian or other Greek who wishes is initiated, and the sound that you hear is the cry "Iacchos," which they raise at this feast.'

The account is interesting because it shows that 'the Iacchos' was a ritual cry, one easily recognizable by an Athenian, just as now-a-days we should recognize Alleluia or Hosanna. That the mysteries at Eleusis were still in the main of local import is clear from the fact that a Spartan did not recognise the cry.

Iacchos gave his name to one of the days of the Eleusinian mysteries—the 20th of Boedromion (Sept., Oct.). On this day he was taken from his sanctuary in Athens, the Iaccheion, and escorted in solemn procession to Eleusis. Plutarch[2], in commenting on lucky and unlucky days, says he is aware that unlucky things sometimes happen on lucky days: for the Athenians had

[1] Herod. VIII. 65, *καί οἱ φαίνεσθαι τὴν φωνὴν εἶναι τὸν μυστικὸν ἴακχον...καὶ τὴν φωνὴν τῆς ἀκούεις ἐν ταύτῃ τῇ ὀρτῇ ἰακχάζουσι.*

[2] Plut. *Cam.* XIX. 15. The word used for the ceremony of escorting is variously *ἐξάγειν*, *προπέμπειν*, and once *ἐξελαύνειν*, see Foucart, *Les Grands Mystères d'Éleusis*, p. 121 (1900), and Roscher, s.v. Iacchos.

to receive a Macedonian garrison 'even on the 20th of Boedromion, the day on which they lead forth the mystic Iacchos.'

Iacchos then was the name by which Dionysos was known at Eleusis, his mystery name *par excellence* for Athens. It is important to note what special form of the god the name expressed.

Strabo[1] says vaguely, 'they call Dionysos, Iacchos, and the spirit (*δαίμονα*) who is leader of the mysteries of Demeter'; but vagueness is pardonable in the particular connection in which he speaks, as he is concerned to show the general analogy of all orgiastic rites. Mythologists have too readily concluded that Iacchos is a vague title denoting a sort of 'genius of the mysteries,' and 'the mystic Iacchos' has come to mean anything and nothing in particular.

But Suidas[2] is quite precise; he notes that Iacchos means 'a certain day,' 'a certain song,' but he puts, first and foremost, what is the root idea of Iacchos, he is 'Dionysos at the breast.' Iacchos at Eleusis is not the beer-god, not the wine-god, but the son-god, 'child of Semele, the wealth-giver[3],' the same as Liknites, 'He of the cradle,' whom, year by year on Parnassos, the Thyiades wakened to new life (p. 401).

Iacchos had his sanctuary at Athens and was received as a guest at Eleusis. Never, so far as we know, had he temple precinct or shrine at Eleusis, and his name occurs very rarely in inscriptions. He is a god made by the Athenians in their own image; they were guests at Eleusis, so their god was a guest. He is as it were a reflection of the influence of Athens at Eleusis.

Another point must be noted. Zagreus, it has been seen, is a god of ritual rather than poetry, Iacchos is of poetry rather than ritual, of poetry touched and deepened by mysticism. He is just so much of the religion of Dionysos as the imaginative Athenian can face. We never hear that Iacchos was a bull, there is no legend that he was torn to pieces. Sophocles[4], the most

[1] Strab. x. 3. 11, *Ἴακχόν τε καὶ Διόνυσον καλοῦσι καὶ τὸν ἀρχηγέτην τῶν μυστηρίων τῆς Δήμητρος δαίμονα.* An inscription of Roman date has *[δαί]μονι πέμψαν ἰάκχωι*, see Ἐφ. Ἀρχ. 1899, p. 215. We are reminded of the Agathos Daimon, the spirit of wealth (p. 33).

[2] Suidas, s.v. Ἴακχος. Lucret. IV. 1160, 'tumida et mammosa Ceres est ipsa ab Iaccho.'

[3] Schol. ad Ar. *Ran.* 479, *Σεμελήι' Ἴακχε πλουτοδότα.*

[4] Soph. frg. 782, ap. Strab. xv. p. 687, see p. 378.

orthodox of poets, knows he has horns, but he sends his horned Iacchos to dwell in fabulous Nysa,

'Where no shrill voice doth sound of any bird,'

and for the rest he is compact of torchlight and dancing.

The learned Nonnus[1], who is steeped in Orphism and a most careful ritualist, seems to hit the mark when he makes Iacchos the latest born of the divine Bacchic incarnations. According to Nonnus, Iacchos is the child of Aura by Bacchus, and is presented by his father to Athene, and Athene adopted him, and gave him the breast that before him none but Erechtheus had sucked. Here we have a manifest reminiscence of Iacchos as 'Dionysos at the breast.' Nonnus goes on to say how the nymphs, the Bacchae of Eleusis, received the new-born child with dance and song, and they hymned first Zagreus son of Persephone, next Bromios son of Semele, and third in order Iacchos.

So shadowy, so poetical are the associations that cluster round the name Iacchos, that, if Iacchos were our only evidence of Dionysos at Eleusis, I should be inclined to believe his influence was in the main late and literary. It is to ritual we must look for evidence more substantial.

It is perhaps worth noting that Pausanias[2], in mentioning a trivial ritual taboo, notes that it is common to the mysteries of Eleusis and the teaching of Orpheus. He is speaking of the temple of the Bean-Man (Cyamites), but is uncertain of the origin of the name and cult, and knows he is treading on delicate ground, so he contents himself with saying darkly, 'Whoever has seen the rite at Eleusis, or has read what are called the sayings of Orpheus, knows what I mean.' More than once, in examining a sanctuary of Demeter or Kore, he stops to note that local tradition attributed its foundation to Orpheus. Thus at Sparta[3] he saw a temple of Kore the Saviour, and 'some say Orpheus the Thracian made it, but others Abaris who came

[1] Nonn. XLVIII. 951 ff.

καὶ τριτάτῳ νέον ὕμνον ἐπεσμαράγησαν Ἰάκχῳ
καὶ χορὸν ὀψιτέλεστον ἀνεκρούσαντο πολῖται
Ζαγρέα κυδαίνοντες ἅμα Βρομίῳ καὶ Ἰάκχῳ.

That the child Iacchos at Eleusis became an element in Orphic teaching is evident from the primitive form of the Baubo legend expressed in an Orphic hymn and quoted in full by Clement, *Protr.* 21. 26.

[2] P. I. 37. 4.

[3] P. III. 13. 2.

from the Hyperboreans.' Here the diverse tradition is unanimous as to Northern influence. The Lacedaemonians believed, he says, that Orpheus taught them to worship Demeter of the Underworld, but Pausanias himself thinks that they, like other people, got it from Hermione[1]. No great importance can be attached to these floating traditions, but they serve to show that popular belief connected the worship of the Mother and the Maid with Orpheus and the North. We are inclined to connect the rise of their worship exclusively with Eleusis, so that local tradition to the contrary is of some value.

But the real substantial evidence as to the presence and influence of Orphic rites and conceptions at Eleusis is drawn from the Eleusinian ceremonial itself. Of the three main Orphic mysteries examined, the Omophagia, the Liknophoria, and the Sacred Marriage, two, the Liknophoria and the Sacred Marriage, are known with absolute certainty to have been practised at Eleusis.

The first and perhaps the most profound and characteristic of Orphic rites, the Omophagia, is wholly absent[2]. The reason is not far to seek. The Omophagia, deep though its spiritual meaning was, is in its actual ritual savage and repulsive. We have seen a rite closely analogous practised by primitive nomadic Arabs. The cultus at Eleusis is, as has already been shown, based on agricultural conditions; the emergence of Eleusis was primarily due to the fertile Rarian corn plain. A god who comes to Eleusis, who is affiliated by this agricultural people, will shed the barbarous side of his worship, and develope only that side of his nature and ritual that is consonant with civilised life. A god can only exist so long as he is the mirror of the people who worship him. Accordingly we find, as might be expected, that it is the Dionysos of agriculture, and of those marriage rites that go with agriculture, who is worshipped at Eleusis, worshipped with the rites of the Liknophoria and of the Sacred Marriage.

[1] P. III. 14. 5.

[2] The singular and very peculiar ritual of bull-sacrifice described in the *Kritias* of Plato, and represented on imperial coins of Ilium, has recently been elucidated by Dr von Fritze ('Troja und Ilium,' *Beiträge*, pp. 514, 563). It probably took place at Eleusis, cf. *C.I.A.* II. 467, *ἤραντο δὲ τοῖς Μυστηρίοις τοὺς βοῦς ἐν Ἐλευσῖνι τῇ θυσίᾳ*. But this ceremony I believe to have been part of the primitive ritual of Poseidon at Eleusis, which, interesting though it is, does not here concern us. Of an Omophagia at Eleusis the 'tokens' contain no trace, though the bull-ritual of Poseidon may have facilitated the affiliation of Dionysos.

b. The Liknophoria at Eleusis.

The Liknophoria as an element in the rites at Eleusis is clearly shown in the monument reproduced in figs. 153—155. The design forms the decoration of a cinerary urn[1] (fig. 153) found in a grave near a Columbarium on the Esquiline Hill. The scenes represented are clearly rites of initiation. In fig. 154 we see Demeter herself enthroned; about her is coiled her great snake caressed by the initiated mystic[2]. To the left stands a female torch-bearer; she is probably Persephone. This scene represents the final stage of initiation (ἐποπτεία), where the *epoptes* is admitted to the presence and converse of the goddesses.

Fig. 153.

The remainder of the design (fig. 155) is occupied by two

Fig. 154.

[1] Helbig, *Cat.* 1168, Museo delle Terme, Rome, published and discussed by E. Caetani Lovatelli, *Ant. Mon. illustr.* p. 25 ff., tav. II—IV.

[2] The mystic initiated holds a club. He is probably Herakles, who, according to tradition, was initiated in the mysteries at Agrae.

preliminary ceremonies of purification, the sacrifice of the 'mystic' pig already discussed (p. 152) and the *liknon* ceremonial. It is on this last that attention must be focussed. The candidate is

Fig. 155.

seated on a low seat (θρόνος); his right foot rests on a ram's head which doubtless stands for the 'fleece of purification' (p. 24); he is veiled and in his left hand carries a torch; above his head a priestess holds a *liknon*. It is remarkable that the *liknon* in this representation, unlike those previously discussed, contains no fruits. This can scarcely, I think, be accidental. When the artist wishes to show fruits in a sacred vessel, he is quite able to do so, as is seen in the dish of poppy heads held by the priest to the right, where perspective is violated to make the content clear. The absence of the fruits is best, I think, explained on the supposition that the *liknon* is by this time mysticized. It is regarded as the winnowing fan, the 'mystic fan of Iacchos,' rather than as the basket of earth's fruits. It is held empty over the candidate's head merely as a symbol of purification. This explanation is the more probable, if the scene be, as is generally supposed, a representation of Eleusinian mysteries, but of Eleusinian mysteries held not at Eleusis but at Alexandria. The vertical corn-ears on the head of Demeter, the fringed garment of the youth who handles the snake, and the scale pattern that decorates the cover of the urn itself (fig. 153), all find their closer analogies in Egyptian rather than indigenous Greek monuments.

A Liknophoria, it is clear, was part of Eleusinian ritual. But the question naturally arises—did not Dionysos borrow the *liknon* from Demeter rather than Demeter from Dionysos? It is almost certain that he did not. Dionysos was worshipped as Liknites at Delphi before he came to Eleusis. Moreover, in the Eleusinian 'tokens' the confession is not 'I have carried the *liknon*,' but 'I have carried the *kernos*.' That Kernophoria and Liknophoria were analogous ceremonies, both being the carrying of first-fruits, is possible; that they were identical is improbable. Dionysos borrowed the *liknon* from his own mother, not from her of Eleusis.

Far more complete and satisfactory is the evidence for the Sacred Marriage and the Birth of the holy child. These were as integral a part of the mysteries of Eleusis as of the rites of Sabazios and Dionysos.

c. *The Sacred Marriage and the Sacred Birth at Eleusis.*

Iacchos, we have seen, was defined as the child Dionysos 'at the breast,' but for any ceremony of his birth or awakening under the name of Iacchos we look in vain. Iacchos is Athenian; no one ventured to say he was born at Eleusis, but by a most fortunate chance the record is left us of another Mother and Son at Eleusis, and we know too that the marriage of this Mother and the birth of this Son were the central acts, the culmination, of the whole ritual of its mysteries. We owe this knowledge to the anonymous treatise which has already furnished the important details as to the Mysteries of Phlya.

The author of the *Philosophoumena*[1] is concerned to prove that

[1] This passage is of such cardinal importance that the text is given below. The birth of Brimos and the 'ear of grain reaped' are often cited separately as elements in Eleusinian rites, but so far as I know their substantial identity has never been noted, nor has attention been called to the fact that they are both Dionysiac (Thraco-Phrygian) elements. The text is that of Cruice, *Philosophoumena*, Paris 1860, p. 170. *Λέγουσι δὲ αὐτόν, φησί, Φρύγες καὶ 'χλοερὸν στάχυν τεθερισμένον' καὶ μετὰ τοὺς Φρύγας 'Αθηναῖοι μυοῦντες 'Ελευσίνια, καὶ ἐπιδεικνύντες τοῖς ἐποπτεύουσι τὸ μέγα καὶ θαυμαστὸν καὶ τελειότατον ἐποπτικὸν ἐκεῖ μυστήριον, ἐν σιωπῇ τεθερισμένον*

the heretical sect of the Naassenes got their doctrine from ceremonials practised by the Phrygians. The Phrygians, the Naassene says, assert that god is 'a fresh ear of grain reaped.' He then goes on to make a statement to us of supreme importance. 'And following the Phrygians the Athenians, when they initiate at the Eleusinian rites, exhibit to the epoptae the mighty and marvellous and most complete epoptic mystery, an ear of grain reaped in silence. And this ear of grain the Athenians themselves hold to be the great and perfect light that is from that which has no form, as the Hierophant himself, who is not like Attis, but who is made a eunuch by means of hemlock and has renounced all carnal generation, he, by night at Eleusis, accomplishing by the light of a great flame the great and unutterable mysteries, says and cries in a loud voice "Holy Brimo has borne a sacred Child, Brimos," that is, the mighty has borne the mighty; and holy, he (i.e. the Naassene) says, is the generation that is spiritual, that is heavenly, that is from above, and mighty is he so engendered.'

The evidence of the writer of the *Philosophoumena* is indefeasible, not indeed as to the mystical meaning either he or the Naassene he quotes attached to the rites, but as to the rites themselves. He describes the rites only to discredit them and he quotes an actual ritual formulary. We may take it then as certain that to the epoptae at Eleusis was shown as the supreme revelation a 'fresh ear reaped' and that by night there was declared to these epoptae the birth of a sacred Child: 'Unto us a Child is born, unto us a Son is given.' The close conjunction in which the two rites are placed makes it highly probable, though not absolutely certain, that the one, the human birth, was but the anthropomorphic form of the other, that in fact we have here the drama of Liknites, child and fruit, reenacted; the thought is the same as that expressed by the vase-painter (fig. 151) where the new-born child rises out of the cornucopia of fruits. And last it is highly satisfactory to learn, and that from the mouth of a Christian writer, that the birth and the begetting were symbolical. The

στάχυν. Ὁ δὲ στάχυς οὗτός ἐστι καὶ παρὰ Ἀθηναίοις ὁ παρὰ τοῦ ἀχαρακτηρίστου φωστὴρ τέλειος μέγας καθάπερ αὐτὸς ὁ ἱεροφάντης, οὐκ ἀποκεκομμένος μέν, ὡς ὁ Ἄττις, εὐνουχισμένος δὲ διὰ κωνείου καὶ πᾶσαν παρῃτημένος τὴν σαρκικὴν γένεσιν νυκτὸς ἐν Ἐλευσῖνι ὑπὸ πολλῷ πυρὶ τελῶν τὰ μεγάλα καὶ ἄρρητα μυστήρια βοᾷ καὶ κέκραγε λέγων 'ἱερὸν ἔτεκε πότνια κοῦρον Βριμὼ Βριμόν,' τουτέστιν ἰσχυρὰ ἰσχυρόν. Πότνια δέ ἐστι, φησίν, ἡ γένεσις ἡ πνευματική, ἡ ἐπουράνιος, ἡ ἄνω· ἰσχυρὸς δέ ἐστιν ὁ οὕτω γεννώμενος. φησίν of course refers to the Naassene not the Hierophant.

express statement that the Hierophant partook of some drug compelling abstinence cannot have been invented[1].

The author of the *Philosophoumena* says nothing of the Sacred Marriage, though from the birth of the holy Child it might be inferred. The confession 'I have gone down into the bridal chamber' is one of the 'tokens' of the mysteries of the Great Mother, but we cannot certainly say that it was a 'token' at Eleusis; neither Clement nor Firmicus nor Arnobius includes it in his enumeration. We cannot therefore assert that each mystic at Eleusis went through a mimetic marriage, but we do know that the holy rite was enacted between the hierophant and the chief priestess of Demeter. Asterius[2], speaking of the various procedures of initiation at Eleusis, asks—'is there not there the descent into darkness and the holy congress of the hierophant and the priestess, of him alone and her alone?'

Lucian[3] adds incidental testimony. In his account of the doings of the false prophet Alexander he describes how the impostor instituted rites that were a close parody of those at Eleusis, and he narrates the details of the blasphemous travesty. Among the mimetic performances were not only the Epiphany and Birth of a god but the enactment of a Sacred Marriage. All preliminaries were gone through, and Lucian says that but for the abundance of lighted torches the marriage rite would actually have been consummated. The part of the hierophant was taken by the false prophet himself. A short time after the parody of the marriage ceremony he came in wearing the characteristic dress of the hierophant, and, amid a deep silence, announced in the usual loud voice 'Hail, Glykon,' and 'some fellows attending him, Paphlagonians, wearing sandals and smelling of garlic and supposed to be Eumolpidae and Kerykes, cried in answer "Hail, Alexander."'

Lucian's account of this scurrilous travesty is not pleasant reading, but it serves one important end—it enables us to put together the two rites, the Sacred Marriage and the Birth of the

[1] So determined are some commentators to see in pagan rites evil where no evil is, that Miller has substituted *ἀπηρτισμένος* for *παρῃτημένος*, thus making nonsense of the passage.

[2] Aster. *Encom. Mart.* p. 113 B, *οὐκ ἐκεῖ καταβάσιον τὸ σκοτεινὸν καὶ αἱ σεμναὶ τοῦ ἱεροφάντου πρὸς τὴν ἱερείαν συντυχίαι μόνου πρὸς μόνην;*

[3] Luc. *Alex.* 38, *εἰ δὲ μὴ πολλαὶ ἦσαν αἱ δᾷδες τάχ' ἄν τι καὶ τῶν ὑπὸ κόλπου ἐπράττετο. μετὰ μικρὸν δὲ πάλιν ἐσῄει ἱεροφαντικῶς ἐσκευασμένος ἐν πολλῇ τῇ σιωπῇ καὶ αὐτὸς μὲν ἔλεγε μεγάλῃ τῇ φωνῇ ἰὴ Γλύκων κ.τ.λ.*

holy Child; but for Lucian the sequence must have remained conjectural. We may now be certain that in silence, in darkness and in perfect chastity the Sacred Marriage was first enacted, and that immediately after the Hierophant came forth, and, standing in a blaze of torchlight, cried aloud that the supreme mystery was accomplished, 'Holy Brimo has borne a sacred Child, Brimos.'

The Sacred Marriage[1] formed part of the ritual of Eleusis, as it formed part of the Orphic mysteries of Sabazios and the Great Mother, but the further question arises—was this Sacred Marriage indigenous at Eleusis or did it, like the religion of Dionysos, come from the North? Was Brimo only a title of the Eleusinian Demeter? This it would seem was the view of Clement[2] who is not strong in ethnography, but it can I think be shown that Clement was wrong. Brimo *is* a form of the Great Mother who is also the Maid, but she is a Northern not an Eleusinian form. This is clearly evidenced by what we know of her apart from the mysteries.

d. Thessalian influence at Eleusis. Brimo.

Of Brimos we know nothing save as the mystery child; he is the attributive son marking by identity of name the function of his mother. Brimo we know as an underworld goddess, and, a fact all important for the argument, she comes from Pherae in Thessaly.

In the *Alexandra* of Lycophron Cassandra thus addresses her mother Hecuba[3]:

'Mother, unhappy mother, not untold
Shall be thy fame, for Brimo, Perses' maid,
The Threefold One, shall for her ministrant
Take thee, to fright men with dire sounds at night,
Yea such as worship not with torchlit rites
The images of her who Strymon holds,
Pherae's dread goddess leaving unassoiled.'

For once Lycophron is intelligible; Hecuba is to be trans-

[1] The Christian Fathers of course regarded the Sacred Marriage as a shameful rape. Tertullian (*ad nat.* II. 7, p. 57 D) asks 'Cur rapitur sacerdos Cereris si non tale Ceres passa est?' That Tertullian's view is wrong is sufficiently evidenced by the author of the *Philosophoumena*, loc. cit.

[2] Clem. Al. *Protr.* I. 15, Δηοῦς δὲ μυστήρια καὶ Διὸς πρὸς μητέρα Δήμητρα ἀφροδίσιοι συμπλοκαὶ καὶ μῆνις...τῆς Δηοῦς ἧς δὴ χάριν Βριμὼ προσαγορευθῆναι λέγεται.

[3] Lyc. *Al.* 1175.

formed into a hound of the triple Hecate, Thessalian goddess of the underworld, and Brimo is but her other name: she is the Thessalian Kore. The mystic child at Eleusis was born of a maiden; these ancients made for themselves the sacred dogma, 'A virgin shall conceive and bear a son.' It was left to Christian Fathers, blending the motherhood of Demeter with the virgin mother and the parentage of Zeus, things they did not and would not understand, to make of the sacred legend a story of vile human incest.

Brimo, though we find her, in late times, in the very heart of the mysteries, belongs with her hell-hounds to a *couche* of mythology obviously primitive. To the popular mind of the uninitiated she lapsed into mere bogeydom. Lucian[1] in his *Oracle of the Dead* brings her in with the rest of the comic horrors of Hades. When the underworld decree is passed the magistrates of Hades record their votes, the populace holds up its hands, 'Brimo snorts approval, Cerberus yelps his aye.'

But Apollonius Rhodius[2], writing of things Thessalian, and by natural temper inclined always to the serious and beautiful, knows of Brimo as terrible and magical, but yet as the Nursing Mother (Kourotrophos). When Medea is about to pluck the awful underworld root for the undoing of Jason,

> 'Seven times bathed she herself in living founts,
> Seven times called she on Brimo, she who haunts
> The night, the Nursing Mother. In black weed
> And murky gloom she dwells, Queen of the dead.'

And the scholiast commenting on the passage says she is Hecate, 'whom sorceresses were wont magically to induce (ἐπάγεσθαι); and they called her Brimo because of the terror and horror of her; and she sent against men the apparitions called Hekataia; and she was wont to change her shape, hence they called her Empusa.' He goes off into fruitless etymology but drops by the way a suggestion that may contain some truth, that the name Brimo is connected with ὄβριμος, 'raging,' the epithet of another Thracian, Ares.

Brimo then, some said, meant the Mighty, some the Angry

[1] Luc. *Menippus*, 20, καὶ ἐνεβριμήσατο ἡ Βριμὼ καὶ ὑλάκτησεν ὁ Κέρβερος. The untranslatable play on the words shows that the name Brimo was taken to imply a loud angry noise.

[2] Apoll. Rhod. III. 861, and schol. ad loc.

One. The two, for minds obsessed by the atmosphere of 'aversion,' are not far apart: the Angry-Raging One is own sister to the Angry Demeter, Demeter Erinys. But by their Angry name it is not well to address the gods, lest by sympathetic magic you rouse the very anger you seek to allay. Brimo may well have been one of the Silent Names.

Brimo is Thessalian, and Thessalian often spells 'later Thracian.' Brimo is near akin to the Mother Kotys, the mystery goddess of the Thracians, but we cannot say that she is herself certainly Thracian. For definite evidence of a Thracian element at Eleusis we must look to its chief hereditary priesthood, the family from which the Hierophant was taken, the Eumolpidae.

e. Thracian influence at Eleusis. Eumolpos.

The Eumolpidae must also be the keystone of any contention as to Thracian influence at Eleusis, and fortunately we are fairly well informed as to their *provenance*.

Sophocles[1] in the *Oedipus Coloneus* makes the Chorus sing:

> 'O to be there
> Upon the sea shore, where,
> Ablaze with light,
> The Holy Ones for mortals their dread rite
> Nurse, and on mortal lips the golden key
> Is set of celebrant Eumolpidae.'

The scholiast[2] asks the very pertinent question—'Why in the world have the Eumolpidae presidency over the rites, when they are foreigners?' He proceeds as usual to make several puzzled and contradictory suggestions. Perhaps the reason is that it was Eumolpos, son of Deiope daughter of Triptolemos, who

[1] Soph. *Oed. Col.* 1048. I have translated *κλῆς* by *key* not by *seal*, although, as Prof. Jebb (ad loc.) points out, 'there is no evidence for the Eleusinian Hierophant putting a key to the lips of the initiated.' In face of the fact that the key was the recognized symbol of priestly office, I incline to think some such ceremony was enacted. We know from Hesychius (s.v.) that there was a festival or ceremony called 'the festival of the keys,' Epikleidia, but unhappily we have no details and cannot use the fact as an argument.

[2] Schol. ad *Oed. Col.* 1048, *ζητεῖται τί δήποτε οἱ Εὐμολπίδαι τῶν τελετῶν ἐξάρχουσι ξένοι ὄντες; εἴποι δ' ἄν τις ὅτι ἀξιοῦσι πρῶτον τὸν Εὔμολπον ποιῆσαι τὸν Δηϊόπης τῆς Τριπτολέμου τὰ ἐν Ἐλευσῖνι μυστήρια καὶ οὐ τὸν Θρᾷκα καὶ τοῦτο ἱστορεῖν Ἴστρον ἐν τῷ περὶ τῶν Ἀτάκτων. Ἀκεσίδωρος δὲ πεμπτὸν ἀπὸ τοῦ πρώτου Εὐμόλπου εἶναι τὸν τὰς τελετὰς καταδείξαντα, γράφων οὕτως 'Κατοικῆσαι δὲ τὴν Ἐλευσῖνα ἱστοροῦσι πρῶτον μὲν τοὺς αὐτοχθόνας εἶτα Θρᾷκας τοὺς μετὰ Εὐμόλπου παραγενομένους πρὸς βοηθείαν εἰς τὸν κατ' Ἐρεχθέως πόλεμον, τινὲς δέ φασι καὶ τὸν Εὔμολπον εὑρεῖν τὴν μύησιν τὴν συντελουμένην κατ' ἐνιαυτὸν ἐν Ἐλευσῖνι Δήμητρι καὶ Κόρῃ.'*

first instituted the mysteries at Eleusis, and not the Thracian, and this was the view taken by Istros in his book on 'Things out of Order,' or perhaps Akesidorus was right; his theory was that the Eumolpos who founded the rites was fifth in descent from the first Eumolpos.

Unpleasant facts are always apt to be classed as 'Things out of Order.' Facts are facts, but Order is what you happen to like yourself. The simple fact cheerfully accepted at Eleusis was that the Eumolpidae were Thracians, but the Athenians did not like the Thracians, so when they came to Eleusis they proceeded to get the unpalatable fact into 'order.' One of two things must be done, either the Eumolpidae, whose respectability was above impeachment, must be provided with a new and local parentage, they must be affiliated to Triptolemos, or the old parentage must be removed to a safe and decorous antiquity. Few people feel very acutely about what happened five generations ago.

But all the time historians knew perfectly well what really had happened, and Akesidorus proceeds to state it quite simply: 'Tradition says that Eleusis was first inhabited by an autochthonous population, and then by those Thracians who came with Eumolpos to help in the war against Erechtheus.' He lets out at last what was at the bottom of the whole complication, a fight between Eleusis and Athens and a contingent of Thracian auxiliaries. The war had been internecine, for the legend says the single combat between Erechtheus and Eumolpos ended in the death of both. Athens ultimately emerged to political supremacy, but Eleusis, to which Eumolpos first brought his rites, maintained her religious hegemony. Athens did what she could. She even built herself an Eleusinion and instituted Lesser Mysteries; there was much to-ing and fro-ing of sacred objects, the *ἱερά* are brought from Eleusis and Iacchos makes a return visit, but the actual final initiation takes place at Eleusis and the chief celebrant is still to all time a Thracian Eumolpid[1].

Art is not without its evidence as to Eumolpos at Eleusis. The simple vase-painter is untroubled by the Eleusinian blend of

[1] I have elsewhere (*Myth. and Mon. Anc. Athens*, p. lvii ff.) discussed the relations of Erechtheus and Eumolpos. The view there expressed as to the Eumolpidae and their relation to Thrace and the incoming of Dionysos is confirmed by the more detailed and independent examination of the legend by Dr Toepffer, *Attische Genealogie*, p. 40.

Dionysos and Demeter, and the Thracian origin of Eumolpos. On the kotyle in fig. 156, signed by the potter Hieron, and now in the British Museum[1], he has brought together in friendly comradeship a group of Eleusinian personages, some of the ancient local stock, some of the northern immigrants. All the figures are carefully inscribed, so that there is no question of doubtful interpretation. On the obverse, and plainly occupying the central important place, the young local hero Triptolemos starts in his winged chariot to carry his ears of corn to the world. Demeter

Fig. 156.

in her splendid robe stands behind him, and 'Pherophatta' pours out the farewell cup. Triptolemos was, as has already been noted (p. 273), originally a local king; it may be he became young out of complimentary rivalry with the child Iacchos. Behind 'Pherophatta' stands a nymph whom, but for the inscription, we should not have dared to name, 'Eleusis.' Beneath one handle, looking back at the group of local divinities, is the seated Eumolpos, and near him is a great swan—for Eumolpos is the

[1] *Cat.* 61, 140; *Wiener Vorlegeblätter* A. 7.

sweet singer. He is the Thracian warrior when he fights Erechtheus, but here he holds the sceptre as priestly king; he is, Thracian-fashion, compounded of Ares and Orpheus. The centre of this reverse picture is occupied by the Thracian Dionysos, with his great vine branch, and behind him comes his father Zeus, with thunderbolt and sceptre. Dionysos a full-grown man, not babe, balances Triptolemos. Eumolpos is *vis à vis* to Poseidon, with whom he had close relations. Amphitrite completes the picture, a veritable little manual of the mythology of Eleusis.

f. The Delphic Dionysos at Eleusis and Agrae.

Another class of vase-paintings, in date nearly a century later than that of Hieron, bring before us Dionysos at Eleusis, but they depict him as an incomer, not from Thrace, but from the half-way station of Delphi. A polychrome vase of the 4th cen-

FIG. 157.

tury B.C., formerly in the Tyskiewicky Collection[1] (fig. 157), puts the matter very clearly. The central figure is Demeter, crowned and sceptred, sitting on an altar-like throne. To the right is Kore with her torches. She turns towards Dionysos. He too is seated, as becomes a god, and he holds his thyrsos. He is seated, but on what a throne! He is seated on the *omphalos*. To the ancient mind no symbolism could speak more clearly; Dionysos is

[1] For polychrome fac-simile see *Coll. Tyskiewicky*, Pl. x. The vase is now in the Museum at Lyons.

accepted at Eleusis; he has come from Delphi and brought his omphalos with him. We are apt to regard the omphalos as exclusively the property of Apollo, and it comes as something of a shock to see Dionysos seated quietly upon it. We have already (p. 319) seen that Apollo took it from Ge, took the ancient symbol of Mother Earth and made it his oracular throne; but at Delphi men knew that it had another and mystical content. It was the tomb of the dismembered Dionysos. The tradition that Dionysos was buried at Delphi is recorded again and again by lexicographers, Christian Fathers, and Byzantine historians; but the common source of their information seems to be the *Atthis* of Philochoros (3rd cent. B.C.). Malalas[1], in his *Chronicles* (6th cent.), tells the story of how Dionysos was chased from Boeotia, and ended his days at Delphi, 'and the remains of him are buried there in a coffin (*ἐν σορῷ*). And his gear is hung up in the sanctuary, as the learned Deinarchus says in his history of him. And the learned Philochoros gives the same account in his exposition about Dionysos himself; his tomb is to be seen near the gold Apollo. It may be conjectured that there is a sort of basis on which he writes "Here lies the dead Dionysos the son of Semele."' We need not attach serious importance to what is 'conjectured,' as the conjecture seems to be rather of Malalas than Philochoros, but it is clear that Philochoros recorded a tradition that the tomb of Dionysos was at Delphi. Tatian[2] identifies the tomb of Dionysos with the omphalos.

The vase in fig 157 does not stand alone. The Ninnion pinax[3], though details in its interpretation remain obscure, is clear on this one point—the influence of Delphi on the Mysteries.

In the discussion of this difficult and important monument I shall confine myself to such points as seem to me certain and immediately relevant. The inscription at the base tells us that it was dedicated by a woman 'Ninnion' to the 'Two Goddesses.' The main field of the pinax is occupied by two scenes, occupying

[1] Malalas, *Chron.* II. p. 45, ed. Bonn. The sources are fully given in Lobeck's *Aglaophamus*, p. 572. The word *βάθρον* is sometimes written *βόθρον*, a detail which does not affect the present argument.

[2] Tatian, c. *Gr.* VIII. 251, *ἐν τῷ τεμένει τοῦ Λητοΐδου καλεῖταί τις ὀμφαλός, ὁ δὲ ὀμφαλὸς τάφος τοῦ Διονύσου.*

[3] *Rev. Internat. d'Archéologie et Numismatique* 1901, pl. I. and Dr Svoronos's interpretation, p. 234.

the upper and lower halves, and divided, according to the familiar convention of the vase-painter, into two parts by an irregular white line, indicating the ground on which the figures in the upper part stand. In each of these two parts some of the figures, distinguished by their larger size, are divine, e.g. the seated goddesses to the right; others, of smaller stature, are human. Among the human figures in both the upper and lower row one

FIG. 158.

is marked out by the fact that she carries on her head a *kernos* (see p. 159). She is a dancing *Kernophoros*[1]. She is the principal figure among the worshippers, and she can scarcely be other than Ninnion[2], who dedicated the pinax. In a word, Ninnion, in her votive offering, dedicates the representation of one, and certainly an important, element in her own initiation, her *Kernophoria*.

[1] Poll. *Onom.* IV. 103, τὸ γὰρ κερνοφόρον ὄρχημα, οἶδα ὅτι λίκνα ἢ ἐσχαρίδας ἔφερον. κέρνα δὲ ταῦτα ἐκαλεῖτο.

[2] Dr Svoronos identifies 'Ninnion,' and I believe correctly, with the hetaira Nannion, whose notorious career is related by Athenaeus (Bk. XIII. pp. 582 and 587), but this question is for my purpose irrelevant.

Of this initiation why does she give a twofold representation? The answer, once suggested, is simple and convincing. Each and every candidate was *twice* initiated, once in the spring, at Agrae, in the Lesser Mysteries; once in the autumn, at Eleusis, in the Greater Mysteries. The scene in the lower half is the initiation at Agrae, that in the upper half the initiation at Eleusis. It is the scene in the lower half that specially concerns us.

The two seated goddesses to the right are clearly the 'Two Goddesses,' and the lower one is, it is equally evident, the younger, Kore. She is seated in somewhat curious fashion on the ground; near her is *an empty throne*. Some interpreters have said that the vase-painter *meant* her to be seated *on* the throne, but by an oversight drew in her figure seated a little above it. But the artist's intention is quite clear. Kore is seated on the ground, indicated by the curved white line beneath her. The empty throne is intentional and emphatic. Demeter, who should be seated on it, who in the upper tier *is* seated on a throne precisely identical, is absent. A vase-painter could not speak more clearly.

The explanation is again as simple as illuminating. The lower tier represents the initiation of Ninnion into the Lesser Mysteries at Agrae. These were sacred to Persephone, not Demeter. The scholiast[1] on the *Plutus* of Aristophanes says: 'In the course of the year two sets of mysteries are performed to Demeter and Kore, the Lesser and the Greater......the Greater were of Demeter, the Lesser of Persephone her daughter.' He further tells us that these Lesser Mysteries were a sort of pre-purification (*προκάθαρσις*) for the Greater, and that they were founded later than the great Eleusinian Mysteries, tradition said, in order that Herakles might be initiated. To these statements Stephen[2] of Byzantium adds an important fact: 'the Lesser Mysteries performed at Agra or Agrae were,' he says, 'an imitation of *what happened about Dionysos*.'

With these facts in our minds we are able to interpret the lower row of figures. Kore alone receives the mystic Ninnion, and Dionysos himself acts as Dadouchos. That the figure holding

[1] Schol. Ar. *Plut.* 845.

[2] Steph. Byz. Ἄγρα καὶ Ἄγραι χωρίον πρὸ τῆς πόλεως, ἐν ᾧ τὰ μικρὰ μυστήρια ἐπιτελεῖται μίμημα τῶν περὶ τὸν Διόνυσον.

the torches is a god is clear from his greater stature, and, if a god, he can be none other than Dionysos, who, as Iacchos, led the mystics in their dance. Dionysos has come from Delphi and found there a great white omphalos[1], like his Delphic grave. Below it are depicted two of the bundles of myrtle twigs, which are frequently the emblems of initiation, and which bore the name of 'Bacchoi[2].'

This interpretation is confirmed when we turn to the upper tier. 'Ninnion,' having been initiated by Dionysos into the mysteries at Agrae, which he shared with Kore, now comes for the Greater Mysteries to Eleusis. Kore herself brings her mystic, and leads her into the presence of Demeter enthroned. The scene is the telesterion of Eleusis marked by two columns, which, be it noted, extend only half-way down the pinax. In the Lesser Mysteries, a later foundation, Dionysos shares the honours with Kore; in the Greater and earlier to the end he is only a visitant.

The direct influence of Delphi on Eleusis as evidenced by these vases, and by many inscriptions, may have been comparatively late, but in a place to which Eumolpos had already brought the worship of Dionysos it would have easy access. At home Delphi became in the lapse of time more and more 'all for Apollo,' but abroad, as Athens, Eleusis, and Magnesia testify, she remembered sometimes to promote the worship of a god greater than Apollo, a god who was before him, and who never ceased, even at Delphi, to be his *paredros*, Dionysos.

Both on the kotylos of Hieron (fig. 156) and on the Tyskiewicky vase (fig. 157) Dionysos at Eleusis is represented as a full-grown man, not as a mystery babe. This fact is highly significant. The son has ceased to be a child, and growing to maturity forgets his relation to his mother. In the old Thracian religion, preserved in its primitive savagery in Asia Minor, the Mother, by whatever name she be called, whether Kotys or Kybele or Rhea or the Great Mother, is the dominant factor; the Son is, as is natural

[1] Dr Svoronos, whose brilliant interpretation of the pinax I follow in the main, sees in the 'omphalos' the πέτρα ἀγέλαστος. Here reluctantly I am obliged to differ; the real significance of the omphalos, its connection with Earth and Baubo worship has been I think conclusively shown by Dr Diels in his *Arcana Cerealia* in *Miscellanea dedicata al Prof. A. Salinas*, p. 14.

[2] Schol. ad Ar. *Eq.* 409, βάκχον ἐκάλουν...τοὺς κλάδους οὓς οἱ μύσται φέρουσι. The name given to these bunches of myrtle is evidence in itself of the intrusion of the worship of Dionysos.

in a matriarchal civilization, at first but the attribute of motherhood. When a cult is mainly in the hands of primitive women they will tend to keep their male god in the only condition they *can* keep him, i.e. as child. But if that cult is to advance with civilization, if the god is to have his male worshippers, he must grow to be a man; and as the power of the Son waxes and he becomes more and more the Father, the power of the Mother wanes, and she that was the Great Mother sinks to be Semele the thunder-stricken. If we bear in mind the old principle that man makes the gods in his own image, that a god only *is* because he reflects the life of his worshipper, the constant shift of Dionysos from child to full-grown man, from Son of his Mother to Son of his Father, becomes intelligible, nay more, necessary.

In all probability the development of Dionysos from child to man was helped and precipitated by his appropriation of the vine—a spirit of intoxication will be worshipped by man as much as and perhaps more than by women. But the interesting thing about Dionysos is that, develope as he may, he bears to the end, as no other god does, the stamp of his matriarchal origin. He can never rid himself of the throng of worshipping women, he is always the nursling of his Maenads. Moreover the instruments of his cult are always not his but his mother's. It is not enough to say that all orgiastic cults have analogies, nor, as is usually maintained, that the worship of Kybele came in classical times from Asia Minor, and was *contaminated* with that of Dionysos. All this is true, but the roots of the analogy lie deeper down. The Mother and the Son were together from the beginning. Brimos never came to Eleusis without Brimo. Demeter at Eleusis did not borrow her cymbals from Rhea; she had her own, and Dionysos shared them. Pindar knows it, if only half consciously:

'Or this, O Thebes, thy soul hath for its pride,
That Dionysos thou to birth didst bring,
Him of the flowing hair, who sits beside
Deo for whom the brazen cymbals ring.'

Strabo[1], as we have already seen (p. 374), knew that the orgies of Thrace and Phrygia and Crete were substantially the same, that Kuretes and Satyrs and Korybants, attendants on the Son, are also satellites of the Mother—and he cites Euripides[2]. The

[1] Strab. x. iii. 13 § 468.

[2] Eur. *Bacch.* 126.

Bacchae never forget that their worship is of the Mother as of the Son:

'But the Timbrel, the Timbrel is another's,
And away to Mother Rhea it must wend;
And to our holy singing from the Mother's
The mad Satyrs carried it, to blend
In the dancing and the cheer
Of our third and perfect Year;
And it serves Dionysos in the end!'

But the modern mind, obsessed and limited by a canonical Olympus, an Olympus which is 'all for the Father,' has forgotten the Great Mother, robbed the Son of half his grace, and left him desolate of all kinship save adoption.

It is not hard to see why at Eleusis the mother of Dionysos should fade into obscurity, fade so all but entirely that save for the one mention in the *Philosophoumena* we should have had no certainty of the birth of the holy child. Eleusis, before the coming of Eumolpos and Dionysos, had its Mother-goddess Demeter, and she would not lightly brook a rival. The old matriarchal couple, the Mother and the Maid, who though they were two persons were yet but one goddess, had for their foster-child now one local hero, now another, now Demophon, now and chiefly Triptolemos. At the coming of the northern Mother and Son, of Brimo and Brimos or Semele and Dionysos, matters had to be adjusted between the immigrant and the indigenous divinities. The northern Mother fades almost wholly, but in the Mysteries her Thessalian name is still proclaimed aloud. The attributive child Brimos is merged, partly in the Athenian Iacchos, partly in the local hero Triptolemos, who, to meet him half way, descended from his high estate as local chieftain to become a beautiful boy in a chariot drawn by snakes.

The hopeless fusion and confusion is well evidenced by monuments like the relief from Eleusis[1] in fig. 159. Here are the Mother and the Maid, the Mother with her sceptre, the Maid with her torch, and between them is a boy, their nursling. Is he Triptolemos, is he Iacchos? The question may be asked, learned monographs may be and have been written in favour of either name, but it is a question that can never certainly be

[1] From a photograph of the relief, now in the National Museum at Athens.

answered. He is the young male divinity of Eleusis, the nursling of the goddesses; beyond that we cannot go.

The rite of the Sacred Marriage and the Birth of the Holy Child have been considered in detail because they were, I believe, *the* central mystery. Asterius[1], in his 'Encomium on the Blessed Martyrs' already cited, protests against the Eleusinian Mysteries as the head and front of heathen idolatry and speaks of the Sacred Marriage as its crowning act. 'Are not the Mysteries at Eleusis the chief act of your worship and does not the Attic people and the whole land of Hellas assemble that it may accomplish a rite of folly? Is there not there performed the descent into darkness, the venerated congress of the Hierophant with the priestess, of him alone with her alone? Are not the torches extinguished and does not the vast and countless assemblage believe *that in what is done by the two in darkness is their salvation*?'

Fig. 159.

Making all allowance for the fact that Christian Fathers naturally focus their attention on rites they chose to regard as immoral, it is yet abundantly clear that at Eleusis the Marriage and the Birth were the culminating ritual acts, acts by which *union with the divine*, the goal of all mystic ceremonial, was at first held to be actually effected, later symbolized. Preceded by

[1] S. Aster. *Amasen. Hom. x. in SS. Martyr.* οὐ κεφάλαιον τῆς σῆς θρησκείας τὰ ἐν Ἐλευσῖνι μυστήρια καὶ δῆμος Ἀττικὸς καὶ ἡ Ἑλλὰς πᾶσα συναίρει ἵνα τελέσῃ ματαιότητα; Οὐκ ἐκεῖ τὸ καταβάσιον τὸ σκοτεινὸν καὶ αἱ σεμναὶ τοῦ ἱεροφάντου πρὸς τὴν ἱερείαν συντυχίαι μόνου πρὸς μόνην; Οὐχ αἱ λαμπάδες σβέννυνται καὶ ὁ πολὺς καὶ ἀναρίθμητος δῆμος τὴν σωτηρίαν αὐτῶν εἶναι νομίζουσι τὰ ἐν τῷ σκότῳ παρὰ τῶν δύο πραττόμενα;

rites of purification such as the Liknophoria, amplified, emphasized by endless subordinate scenes, reenacted in various mythological forms, as e.g. in the rape of Persephone, they yet remained at Eleusis, at Samothrace and elsewhere, *the* cardinal mysteries. Man makes the rites of the gods in the image of his human conduct. The mysteries of these man-made gods are but the eternal mysteries of the life of man. The examination of endless various and shifting details would lead us no further.

Before we leave the Sacred Marriage, an ethnographical point of some interest remains to be considered.

g. Cretan influence on the mysteries at Eleusis.

In Crete we found the *Omophagia* and the Mother, but no marriage rite, and yet there is evidence that makes it highly probable that Demeter and her marriage developed in Crete and came thence to Eleusis.

Such is the tradition of the Homeric Hymn[1]:

> 'Dos is the name that to me my holy mother gave,
> And I am come from Crete across the wide sea-water wave.'

This may be a mere chance pirate legend, but such legends often echo ethnographical fact.

Again at the close of the Hymn[2] the poet seems to remember the island route by which Demeter passed to Thessaly:

> 'Goddess who holdst the fragrance of Eleusis in thy hands,
> Mistress of rocky Antron and Paros' sea-girt strand,
> Lady revered, fair Deo, gift-giver year by year,
> Thou and thy fair Persephone, to us incline thine ear.'

Whether Demeter brought her daughter from Crete must remain for the present unconsidered; but from mythology, not ritual, we learn that in Crete she had a Sacred Marriage. Calypso, recounting the tale of ancient mortal lovers of whom the gods were jealous, says[3]:

> 'So too fair-haired Demeter once in the spring did yield
> To love, and with Iasion lay in a new-ploughed field.
> But not for long she loved him, for Zeus high overhead
> Cast on him his white lightning and Iasion lay dead.'

[1] *Hymn. ad Cer.* 122. [2] *v.* 490.

[3] *Od.* v. 125, *νειῷ ἔνι τριπόλῳ.* I venture to render *τριπόλῳ* by 'in the spring,' because Theophrastos (*H.P.* VII. 1) says there were three ploughings, one in the winter, one in the summer and a third between the two (*ἄροτος τρίτος ὁ μεταξὺ τούτων*) which must have been in the spring before the seed was sown. *Triptolemos* is the Eleusinian Iasion.

It is one of the lovely earth-born myths that crop up now and again in Homer, telling of an older simpler world, of gods who had only half emerged from the natural things they are, real earth-born flesh and blood creatures, not splendid phantoms of an imagined Olympic pageant. To smite and slay these primitive divinities of the order he supersedes, Zeus is always ready with his virtuous thunderbolt.

Hesiod[1], if later in date, is almost always earlier in thought than Homer. He knows of the Marriage and knows that it was in Crete:

> 'Demeter brought forth Ploutos; a glorious goddess she,
> And yet she loved Iasion, a mortal hero he.
> In Crete's rich furrows lay they; glad and kindly was the birth
> Of him whose way is on the sea and over all the Earth.
> Happy, happy is the mortal who doth meet him as he goes,
> For his hands are full of blessings and his treasure overflows.'

Theocritus[2] knows that this Marriage of Iasion was a Mystery:

> 'Oh, happy, happy, in his changeless fate,
> Endymion dreaming: happy, Love, and great
> Iasion, who won the mystic joy
> That ye shall never learn, Unconsecrate!'

Hesiod is all husbandman; he knows of no mystery child[3], only of the old agricultural mimetic rite and the child who is the fruits of the earth and of the sea. Zeus with his thunder has not yet come to make of innocent bliss a transgression. Hesiod might have written the ancient tag preserved for us by his scholiast[4]:

> 'Ah for the wheat and barley, O child Ploutos.'

The writer of the Homeric Hymn[5] is altogether Zeus-ridden, hence many of the anomalies and absurdities of the tale he so beautifully tells; he is Homeric in his aloofness from things primitive, he is also Orphic in his emphasis on the spiritual bliss of the initiated and in his other-worldliness. He is concerned to show their future weal rather than their present wealth:

> 'Blessed is he among men who is given these rites to know,
> But the uninitiate man, the man without, must go
> To no such happy lot when dead in the dusk below.'

1 Hes. *Theog.* 969.

2 Theocr. *Id.* III. 50. Translated by Mr Gilbert Murray.

3 In Samothrace, Iasion becomes a mystery-figure. He is the father of Korybas, and his sister Harmonia takes her *ἱερὸς γάμος* to Thebes. Again the route is by the islands, see Diod. v. 45.

4 Schol. ad Hes. *Theog.* 971, *καὶ γὰρ ἡ παροιμία* '*πυρῶν καὶ κριθῶν, ὦ νήπιε Πλοῦτε.*'

5 *Hom. Hymn. ad Cer.* 480.

And yet, so strong is the ancient agricultural tradition and association of the rites that the primitive sacred child of Crete, the Wealth-god, reemerges[1] almost automatically at the close, though in half abstracted fashion, born of heaven not earth:

'Then when the goddess all things had ordered of her grace,
She fared to high Olympus, their great assembly place.
There do they dwell with Father Zeus, who thunders through the sky,
Holy and reverend are their names, and great his earthly joy
Whom they vouchsafe to love. Above all mortals is he blest,
Swiftly they send to his great home Ploutos to be his guest.'

The mimetic marriage of Crete, a bit of sympathetic magic common to many primitive peoples, became a cardinal *mystic* rite. Diodorus[2] in a very instructive passage tells us that in Crete 'mysteries' were not mysterious, and we shall not, I think, be far wrong if we suppose that the Cretan non-mysterious form was the earlier. After discussing Cretan mythology he says: 'The Cretans in alleging that they from Crete conferred on other mortals the services of the gods, sacrifices and rites appertaining to mysteries, bring forward this point as being to their thinking the principal piece of evidence. The rite of initiation, which is perhaps the most celebrated of all, is that which is performed by the Athenians at Eleusis, and the rite at Samothrace and that in Thrace among the Cicones, the country of Orpheus, inventor of rites, all these are imparted as mysteries; whereas in Crete at Cnossos the custom from ancient times was that these rites should be communicated openly and to all, and things that among the other peoples were communicated in secrecy among the Cretans no one concealed from any one who wished to know.'

The Cretans, like most patriots, went a little too far. The gods had not left themselves without witness among other peoples till they, the elect Cretans, started on their missionary enterprise. But, as regards certain mystery rites, as regards two of those discussed in detail, the Omophagia and the Sacred Marriage, may not their statement have been substantially true? Before the downward movement of Dionysos from the North, may there not have been an upward movement of (shall we say) Orpheus from the South? May not the Orphic mysteries of the Mother

[1] *v*. 483.

[2] Diod. v. 77, and see Diod. v. 64. For relations between Crete and Eleusis and the Cretan origin of the 'pig-Demeter' see Athenaeus, p. 375, discussed by Dr Neustadt in his *De Jove Cretico*, p. 54.

have started, or at least fully developed, in matriarchal Crete[1], Crete that was to the end 'of the Mother,' that refused even in her language to recognise the foolish empty patriarchalism, 'Father-land'? In Crete the discoveries of Mr Arthur Evans have shown us a splendid and barbarous civilization, mature, even decadent, before the uprising of Athens. From Crete to Athens came Epimenides, who is but a quasi-historical Orpheus, and with him he brought rites of cleansing. In Cretan 'Mycenaean' civilization[2] and only there, is seen that strange blend of Egyptian and 'Pelasgian' that haunted Plutarch and made him say that Osiris was one with Dionysos, Isis with Demeter.

Diodorus, quoting the local tradition, knows the very route by which the rites of Crete went northward, by way of the islands, by Samothrace home of the mysteries, up to the land of the Cicones. There, it would seem, Orpheus the sober met the raging wine-god, there the Maenads slew him, and repented and upraised his sanctuary. Thence the two religions, so different yet so intimately fused, came down to Greece, a conjoint force, dominant, irresistible. Mysticism and 'Enthusiasm' are met together, and, for Greek religion, the last word is said.

Orpheus for all his lyre-playing is a priest or rather a 're-ligious.' Dionysos is, at least as we know him at Athens, less priest than artist. Most primitive religions have *δρώμενα*, but from the religion of Dionysos sprang the drama. The analogy between *δρώμενα*, things done, actions, and *δρᾶμα*, a Thing Acted in the stage sense, has been often observed, but the problem still remains—why was the transition effected in the religion of Dionysos and in his only, why have Athene and Zeus and Poseidon no drama, only *δρώμενα*?

h. The Drama of Dionysos and the δρώμενα of Eleusis.

The question would not be raised here but that the answer I would suggest comes mainly from religion, and some stages of the transition are, I believe, to be found in the ritual of Eleusis[3].

[1] Plut. *An. sen. est ger. resp.* XVII. ἡ δὲ πατρὶς καὶ μητρὶς (ὡς Κρῆτες καλοῦσι).

[2] A. J. Evans, *The Palace of Knossos in its Egyptian relations*, Egypt Exploration Fund, Arch. Report, 1899—90, p. 60.

[3] I would only be understood as indicating one strand in the many that may have gone to the weaving of the drama. For other Dionysiac elements see K. T. Preuss, 'Der Dämonische Ursprung d. gr. Dramas erläutert durch Mexicanische Parallelen,' in *Neue Jahrbücher f. das kl. Altertum*, 1906, p. 161.

Epic, lyric and dramatic poetry succeed each other in our handbooks and our minds in easy and canonical fashion. Lyric poetry asks no explanation, or finds it instantly in our common human egotism. But we are apt to forget that from the *epos*, the narrative, to the *drama*, the enactment, is a momentous step, one, so far as we know, not taken in Greece till after centuries of epic achievement, and then taken suddenly, almost in the dark, and irrevocably. All we really know of this momentous step is that it was taken some time in the sixth century B.C. and taken in connection with the worship of Dionysos. Surely it is at least possible that the real impulse to the drama lay not wholly in 'goat-songs' and 'circular dancing places' but also in the cardinal, the essentially dramatic, conviction of the religion of Dionysos, that the worshipper can not only worship, but can become, can *be*, his god[1]. Athene and Zeus and Poseidon have no drama because no one, in his wildest moments, believed he could become and be Athene or Zeus or Poseidon. It is indeed only in the orgiastic religions that these splendid moments of conviction could come, and, for Greece at least, only in an orgiastic religion did the drama take its rise.

In the rites at Eleusis of which most details are known we have the very last stage of the development before the final step was actually taken, we have δρώμενα on the very verge of *drama*.

Late authors in describing the Eleusinian rites use constantly the vocabulary of the stage. Take the account of Psellus[2], whose

[1] An instance of a sacred pantomime in which the parts of gods were taken by 'Iobacchoi' is given in another connection (p. 474), but this pantomime cannot be used as evidence. Its date is long after the rise of the drama.

[2] Psellus, *Quaenam sunt Graecorum opiniones de daemonibus*, 3 (ed. Migne), ἃ δέ γε μυστήρια τούτων οἷα αὐτίκα τὰ Ἐλευσίνια τὸν μυθικὸν ὑποκρίνεται Δία μιγνύμενον ἤγουν τῇ Δηοῖ ἢ τῇ Δημήτερι καὶ τῇ θυγατρὶ ταύτης Φερεφάττῃ, τῇ καὶ Κόρῃ. Ἐπειδὴ δὲ ἔμελλον καὶ ἀφροδίσιοι ἐπὶ τῇ μυήσει γίνεσθαι συμπλοκαί, ἀναδύεταί πως ἡ Ἀφροδίτη ἀπό τινων πεπλασμένων μηδέων πελάγιος. Εἶτα δὲ γαμήλιος ἐπὶ τῇ Κόρῃ ὑμεναῖος. Καὶ ὑπᾴδουσιν οἱ τελούμενοι 'ἐκ τυμπάνου ἔφαγον, ἐκ κυμβάλων ἔπιον, ἐκιρνοφόρησα, ὑπὸ τὸν παστὸν εἰσέδυν.' Ὑποκρίνεται δὲ καὶ τὰς Δηοῦς ὠδῖνας. Ἱκετηρίαι γοῦν αὐτίκα Δηοῦς. καὶ χολῆς πόσις καὶ καρδιαλγίαι. Ἐφ' οἷς καὶ τραγόσκελες μίμημα παθαινόμενον περὶ τοῖς διδύμοις ὅτι περ ὁ Ζεὺς δίκας ἀποτιννὺς τῆς βίας τῇ Δήμητρι τράγου ὄρχεις ἀποτεμὼν τῷ κόλπῳ ταύτης κατέθετο ὥσπερ δὴ καὶ ἑαυτοῦ. Ἐπὶ πᾶσιν αἱ τοῦ Διονύσου τιμαὶ καὶ ἡ κίστις καὶ τὰ πολυόμφαλα πόπανα καὶ οἱ τῷ Σαβαζίῳ τελούμενοι καὶ οἱ μητριάζοντες Κλώδωνές τε καὶ Μιμαλλόνες, καί τις ἠχῶν λέβης Θεσπρώτειος καὶ Δωδώναιον χαλκεῖον καὶ Κορύβας ἄλλος καὶ Κούρης ἕτερος δαιμόνων μιμήματα. Ἐφ' οἷς ἡ Βαυβὼ τοὺς μηροὺς ἀνασυρομένη καὶ ὁ γυναικεῖος κτείς· οὕτω γὰρ ὀνομάζουσι τὴν αἰδῶ αἰσχυνόμενοι. Καὶ οὕτως ἐν αἰσχρῷ τὴν τελετὴν καταλύουσιν.

I owe this reference to Taylor's *Eleusinian Mysteries*. The book is by modern authorities as a rule contemptuously ignored, probably because Taylor's construing is always vague and often inaccurate and he entirely declines to accentuate his Greek. In spite of these minor drawbacks his attitude towards the interpretation of the Mysteries is far in advance of that of many better furnished scholars.

testimony has been too much neglected. Psellus is recording 'what the Greeks believe about demons' and he passes from theology to ritual. 'Yes and the mysteries of these (demons), as for example those of Eleusis, enact the double story of Deo or Demeter and her daughter Pherephatta or Kore. As in the rite of initiation love affairs are to take place, Aphrodite of the Sea is represented as uprising. Next there is the wedding rite for Kore. And the initiated sing as an accompaniment "I have eaten from the timbrel, I have drunk from the cymbals, I have carried the *kernos*, I have gone down into the bridal chamber." Then also they enact the birth-pains of Deo. At least there are cries of entreaty of Deo, and there is the draught of gall and the throes of pain. After these there is a goat-legged mime because of what Zeus did to Demeter. After all this there are the rites of Dionysos and the cista and the cakes with many bosses and the initiated to Sabazios and the Klodones and Mimallones who do the rites of the Mother and the sounding cauldron of Thesprotia and the gong of Dodona and a Korybas and a Koures, separate figures, mimic forms of demons. After this is the action of Baubo[1].'

Psellus shows us the sacred pantomime in full complexity. From other sources we know that it was not all dumb-show, that other words were spoken besides the confession of the 'tokens.' Galen[2] when he is urging his readers to attend to natural science no less than theology says: 'Lend me then your whole attention even more than you did supposing you were initiated in the Eleusinian and Samothracian mysteries or any other holy rite and gave yourself up wholly *to the things done and the things spoken* by the Hierophants.'

The fashion in which the 'things spoken' supplemented and

[1] The account of Psellus is for obvious reasons rather resumed than translated. Some of the rites recorded by Psellus are not in harmony with modern conventions, and for my purpose it is not needful to discuss them. But once for all I wish to record my conviction that such evil as we find in these mysteries we bring with us. The mind of Herondas is not the measure of primitive sanctities. The story of Babo or Baubo has always been a stumbling-block, but it has now been clearly proved by Dr Diels in his *Arcana Cerealia* (in Miscellanea di Archeologia di Storia et di Filologia dedicata al Prof. A. Salinas) that Baubo, as Hesychius s.v. *βαυβώ* says, is not only *τιθήνη Δήμητρος—σημαίνει δὲ καὶ κοιλίαν, ὡς παρ' Ἐμπεδοκλεῖ*. The true mystic said with Heracleitos (ap. Clem. *Protr.* II. p. 30): *Εἰ μὴ γὰρ Διονύσῳ πομπὴν ἐποίευντο καὶ ὕμνεον ᾆσμα αἰδοίοισιν, ἀναιδέστατα εἴργαστ' ἄν· αὐτὸς δὲ Ἀΐδης καὶ Διόνυσος ὅτεῳ μαίνονται καὶ ληναΐζουσιν.* See Pfleiderer, *Die Philosophie des Heraklit im Lichte der Mysterienidee*, p. 28.

[2] Galen, *de Usu Part.* VII. 14 § 469; see Lobeck, *Aglaoph.* p. 63.

helped out the 'things done' comes out very clearly in the curious fictitious legal case which occurs among the collection of rhetorical exercises made by Sopater[1]. A young man dreams that he is initiated, and sees the 'things done.' He recounts the 'things done' to an initiated friend and asks if they correspond to the actual Eleusinian rite. The friend nods assent. Is the friend guilty of impiety, i.e. has he revealed the 'things done' to one uninitiated? No, argues the initiated man, for the dreamer was really initiated by the goddesses themselves; only one thing was lacking to him, he had not heard the voice of the hierophant so as to understand clearly the sense of the symbols uttered by him. The symbols uttered must have been words corresponding to, explanatory of, the things done, dark enough no doubt, but felt to be illuminating. The hierophant acted as sacred showman to the pantomime. Here we have brought into close, inevitable conjunction the narrative element of the epos and the action element of the drama. We have all the apparatus of the stage, the appearances and disappearances, the dancing and the singing, the lights, the voices and the darkness. Religion gave all the circumstances and the scenery, religion woke the instinct of intense impersonation, some genius made the dumb figures speak themselves and tragedy was born.

Dionysos gave men tragedy to gladden and to greaten their toilsome life on earth. His other great gift was, as has been already shown, the hope that by attaining divinity they would as a necessary consequence attain immortality. To the dim forecast of some sort of after guerdon that Demeter gave, he brought something as near conviction as the human mind can get. Plutarch[2] writes to his wife when they have lost their little girl, who was so like the father and so dear to the mother, and he bids her remember both her traditional faith and 'the mystic symbols of the rites of initiation to Dionysos.' These, he says, will prevent her from thinking that the soul suffers nothing after death, that it ceases to be. He reads into these rites of course his own Platonism; they teach him that the soul is like a bird caught in a cage,

[1] Sopat. *Dist. Quaest.* Walz, *Rhet. Graec.* vol. VIII. p. 1.

[2] Plut. *Consol. ad uxor.* X. ὅτι κωλύει σε πιστεύειν ὁ πάτριος λόγος καὶ τὰ μυστικὰ σύμβολα τῶν περὶ τὸν Διόνυσον ὀργιασμῶν ἃ σύνισμεν ἀλλήλοις οἱ κοινοῦντες.

caught and recaught ever in new births, that the evil of old age is not its wrinkles and grey hairs but, hardest thing of all, the dimness and staleness of the soul to the memory of things 'there' not here; and the soul that leaves the body soon is not cramped and bent but only softly and pliantly moulded and soon shakes its mane and is free, just as fire that is quenched and relighted forthwith flames and sparkles anew. The customs of his country forbade him to make libations for children, and he reads into the old barbarous convention, based on the harmlessness of the child-ghost, the doctrine that children have no part in earth and earthly things, but have passed straightway to a better and more divine fate. Still in the mystic symbols of Dionysos he sees only what was there implicit if only in dim fashion.

It has been thought that the rites of Eleusis and other Orphic mysteries contained among these 'things done' mimetic presentations of a future life, a sort of revelation and instruction for the conduct of the soul in the world below. Elements of this kind, it will later be seen, may easily have been interpolated from Egypt, but for Eleusis we have no certain evidence. The best witness to the faith of the Orphic as to the future life are his own confessions buried with him in his tomb, inscribed happily for us on imperishable gold, and to this witness we must now turn.

CHAPTER XI.

ORPHIC ESCHATOLOGY.

'Χαίρετ', ἐγὼ δ' ὔμμιν θεὸς ἄμβροτος, οὐκέτι θνητός.'

α. THE ORPHIC TABLETS.

THE monuments in question are a series of eight inscribed tablets all of very thin gold, which have come to light in tombs. Six out of the eight were found in Lower Italy, in the neighbourhood of ancient Sybaris, one near Rome, one in Crete. In the first and third cases, it should be noted, the place *provenance* is an ancient home of Orphism. These tablets are of such cardinal importance that they will need to be examined separately and in detail. But all have this much in common: buried with the dead they contain instructions for his conduct in the world below, exhortations to the soul, formularies to be repeated, confessions of faith and of ritual performed, and the like. They belong to the domain of ritual rather than of literature, and therefore offer evidence the more unimpeachable; but, though defective in style and often regardless of metre, they are touched with a certain ecstasy of conviction that lifts them sometimes to a high level of poetry.

The Orphic tablets have frequently been discussed[1], but their full importance as documents for the history of Greek religion has perhaps as yet not been fully realized. Their interpretation presents exceptional difficulties; the shining surface and creased condition of the gold-leaf on which they are written make them difficult to photograph and irksome to decipher; moreover the text, even when deciphered, is in some cases obviously fragmentary. It has been thought best to reserve all textual difficulties for separate discussion[2].

[1] See especially A. Dieterich, *Nekuia*, pp. 84 ff., and *De Hymnis Orphicis*, pp. 31 ff. Other references are given in the notes and Appendix.

[2] In the Appendix kindly written for me by Mr Gilbert Murray.

The series of tablets or scrolls is as follows:

I. *The Petelia tablet*[1] (fig. 160).

FIG. 160.

'Thou shalt find on the left of the House of Hades a Well-spring,
And by the side thereof standing a white cypress.
To this Well-spring approach not near.
But thou shalt find another by the Lake of Memory,
Cold water flowing forth, and there are Guardians before it.
Say: "I am a child of Earth and of Starry Heaven;
But my race is of Heaven (alone). This ye know yourselves.
And lo, I am parched with thirst and I perish. Give me quickly
The cold water flowing forth from the Lake of Memory."
And of themselves they will give thee to drink from the holy Well-spring,
And thereafter among the other Heroes thou shalt have lordship....'

The text breaks off at this point. The scattered words that remain make no consecutive sense. Of the last line, written from bottom to top of the right edge of the tablet, the two last words only are legible, 'darkness enfolding' (σκότος ἀμφικαλύψας).

[1] Brit. Mus. Gold Ornament Room, Table-Case H. Kaibel, *CIGIS*, No. 641. The tablet had been rolled up and placed in a hexagonal cylinder hanging from a delicate gold chain and doubtless worn by the dead person as an amulet. The facsimile reproduced here and first published *J.H.S.* III. p. 112 was verified for Prof. Comparetti by Mr Cecil Smith and supersedes Kaibel's publication. As the letters in the original are small and in places not easily legible, Mr Smith's reading is given below:

Εὑρήσσεις δ' 'Αίδαο δόμων ἐπ' ἀριστερὰ κρήνην
πὰρ δ' αὐτῆι λευκὴν ἑστηκυῖαν κυπάρισσον·
ταύτης τῆς κρήνης μηδὲ σχεδὸν ἐμπελάσειας.
Εὑρήσεις δ' ἑτέραν τῆς Μνημοσύνης ἀπὸ λίμνης
ψυχρὸν ὕδωρ προρέον· φύλακες δ' ἐπίπροσθεν ἔασιν.
Εἰπεῖν· γῆς παῖς εἰμι καὶ οὐρανοῦ ἀστερόεντος,
αὐτὰρ ἐμοὶ γένος οὐράνιον· τόδε δ' ἴστε καὶ αὐτοί·
δίψηι δ' εἰμὶ αὔη καὶ ἀπόλλυμαι· ἀλλὰ δότ' αἶψα
ψυχρὸν ὕδωρ προρέον τῆς Μνημοσύνης ἀπὸ λίμνης·
καὔ[τοί σο]ι δώσουσι πιεῖν θείης ἀπ[ὸ κρήν]ης
καὶ τότ' ἔπειτ' ἄ[λλοισι μεθ'] ἡρώεσσιν ἀνάξει[s]
............ιης τόδε..................................θανεῖ[σ]θαι
.....................τοδ' ἔγραψ[εν ?]...
...................................σκότος ἀμφικαλύψας.

As a sequel to this tablet comes a second found in Crete:

II. *The Eleuthernae tablet*[1].

'I am parched with thirst and I perish.—Nay, drink of Me,
The Well-spring flowing for ever on the Right, where the Cypress is.
Who art thou?......
Whence art thou?—I am son of Earth and of Starry Heaven.'

The soul itself speaks to the Well of Mnemosyne and the Well makes answer.

Both tablets contain the same two elements, the Well of Remembrance, and the avowal of origin. The avowal of origin constitutes in each the claim to drink of the Well.

The origin claimed is divine. Hesiod[2] uses exactly the same words in describing the parentage of the gods. He bids the Muse

'Sing the holy race of Immortals ever existing,
Who from Earth were born and born from Starry Heaven.'

We have in the avowal of the soul the clearest possible statement of the cardinal doctrine of Orphic faith—immortality is possible only in virtue of the divinity of humanity. The sacrament of this immortality is the drinking of a divine well.

THE WELL OF MNEMOSYNE.

On the first tablet the soul is bidden to avoid a well on the left hand. This well is left nameless, but contrasted as it is with the Well of Mnemosyne or Remembrance, we may safely conclude that the forbidden well is Lethe, Forgetfulness.

The notion that in death we forget, forget the sorrows of this troublesome world, forget the toilsome journey to the next, is not Orphic, not even specially Greek; it is elemental, human, and may occur anywhere.

The Fiji islanders[3] have their 'Path of the Shades' beset with perils and their Wai-na-dula, a well from which the dead man drinks and forgets sorrow. 'He passed the twin goddesses Nino

[1] Joubin, *Bull. de Corr. Hell.* XVII. 1893, p. 122. This tablet, with two others which are duplicates of the one here given, are now in the National Museum at Athens. For facsimiles and discussion of text see Appendix.

[2] Hes. *Theog.* 135.

[3] Basil Thomson, 'The Kalou-Vu' (*Journal Anthrop. Inst.* May 1895, p. 349). I am indebted for this reference to Mr Andrew Lang's *Homeric Hymns*, p. 91.

who peered at him and gnashed their terrible teeth, fled up the path and came to a spring and stopped and drank, and, as soon as he tasted the water, he ceased weeping, and his friends also ceased weeping in his home, for they straightway forgot their sorrows and were consoled. Therefore this spring is called the Wai-na-dula, Water of Solace.' After many other perils, including the escape from two savage Dictynnas who seek to catch him in their nets, the soul at last is allowed to pass into the dancing grounds where the young gods dance and sing.

This Fiji parallel is worth noting because it is so different. The Fiji soul drinks of forgetfulness, and why? Because his friends and relations must put a term to their irksome mourning, and till the soul sets the example and himself forgets they must remember. His confession of faith is also somewhat different. Before he can be admitted to his Happy Land he must prove that he has died a violent death, otherwise he must go back to the upper air and die respectably, i.e. violently.

I have noted the Lethe of the Fiji islands to show that I am not unaware that savage parallels exist, that a well may be drunk on the 'Path of the Shades' in any land, and that there is no need to suppose that the Greeks borrowed their well either from Fiji or from Egypt: and yet in this particular case it can, I believe, be shown that the Orphic well came from Egypt[1], came I believe to Crete, and passed with Orpheus from Crete by the islands to Thrace and to Athens, and thence to Magna Graecia.

Osiris in Egypt had a 'cold' well or water of which he gave the souls to drink. On tombs of Roman date[2] the formulary appears: 'May Osiris give thee the cold water.' Sometimes it is Aidoneus sometimes Osiris who is invoked, for by that time

[1] Mr Lang, op. cit. p. 81, examines 'the alleged Egyptian origins' of the Eleusinian mysteries and decides against M. Foucart's theory *in toto*. Mr Lang certainly succeeds in showing that for all Greek mysteries a satisfactory savage analogy can be found; but this surely does not preclude the possibility of occasional borrowing. Crete has shown conclusively that 'Mycenaean' art borrowed from Egypt: why not 'Mycenaean' religion? See *Classical Review*, Feb. 1903, p. 84.

[2] Kaibel, *CIGIS* 1842:

ψυχρὸν ὕδωρ δοίη σοι ἄναξ ἐνέρων Ἀιδωνεύς,
ὦ Μέλαν· ἥβης γάρ σοι ἀπώλετο φίλτατον ἄνθος

and 1488 Θ(εοῖς) Κ(αταχθονίοις). εὐψύχει, κυρία, καὶ δοῖ σοι ὁ Ὄσιρις τὸ ψυχρὸν ὕδωρ. For the analogy of the Christian *refrigerium* see Mr J. A. Stewart's interesting note in the *Classical Review* for March 1903, p. 117, published since the above was written. See Dieterich, *Nekuia*, p. 95, and Foucart, *Recherches sur l'Origine et la Nature des Mystères d'Éleusis*, Paris, 1895, p. 68.

the two were not clearly distinguished. In so far as Osiris was a sun-god the well became a well of light, in which the sun-god Ra was wont to wash his face. In one of the magical papyri[1] the line occurs

'Hail to the water white and the tree with the leaves high hanging,'

which seems to echo vaguely the white cypress and the forbidden well. The well of Osiris, whatever the precise significance of its Egyptian name, would easily to the Greeks become of double significance; ψυχρόν would suggest ψυχή, and the well would be both cool and fresh and *life*-giving; by it the soul would *revive* (ἀναψύχειν), it would become 'a living water, springing up into everlasting life.'

A 'living water' given by Osiris to the thirsty soul was part of the eschatology of Egypt, but, so far as we know, Egypt had neither Lethe nor Mnemosyne. In the *Book of the Dead* there occurs indeed the *Chapter of making a man possess memory in the underworld* (No. XXV.), but the process has no connection with the drinking from a well. The *Chapter of drinking water in the underworld* (No. LXII.) is quite distinct. Lethe and Mnemosyne are, I think, Greek developments from the neutral *fonds* of Egypt, and developments due to the influence of Orpheus.

Lethe as a person is as old as Hesiod[2]. She is bad from the beginning:

'Next hateful Strife gave birth to grievous Toil,
Forgetfulness and Famine, tearful Woes,
Contests and Slaughters.'

By the time of Aristophanes the 'plain of Lethe' is part of the stock furniture of Hades. In the *Frogs*[3] Charon on the look-out for passengers asks:

'Who's for the plain of Lethe? Who's for the Donkey-shearings?
Who's for the Cerberus folk? or Taenarus? Who's for the Rookeries?'

The mystic comic Hades of Aristophanes is thoroughly Orphic. He mentions no well, but he knows of a *Stone of Parching*[4], where it may be the thirsty soul sat down to rest.

[1] Dieterich, *Abraxas*, p. 97:
χαῖρε δὲ λευκὸν ὕδωρ καὶ δένδρεον ὑψιπέτηλον.
It is perhaps worth noting that in the Egyptian *Book of the Dead* (Vignette to Chapter LXIII. A.) the dead man receives water from a goddess in a tree growing out of a pool of water.

[2] Hes. *Theog.* 227. [3] Ar. *Ran.* 186. [4] *Ib.* 194, παρὰ τὸν Αὑαίνου λίθον.

Lethe as a water, a river, first appears in the *Republic* of Plato[1] and in such fashion that it seems as though it was by that time proverbial. 'Our story,' says Socrates, 'has been saved and has not perished, and it will save us if we are obedient to it, and we shall make a good passage of the river of Lethe and shall not be defiled in our souls.' It is noticeable that to Plato Lethe is of death and pollution. Just before, Socrates has recounted the myth of Er, a myth steeped in Orphic eschatology of metempsychosis and retribution. The souls have been forced to pass each one into the plain of Lethe through scorching suffocating heat, for the plain of Lethe was devoid of trees and of plants that spring from the earth. Towards evening they took shelter by the river of Unmindfulness whose water no vessel can hold[2]. Of this all were compelled to drink a certain measure, and those who were not safe-guarded by wisdom drank more than the measure, and each one as he drank forgot all things. The river *Ameles*, Unmindfulness, is of course Lethe: Plato likes to borrow a popular notion and slightly rechristen it. Just so he takes Mnemosyne, Remembrance, and makes of her Anamnesis, Remembering-again. It was not the fashion of his day to give chapter and verse for your borrowings, and Plato so detested the lower side of Orphic rites that perhaps he only half realized the extent of his debts. It is a human and rather malicious touch, that in the order of those who remember again, the man who lives the 'initiated life' comes only fifth, side by side with the seer, below the philosopher and the lover and the righteous king and the warrior, below even the economist and the man of business; but after all he cannot much complain, for low though he is, he is above the poet and the artist. Moreover Plato would take as clearly and vividly known to the initiated all that through lapse of time has become dim to us, and his constant use of the technical terms of initiation is adequate acknowledgment. He tells[3] of the uninitiate (ἀμύητος), the partly initiate (ἀτέλεστος), the newly initiate (νεοτελής), wholly initiate (ἀρτιτελής), of the man rapt by the divine (ἐνθουσιάζων), whom the vulgar deem distraught, of how before we were caught in the prison of the body we celebrated (ὠργιάζομεν) a most blessed rite, being initiated to

[1] Plat. *Rep.* x. 621.
[2] A reminiscence of Styx, see Pausanias VIII. 18. 5 and Dr Frazer's commentary.
[3] Plat. *Phaedr.* 249 ff.

behold dimly and see perfectly (μυούμενοι καὶ ἐποπτεύοντες) apparitions complete, simple, quiet and happy, shining in a clear light.

For Mnemosyne and Lethe in Greek religion we are not however dependent on the myths and philosophy of Plato. We have definite evidence in local ritual. Mnemosyne herself takes us straight to the North, the land of Eumolpos and the Muses, to Pangaion, to Pieria, to Helicon. If Orpheus found in Egypt, or as is more probable in Crete, a well of living water, that well was I think nameless, or at least did not bear the name of Mnemosyne. It may of course be accidental, but in the tablet from Crete the well, though obviously the same as that in the Petelia tablet, is unnamed. The name Mnemosyne was found for the well when Orpheus took it with him to the land of the Muses, where he himself got his magic lyre. Not ten miles away from the slopes of Helicon, at the sanctuary of Trophonios at Lebadeia, we find a well not only of Mnemosyne but also of Lethe, and we find the worshipper is made to drink of these wells not in the imagined kingdom of the dead, but in the actual ritual of the living. Man makes the next world in the image of this present.

Pausanias[1] has left us a detailed account of the ritual of the oracle of Trophonios of which only the essential points can be noted here. Before the worshipper can actually descend into the oracular chasm, he must spend some days in a house that is a sanctuary of the Agathos Daimon and of Tyche; then he is purified and eats sacrificial flesh. After omens have been taken and a black ram sacrificed into a trench, the inquirer is washed and anointed and led by the priests to certain 'springs of water which are very near to one another, and then he must drink of the water called Forgetfulness (Λήθης), that there may be forgetfulness of everything that he has hitherto had in his mind, and after that he drinks of yet another water called Memory (Μνημοσύνης), by which he remembers what he has seen when he goes down below.' He is then shown an image which Daedalus made, i.e. a very ancient xoanon, and one which was only shown to those who are going to visit Trophonios; this he worships and prays to, and then, clad in a linen tunic—another Orphic touch—and girt with taeniae and shod with boots of the country he goes to the

[1] P. IX. 39. 5—14.

oracle. The ritual that follows is of course a descent into the underworld, the man goes down into the oven-shaped cavity, an elaborate artificial chasm, enters a hole, is dragged through by the feet, swirled away, hears and sees 'the things that are to be' (*τὰ μέλλοντα*), he comes up feet foremost and then the priests set him on the seat, called the seat of Memory, which is near the shrine. They question him and, when they have learnt all they can, give him over to his friends, who carry him possessed by fear and unconscious to the house of Agathe Tyche and Agathos Daimon where he lodged before. Then he comes to himself and, one is relieved to hear, is able to laugh again. Pausanias says expressly that he had been through the performance himself and is not writing from hearsay.

The Orphic notes in this description are many. To those already discussed we may add that Demeter at Lebadeia was known as Europa, a name which points to Crete. Another Cretan link indicates that the worship of Trophonios was, as we should expect if it is Dionysiac, of orgiastic character. Plutarch[1], in a passage that has not received the attention it deserves, classes together certain daemons who 'do not always stay in the moon, but descend here below to have the supervision of *oracular shrines,* and they are present at and *celebrate the orgies of the most sublime rites.* They are punishers of evil deeds and *watchers* over such.' The word watchers (*φύλακες*) is the same as that used in the tablet of the guardians of Mnemosyne's well. If in the performance of their office they themselves do wrong either through fear or favour, they themselves suffer for it, and in characteristically Orphic fashion they are thrust down again and tied to human bodies. Then comes this notable statement. 'Those of the age of Kronos said that they themselves were of the better sort of these daemons, and the Idaean Daktyls who were formerly in Crete, and the Korybantes who were in Phrygia, and the Trophoniads in Lebadeia, and thousands of others throughout the world whose titles, sanctuaries and honours remain to this day.' The rites of Daktyls, Korybants and Trophoniads are all the same and all are orgiastic and of the nature of initiation, all deal with

[1] Plut. *de fac. in orb. lun.* XXX. *ἀλλὰ χρηστηρίων δεῦρο κατίασιν ἐπιμελησόμενοι καὶ ταῖς ἀνωτάτω συμπάρεισι καὶ συνοργιάζουσι τῶν τελετῶν. κολασταί τε γίνονται καὶ φύλακες ἀδικημάτων.*

purgation and the emergence of the divine. All have rites that tell of 'things to be' and prepare the soul to meet them.

Pausanias of course understands 'things to be' (τὰ μέλλοντα) as merely the future, his attention is fixed on what is merely oracular and prophetic. The action of Lethe is to prepare a blank sheet for the reception of the oracle of Mnemosyne, to make the utterance of the oracle indelible. In point of fact, no doubt, the Trophoniads, the Orphics, found when they came to Lebadeia an ancient hero-oracle. That is clear from the sacrifice of the ram in the trench, a sacrifice made, be it observed, not to Trophonios but to Agamedes, the old hero. That the revelation at Lebadeia of 'things to be' was to the Orphic a vision of and a preparation for the other world (τὰ ἐκεῖ) is clear from the experiences recounted by Timarchos[1] as having occurred to him in the chasm of Trophonios. Socrates, it is said, was angry that no one told him about it while Timarchos was alive, for he would have liked to hear about it at first hand. What Timarchos saw was a vision of heaven and hell after the fashion of a Platonic myth, and his guide instructed him as to the meaning of things and how the soul shakes off the impurities of the body. The whole ecstatic mystic account beginning with the sensation of a blow on the head and the sense of the soul escaping, reads like a trance-experience or like the revelation experienced under an anaesthetic. It may be, and probably is, an invention from beginning to end. The important point is that this vision of things invisible is considered an appropriate experience to a man performing the rites of Trophonios.

The worshipper initiated at Lebadeia drank of Lethe; there was evil still to forget. The Orphic who, after a life spent in purification, passed into Hades, had done with forgetting; his soul drinks only of Remembrance. It is curious to note that in the contrast between Lethe and Mnemosyne we have what seems to be an Orphic protest against the lower, the sensuous side of the religion of Dionysos. To Mnemosyne, it will be remembered (p. 508), as to the Muses, the Sun and the Moon and the other primitive potencies affected by the Orphics, the Athenians offered only wineless offerings, but 'ancestral tradition,' Plutarch[2] tells us,

[1] Plut. *de Gen. Soc.* XXI. ff.

[2] Plut. *Symp.* Proem. and VII. 5. 3.

'consecrated to Dionysos, Lethe, together with the narthex.' It is this ancestral tradition that Teiresias[1] remembers when he tells of the blessings brought by the god, and how

'He rests man's spirit dim
From grieving, when the vine exalteth him.
He giveth sleep to sink the fretful day
In cool forgetting. Is there any way
With man's sore heart save only to forget?'

To man entangled in the flesh, man to whom sleep for the body, death for the soul was the only outlook, Lethe became a Queen of the Shades, Assessor of Hades[2]. Orestes[3], outworn with madness, cries

'O magic of sweet sleep, healer of pain,
I need thee and how sweetly art thou come.
O holy Lethe, wise physician thou,
Goddess invoked of miserable men.'

Orpheus found for 'miserable men' another way, not by the vine-god, but through the wineless ecstasy of Mnemosyne. The Orphic hymn[4] to the goddess ends with the prayer

'And in thy mystics waken memory
Of the holy rite, and Lethe drive afar.'

Lethe is to the Orphic as to Hesiod wholly bad, a thing from which he must purge himself. Plato[5] is thoroughly Orphic when he says in the *Phaedrus* that the soul sinks to earth 'full of forgetfulness and vice.' The doctrine as to future punishment which Plutarch[6] expounds in his treatise 'On Living Hidden' touches the high water mark of Orphic eschatology. The extreme penalty of the wicked in Erebos is not torture but unconsciousness (ἄγνοια). Pindar's 'sluggish streams of murky night,' he says, receive the guilty, and hide them in unconsciousness and forgetfulness. He denies emphatically the orthodox punishments, the gnawing vulture, the wearisome labours; the body cannot suffer torment or bear its marks, for the body is rotted away or consumed by fire; 'the one and only instrument of punishment is unconsciousness and obscurity, utter disappearance, carrying a man into

[1] Eur. *Bacch.* 280.
[2] Apollod. *Epit. Vat.* 6. 3.
[3] Eur. *Or.* 211.
[4] *Orph. Hymn.* LXXVII.
[5] Plat. *Phaedr.* p. 248 c.
[6] Plut. *de occult. viv.* sub fin. δεχόμενοι καὶ ἀποκρύπτοντες ἀγνοίᾳ καὶ λήθῃ τοὺς κολαζομένους...ἓν κολαστήριον...ἀδοξία καὶ ἄγνοια καὶ παντελῶς ἀφανισμὸς αἴρων εἰς τὸν ἀμειδῆ ποταμὸν ἀπὸ τῆς λήθης.

the smileless river that flows from Lethe, sinking him into an abyss and yawning gulf, bringing in its train all obscurity and all unconsciousness.'

The Orphic well of Mnemosyne lives on not only in the philosophy of Plato, but also, it would seem, in the inspired vision of Dante. At the close of the *Purgatorio*, when Dante[1] is wandering through the ancient wood, his steps are stayed by a little stream so pure that it hid nothing, and beside it all other waters seemed to have in them some admixture. The lady gathering flowers on the further bank tells him he is now in the Earthly Paradise: the Highest Good made man good and for goodness and gave him this place as earnest of eternal peace. Man fell away,

> 'changed to toil and weeping
> His honest laughter and sweet mirth.'

Then she tells of the virtue of the little stream. It does not rise, like an earthly water, from a vein replenished by evaporation, losing and gaining force in turn, but issues from a fountain sure and safe, ever receiving again by the will of God as much as on two sides it pours forth.

> 'On this side down it flows and with a virtue
> That takes away from man of sin the memory,
> On that the memory of good deeds it bringeth.
> Lethe its name on this side and Eunoë
> On that, nor does it work its work save only
> If first on this side then on that thou taste it.'

Dante hears a voice unspeakable say *Asperges me*, and is bathed in Lethe, and thereafter cannot wholly remember what made him to sin. Beatrice says to him smiling,

> 'And now bethink thee thou hast drunk of Lethe;
> And if from smoke the flame of fire be argued,
> This thine oblivion doth conclude most clearly
> A fault within thy Will elsewhere intended.'

And she turns to her attendant maid saying,

> 'See there Eunoë from its source forth flowing.
> Lead thou him to it, and as thou art wonted
> His virtue partly dead do thou requicken.'

[1] Dante, *Purg.* XXVIII. 130, XXXI. 98, XXXIII. 127. I owe this reference to Dante's well to the kindness of Mr F. M. Cornford. He tells me that the source from which Dante took *Eunoë* is not known.

And Dante comes back from 'that most holy wave':

> 'Refect was I, and as young plants renewing
> Their new leaves with new shoots, so I in spirit
> Pure, and disposed to mount towards starry heaven.'

The Eunoë[1] of Dante is Good-Consciousness, or the Consciousness of Good. It is the result of a purified, specialized memory, from which evil has fallen away. On the tomb-inscriptions the formulary occurs *εὐνοίας καὶ μνήμης χάριν* 'for good thought and remembrance' sake,' where the two are very near together. It is just what the Orphic meant by his Remembrance of the Divine, and, when we come to the next tablet, it will seem probable that not only the idea of Good-Consciousness but the very name *Eunoia* may perhaps have been suggested to Dante by an analogous Orphic well *En*noia.

THE SYBARIS TABLETS.

Six tablets still remain to be considered. Of these five were all found in tombs in the territory of ancient Sybaris, in the modern commune of Corigliano-Calabro. Two of them (III and IV) were found together in a tomb known locally as the *Timpone grande.* They were folded closely together, and lay near the skull of the skeleton. Their contents, so far as they can be deciphered, are as follows:

III. *Timpone grande tablet* (*a*)[2].

> 'But so soon as the Spirit hath left the light of the sun,
> To the right..of Ennoia
> Then must man.................being right wary in all things.
> Hail, thou who hast suffered the Suffering. This thou hadst never suffered before.
> Thou art become God from Man. A kid thou art fallen into milk.
> Hail, hail to thee journeying on the right........
> ...Holy meadows and groves of Phersephoneia.'

The second line seems to be a fragment of a whole sentence or set of sentences put for the whole, as we might put 'Therefore with Angels and Archangels,' leaving those familiar with our ritual to supply the missing words. Popular quotations and extracts always tend to make the grammar complete or at least intelligible.

[1] Εὐνόη is the name of a Nymph, apparently a Naiad; see Roscher, s.v.

[2] Naples Museum, Kaibel, *CIGIS* 642. For facsimiles of this and the following tablets, the text of which presents many difficulties, see Appendix, pp. 662, 664.

The name of the well, 'Ennoia,' depends on a conjectural emendation. The tablet of course cannot be the actual source of Dante's Eunoë. It is, however, very unlikely that Dante invented the name; he may have known of *En*noia and modified it to *Eu*noia. It has been seen that Lethe is regarded as the equivalent of Agnoia, Unconsciousness, and to *Ag*noia *En*noia would be a fitting contrast.

The formularies that occur at the end, the 'Suffering,' the 'kid' and the 'groves of Phersephoneia,' will be considered in relation to other and more complete tablets (p. 585).

With the 'Ennoia' tablet was found

IV. *Timpone grande tablet* (*b*)[1]. The inscription on this tablet is unhappily as yet only partially read. It appears to be in some cryptic script.

The broken formularies of tablet (*a*) and the cryptic script of (*b*) mark a stage in which the Orphic prescriptions are ceasing to be intelligent and intelligible, and tending to become cabalistic charms. Orphism shared the inevitable tendency of all mystic religions to lapse into mere mechanical magic. In the *Cyclops* of Euripides[2], the Satyr chorus, when they want to burn out the eye of the Cyclops, say they know

> 'A real good incantation
> Of Orpheus, that will make the pole go round
> Of its own accord'

Three tablets found near Sybaris yet remain. All these were found in different tombs in the same district as the *Timpone grande* tablets. In each case the tablet lay near the hand of the skeleton. The tombs were on the estate of Baron Compagno, who presented the tablets to the National Museum at Naples. In form of letters and in content they offer close analogies. They are all three reproduced in the Appendix, and will be considered together[3].

[1] See Appendix, p. 664.
[2] Eur. *Cycl.* 646.
[3] *Notizie degli Scavi*, 1880, Tav[a] III[a], Figs. 1, 2, 3. With these three tablets was found a red-figured plate of Lucanian fabric on which was represented a winged genius bearing a crown.

V. *Compagno tablet (a)*[1].

'Out of the pure I come, Pure Queen of Them Below,
Eukles and Eubouleus and the other Gods immortal.
For I also avow me that I am of your blessed race,
But Fate laid me low and the other Gods immortal
....................starflung thunderbolt.
I have flown out of the sorrowful weary Wheel.
I have passed with eager feet to the Circle desired.
I have entered into the bosom of Despoina, Queen of the Underworld.
I have passed with eager feet from the Circle desired.
Happy and Blessed One, thou shalt be God instead of mortal.
A kid I have fallen into milk.'

VI. *Compagno tablet (b)*[2].

'Out of the pure I come, Pure Queen of the Pure below,
Eukles and Eubouleus and the other Gods and Daemons.
For I also, I avow me, am of your blessed race.
I have paid the penalty for deeds unrighteous
Whether Fate laid me low or......
with starry thunderbolt.
But now I come a suppliant to Holy Phersephoneia
That of her grace she receive me to the seats of the Hallowed.'

VII. *Compagno tablet (c)*[3].

But for one or two purely verbal differences tablet (*c*) is precisely the same as (*b*). It is written carelessly on both sides of the gold plate, and but for the existence of (*b*) could scarcely have been made out. Tablet (*b*) has itself so many omissions that its interpretation depends mainly on the more complete contents of (*a*).

The last tablet to be considered presents two features of special interest. First, the name of its owner Caecilia Secundina[4] is inscribed, and from this fact, together with the loose cursive script in which it is written, the tablet can be securely dated as of Roman times. Second, the contents show but too plainly that the tablet was buried with magical intent.

VIII. *Caecilia Secundina tablet.*

'She comes from the Pure, O Pure Queen of those below
And Eukles and Eubouleus.—Child of Zeus, receive here the armour
Of Memory ('tis a gift songful among men).
Caecilia Secundina, come, by due rite grown to be a goddess.'

---

[1] Kaibel, *CIGIS* 641: see Appendix, p. 667.
[2] Kaibel, *CIGIS* 2: see Appendix, p. 668.
[3] Kaibel, *CIGIS* 641. 8: see Appendix, p. 668.
[4] Nothing certain is known of Caecilia Secundina, though her name suggests connection with the family of Pliny the Younger, whose original name before his adoption by his uncle C. Plinius Secundus was Publius Caecilius Secundus.

The tablet reads like a brief compendium from the two sets of formularies already given. We have the statement made to Despoina, Eukles and Eubouleus on behalf of Caecilia that she comes from the congregation of the pure, but it is not followed by the detailed confession of ritual performed—that is, so to speak, 'taken as read.' Mention is further made of the divine origin of Caecilia and of Mnemosyne, but in both cases after significant fashion. The 'gift of Mnemosyne' is now not water from a well, but rather the tablet itself, a certificate of Caecilia's purity, in verse (ἀοίδιμον), and graven on imperishable gold. Caecilia claims divine descent not from the Orphic Zagreus but from Zeus, who as has already been shown (p. 479) took on, in popular monotheism, something of the nature and functions of Zagreus. Caecilia's theology, like that of the Lower Italy vases (pp. 601, 602), is Orphism made orthodox, Olympicized, conventionalized. The last lines are spoken not by the Soul but by those who receive the Soul, as in *Timpone grande* (*a*). Caecilia is bidden to 'come,' since 'by due rite,' or 'by the law' she has become divine. It is the usual priestly confusion. The Soul *is* divine—that no Orphic priest dare deny—yet this divine soul needs the 'due ritual,' or the 'law,' to make sure of its divinity—needs apparently also the ὅπλα, the 'armour' forged by mortal hands. The reading of this word is very uncertain; it may be merely an epithet 'glorious' agreeing with the preceding 'Child of Zeus.' The word ὅπλα means 'gear' or 'tackle' as much as 'armour,' though we are accustomed to translate it as 'armour' in St Paul's phrases, 'the armour of righteousness,' 'the armour of light.' It is the language of symbolism. The spiritual 'armour of memory' is typified by, or even identified with, the magic gear of the charlatan.

If the mutilated condition of tablet VII, the illegible character of IV and the express statement of VIII are evidence of the lower, the magical side of Orphism, the complete text of tablets V and VI are the expression of its highest faith, of a faith so high that it may be questioned whether any faith, ancient or modern, has ever out-passed it.

Tablets V and VI both begin with a prayer or rather a claim addressed to the queen of the underworld, later defined as Phersephoneia or Despoina, and to two gods called Eukles and Eubouleus. The two are manifestly different titles of the same divinity. Eukles, 'Glorious One,' is only known to us from a gloss in Hesychius[1], who defines it as a euphemism for Hades. Eubouleus, 'He of good Counsel,' the local hero and underworld divinity of Eleusis, the equivalent of Plouton, occurs frequently in the Orphic Hymns as an epithet of Dionysos[2]. Eukles and Eubouleus are in fact only titles of the one god of Orphism who appears under many forms, as Hades, Zagreus, Phanes and the like. The gist of this monotheism will fall to be discussed when we come to the theogony of Orpheus (Chap. XII.). For the present it is sufficient to state that the Eukles-Eubouleus of the tablets, whom the Orphic invokes, is substantially the same as the Zagreus to whom the Cretan Orphic (p. 479) was initiated. To the names named, i.e. the Queen of the Underworld, Eukles and Eubouleus, the Orphic adds 'the other gods and daemons.' This is a somewhat magical touch. The ancient worshipper was apt to end his prayer with some such formulary; it was dangerous to leave any one out. The word δαίμονες, daemons or subordinate spirits, is significant at once of the lower, the magical side of Orphism, and as will be seen later (p. 655) of its higher spirituality. Orphism tended rather to the worship of potencies (δαίμονες) than of anthropomorphic divinities (θεοί).

The Orphic then proceeds to state the general basis of his claim: he is of divine birth,

'For I also avow me that I am of your blessed race.'

By this he means, as has been shown in examining the legend of Zagreus, that some portion of the god Zagreus or Eubouleus or whatever he be called was in him; his fathers the Titans had eaten the god and he sprang from their ashes. That this is the meaning of the tablets is quite clear from the words

'But Fate laid me low...starflung thunderbolt.'

He identifies himself with the whole human race as 'dead in trespasses and sins.' If this were all, his case were hopeless; 'dust we are and unto dust we must return.' He urges at the outset another claim,

'Out of the pure I come.'

1 Hesych. s.v. Εὐκλῆς.
2 *Orph. Hymn.* XXX. 6, 7, and see Abel, *Orphica* s.v.

That is, as an Orphic I am purified by the ceremonials of the Orphics. He presents as it were his certificate of spiritual health, he is free from all contagion of evil. 'Bearer is certified pure, coming from a congregation of pure people.' In like fashion in the Egyptian *Book of the Dead* (No. CXXV.) after the long negative confession made to Osiris the soul says, 'I am pure,' 'I am pure,' 'I am pure,' 'I am pure.' He then proceeds to recite his creed, or rather in ancient fashion[1] to confess or acknowledge the ritual acts he has performed. The gist of them each and all is, 'Bad have I fled, better have I found,' or as we should put it, 'I have passed from death unto life.' He does not himself say, I am a god—that might be overbold—but the answer he looks for comes clear and unmistakeable,

'Happy and Blessed One, thou shalt be God instead of mortal.'

The confession he makes of ritual acts is so instructive as to his convictions, so expresses his whole attitude towards religion that it must be examined sentence by sentence.

I say advisedly confession of *ritual acts*, because each of the little sentences describes in the past tense an action performed, 'I have escaped,' 'I have set my feet,' 'I have crept,' 'I have fallen.' These several acts described are, I believe, statements of actual ritual performed on earth by the Orphic candidate for initiation, and in the fact that they have been performed lies his certainty of ultimate bliss. They are the exact counterpart of the ancient Eleusinian confession formularies, 'I have fasted, I have drunk the *kykeon*' (p. 154).

THE RITUAL FORMULARIES.

The first article in the creed or confession of the Orphic soul is

κύκλου δ' ἐξέπταν βαρυπενθέος ἀργαλέοιο.
'I have flown out of the sorrowful weary Wheel.'

The notion of existence as a Wheel, a cycle of life upon life ceaselessly revolving, in which the soul is caught, from the tangle

[1] In magical papyri the utterance of certain σύμβολα or tokens is urged as a plea for acceptance:

νεῦσον ἐμοί, λίτομαι, ὅτι σύμβολα μυστικὰ φράζω.

See Dieterich, *Abraxas*, p. 97.

and turmoil of which it seeks and at last finds rest, is familiar to us from the symbolism of Buddha. Herodotus[1] expressly says that the Egyptians were the first to assert that the soul of man was immortal, born and reborn in various incarnations, and this doctrine he adds was borrowed from the Egyptians by the Greeks. To Plato[2] it was already 'an ancient doctrine that the souls of men that come Here are from There and that they go There again and come to birth from the dead.' It was indeed a very ancient saying or doctrine. It has already been observed in discussing (p. 179) the mythology of the Keres and Tritopatores. Orpheus took it as he took so many ancient things that lay to his hand, and moralized it. Rebirth, reincarnation, became for him *new* birth. The savage logic which said that life could only come from life, that new souls are old souls reborn in endless succession, was transformed by him into a Wheel or cycle of ceaseless purgation. So long as man has not severed completely his brotherhood with plants and animals, not realized the distinctive marks and attributes of his humanity, he will say with Empedocles[3]:

> 'Once on a time a youth was I, and I was a maiden,
> A bush, a bird, and a fish with scales that gleam in the ocean.'

To Plato the belief in the rebirth of old souls was 'an ancient doctrine,' but because the Orphics gave it a new mystical content the notion was for the most part fathered on Orpheus or Pythagoras. Diogenes Laertius[4], who is concerned to glorify Pythagoras, said that he was the first to assert that 'the soul went round in a changing Wheel of necessity, being bound down now in this now in that animal.' A people who saw in a chance snake the soul of a hero would have no difficulty in formulating a doctrine of metempsychosis. They need not have borrowed it from Egypt, and yet it is probable that the influence of Egypt, the home of animal worship, helped out the doctrine by emphasizing the sanctity of animal life. The almost ceremonial tenderness shown to animals by the Pythagorean Orphics is an Egyptian rather than a Greek characteristic. The notion of kinship with

[1] Herod. II. 122.

[2] Plat. *Phaedo*, 70 C. Plato may have had some Orphic rite vaguely in his mind in the *Phaedrus*. The soul escapes by wings from the inside of the sphere into heavenly places (248 C).

[3] Emped. ap. Diog. Laert. VII. 77.

[4] Diog. Laert. VII. 12.

the brute creation harmonized well with the somewhat elaborate and self-conscious humility of the Orphic.

What precisely the ritual of the Wheel was we do not know. That there was an actual Wheel[1] in the rites and that some form of symbolical release was enacted is probable. It is indeed almost certain, as we know that Wheels formed part of the sacred furniture of certain sanctuaries. It is worth noting that on Orphic vases of Lower Italy to be discussed later (p. 599) wheels are suspended in the palace of Hades and Persephone, and these are of two kinds, solid and spoked, designed probably for quite different uses. The grammarian Dionysios, surnamed the Thracian, wrote a book on 'The Interpretation of the Symbolism that has to do with Wheels,' which probably contained just the necessary missing information. Clement[2] has preserved for us one valuable sentence which makes the ritual use of Wheels a certainty. 'People signify actions,' he says, 'not only by words but by symbols, by words as in the case of the Delphic utterances "Nothing too much" and "Know thyself," and in like manner by symbols as in the case of the Wheel that is turned round in the precincts of the gods and that was derived from the Egyptians.' Dionysios is probably right. The Wheel like the Well may have come from Egypt, or from Egyptianized Crete.

Hero of Alexandria[3] in his curious treatise on 'Machines moved by air' twice mentions Wheels as in ritual use. 'In Egyptian sanctuaries there are Wheels of bronze against the door-posts, and they are moveable so that those who enter may set them in motion, because of the belief that bronze purifies; and there are vessels for purifying so that those who enter may

[1] The *κύκλος* of the rites was probably a real wheel, but it is also possible that it was a circle drawn round the neophyte out of which he escaped. Psellus (*περὶ δαιμόνων*) records an old Bacchic rite in which demons were expelled by the action of leaping out of a circle of fire: *πυρὰ δὲ πολλὰ κύκλῳ τινὶ περιγράφοντες ἐξάλλονται τῆς φλογός. ἦν δὲ καὶ τοῦτο τῆς παλαιᾶς βακχείας, ἵνα μὴ λέγω μανίας μέρος...ὁ δέ γε κύκλος κατοχῆς ἔχει δύναμιν.* The wheel and the magic mesmeric circle may have got 'contaminated.'

[2] Clem. Alex. *Strom.* v. p. 242, *διὰ δὲ συμβόλων, ὡς ὅ τε τροχὸς ὁ στρεφόμενος ἐν τοῖς τῶν θεῶν τεμένεσιν εἱλκυσμένος παρὰ Αἰγυπτίων.*

I have throughout translated *κύκλος* by wheel. The same idea is rendered indifferently by *τροχός* and *κύκλος*, though *κύκλος* occurs more frequently: cf. Proclus, *ad Tim.* p. 330 A, *κύκλος τῆς γενέσεως, ἐν τῷ τῆς εἱμαρμένης...τροχῷ.* The same thing is in English a 'cycle,' in American a 'wheel.' In the Orphic Hades of Vergil the *κύκλος* is a *rota*.

[3] Hero Alex. *Pneum.* I. 32 and II. 32, *θησαυροῦ κατασκευὴ τροχὸν ἔχοντος στρεφόμενον χάλκεον ὃς καλεῖται ἁγνιστήριον.*

purify themselves. The problem is how to arrange so that when the Wheel is turned the water may flow mechanically so that as aforesaid it may be sprinkled for purifying.' The problem which Hero faced mechanically the Orphics solved in metaphor—how to connect the Wheel with purification. It was not difficult. Bronze, as Hero notes, was supposed to be a purifier; in another section he says the Wheel was actually called *Hagnisterion*, the thing for purification. Each metal when first it comes into use is regarded as having magical properties. A resonant metal was of special use because it frightened away bogeys. Simaetha[1] in her incantations cries

> 'The goddess at the Crossways. Sound the gong'

and the scholiast on the passage remarks instructively that bronze was sounded at eclipses of the moon, inasmuch as it was held to be pure and to have the power of warding off pollutions, and he quotes the treatise of Apollodorus 'Concerning the Gods' as his authority for the statement that bronze was in use in all kinds of consecration and purification. It was appropriate to the dead, he adds, and at Athens the Hierophant beats a gong when Kore is invoked.

Here again we have a primitive superstition ready to the hand of the Orphic. He is familiar with bronze-beating as a piece of apotropaic ritual; he sees, probably in an Egyptian temple, a bronze wheel known by some name that he translates as 'a thing for purifying'; he has a doctrine of metempsychosis and an ardent longing after purification; he puts them all together and says with Proclus[2] the one salvation offered by the creator is that the spirit free itself from the wheel of birth. 'This is what those who are initiated by Orpheus to Dionysos and Kore pray that they may attain, to

> "Cease from the Wheel and breathe again from ill."'

The notion of escape whether from the tomb of the body, or from the restless Wheel or from the troubled sea, haunts the

[1] Theocr. II. 36 schol. *διόπερ πρὸς πᾶσαν ἀφοσίωσιν καὶ ἀποκάθαρσιν αὐτῷ ἐχρῶντο ὥς φησι καὶ Ἀπολλόδωρος ἐν τῷ περὶ θεῶν.* For a full discussion of the apotropaic uses of bronze gongs see Mr A. B. Cook, 'The Gong at Dodona,' *J.H.S.* vol. XXII. 1902, p. 5.

[2] Procl. in Plat. *Tim.* v. 330, *ἧς καὶ οἱ παρ' Ὀρφεῖ τῷ Διονύσῳ καὶ τῇ Κόρῃ τελούμενοι τυχεῖν εὔχονται·*

Κύκλου τ' αὖ λῆξαι καὶ ἀναπνεῦσαι κακότητος.

Orphic, haunts Plato, haunts Euripides, lends him lovely metaphors of a fawn escaped, makes his Bacchants sing[1],

> 'Happy he, on the weary sea
> Who hath fled the tempest and won the haven.
> Happy whoso hath risen free
> Above his striving.'

The downward steps from purification to penance, from penance to vindictive punishment, were easy to take and swiftly taken. Plato, in the vision of Er, though he knows of purification, is not free from this dismal and barren eschatology of vengeance and retribution. On Lower Italy vases under Orphic influence, as will later be seen (p. 605), great Ananke, Necessity herself, is made to hold a scourge and behave like a Fury. That such notions were not alien to Orphism is clear from the line in tablet VI:

> 'I have paid the penalty for deeds unrighteous.'

The deeds unrighteous are not only the soul's own personal sins but his hereditary taint, the 'ancient woe' that is his as the heir of the earth-born Titans.

The next avowal is

> ἱμερτοῦ δ' ἐπέβαν στεφάνου ποσὶ καρπαλίμοισι.
> 'I have passed with eager feet to the Circle desired.'

It occurs in a second form, thus:

> ἱμερτοῦ δ' ἀπέβαν στεφάνου ποσὶ καρπαλίμοισι.
> 'I have passed with eager feet *from* the Circle desired.'

It is impossible to say which form is correct. It may be that both were indispensable, that the neophyte had to pass first *into* and then *out of* a ring or circle.

The word ἐπιβαίνω (I step on or over) is of course frequently used metaphorically with the meaning 'I entered on, embarked on.' It might therefore be possible to translate the words as 'with eager feet I entered on, i.e. I obtained, the crown I longed for.' But as the word στέφανος means not only a crown for the head, but a ring or circle, a thing that encloses, it is perhaps better to take it here in its wider sense[2]. The mystic has escaped

[1] Eur. *Bacch.* 901.

[2] Dr Dieterich in his valuable tract *De Hymnis Orphicis capitula quinque* says (p. 55): στέφανος est qui cingit loca beatorum, vel prata illa ipsa desiderata. Simili notione vox στέφανος usurpatur in Orphicorum Argonauticorum versu 71

> αὐτίκα οἱ στέφανος καὶ τεῖχος ἐρυμνὸν
> Αἰητέω κατέφαινε καὶ ἄλσεα.

His interpretation suggested that given in the text, though the two are not identical.

from the Wheel of Purgation, he passes with eager feet over the Ring or circle that includes the bliss he longs for, he enters and perhaps passes out of some sort of sacred enclosure. As to the actual rite performed we are wholly in the dark. Possibly the innermost shrine was garlanded about with mystic magical flowers. This is however pure conjecture. We know[1] that the putting on of garlands or *στέμματα* was the final stage of initiation for Hierophants and other priests, a stage that was as it were Consecration and Ordination in one; but the putting on of garlands is not the entering of a garlanded enclosure, and it is the entering of an enclosure that the 'eager feet' seem to imply.

Next comes the clause,

δεσποίνας δ' ὑπὸ κόλπον ἔδυν χθονίας βασιλείας.
'I have sunk beneath the bosom of Despoina, Queen of the Underworld.'

That this clause is an avowal of an actual rite performed admits of no doubt. It is the counterpart of the 'token' of the mysteries of the Mother: 'I have passed down into the bridal-chamber,' but here the symbolism seems to be rather of birth than marriage. In discussing the ritual of the Semnae (p. 244), it has been seen that the 'second-fated man' had to be reborn before he could be admitted to the sanctuary, and the rebirth was a mimetic birth[2]. The same ceremony was gone through among some peoples at adoption[3]. Dionysos himself in Orphic hymns is called *ὑποκόλπιε*, 'he who is beneath the bosom.' If the rites are enumerated in the order of their performance this rite of birth or adoption must have taken place *within* the Circle, after the entrance *into* and before the exit *from*.

In the highest grades of initiation not only was there a new birth but also a new name given, a beautiful custom still preserved in the Roman Church. Lucian[4] makes Lexiphanes tell of a man called Deinias, who was charged with the crime of having addressed the Hierophant and the Dadouchos by name, 'and that when he

[1] Theo. Smyrn. *Mathem.* I. p. 18, τετάρτη δὲ ὃ δὴ καὶ τέλος τῆς ἐποπτείας ἀνάδεσις καὶ στεμμάτων ἐπίθεσις...δᾳδουχίας τυχόντα ἢ ἱεροφαντίας ἢ τινος ἄλλης ἱεροσύνης.

[2] Hesych. s.v. δευτερόποτμος· ἢ ὁ δεύτερον διὰ γυναικείου κόλπου διαδύς· ὡς ἔθος ἦν παρὰ Ἀθηναίοις ἐκ δευτέρου γεννᾶσθαι.

[3] Diod. IV. 39.

[4] Luc. *Lexiph.* 10, καὶ ταῦτα εὖ εἰδὼς ὅτι ἐξ οὗπερ ὡσιώθησαν ἀνώνυμοί τέ εἰσι καὶ οὐκέτι ὀνομαστοὶ ὡς ἂν ἱερώνυμοι ἤδη γεγενημένοι. ὡσιώθησαν here clearly marks the final stage of initiation only open to priests: it is practically 'ordination.'

well knew that from the time they are consecrated they are nameless and can no longer be named, on the supposition that they have from that time holy names.'

The last affirmation of the mystic is

ἔριφος ἐς γάλ' ἔπετον,
'A kid I have fallen into milk,'

a sentence which occurred, it will be remembered, in the second person, on tablet III.

The quaint little formulary is simple almost to fatuity. Mysticism, in its attempt to utter the ineffable, often verges on imbecility.

Before we attempt to determine the precise nature of the ritual act performed, it may be well to consider the symbolism of the kid and the milk. It is significant that in both cases the formulary occurs immediately after another statement:

'Thou shalt be God instead of mortal.'

It would seem that about the kid there is something divine. Eriphos according to Hesychius[1] was a title of Dionysos. Stephanus[2] the Byzantine says that Dionysos bore the title Eriphios among the Metapontians, i.e. in the very neighbourhood where these Orphic tablets were engraved. It is clear that there was not only a Bull-Dionysos (Eiraphiotes) but a Kid-Dionysos (Eriphos), and this was just the sort of title that the Orphics would be likely to seize on and mysticize. In the *Bacchae* it has been seen (p. 445) that there seems to attach a sort of special sanctity to young wild things, a certain mystic symbolism about the fawn escaped, and the nursing mothers who suckle the young of wolves and deer. It may be that each one thought her nursling was a Baby-God. Christian children to this day are called Christ's Lambs because Christ is the Lamb of God, and Clement[3] joining new and old together says: 'This is the mountain beloved of God, not the place of tragedies like Cithaeron but consecrated to the dramas of truth, a mount of

[1] Hesych. s.v. Ἔριφος· Διόνυσος.

[2] Steph. Byz. s.v. Διόνυσος· Ἐρίφιος παρὰ Μεταποντίοις.

[3] Clem. Al. *Protr.* XII. 119, βακχεύουσι δὲ ἐν αὐτῷ οὐχ αἱ Σεμέλης τῆς κεραυνίας ἀδελφαὶ αἱ μαινάδες αἱ δύσαγνον κρεανομίαν μυούμεναι ἀλλὰ τοῦ θεοῦ θυγατέρες αἱ ἀμνάδες αἱ καλαὶ τὰ σεμνὰ τοῦ λόγου θεσπίζονται ὄργια χορὸν ἐγείρουσαι σώφρονα.

sobriety shaded with the woods of purity. And there revel on it not the Maenads, sisters of Semele the thunderstruck, initiated in the impure feast of flesh, but the daughters of God, fair Lambs who celebrate the holy rites of the Word, raising a sober choral chant.'

The initiated then believed himself new born as a young divine animal, as a kid, one of the god's many incarnations; and as a kid he falls into milk. Milk was a god-given drink before the coming of wine, and the Epiphany of Dionysos was shown not only by wine but by milk and honey[1]:

> 'Then streams the earth with milk, yea streams
> With wine and honey of the bee.'

Out on the mountain of Cithaeron he gives his Maenads draughts of miraculous wine, and also[2]

> 'If any lips
> Sought whiter draughts, with dipping finger-tips
> They pressed the sod, and gushing from the ground
> Came springs of milk. And reed-wands ivy-crowned
> Ran with sweet honey.'

The symbolism of honey, the nectar of gods and men, does not here concern us, but it is curious to note how honey, used in ancient days to embalm the dead body, became the symbol of eternal bliss. A sepulchral inscription of the first century A.D. runs as follows[3]:

> 'Here lies Boethos Muse-bedewed, undying
> Joy hath he of sweet sleep in honey lying.'

Boethos lies in honey, the mystic falls into milk, both are symbols taken from the ancient ritual of the *Nephalia* and mysticized.

The question remains—what was the exact ritual of the falling into milk? The ritual formulary is not ἔπιον γάλα 'I *drank* milk,' but ἔπετον ἐς γάλα 'I *fell into* milk.' Did the neophyte actually fall into[4] a bath of milk, or, as in the case of 'I stepped on the

[1] Eur. *Bacch.* 142. [2] Eur. *Bacch.* 706.

[3] O. Benndorf, *Grabschrift von Telmessos* (Sonderabdruck aus der Festschrift für Th. Gomperz), p. 404:

> '῞Ενθα Βόηθος ἀνὴρ μουσόρρυτος ὕπνον ἰαύει
> αἰῶνος γλυκερῷ κείμενος ἐν μέλιτι.'

[4] M. Salomon Reinach ('Une formule Orphique,' *Rev. Arch.* XXXIX. 1901, p. 202) takes πίπτειν ἐς to be metaphorical and compares *incidere in* and the French *tomber sur*. But the division of verb and preposition and the fact that the sentence is a religious formulary are against this light colloquial sense. If the expression

crown I longed for,' is the ritual act of drinking milk from the beginning metaphorically described? The question unhappily cannot with certainty be decided. The words 'I fell into milk' are not even exactly what we should expect if a rite of Baptism were described; of a rite of immersion in milk we have no evidence.

It is however from primitive rites of Baptism that we get most light as to the general symbolism of the formulary. In the primitive Church the sacrament of Baptism was immediately followed by Communion. The custom is still preserved among the Copts[1]. The neophyte drank not only of wine but also of a cup of milk and honey mixed[2], those 'new born in Christ' partook of the food of babes. Our Church has severed Communion from Baptism and lost the symbolism of milk and honey, nor does she any longer crown her neophytes after Baptism[3].

S. Jerome[4] complains in Protestant fashion that much was done in the Church of his days from tradition that had not really the sanction of Holy Writ. This tradition which the early Church so wisely and beautifully followed can only have come from pagan sources. Among the unsanctioned rites S. Jerome mentions the cup of milk and honey. That the cup of milk and honey was pagan we know from a beautiful prescription preserved in one of the magic papyri[5] in which the worshipper is thus instructed: 'Take the honey with the milk, drink of it before the rising of the sun, and there shall be in thy heart something that is divine.'

is metaphorical it has a close analogy in *πίπτειν ἐς γένεσιν*. Porphyry says (*De Antr. Nymph.* 13) of the souls *ὅταν ἐς γένεσιν πέσωσιν*. It may I think be worth noting that in Egypt, when the soles of the feet (of the mummy) which had trodden the mire of earth were removed, the gods were prayed to grant milk to the Osiris that he might bathe his feet in it. See Wiedemann, *Ancient Egyptian Doctrine of Immortality*, p. 48.

[1] Usener, 'Milch und Honig,' *Rhein. Mus.* 1902, Heft 2, p. 177.

[2] Tertull. *de corona militis* 3: dehinc ter mergitamur...unde suscepti lactis et mellis concordiam praegustamus.

[3] For a full account of the complex and beautiful ceremony of primitive Baptism see *Didaskaliae fragmenta Veronensia latina*, ed. Ettauler (Lips. 1900), pp. 111—113, and E. Trumpf, *Abh. d. philos.-philol. Cl. der K. Bayer. Ak. d. Wiss.* XIV. 3, p. 180.

[4] S. Hieron. *Altercat. Lucif. et orthodox.* c. 8, t. 11, p. 180e: 'nam et multa alia quae per traditionem in ecclesiis observantur auctoritatem sibi scriptae legis usurpaverunt, velut in lavacro ter caput mergitare deinde egresso lactis et mellis praegustare concordiam.

[5] 'Berliner Zauber-papyrus,' *Abh. d. Berl. Akad.* 1865, p. 120. 20: *καὶ λαβὼν τὸ γάλα σὺν τῷ (μέλι)τι ἀπόπιε πρὶν ἀνατολῆς ἡλίου καὶ ἔσται τι ἔνθεον ἐν τῇ σῇ καρδίᾳ.*

The milk and honey can be materialized into a future 'happy land' flowing with milk and honey, but the promise of the magical papyrus is the utmost possible guerdon of present spiritual certainty. We find in every sacrament what we bring.

If the formularies inscribed on the tablets have been actually recited while the Orphic was alive we naturally ask—When and at what particular Mysteries? To this question no certain answer can be returned. Save for one instance,

'I have sunk beneath the bosom of Despoina, Queen of the Underworld,'

the formularies of the tablets bear no analogy either to the tokens of Eleusis or to those of the Great Mother. The Greater Mysteries at Eleusis were preceded, we know, by Lesser Mysteries celebrated at Agra[1], a suburb of Athens. These mysteries were sacred to Dionysos and Kore rather than to Demeter, and it is noticeable that in the tablets there is no mention of Demeter, no trace of agricultural intent; the whole gist is eschatological. But, found as they are in Crete and Lower Italy, it is more probable that these tablets refer to Orphic mysteries pure and simple before Orphic rites have blended with those of the Wine-God. Pythagoras, tradition[2] says, was initiated in Crete; he met there 'one of the Idaean Daktyls and at their hands was purified by a thunderbolt; he lay from dawn outstretched face-foremost by the sea and by night lay near a river covered with fillets from the fleece of a black lamb, and he went down into the Idaean cave holding black wool and spent there the accustomed thrice nine hallowed days and beheld the seat bedecked every year for Zeus, and he engraved an inscription about the tomb with the title "Pythagoras to Zeus" of which the beginning is:

"Here in death lies Zan, whom they call Zeus,"

and after his stay in Crete he went to Italy and settled in Croton.'

The story looks as if Pythagoras had brought to Italy from Crete Orphic rites in all their primitive freshness. The religion

[1] Steph. Byz. s.v. Ἄγρα· χωρίον...πρὸ τῆς πόλεως ἐν ᾗ τὰ μικρὰ μυστήρια ἐπιτελεῖται μίμημα τῶν περὶ τὸν Διόνυσον. These Lesser Mysteries were celebrated in the month Anthesterion sacred to Dionysos, see p. 559. For Persephone see Schol. Ar. *Plut.* 845, ἦσαν δὲ τὰ μὲν μεγάλα τῆς Δήμητρος τὰ δὲ μικρὰ Περσεφόνης.

[2] Porphyr. *Vit. Pythag.* 17.

of Dionysos was not the only faith that taught man he could become a god. The Egyptian also believed that when dead he could become Osiris. The Orphic in Crete and Lower Italy may have had rites dealing with his conduct in the next world more directly than those of the Great Mother or of Eleusis.

This is made the more probable from the fact that we certainly know that the sect of the Pythagoreans had special burial rites, strictly confined to the initiated. Of this Plutarch[1] incidentally gives clear evidence in his discourse of 'The Daemon of Socrates.' A young Pythagorean, Lysis, came to Thebes and died there and was buried by his Theban friends. His ghost appeared in a dream to the Pythagorean friends he had left in Italy. The Pythagoreans, more skilled in these matters than modern psychical experts, had a certain sign by which they knew the apparition of a dead man from the phantasm of the living. They got anxious as to how Lysis had been buried, for 'there is something special and sacrosanct (*ὅσιον*) that takes place at the burial of the Pythagoreans and is peculiar to them, and if they do not attain this rite they think that they will fail in reaching the very happy end that is proper to them.' So concerned were some of the Pythagoreans that they wished to have the body of Lysis disinterred and brought to Italy to be reburied. Accordingly one of them, Theanor, started for Thebes to make enquiries as to what had been done. He was directed by the people of the place to the tomb and went in the evening to offer libations, and he invoked the soul of Lysis to give inspired direction as to what was to be done. 'As the night went on,' Theanor recounts, 'I saw nothing, but I thought I heard a voice say "Move not that which should not be moved," for the body of Lysis was buried by his friends with sacrosanct ceremonies (*ὁσίως*), and his spirit is already separated from it and set free into another birth, having obtained a share in another spirit.' On enquiry next morning Theanor found that Lysis had imparted to a friend all the secret of the mysteries so that the funeral rites had been performed after Pythagorean fashion.

What precisely the *ὅσια*, the sacrosanct rites, were we cannot

[1] Plut. *de Gen. Socr.* XVI. *ἔστι γάρ τι γενόμενον ἰδίᾳ περὶ τὰς ταφὰς τῶν Πυθαγορικῶν ὅσιον οὗ μὴ τυχόντες οὐ δοκοῦμεν ἀπέχειν τὸ μακαριστὸν καὶ οἰκεῖον τέλος...ὁσίως γὰρ ὑπὸ τῶν φίλων κεκηδεῦσθαι τὸ Λύσιδος σῶμα.*

in detail say, but we may be tolerably sure that something special was done for the man who had been finally initiated, who was like the Cretan mystic ὁσιωθείς, 'consecrated.' This something may have included the burial with his body of tablets inscribed with sentences from his 'Book of the Dead.' This I think is implied in a familiar passage of Plato. Socrates in the *Phaedo*[1] says that 'the journey to Hades does not seem to him a simple road like that described by Aeschylus in the *Telephos*. On the contrary it is neither simple nor one. If it were there would be no need of guides. But it appears in point of fact to have many partings of the ways and circuits. And this,' he adds, 'I say conjecturing it from the customary and sacrosanct (ὁσίων) rites which we observe in this world.' The customary rites (νόμιμα) were for each and all; the sacrosanct rites (ὅσια) were for the initiated only, for they only were sacrosanct (ὅσιοι).

The Pythagoreans we know revived the custom of burial in the earth, which had been at least in part superseded by the Northern practice of cremation. It was part of their general return to things primitive. Earth was the kingdom of 'Despoina, Queen of the underworld,' who was more to them than Zeus of the upper air. To their minds bent on symbolism burial itself would be a consecration, they would remember that to the Athenians the dead were Δημητρεῖοι[2], Demeter's people, that burial was refused to the traitor because he was unworthy 'to be consecrated by earth[3],' and burial in itself may well have been to them as to Antigone a mystic marriage:

'I have sunk beneath the bosom of Despoina, Queen of the Underworld.'

b. Orphic Vases of Lower Italy.

Orphic religion, as seen on the tablets just discussed, is singularly free from 'other-worldliness.' It is a religion promising, indeed, immortality, but instinct not so much with the hope of future rewards as with the ardent longing after perfect purity; it is concerned with the state of a soul rather than with its circum-

[1] Plat. *Phaedo*, 108 A, ἀπὸ τῶν ὁσίων τε καὶ νομίμων τῶν ἐνθάδε.
[2] Plut. *de fac. in orb. lun.* XXVIII.
[3] Philostr. *Her.* 714, ὠμὸν γὰρ τὸ ἐπ' αὐτῷ κήρυγμα· μὴ γὰρ θάπτειν τὸν Παλαμήδην μηδὲ ὁσιοῦν τῇ γῇ.

stances. We have the certainty of beatitude for the initiated, the 'seats of the blessed,' the 'groves of Phersephoneia,' but the longing uttered is ecstatic, mystic not sensuous; it is summed up in the line:

'Happy and Blessed One, thou shalt be God instead of mortal.'

None knew better than the Orphic himself that this was only for the few: 'Many are they that carry the narthex, few are they that are made one with Bacchus.' For the many there remained other and lower beatitudes, there remained also—a thing wholly absent from the esoteric Orphic doctrine—the fear of punishment, punishment conceived not as a welcome purification, but as a fruitless, endless vengeance. Of the existence of this lower faith or rather *un*faith in the popular forms of Orphism we have definite and curious evidence from a class of vases, found in Lower Italy, representing scenes in the underworld and obviously designed under Orphic influence.

Two specimens[1] of these 'Apulian' vases are given in figs. 161 and 162. It will be obvious at the first glance that the composition of both designs is substantially the same. This need not oblige us to conjecture any one great work of art of which these two and the other designs not figured here are copies; it only shows that some vase-painter of note in the 4th century B.C. conceived the scheme and it became popular in his factory.

The main lines of both compositions are as follows: in the centre the palace of Hades with Plouton and Persephone. Immediately below, and also occupying a central position, is Herakles, carrying off Cerberus. Immediately to the left of the temple and therefore also fairly central, is the figure of Orpheus. About these central figures various groups of criminals and other denizens of Hades are diversely arrayed.

With this scheme in our minds we may examine the first specimen, the most important of the series, because inscribed. The vase itself, now in the Naples Museum and usually known from the place where it was found as the 'Altamura' vase[2], is in a disastrous

[1] The whole series is published in the *Wiener Vorlegeblätter*, Serie E, Taf. I—VII.

[2] Heydemann, *Cat.* 3222. *Wiener Vorlegeblätter*, Serie E, Taf. II. This vase was carefully examined by Dr Studniczka in 1887. On his report is based the full discussion by Dr Winkler, 'Unter-italische Unterweltsdarstellungen,' *Breslauer Philolog. Abhandlungen*, Band III. Heft 5, 1888. I verified Dr Studniczka's report

condition. It was put together out of hundreds of fragments, painted over and freely restored after the fashion of the day, and it has never yet been subjected to a proper chemical cleaning. Much therefore in the drawing remains uncertain, and only such parts and inscriptions will be dealt with as are above suspicion.

The palace of Hades, save for the suspended wheels (p. 590), presents no features of interest. In the 'Altamura' vase many of its architectural features are from the hand of the restorer, but from the other vases the main outlines are sure. In the Altamura

Fig. 161.

vase both Hades and Persephone are seated—in the others sometimes Persephone, sometimes Plouton occupies the throne. Had the designs been exclusively inspired by Orphic tradition, more uniform stress would probably have been laid on Persephone.

The figure of Orpheus, common to both vases, is interesting from its dress, which reminds us of Virgil's[1] description,

'There too the Thracian priest in trailing robe.'

The vase-painter of the late 4th cent. B.C. was more archaeologist than patriot. In the Lesche picture of Polygnotus, Pausanias[2]

of the inscriptions in 1902. Nothing further can be done till the vase is properly cleaned, and, now that the Naples Museum is under new direction, this, it may be hoped, will be done.

[1] Virg. *Aen.* VI. 644.

[2] P. X. 30. 6.

expressly notes that Orpheus was 'Greek in appearance,' and that neither his dress nor the covering he had on his head was Thracian. The Orpheus of Polygnotus must have been near akin to the beautiful Orpheus of the vase-painter in fig. 140. Polygnotus, too, made him 'seated as it were on a sort of hill, and grasping his cithara with his left hand; with the other he was touching some

FIG. 162.

sprays of willow, and he leant against a tree.' Very different this from the frigid ritual priest.

About this figure of Orpheus an amazing amount of nonsense has been written. The modern commentator thinks of Orpheus as two things—as magical musician, which he *was*, as passionate lover, which in early days he was *not*. The commentator's mind is obsessed by 'Che farò senza te, Eurydice?' He asks himself the question, 'Why has Orpheus descended into Hades?' and the answer rises automatically, 'To fetch Eurydice.' As regards these Lower Italy vases there is one trifling objection to this interpretation, and that is that *there is no Eurydice*. Tantalos, Sisyphos, Danaides, Herakles, but no Eurydice. This does not deter the commentator. The figure of Eurydice is 'inferred rather than expressed.' Happily this line of interpretation, which might lead us far, has been put an end to by the discovery of a vase in which Eurydice *does* appear; Orpheus leads her by the wrist and a love-god floats above. It is evident that when the vase-painter wishes to 'express' Eurydice he does not leave her to be 'inferred.'

It may be taken as an axiom in Greek mythology that passionate lovers are always late. The myth of Eurydice is of considerable interest, but not as a love-story. It is a piece of theology taken over from Dionysos, and, primarily, has nothing to do with Orpheus. Anyone who realizes Orpheus at all would feel that the intrusion of desperate emotion puts him out of key. Semele, the green earth, comes up from below, year by year; with her comes her son Dionysos, and by a certain instinct of chivalry men said he had gone to fetch her. The mantle of Dionysos descends on Orpheus.

Eurydice is one of those general, adjectival names that are appropriate to any and every goddess: she is the 'Wide-Ruler.' At Trozen, Pausanias[1] saw 'a Temple of Artemis the Saviour, and in it were altars of those gods who are said to rule below the earth, and they say that in this place Semele was brought up from Hades by Dionysos, and that here Herakles dragged up the hound of Hades.' Pausanias is sceptical: 'But I do not the least believe that Semele died, she who was the wife of Zeus, and as to the beast called the hound of Hades, I shall state what I am sure is the truth about him in another place.' The cult of Artemis is clearly superposed over an ancient, perhaps nameless, anyhow forgotten cult of underworld gods. There was probably a cleft at hand and a legend of a rising Earth-goddess, as at the rock of Recall, *Anaklethra* (p. 283), and the Smileless Rock at Eleusis (p. 127); and of course, given somebody's *Anodos*, a Kathodos is soon supplied, and then a formal descent into Hades. At the Alcyonian lake, near Argos, which Nero tried in vain to sound, the Argives told Pausanias[2] that Dionysos went down to Hades to fetch Semele, and Polymnos, a local hero, showed him the way down, and 'there were certain rites performed there yearly.' Unfortunately, as is mostly the case when he comes to the real point, Pausanias found it would 'not be pious' to reveal these rites to

[1] P. II. 31. 1.

[2] P. II. 37. 5.

the general public. At Delphi, too, it will be remembered (p. 402), the Thyiades knew the mystic meaning of the festival of Herois, and 'even an outsider could conjecture,' Plutarch says, 'from what was done, that it was an upbringing of Semele.'

Orpheus, priest of Dionysos, took on his resurrection as well as his death; that is the germ from which sprang the beautiful love-story. A taboo-element, common to many primitive stories, is easily added. You may not look back when spirits are about from the underworld. If you do you may have to join them. Underworld rites are often performed 'without looking back' (*ἀμεταστρεπτί*, see p. 24 note 2).

There is another current fallacy about these underworld vases. Commentators are not only prone to the romantic tendency to see a love-story where none is, but, having once got the magical musician into their minds, they see him everywhere. In these vases, they say, we have 'the power of music to stay the torments of hell.' They remember, and small wonder, the amazing scene in Gluck's opera, where Orpheus comes down into the shades playing on his lyre, and the clamour of hell is spell-bound; or they bethink them of Virgil:

> 'The very house itself, the inmost depths
> Of Death stood still to hearken.'

But the vase-painter of the 4th cent. B.C. is necessarily guiltless of Virgil as of Gluck. Moreover his work is untinged by any emotion, whether of poetry or religion; his composition is simply an *omnium gatherum* of conventional orthodox dwellers in Hades. Orpheus is there because, by that time, convention demanded his presence. The vase-painter's wealthy clients—these Apulian vases were as expensive as they are ugly—would have been ill-pleased had the founder of popular mysteries not had his fitting place. But if interest focusses anywhere in a design so scattered and devitalized, it is on the obvious 'record' of Herakles, who, tradition said, had been initiated, not on the secret magic of Orpheus. It is true that the 'Danaides,' when they appear, are doing nothing but dangling their pitchers in attitudes meant to be decorative, but Tantalos still extends a hand to keep off his rock, and Sisyphos still uprolls the 'pitiless' stone; there is no pause in their torments.

It remains to note the figures in the side groups. In the top row to the left are Megara and her sons, placed there by a pardonable anachronism, out of compliment to Herakles and Athens. We should never have guessed their names, but the inscriptions are certain. Opposite them to the right a group which on the Altamura vase is almost certainly due to restoration. The figures are Myrtilos, Pelops, and Hippodameia. To the left of Orpheus are two *Poinae*, developments, as has been seen (p. 231), of the tragic Erinyes. Above Sisyphos is another figure, a favourite of the Orphics, Ananke, Necessity. Only three letters (*ναν*) of the name remain, but the restoration is practically certain. Opposite Orpheus are the three 'Judges' of Hades, Triptolemos, Aiakos, Rhadamanthys. Below the Judges are women bearing water-vessels, to whom provisionally we may give the canonical name of 'Danaides.' The sea horse is probably due to the restorer.

Turning to the Canosa vase, now in the Old Pinakothek at Munich[1], we find that, though none of the figures are inscribed, most can easily be traced. Some modifications of the previous scheme must be noted. Tantalos the Phrygian takes the place of the Danaides. Near Orpheus, in place of the *Poinae*, is a group, man, wife and child, who are hard to interpret. No mythological figures quite suit them, and some authorities incline to see in the group just a human family initiated by Orpheus in his rites. In face of the fact that all the other figures present are mythological, this is, I think, difficult to accept. The figures are best left unnamed till further evidence comes to light. On the right hand, in the top row, is a group of great interest, Theseus, Peirithoös and Dike, armed with a sword.

To resume, we have as certain elements in these vases Orpheus, the three Judges of Hades, two heroes, Herakles and Theseus, who go down into Hades and return thence, two standard Homeric criminals, Sisyphos and Tantalos, and, in the case of the Altamura vase, the Danaides. The question naturally rises, is there in all these figures any common factor which determines their selection, or is it a mere haphazard aggregate?

The answer is as simple as instructive, and may be stated at the outset: *All the canonical denizens of the underworld are heroic*

[1] Jahn, *Cat.* 849. *Wiener Vorlegeblätter*, Serie E, Taf. I.

or divine figures of the older stratum of the population. Hades has become a sort of decent Lower-house to which are relegated the divinities of extinct or dying cults.

In discussing hero-worship, we have already seen (p. 335) that Tityos and Salmoneus are beings of this order. Once locally the rivals of Zeus, they paled before him, and as vanquished rivals became typical aggressors, punished for ever as a warning to the faithful. Tityos does not appear on Lower Italy vases, but Pausanias[1] saw him on the fresco of Polygnotus at Delphi, a 'dim and mangled spectre,' and Aeneas[2] in the underworld says:

'I saw Salmoneus cruel payment make,
For that he mocked the lightning and the thunder
Of Jove on high.'

It was an ingenious theological device, or rather perhaps unconscious instinct, that took these ancient hero figures, really regnant in the world below, and made the place of their rule the symbol of their punishment. According to the old faith all men, good and bad, went below the earth, great local heroes reigned below as they had reigned above; but the new faith sent its saints to a remote Elysium or to the upper air and made this underworld kingdom a place of punishment; and in that place significantly we find that the tortured criminals *are all offenders against Olympian Zeus.*

We must confine our examination to the two typical instances selected by the vase-painter, Sisyphos and Tantalos.

We are apt to think of Sisyphos and Tantalos as punished for overweening pride and insolence, and to regard their downfall as a warning of the ephemeral nature of earthly prosperity.

'Oh what are wealth and power! Tantalos
And Sisyphos were kings long years ago,
And now they lie in the lake dolorous;
The hills of hell are noisy with their woe,
Aye swift the tides of empire ebb and flow.'

Kings they were, but kings of the old discredited order. Homer says nothing of their crime, he takes it as known; but in dim local legends we can in both cases track out the real gist of their ill-doing: they were rebels against Zeus.

This is fairly clear in the case of Tantalos. According to one

[1] P. x. 29. 3. [2] Virg. *Aen.* VI. 585.

legend[1] he suffered because he either stole or concealed for Pandareos the golden hound of Zeus. According to the epic author[2] of the 'Return of the Atreidae,' he had been admitted to feast with the gods, and Zeus promised to grant him whatever boon he desired. 'He,' Athenaeus says, 'being a man insatiable in his desire for enjoyment, asked that he might have eternal remembrance of his joys and live after the same fashion as the gods.' Zeus was angry; he kept his promise, but added the torment of the imminent stone. It is clear that in some fashion Tantalos, the old hero-king, tried to make himself the equal of the new Olympians. The insatiable lust is added as a later justification of the vengeance. Tantalos is a real king, with a real grave. Pausanias[3] says, 'In my country there are still signs left that Pelops and Tantalos once dwelt there. There is a famous grave of Tantalos, and there is a lake called by his name. The grave, he says elsewhere[4], he had himself seen in Mount Sipylos, and 'well worth seeing it was.' He mentions no cult, but a grave so noteworthy would not be left untended.

The legend of Sisyphos, if more obscure than that of Tantalos, is not less instructive. The *Iliad* knows of Sisyphos as an ancient king. When Glaukos would tell his lineage to Diomede he says[5]:

> 'A city Ephyre there was in Argos' midmost glen
> Horse-rearing, there dwelt Sisyphos the craftiest of all men,
> Sisyphos son of Aiolos, and Glaukos was his son,
> And Glaukos had for offspring blameless Bellerophon.'

Ephyre is the ancient name of Corinth, and on Corinth Pausanias[6] in his discussion of the district has a highly significant note. He says, 'I do not know that anyone save the majority of the Corinthians themselves has ever seriously asserted that Corinthos was the son of Zeus.' He goes on to say that according to Eumelus (circ. B.C. 750), the 'first inhabitant of the land was Ephyra, daughter of Okeanos.' The meaning is transparent. An ancient pre-Achaean city, with an eponymous hero, a later attempt —discredited of all but the interested inhabitants—to affiliate the

[1] Schol. ad Pind. *Ol.* I. 89.
[2] Athen. VII. 14 p. 281. The sources for the punishment of Tantalos are fully collected by Dr Frazer ad Paus. x. 31.
[3] P. v. 13. 7.
[4] P. II. 22. 3.
[5] Hom. *Il.* VI. 152.
[6] P. II. 1. 1.

indigenous stock to the immigrant conquerors by a new eponymous hero, a son of Zeus.

The epithet 'craftiest,' κέρδιστος, is, as Eustathius[1] observes, a 'mid-way expression,' i.e. for better for worse. 'Glaukos,' he says in his observant way, 'does not wish to speak evil of his ancestor.' The word he uses means very clever (συνετώτατος), very ready and versatile (εὐτρεχέστατος). It is in fact no more an epithet of blame than πολύμητις, 'of many wiles,' the stock epithet of Odysseus. Eustathius goes on to explain the meaning of the name Sisyphos. Sisyphos, he says, was among the ancients a word of the same significance as θεόσοφος, divinely wise, σιός being among the Peloponnesians a form of θεός. He cites the oath used by comic poets, ναὶ τὼ σιώ for νὴ τοὺς θεούς, 'by the gods.' Whether Eustathius is right, and Sisyphos means 'divinely wise,' or whether we adopt the current etymology[2] and make Sisyphos a reduplicated form of σοφός, i.e. the 'Very Very Wise One,' thus much is clear. The title was traditionally understood as of praise rather than blame, and it is not rash to see in it one of the cultus epithets of the old religion like 'The Blameless One.'

It is as a benefactor that Sisyphos appears in local legend. It was Sisyphos, Pausanius[3] says, who found the child Melicertes, buried him, and instituted in his honour the Isthmian games. It was to Sisyphos that Asopos[4] gave the fountain behind the temple of Aphrodite, and for a reason most significant. 'Sisyphos,' the story says, 'knew that it was Zeus who had carried off Aegina, the daughter of Asopos, but he would not tell till the spring on Acrocorinthus was given him. Asopos gave it him, and then he gave information, and for that information he, if you like to believe it, paid the penalty in Hades.' Pausanias is manifestly sceptical, but his story touches the real truth. Sisyphos is the ally of the indigenous river Asopos. Zeus carries off the daughter of the neighbouring land; Sisyphos, hostile to the conqueror, gave information, and for that hostility he suffers in Hades. But though he points a moral in Olympian eschatology, he remains a great local power. The stronghold of the lower city bore his name, the Sisypheion. Diodorus[5] relates how it was besieged by Demetrius,

[1] Eustath. ad *Il.* vi. 153, 631 and ad *Od.* xi. 592, 1702.

[2] By substitution of the Aeolic υ for ο. See Vaniček, *Etym. Wörterbuch*, p. 592.

[3] P. ii. 1. 3.

[4] P. ii. 5. 1.

[5] Diod. xx. 103.

and when it was taken the garrison surrendered. It must have been a place of the old type, half fortress half sanctuary. Strabo[1] notes that in his day extensive ruins of white marble remained, and he is in doubt whether to call it temple or palace.

As to the particular punishment selected for Sisyphos, a word remains to be said. It bears no relation to his supposed offence, whether that offence be the cheating of Death or the betrayal of Zeus. His doom is ceaselessly to upheave a stone. Reluctant though I am to resort to sun-myths, it seems that here the sun counts for something. The sun was regarded by the sceptical as a large red-hot stone: its rising and setting might very fitly be represented as the heaving of such a stone up the steep of heaven, whence it eternally rolls back. The worship of Helios was established at Corinth[2]; whether it was due to Oriental immigration or to some pre-Hellenic stratum of population cannot here be determined. Sisyphos was a real king, the place of his sepulture on the Isthmus was known only to a few. It may have been kept secret like that of Neleus[3] for prophylactic purposes. But a real king may and often does take on some of the features and functions of a nature god[4].

On the 'Canosa' vase, immediately above Tantalos, is a group of three Judges, carrying sceptres. On the Altamura vase are also three Judges, occupying the same place in the composition, and happily they are inscribed—Triptolemos, Aiakos, and Rhadamanthys. Two of the three, Triptolemos and Aiakos, certainly belong to the earlier stratum.

Triptolemos had never even the shadowest connection with any Olympian system; there is no attempt to affiliate him; he ends as he began, the foster-child of Demeter and Kore, and by virtue of his connection with the 'Two Goddesses' of the underworld he reigns below. Demeter and Kore, the ancient Mother and Maid, were strong enough to withstand, nay to out-top, any

[1] Strab. VIII. 21 § 379.

[2] P. II. 5. 1.

[3] P. II. 2. 2.

[4] My present object is not to discuss the origin of the particular forms of punishment inflicted in Hades, but it may be noted in passing that the stone overhanging Tantalos and the lake in which he is submerged may have contained a reminiscence of some natural precipice and actual catastrophe, see Eustath. ad *Od.* XI. 592, 1701. In the *Aeneid* (VI. 601) the Lapithae, Ixion and Peirithoös all alike suffer the penalty of the imminent stone.

number of Olympian divinities. To tamper with the genealogy of their local hero was felt to be useless and never attempted.

In striking contrast to Triptolemos, Aiakos seems at first sight entirely of the later stratum. He is father of the great Homeric heroes, Telamon and Peleus, and when a drought afflicts Greece it is he who by sacrifice and prayer to Pan-Hellenian Zeus procures the needful rain. Recent investigation[1] has, however, clearly shown that Aiakos is but one of the countless heroes taken over, affiliated by the new religion, and his cult, though overshadowed, was never quite extinguished. One fact alone suffices to prove this. Pausanias[2] saw and described a sanctuary in Aegina known as the Aiakeion. 'It stood in the most conspicuous part of the city, and consisted of a quadrangular precinct of white marble. Within the precinct grew ancient olives, and there was there also an altar rising only a little way from the ground, and it was said, as a secret not to be divulged, that this altar was the tomb of Aiakos.' The altar-tomb was probably of the form already discussed (p. 63) and seen in fig. 8. Such a tomb, as altar, presupposes the cult of a hero.

Minos does not appear on these Lower Italy vases. In his place is Rhadamanthys, his brother and like him a Cretan. The reason of the substitution is perhaps not far to seek. Eustathius[3] notes that some authorities held that Minos was a pirate and others that he was just and a lawgiver. It is not hard to see to which school of thinkers the Athenians would be apt to belong, and the Lower Italy vases are manifestly under Attic influence. If the old Cretan tradition had to be embodied, Rhadamanthys was a safe non-committal figure. He is most at home in the Elysian fields, a conception that was foreign to the old order. As brother of Minos, Rhadamanthys must have belonged to the old Pelasgian dark-haired stock, but we find with some surprise that he is in the *Odyssey* 'golden-haired' (ξανθός), like any other Achaean. Eustathius hits the mark when he says[4], 'Rhadamanthys is golden-haired, out of compliment to Menelaos, for Menelaos had golden hair.'

Herakles and Theseus remain, and need not long detain us.

[1] W. M. L. Hutchinson, *Aeacus, a Judge of the Underworld*, p. 25.

[2] P. II. 29. 6.

[3] Eustath. ad *Il.* XIV. 321, 989.

[4] Eustath. ad *Od.* IV. 564. 187, τὸ δὲ ξανθὸς Ῥαδάμανθυς πρὸς ἡδονὴν Μενελάῳ πέφρασται, ξανθὸς γὰρ καὶ αὐτός.

Herakles is obviously no permanent denizen of Hades; he is triumphant, not tortured; he hales Cerberus to the upper air, and that there may be no mistake Hermes points the way. It has already been seen (p. 55) that Herakles was a hero, *the* hero well worth Olympianizing though he never became quite Olympianized. In the *Nekuia*, when the poet is describing Herakles, he is caught on the horns of a dilemma between the old and the new faith, and instinctively he betrays his predicament. Odysseus[1] says:

> 'Next Herakles' great strength I looked upon,
> His shadow, for the man himself is gone
> To join him with the gods immortal; there
> He feasts and hath for bride Hebe the fair.'

The case of Theseus is different. In the Hades of Virgil[2] he is a criminal condemned for ever:

> 'There sits, and to eternity shall sit,
> Unhappy Theseus.'

But on these Lower Italy vases we have again to reckon with Athenian influence. Theseus is of the old order, son of Poseidon, but Athens was never fully Olympianized, and she will not have her hero in disgrace. Had he not a sanctuary at Athens, an ancient asylum[3]? Were not his bones brought in solemn pomp from Skyros[4]? So the matter is adjusted with considerable tact. Theseus, never accounted as guilty as Peirithoös, is suffered to return to the upper air, Peirithoös has to remain below; and this satisfies Justice, Dike, the woman seated by his side. That the woman holding the sword is none other than Dike herself is happily certain, for she appears inscribed on the fragment of another and similar amphora in the Museum at Carlsruhe[5]. Near her on this fragment is Peirithoös, also inscribed.

So far in our consideration of the criminals of Hades it might seem as though they owed their existence purely to theological *animus*. They are, we have seen, figures of the old religion degraded by the new. But to suppose that this was the sole clue to their presence would be a grave mistake. The notion of punishment, and especially eternal punishment, cannot be fairly charged to the account of Homer and the Olympian religion

[1] Hom. *Od.* XI. 601.
[2] Virg. *Aen.* VI. 617.
[3] P. I. 17. 2, and Ar. *Eq.* 1311 schol. ad loc.
[4] P. III. 3. 7.
[5] *Cat.* 258. Hartung, *Arch. Zeit.* p. 263, Taf. XIX. and *Wiener Vorlegeblätter*, Serie E, Taf. VI. 3.

he represents. This religion was too easy-going, too essentially aristocratic to provide an eternity even of torture for the religious figures it degraded and despised. Enough for it if they were carelessly banished to their own proper kingdom, the underworld. It is, alas, to the Orphics, not to the Achaeans, that religion owes the dark disgrace of a doctrine of eternal punishment. The Orphics were concerned, as has fully been seen, with two things, immortality and purification; the two notions to them were inseparable, but by an easy descent the pains that were for purification became for vengeance. The germ of such a doctrine is already in the line:

'I have paid the penalty for deeds unrighteous.'

The lower kind of Orphic could not rid of vengeance the Hades he made in his own vindictive image. We have seen (p. 506) the heights to which Dike could rise as Heavenly Justice, as Purity; here in Hades she descends to another and more human level.

The figure of Dike in art was not invented by the artist of the Lower Italy vases. She is quaintly figured in the design in fig. 163, from an amphora in the Museum at Vienna[1]. Dike, with uplifted mallet, is about to pound the head of an ugly speckled woman, Adikia, Injustice. The vase, though not signed by Nikosthenes, is manifestly of his school, and therefore dates about the turn of the 6th and 5th centuries B.C. The figure of Dike smiting with the mallet or club was familiar to literature. Theseus, when he learns the death of Hippolytos, asks:

FIG. 163.

'How then did Justice smite him with her club,
My son who shamed me?'

[1] *Cat.* 319. Masner, p. 39, fig. 22.

The Hades, then, of the Lower Italy vases is a popular blend of Orphism and of Olympian theology, or rather of ancient Pelasgian figures viewed through the medium of Olympianism. The old stratum provides the material, the new stratum degrades it, and Orphism moralises it.

The Danaides.

We have left to the end the figures of the 'Danaides,' the maiden-figures carrying water-jars, who on the Altamura vase[1] stand in the lowest row on the right hand. The 'Danaides' have been reserved advisedly, because in their case we have positive evidence of the blend between new and old.

When mention is made of the water-carriers in Hades, maidens who carry water in a leaky vessel, to the modern mind the name 'Danaides' instantly occurs:

'O Danaides, O sieve.'

The association is real and valid, but its cause and origin have been misunderstood, and thereby much confusion has arisen.

The water-carriers of Hades are familiar to us mainly through the famous attack made by Plato[2] in the *Republic* on Orphic eschatology. Seizing, according to his fashion, on the lower side of Orphism, Plato complains that it is riddled through and through with other-worldliness. Homer and Hesiod promise to the just man good in this life, 'bees' and 'woolly sheep,' and 'trees laden with fruit,' and 'wealthy marriages' and 'high offices.' That in Plato's eyes is bad enough, but religious poets, among them Orpheus, do worse. 'Still more lusty are the blessings that Musaeus and his son give on behalf of the gods to the just, for on their showing they take them down into Hades and set them on couches and prepare a Banquet of the Blest; they crown them with garlands and make them spend their whole time being drunk, accounting eternal drunkenness to be the fairest reward of virtue; and others lengthen out still longer the recompense given by the gods, saying that there shall be children's children and

[1] In a vase in the Museum at Carlsruhe (*Cat.* 388) one 'Danaid' appears in the second tier of figures, see Winkler, *Darstellungen der Unterwelt*, p. 13.

[2] Plat. *Rep.* 363 D and E.

a posterity of the blessed and those who keep faith. In such and the like fashion do they sing the praise of justice. But the impious and unjust they bury in a kind of mud in Hades, and compel them to carry water in a sieve.'

The 'immortal drunkenness' promised as guerdon to the blessed was of course conceived of by the higher sort of Orphic as a spiritual ecstasy, by the lower Orphic as merely eternal banqueting. The notion was easily popularized, for the germ of it existed in the 'Hero-feast' already discussed (p. 349), and these 'Hero-feasts,' we have seen, were taken over by Dionysos.

The mud and the sieve to which the impious were condemned remain to be considered. They can only be understood in relation to Orphic ritual, and in this relation are instantly clear. Daubing with mud was, we have seen (p. 491), an integral rite in certain Orphic mysteries. The rite neglected on earth by the impious must be performed for ever in Hades. The like notion lies at the bottom of the water-carrying. He who did not purify himself on earth by initiation must for ever purify himself in Hades. But the vindictive instinct, always alive in man, adds, it is too late, he carries water in a pierced vessel, a sieve, and carries it for ever.

It is often said by modern commentators who have made no trial of eternal burning that fruitless labour is the greatest of all punishments. Goethe was the first offender. 'The ancients,' he says, 'rightly considered fruitless labour as the greatest of all torments, and the punishments which Tantalos, Sisyphos, the Danaides and the Uninitiated undergo in Hades bear witness to this.' But it is not in this reflective fashion that primitive mythology and eschatology are made.

The word used by Plato for those who carry the water in the sieve is noteworthy, it is *ἀνόσιοι*, which perhaps is best translated 'unconsecrated ones.' The word *ὅσιοι* we have already seen denoted complete initiation, the full and final stage; *ἀνόσιοι* is almost, though not quite, 'uninitiated.' In the *Phaedo*, Plato does not mention the water-carriers, but he says explicitly what he here implies, that those who lie in mud are those uninitiated in the mysteries. 'I think,' says Socrates, 'that those who founded our mysteries were not altogether foolish, but from old had a hidden meaning when they said that whoso goes to Hades uninitiated (ἀμύητος), and not having finally accomplished the rites (ἀτέλεστος), will lie in mud.'

Again, when in the *Gorgias* Plato[1] notes the moralization of the notion of the water-carrying, he quite clearly states that the water-carriers are the uninitiated. Socrates is refuting the notion propounded by Callicles that the full satisfaction of the passions is virtue. 'You make of life a fearful thing,' he says, and I think perhaps Euripides was right when he said:

'Life may be death, death life—who knows?'

'A certain philosopher,' he goes on, 'has said we are dead, and that the body (σῶμα) is a tomb (σῆμα).' This doctrine, it will be remembered, was fathered in the *Cratylus* on the Orphics. Then with the notion of the tomb-body (σῶμα σῆμα) still in his mind, Socrates continues: 'A certain ingenious man, probably an Italian or a Sicilian, playing on the word, invented a myth in which he called that part of the soul which is the seat of the desires a *pithos*, because it was *bid*able (πίθανον) and persuadable, and he called the ignorant "unshutting" (ἀμυήτους)...and he declared that of the souls in Hades the uninitiated were most miserable, for they carry water into a *pithos* which is pierced, with a sieve that is pierced in like manner.' Whether the 'ingenious man' was Empedocles or Pythagoras is not for our purpose important; both held Orphic doctrines, and one of these doctrines was that the uninitiated carried water in Hades. It has not, I think, been noticed that the tomb (σῆμα) as a symbol of the body evidently suggests the *pithos* or jar as symbol of the seat of the desires. We have seen in discussing the Anthesteria (p. 43) that the souls rise from a grave-*pithos*.

So far it must be distinctly noted that Plato nowhere calls the water-carriers in Hades *Danaides*. The first literary source for the Danaides *as water-carriers in Hades* is the pseudo-Platonic dialogue the *Axiochus*[2]. In Hades, we are there told, is the region of the unholy (χῶρος ἀσεβῶν) and the 'unaccomplished water-carryings of the Danaides' (Δαναΐδων ὑδρεῖαι ἀτελεῖς). The word ἀτελεῖς, 'unaccomplished,' means also uninitiated, and we are left in doubt—a doubt probably intentional, as to which meaning is

[1] Plat. *Gorg.* 493.

[2] Ps.-Plat. *Axioch.* 573 E. In Xenophon (*Oec.* VII. 40) the water-carriers are unnamed and masculine: οἱ εἰς τὸν τετρημένον πίθον ἀντλεῖν λεγόμενοι.

here proposed. The whole purport of the *Axiochus* is to prepare a coward to face death decently, and the dialogue is full of mysticism. We have as the meed of the blessed 'flowery meadows,' streams of 'pure water,' 'drinking feasts with songs,' and the like. Moreover and most significant of all, the initiated have 'some sort of *proedria*' or right of the first place, and even in Hades they '*go on performing their pure and sanctified rites.*' It is the very mirror of the heaven where

'Congregations ne'er break up and Sabbaths have no end.'

To Plato, then, the water-carriers of Hades are 'uninitiated'; by the time of the *Axiochus* they are Danaides: what is the connecting link? The answer must wait till the evidence of art has been examined.

The evidence of vase-painting is of high importance, because we possess two black-figured vases which antedate Plato by more than a century. The design in fig. 164 is from an amphora in

FIG. 164.

the old Pinakothek[1] in Munich. The scene is laid in the underworld; of that we are sure from the figure of Sisyphos. On the reverse of the vase (not figured here) Herakles is represented with Cerberus. On the obverse (fig. 164), four little winged *eidola* (ghosts) are climbing carefully up a huge *pithos*, and into it they pour water from their water-jars. The *pithos*, it should be noted, is sunk deep into the earth; it is in intent the mouth of a well. Such *pithoi* are still to be found sunk in the earth at Athens, and served the Turks for cisterns. The upper part of the *pithos* is intact, so are the water-jars, but it is possible and indeed almost

[1] Jahn, *Cat.* 153. Baumeister, II. 866.

certain that the *pithos* is thought of as pierced at the bottom so that the water poured in flows away into the ground;

'inane lymphae
dolium fundo pereuntis *imo.*'

The vase in fig. 164 is usually figured as an illustration of the 'Danaid' myth, but there is not the faintest adducible evidence that the winged *eidola* are Danaides.

The design in fig. 165, from a black-figured lekythos in the Museum at Palermo[1], allows us to go a step further. The water-

Fig. 165.

carriers are emphatically *not* Danaides. Of the six figures who rush in grotesque hurry to fill the *pithos*, three are men, three women. If we give them a name, it must be not Danaides but 'Uninitiated.' They are burlesqued, in the spirit of Aristophanes; the uninitiated soul pauses to refresh his mind by pulling the donkey's tail. The donkey, it may be noted, is further evidence that the vase-painter has the mysteries in his mind. He has fallen on his knees, and his burden has dropped from his back. The seated old man gazes at it helplessly. There seems a reminiscence of the 'ass who carried the mysteries,' and in this topsy-turvy Hades, as in Aristophanes, he turns and will carry them no more. The ass and the old man, sometimes called Oknos, are stock figures in the comic Hades, and they are variously moralized. The closest literary analogy to our picture is offered centuries later by Apuleius[2]. Psyche, when about to descend into the lower

[1] *Arch. Zeit.* 1871, Taf. 31. The objects in front of the seated old man are apparently a collection of loose sticks. I had doubts as to the accuracy of the reproduction, but the original at Palermo was examined for me by the late Mr R. A. Neil, and he pronounced the reproduction substantially correct.

[2] Apul. *Met.* VI. 18. Prof. Furtwängler was, I believe, the first to call attention to the passage of Apuleius in connection with this vase. See *Jahrbuch d. Inst.* 1890, Anz. p. 24, and for the whole question of Oknos, which does not here immediately concern us, see O. Rossbach, 'Dämonen der Unterwelt,' *Rhein. Mus.* 1893, p. 593.

world, is warned that when she has gone some distance on the 'deadly way' she will come upon a lame ass and a lame ass-driver. The driver will ask her to pick up for him some of the bundles that have fallen from the ass's pack. She is to remain silent and pass on.

It is of course matter for regret that neither of the black-figured vases that we possess is inscribed. It would have been most instructive to learn what that echo of popular tradition, the vase-painter, actually *called* the water-carriers. Happily we have, not indeed a work of art itself, but the literary record of such a work in which an inscription *did* occur—the painting by Polygnotus of the descent of Odysseus into Hades, frescoed on the wall of the Lesche of Delphi, and minutely described by Pausanias.

'Above the figure of Penthesilea,' Pausanias[1] says, 'are women carrying water in broken earthen sherds.' The vessels are here described as broken, not pierced, and Pausanias says nothing about whether the vessel into which they pour is pierced or not. 'One of the women is represented as in the flower of her youth, the other of advanced years.' There were certainly no *old* Danaides. 'There is no separate inscription over each woman, but there is an inscription common to both which says they are 'of those who have not been initiated.' Pausanias then goes on to describe some other mythological figures unconnected with these women, among them Sisyphos, who is 'struggling to push a rock up a precipice.' He then adds, 'There is also in the picture a *pithos* and an elderly man, a boy and two women, one just below the rock, who is young, and near to the old man a woman of similar age. The others are going on carrying water, but the old woman seems to have broken her hydria, but what is left in the potsherd she is pouring into the *pithos*.' As in the black-figured vase-paintings it is a hydrophoria into a *pithos*, but the hydriae are in some cases at least broken. How many figures in all Pausanias saw is not clear, owing to his disjointed account, nor does it matter, the essential thing is that they are of both sexes and any age—they are nowise Danaides. Nor did Pausanias, charged though he was with later mythological associations, suppose them to be so—that the inscription forbade. He concludes his account thus: 'We inferred that these also

[1] P. x. 31. 9—11.

(i.e. the last group mentioned by him) were persons who held the rites at Eleusis to be of no account. For the Greeks of early days held initiation at Eleusis to be of as much more account than any other matter as the gods are compared to the heroes.'

Polygnotus and Plato certainly, the black-figured vase-painter probably, regarded the water-carriers of Hades not as mythical Danaides, but as real human persons uninitiated. By the date of the *Axiochus* the fruitless water-carriers are Danaides. The question still remains to be answered, Why are the Danaides selected as typically Uninitiate? It was, it must be noted, perfectly natural that popular theology, when it made of the Uninitiate water-carriers in Hades, should seek a mythical prototype, but why were the Danaides selected? The reason is primarily simple and obvious, though later it became curiously complex.

The Danaides of mythology were *well-nymphs*. One of the sisterhood was called Amymone: she gave her name to the spring near Lerna, still called in Strabo's time Amymone. Strabo[1] preserves for us a line from an epic poet,

> 'Argos, waterless once, the Danai made well-watered.'

Long before the tragedy about their husbands, the Danaides were at work watering, fertilizing thirsty Argos. The Danaides, *as merely Danaides*, might fitly be represented as filling a great well-*pithos*.

But, it must next be observed, the Danaides belong to the old stratum of the population, the same stratum as Tantalos, as Sisyphos, as Tityos: they are of the old matriarchal order, their prayer persistently iterated is:

> 'We, the great seed of a Holy Mother, ah me!
> Grant us that we
> Unwed, unsubdued, from marriage of men may flee[2].'

In the *Suppliants* of Aeschylus it is from a marriage they deem lawless that the Danaides flee, and their act is justified. Behind the legend we seem to discern, though dimly, the reflection of some shift of old to new, some transition from matriarchal freedom to patriarchal marriage enactments. In any case, in the late orthodox

[1] Strab. VIII. § 256. Eustathius, ad *Il.* IV. 171. 351, attributes the verse in slightly different form to Hesiod: ἢ καὶ ἀπὸ τῶν Δαναΐδων αἳ παραγενόμεναι ἐξ Αἰγύπτου φρεωρυχίαν ἐδίδαξαν ὡς Ἡσίοδος
"Ἄργος ἄνυδρον ἐὸν Δαναὸς ποίησεν ἔνυδρον.

[2] Aesch. *Supp.* 158.

form of the myth, we meet the Danaides as criminals, and their crime is clearly not only that of murder, but of rejection of marriage. What was justified by the old order was criminal in the new. Here was an opportunity for the moralist. Of old the Danaides carried water because they were well-nymphs; the new order has made them criminals, and it makes of their fruitful water-carrying a fruitless punishment—an atonement for murder[1].

It will readily be seen that the well-nymphs, regarded by the new order as guilty maidens seeking purification, offered just the mythological prototype needed for the uninitiated water-carriers. Once the analogy was seized, many further traits of resemblance would eagerly be added. At the lake of Lerna, near which was the spring known as Amymone, expiatory purifications were, Strabo[2] tells us, actually performed. Hence, he says, arose the expression 'a Lerna of ills.' It was the custom no doubt at Lerna as in many another swamp and lake to bury 'purifications' (καθάρματα). Such rites of the old order were the 'mysteries' of primitive religion. Herodotus[3] expressly tells us that it was the Danaides who taught to the Pelasgian women the sacred rites of Demeter, which the Greeks called Thesmophoria, and of which Herodotus dares not disclose the full details. The Danaides, who later became types of the Uninitiated, were, it would seem, the prime Initiators. So does theology shift.

Another ritual fact helped out the fusion and confusion. To the Roman Church marriage is a sacrament, to the Anglican still 'an excellent mystery.' In like fashion to the Greeks marriage was conceived of as a rite of initiation, and through initiation of consummation; the word τέλη in its plural form was used of all mysteries, the singular form was expressly applied to marriage. Pollux[4], in discussing wedding ceremonies, says, 'and

[1] The story that the *heads* of the murdered husbands were buried in or near Lerna apart from their bodies may have been merely aetiological and based on the practice of calling the brim of a well κεφαλή. Cf. our 'well-head,' 'fountain-head.' Latin *caput aquae*. It is not my purpose here to examine completely the Danaid myth save in so far as the Danaides were *contaminated* with the Uninitiated in Hades. The folklore of the subject has been well collected by Dr Campbell Bonner, *Trans. American Philol. Ass.* vol. XXXI. 1900, II. p. 27.

[2] Strab. loc. cit. supra.

[3] Herod. II. 171.

[4] Poll. *On.* III. 38, καὶ τέλος ὁ γάμος ἐκαλεῖτο καὶ τέλειοι οἱ γεγαμηκότες διὰ τοῦτο καὶ Ἥρα τελεία ἡ ζυγία. The play on the word τέλος cannot be reproduced in English.

marriage is called τέλος, i.e. a rite that completes, and those who have been married are called complete, and on this account the Hera of marriage is called Teleia, the Complete One.' It has already been seen (p. 532) that one special rite of purification, the *Liknophoria*, was common to marriage and the mysteries. The same is true of the *Loutrophoria*, carrying of the bath. Is it surprising that in the figures of the well-nymphs some ingenious person saw the Danaides as ἀτελεῖς γάμου, 'uninitiated in marriage,' and therefore condemned in Hades to carry for ever in vain the water for their bridal bath? The more so as, if we may trust Eustathius[1], it was the custom to place 'on the grave of those who died unmarried a water jar called *Loutrophoros*[2] in token that the dead had died unbathed and without offspring.' Probably these vases, as Dr Frazer[3] suggests, were at first placed on the graves of the unmarried with the kindly intent of helping the desolate unmarried ghost to accomplish his wedding in the world below. But once the custom fixed, it might easily be interpreted as the symbol of an underworld punishment.

Some versions of the story say that the water was carried in a sieve (κοσκίνῳ). This notion may have arisen from another ritual practice. It is noticeable that the sieves of the stone age seem to have been simply pierced jars. Sieve and *pithos* were one and the same. Carrying water in a sieve was an ancient test of virginity. Pliny[4] tells us that the test of the sieve was applied to the Vestal Tuccia. If the water-carrying of the Danaides was conceived as a virginity test, the forty-nine sisters married before the murder would fail at the test, and Hypermnestra alone would carry the water in the leaky sieve:

> 'Splendide mendax et in omne *virgo*
> Nobilis aevum[5].'

Finally, it will be remembered (p. 574) that the Orphics had their Well of Memory, which was in effect a Well of Life. It would

[1] Eustath. ad *Il.* XXIII. 141, p. 1293.

[2] For the vases known as Loutrophoroi see Milchhoeffer, *A. Mitt.* V. 1880, p. 174, and P. Wolters, *A. Mitt.* XVI. 1891, p. 371, and *ib.* XVIII. 1893, p. 66. These vases were sometimes pierced at the bottom but it is not certain that the pierced vases were placed only on the graves of the unmarried.

[3] Dr Frazer, ad P. X. 31. 9, collects a number of interesting modern parallels.

[4] Plin. *N.H.* XXVIII. 2. 3.

[5] Hor. *Od.* 3. 11. 35. Apollodorus, II. 1. 14, says of Hypermnestra, αὕτη δὲ Λυγκέα διέσωσε παρθένον αὐτὴν φυλάξαντα.

not escape a mystic who saw the figures of the water-carriers that these were drawing water for ever but in vain from the Well of Life. So the scholiast[1] to Aristides in quaint fashion interprets the myth: 'the pierced *pithos* of the Danaides,' he says, 'signifies that the Danaides after the murder of their dearest can never obtain from another man the grace of the living water of marriage.' The notion of a 'Water of Life' haunts him, but he knows the real gist of the symbolism, for he adds: they have 'become suspected on account of their pollution.' Of the making of such mysticism there is clearly no end.

The symbolism of marriage, of virginity tests, of living water might, doubtless did, gather about the figures of the Danaides, but the primary notion that fitted them to be mythical prototypes of the 'Uninitiated' was that they were polluted, uncleansed. They are Choephoroi, but in vain; the libations that they pour into the grave-*pithoi* of their husbands are a *χάρις ἄχαρις*, an attempted offscouring, *ἀπόνιμμα*, but no real purification. Of such a vain Choephoria performed by Clytaemnestra Electra[2] says:

> 'It is not right or meet
> By law of gods or men that from a hateful wife
> Grave-dues and washings should be brought my father.
> Give them the winds, or in the deep dug earth
> Go hide them.'

The water-carriers in Hades have been discussed at some length[3], because they afford an instance typical of the methods of Orphic procedure. In discussing the mysteries it has been repeatedly seen that Orphism did not invent new rites, but mysticized and moralized old ones. In like fashion when Orphism developes eschatology, it takes for its material the

[1] Schol. ad Arist. *Orat.* II. p. 229, τῶν δὲ Δαναΐδων ὁ τετρημένος πίθος τὸ μήποτε ταύτας μετὰ τὸν φόνον τῶν φιλτάτων τὴν ἀναψύχουσαν αὐτὰς ἐκ τῆς ἀνδρείας κηδεμονίας χάριν παρ' ἄλλων τυγχάνειν, πᾶσι γενομένας ὑπόπτους διὰ τὸ ἄγος.

[2] Soph. *El.* 433.

[3] It is scarcely necessary to say that in my interpretation of this myth I owe much to my predecessors, though my view is slightly different from any previously given. Controversy has raged as to whether the mythical Danaides gave rise to the 'Uninitiated' or *vice versâ*. This seems to me a fruitless question with no possible answer. Each form arose separately, and the point is their ultimate *contaminatio*. The literature of the controversy is given by Dr Frazer ad P. x. 31. 9. To his references may be added, Dümmler, *Delphika*, p. 22, and Mr A. B. Cook, *J.H.S.* XIII. 1892, p. 97.

mythology of the older stratum[1], invents no new figures but gives to the old ones an intensified and moralized significance.

The Orphic tablets showed us the heights to which Orphism could rise. If we are inclined to estimate over highly the general level of the Orphic faith, the Lower Italy vases may correct the error. They mirror Orphism as it seemed to the many. In the matter of doctrine, instead of or at best in addition to purification, we have vindictive punishment; in the matter of theology, in place of what was practically monotheism on the tablets, the vases restore the old popular polytheism.

It is natural to ask, Is this the end? Did Orphism create no new figure, make no new god in its own purified image? The answer to this question will be found in our concluding enquiry as to the nature of Orphic Cosmogony.

[1] Between the issue of my first and second editions much light has been thrown on the figures of the criminals in Hades by the publication of M. Salomon Reinach's brilliant paper 'Sisyphe aux enfers et quelques autres damnés' (*Rev. Arch.* 1903, p. 1). He has shown conclusively that 'l'idée orphique de la perpétuité des peines est venue se greffer sur des images populaires représentant des morts, soit dans l'exercice de leur activité familière, soit dans les attitudes caractéristiques de leur trépas,' e.g. Sisyphus rolls a stone up a hill because he was on earth a Master-Builder. True and illuminating, but to make the view complete we have to add that one familiar function of an ancient king was to be vice-gerent of his tribal god. Salmoneus, M. Reinach sees, counterfeits the weather; Sisyphus he fails to note is not merely as mortal a Master-Builder, but as vice-gerent of the Corinthian Helios he rolls the sun day by day up the steep of heaven. Both ideas went to make the image of the stone-roller.

CHAPTER XII.

ORPHIC COSMOGONY.

‘Ὡραῖος καὶ Ἔρως ἐπιτέλλεται...’

If, in attempting to understand Orphic Theogony, we turn to the collection of hymns known as ‘Orphic,’ hymns dating for the most part about the 4th century A.D., we find ourselves at once in an atmosphere of mystical monotheism. We have addresses to the various Olympians, to Zeus and Apollo and Hera and Athene and the rest, but these are no longer the old, clear-cut, departmental deities, with attributes sharply distinguished and incommunicable; the outlines are all blurred; we feel that everyone is changing into everyone else. A few traditional epithets indeed remain; Poseidon is still ‘dark-haired,’ and ‘Lord of Horses’—he is a stubborn old god and hard to fuse; but, for the most part, sooner or later, all divinities greater or less, mingle in the mystery melting-pot, all become ‘multiform,’ ‘mighty,’ ‘all-nourishing,’ ‘first-born,’ ‘saviours,’ ‘all-glorious,’ and the like. In a word the several gods by this time are all really one, and this one god is mystically conceived as a potency (*δαίμων*) rather than a personal divinity (*θεός*).

The doctrine of the mutation of the gods, now into one shape, now into another, was, it would seem, part of the regular symbolic teaching of the mysteries. It is easy to see that such a doctrine would lend itself readily to the notion of their interchangeability. Proclus says[1]: ‘In all the rites of initiation and mysteries the gods exhibit their shapes as many, and they appear changing often from one form to another, and now they are made manifest in the

[1] Procl. *Ennead.* I. 6. 9, *ἐν ἅπασι ταῖς τελεταῖς καὶ τοῖς μυστηρίοις οἱ θεοὶ πολλὰς μὲν ἑαυτῶν προτείνουσι μορφάς, πολλὰ δὲ σχήματα ἐξαλλάττοντες φαίνονται καὶ τοῖς μὲν ἀτύπωτον αὐτῶν προβέβληται φῶς τοῖς δὲ εἰς ἀνθρώπειον μορφὴν ἐσχηματισμένον, τότε δὲ εἰς ἀλλοῖον τύπον προεληλυθός.*

emission of formless light, now taking human shape, now again in other and different form.'

By the date of the 'Hymns' monotheism was of course in some degree the common property of all educated minds, and cannot therefore be claimed as distinctive of Orphism. Wholly Orphic, however, is the mystical joy with which the Hymns brim over; they are 'full of repetitions and magniloquence, and make for emotion[1].' They are like learned, self-conscious, even pretentious echoes of the simple ecstasy of the tablets.

It would therefore be idle to examine the Orphic Hymns severally and in detail, in order to extract from them the Orphic characteristics of each particular god. Any one who reads them through will speedily be conscious that, save for the prooemium, and an occasional stereotyped epithet, it would usually be impossible to determine which hymn was addressed to what god. With whatever attempt at individualization they begin, the poet is soon safe away into a mystical monotheism. A more profitable enquiry is, how far did primitive Orphism attempt monotheism, and of what nature was the one God whom the Orphic made in his own image? Here, fortunately, we are not left wholly without evidence.

THE WORLD-EGG.

In the *Birds* of Aristophanes[2], the chorus tells of a time, when Earth and Air and Heaven as yet were not, only Chaos was, and Night and black Erebos:

'In the beginning of Things, black-winged Night
  Into the bosom of Erebos dark and deep
Laid a wind-born egg, and, as the seasons rolled,
Forth sprang Love, gleaming with wings of gold,
Like to the whirlings of wind, Love the Delight—
  And Love with Chaos in Tartaros laid him to sleep;
And we, his children, nestled, fluttering there,
Till he led us forth to the light of the upper air.'

This is pure Orphism. Homer knows of no world-egg[3], no birth of Love. Homer is so dazzled by the splendour of his

[1] Mr Gilbert Murray, *Greek Literature*, p. 66.

[2] Ar. *Av.* 692.

[3] ὑπηνέμιον—literally 'wind-begotten.' The beautiful doctrine of the Fatherhood of the Wind or the Virgin Birth was Orphic, and connected with the ancient Attic cult of the Tritopatores, worshipped by bride and bridegroom before marriage, see p. 179. The Scholiast half understanding says *ὑπηνέμια καλεῖται τὰ δίχα συνουσίας καὶ μίξεως.* For Egyptian egg-cosmogonies see Diodorus, I. 27, and Eusebius, *de praep.-evang.* 3. 11.

human heroes and their radiant reflections in Olympus that his eyes never look back to see from whence they sprang. He cares as little, it seems, for the Before as for the Hereafter. The two indeed seem strangely linked together. An eschatology and a cosmogony are both pathetic attempts to answer the question Homer never cared to raise, Whence came Man and the Good and Evil of humanity?

We have of course a cosmogony in Hesiod, Hesiod who is a peasant and a rebel, a man bitter and weary with the hardness of life, compelled by rude circumstances to ask why things are so evil, and always ready, as in the myth of Pandora, to frame or borrow a crude superstitious hypothesis. How much Hesiod borrowed from Orphism is hard to say. He knows of Night and Chaos and the birth of Eros, but he does *not* know, or does not care to tell, of one characteristic Orphic element, the cosmic egg. He only says[1]:

'First Chaos came to be and Gaia next
Broad-bosomed, she that was the steadfast base
Of all things—Ge, and murky Tartaros
Deep in the hollow of wide earth. And next
Eros, most beautiful of deathless gods,
Looser of limbs, Tamer of heart and will
To mortals and immortals.'

Hesiod is not wholly Orphic, he is concerned to hurry his Eros up into Olympus, one and most beautiful among many, but not for Hesiod the real source of life, the only God.

By common traditional consent the cosmic egg was attributed to Orpheus. Whether the father was Tartaros or Erebos or Chronos is of small moment and varies from author to author. The cardinal, essential doctrine is the world-egg from which sprang the first articulate god, source and creator of all, Eros.

Damascius[2], in his 'Inquiry concerning first principles,' attributes the egg to Orpheus. For Orpheus said:

'What time great Chronos fashioned in holy aether
A silver-gleaming egg.'

It is fortunate that Damascius has preserved the actual line,

[1] Hes. *Theog.* 116.

[2] Damasc. *Quaest. de prim. princ.* p. 147. The sources are fully given in Abel's *Orphica*, p. 173. I am also indebted for references to Schömann's *De Cupidine Cosmog.*, see Schömann, *Opuscula*, vol. II. p. 60.

though of course we cannot date it. Clement of Rome[1] in his Homilies contrasts the cosmogonies of Hesiod and Orpheus. 'Orpheus likened Chaos to an egg, in which was the commingling of the primaeval elements; Hesiod assumes this chaos as a substratum, the which Orpheus calls an egg, a birth emitted from formless matter, and the birth was on this wise....' Plato, usually so Orphic, avoids in the *Timaeus* all mention of the primaeval egg; his mind is preoccupied with triangles, but Proclus in his commentary[2] says 'the "being" (τὸ ὄν) of Plato would be the same as the Orphic egg.'

The doctrine of the egg was not a mere dogmatic dead-letter. It was taught to the initiated as part of their mysteries, and this leads us to suspect that it had its rise in a primitive taboo on eggs. Plutarch[3], in consequence of a dream, abstained for a long time from eggs. One night, he tells us, when he was dining out, some of the guests noticed this, and got it into their heads that he was 'infected by Orphic and Pythagorean notions, and was refusing eggs just as certain people refuse to eat the heart and brains, because he held an egg to be taboo (ἀφοσιοῦσθαι) as being the principle of life.' Alexander the Epicurean, by way of chaff, quoted,

'To feed on beans is eating parents' heads.'

'As if,' Plutarch says, 'the Pythagoreans meant eggs by *be*ans because of *be*ing (ὡς δὴ κυάμους τὰ ᾠὰ διὰ τὴν κύησιν αἰνιττομένων τῶν ἀνδρῶν), and thought it just as bad to eat eggs as to eat the animals that laid them.' It was no use, he goes on, in talking to an Epicurean, to plead a dream as an excuse for abstinence, for to him the explanation would seem more foolish than the fact; so, as Alexander was quite pleasant about it and a cultivated man, Plutarch let him go on to propound the interesting question, which came first, the bird or the egg? Alexander in the course of the argument came back to Orpheus and, after quoting Plato about matter being the mother and nurse, said with a smile,

'I sing to those who know

[1] Clem. Rom. *Homil.* VI. 4. 671, καὶ Ὀρφεὺς δὲ τὸ Χάος ᾠῷ παρεικάζει, ἐν ᾧ τῶν πρώτων στοιχείων ἦν ἡ σύγχυσις, τοῦτο Ἡσίοδος Χάος ὑποτίθεται, ὅπερ Ὀρφεὺς ᾠὸν λέγει, γεννητὸν ἐξ ἀπείρου τῆς ὕλης προβεβλημένον, γεγονὸς δὲ οὕτω, κ.τ.λ.
[2] Procl. in Plat. *Tim.* 2, p. 307, εἴη ἂν ταὐτὸν τό τε Πλάτωνος ὂν καὶ τὸ Ὀρφικὸν ᾠόν.
[3] Plut. *Quaest. Symp.* II. 3. 1.

the Orphic and sacred dogma (λόγος) which not only affirms that the egg is older than the bird, but gives it priority of being over all things.' Finally, the speaker adds to his theorizing an instructive ritual fact: 'and therefore it is not inappropriate that in the orgiastic ceremonies in honour of Dionysos an egg is among the sacred offerings, as being the symbol of what gives birth to all things, and in itself contains all things.'

Macrobius[1] in the *Saturnalia* states the same fact, and gives a similar reason. 'Ask those who have been initiated,' he says, 'in the rites of Father Liber, in which an egg is the object of reverence, on the supposition that it is in its spherical form the image of the universe'; and Achilles Tatius[2] says, 'some assert that the universe is cone-shaped, others egg-shaped, and this opinion is held by those who perform the mysteries of Orpheus.'

But for the bird-cosmogony of Aristophanes we might have inclined to think that the egg was a late importation into Orphic mysteries, but, the more closely Orphic doctrines are examined, the more clearly is it seen that they are for the most part based on very primitive ritual. A ritual egg was good material; those who mysticized the kid and the milk would not be likely to leave an egg without esoteric significance.

How, precisely, the egg was used in Orphic ritual we do not know. In ordinary ceremonial it served two purposes: it was used for *purification*, it was an *offering to the dead*. It has been previously shown in detail (p. 53) that in primitive rites purgation often *is* propitiation of ghosts and sprites, and the two functions, propitiation and purgation, are summed up in the common term *devotions* (ἐναγίσματα). Lucian[3] in two passages mentions eggs, together with Hecate's suppers, as the refuse of 'purification.' Pollux is bidden by Diogenes to tell the Cynic Menippus, when he comes down to Hades, to 'fill his wallet with beans, and if he can he is to pick up also a Hecate's supper or an egg from a purification or something of the sort'; and in another dialogue, the 'Landing,' Clotho, who is waiting for her victims, asks 'Where is Kyniskos the philosopher who ought to be dead from eating Hecate's suppers and eggs from purification and raw cuttle

[1] Macrob. *Sat.* VII. 16. 691.
[2] Achill. Tat. Isag. ad Arati, *Phenom.* p. 77.
[3] Luc. *Dial. Mort.* I. 1 and *Catapl.* 7.

fish too?' Again in Ovid's *Art of Love*[1] the old hag who makes purifications for the sick woman is to bring sulphur and eggs:

'Then too the aged hag must come,
And purify both bed and home,
And bid her, for lustration, proffer
With palsied hands both eggs and sulphur.'

That eggs were offered not only for a purification of the living, but as the due of the dead, is certain from the fact that they appear on Athenian white lekythoi among the objects brought in baskets to the tomb[2].

We think of eggs rather as for nourishment than as for purification, though the yolk of an egg is still used for the washing of hair. Doubtless, in ancient days, the cleansing action of eggs was more magical than actual. As propitiatory offerings to the dead (*ἐναγίσματα*) they became 'purifications' in general; then connection with the dead explains of course the taboo on them as food.

Still, primitive man though pious is also thrifty. A Cynic may show his atheism, and also eke out a scanty subsistence by eating 'eggs from purification'; and even the most superstitious man may have hoped that, if he did not break the egg, he might cleanse himself and yet secure a chicken. Clement[3] says, 'you may see the eggs that have been used for purifications hatched, if they are subjected to warmth': he adds instructively, 'this could not have taken place if the eggs had taken into themselves the sins of the man who had been purified.' Clement's own state of mind is at least as primitive as that of the 'heathen' against whom he protests. The Orphics themselves, it is clear, merely mysticized an ancient ritual. Orphism is here as elsewhere only the pouring of new wine into very old bottles.

We may say then with certainty that the cosmic egg was Orphic, and was probably[4] a dogma based on a primitive rite. The origin of the winged Eros who sprang from it is more complex. Elements many and diverse seem to have gone to his making.

[1] Ov. *Ars Am.* II. 330. Cf. Juvenal VI. 518.

[2] This fact, that eggs were offered to the dead, has been clearly established by Dr Martin Nilsson in his tract *Das Ei im Totenkultus der Griechen*. The 'Sonderabdruck' he has kindly sent me appeared in the *Från Filologiska Föreningen i Lund Språkliga uppsatser* II. (Lund, 1902).

[3] Clem. Al. *Str.* VII. 4, p. 713, ὁρᾶν γοῦν ἔστι τὰ ᾠὰ ἀπὸ τῶν περικαθαρθέντων, εἰ θαλφθείη, ζωογονούμενα, οὐκ ἂν δὲ τοῦτο ἐγένετο εἰ ἀνελάμβανεν τὰ τοῦ περικαθαρθέντος κακά.

[4] It is possible that the cosmic egg may have been imported from Egypt and *contaminated* later with the egg of purification.

EROS AS HERM.

Homer knows nothing of Eros as a person; with him love is of Aphrodite. From actual local cultus Eros is strangely and significantly absent. Two instances only are recorded. Pausanias[1] says, 'The Thespians honoured Eros most of all the gods from the beginning, and they have a very ancient image of him, an unwrought stone.' 'Every four years,' Plutarch[2] says, 'the Thespians celebrated a splendid festival to Eros conjointly with the Muses.' Plutarch went to this festival very soon after he was married, before his sons were born. He seems to have gone because of a difference that had arisen between his own and his wife's people, and we are expressly told by his sons that he took his newly-married wife with him, 'for both the prayer and the sacrifice were her affair.' Probably they went to pray for children. Plutarch, if we may trust his own letter to his wife, was a kind husband, but the intent of the conjoint journey was strictly practical, and points to the main function of the Thespian Eros. The 'unwrought stone' is very remote from the winged Eros, very near akin to the rude Pelasgian Hermes himself, own brother to the Priapos[3] of the Hellespont and Asia Minor. There seems then to have gone to the making of Eros some old wide-spread divinity of generation[4].

Pausanias did not know who instituted the worship of Eros among the Thespians, but he remarks that the people of Parium on the Hellespont, who were colonists from Erythrae in Ionia, worshipped him equally. He knew also of an older and a younger Eros. 'Most people,' he says, 'hold that he is the youngest of the gods and the son of Aphrodite; but Olen the Lycian (again Asia Minor), maker of the most ancient hymns among the Greeks, says in a hymn to Eileithyia that she is the mother of Eros.' 'After Olen,' he goes on, 'Pamphos and Orpheus composed epic verses, and they both made hymns to Eros to be sung by the Lycomids at their rites.'

[1] P. IX. 27. 1. [2] *Amat.* 1.

[3] Diod. IV. 6, μυθολογοῦσιν οὖν οἱ παλαιοὶ τὸν Πρίαπον υἱὸν εἶναι τοῦ Διονύσου καὶ Ἀφροδίτης.

[4] For this whole question see Dr Kaibel's 'Dactyloi Idaioi' in *Nachrichten von der Königl. Gesellschaft der Wissenschaften zu Göttingen Phil. Hist. Kl.* 1901, Heft 4; and for Eros as Adonis see J. Böhlan, 'Ein neuer-Erosmythus' in *Philologos* LX. 1901, Heft 3.

Eros as Ker of Life.

The Orphic theologist found then to his hand in local cultus an ancient god of life and generation, and in antique ritual another element quite unconnected, the egg of purification. Given an egg as the beginning of a cosmogony, and it was almost inevitable that there should emerge from the egg a bird-god, a winged thing, a source of life, more articulate than the egg yet near akin to it in potency. The art-form for this winged thing was also ready to hand. Eros is but a specialized form of the Ker; the Erotes are Keres of life, and like the Keres take the form of winged *Eidola*. In essence as in art-form, Keres and Erotes are near akin. The Keres, it has already been seen, are little winged bacilli, fructifying or death-bringing; but the Keres developed mainly on the dark side; they went downwards, deathwards; the Erotes, instinct with a new spirit, went upwards, lifewards.

The close analogy, nay, the identity of the art-form of Keres and Erotes is well seen in the two vase-paintings in figs. 166 and 167. The design in fig. 166 is from a vase-fragment in the Museum at Palermo[1]. A warrior lies fallen in death. From his open mouth the breath of life escapes. Over him hovers a winged Ker, and with his right hand seems as though he would tenderly collect the parting soul. A ghost has come to fetch a ghost. Among the Romans this gentle office of collecting the parting breath was done with the lips, by the nearest of kin. So Anna[2] for Dido:

Fig. 166.

> 'Give water, I will bathe her wounds, and catch
> Upon my lips her last stray breath.'

[1] *Inv.* 2351. P. Hartwig, *J.H.S.* XII. 1891, p. 340.

[2] Virg. *Aen.* IV. 684. If we may trust Servius (ad loc.), with strictly practical intent, 'Muliebriter tanquam possit animam sororis excipere et in se transferre. Sic

The design in fig. 167 is from a red-figured cylix[1] in the Municipal Museum at Corneto. Theseus, summoned by Hermes,

FIG. 167.

is in the act of deserting Ariadne; he picks up his sandal from the ground and in a moment he will be gone. Ariadne is sunk in sleep beneath the great vine of Dionysos. Over her hovers a winged genius to comfort and to crown her. He is own brother to the delicate Ker in fig. 166. Archaeologists wrangle over his name. Is he Life or Love or Sleep or Death? Who knows? It is this shifting uncertainty we must seize and hold; no doubt could be more beautiful and instructive. All that we can certainly say is that the vase-painter gave to the ministrant the form of a winged Ker, and that such was the form taken by Eros, as also by Death and by Sleep.

If we would understand at all the spirit in which the Orphic Eros is conceived we must cleanse our minds of many current conceptions, and in effecting this riddance vase-paintings are of no small service. To black-figured vase-paintings Eros is unknown. Keres of course appear, but Eros has not yet developed personality in popular art. As soon as Eros takes mythological shape in art, he leaves the Herm-form under which he was worshipped at Thespiae, leaves it to Hermes himself and to Dionysos and Priapos,

Cicero in Verrinis "ut extremum filiorum spiritum ore excipere liceret." So according to the thinking of many primitive people are new souls born of old souls, see Tylor, *Primitive Culture*, II. p. 4.

[1] *Wiener Vorlegeblätter*, Serie D, Taf. VIII.

and, because he is the egg-born cosmic god, takes shape as *the* winged Ker. Early red-figured vase-paintings are innocent alike of the fat boy of the Romans and the idle impish urchin of Hellenism. Nor do they know anything of the Eros of modern romantic passion between man and woman. If we would follow the safe guiding of early art, we must be content to think of Eros as a Ker, a life-impulse, a thing fateful to all that lives, a man because of his moralized complexity, terrible and sometimes intolerable, but to plants and flowers and young live things in spring infinitely glad and kind. Such is the Eros of Theognis[1]:

'Love comes at his hour, comes with the flowers in spring,
 Leaving the land of his birth,
Kypros, beautiful isle. Love comes, scattering
 Seed for man upon earth.'

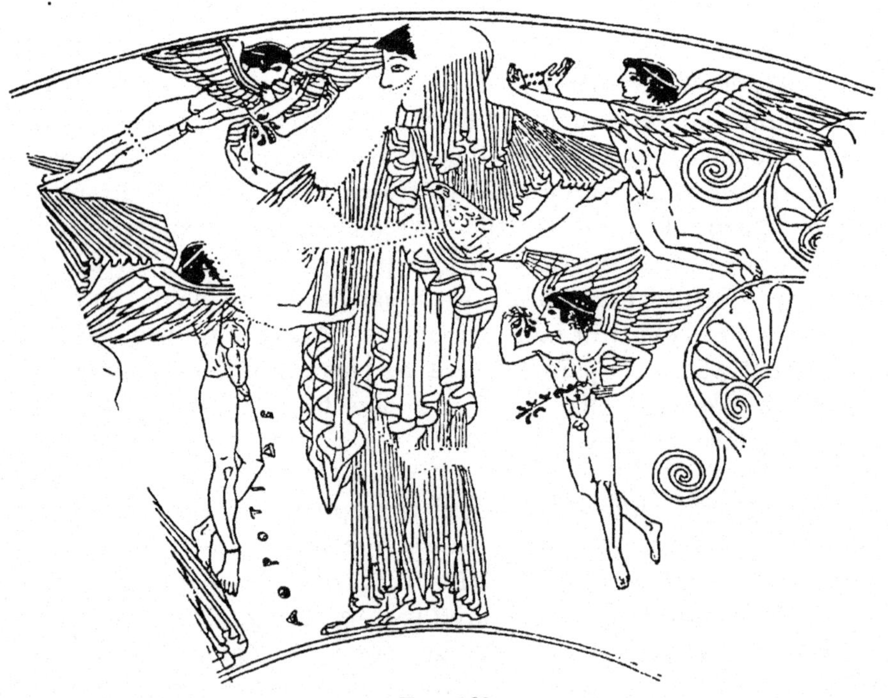

Fig. 168.

Such little spirits of life the vase-painter Hieron makes to cluster round their mother and mistress, Aphrodite. The design in fig. 168 is from a cylix in the Berlin Museum[2] and is part

[1] *Theog.* 1275. [2] *Cat.* 2291. *Wiener Vorlegeblätter*, Serie A, Taf. V.

of a scene representing the Judgment of Paris. Aphrodite, she the victorious Gift-Giver, greatest of the Charites, stands holding her dove. About her cluster the little solemn worshipping Erotes, like the winged Keres that minister to Kyrene (fig. 22): they carry wreaths and flower-sprays in their hands, not only as gifts to the Gift-Giver, but because they too are spirits of Life and Grace.

Just such another Eros is seen in fig. 169, from the centre

FIG. 169.

of a beautiful archaic red-figured cylix[1] in the Museo Civico at Florence. The cylix is signed by the master Chachrylion: he signs it twice over, proudly, as well he may, 'Chachrylion made it, made it, Chachrylion made it.' His Eros too carries a great branching flower-spray, and as the spirit of God moves upon the face of the waters. So Sophocles[2]:

'O Thou of War unconquered, thou, Erôs,
  Spoiler of garnered gold, who liest hid
  In a girl's cheek, under the dreaming lid,
While the long night time flows:

[1] *Museo Ital. di Antichita*, vol. III. 1, pl. 2.
[2] Soph. *Ant.* 781, trans. by Mr Gilbert Murray.

O rover of the seas, O terrible one
In wastes and wildwood caves,
None may escape thee, none:
Not of the heavenly gods who live alway,
Not of low men, who vanish ere the day;
And he who finds thee, raves.'

The Erotes retain always the multiplicity of the Keres, but as Eros developes complete personality he becomes one person, and he changes from a delicate sprite to a beautiful youth. But down to late days there linger about him traces of the Life-Spirit, the Grace-Giver. The design in fig. 170 is from a late red-figured vase in the Museum at Athens[1]. Here we find Eros

FIG. 170.

employed watering tall slender flowers in a garden. Of course by this time the Love-God is put to do anything and everything: degraded to a god of all work, he has to swing a maiden, to trundle a hoop, to attend a lady's toilet; but here in the flower-watering there seems a haunting of the old spirit. We are reminded of Plato[2] in the *Symposium* where he says 'The bloom of his body is shown by his dwelling among flowers, for Eros has his abiding, not in the body or soul that is flowerless and fades, but in the place of fair flowers and fair scents, there sits he and abides.'

[1] *Cat.* 1852. Fig. 170 is reproduced from a hasty sketch kindly made for me by Mrs Hugh Stewart; it is only intended as a note of subject and not as a substitute for complete publication.

[2] Plat. *Symp.* 196 A.

EROS AS EPHEBOS.

Vase-paintings with representations of Eros come to us for the most part from Athens, and it was at Athens that the art-type of Eros as the slender ephebos was perfected. This type appears with marked frequency on the vases of early red-figured technique which bear the inscription *καλός* 'beautiful,' vases probably made to sell as love-gifts. Eros is represented bearing a torch, a lyre, a hare, sometimes still a flower. Perhaps the finest of these representations left us is the Eros in fig. 171. The design is from

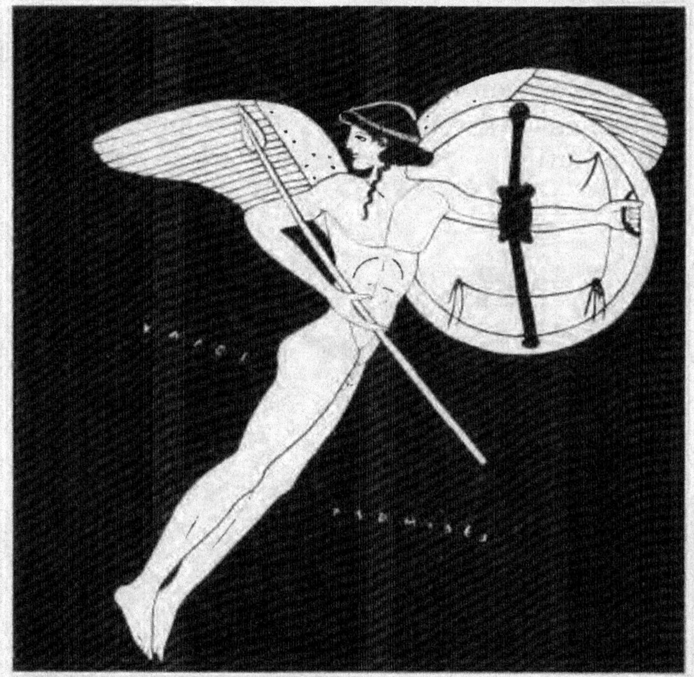

FIG. 171.

an amphora[1] which bears the inscription 'Charmides is beautiful.' Eros is armed, he carries shield and spear, he flies straight downward, the slender naked body making a clean lovely line. A poet thinks as he will, but these Love-gods of the vase-painter, these Keres of Life and Death, and most of all this Eros, armed,

[1] Now in the Bibliothèque Nationale, Paris, De Ridder, *Cat.* 366; see Lenormant et de Witte, *Élite des Monuments Céramographiques*, IV. Pl. LI.

inevitable, recall the prayer of the chorus in the *Hippolytus* of Euripides[1]:

> 'Erôs, Erôs, who blindest, tear by tear,
>   Men's eyes with hunger, thou swift Foe that pliest
> Deep in our hearts joy like an edged spear;
> Come not to me with Evil haunting near,
> Wrath on the wind, nor jarring of the clear
>   Wing's music as thou fliest.
> There is no shaft that burneth, not in fire,
> Not in wild stars, far off and flinging fear
> As in thine hands the shaft of All Desire,
>   Erôs, Child of the Highest.'

Most often the presentments of painting hinder rather than help the imagery of poetry, but here both arts are haunted by the same august tradition of Life and Death.

The Eros of the vase-painter is the love, not untouched by passion, of man for man, and these sedate and even austere Erotes help us to understand that to the Greek mind such loves were serious and beautiful, of the soul, as Plato says, rather than of

FIG. 172.

the body[2], aloof from common things and from the emotional squalor of mere domestic felicity. They seem to embody for him that white heat of the spirit before which and by which the flesh shrivels into silence.

[1] Eur. *Hipp.* 525.

[2] For the religious *origin* of the institution of παιδεραστία and its connection with primitive initiation ceremonies see E. Bethe, 'Die dorische Knabenliebe, ihre Ethik und ihre Idee' in *Rhein. Mus.* 1907.

It is curious to note that, as the two women Charites, Mother and Daughter, became three, so there is a distinct effort to form a trinity of Erotes. On the vase-painting in fig. 172 from a red-figured *stamnos* in the British Museum[1] we have three beautiful Erotes flying over the sea. The foremost is inscribed Himeros; he carries a long taenia, and he looks back at the others; one of these carries a tendril, the other a hare. Near each of them is written καλός. But the triple forms, Eros, Himeros and Pothos, never really obtain. The origin of the countless women trinities has been already examined. Male gods lack the natural tie that bound the women types together; the male trinity is in Greek religion felt to be artificial and lapses.

Eros and the Mother.

The mention of these women trinities brings us back to the greatest of the three Grace-Givers, Aphrodite. At the close of the chapter on *The Making of a Goddess* her figure reigned supreme, but for a time at Athens she suffered eclipse; we might almost say with Alcman[2]:

> 'There is no Aphrodite. Hungry Love
> Plays boy-like with light feet upon the flowers.'

We cannot fairly charge the eclipse of Aphrodite wholly to the count of Orphism. Legend made Orpheus a woman-hater and credited him with Hesiodic tags about her 'dog-like' nature; but such tradition is manifestly coloured and distorted by two influences, by the orthodox Hesiodic patriarchalism, and by the peculiar social conditions of Athens and other Greek states. Both these causes, by degrading women, compelled the impersonation of love to take form as a youth.

To these we must add the fact that as Orphism was based on the religion of Dionysos, and as that religion had for its god Dionysos, son of Semele, so Orphism tended naturally to the formulation of a divinity who was the Son of his Mother. By the time the religion of Dionysos reached Athens the Son had

[1] *Cat.* E 440. *Mon. d. Inst.* I. Pl. VIII. The design in fig. 37, Odysseus passing the Sirens, is from the obverse of this vase. The three Sirens probably suggested the triple Erotes.

[2] Alcman, frg. 38 (34).

well nigh effaced the Mother, and in like fashion Eros was supreme over Aphrodite; and significantly enough the woman-goddess, in so far as she was worshipped by the Orphics, was rather the old figure of Ge, the Earth-goddess, than the more specialized departmental Love-goddess Aphrodite.

This blend of the old Earth-goddess and the new Love-god is shown in very instructive fashion by representations on late red-figured vases. The design in fig. 173 is from a late red-

Fig. 173.

figured hydria[1]. It will at once be seen that we have the representation of a scene exactly similar to that in figs. 67 and 69, the Anodos of an Earth-goddess. The great head rises from the ground, the Satyr worshippers of the Earth-goddess are there with their picks. But a new element is introduced. Two Erotes hover over the goddess to greet her coming. In like fashion in fig. 71 Eros receives Pandora, and in fig. 86 receives Aphrodite at her Birth or Bath. It is usual to name the goddess in fig. 173 Aphrodite. This is, I think, to miss the point. She is an Earth spirit like Persephone herself. She is the new life rising from the ground, and she is welcomed by the spirits of life, the Keres-Erotes. Beyond that we cannot go. Nothing could better embody the shift from old to new, and the blend of both, than the presence together of the Satyrs, the primitive Ge-worshippers, and the Erotes, the new spirits of love and life.

[1] Fröhner, *Choix de vases grecs*, Pl. VI. p. 24. The vase is now as M. Hébert kindly informs me in the Musée du Cinquantenaire at Brussels.

If we bear in mind the simple fact that Aphrodite and Persephone are each equally and alike Kore, the Maiden form of the Earth-goddess, it is not hard to realise how easily the one figure passes into the other. The Orphic, we have seen (p. 593), put his faith in the Kore who is Persephone; to her he prays:

'Out of the pure I come, Pure Queen of Them Below';

his confession is

'I have sunk beneath the bosom of Despoina, Queen of the Underworld,'

and again

'But now I come a suppliant to holy Phersephoneia
That of her grace she receive me to the seats of the Hallowed';

but from the fragment of an epic poet preserved for us by the anonymous author of the *Philosophoumena*[1], we learn that, according to some, in the underworld grove another Kore, or rather Kore by another name, was believed to rule. 'The Lesser Mysteries,' he says, 'are of Persephone below, in regard to which Mysteries and the path that leads there, which is wide and large and leads the dying to Persephone, the poet also says:

"And yet 'neath it there is a rugged track,
Hollow, bemired; yet best whereby to reach
All-hallowed Aphrodite's lovely grove."'

The figures of the two Maidens, Persephone and Aphrodite, acted and reacted on each other; Persephone takes on more of Love, Aphrodite more of Death; as Eros the Son waxes, Aphrodite the Mother wanes into Persephone the underworld Maid.

The blend of the two notions, the primitive Earth-goddess and the Orphic Eros, is for art very clearly seen on the vase in fig. 173. Happily we have definite evidence that in local *cultus* there was the like fusion, and that at a place of associations specially sacred, the deme of Phlya in Attica, the birthplace of Euripides[2].

THE MYSTERIES OF EROS AND THE MOTHER AT PHLYA.

Phlya, as the birthplace of Euripides, has special claims on our attention. Here, it will be shown, were mysteries reputed to be more ancient than those of Eleusis, mysteries not only of the Mother and the Maid but of Eros the cosmic spirit of the Orphics.

[1] *Philosoph.* v. 8, ed. Cruice. The 'poet' is *probably* Parmenides; see Diels, *Frag. d. Vorsokratiker*, *Parm.* 20 (dub.).
[2] Harpocrat. s.v. Φλυεῖς.

Euripides, obviously hostile as he is to Orthodox Olympian theology, handles always with reverence the two gods or spirits of Orphism, Dionysos and Eros: it seems not improbable that, perhaps unconsciously, the mysteries of his early home may have influenced his religious attitude.

From Pausanias[1] we learn that Phlya had a cult of the Earth-goddess. She was worshipped together with a number of other kindred divinities. 'Among the inhabitants of Phlya there are altars of Artemis the Light-Bearer, and of Dionysos Anthios, and of the Ismenian Nymphs, and of Ge, whom they call the Great Goddess. And another temple has altars of Demeter Anesidora, and of Zeus Ktesios, and of Athene Tithrone, and of Kore Protogene, and of the goddesses called Venerable.'

The district of Phlya[2] is still well watered and fertile, still a fitting home for Dionysos 'of the Flowers,' and for Demeter 'Sender up of Gifts'; probably it took its name from this characteristic fertility[3]. Plutarch[4] discussed with some grammarians at dessert the reason why apples were called by Empedocles *ὑπέρφλοα*, 'very fruitful.' Plutarch made a bad and unmetrical guess; he thought the word was connected with *φλοιός*, husk or rind, and that the apple was called *ὑπέρφλοιον* 'because all that was eatable in it lay outside the inner rind-like core.' The grammarians knew better; they pointed out that Aratus[5] used the word *φλόον* to mean verdure and blossoming, the 'greenness and bloom of fruits,' and they added the instructive statement that 'certain of the Greeks sacrificed to Dionysos Phloios, 'He of blossom and growth.' Dionysos Phloios and Dionysos Anthios are one and the same potency.

[1] P. I. 31. 4. Attention was first drawn to this passage in connection with the 'Anodos' vase-paintings by Prof. Furtwängler, *Jahrbuch d. Inst.* 1891, pp. 117—124, but with his interpretation of the vases I find myself unable to agree (see p. 282, n. 2) and the evidence from the *Philosophoumena* seems to be unknown to him.

[2] See Dr Frazer, *Pausanias*, vol. II. p. 412.

[3] The roots *φλε*, *φλι*, *φλυ* and the guttural form *χλι* (cf. *χλιδή*) all express the same notion of bursting, bubbling, germinating, see Vaniček, ad voc. and cf. Hesych. *φλεῖ· γέμει, εὐκαρπεῖ, πολυκαρπεῖ*, and the words *φλύκταινα*, *φλύζει*.

[4] Plut. *Symp.* v. 8. 2 and 3, *τοῦ δὲ Ἐμπεδοκλέους εἰρηκότος·*

οὕνεκεν ὀψίγονοί τε σίδαι καὶ ὑπέρφλοια μῆλα.

The text has *ὑπέρφλοια*: the superfluous *ι* may have crept in owing to Plutarch's guess.

[5] Plut. loc. cit. *ὁμοίως τὸν Ἄρατον ἐπὶ τοῦ Σειρίου λέγοντα·*

καὶ τὰ μὲν ἔρρωσεν τὸν δὲ φλόον ὤλεσε πάντα,

τὴν χλωρότητα καὶ τὸ ἄνθος τῶν καρπῶν φλόον προσαγορεύειν...εἶναι δὲ καὶ τῶν Ἑλλήνων τινὰς οἳ Φλοίῳ Διονύσῳ θύουσιν.

Among this family group of ancient earth divinities Artemis and Zeus read like the names of late Olympian intruders. Artemis as Light-Bearer may have taken over an ancient mystery cult of Hecate, who also bore the title of Phosphoros; Zeus Ktesios, we are certain, is not the Olympian. Like Zeus Meilichios he has taken over the cult of an old divinity of 'acquisition' and fertility. 'Zeus' Ktesios was the god of the storeroom. Harpocration[1] says, 'they set up Zeus Ktesios in storerooms.' The god himself lived in a jar. In discussing the various shapes of vessels Athenaeus[2] says of the *kadiskos*, 'it is the vessel in which they consecrate the Ktesian Zeuses, as Antikleides says in his "Interpretations," as follows: the symbols of Zeus Ktesios are consecrated as follows: "the lid must be put on a new *kadiskos* with two handles, and the handles crowned with white wool...... and you must put into it whatever you chance to find and pour in ambrosia. Ambrosia is pure water, olive oil and all fruits (*παγκάρπια*). Pour in these."' Whatever are the obscurities of the account of Antikleides, thus much is clear—Zeus Ktesios is not the Olympian of the thunderbolt, he is Zeus in nothing but his name[3]. *Ktesios* is clearly an old divinity of fertility, of the same order as Meilichios; his *σημεῖα* are symbols not statues, symbols probably like the *sacra* carried in chests at the Arrephoria; they are *θεσμοί*, magical spells kept in a jar for the safe guarding of the storeroom. Zeus Ktesios is well in place at Phlya. The great *pithoi* that in Homer stand on the threshold of Olympian Zeus (p. 47) may be the last reminiscence of this earlier *Dian* daemon who had his habitation, genius-like, in a jar.

But this old daemon of fertility who took on the name of Zeus only concerns us incidentally. In the complex of gods enumerated by Pausanias as worshipped at Phlya, the Great Goddess is manifestly chief. The name given to Kore, *Protogene*, suggests Orphism, but we are not told that it was a mystery cult, and of Eros there is no notice. Happily from other sources we know

[1] Harp. s.v. Κτησίου Διός·...Κτήσιον Δία ἐν τοῖς ταμείοις ἵδρυντο.

[2] Athen. XI. 46 p. 473: the portions omitted *καὶ ἐκ τοῦ ὤμου τοῦ δεξιοῦ καὶ ἐκ τοῦ μετώπου τοῦ κροκίου* are unintelligible as they stand, but their meaning does not affect the present argument.

[3] Probably not even in name; if my conjecture be correct the 'Zeuses' set up are of the same nature as the *dirae* and the *δῖον κῴδιον*, see p. 23, note 2.

further particulars. In discussing the parentage of Themistocles Plutarch[1] asserts that Themistocles was related to the family of the Lycomids. 'This is clear,' he says, 'for Simonides states that, when the Telesterion at Phlya, which was the common property of the gens of the Lycomids, was burnt down by the barbarians, Themistocles himself restored it and decorated it with paintings.' In this Telesterion, this 'Place of Initiation,' the cult of Eros was practised. The evidence is slight but sufficient. In discussing the worship of Eros at Thespiae Pausanias states incidentally, we already noted (p. 470), that the poets Pamphos and Orpheus both composed 'poems about Eros to be chanted by the Lycomids over their rites.'

This mystery cult, we further know, was also addressed to a form of the Earth goddess. When actually at Phlya, Pausanias, as already noted, curiously enough says nothing of *mysteries*; he simply notes that the Great Goddess and other divinities were worshipped there. Probably by his time the mystery cult of Phlya was completely overshadowed and obscured by the dominant, orthodox rites at Eleusis. But, *apropos* of the mysteries at Andania in Messene[2], he gives significant details about Phlya. He tells us three facts which all go to show that the cult at Phlya was a mystery-cult. First, the mysteries of Andania were, he says, brought there by a grandson of Phlyos; and this Phlyos, we may conclude, was the eponymous hero of Phlya. Second, for the Lycomids, who, we have seen, had a 'Place of Initiation' at Phlya and hymns to Eros, Musaeus wrote a hymn to Demeter, and in this hymn it was stated that Phlyos was a son of Ge. Third, Methapos, the great 'deviser of rites of initiation,' had a statue in the sanctuary of the Lycomids, the metrical inscription on which Pausanias quotes. In view of this evidence it cannot be doubted that the cult of Phlya was a mystery-cult, and the divinities worshipped among others were the Mother and the Maid and Eros.

At Phlya then, it is clear, we have just that blend of divinities that appears on the vase-painting in fig. 173. We have the

[1] Plut. *Them.* I. Pausanias (IV. 1. 7) in speaking of this same *telesterion*, which was the sanctuary of the Lycomids, calls it by the very peculiar name κλίσιον. Dr Frazer translates κλίσιον 'chapel.' The word *may* mean a 'lean to,' a rough annexe, but I would conjecture that here it means the same as παστάς, i.e. 'bridal chamber,' the place of the ἱερὸς γάμος, see p. 535. For the relations of the Lycomids to the cult of the Phrygian Great Mother see Leo Bloch, 'Zur Geschichte des Meterkultes,' *Philologos*, 1894, p. 579.

[2] P. IV. 1. 7 and 8.

worship of the great Earth-goddess who was Mother and Maid in one, and, conjointly, we have the worship of the Orphic spirit of love and life, Eros. It is probable that the worship of the Earth-goddess was primaeval, and that Eros was added through Orphic influence.

The Eros of the Athenian vase-painting is the beautiful Attic boy, but there is evidence to show that the Eros of Phlya was conceived of as near akin in form to a Herm. In discussing the Orphic mysteries (p. 535), we found that at Phlya according to the anonymous author of the *Philosophoumena* there was a παστάς or bridal chamber decorated with paintings. This bridal chamber was probably the whole or a part of that Telesterion which was restored and decorated by Themistocles. The subjects of these paintings Plutarch had fully discussed in a treatise now unhappily lost. The loss is to be the more deeply regretted because the account by Plutarch of pictures manifestly Orphic would have been sympathetic and would greatly have helped our understanding of Orphism. The author of the *Philosophoumena*[1] describes briefly one picture and one picture only, as follows: 'There is in the gateway the picture of an old man, white-haired, winged; he is pursuing a blue-coloured woman who escapes. Above the man is written φάος ῥυέντης, above the woman περεηφικόλα. According to the doctrine of the Sethians, it seems that φάος ῥυέντης is "light" and that φικόλα is "dark water."' The exact meaning of these mysterious paintings is probably lost for ever; but it is scarcely rash to conjecture that the male figure is Eros. He pursues a woman; he is winged; that is like the ordinary Eros of common mythology. But this is the Eros of the mysteries; not young, but very ancient, and white-haired, the ἀρχαῖος ἔρως[2] of Orphic tradition, eldest of all the Gods. And the name written above him as he pursues his bride inscribed 'Darkness' or 'Dark Water' is 'Phaos Ruentes,' 'The rushing or streaming Light.' We are reminded of the time when 'the Spirit of God moved

[1] *Philosophoum.* v. 3 ed. Cruice, ἔστι δ' ἐν τοῖς πυλεῶσι καὶ πρεσβύτης τις ἐγγεγραμμένος, πολιὸς, πτερωτὸς, γυναῖκα ἀποφεύγουσαν διώκων κυανοειδῆ (κυνοειδῆ the MS.: but Schneidewin's correction is generally admitted). ἐπιγέγραπται δὲ ἐπὶ τοῦ πρεσβύτου· φάος ῥυέντης, ἐπὶ δὲ τῆς γυναικός· περεηφικόλα. ἔοικε δὲ εἶναι κατὰ τὸν Σηθιανῶν λόγον ὁ φάος ῥυέντης τὸ φῶς, τὸ δὲ σκοτεινὸν ὕδωρ ἡ φικόλα, τὸ δὲ ἐν μέσῳ τούτων διάστημα ἁρμονία πνεύματος μεταξὺ τεταγμένου.

[2] Luc. *de Salt.* 7, and Xen. *Symp.* VIII. 1.

upon the face of the waters.' The ancient Eros of Thespiae, who was in intent a Herm, has become the principle not only of Life but of Light—Light pursuing and penetrating Darkness. Exactly such a being, such a strange blend of animal and spiritual, is the egg-born, wind-born Protogonos of the Orphic hymn[1]:

'Thou tempest spirit in all the ordered world
On wild wings flashing; bearer of bright light
And holy; therefore Phanes named, and Lord
Priapos, and the Dawn that answereth Dawn.'

So chants the mystic, seeking to utter the unutterable, and the poet[2], born in the home of mysticism, sings to Mother and Son:

'Thou comest to bend the pride
Of the hearts of God and man,
Cypris; and by thy side
In earth's encircling span
He of the changing plumes,
The Wing that the world illumes,
As over the leagues of land flies he,
Over the salt and sounding sea.

For mad is the heart of Love,
And gold the gleam of his wing;
And all to the spell thereof
Bend, when he makes his spring;
All life that is wild and young,
In mountain and wave and stream,
All that of earth is sprung
Or breathes in the red sunbeam.
Yea and Mankind. O'er all a royal throne,
Cyprian, Cyprian, is thine alone.'

Pythagorean Revival of the Mother.

The development of the male Eros, the beautiful youth, was due, we may be sure, to influences rather Athenian than Orphic. In this connection it is important to note that the Orphic Pythagoreans tended to revive religious conceptions that were matriarchal rather than patriarchal. The religion of Dionysos, based on the worship of Mother and Son, gave to women a freedom and a consequence possible only perhaps among the more spiritual peoples of the North. Under Pythagoras we have clear

[1] *Orph. Hymn.* VI. 7 (trans. by Mr Gilbert Murray):
πάντη διvηθεὶς πτερύγων ῥιπαῖς κατὰ κόσμον
λαμπρὸν ἄγων φάος ἁγνόν, ἀφ' οὗ σε Φάνητα κικλήσκω
ἠδὲ Πρίηπον ἄνακτα καὶ 'Ανταύγην ἑλίκωπον.

[2] Eur. *Hipp.* 1269.

indications of a revival of the like conditions, of course with a difference, a resurgence as it were of matriarchal conditions, and with it a realization of the appeal of women to the spirit as well as the flesh.

According to Aristoxenus[1] Pythagoras got most of his ethical lore from a woman, Themistoclea, a priestess of Delphi. We are reminded of Socrates and Diotima, Diotima the wise woman of Mantinea, which has yielded up to us the great inscription dealing with the mysteries of Demeter at Andania[2]. We are reminded too of the close friendship between Plutarch and the Thyiad, Clea. It was to a woman, his daughter Damo, that Pythagoras entrusted his writings with orders to divulge them to no outside person. Diogenes further[3] records with evident surprise that men 'gave their wives into the charge of Pythagoras to learn somewhat of his doctrine,' and that these women were called 'Pythagoreans.' Kratinos wrote a comedy on these Pythagorean women in which he ridiculed Pythagoras; so we may be sure his women followers were not spared. This Pythagorean woman movement probably suggested some elements in the ideal state of Plato, and may have prompted the women comedies of Aristophanes. Of a woman called Arignote we learn[4] that 'she was a disciple of the famous Pythagoras and of Theano, a Samian and a Pythagorean philosopher, and she edited the Bacchic books that follow: one is about the mysteries of Demeter, and the title of it is the *Sacred Discourse*, and she was the author of the *Rites of Dionysos* and other philosophical works.' That this matriarchalism of Pythagoras was a revival rather than an innovation seems clear. Iamblichus[5] says, 'whatever bore the name of Pythagoras bore also the stamp of antiquity and was crusted with the patina of archaism.'

It is not a little remarkable that, in his letter[6] to the women of Croton, Pythagoras says expressly that 'women as a sex are more naturally akin to piety.' He says this reverently, not as Strabo[7] does taking it as evidence of ignorance and superstition.

1 Diog. Laert. *Vit. Pyth.* v.

2 Sauppe, *Die Mysterieninschrift von Andania.*

3 Diog. Laert. *Vit. Pyth.* xxi.

4 Clem. Al. *Strom.* iv. 19 § 583.

5 Iambl. *de Myst.* § 247, χαρακτὴρ παλαιότροπος...ἀρχαιοτρόπου δὲ καὶ παλαιοῦ πίνου διαφερόντως ὥσπερ τινὸς ἀχειραπτήτου νοῦ προσπνέοντα.

6 Diog. Laert. *Vit. Pyth.* 8. 1. 10.

7 Strab. vii. § 297.

Strabo in discussing the celibate customs of certain among the Getae remarks, 'all agree that women are the prime promoters of superstition, and it is they who incite men to frequent worshippings of the gods and to feasts and excited celebrations (ποτνιασμούς).' He adds with charming frankness 'you could scarcely find a man living by himself who would do this sort of thing.' It is to Pythagoras, as has already been noted (p. 262), that we owe the fertile suggestion that in the figures of the women-goddesses we have the counterpart of the successive stages of a woman's life as Maiden, Bride and Mother.

The doctrine of the Pythagoreans in their lifetime was matriarchal and in their death they turned to Mother Earth. The house of Pythagoras[1] after his death was dedicated as a sanctuary to Demeter, and Pliny[2] records—significant fact—that the disciples of Pythagoras reverted to the ancient method of inhumation long superseded by cremation and were buried in *pithoi*, earth to earth.

EROS AS PHANES, PROTOGONOS, METIS, ERIKAPAIOS.

The Eros of Athenian poetry and painting is unquestionably male, but the Protogonos of esoteric doctrine is not male or female but bisexed, resuming in mystic fashion Eros and Aphrodite. He is an impossible, unthinkable cosmic potency. The beautiful name of Eros is foreign to Orphic hymns. Instead we have Metis, Phanes, Erikapaios, 'which being interpreted in the vulgar tongue are Counsel, Light and Lifegiver[3].' The commentators on Plato are conscious of what Plato himself scarcely realizes, that in his philosophy he is always trying to articulate the symbolism of these and other Orphic titles, trying like Orpheus to utter the unutterable; he puts νοῦς for Metis, τὸ ὄν for Erikapaios, but, in despair, he constantly lapses back into myth and we have the winged soul, the charioteer, the four-square bisexed man. Proklos[4]

[1] Valer. Max. 8. 15. 1.

[2] Plin. *Nat. Hist.* XXXVI. 46.

[3] Johannes Malala, *Chronogr.* IV. 74, οὗ ὄνομα ὁ αὐτὸς Ὀρφεὺς ἀκούσας ἐκ τῆς μαντείας ἐξεῖπε Μῆτιν, Φάνητα, Ἠρικαπαῖον ὅπερ ἑρμηνεύεται τῇ κοινῇ γλώσσῃ βουλή, φῶς, ζωοδότηρ.

[4] Prokl. in Plat. *Tim.* II. 207, εἴη ἂν ταὐτὸν τό τε Πλάτωνος ὂν καὶ τὸ Ὀρφικὸν ᾠόν.

knows that τὸ ὄν is but the primaeval egg, knows too that Erikapaios was male and female[1]:

'Father and Mother, the mighty one Erikapaios,'

and Hermias[2] knows that Orpheus made Phanes four-square:

'He of the fourfold eyes, beholding this way, that way.'

It was 'the inspired poets,' Hermias[3] says, 'not Plato, who invented the charioteer and the horses,' and these inspired poets are according to him Homer, Orpheus, Parmenides.

The mention of Homer comes as something of a shock; but it must be remembered that the name *Homer* covered in antiquity a good deal more than our *Iliad* and *Odyssey*. It is not unlikely that some of the 'Homeric' poems were touched with Orphism. The name *Metis* suggests it. The strange denaturalized birth of Athene from the brain of Zeus is a dark, desperate effort to make *thought* the basis of being and reality, and the shadowy parent in the *Kypria* is the Orphic Metis. Athene, as has already been shown (p. 300), was originally only one of the many local Korae; she was ἡ Ἀθηναία (Κόρη), the 'maiden of Athens,' born of the earth, as much as the Kore of Eleusis. Patriarchalism wished to rid her of her matriarchal ancestry, and Orphic mysticism was ready with the male parent Metis. The proud rationalism of Athens, uttering itself in a goddess who embodied Reason, did the rest.

There is a yet more definite tinge of Orphism in the story of Leda and the swan. Leda herself is all folklore and fairy story based probably on a cultus-object. In the sanctuary of the ancient Maidens Hilaira and Phoebe at Sparta[4] there hung from the roof suspended by ribbons an egg, and tradition said it was the egg of Leda. But the author of the *Kypria*[5] gave to Zeus another bride, Nemesis, who belongs to the sisterhood of shadowy Orphicized female impersonations, Dike, Ananke, Adrasteia and the like. The birth of the child from the egg appears on no black-figured vase-painting, and though it need not have been originated by the Orphics, the birth of Eros doubtless lent it new

[1] Prokl. in Plat. *Tim.* II. 130, θῆλυς καὶ γενέτωρ κρατερὸς θεὸς Ἠρικαπαῖος.

[2] Herm. in Plat. *Phaedr.* p. 135, τετρὰς δὲ ὁ Φάνης, ὡς Ὀρφεύς φησι
τετράσιν ὀφθαλμοῖσιν ὁρώμενος ἔνθα καὶ ἔνθα.

[3] Herm. in Plat. *Phaedr.* p. 125, οὐ πρῶτος δὲ ὁ Πλάτων ἡνίοχον καὶ ἵππους παρέλαβεν ἀλλὰ καὶ πρὸ αὐτοῦ οἱ ἔνθεοι τῶν ποιητῶν Ὅμηρος, Ὀρφεύς, Παρμενίδης. The 'Orphic' element in 'Homer' has just been strikingly illustrated by the Orphic papyrus (just published in the fifth volume of the *Berliner-Klassiker Hefte*).

[4] P. III. 16. 1.

[5] *Kypria*, frg. ap. Athen. VIII. p. 334.

prestige. The charming little design in fig. 174 is from a red-figured lekythos in the Berlin Museum[1]. On an altar lies a huge egg. Out of it breaks the figure of a boy. The boy is not winged; otherwise we should be inclined to call him Eros. The woman

FIG. 174.

to whom the child stretches out his hands must be Leda. The scene is the birth of one of the Dioscuri, but probably with some reminiscence of Eros. On most vases in which the birth from the egg is represented it takes place in a sanctuary.

Homeric theology, as we know it in our canonical Homer, was wholly untouched by Orphism. The human figures of the Olympians, clear-cut and departmental as they are, have no kinship with the shifting mystical Protogonos. The Olympians lay no claim to be All in All, nor are they in any sense Creators, sources of life. Homer has no cosmogony, only a splendid ready-made human society. His gods are immortal because death would shadow and mar their splendour, not because they are the perennial sources of things. It is noticeable that Zeus himself, the supreme god of Homeric theology, can only be worked into the Orphic system by making him become Eros[2], and absorb

[1] *Cat.* 2254. Kekulé, *Ueber ein griechisches Vasengemälde im akademischen Kunstmuseum zu Bonn*, 1879, p. 1.

[2] Pherekydes ap. Prokl. in Plat. *Tim.* III. 368, ὁ δὲ Φερεκύδης ἔλεγεν εἰς Ἔρωτα μεταβεβλῆσθαι τὸν Δία μέλλοντα δημιουργεῖν.

Phanes[1]; only so can he become *demiourgos*, a feat which, to do him justice, he never on his own account attempted. Proklos says 'Orpheus in inspired utterance declares that Zeus swallowed Phanes his progenitor, and took into his bosom all his powers.' This mysticism was of course made easy by savage cosmogonies of Kronos and the swallowing of the children.

The Olympians concern themselves as little with the Before as with the Hereafter; they are not the source of life nor are they its goal. Moreover, another characteristic is that they are, with the strictest limitations, *human*. They are not one with the life that is in beasts and streams and woods as well as in man. Eros, 'whose feet are on the flowers,' who 'couches in the folds,' is of all life, he is Dionysos, he is Pan. Under Athenian influence Eros secludes himself into purely human form, but the Phanes[2] of Orpheus was polymorphic, a beast-mystery-god:

'Heads had he many,
Head of a ram, a bull, a snake, and a bright-eyed lion.'

He is like Dionysos, to whom his Bacchants cry[3]:

'Appear, appear, whatso thy shape or name,
O Mountain Bull, Snake of the Hundred Heads,
Lion of the Burning Flame!
O God, Beast, Mystery, come!'

In theology as in ritual Orphism reverted to the more primitive forms, lending them deeper and intenser significance. These primitive forms, shifting and inchoate, were material more malleable than the articulate accomplished figures of the Olympians.

The conception of Phanes Protogonos remained always somewhat esoteric, a thing taught in mysteries, but his content is popularized in the figure of the goat-god who passed from being ὁ Πάων the feeder, the shepherd, to be τὸ πᾶν Pan the All-God.

Pan came to Athens[4] from Arcadia after the Persian War, came at a time when scepticism was busy with the figures of the

[1] Prokl. in Plat. *Cratyl.* p. 66, ὡς ὁ 'Ορφεὺς ἐνθέῳ στόματι λέγει καὶ καταπίνει τὸν πρόγονον αὐτοῦ τὸν Φάνητα καὶ ἐγκολπίζεται πάσας αὐτοῦ τὰς δυνάμεις ὁ Ζεύς.

[2] Prokl. in Plat. *Tim.* II. p. 130 B, τοιαῦτα γὰρ περὶ αὐτοῦ καὶ 'Ορφεὺς ἐνδείκνυται περὶ τοῦ Φάνητος θεολογῶν. πρῶτος γὰρ ὁ θεὸς παρ' αὐτῷ ζῴων κεφαλὰς φέρει
πολλὰς
κρίας, ταυρείας, ὄφιος χαροποῦ τε λέοντος,
καὶ πρόεισιν ἀπὸ τοῦ πρωτογενοῦς ᾠοῦ, ἐν ᾧ σπερματικῶς τὸ ζῷόν ἐστι, and p. 131 E, διὸ καὶ ὁλικώτατον ζῷον ὁ θεόλογος ἀναπλάττει κριοῦ καὶ ταύρου καὶ λέοντος καὶ δράκοντος αὐτῷ περιθεὶς κεφαλάς.

[3] Eur. *Bacch.* 1017.

[4] *Myth. and Mon. Anc. Athens*, p. 538.

Olympians and their old prestige was on the wane. Pan of course had to have his reception into Olympus, and a derivation duly Olympian was found for his name. The Homeric Hymn[1], even if it be of Alexandrian date, is thoroughly Homeric in religious tone: the poet tells how

'Straight to the seats of the gods immortal did Hermes fare
With his child wrapped warmly up in skins of the mountain hare,
And down by the side of Zeus and the rest, he made him to sit,
And showed him that boy of his, and they all rejoiced at it.
But most of all Dionysos, the god of the Bacchanal,
And they called the name of him PAN because he delighted them ALL.'

Dionysos the Bull-god and Pan the Goat-god both belong to early pre-anthropomorphic days, before man had cut the ties that bound him to the other animals; one and both they were welcomed as saviours by a tired humanity. Pan had no part in Orphic ritual, but in mythology as the All-god[2] he is the popular reflection of Protogonos. He gave a soul of life and reality to a difficult monotheistic dogma, and the last word was not said in Greek religion, until over the midnight sea a voice[3] was heard crying 'Great Pan is dead.'

Our evidence for the mystic Phanes Protogonos, as distinguished from the beautiful Eros of the Athenians, has been, so far, drawn from late and purely learned authors, commentators on Plato, Christian Fathers, and the like. The suspicion may lurk in some minds that all this cosmogony, apart from the simple myth of the world-egg vouched for by Aristophanes, is a matter of late mysticizing, and never touched popular religion at all, or if at all, not till the days of decadence. It is most true that 'the main current of speculation, as directed by Athens, set steadily contrariwise, in the line of getting bit by bit at the meaning of things through hard thinking,' but we need constantly to remind ourselves of the important fact 'that the mystical and "enthusiastic" explanation of the world was never without its apostles in Greece[4].' That the common people heard this doctrine gladly is curiously

[1] *Hom. Hym.* XIX. 42, trans. by Mr D. S. MacColl.

[2] The Orphic conception of Pan as All-god was no doubt helped out by the fact that as early as the time of Herodotus (II. 46) the analogy was noted between the Greek Pan and the Egyptian Mendes, who was both Goat-god and All-god; see Roscher, 'Pan als Allgott' in *Festschrift f. Overbeck*, 1893, p. 56 ff., and for Mendes, Roscher, s.v.

[3] Plut. *de defect. orac.* 17. For the probable origin of the story, which does not here concern us, see S. Reinach, *Bull. de Corr. Hell.* 1907, p. 5; and F. Liebrecht, *Gervasius von Tilbury*, p. 180.

[4] Murray, *Ancient Greek Literature*, p. 68.

evidenced by the next monument to be discussed, a religious document of high value, the fragment of a black-figured vase-painting[1] in fig. 175.

In the sanctuary of the Kabeiroi near Thebes[2] there came to light a mass of fragments of black-figured vases, dating about the

FIG. 175.

end of the 5th or the beginning of the 4th century B.C., of local technique and obviously having been used in a local cult. The important inscribed fragment is here reproduced. The reclining man holding the kantharos, would, if there were no inscription, be named without hesitation Dionysos. But over him is clearly written *Kabiros*.

Goethe makes his Sirens say of the Kabeiroi that they

'Sind Götter, wundersam eigen,
Die sich immerfort selbst erzeugen
Und niemals wissen was sie sind.'

They have certainly a wondrous power of taking on the forms of other deities; here in shape and semblance they are Dionysos, the father and the son. Very surprising are the other inscribed figures, a man and a woman closely linked together, Mitos and Krateia, and a child Protolaos. What precisely is meant by the conjunction is not easy to say, but the names Mitos and Protolaos take us straight to Orphism. Clement[3] says in the *Stromata* that Epigenes wrote a book on the poetry of Orpheus and 'in it noted certain characteristic expressions.' Among them was this, that by warp (στήμοσι) Orpheus meant furrow, and by woof (μίτος) he meant seed (σπέρμα).

Did this statement stand alone we might naturally dismiss it as late allegorizing, but here, on a bit of local pottery of the

[1] *A. Mitth.* XIII. pl. IX. To the fuller discussion of the Kabiric and Dactylic cults which I now believe to underlie much of Orphic mysticism I hope to return on some future occasion.

[2] P. IX. 25. 5.

[3] Clem. Al. *Strom.* v. 8 § 231.

5th or 4th century B.C., we have the figure of Mitos in popular use. All the Theban Kabeiroi vases are marked by a spirit of grotesque and sometimes gross caricature. Mitos, Krateia and Protolaos it will be noted have snub negro faces. This gives us a curious glimpse into that blending of the cosmic and the mystic, that concealing of the sacred by the profane, that seems inherent in the anxious primitive mind. It makes us feel that Aristophanes, to his own contemporaries, may have appeared less frankly blasphemous than he seems to us.

The vase fragment has another interest. The little Orphic cosmogonic group, *Seed* and *Strong One* and *First people*, the birth of the human world as it were, is in close connection with Dionysos, the father and the son. It is all like a little popular diagram of the relation of Orphic and Bacchic rites, and moreover it comes to us from the immediate neighbourhood of Thebes, the reputed birthplace of the god.

The vase fragment from Thebes shows plainly the influence of mystery doctrines on popular conceptions of Dionysos. It is worth noting that in red-figured vase-paintings of a somewhat late style Eros comes to be a frequent attendant on Dionysos, whereas in vases of severe style he is wholly absent. Maenads and Satyrs revel either together or alone. The design in fig. 177, from the lid of a red-figured lekane (fig. 176) in the Museum at Odessa[1], is a singularly beautiful instance of Eros as present at a Bacchic revel. A Maenad and a Satyr dance in ecstasy, holding between them a little fawn, as though in the act of rending it asunder. Over her long chiton, that trails and swirls about her feet in oddly modern fashion, the Maenad wears a fawn-skin; a second dancing Maenad strikes her timbrel. One half of the design is all ecstasy and even savagery, the other half is perfectly quiet. Two

Fig. 176.

[1] Reproduced by kind permission of Dr E. von Stern from the *Mémoires de la Société Impériale d'histoire et des antiquités*, vol. xviii. pl. i. The vase was found at Kertsch.

Maenads stand talking, at rest; the god Dionysos is seated and Eros offers him the wine-cup. Here it is Eros the son, not Aphrodite the mother, who is linked with Dionysos, but we remember how in the *Bacchae* of Euripides[1] the Messenger thus pleads with Pentheus:

> 'Therefore I counsel thee,
> O King, receive this Spirit whoe'er he be
> To Thebes in glory. Greatness manifold
> Is all about him—and the tale is told
> That this is he who first to man did give
> The grief-assuaging vine.—Oh, let him live,
> For if he die, then Love herself is slain;
> And nothing joyous in the world again.'

FIG. 177.

Eros and Dionysos, the poet sees, are near akin; both are spirits of Life and of Life's ecstasy.

[1] Eur. *Bacch.* 769.

Dionysos like Eros is a *daimon*, a spirit rather than a clear-cut crystallized god; he is as has been already seen of many shapes, of plants and animals as well as man, so he like Eros becomes Phanes:

> 'Therefore him we call both Phanes and Dionysos[1].'

Dionysos is but a new ingredient in the monotheistic mystery melting-pot:

> 'One Zeus, one Hades, one Helios, one Dionysos,
> Yea in all things One God, his name why speak I asunder[2]?'

In becoming the Orphic Phanes Dionysos lost most of his characteristics. In spite of his persistent monotheism we are somehow conscious that Orpheus did not feel all the gods to be really one, all equal manifestations of the same potency. He is concerned to push the claims of the cosmic Eros as against the simpler wine god. Possibly he felt that Dionysos needed much adjustment and was not always for edification. Of this we have some hint in the last literary document to be examined.

In the statutes of the Iobacchoi[3] at Athens, we have already seen (p. 475), the thyrsos became the symbol not of revel but of quiet seemliness. We shall now find that though by name and tradition they are pledged to the worship of Dionysos the Iobacchoi have introduced into their ceremonies a figure more grave and orderly, a figure bearing in the inscription a name of beautiful significance, Proteurhythmos. A part of their great festival consisted in a sacred pantomime, the *rôles* in which were distributed by lot. The divine persons represented were 'Dionysos, Kore, Palaimon, Aphrodite, and Proteurhythmos[4].' Who was Proteurhythmos, First of fair rhythm? The word defies translation into English, but its initial syllable *πρωτ*, first, at once inclines us to see in it an Orphic

[1] Diod. Sic. I. 11. 3, Εὔμολπος μὲν ἐν τοῖς Βακχικοῖς ἔπεσί φησιν Ἀστροφαῆ Διόνυσον ἐν ἀκτίνεσσι πυρωτόν. Ὀρφεὺς δὲ
'Τοὔνεκά μιν καλέουσι Φάνητά τε καὶ Διόνυσον.'

[2] Justinus, *Cohort.* c. 15, καὶ αὖθις ἀλλαχοῦ που οὕτως λέγει
εἷς Ζεύς, εἷς Ἀΐδης, εἷς Ἥλιος, εἷς Διόνυσος,
εἷς θεὸς ἐν πάντεσσι· τί σοι δίχα ταῦτ' ἀγορεύω;

[3] Dr Sam. Wide, *A. Mitt.* XIX. 1894, p. 248 ff.

[4] Inscr. line 120, Μερῶν δὲ γεινομένων αἱρέτω ἱερεὺς ἀνθιερεύς, ἀρχίβακχος ταμίας, βουκολικός, Διόνυσος, Κόρη, Παλαίμων, Ἀφροδείτη, Πρωτεύρυθμος, τὰ δὲ ὀνόματα αὐτῶν συνκληρούσθω πᾶσι.

title like Protogonos or Protolaos. The word has indeed been interpreted[1] as a title of Orpheus himself, Orpheus Proteurhythmos, First dancer or singer. Such an interpretation argues, I think, a grave misunderstanding. It ignores the juxtaposition of Proteurhythmos with Aphrodite and rests for support on the initial error that Orpheus himself is a faded god. Proteurhythmos is, I think, not Orpheus, but a greater than he, the god whom he worshipped, Eros Protogonos. Orpheus is a musician, but it was Eros, not Orpheus, who gave impulse and rhythm to the great dance of creation when 'the Morning Stars sang together.' Eros, not Orpheus, is demiourgos.

Lucian[2] knew this. 'It would seem that dancing came into being at the beginning of all things, and was brought to light together with Eros, that ancient one, for we see this primaeval dancing clearly set forth in the choral dance of the constellations, and in the planets and fixed stars, their interweaving and interchange and orderly harmony.'

It is the primaeval life that Eros, not Orpheus, begets within us, that wakes now and again, that feels the rhythm of a poem, the pulse of a pattern and the chime of a dancer's feet.

> 'In the beginning when the sun was lit
> The maze of things was marshalled to a dance.
> Deep in us lie forgotten strains of it,
> Like obsolete, charmed sleepers of romance.
>
> And we remember, when on thrilling strings
> And hollow flutes the heart of midnight burns,
> The heritage of splendid, moving things
> Descends on us, and the old power returns.'

Eros is Lord of Life and Death, he is also Proteurhythmos, but because of the bitter antinomy of human things to man he is also Lord of Discord and Misrule. And therefore the chorus in the *Hippolytus*[3], brooding over the sickness and disorder of Phaedra, prays:

> 'When I am thine, O Master, bring thou near
> No spirit of evil, make not jarred the clear
> Wings' music as thou fliest.'

---

[1] E. Maass, *Orpheus*, p. 64. The theory that Orpheus is a god seems to me to vitiate much of Dr Maass's interesting and valuable book.

[2] Lucian, *De Salt.* 7 § 271, ...καὶ εὔρυθμος αὐτῶν κοινωνία καὶ εὔτακτος ἁρμονία τῆς πρωτογόνου ὀρχήσεως δείγματά ἐστι.

[3] Eur. *Hipp.* 527.

The gods whose worship Orpheus taught were two, Bacchus and Eros; in actual religion chiefly Bacchus, in mystical dogma Eros, and in ancient Greek religion these are the only real gods. Orpheus dimly divined the truth, later to become explicit through Euripides of Phlya:

'I saw that there are first and above all
The hidden forces, blind necessities
Named Nature, but the things self-unconceived.
We know not how imposed above ourselves,
We well know what I name the god, a power
Various or one.'

Through all the chaos of his cosmogony and the shifting, uncertain outlines of his personifications, we feel, in these two gods lies the real advance of the religion of Orpheus—an advance, not only beyond the old *riddance* of ghosts and sprites and demons, but also beyond the gracious and beautiful *service* of those magnified mortals, the Olympians. The religion of Orpheus *is* religious in the sense that it is the worship of the real mysteries of life, of potencies (δαίμονες) rather than personal gods (θεοί); it is the worship of life itself in its supreme mysteries of ecstasy and love. '*Reason is great, but it is not everything. There are in the world things, not of reason, but both below and above it, causes of emotion which we cannot express, which we tend to worship, which we feel perhaps to be the precious things in life. These things are God or forms of God, not fabulous immortal men, but "Things which Are," things utterly non-human and non-moral which bring man bliss or tear his life to shreds without a break in their own serenity*[1].'

It is these real gods, this life itself, that the Greeks, like most men, were inwardly afraid to recognize and face, afraid even to worship. Orpheus too was afraid—the garb of the ascetic that he always wears is the token at once of his realization and his fear—but at least he dares to worship. Now and again a philosopher or a poet, in the very spirit of Orpheus, proclaims these true gods, and asks in wonder why to their shrines is brought no sacrifice. Plato[2] in the *Symposium* makes Aristophanes say, 'Mankind would seem to have never realized the might of Eros, for if they had really felt it they would have built him great sanctuaries and altars and offered solemn sacrifices, and none of these things are

[1] Murray, *Ancient Greek Literature*, p. 272.
[2] Plat. *Symp.* 189.

done, but of all things they ought to be done.' Euripides[1] in the *Hippolytus* makes his chorus sing:

'In vain, in vain by old Alpheus' shore,
The blood of many bulls doth stain the river,
And all Greece bows on Phoebus' Pythian floor,
Yet bring we to the Master of Man no store,
The Keybearer that standeth at the door
Close barred, where hideth ever
Love's inmost jewel. Yea, though he sack man's life,
Like a sacked city and moveth evermore,
Girt with calamity and strange ways of strife,
Him have we worshipped never.'

To resume: the last word in ancient Greek religion was said by the Orphics, and the beautiful figure of Orpheus is strangely modern. Then, as now, we have, for one side of the picture, a revived and intensified spirituality, an ardent, even ecstatic enthusiasm, a high and self-conscious standard of moral conduct, a deliberate simplicity of life; abstinence from many things, temperance in all, a great quiet of demeanour, a marvellous gentleness to all living things.

And, for the reverse, we have formalism, faddism, priggishness, a constant, and it would seem inevitable lapse into arid symbolism, pseudo-science, pseudo-philosophy, the ignorant revival of obsolete rites, the exhibition of all manner of ignoble thaumaturgy and squalid credulity. The whole strange blend redeemed, illuminated but confounded, in practice by the strenuous effort after purity of life, in theory by the 'further determination of the Absolute' into the mysticism of Love.

[1] Eur. *Hipp.* 535.

CRITICAL APPENDIX ON THE ORPHIC TABLETS.

I. *The Petelia Tablet.*

Found in excavations near Petelia, S. Italy: now in the British Museum. Kaibel, *CIGIS*, No. 638. Cf. Comparetti, *J.H.S.* III. p. 112.

ΕΥΡΗΣΣΕΙΣ Δ' ΑΙΔΑΟ ΔΟΜΩΝ ΕΠ' ΑΡΙΣΤΕΡΑ ΚΡΗΝΗΝ,
ΠΑΡ Δ' ΑΥΤΗΙ ΛΕΥΚΗΝ ΕΣΤΗΚΥΙΑΝ ΚΥΠΑΡΙΣΣΟΝ·
ΤΑΥΤΗΣ ΤΗΣ ΚΡΗΝΗΣ ΜΗΔΕ ΣΧΕΔΟΝ ΕΜΠΕΛΑΣΕΙΑΣ.
ΕΥΡΗΣΕΙΣ Δ' ΕΤΕΡΑΝ ΤΗΣ ΜΝΗΜΟΣΥΝΗΣ ΑΠΟ ΛΙΜΝΗΣ
ΨΥΧΡΟΝ ΥΔΩΡ ΠΡΟΡΕΟΝ, ΦΥΛΑΚΕΣ Δ' ΕΠΙΠΡΟΣΘΕΝ ΕΑΣΙΝ.
ΕΙΠΕΙΝ· ΓΗΣ ΠΑΙΣ ΕΙΜΙ ΚΑΙ ΟΥΡΑΝΟΥ ΑΣΤΕΡΟΕΝΤΟΣ,
ΑΥΤΑΡ ΕΜΟΙ ΓΕΝΟΣ ΟΥΡΑΝΙΟΝ· ΤΟΔΕ Δ' ΙΣΤΕ ΚΑΙ ΑΥΤΟΙ·
ΔΙΨΗΙ Δ' ΕΙΜΙ ΑΥΗ ΚΑΙ ΑΠΟΛΛΥΜΑΙ· ΑΛΛΑ ΔΟΤ' ΑΙΨΑ
ΨΥΧΡΟΝ ΥΔΩΡ ΠΡΟΡΕΟΝ ΤΗΣ ΜΝΗΜΟΣΥΝΗΣ ΑΠΟ ΛΙΜΝΗΣ.
ΚΑΥΤ⟨ΟΙ ΣΟ⟩Ι ΔΩΣΟΥΣΙ ΠΙΕΙΝ ΘΕΙΗΣ ΑΠ⟨Ο ΛΙΜΝ⟩ΗΣ
ΚΑΙ ΤΟΤ' ΕΠΕΙΤ' Α⟨ΛΛΟΙΣΙ ΜΕΘ'⟩ ΗΡΩΕΣΣΙΝ ΑΝΑΞΕΙΣ
· · · · · ΙΗΣ ΤΟΔΕ · · · · · ΘΑΝΕΙΣΘ · · · ·
· · · · · · · ΤΟΔΕΓΡΑΨ · · · · ·
· · · ΓΛΩΣΕΙΠΑ (?) · · · ΣΚΟΤΟΣ ΑΜΦΙΚΑΛΥΨΑΣ

'Thou shalt find to the left of the House of Hades a Well-spring,
And by the side thereof standing a white cypress.
To this Well-spring approach not near.

But thou shalt find another by the Lake of Memory,
Cold water flowing forth, and there are Guardians before it.
Say: "I am a child of Earth and of Starry Heaven;
But my race is of Heaven (alone). This ye know yourselves.
And lo, I am parched with thirst and I perish. Give me quickly
The cold water flowing forth from the Lake of Memory."
And of themselves they will give thee to drink from the holy Well-spring,
And thereafter among the other Heroes thou shalt have lordship....'

Kaibel (l.c.) says "pertinet lammina, ut nunc apparet, ad saeculum iii vel summum iv ante Chr. n." It had formerly been supposed to be much later. He confidently attributes the accompanying tablet (No. V.) to the fourth century, and this one seems to me to be quite as early or earlier. It is altogether more carefully written, which detracts from its appearance of age. The use of the diphthong *ου* for instance, where No. V. has *ο*, is probably a sign of careful writing, not of lateness. The letters are very well formed and early in shape. Subscript *ι* is never neglected. Elision only once (*εἰμὶ αὔη*), and then, it would seem, of set purpose to avoid ambiguity. Weight must also be allowed to the completeness and accuracy with which the text of the "ancient Orphic poem" (see below on No. V.) is given, with no compendia or corruptions. The dialect, also, is pure literary epic; i.e., one may presume, the pure dialect of the "ancient poem" itself, with no admixture of local forms such as have crept by process of time into the formulae on the other tablets. The double *σ* of *εὑρήσσεις* in l. 1 may indeed be dialectical; cf. *ἀσστεροβλῆτα*, *Δεσσποίνας* in V., but that scarcely affects the main impression.

II. Three tablets from Crete (Eleuthernae?) now in the National Museum at Athens.

A.

ΔΙΨΑΙΑΥΟϹΛΑΙϹϹΕΓΩΚΙΙΑΠ·ΛΛΥΜΑΙΑΛΛΑΠΙΕΜΙΥΟΥ
ΚΡΑΝΑϹΑΙΕΝΑΩΕΠΙΔΕ-ΙΑΤΗΚΥΦΑΡ\'ΣΟϹ
ΤΙϹΔϹΖΙΠΩΔΕΖΙΓΑϹΥΙΟϹΗΜΙΚΑΙΩΡΑΝΩ
ΑϹΤΕΡΟΕΝΤΟϹ

Length 55 mm.; breadth 7 mm.

B.

ΔΙΨΑΙΑΥΟϹΕΓΩΚΑΙΑΠΟΛΛΥΜΑΜΑΙΑΛΛΑΠΙΕΜΟΥ
ΚΡΑΝΑϹΑΙΕΙΡΟΩΕΠΙΔΕΞΙΑΤΗΚΥΦΑΡΙΣΟϹ
ΤΙϹΔΕΣΙΠΩΔΕΙΙΤΑϹΥΙΟϹΗΜΙΚΑΙΩΡΑΝΩ
ΑϹΤΕΡΟϹΝΤΟϹ

Length 62 mm.; breadth 8 mm.

C.

ΔΙΨΑΙΑΥΟΣΕΓΩ ΚΑΙΑΠΟΛΛΥΜΑΙΑΛΛΑΠΙΕΜΟΙ
ΚΡΑΝΑΣΑΙΕΙΡΟΩΕΠΙΔΕΞΙΑΤΗ ΚΥΦΑΡΙΣΟΣ
ΤΙΣΔΕΣΙΠΩΔΕΣΙΓΑΣΥΙΟΣΗΜΙΚΑΙΩΡΑΝΩ
ΑΣΤΕΡΟΕΝΤΟΣ

Length 56 mm.; breadth 10 mm.

The general formula represented by these tablets is:

Δίψαι αὖος ἐγὼ καὶ ἀπόλλυμαι—'Αλλὰ πίε μμου
Κράνας αἰερόω [or αἰενάω] ἐπὶ δεξιὰ, τῇ κυφάρισος.
Τίς δ' ἐσι;....................
πῶ δ' ἐσι;...Γᾶς υἱὸς ἠμὶ καὶ ὠρανῶ ἀστερόεντος.

'I am parched with thirst and I perish.—Nay, drink of Me,
The Well-spring flowing for ever on the Right, where the Cypress is.
Who art thou?.................
Whence art thou?—I am son of Earth and of Starry Heaven.'

Tablet C was published, with some inaccuracies, by M. Joubin in *Bull. de Corr. Hell.* xvii. p. 122, where it is said to have been found at Eleuthernae in Crete. I subjoin an account of the three tablets kindly sent by Mr Marcus Tod, Assistant Director of the British School at Athens, to whom are also due the above fac-similes.

"The inscription is at present in the *Ethnikon Mouseion* here, and along with it are two others almost exactly similar. I could get no information about them, save that they also, according to the Εὑρετήριον of the Museum, are 'from Crete.' All three are on thin strips of gold, roughly rectangular, and are traced in very small and fine letters with a needle point. The execution is in all three instances rough, but C is considerably better in this respect than A; B holds an intermediate position. I worked with a powerful magnifying glass, and in most cases am quite sure of my readings even where I differ from *Bull. Corr. Hell.*"

NOTES: l. 1. What comes between αὖος and ἐγὼ in A, Mr Tod cannot decipher. Was it αὖος written twice?

πιε μοι C: πιε μου B (and C, according to Joubin). I had conjectured from Joubin's reading πίε μμου, the initial μ being doubled as in ἐνὶ μμεγάροισιν, etc., in the so-called Aeolic poetry (Cretan = Arcadian = 'Urgriechisch'), and this proves to be the reading of A.

l. 2. αιειροω C and B. Joubin gave αἰεὶ ῥέω: αιεναω A. Evidently the Doric genitive of an adj. αἰέροος or αἰέναος. Mr Tod (and I also) had conjectured αἰὲ ῥέω, and he would also take αἰενάω as a verb.

τῇ κυφάρισος: sc. ἐστί.

As to the metre and reading of the last line, see below p. 671.

III. *Timpone Grande Tablet* (*a*).

A thin rectangular slip of gold, like the others, found in a large tomb in the commune of Corigliano-Calabro, S. Italy. (Published in the *Atti d. R. Accad. dei Lincei*, Serie III. 1878—79; *Memorie*, p. 328: cf. Kaibel, *CIGIS*, 642.) The fac-simile that follows was kindly furnished by Prof. Comparetti.

ΑΛΛΟΠΟΤΑΜΨΥΧΗΠΡΟΛΙΠΗΙΦΑΟΣΑΕΛΙΟΙΟ
ΔΕΞΙΟΝΕ ΟΙΑΣ ΔΕΙΤΙΝΑΠΕΦΥΛΑΓΜΕΝΟΝ
ΕΥΜΑΛΑΠΑΝΤΑΧ ΑΙΡΕΠΑΘΩΝΤΟΠΑΘΗ
ΜΑΤΟΔΟΥΠΩΙ ΟΣ ΘΕΕΠΕΠΟΝΘΕΙΣΘΕΟΣΕΙ
ΕΝΟΥΕΞ ΑΝΘΡΩΠΟΥΕΡΙΦΟΣΕΣΓΑΛΑ
ΕΠΕΤΕΣΧΑΙΡΧΑΙΡΕΔΕΞΙΑΝΟΔΟΙΠΟΡ
ΛΕΙΜΩΝΑΣΤΕΙΕΡΟΥΣΚΑΤΑΑΣΕΑ
ΦΕΣΕ ΝΕΙΑΣ

'Αλλ' ὁπόταμ ψυχὴ προλίπηι φάος ἀελίοιο
δεξιὸν εν·οιας δειτινα
............πεφυλαγμένον εὖ μάλα πάντα.
Χαῖρε παθὼν τὸ πάθημα, τόδ' οὔπω πρόσθε ἐπεπόνθεις.
θεὸς ἐγένου ἐξ ἀνθρώπου.
ἔριφος ἐς γάλα ἔπετες.
χαῖρε, χαῖρε, δεξιὰν ὁδοιπορ<ῶν>
λειμῶνάς τε ἱεροὺς κατά <τ'> ἄ<λ>σεα Φεσε<φο>νείας.

'But so soon as the Spirit hath left the light of the sun,
To the right......................................of Ennoia
Then must man...............being right wary in all things.
Hail, thou who hast suffered the Suffering. This thou hadst never suffered before.
Thou art become God from Man. A kid thou art fallen into milk.
Hail, hail to thee journeying on the right.........
...Holy meadows and groves of Phersephoneia.'

l. 2. The reading is doubtful. The strip of gold has been folded over and over, making eight little divisions by vertical lines and four by horizontal. The curious thing is that in some cases the fold has been allowed for in the writing, in others not. For instance, the first vertical fold would cut, as a rule, the seventh or eighth letter from the beginning. A large space has been left for it between *ἐξ* and *ἀνθρώπου* in line 5 (the gold is worn into a little hole at this point, and may have been somehow injured before the writing was made); and in lines 1, 3, 4 and 7 the letters successfully dodge it. But the *χ* of *χαῖρε* is half obliterated, and the letter following *ε* in l. 2 is lost in a mass of crumpled gold. It might be ΕΙΟΙΑΣ = *ἠοίας*, supposing a space to be vacant in the crumple, as between *ἐξ* and *ἀνθρώπου*. But ΕΝΟΙΑΣ is the most probable, standing presumably for ΕΝΝΟΙΑΣ. The following word has generally been read as ΔΕΙ, though ΑΕΙ is equally probable.

l. 3. *τόδ' οὔπω*: *τό τ' οὔπω* coni. Kaibel.

ἐγένου. The γ is clear.

As to the interpretation of l. 2, we may accept Kaibel's judgment: "videtur versus ex duobus coaluisse: nam hoc quoque carmen ex antiquiore archetypo derivatum est." But any attempt to restore the original "carmen antiquum" is utterly uncertain. How uncertain, it may be worth while illustrating from a parallel instance.

There is a small oval Christian amulet (*CIGIS* 2413, 18) containing verses from an elegiac poem of Gregory Nazianzene in an abbreviated form. One passage, for instance, runs in the original

> *Χριστὸς ἄναξ κέλεταί σε φυγεῖν ἐς λαῖτμα θαλάσσης*
> *ἠὲ κατὰ σκοπέλων ἠὲ συῶν ἀγελήν,*
> *ὡς Λεγεῶνα πάροιθεν ἀτάσθαλον.*

This appears on the amulet (I divide the words):

> *Χσ ἄναξ κέλετέ σε φυγὲν ἐσ λἐτμα θαλάσσης*
> *ἐ ἀ σκοπέλων ἐ συῶ ἀὴν*
> *ὠ εενα πάροι ἀτάσθαλον.*

The accented letter alone, or the first and last, or a group of letters in the middle are made to stand for a word. On this principle we might find in ΔΕΙΤΙΝΑ

> *Δεξιόν, Ἐννοίας Δεσποίνας ὕδατι λίμνας*

or various other formulae built up in the same manner. (I mark the letters which occur, not those which are omitted.)

But, is this the process that has taken place at all? The same amulet, a few lines earlier, in place of

> *φεῦγ' ἀπ' ἐμῶν μελέων, φεῦγ' ἀπ' ἐμοῦ βιότου,*
> *κλώψ, ὄφι, πῦρ, βελιάρ, κακίη, μόρε*

gives

> *φεῦγ' ἀπ' ἐμῶν μελέων ψόφι πῦρ βελιάρ κακίη μόρε*

through mere lipography, the writer's eye having wandered from φ to ψ.

On this principle we may here be dealing with an original such as

> *Δεξιόν, Ἐννοίας ἀεί τινα ποσσὶ φέρεσθαι*
> *χριμπτόμενον κρανᾶς, πεφυλαγμένον εὖ μάλα πάντα.*

Such conjectures are merely illustrative. The basis of sound conclusion seems to be that we have here fragments of formulae, not a complete sentence. (See below p. 671.)

The word *δεξιὸν* must, I think, certainly bear its ordinary meaning "right," "on the right": cf. l. 6 *δεξιὰν ὁδοιπορῶν*, and, for the syntax, *δεξιὸς ἀΐξας ὑπὲρ ἄστεος* Ω 320; *ὧδε καταστὰς, δεξιὸς, ἀθανάτοις θεοῖσιν ἐπευχόμενος* Theogn. 943. "On the right, by the Spring of Ennoia" means, perhaps "by the Spring of Thought issuing from the Lake of Memory."

Such a sense would suit the doctrines of tablets I. and II., and might even help to explain the origin of Dante's *Eunoë*. (Professor Comparetti, who takes *δεξιὸν* in the metaphorical prose sense of "clever," considers the introduction of such a word to be due to Euripidean or sophistic influence.)

IV. *Timpone Grande Tablet (b).*

ΠΡΑΤΟΤΟΝΟΤΗΜΑΙΤΙΕΤΗΤΑΜΜΑΤΡΙΕΠΑΚΥΒΕΛΕΙΑΚΟΡΡΑΙΣ ΕΝΤΑΙΝΑΗΜΗΤΡΟΣΗΤ
ΤΑΤΑΙΤΤΑΤΑΠΤΑΣΕΥΡΑΤΗΤΥ ΔΕΡΣΑΠΑΗΔΙΕΠΥΙΝΗΙΑΝΤΑΣ ΤΗΙΝΤΑΣ ΤΗΝ ΚΑΤΟΠΕΥΙΚΑΙΙ
ΣΗΔΕΤΥΧΑΗΕΦΑΝΗΣΠΑΜΜΗΕΥΙΜΟΗΑΙΣ ΣΤΗΤΟΙΤΑΝΝΥΑΝΑΝΤΗΣΥΚΛΗΤΕΔΑΡΜΟΝΔΕ
ΣΠΑΤΡΑΤΙΣΠΑΝΤΑΔΑΜΑΣΤΑΡΑΝ ΤΗΡΝΥΝ ΤΑΙΣΕΛΑΒΔΟΝΤΑΣΕΠΑΝΙΕΜΟΙΒΝΣΤΑΗΣΕΑΠΑ
ΤΗΜΗΑΕΡΙΠΥΟΜΕΜΜΑΙΕΔΑΥΕΣΤΙΣ ΗΔΥΕΠΤΑ ΤΟΝΗΣΣΙΝΝ ΝΕ ΙΝΗΜΕΘΗΜΕΡΑΝΕΓΛΥΥΕ
ΕΠΤΙΗΜΑΡΤΙΝΙΟΙΣ ΙΑΣΤΑΝΙΕΥΕΝΥΡΥΤΤΙΕ ΚΑΙΗΑΝΟΠΤΑΔΙΕΝΑΜΙ ΥΡΜΑΤΕΙΟΜΑΣΕΠ
ΙΔΥΣΡΙ ΕΒΕΥΝΑΣΤΑΚΤΑΠΥΡΟΣΥΛΚΑΠΕΧΙΟΥΑΜΗΙΕΜΟΝ ΚΑΥΝΑΝΕΡΑ ΔΑΜΝΕΥΔΑ ΜΝΥΙ
ΤΑΣΤΗΟΤΕΧΑΜΑ ΠΙΕΙΑΦΝΤΕΑΡΥΙΖΕΥΚΕΤΗΧΕΙΔΑ ΤΡΑΒΣ ΙΗΤΡΟΣΗΥΣ ΤΗΟΠΤΕΙ
ΗΙΞΣΝΗΤΣΥΝΝΑΟΣ ΕΣΠΙΕΝΑΜΑΤΑΜΗΤΝΝ ΤΗΣΝΝΣΥΜΜΕΣΤΟΡΓΜΕΙΣΩΡΗΛΣ
Α ΙΗΡ-ΣΝΟΣΣΧ ΕΥΤΟΛΑΕΡΤΑΙΙ ΜΥΗ· ΦΡΕΝΑΙΛΑΙ

Prof. Comparetti examined the tablet when it was discovered in 1879, and reported (*Notizie d. Scavi*, 1880, p. 328) that it contained names of divinities belonging to the Orphic theology. Of these he then read *Protogonos*, *Gê*, *Pammêtor*, *Kybelê*, *Korê*, *Dêmêtêr* and *Tychê*. For his later results we must await his publication and discussion of the new fac-simile which, by his kindness, is reproduced above. Prof. Diels published the tablet with a full discussion in 1902 (*Ein Orphischer Demeter-Hymnus, Festschrift Theodor Gomperz*, p. 1). He also with great kindness has allowed his photographs of the tablet to be used for the purposes of the present book.

I examined the tablet itself in the Naples Museum and was able here and there to make out a few more letters than Prof. Diels; but, as it evidently did not contain any special Orphic doctrines, and was besides very trying to the eyes, I did not attempt a complete transcript. This note is based chiefly on Prof. Comparetti's fac-simile.

That the tablet is unintelligible as it stands, no one will deny. It seems indeed to belong to that class of magical or cryptic writings in which, as Wünsch puts it, "singulari quadam scribendi ratione id agitur ne legi possint."

Prof. Diels, however, did not view it in this light. He adopted the hypothesis that the tablet was the simple and *bonâ fide* work of an Apulian engraver who knew very little Greek, but was copying a Greek original which already contained various readings. He often got his letters down in the wrong order; often mistook one letter for another; often tried to correct his mistakes by repeating words or syllables.

Much of this seems perfectly true. Cf. for transpositions ισελαβροντα = ἐλασίβροντα, ρσαπια = σάραπι, πτεν αματα = πέντ' ἄματα, μαιτιετη = μητίετα, οσειιταιν = ὁσίη παῖς (?).

Confusions: τλταιττατaπτα Ζεῦ (= πάντοπτα? or ἄττα, ἶᾶτα written backward?), so παννυανταυτης, if that is what is written, must be an attempt to get some word right by repeated correction.

Ignorance of Greek: Ηανοπτα = Πανόπτα, επιτιημαρ = ἐπτῆμαρ are typical, but the above transpositions and confusions point to the same conclusion. On the other hand, there is knowledge of the Greek alphabet, as is shown by the varying shapes of many letters, e.g. δ, ρ [sometimes *R*], π [sometimes P], and the use of compendia: cf. especially the curious compounds with N.

Prof. Diels, however, goes a good deal further than this. He attempts to show that the original from which the tablet is copied is a Hymn to Demeter, written in hexameters; and he proceeds to its conjectural reconstruction—

while observing that "*Niemand die Unsicherheit der Ergänzung verkennen oder die Barbarei der Formen beanstanden wird.*"

The conjecture was worth making, and is carried out with the learning and ability which mark all Prof. Diels's work. So it is less surprising than it would otherwise be, to find the tablet described by scholars[1], without further qualification, as a *Demeter-hymnus*! But it remains a highly improbable hypothesis, not only because of the violent changes necessary to get any consecutive sense suitable to a *Demeter-hymnus*, but more definitely because among the few really legible passages in the tablet, the very clearest are certainly not in dactylic metre; *νυξὶν ἢ μεθ' ἡμέραν, ἰητρὸς Ἥλιε, εὔκλητε δαῖμον*. True, there are fragments also which seem dactylic; *ῥεῦμ' ἄστακτα πυρός, Νίκαις ἠδὲ Τύχαις ἐφάνης παμμήδεσι Μοίραις* (?). But this need not surprise us. The words of a charm, for instance, are sometimes found set in the midst of a hexameter verse: cf. the Tanagra Tablet in Wünsch, *App. CIA*, Praef. p. viii:

> *Ἑρμῆν κικλήσκω χθόνιον*
> *(καταδίδημι Διονυσίαν)*
> *καὶ Φερσεφόνηαν. (δῆσαι Διο-*
> *νυσίας γλῶσαν κτλ.)*

This parallel would account easily for all the hexameter fragments that we have in this tablet.

On the other hand, the strange corruptions and repetitions of the tablet are more than can be explained by the mere ignorance of a copy-maker. They are not indeed similar to the rows of abracadabra-like syllables found in magical papyri (cf. Dieterich, *Abraxas*, p. 178 *θηθουθη ααθω αθηρουωραμια θαρ μιγαρναχφουρι κτλ.*), but they do bear a fairly close resemblance to some of the cryptic curses, in which, as said above, the writing is deliberately confused by transpositions and the like, so as to be unintelligible. Cf. Wünsch, 110:

ΠΡΩΤΟΝΩΣΠΕΡΤΑΥΤΑΑΝΑΤΙ ΟΤΩΣΚΑΙΤΟΣΑΓΟΡΑΙΑΣΠΡΩΤΟ
ΝΑΝΑΤΙΑΕΗΑΠΑΤΑΚΑΙΗΜΑΙΟΙΤΟΙΣΤΟΙΣΤΙΜΑΤΙ ΙΤΑΤΟΠΩΑΕ
ΤΟΙΠΑΡΑΠΡΩΤΟΙΟΤΟΚΑΙΟΤΟΠΩΛΟΤΙΚΑΝΔΕΚΑΙΑΥΤΟΣΚΑΙΤΗ
ΤΗΧΝΗ

(*Πρῶτον ὥσπερ ταῦτα* ..... *οὕτως καὶ ὁ Ἀρισταγόρας* ..... then at the end *καταδέω* (?) *αὐτοὺς καὶ τὴν τέχνην*.)

ΤΟΣΑΓΟΡΑΙΑΣ = *ὁ Ἀρισταγόρας* is just like what we find in our tablet, and examination will show many other resemblances.

I have here attempted no reconstruction. I have merely copied the inscription and tried to collect such intelligible words or phrases as presented themselves at once or were to be reached by very slight emendations. The result so obtained is a patchwork of a few ritual phrases and fragmentary formulae; rows of titles of gods, heroes and daemons, including possibly Phanes and certainly Rhadamanthys; and lastly, an unintelligible residuum.

The whole seems to be a charm of some kind, concerned with healing and fasting. I can find no signs of its being a curse; nor indeed was gold, unless I am mistaken, used for writing curses. The long lists of titles of gods can be paralleled in abundance from magical inscriptions and papyri.

[1] E.g. Maass, *Die Tagesgötter*, p. 288.

Transcript:

ΠΡΩΤΟΤΟΝΟΤΗΜΑΙΤΙΕΤΗΓΑΜΜΑΤΡΙΕΠΑΚΥΒΕΛΕΙΑΚΟΡΡΑΟΣ
ΕΝΤΑΙΝΔΗΜΗΤΡΟΣΗΤ |
ΤΛΤΑΠΤΑΤΑΠΤΑΖΕΥΙΑΤΗΤΥΔΕΡΣΑΠΙΑΗΔΙΕΠΥΡΑΥΗΙΑΝΤΑΣΤ
ΗΙΑΝΤΑΣΤΗΝΚΑΤΟΤΙΕΝΙΚΑΙΙ
ΣΗΔΕΤΥΧΑΙΤΕΦΑΝΗΣΠΑΜΜΗ·ΕΟΙΜΟΙΡΑΙΣΣΤΗΤΟΙΓΑΝΝΥΑΝ
ΑΝΤΗΣΥΚΛΗΤΕΔΑΙΜΟΝΔΕ
ΣΠΑΤΡΙΑΤΙ·ΠΑΝΤΑΔΑΜΑΣΤΑΡΑΝΤΗΡΝΥΝΤΑΙΣΕΛΑΒΡΟΝΤΑ
ΔΕΠΑΝΙΕΜΟΙΒΝΤΣΤΛΗΤΕΑΠΑ
·ΤΗΜΗΑΕΡΙΠΥΟΜΕΜΜΑΙΕΡΑΥΕΣΤΙΣ··Δ·ΕΠΤΑΤΟΝΗΣΣΙΝ
ΝΥΞΙΝΗΜΕΘΗΜΕΡΑΝΕΓΩ···
ΕΠΙΤΙΗΜΑΡΤΙΝΝ·Σ·ΙΑΣΤΑΝΖΕΥΕΝΟΡΥΤΤΙΕΚΑΙΗΑΝΟΠΤΑ
ΔΙΕΝΑΜΙΝΑΜΑΤΕΙΟΜΑΣΕΠ
·ΠΙΔΥΣΕΙ·ΕΡΕΥΜΑΣΤΑΚΤΑΠΥΡΟΣ·ΛΚΑΠΕΔΙΟΝΑΜΗΓΕΜΟΝ
ΚΑΝΝΑΔΙΕΡΑΔΑΜΑΝΘΥΔΑΜΝΥΙ
ΤΑΣΤΗΟΤΕΞΑΜΑΡΙΕ···ΝΤΕΑΡΓΙΖΕΥΚΕΤΗΞΕΙΔΑ···ΤΡΑΒ··
ΙΗΤΡΟΣΗΛΙΣΤΙΙΟΝΤΕΙ
ΗΙ·ΩΣΝΗΓΣΥΝΝΑΟΣΕΣΠΤΕΝΑΜΑΤΑΜΗΤΗΝ··ΤΗΣΝΝΣΥΜ
ΜΕΣΤΟΡΕΜΕ··ΩΡΗΜ
·Α····ΗΡ···ΝΟΣΣ·····ΕΥΤΟΛΑΕΡΤΑΙ· ΜΥΗ·ΦΑΕΝΑ
ΙΝΑΙ

Πρωτόγονε Γῆ Μητίετα παμματριεία(?) Κυβελεία Κόρρα, ὁσίη παῖς(?) Δήμητρος ηταται (?) παταπτα (= παντόπτα ?) Ζεῦ Ἰάτη, τὺ δὲ Σάραπι (?) Ἥλιε πυραύη φανταστὴ φανταστὴ ἑκατο··ιε (?) Νίκα ἴση δὲ Τύχα· ἴτε Φάνης πάμμηστοι Μοῖραι [or Νίκαις ἠδὲ τύχαις ἐφάνης παμμήδεσι Μοίραις] Στῆτοι (?) παντανυσταὶ (?) εὔκλητε Δαῖμον δέσποτα Ἰάτη (?) παντοδάμαστα παντήρνυντα (= παντοκράτυντα ?) ἐλασίβροντα δρεπάνιε (?)····· τλητέα πάντη. Μὴ ἀέρι πύωμ' ἔμ μοι ἐπαύης, (?) τίσω···· ἑπτατόνησιν. Νυξὶν ἢ μεθ' ἡμέραν ἐγὼ····ἑπτῆμαρ τὴν νηστιαστὺν (?) Ζεῦ ἐνορύττιε καὶ πανόπτα δῖε ναματιαῖε (?)···ἐκπιδύσετε ῥεῦμ' ἄστακτα πυρὸς···καπ πεδίον (?)··· ἡγεμὸν ····· δῖε Ῥαδάμανθυ ······· ἑξάμαρ····· Ζεῦ ··· Δά⟨μα⟩τρα ··· ἰητρὸς Ἥλιε (?) ············ ὡς ⟨ἂ⟩ν ἡ σύνναος πέντ' ἄματα μὴ ········ συμμηστόρε (?)··· ωρην ··················

One might translate tentatively: "O First-Born, Earth, Counsellor, All-Motherly, Cybelean, Kora, Holy Child of Demeter (?)......, All-Seeing Zeus, Healer, and thou Sarapis, Sun, Fire-Kindler, Maker-of-Appearances, Far-Seeing (??)

Victory and equal Fortune; come ye, Phanes, All-Counselling Fates (or With victories and Fortunes thou didst appear, with the All-Devising Fates)

Stayers (?), All-Accomplishers (?), Well-named Daemon, Master, Healer (?), All-Subduer, All-Controller, Driver of Thunder, Sickle-Bearer (?),...........to be endured in all wise. That thou mayest not with vapour make to burn a tumour in me (??) ... I will pay ... sevenfold fasting. In the nights or after daybreak I ...... for seven days the fasting.

Zeus Penetrator (?) and All-seeing, Divine, Ruler of Streams, ... ye will make to spring a stream not in drops of fire.........

Plain ...... guide ... Divine Rhadamanthys ...... for six days...... Zeus...... Demeter ...... Healer, Sun ...... that She sharing the Shrine for five days may not................. "

V., VI. and VII. *The Compagno Tablets.*

Published *Notizie degli Scavi*, 1880. Cf. Kaibel, *CIGIS*, 481, *a*, *b*, *c*. These three tablets were found on the estate of the Baron Compagno, near Naples, not far from the Timpone Grande. The tablets were close to the hand of the skeleton in each case.

V. *Compagno Tablet* (*a*).

ΕΡΧΟΜΑΙ ΕΚ ΚΟΘΑΡΟΝ, ΚΟΘΑΡΑ ΧΘΟΝΙ(ων) ΒΑΣΙΛΕΙΑ,
ΕΥΚΛΗΣ ΕΥΒΟΛΕΥΣ ΤΕ ΚΑΙ ΑΘΑΝΑΤΟΙ ΘΕΟΙ ΑΛΛΟΙ.
ΚΑΙ ΓΑΡ ΕΓΩΝ ΥΜΩΝ ΓΕΝΟΣ ΟΛΒΙΟΝ ΕΥΧΟΜΑ(ι) ΕΙΜΕΝ,
ΑΛΑ ΜΕ ΜΟΡΑ ΕΔΑΜΑΣΕ ΚΑΙ ΑΘΑΝΑΤΟΙ ΘΕΟΙ ΑΛΛΟΙ
········ ΚΑΙ ΑΣΣΤΕΡΟΒΛΗΤΑ ΚΕΡΑΥΝΟΝ.
ΚΥΚΛΟ Δ' ΕΞΕΠΤΑΝ ΒΑΡΥΠΕΝΘΕΟΣ ΑΡΓΑΛΕΟΙΟ·
ΙΜΕΡΤΟ Δ' ΕΠΕΒΑΝ ΣΤΕΦΑΝΟ ΠΟΣΙ ΚΑΡΠΑΛΙΜΟΙΣΙ·
ΔΕΣΣΠΟΙΝΑΣ ΔΕ ΥΠΟ ΚΟΛΠΟΝ ΕΔΥΝ ΧΘΟΝΙΑΣ ΒΑΣΙΛΕΙΑΣ·
ΙΜΕΡΤΟ Δ' ΑΠΕΒΑΝ ΣΤΕΜΑΝΟ ΠΟΣΙ ΚΑΡΠΑΣΙΜΟΙΣΙ.
ΟΛΒΙΕ ΚΑΙ ΜΑΚΑΡΙΣΤΕ, ΘΕΟΣ Δ' ΕΣΗΙ ΑΝΤΙ ΒΡΟΤΟΙΟ.
ΕΡΙΦΟΣ ΕΣ ΓΑΛ' ΕΠΕΤΟΝ.

Kaibel remarks with regard to these three documents: "Fuit aliquando Saeculo Quarto antiquius apud Sybaritas carmen, quod Orphico, ut ita dicam, dicendi genere conceptum lamminis aureis inscriptum defunctorum corporibus imponi solebat, quo ipsi vitae ante actae quasi testimonio fidei deorum inferorum commendarentur. Quod carmen cum in usum sepulcrorum saepius describeretur, sensim corrumpebatur et in brevius redigebatur, omissis aliis, aliis additis, pluribus denique mutatis, ut tamen primaria indoles non oblitteraretur. Tria nunc exempla inventa sunt....Antiquius primum est, quod ad IV a. Chr. n. saeculum referri iubet ipsa ratio orthographica (ΚΥΚΛΟ, ΙΜΕΡΤΟ, ΣΤΕΦΑΝΟ) sed haud ita multo recentiora reliqua duo, quod docet scripturae genus simillimum."

The letters are ancient and well formed, approaching more closely to those of fourth and fifth century inscriptions than to the papyrus of, say, Timotheus.

l. 1. The form *κοθαρός* is dialectical. It occurs in Elean and Thurian inscriptions, e.g. the Heraclean Tables. Contrast this peculiarity with the style of Tablet I.

I punctuate after *κοθαρῶν*: "I come from the Pure, O Pure Queen," not "Pure I come from the Pure, O Queen." The rhythm of the line points strongly to this. Only by a definite system of punctuation, such as did not exist in ancient Greek, could you in such a sentence make a reader pause elsewhere than in the natural pause of the metre. The sense is : "I come from the Orphically-initiated, O Queen of the Orphically-initiated."

3, 4, 5, 8. εἶμεν, Μôρα (=Μοῖρα: cf. the next tablet), ἀσστεροβλῆτα, Δεσποίνας are all dialectical forms.

7 and 9. Observe the difference of reading. *V.* 9 is wrong in στεμάνο and καρπασίμοισι, so ἀπέβαν, in itself an interesting variant, must be suspected to be mere mistake also.

VI. *Compagno Tablet* (*b*).

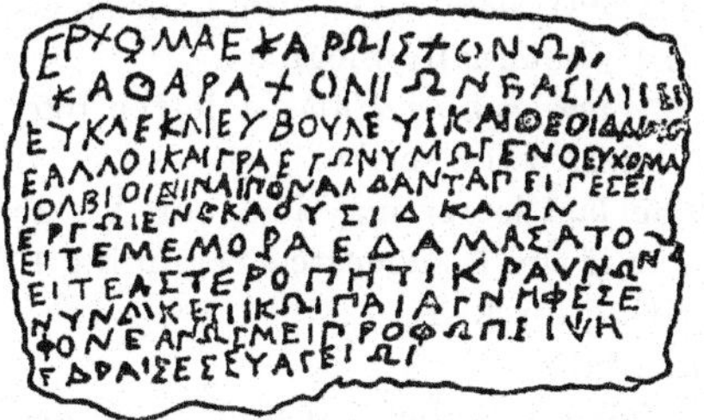

ΕΡΧΟΜΑ Ε ΚΑΡΩΙΣ ΧΟΝΩΝ ΚΑΘΑΡΑ ΧΟΝΙΩΝ ΒΑΣΙΛΗΕΙ
ΕΥΚΛΕ ΚΑΙ ΕΥΒΟΥΛΕΥΙ ΚΑΙ ΘΕΟΙ ⟨και⟩ ΔΑΙΜΟΝΕ⟨c⟩ ΑΛΛΟΙ
ΚΑΙ ΓΡΑ ΕΓΩΝ ΥΜΩ ΓΕΝΟ ΕΥΧΟΜΑΙ ΟΛΒΙΟΙΝ Ε̣ΙΝΑΙ
ΠΟΝΑΝ̣ Δ ΑΝΤΑΠΕΙΓ̣ΕΣΕΙ ΕΡΓΩΙ ΕΝΕΚΑ ΟΥΣ̣Ι Δ⟨ι⟩ΚΑΩΝ
ΕΙΤΕ ΜΕ ΜΟΡΑ ΕΔΑΜΑΣΑΤΟ ΕΙΤΕ ΑΣΤΕΡΟΠΗΤΙ Κ⟨ε⟩ΡΑΥΝΩΝ
ΝΥΝ Δ ΙΚΕΤΙ ΙΚΩΙ ΠΑΙ̣ ΑΓΝΗν ΦΕΣΕΦΟΝΕΑΝ
ΩΣ ΜΕΙ ΠΡΟΦΩ ΠΕΙΨΗ Ε̣ΔΡΑΙ̣Σ ΕΣ ΕΥΑΓΕΙΩΙ

1. Κ may be compendium for ΚΘ; ΙΣ seems to be a mistake for Ν.

3. ΕΙΝΑΙ either begun *per compendium* and then written in full, or else the Ν of ολβιον is compounded with the Ε. Cf. the next tablet.

4. Sc. ποινὰν δ' ἀνταπέτεισ' ἔργων ἕνεκ' οὐχὶ δικαίων.

6, 7. Sc. Νῦν δ' ἱκέτης ἵκω παρ' ἁγνὴν (or ἀγαυὴν ?) Φερσεφόνειαν
ὥς με πρόφρων πέμψῃ ἕδρας ἐς εὐαγέων.

VII. *Compagno Tablet* (*c*).

ΕΡΧΟΜΑΙ Ε ΚΑΘΑΡΩ ΚΑ₰ Ο ΒΑΣΙΛΕΑΕ̣
Ε̣ΥΚΛΕ⟨ΥΑ⟩ ΚΑ ΕΥΒΟΛΕΥ ΚΑΙ ΘΕΟΙ ΟΣΟΙ ΔΜΟΝΕΣ ΑΛΛΟ
ΚΑΙ ΓΑΡ ΕΩ ΥΩ̣ ΓΕΝΟΣ ΕΥΧΟΜΑΙ ΕΙΝΑΙ ΟΛΒΙΟ
ΠΟΙΝΑΝ ΝΑΤΑΠΕΤΕ ΕΡΓΩ ΟΤΙ ΔΙΚΑΩΝ
ΕΤ ΜΕ ΜΟΙΡ·······ΑΣΤΕΡΟΠΗΤΙ ⟨ΚΑ̣Ι⟩ ΚΕΡΑΥΝΟ
ΝΥΝ ΔΕ ΚΕ ΙΚΩ ΛΚΩ ΠΑΡΑ ΦΣΕΦ
ΩΣ ΜΕ ΡΟΦ ΠΕΨΕ Μ ΕΔΡΑΣ ΕΣ ΕΥΓΩ

1. Perhaps ΕΚΚΑΘΑΡΩ, a double Κ being written *per compendium.*

ΚΑ₰ apparently ΚΑΘΡΟ *per compendium*, or even *καθαρά*. The letter given as Ο is more like Π, but really illegible.

After ΒΑΣΙΛΕΑ (ΕΑ *per compendium*) a letter like Ε or R. The name Eukles seems to have puzzled the scribe.

2. ΕΥΚΛΕΥΛ. The last letter may be Α or Λ. Probably there is some confused dittography, as if the Ε suggested beginning ΕΥΚΛΕ again.

ΟΣΟΙ seems miswriting for ΚΑΙ.

3. ΥΩ or ΥΜ: uncertain.

Εἶναι *per compendium*: cf. the foregoing. Kaibel says of (*b*) and (*c*): "Haec duo carmina videntur ex communi archetypo esse descripta non solum quod inter se magis similia sunt quam utrumque primo, sed etiam propterea quod eadem ligatura in utroque verba ὄλβιον εἶναι scripta sunt."

4. Or ΝΑΤΑΠΕΤΕΙΣ ΡΓΩ for ἀνταπέτεισ'.

5. ΕΤ: perhaps *compendium* for εἴτε.

The Σ of ἀστεροπῆτι is like Ε. Before κεραυνô there seems to be καὶ by dittography.

The general formulae represented by the three tablets together, may be translated:

'Out of the Pure I come, Pure Queen of Them Below,
And Eukles and Eubouleus, and other Gods and Daemons:
For I also avow me that I am of your blessed race.
And I have paid the penalty for deeds unrighteous,
Whether it be that Fate laid me low or the Gods Immortal
Or.................. with star-flung thunderbolt.
I have flown out of the sorrowful weary Wheel;
I have passed with eager feet to the Circle desired;
I have sunk beneath the bosom of Despoina, Queen of the Underworld;
I have passed with eager feet to (*or* from) the Circle desired;
And now I come a suppliant to Holy Phersephoneia
That of her grace she receive me to the seats of the Hallowed.—
Happy and Blessèd One, thou shalt be God instead of Mortal.'

(The prose formula: 'A kid I have fallen into milk': is once inserted in the midst of the poem.)

To sum up, we find in these three tablets some common characteristics. They all show traces of the influence of some colloquial Italian dialect. The form κοθαρὸς is Thurian. The free omission and addition of final Ν is probably another Italian symptom, having its analogy in the treatment of final M in Latin. It seems not to have been pronounced. We find ΥΜΩ (ὑμῶν), ΠΡΟΦΩ (*πρόφρων*), ΑΓΝΗ (*ἁγνὴν*), ΕΥΑΓΕΙΩ (*εὐαγεῶν*) and *vice versa* ΚΡΑΥΝΩΝ (*κεραυνῷ*). There is the same uncertainty about Ι following another vowel: we have ΕΡΧΟΜΑ, ΜΕΙ (*με*), ΙΚΩΙ. The writer of (*b*), and perhaps of (*c*) also, did not understand what words he was writing. One could be more sure about (*c*) if it were not that some of his most glaring apparent mistakes prove on examination to be compendiary forms and possibly accurate.

But another form of compendiary writing occurs, I think, in all of these tablets, and is of more interest.

There is a sentence which appears in (*c*) as

ΕΤ ΜΕ ΜΟΙΡ ············ ΑΣΤΕΡΟΠΗΤΙ (ΚΑΙ) ΚΕΡΑΥΝΟ.

Evidently not a complete sentence, any more than it is a complete verse, but a beginning and end with the middle omitted.

In (*b*) we have it a little fuller.

ΕΙΤΕ ΜΕ ΜΟΡΑ ΕΔΑΜΑΣΑΤΟ ···· ΕΙΤΕ ΑΣΤΕΡΟΠΗΤΙ ΚΡΑΥΝΩΝ.

This, with a little necessary emendation, might seem to be a complete sentence, as indeed Kaibel takes it, were it not for a fuller version still in (*a*).

ΑΛΑ ΜΕ ΜΟΡΑ ΕΔΑΜΑΣΕ ΚΑΙ ΑΘΑΝΑΤΟΙ ΘΕΟΙ ΑΛΛΟΙ
······· ΚΑΙ ΑΣΣΤΕΡΟΒΛΗΤΑ ΚΕΡΑΥΝΟΝ.

This fuller and correcter version is obviously incomplete, both in sense and in metre. The conclusion seems to be that we have in all three cases a confessedly incomplete collection of words, standing for a complete and well-known formula. The words seem to be from the beginning and end of the sentences. It is as though, in a community accustomed to the Anglican Church Service, we found, first: "*When the wicked man his soul alive.*" Second, and deceptively complete in appearance: "*When the wicked man shall save his soul alive.*" Third, fuller and betraying its incompleteness: "*When the wicked man turneth from save his soul alive.*"

Instances of this sort of abbreviation can be found in most liturgies, though of course in modern times we should put dots to mark the gap in the middle. But it is certainly not common in Greek inscriptions. Ordinary abbreviations are common enough—Θ Κ = Θεοὶ Καταχθόνιοι, δμονες = δαίμονες, and the like. And there is the system, if system it can be called, illustrated by the quotation from Gregory Nazianzene in the note on Tablet III. The case most closely resembling the present that is known to me is that of the Cyprian Curses, published by Miss Macdonald in the *Proceedings of the Soc. Bibl. Archaeology*, 1890, p. 160 sqq. Cf. Wünsch, *Append. CIA*, Praef. p. xviii sqq. They are prayers to all Ghosts and Daemons to hamper and paralyse and "take away the *θυμὸς* from" some adversary, of whom the writer is in mortal fear. They begin with metrical formulae.

The first starts:

ΟΙΚΑΤΑΓΗΝΚΔΜΟΝΕΣΟΙ
ΚΠΑΤΕΡΕΣΠΑΤΕΡΩΝΚΜΗΤΕΡΕ
ΟΙΚΟΙΤΙΝΕΣΕΝΘΑΔΕΚΕΙΣΘΕΚΟΙΤΙΝΕΣ
ΘΕΘΥΜΟΝΑΠΟΚΡΑΔΙΗΣΠΟΛΥΚΗΔΕΑ
ΟΝΤΕΣ

Another, No. IV.:

> ΑΤΑ—ΓΗΝΚΔΜΟΝΕΣΟΙΤΕΣΤΕΚ
> ΩΝΚΜΗΤΕΡΕΣΑΝΤΙΕΝΙΡΟΙΑΝΔΡΙΟΙ
> ΝΕΣΤΙΝΕΣΕΣΤΕΚΟΙΤΙΝΕΣΕΝΘΑ
> ΕΑ

These seem to represent two very similar formulae. The first will run:

> *Δαίμονες οἱ κατὰ γῆν καὶ δαίμονες οἵτινες ἔστε,*
> *καὶ Πατέρες πατέρων καὶ Μητέρες ἀντιένειροι* (?),
> *χοἵτινες ἐνθάδε κεῖσθε καὶ οἵτινες ἔνθα καθῆσθε,*
> ....
> *θυμὸν ἀπὸ κραδίης πολυκηδέα πρόσθε λαβόντες.*

The other:

> *Δαίμονες οἱ κατὰ γῆν καὶ δαίμονες οἵτινες ἔστε,*
> *καὶ Πατέρες πατέρων καὶ Μητέρες ἀντιένειροι,*
> .... *ἄνδριοι ἠδὲ γύναιοι,*
> *δαίμονες οἵτινες ἔστε καὶ οἵτινες ἐνθάδε κεῖσθε*
> ....
> <*θυμὸν ἀπὸ κραδίης*> *πολυκηδέα* <*πρόσθε λαβόντες.*>

The reconstruction of the verses is helped out by several other smaller fragments. I have followed, with slight variations, Dieterich and Wünsch.

Now here we find several points closely reminding us of the Compagno Tablets. (1) The different documents are all quoting the same magical poem. (2) Since the prayer is a prayer to take away somebody's *θυμός*, and otherwise weaken and paralyse him, I think we may conclude that the line *θυμὸν ἀπὸ κραδίης πολυκηδέα πρόσθε λαβόντες* (*λιπόντες* is added as a v. l. in one only of the fragments) is the final line of the prayer. "Do this, that, and the other, having first taken away the hurtful spirit out of his heart."

(3) The second tablet (No. IV.) gives a half line *ἄνδριοι ἠδὲ γύναιοι*, for which there is no place, and which therefore shows the incompleteness of a formula which, as written in No. I., might have seemed complete, exactly like *καὶ ἀθάνατοι θεοὶ ἄλλοι* in Compagno (*a*).

There is possibly a case of the same phenomenon in the Eleuthernae tablets (II.). There is one place at the end where the metre is broken. It may be the full formula contained a series of questions, beginning with *Τίς δ' ἐσι;* and ending with *Πῶ δ' ἐσι;—Γᾶς υἱὸς ἠμὶ καὶ ὠρανῶ ἀστερόεντος.* If there were only one tablet containing the formula, one would prefer to suppose that *Τίς δ' ἐσι; πῶ δ' ἐσι;* was mere dittography, a scribe having first written the phrase slightly wrong and then re-written it right without deleting the first version. But this hypothesis becomes more difficult when there are three tablets differing in several particulars but agreeing in this unmetrical double question.

In any case, it would probably be wisest to regard the tablets as each consisting of a series of formulae, mostly in verse but some in prose, some apparently complete, others compendiary.

VIII. *The Tablet of Caecilia Secundina.*

A thin gold tablet (75 mm. by 24 mm. in size) found in Rome about the year 1899, probably in one of the ancient tombs on the Ostia Road; now in the British Museum. The script, though generally clear, is peculiar. The form of ε (cf. ευκλεεσευ in line 2) is new to me, but in general the writing is like that of a cursive papyrus of Roman times. The tablet was first published by Prof. Comparetti in *Atene e Roma*, LIV. and LV. (1903). He considered it certainly later than the Herculanean papyri, but would place it in the second century or possibly the first, A.D.

[It has since been discussed by Prof. Hermann Diels in the *Philotesia für Paul Kleinert* (Berlin, 1907). The veteran scholar has succeeded, as was to be expected, in deciphering and explaining the tablet better than his predecessors. He attributes it to the third century A.D., and Dr Kenyon agrees.]

I read it thus:

ἔρχεται ἐκ καθαρῶν, καθαρὰ χθονίων βασίλεια,
Εὔκλεες Εὐβουλεῦ τε. Διὸς τέκος, ὅπλα δ' ἔχ' ὧδε
Μνημοσύνης· τὸ δὲ δῶρον ἀοίδιμον ἀνθρώποισιν·
Καικιλία Σεκουνδεῖνα, νόμῳ ἴθι θία γεγῶσα.

'She comes from the Pure, O Pure Queen of those below
And Eukles and Eubouleus.—Child of Zeus, receive here the armour
Of Memory, ('tis a gift songful among men):
Thou Caecilia Secundina, come, by Law grown to be divine.'

v. 2. Probably Εὔκλεες as Comparetti: not εὔκλεέ τ'. The rest of this line is certain as far as Διὸς τέκος: after that, I make out οπλαδεχωδε, the first δ being (cf. that in τόδε below) very like α, and the ο not well finished. Repeated examination of the tablet still inclines me to think that these are the inscribed letters; and I may add that Dr A. S. Murray and Mr Cecil Smith, as well as Dr Hartwig, who formerly possessed the tablet, all independently read the same.

Taking these letters as they stand, we may obtain sense, grammar and metre by dividing ὅπλα δ' ἔχ' ὧδε: "*Have here the armour of Memory*," and I believe that this interpretation, though curious, is right. The change to the second person and the imperative addressed to the Soul are just like phrases in the other tablets: ὄλβιε καὶ μακάριστε, ἀλλὰ πίε μου, κτλ. The peculiar use of ὅπλα, to which I can find nothing quite similar in our fragments of Orphic literature, has its exact parallel in St Paul's repeated metaphors ὅπλα δικαιοσύνης (Rom. vi. 12; 2 Cor. vi. 7), ὅπλα φωτός (Rom. xiii. 2). The "armour of Mnemosyne" to an Orphic would probably bear just the same shade of meaning as the "armour of light" to a Christian. Lethe was the Orphic "Darkness." The use of ὧδε might be paralleled by Homer's πρόμολ' ὧδε, and the scholiasts have remarked long since that in the later Epic language ὧδε was used more freely than in Homer. The Cyprian Curses just quoted give ὑμεῖς οἱ ὧδε κείμενοι.

A further question here suggests itself. Who is the Διὸς τέκος? A comparison of the phrases applied to the pure soul in the other tablets (θεὸς ἐγένου, ὑμῶν γένος ὄλβιον εὔχομαι εἶναι, etc.) suggests that "Child of Zeus" is vocative and addressed to the soul of the departed. "Child of Zeus, receive here thine armour of Memory." The doctrine is orthodox in Orphism: the completely pure soul is the pure blood of Zagreus, freed from the dross of charred Titan corpses, and as such is the child of Zeus. In an earlier stage it was Γᾶς παῖς καὶ Ὠρανῶ.

Prof. Diels reads Διὸς τέκος, ἀγλαά· ἔχω δε
Μνημοσύνης τόδε δωρὸν κτλ.

and Kenyon agrees. This certainly gives a simpler sense, and is very likely right. I leave my original interpretation standing however, because at the time I carefully considered αγλαα, and decided that the letters on the tablet were οπλαα or οπλαδ.

v. 3. Should we divide τὸ δὲ or τόδε in apposition to ὅπλα?

v. 4. Scanned, apparently, Σ'κουνδεῖνα: such licenses are of course common. Cf. the short α of θ(ε)ία below. The last three words, forming l. 6 on the tablet, are difficult, but have at last been deciphered by Diels. (Kenyon however thinks that ΕΙΑ is written, not ΘΙΑ.) θία of course stands for θεία. My previous interpretation was evidently wrong, and I withdraw it.

The "armour of Memory (!)," the "gift songful among men," is firstly perhaps the spiritual gift, and then in a secondary sense the actual tablet which both symbolises and *preserves from oblivion* Cecilia's claims to immortality; and does so *in song*.

Caecilia Secundina is not otherwise known, but must have belonged in some way to the clan of Caecilii Secundi. The name of the Younger Pliny before his adoption was Publius Caecilius Secundus.

G. M.

INDEX OF CLASSICAL PASSAGES.

GREEK.

INDEX.

I. GREEK.

II. GENERAL.

CAMBRIDGE: PRINTED BY JOHN CLAY, M.A. AT THE UNIVERSITY PRESS.

AT

CPSIA information can be obtained
at www.ICGtesting.com
Printed in the USA
LVOW13s0117160617
538330LV00032B/1510/P

9 781314 279924